A-Z BIRMINGHAM

CONTENTS

Key to Map Pages	2-3	Index to Streets, Towns, Villages and selected Places of Interest	171-292
Large Scale City Centres	4-5,170		
Map Pages	6-169	Index to Hospitals and Hospices	293-295

REFERENCE

Motorway — **M6**

A Road — A

    Under Construction

    Proposed

B Road — **B4284**

Dual Carriageway

One-way Street
Traffic flow on A Roads is also indicated by a heavy line on the driver's left

City Centre Ring Road & Junction Numbers — (1)

Restricted Access

Pedestrianized Road

Track / Footpath

Cycleway (Selected)

Railway
Station   Heritage Station   Level Crossing   Tunnel

Midland Metro
The boarding of Metro trams at stops may be limited to a single direction, indicated by the arrow. — Stop

Built-up Area — NEWTON PL

Local Authority Boundary

Posttown Boundary

Postcode Boundary (within Posttown)

Map Continuation — **20**   Large Scale City Centre — **4**

A and B Roads only

Information Centre — 🛈

Junction Name (M6 Toll only) — BURNTWOOD JUNCTION

National Grid Reference — ⁴15

Park & Ride — Monkspath P+🚍

Police Station — ▲

Post Office — ★

Toilet:
  without facilities for the Disabled — ▽
  with facilities for the Disabled — ▽
  for exclusive use by the Disabled — ▽

Viewpoint — ☀ ☀

Educational Establishment

Hospital or Hospice

Industrial Building

Leisure or Recreational Facility

Place of Interest

Public Building

Shopping Centre or Market

Other Selected Buildings

P
†
■
Ⓗ

SCALE

Map Pages 6-169	Map Pages 4-5,170
1:18,103 3½ inches to 1 mile	1:9,051 7 inches to 1 mile

0   ¼   ½ Mile   0   ⅛   ¼ Mile

0   250   500   750 Metres   0   100   200   300 Metres

5.52 cm to 1 km   8.89 cm to 1 mile   11.05 cm to 1 km   17.78 cm to 1 mile

Copyright of Geographers' A-Z Map Company Limited

Fairfield Road, Borough Green, Sevenoaks, Kent TN15 8PP
Telephone: 01732 781000 (Enquiries & Trade Sales)
          01732 783422 (Retail Sales)
www.a-zmaps.co.uk
Copyright © Geographers' A-Z Map Co. Ltd.

EDITION 5   2008

Every possible care has been taken to ensure that, to the best of our knowledge, the information contained in this atlas is accurate at the date of publication. However, we cannot warrant that our work is entirely error free and whilst we would be grateful to learn of any inaccuracies, we do not accept any responsibility for loss or damage resulting from reliance on information contained within this publication.

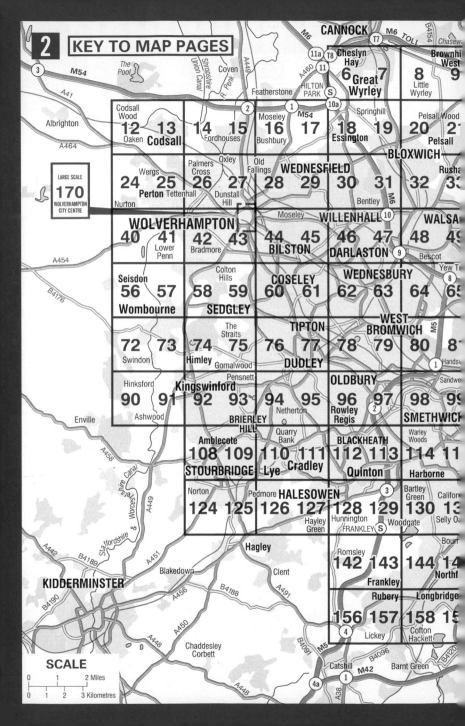

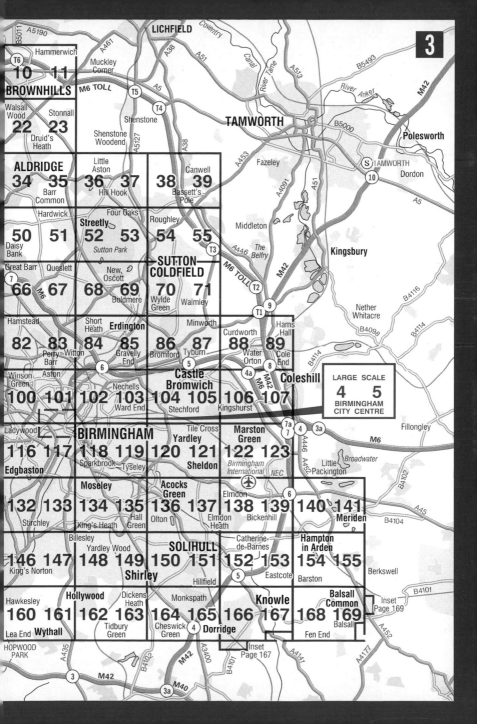

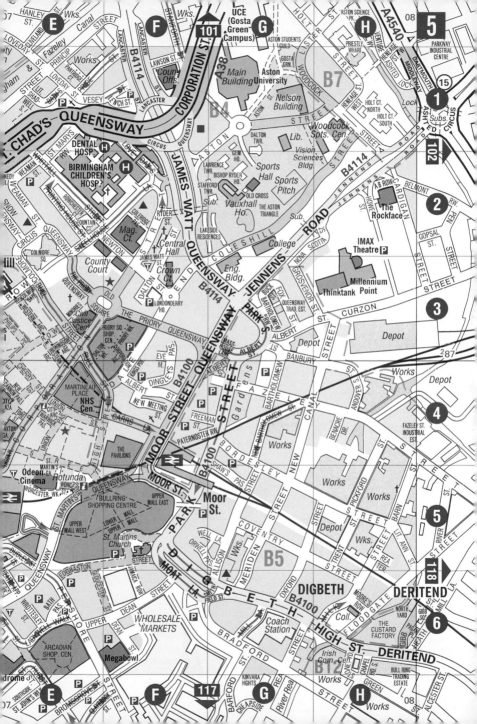

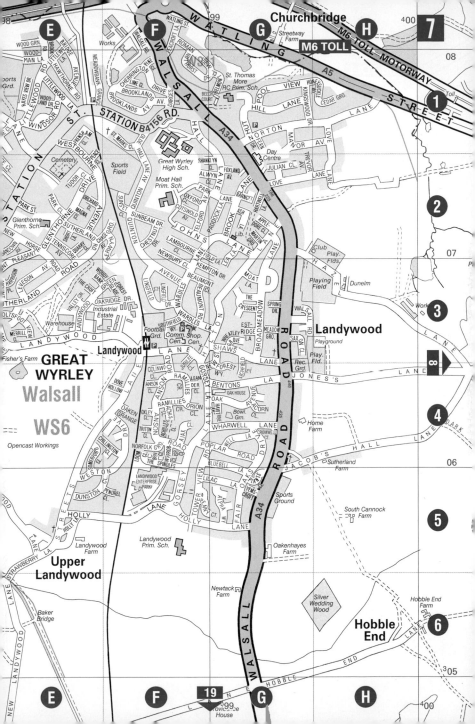

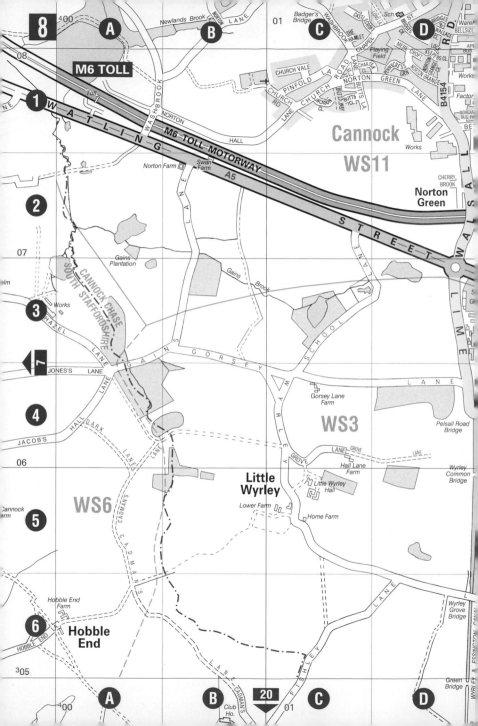

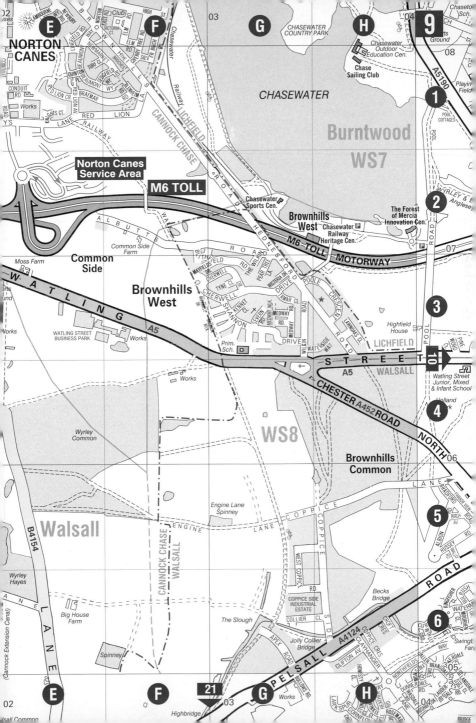

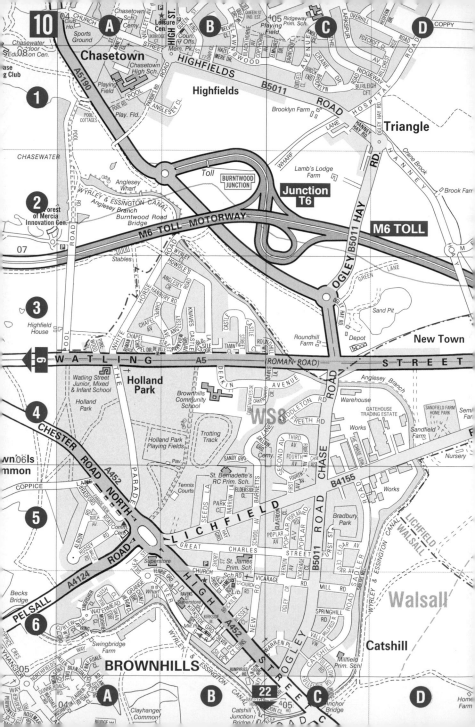

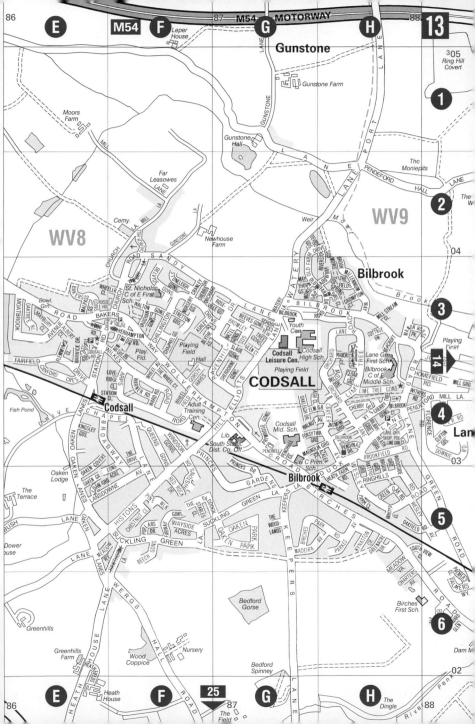

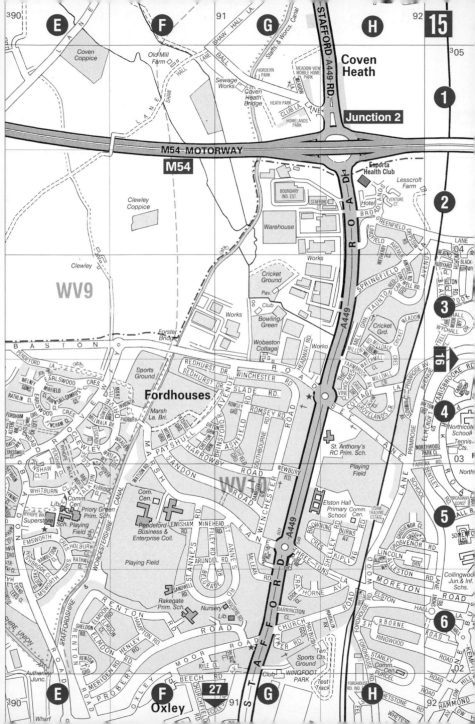

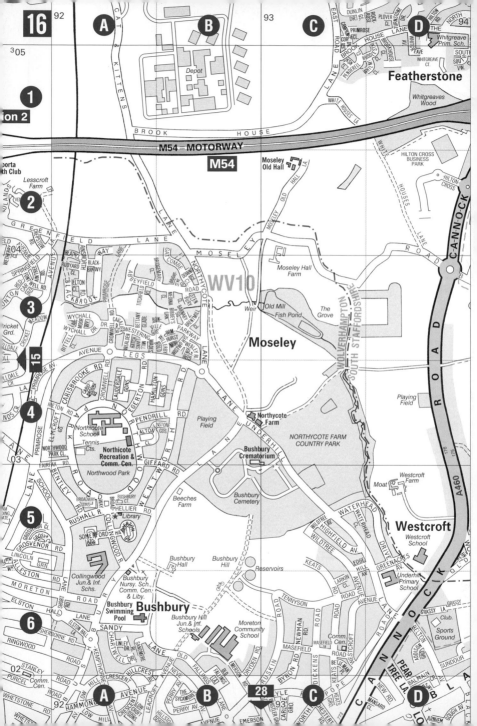

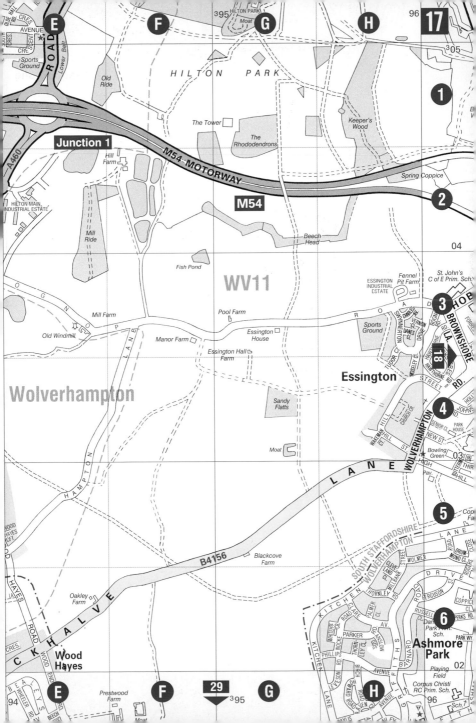

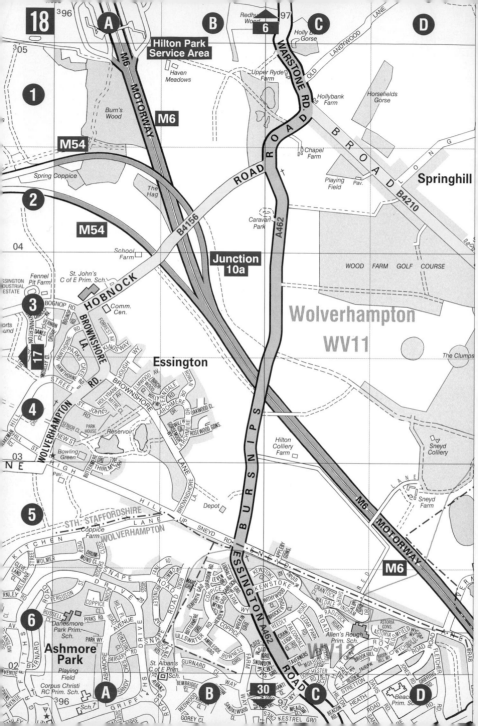

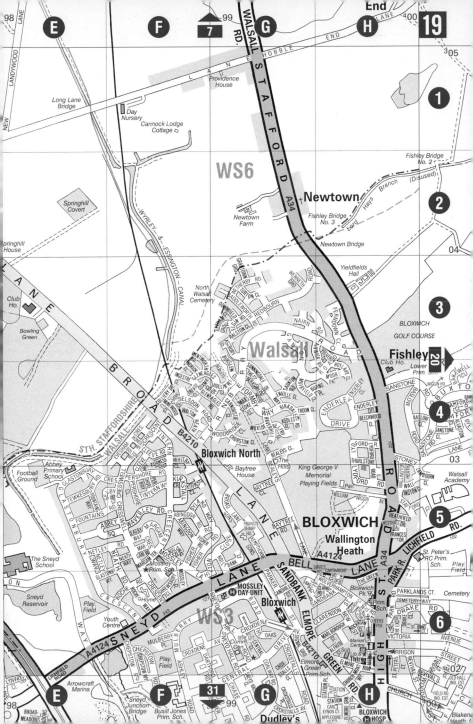

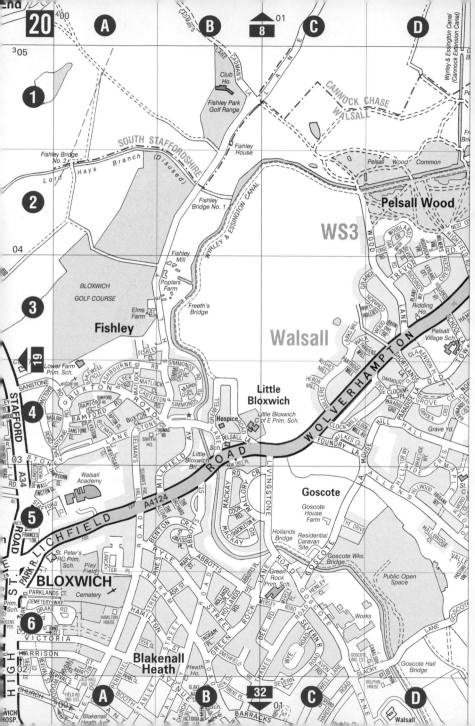

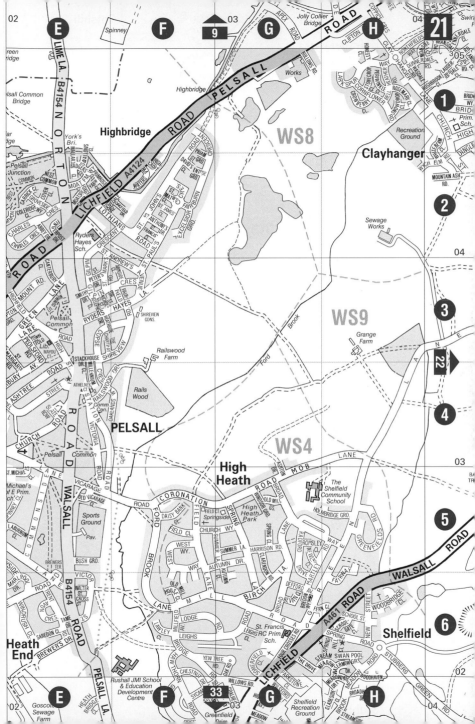

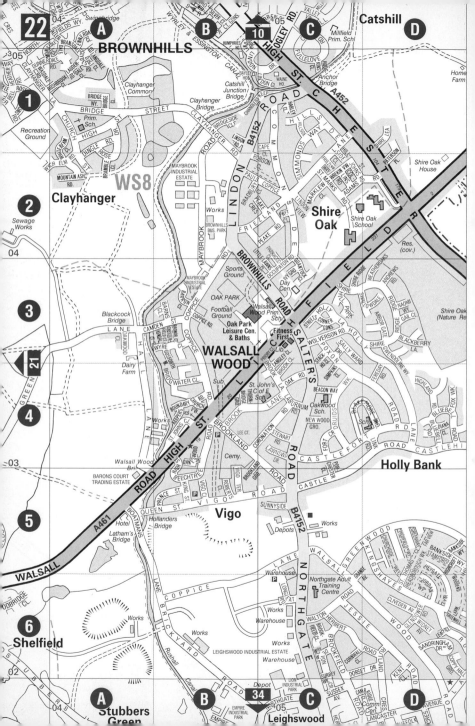

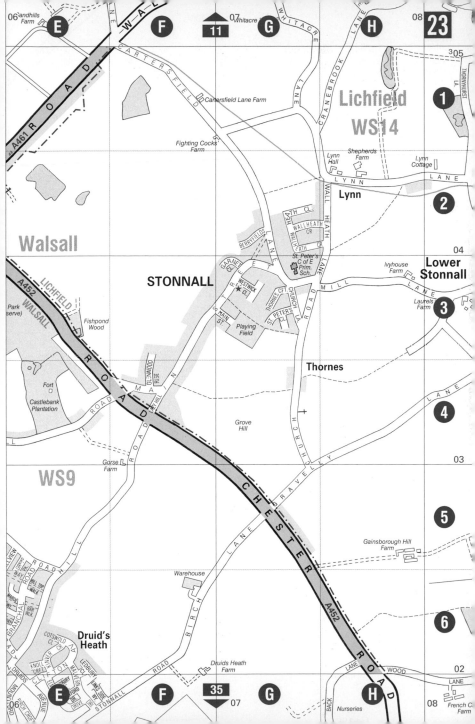

Lichfield WS14

Walsall

STONNALL

Lynn

Lower Stonnall

Thornes

WS9

Druid's Heath

E **F** **11** Whitacre **G** **H** 08

Sandhills Farm 06 07

305

Cartersfield Lane

Canersfield Lane Farm

Fighting Cocks' Farm

Lynn Hall

Shepherds Farm

Lynn Cottage

LYNN LANE

WALL HEATH CR

WALLHEATH CR

HEATH CL.

BERRYFIELDS LANE

Ivyhouse Farm

St. Peter's C of E Prim. Sch.

WESTWICK CL.

GARNET

THORNES CFT

ST. PETER'S CL.

CHURCH LA

MILL ROAD

Laurels Farm

04

MAIN ST.

GLENWOOD RISE

Playing Field

Grove Hill

Park (Reserve)

Fishpond Wood

Fort

Castlebank Plantation

CHURCH LANE

GRAVELLY LANE

LANE

LICHFIELD A452

A461 ROAD

ROAD

Gorse Farm

CHESTER

Gainsborough Hill Farm

03

Warehouse

BIRCH LANE

A452 ROAD

Druids Heath Farm

French Cl. Farm

Nurseries

BACK LANE

WOOD LANE

02

STONNALL ROAD

E **F** **35** 07 **G** **H** 08

06

1

2

3

4

5

6

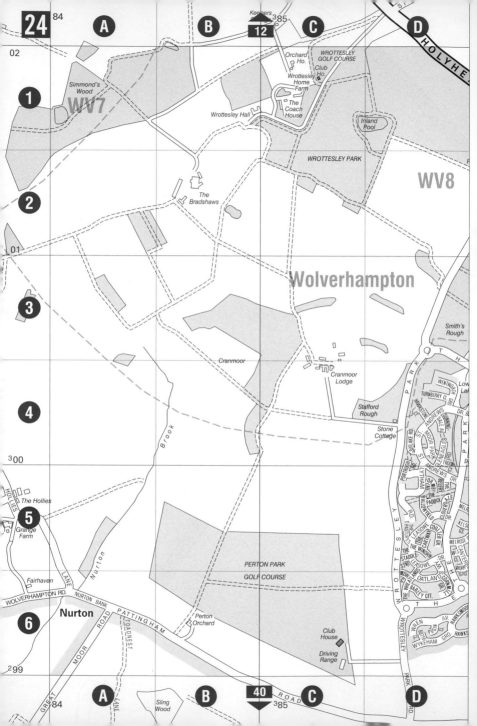

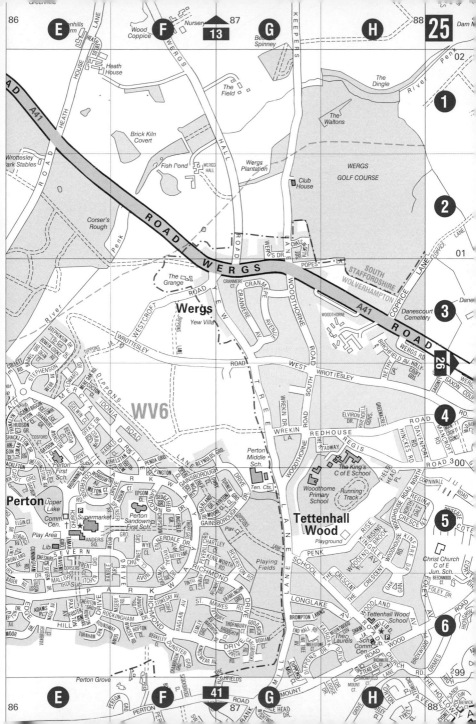

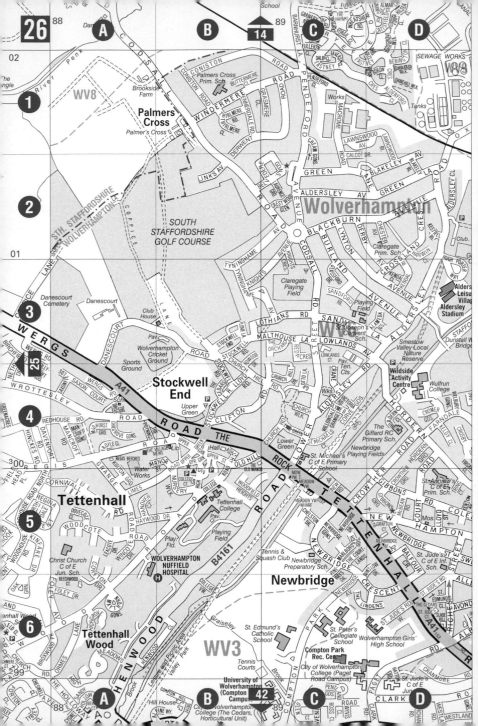

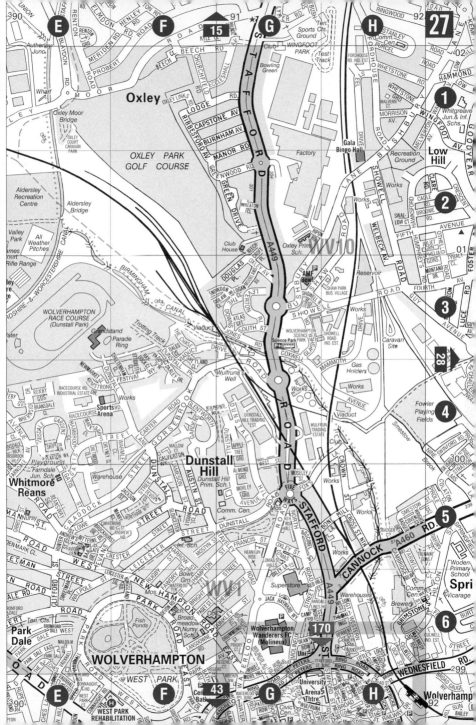

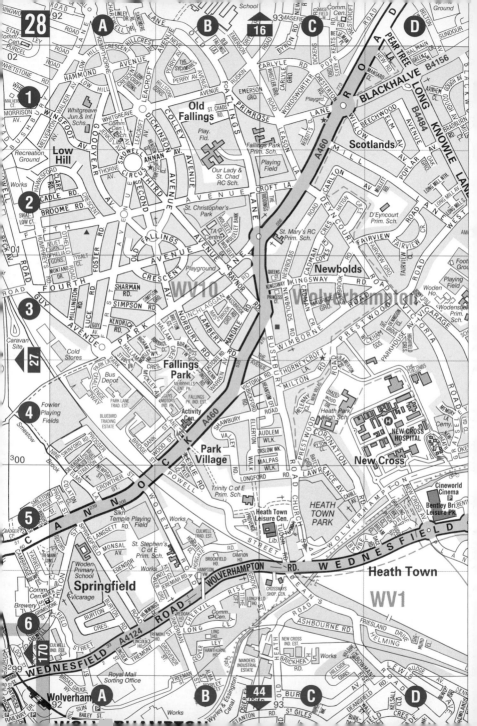

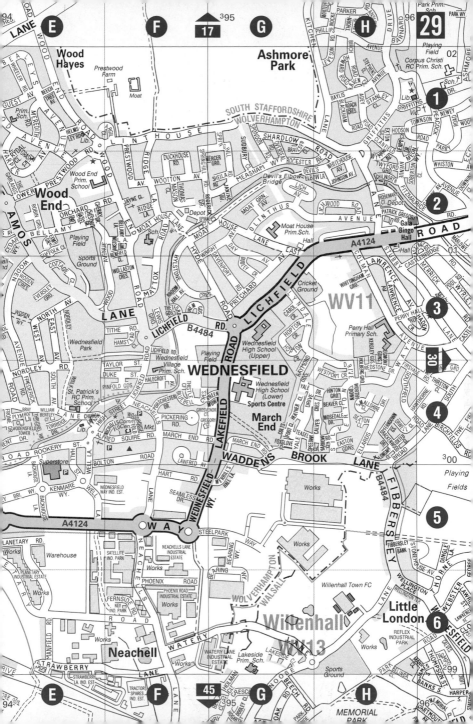

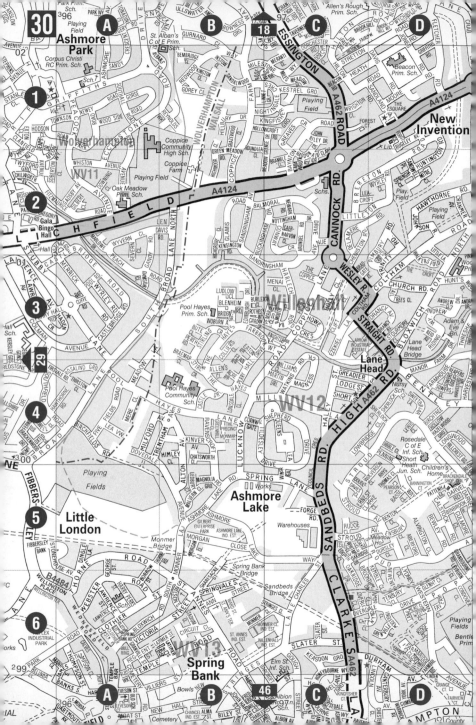

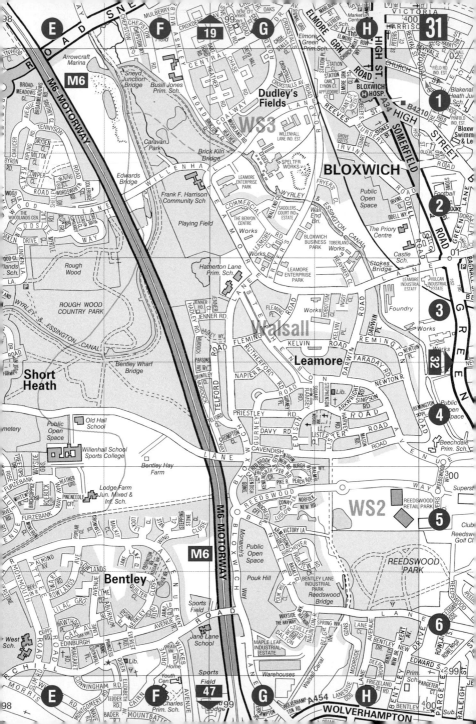

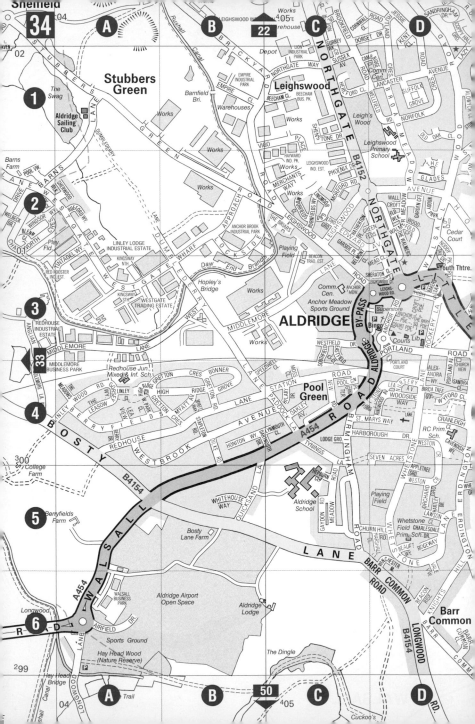

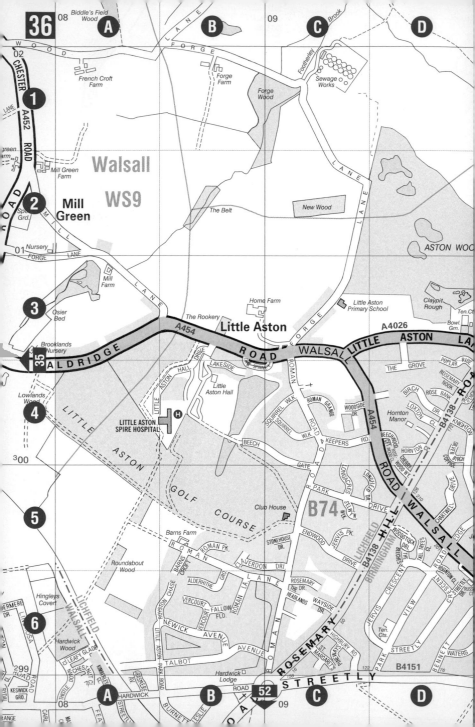

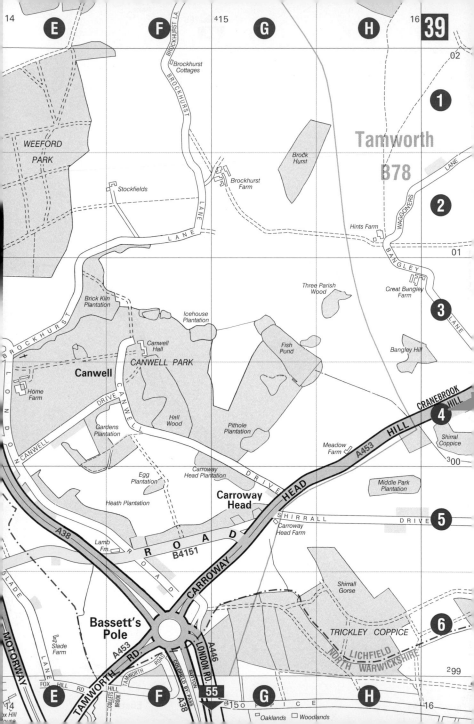

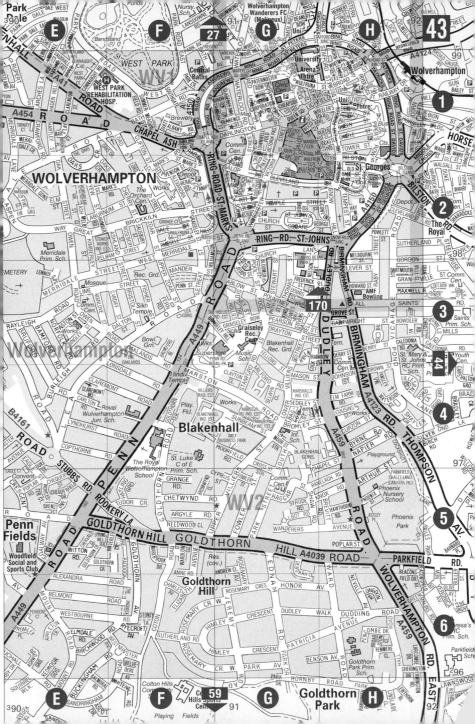

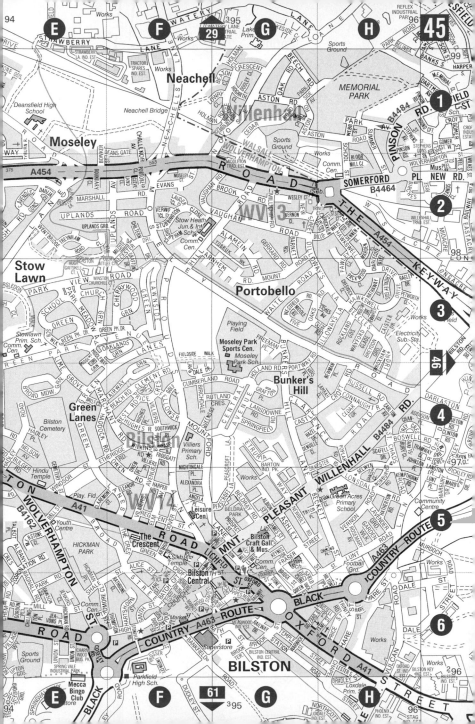

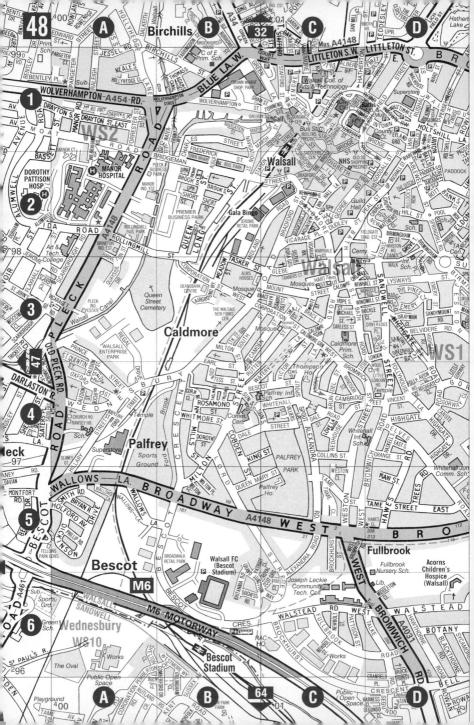

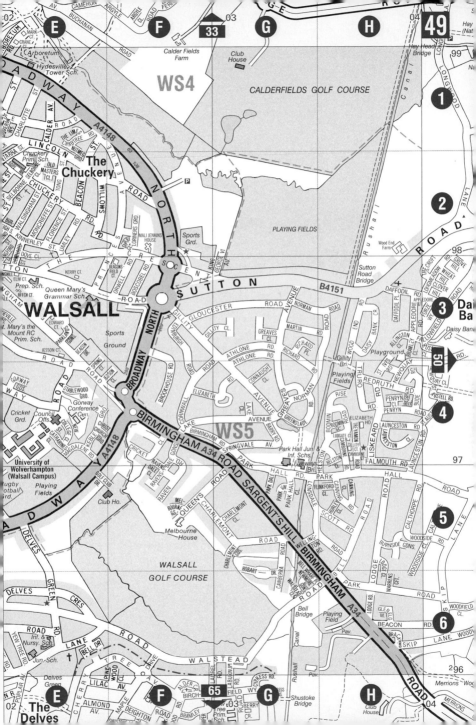

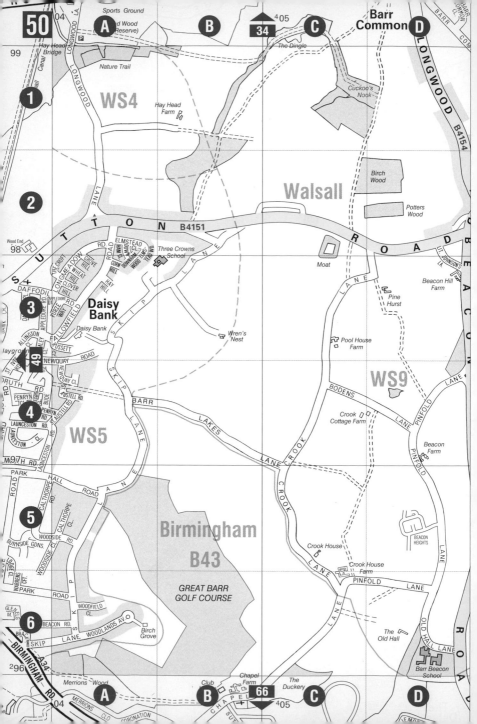

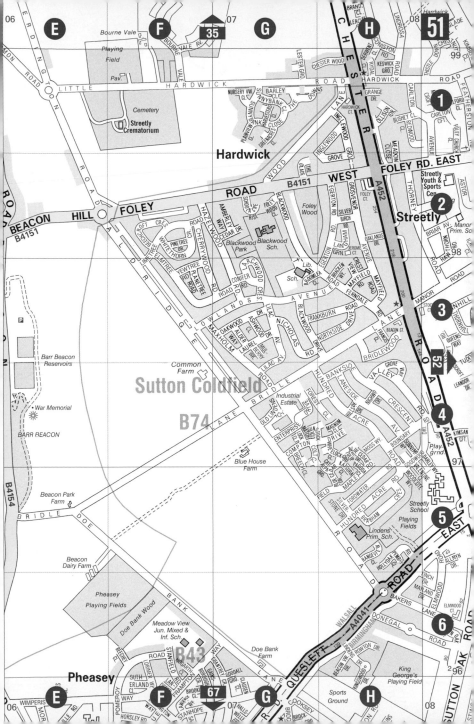

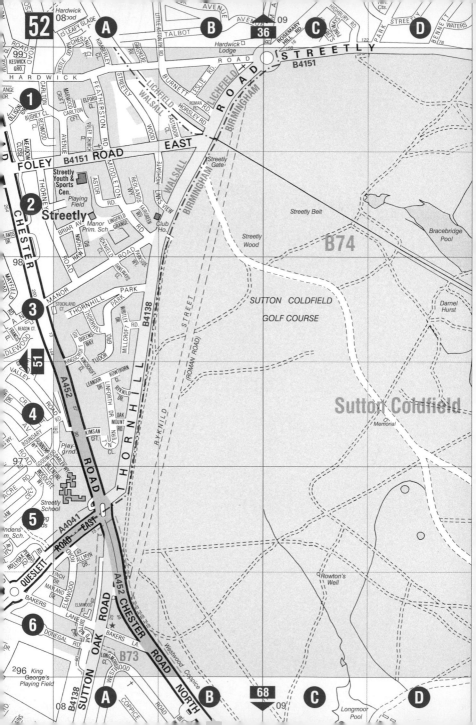

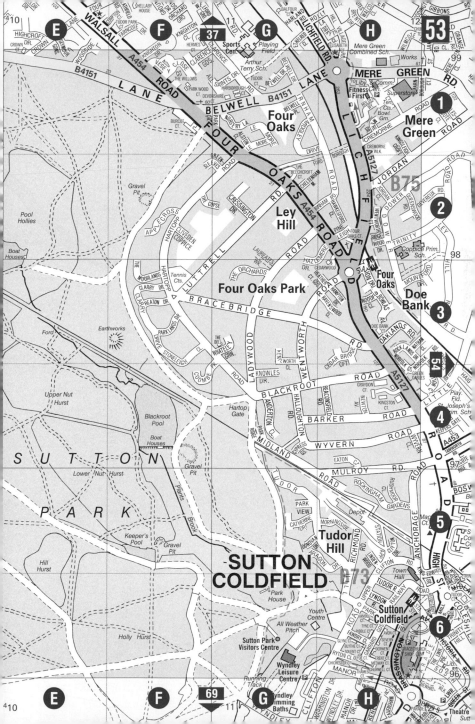

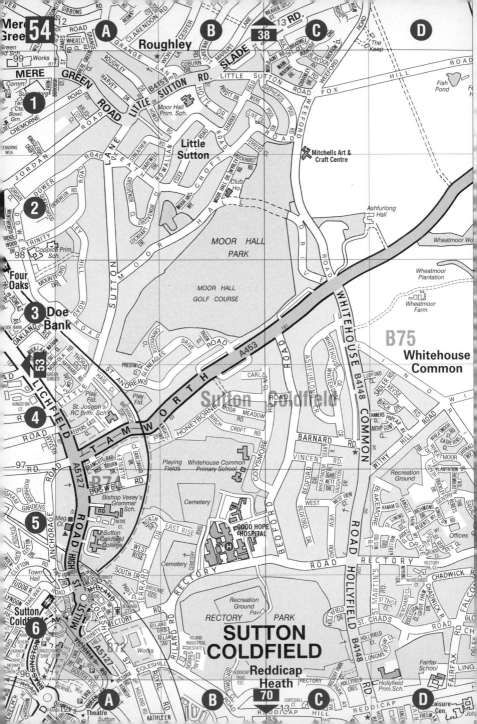

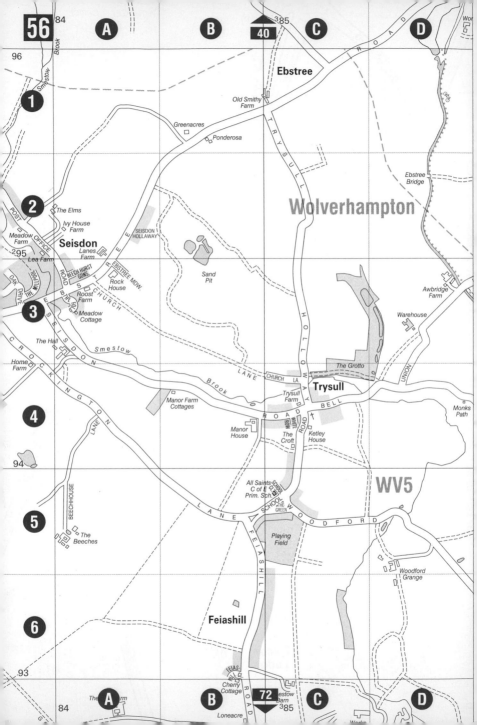

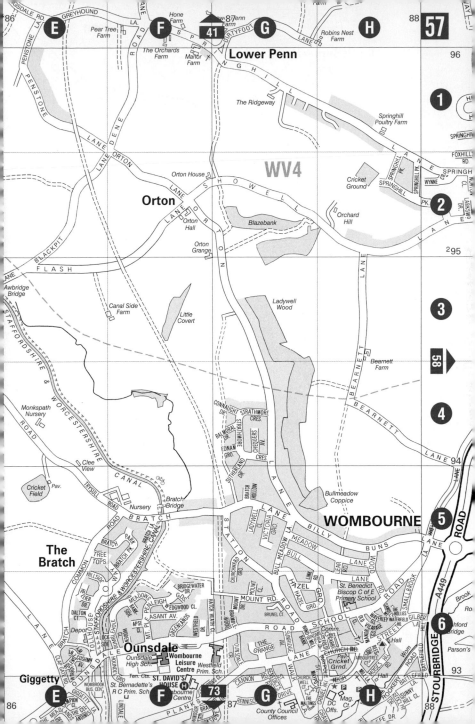

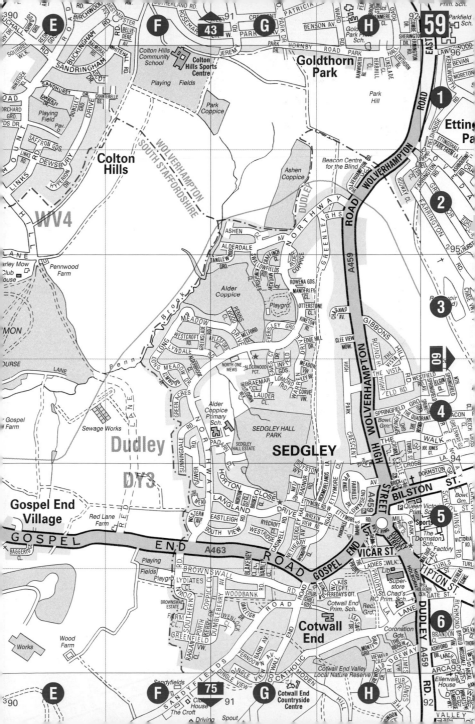

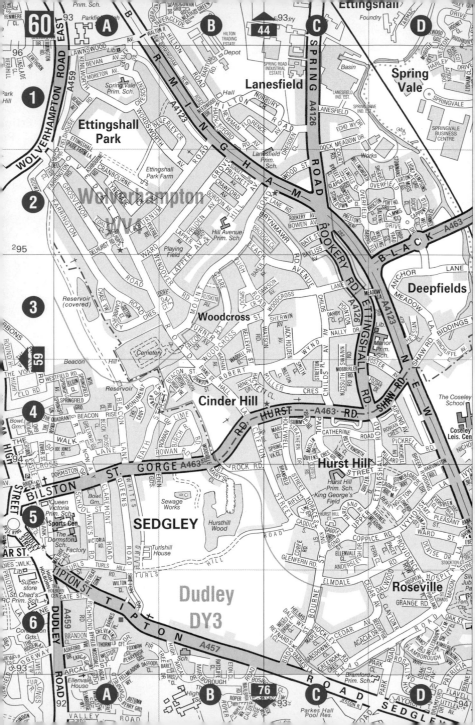

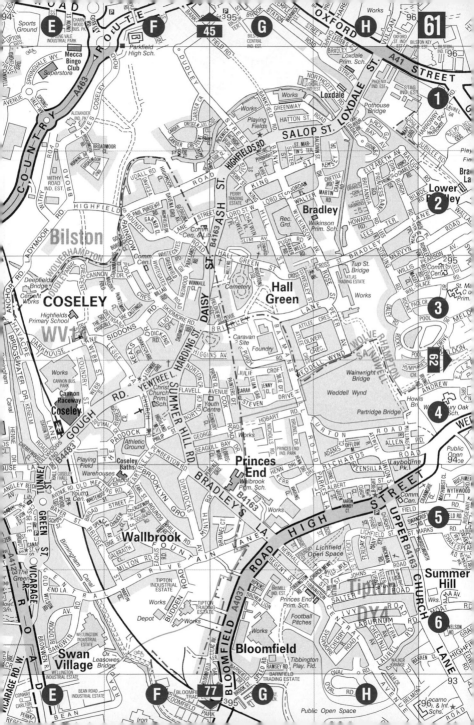

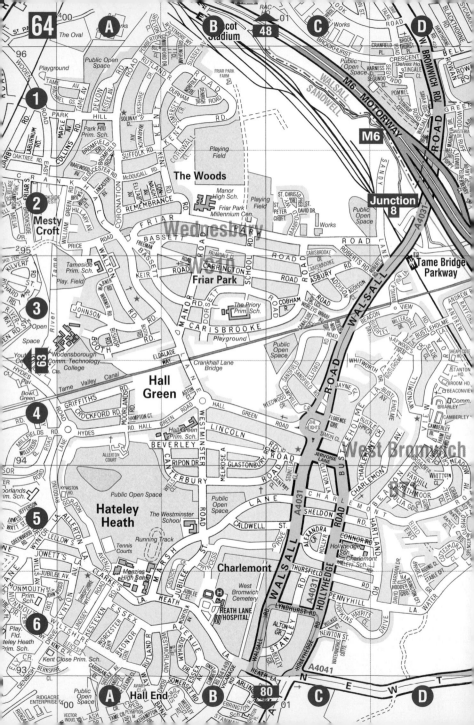

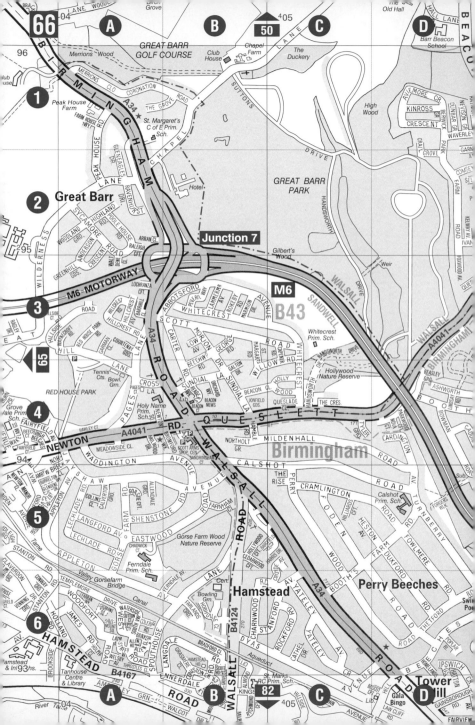

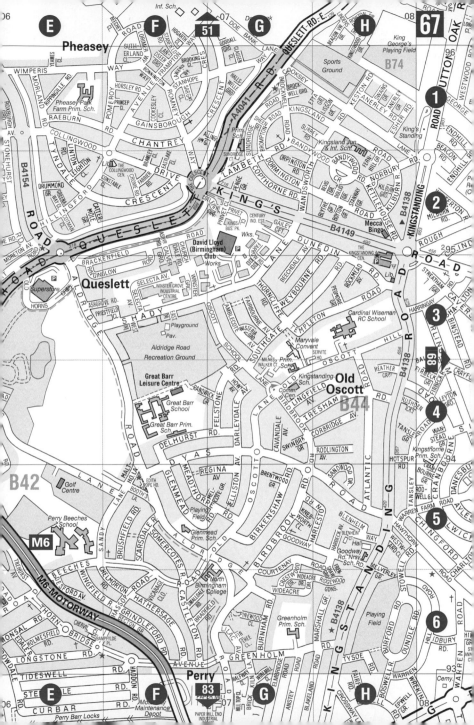

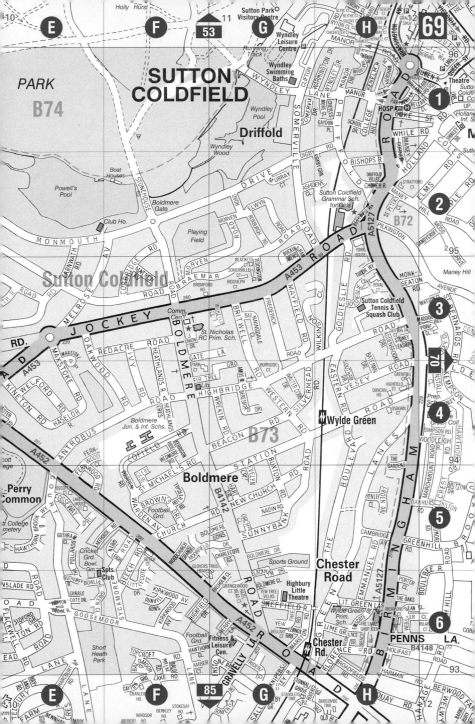

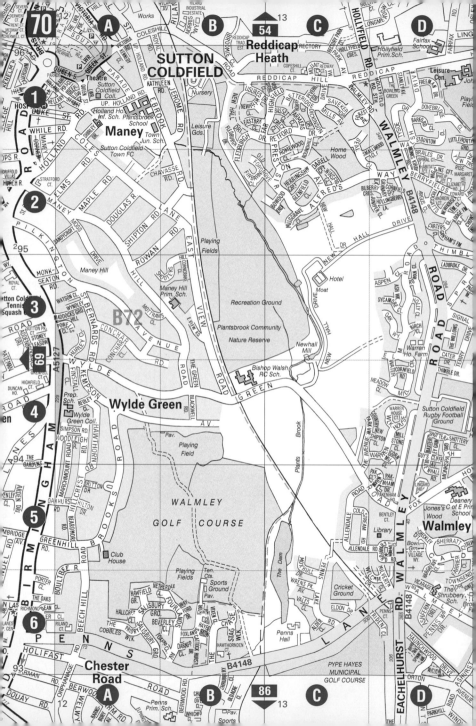

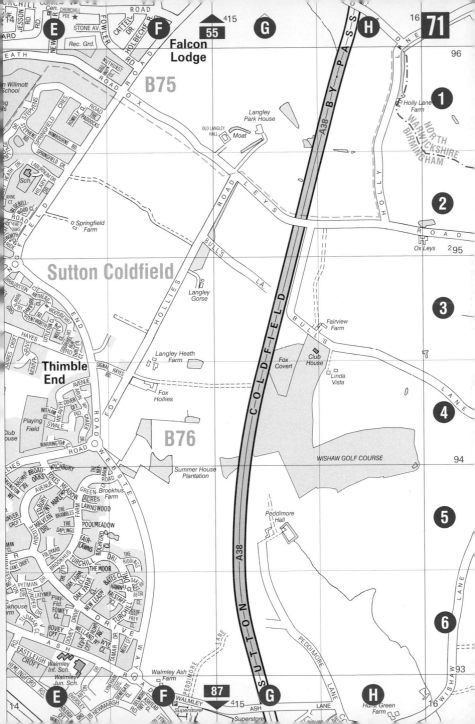

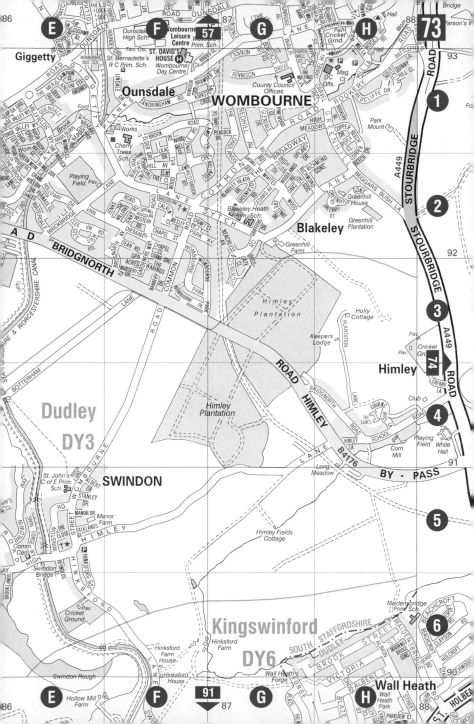

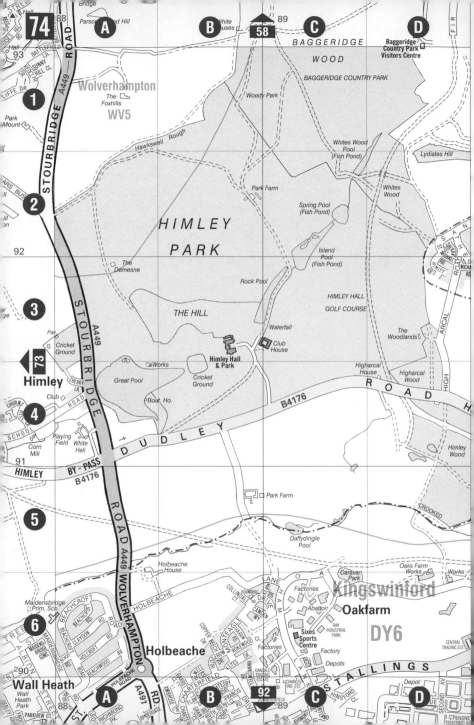

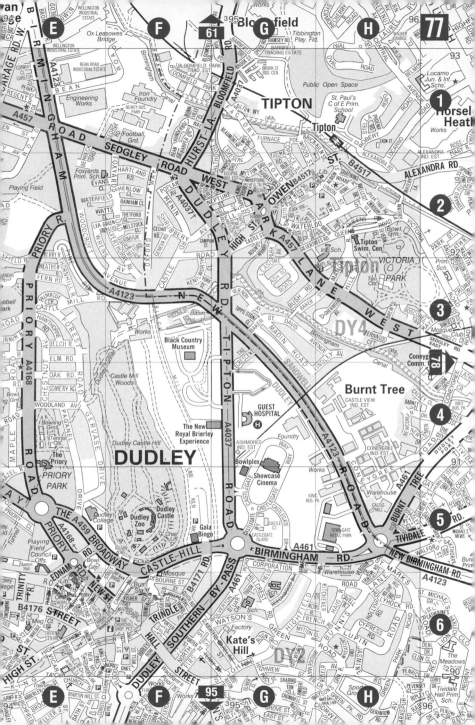

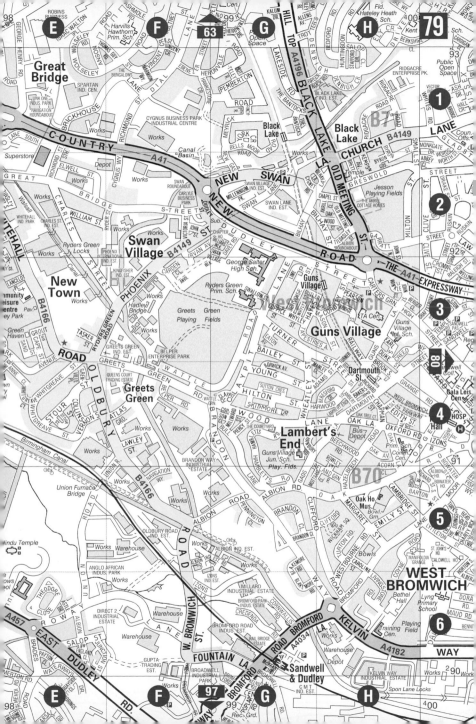

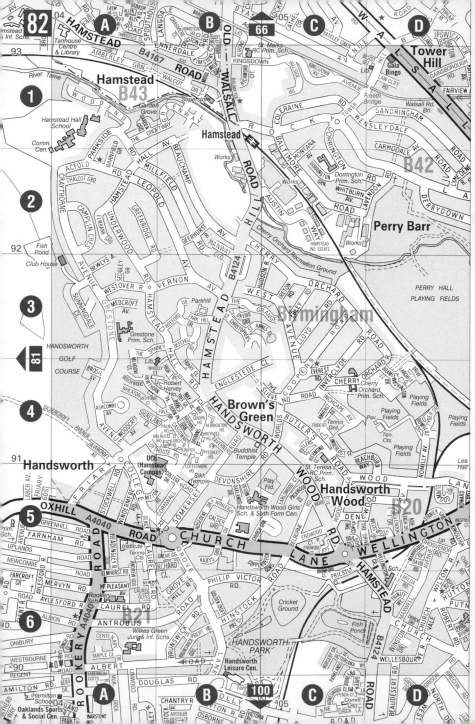

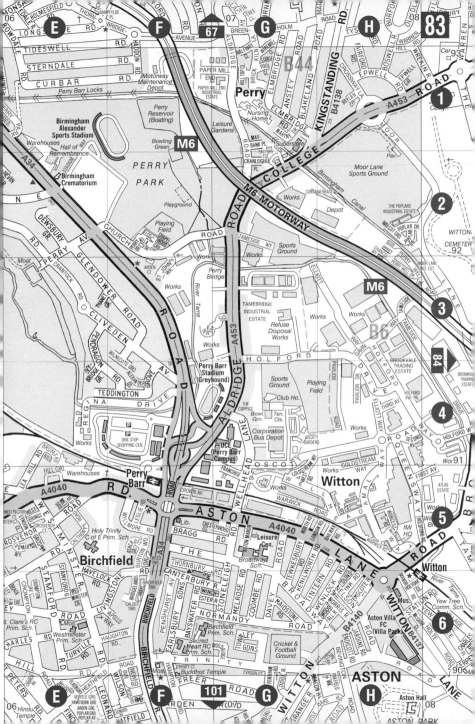

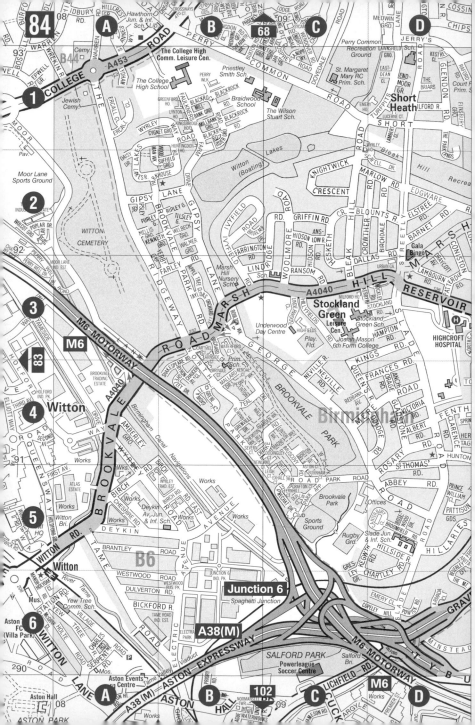

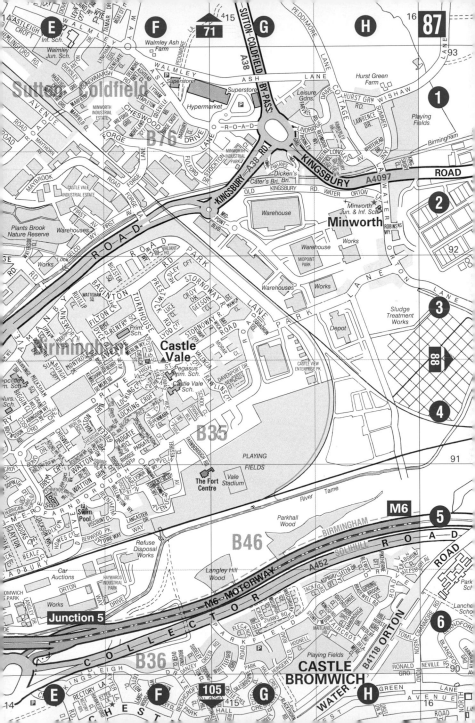

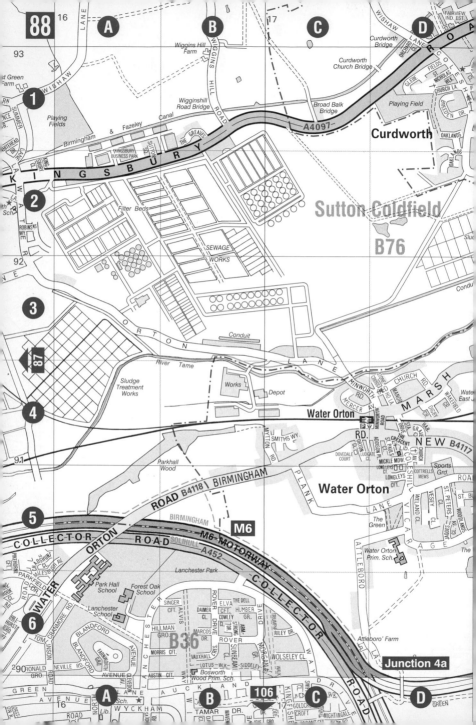

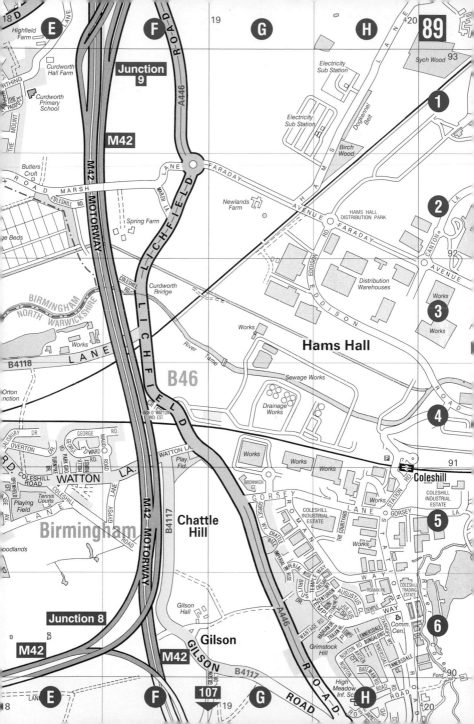

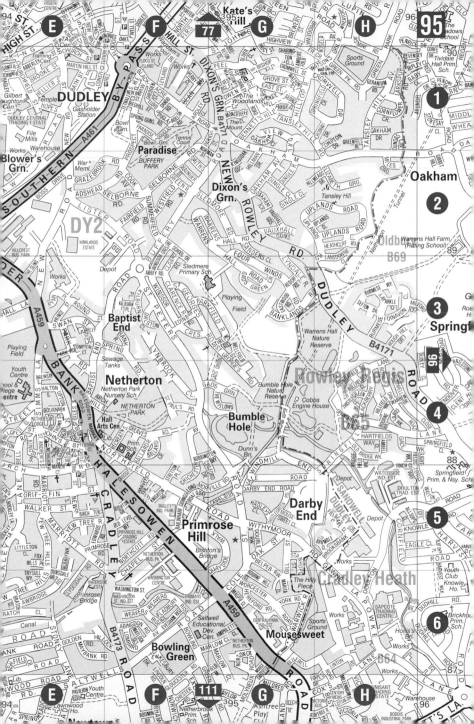

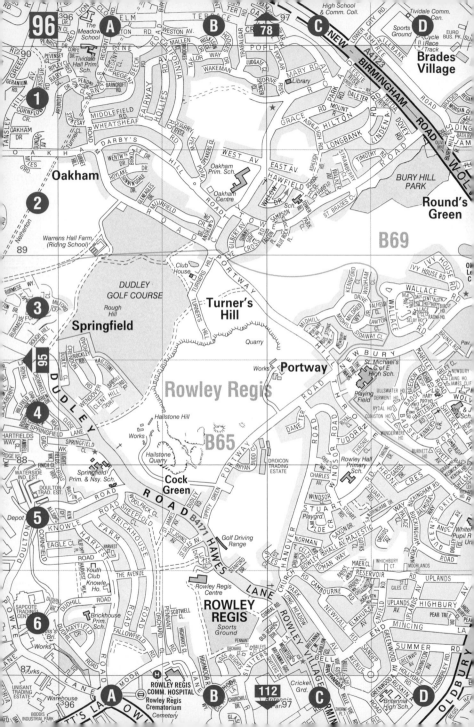

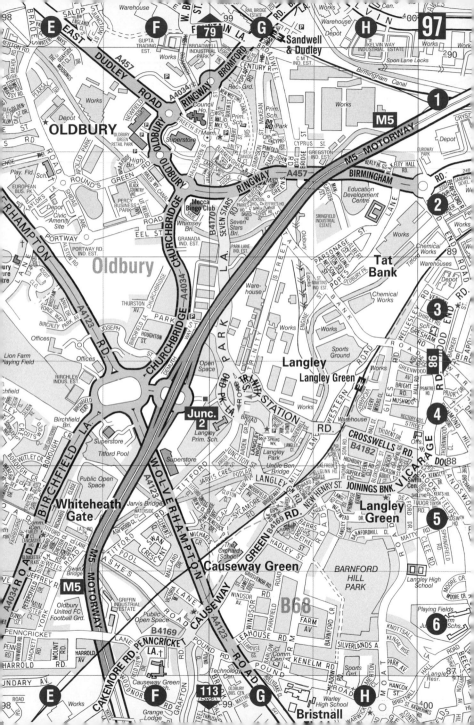

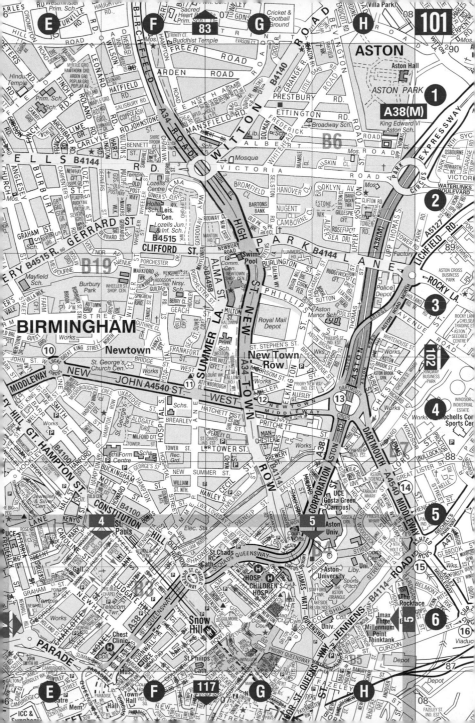

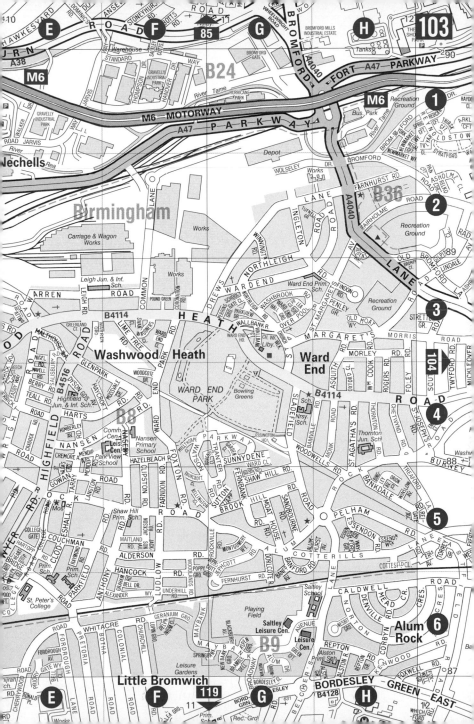

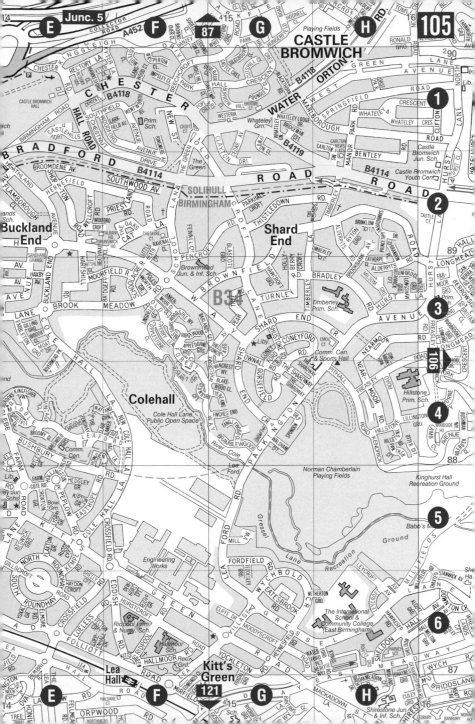

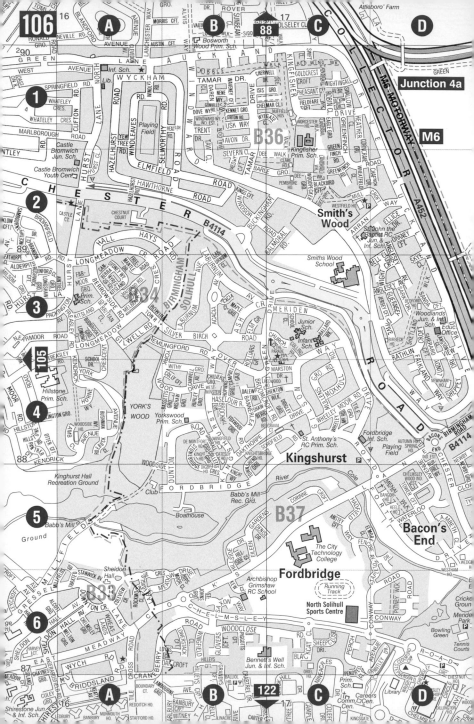

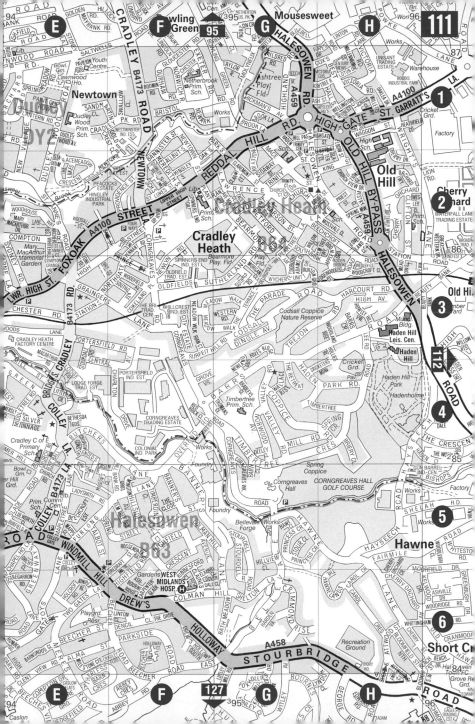

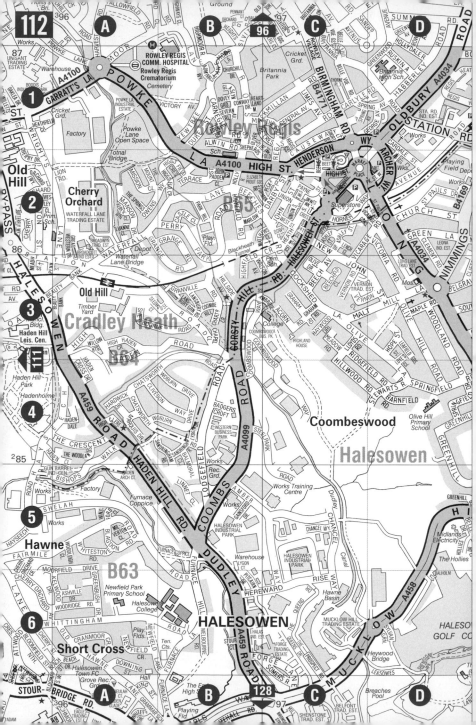

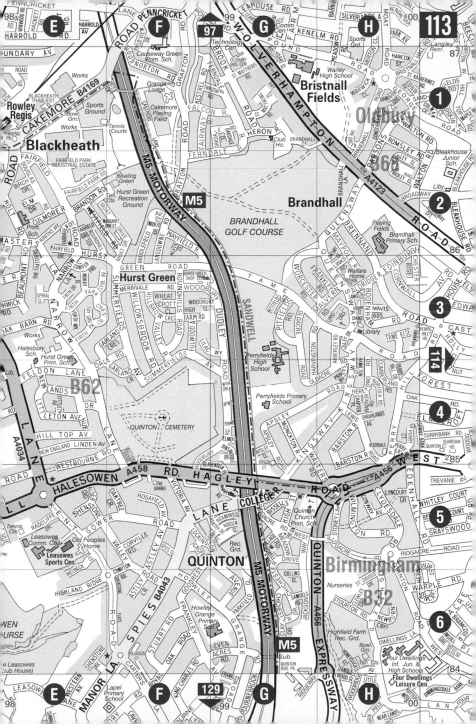

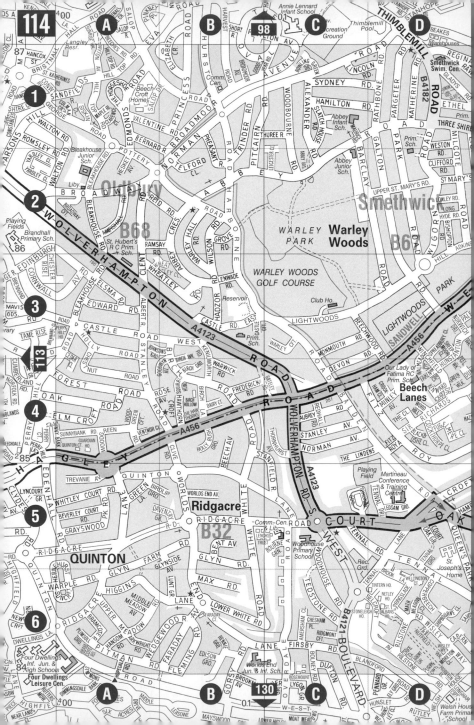

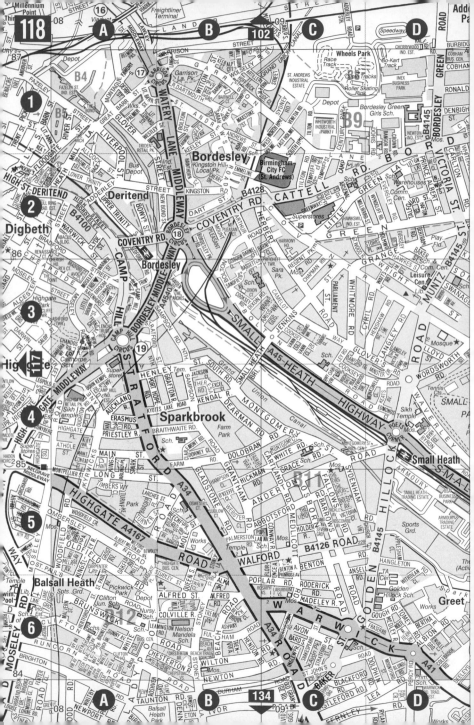

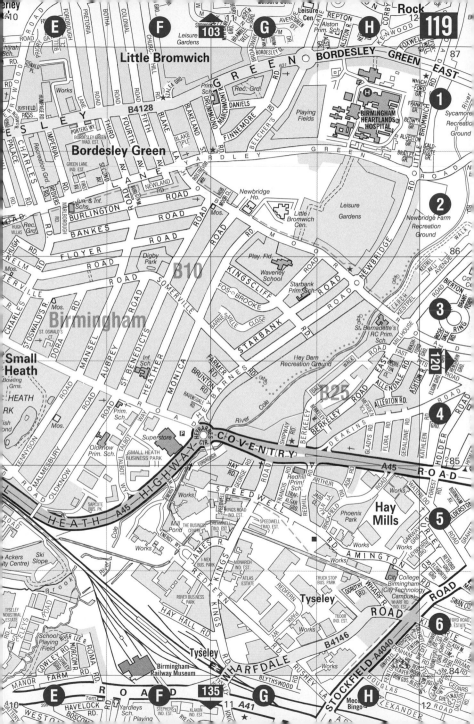

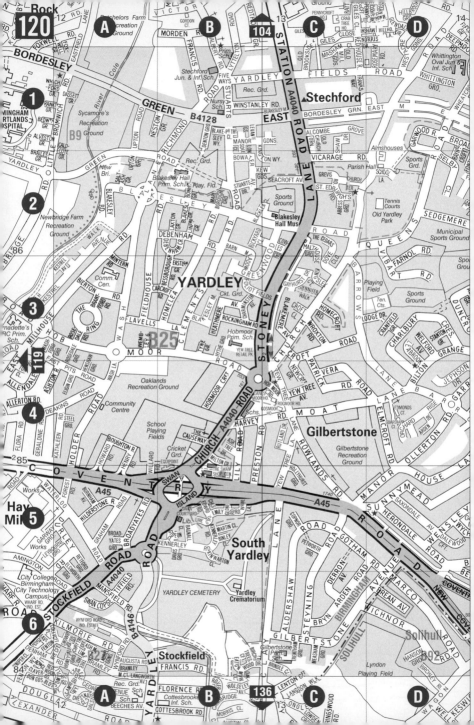

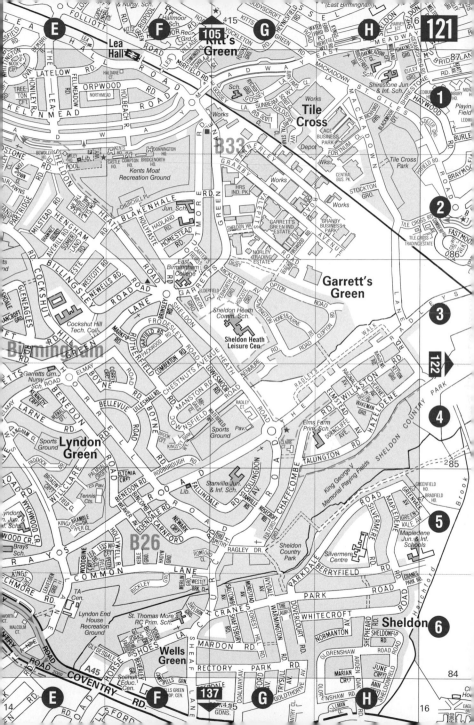

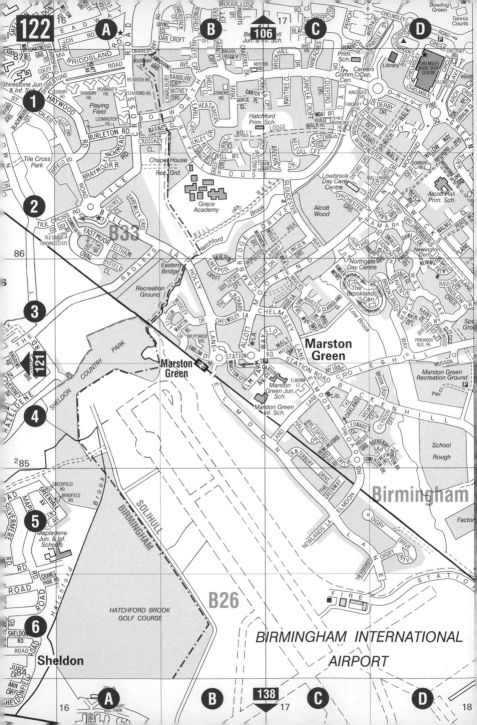

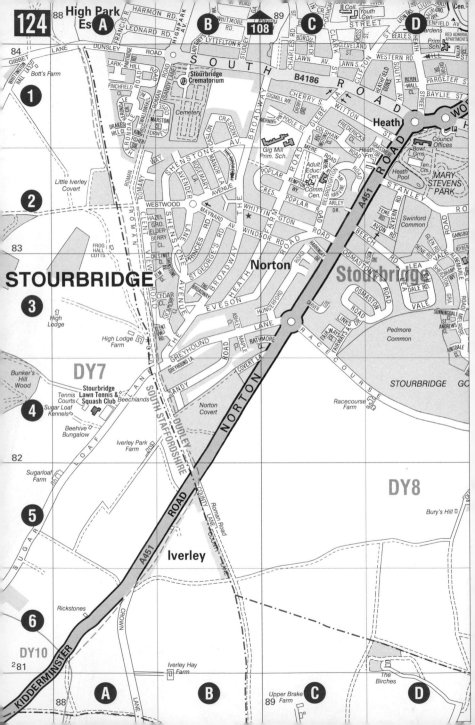

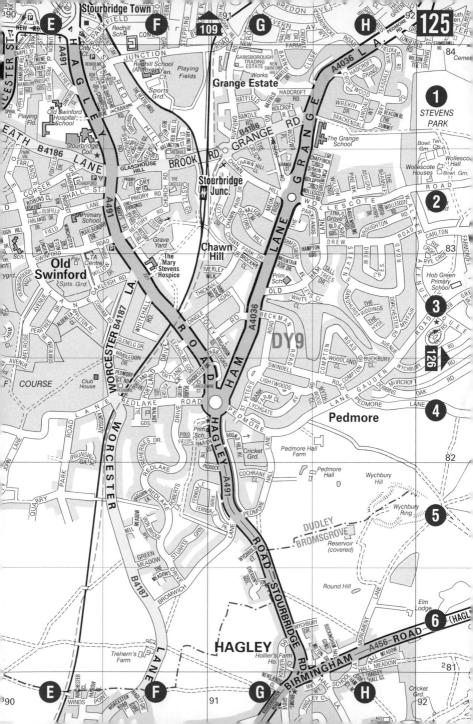

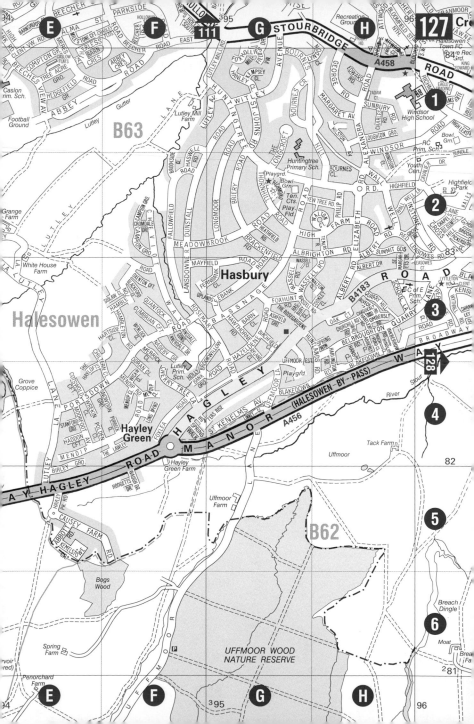

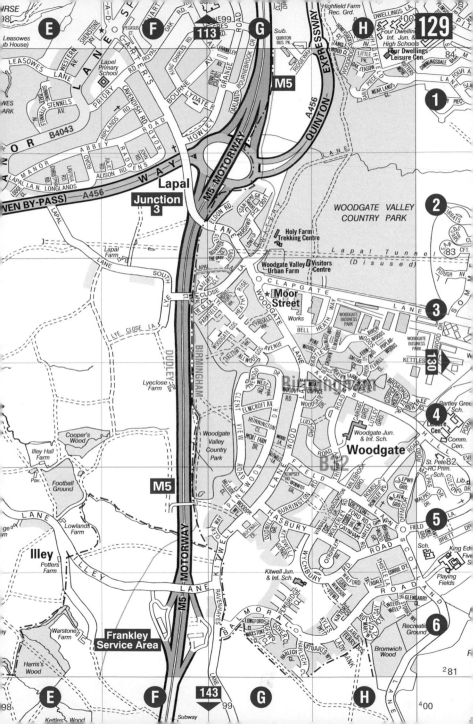

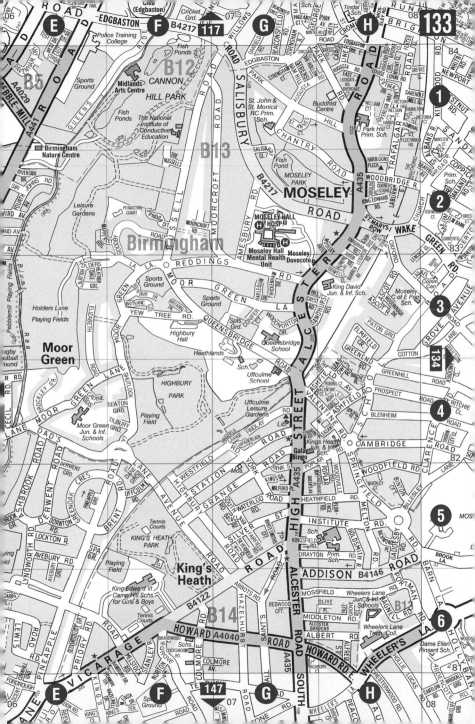

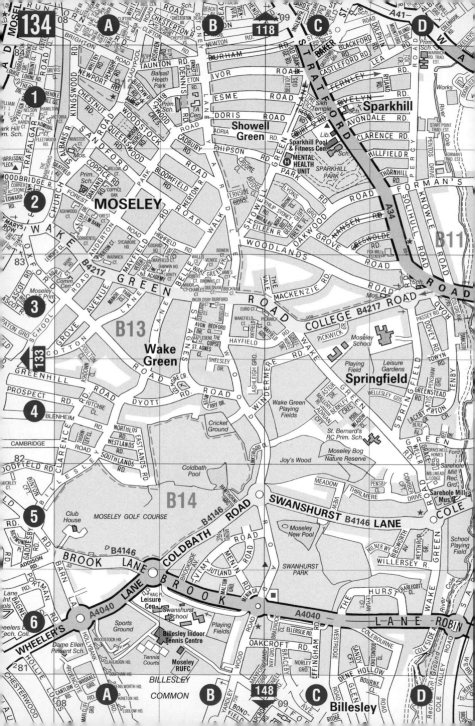

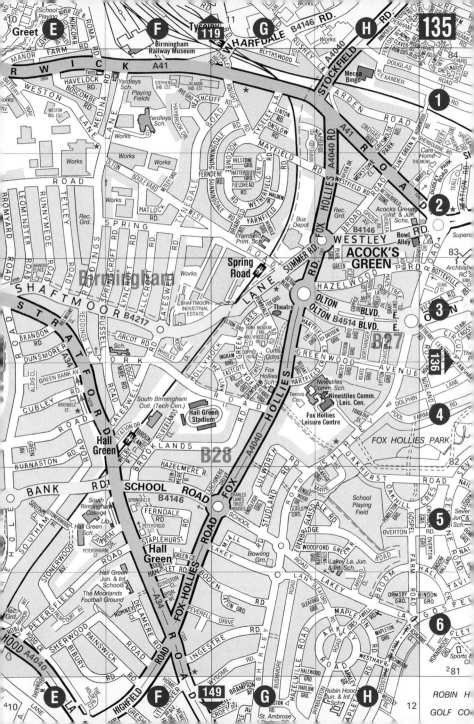

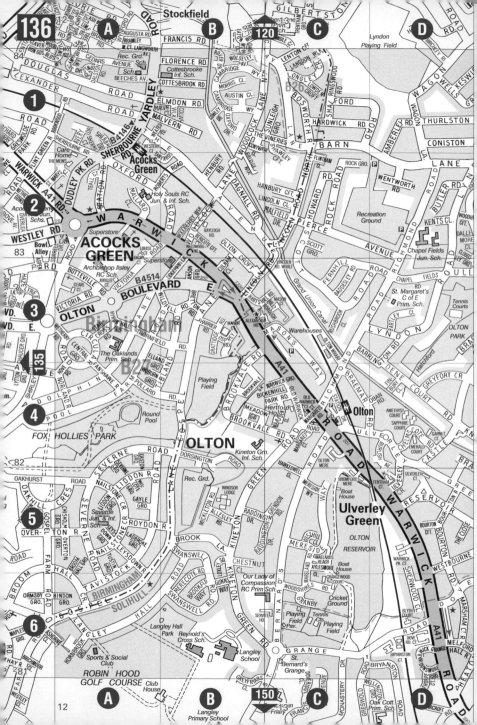

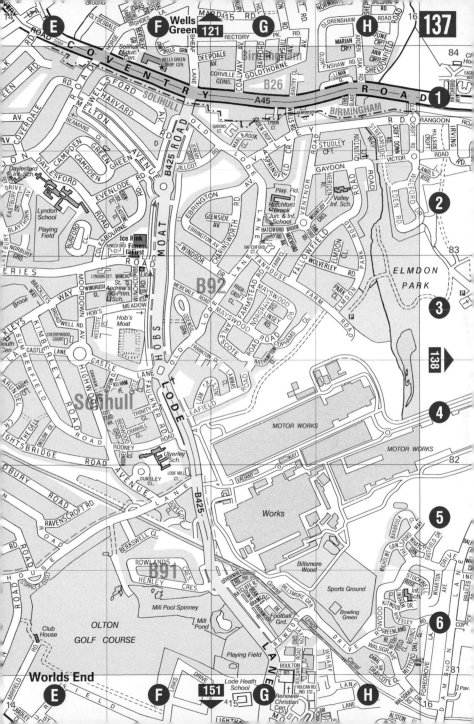

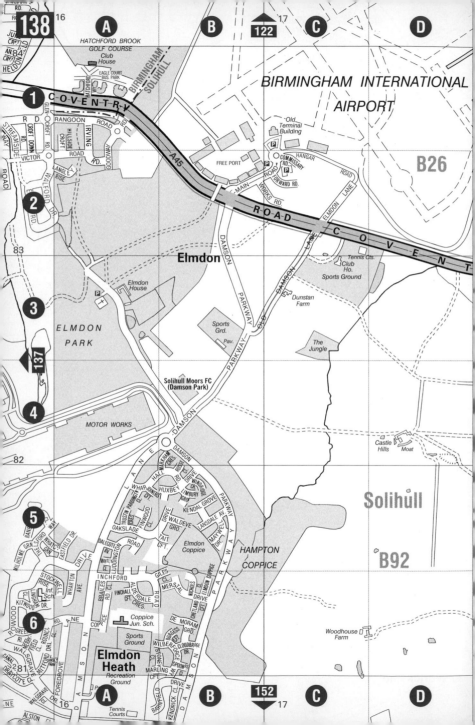

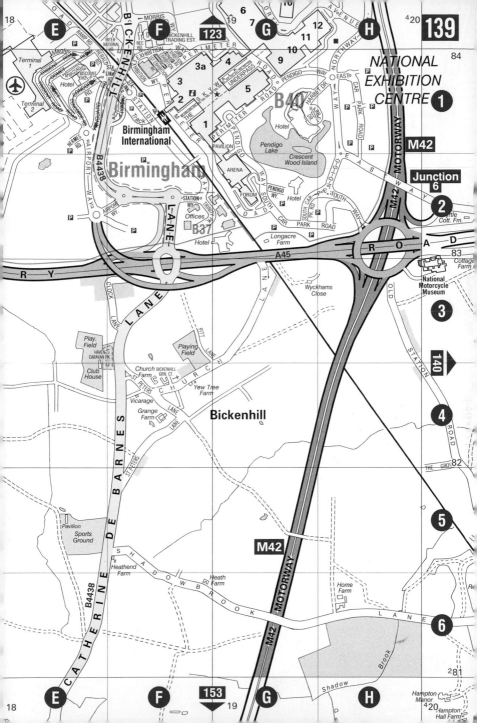

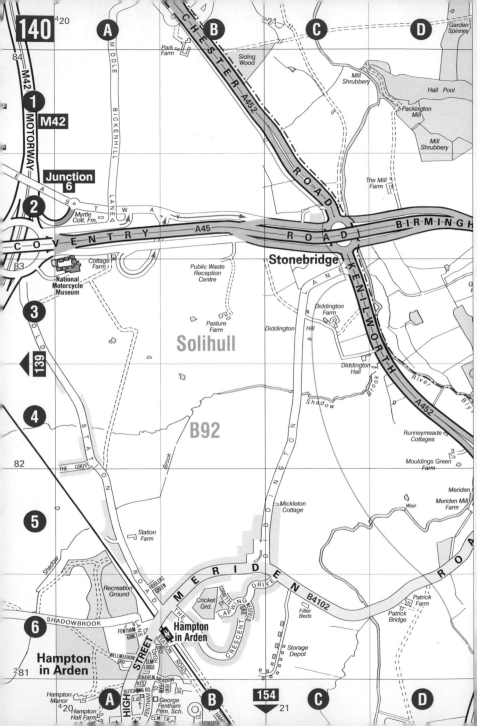

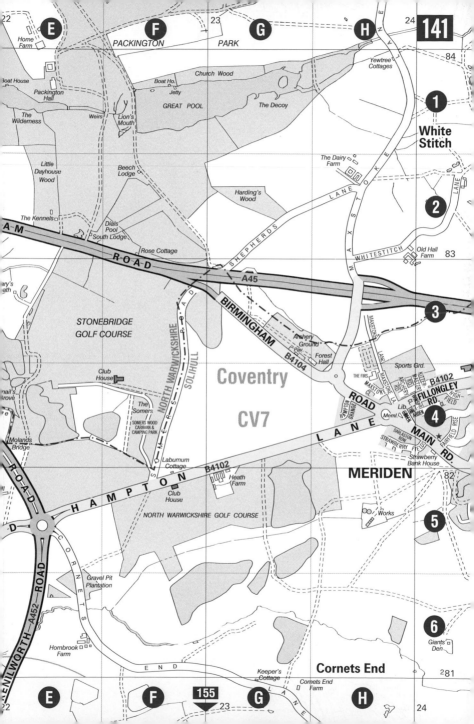

22 **E** | **F** 23 | **G** | **H** 24

PACKINGTON PARK

Home Farm

Boat House

Packington Hall

Church Wood

Boat Ho.

Jetty

GREAT POOL

The Decoy

Lion's Mouth

Weirs

The Wilderness

Little Dayhouse Wood

Beech Lodge

Harding's Wood

Yewtree Cottages

84

1

White Stitch

The Dairy Farm

2

The Kennels

Dials Pool South Lodge

Rose Cottage

A M

R O A D

A45

SHEPHERDS LANE

MAXSTOKE LANE

WHITESTITCH

Old Hall Farm 83

3

STONEBRIDGE GOLF COURSE

Club House

NORTH WARWICKSHIRE

SOLIHULL

BIRMINGHAM

B4104

Archery Ground Pav.

Forest Hall

Coventry

CV7

Sports Grd.

THE FIRS

MAXSTOKE LANE

ARCHERY RD.

MASTERSON

B4102

FILLONGLEY RD.

HIGH FIELD

4

The Somers

SOMERS WOOD CARAVAN & CAMPING PARK

Molands Bridge

Laburnum Cottage

B4102

Heath Farm

Club House

HAMPTON

L A N E

R O A D

HAMPTON ROAD

GRANGE

Lib.

Meml.

DARLASTON ROW

STRAWBERRY

FAIRFIELD RISE

MAIN RD.

Strawberry Bank House

MERIDEN 82

NORTH WARWICKSHIRE GOLF COURSE

Works

5

KENILWORTH A452 ROAD

CORNETS

Gravel Pit Plantation

Hornbrook Farm

END

6

Giants' Den

Keeper's Cottage

Cornets End Farm

Cornets End 281

22 **E** | **F** 155 ▼ 23 | **G** | **H** 24

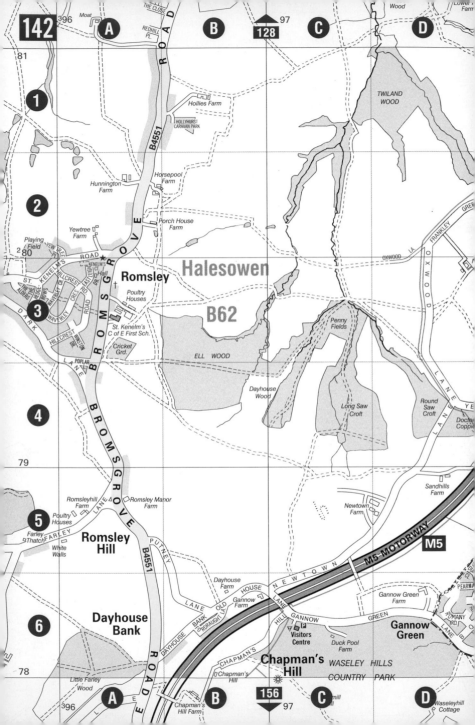

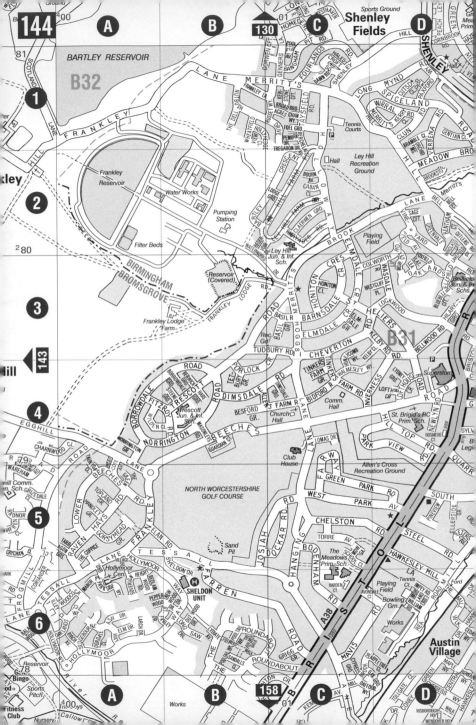

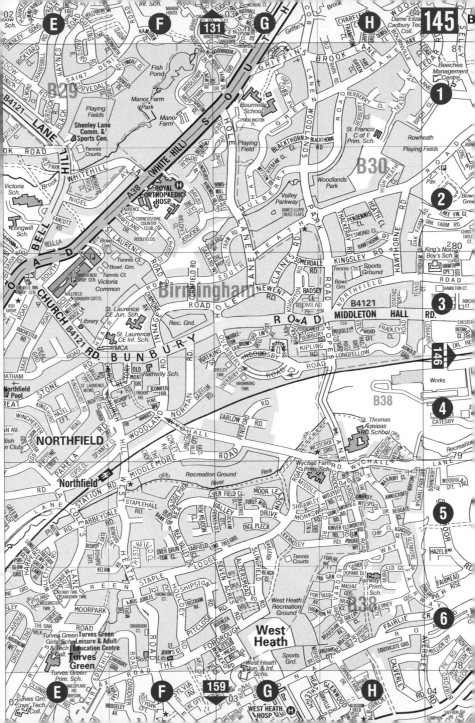

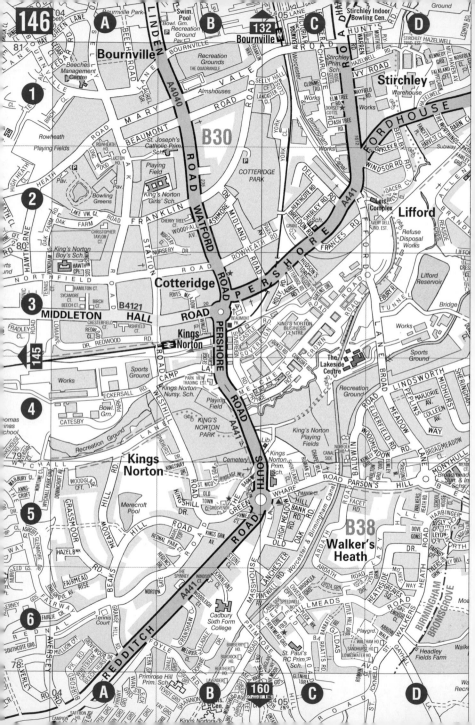

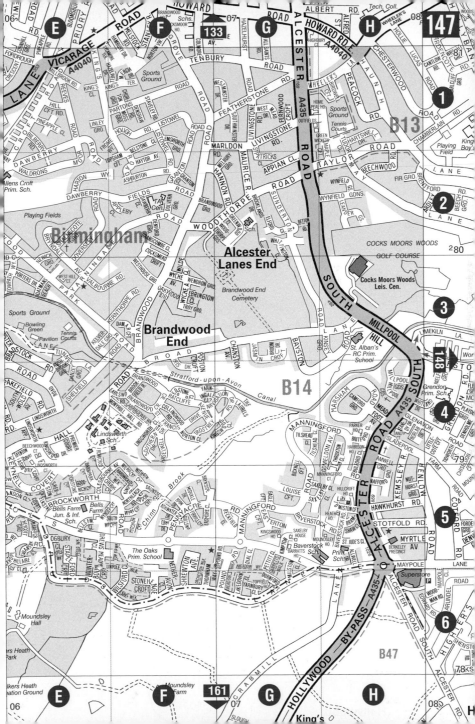

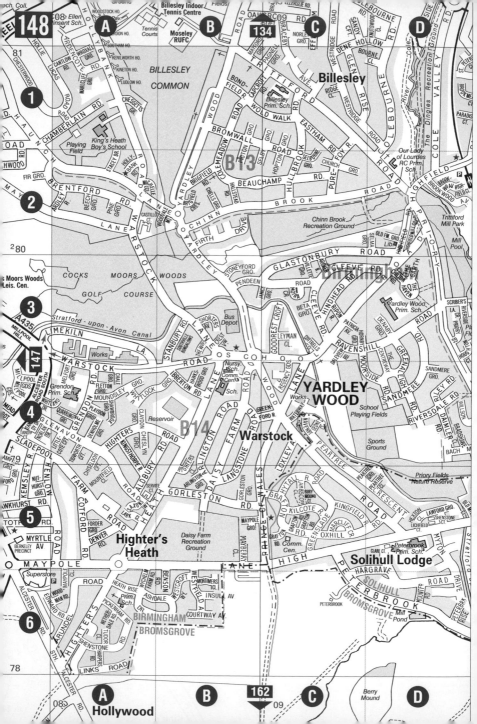

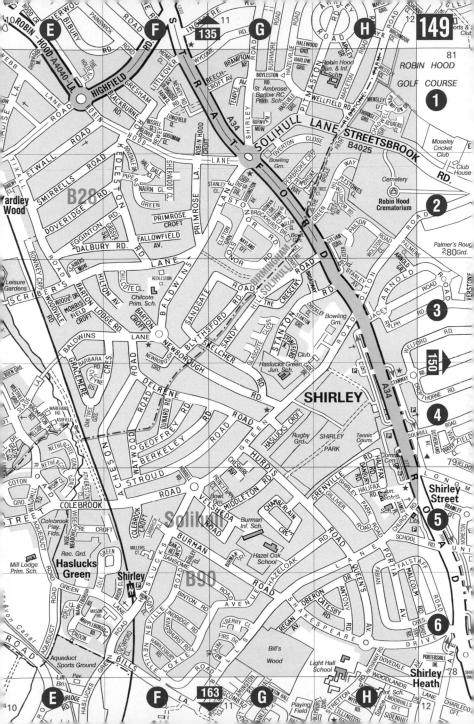

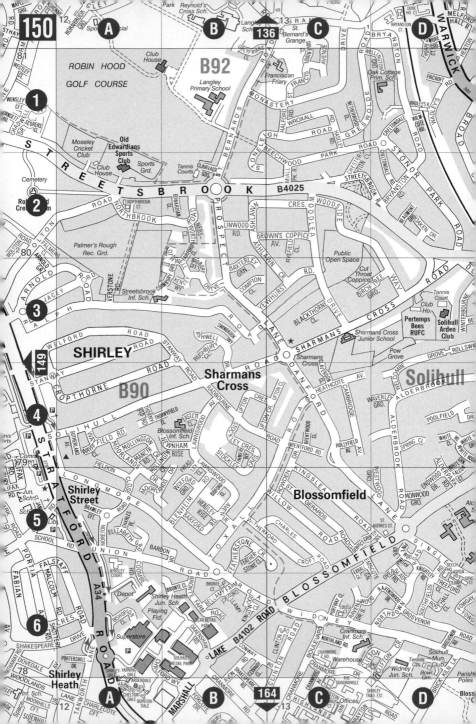

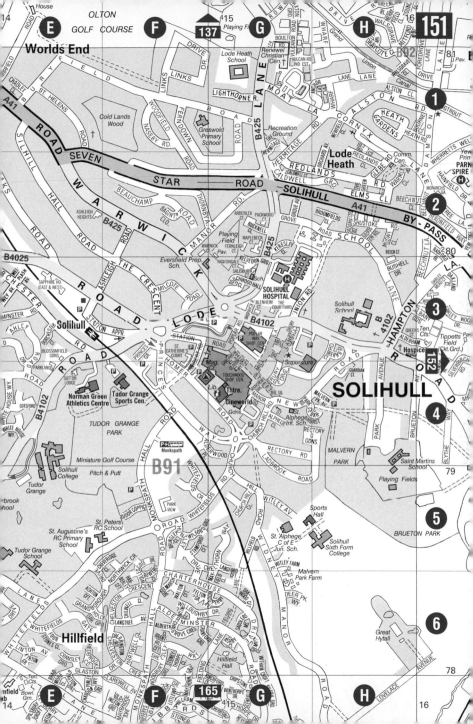

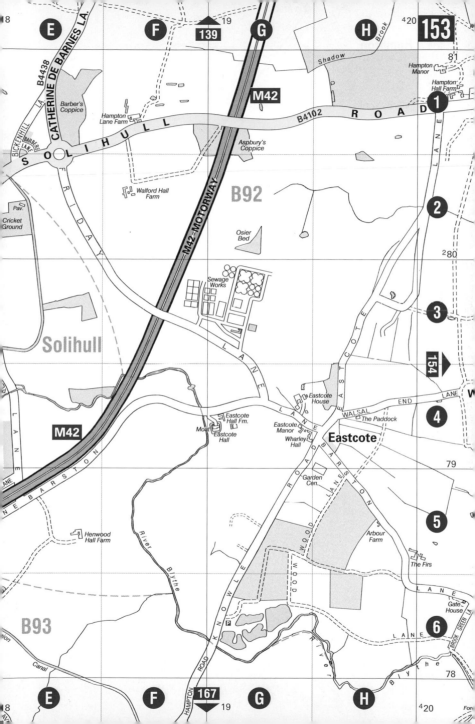

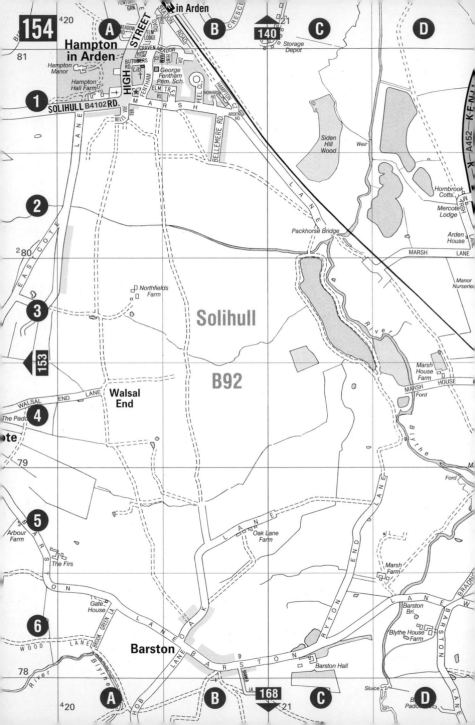

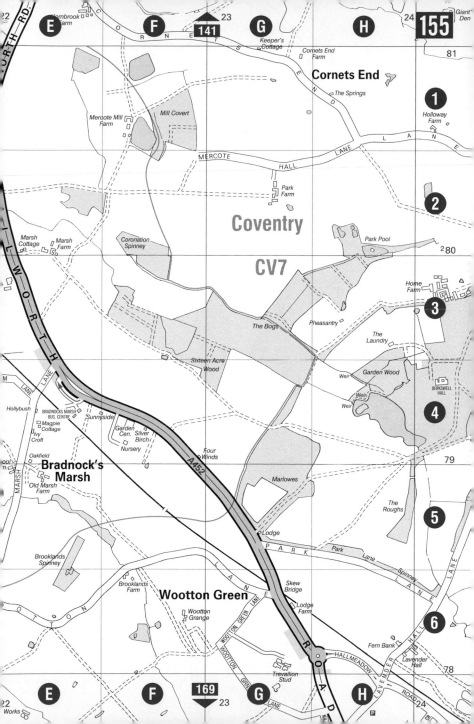

Cornets End

Coventry

CV7

Bradnock's Marsh

Wootton Green

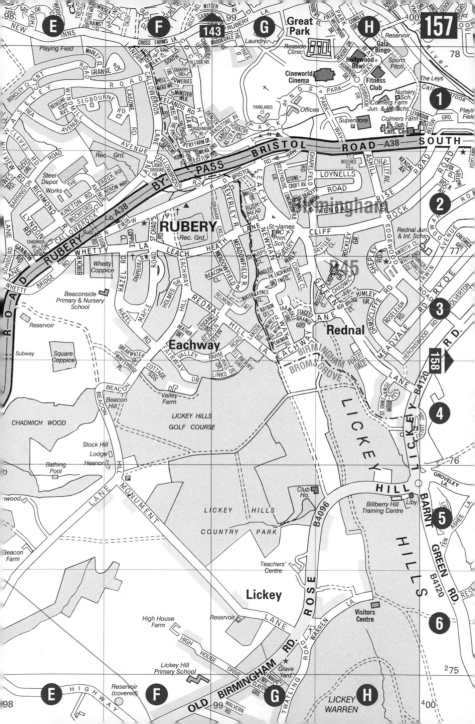

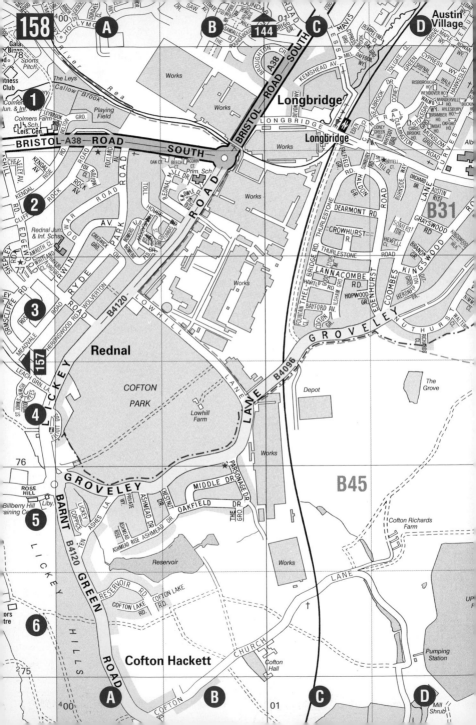

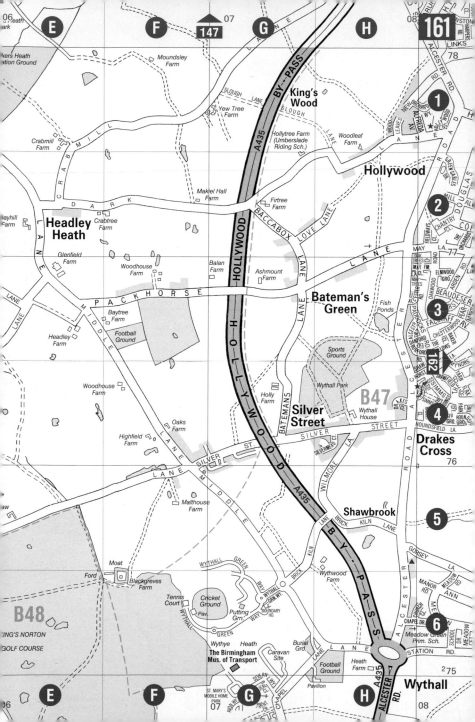

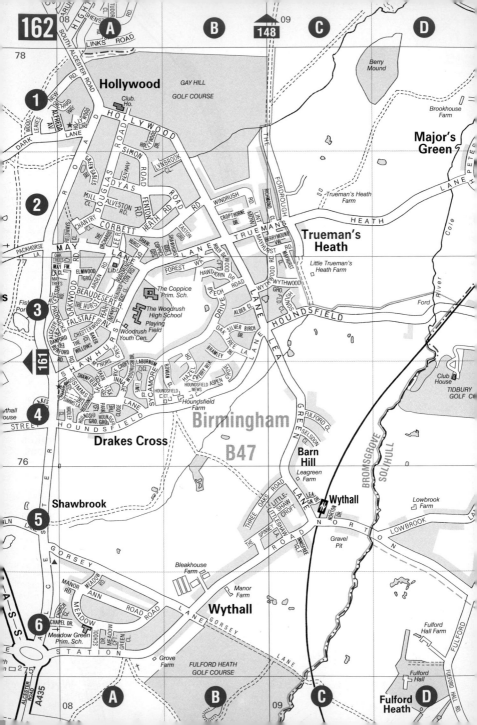

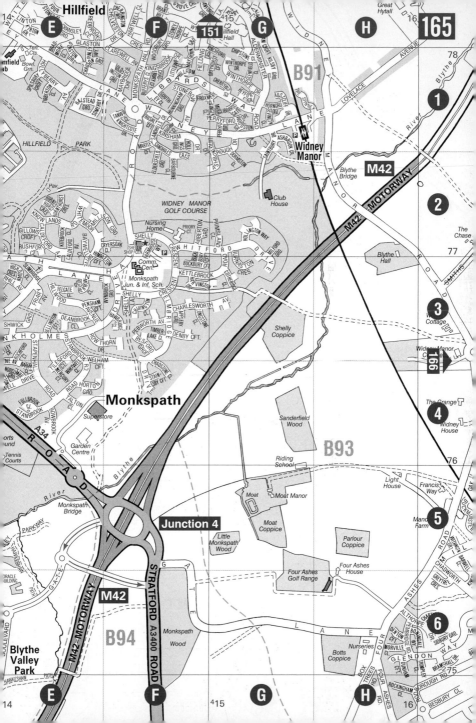

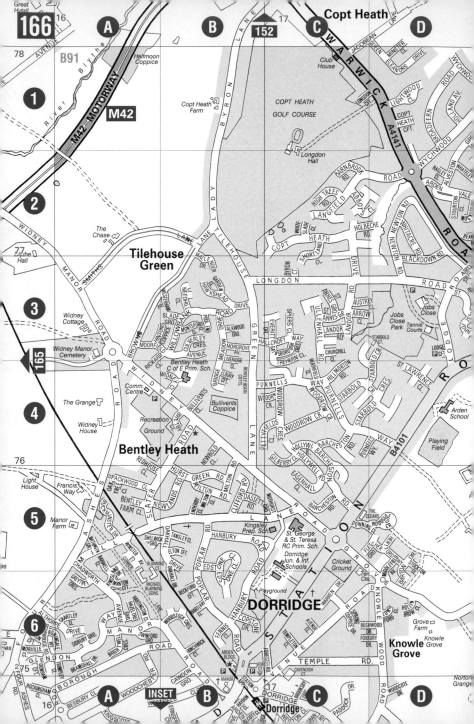

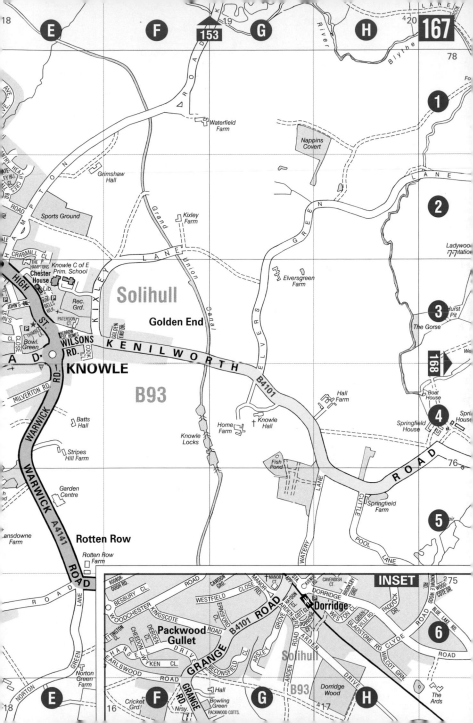

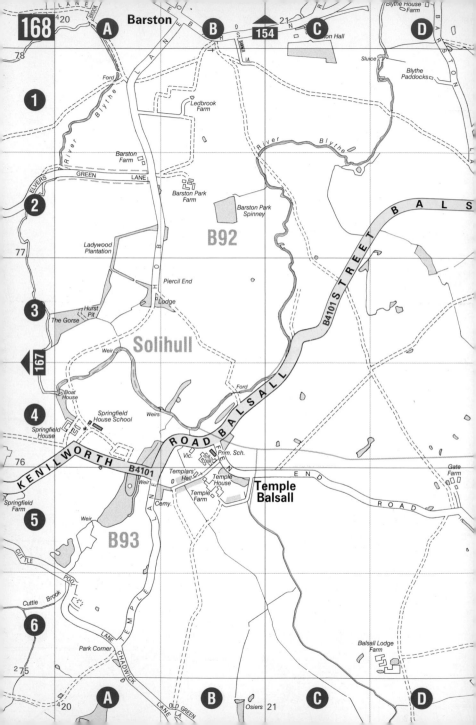

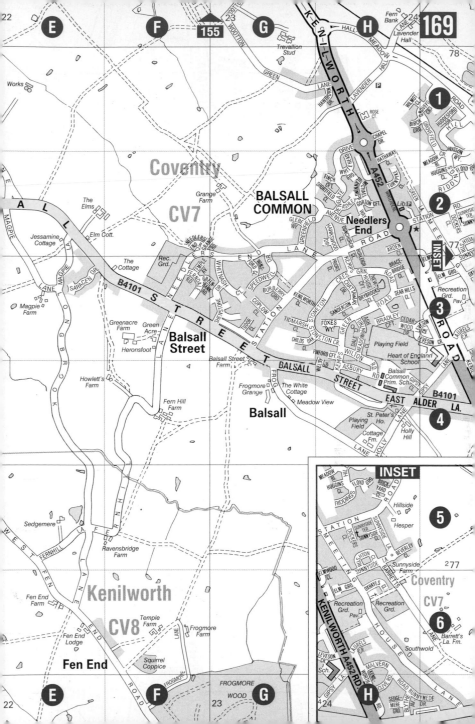

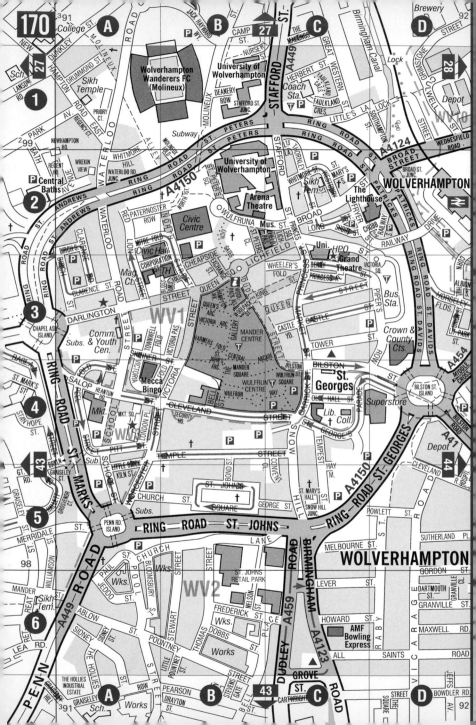

INDEX

Including Streets, Places & Areas, Industrial Estates, Selected Flats & Walkways,
Junction Names & Service Areas, Stations and Selected Places of Interest.

HOW TO USE THIS INDEX

1. Each street name is followed by its Postcode District, then by its Locality abbreviation(s) and then by its map reference;
   e.g. **Abbey Rd.** B67: Smeth . . . .2B **114** is in the B67 Postcode District and the Smethwick Locality and is to be found in
   square 2B on page **114**. The page number is shown in bold type.

2. A strict alphabetical order is followed in which Av., Rd., St., etc. (though abbreviated) are read in full and as part of the street name;
   e.g. **Ash Bri. Ct.** appears after **Ashbourne Way** but before **Ashbrook Cres.**

3. Streets and a selection of flats and walkways too small to be shown on the maps, appear in the index with the thoroughfare to which it is
   connected shown in brackets; e.g. **Abberton Ct.** B23: Erd . . . .5C **84** (off Dunlin Cl.)

4. Addresses that are in more than one part are referred to as not continuous.

5. Places and areas are shown in the index in **BLUE TYPE** and the map reference is to the actual map square in which the town centre or area is
   located and not to the place name shown on the map; e.g. **ALDRIDGE 3D 34**

6. An example of a selected place of interest is **Aston Manor Transport Mus. 6H 83**

7. An example of a station is **Acocks Green Station (Rail) . . . .1A 136.** Included are Rail **(Rail)**, Midland Metro **(MM)** and **Park & Ride**

8. Junction Names and Service Areas are shown in the index in **BOLD CAPITAL TYPE**; e.g. **BURNTWOOD JUNC. 2B 10**

9. Map references for entries that appear on large scale pages **4**, **5** & **170** are shown first, with small scale map references shown in brackets;
   e.g. **Ablow St.** WV2: Wolv 6A **170** (3G **43**)

GENERAL ABBREVIATIONS

All. : Alley	**Ent.** : Enterprise	**Mus.** : Museum
App. : Approach	**Est.** : Estate	**Nth.** : North
Arc. : Arcade	**Ests.** : Estates	**Pde.** : Parade
Av. : Avenue	**Fld.** : Field	**Pk.** : Park
Blvd. : Boulevard	**Flds.** : Fields	**Pas.** : Passage
Bri. : Bridge	**Gdns.** : Gardens	**Pl.** : Place
Bldg. : Building	**Ga.** : Gate	**Pct.** : Precinct
Bldgs. : Buildings	**Gt.** : Great	**Res.** : Residential
Bungs. : Bungalows	**Grn.** : Green	**Ri.** : Rise
Bus. : Business	**Gro.** : Grove	**Rd.** : Road
Cvn. : Caravan	**Hgts.** : Heights	**Rdbt.** : Roundabout
C'way. : Causeway	**Ho.** : House	**Shop.** : Shopping
Cen. : Centre	**Ho's.** : Houses	**Sth.** : South
Chu. : Church	**Ind.** : Industrial	**Sq.** : Square
Circ. : Circle	**Info.** : Information	**Sta.** : Station
Cir. : Circus	**Intl.** : International	**St.** : Street
Cl. : Close	**Junc.** : Junction	**Ter.** : Terrace
Coll. : College	**La.** : Lane	**Twr.** : Tower
Comn. : Common	**Lit.** : Little	**Trad.** : Trading
Cnr. : Corner	**Lwr.** : Lower	**Up.** : Upper
Cott. : Cottage	**Mnr.** : Manor	**Va.** : Vale
Cotts. : Cottages	**Mans.** : Mansions	**Vw.** : View
Ct. : Court	**Mkt.** : Market	**Vs.** : Villas
Cres. : Crescent	**Mdw.** : Meadow	**Vis.** : Visitors
Cft. : Croft	**Mdws.** : Meadows	**Wlk.** : Walk
Dr. : Drive	**M.** : Mews	**W.** : West
E. : East	**Mt.** : Mount	**Yd.** : Yard

LOCALITY ABBREVIATIONS

A Grn : **Acock's Green**	B'hth : **Blackheath**	C Hay : **Cheslyn Hay**
Alb : **Albrighton**	Blox : **Bloxwich**	Ches G : **Cheswick Green**
A'rdge : **Aldridge**	Bly P : **Blythe Valley Park**	Clay : **Clayhanger**
A'chu : **Alvechurch**	Bold : **Boldmere**	Cod : **Codsall**
Amb : **Amblecote**	Bord G : **Bordesley Green**	Cod W : **Codsall Wood**
Aston : **Aston**	B'vlle : **Bournville**	Coft H : **Cofton Hackett**
Bal C : **Balsall Common**	Brie H : **Brierley Hill**	Col : **Coleshill**
Bal H : **Balsall Heath**	B'frd : **Brinsford**	Cose : **Coseley**
B Grn : **Barnt Green**	Bwnhls : **Brownhills**	Coven : **Coven**
Bars : **Barston**	Burn : **Burntwood**	Cov H : **Coven Heath**
Bart G : **Bartley Green**	Bush : **Bushbury**	Crad : **Cradley**
Bass P : **Bassetts Pole**	Cann : **Cannock**	Crad H : **Cradley Heath**
Belb : **Belbroughton**	Can : **Canwell**	Curd : **Curdworth**
Ben H : **Bentley Heath**	Cas B : **Castle Bromwich**	Darl : **Darlaston**
Berk : **Berkswell**	Cas V : **Castle Vale**	Dic H : **Dickens Heath**
Bick : **Bickenhill**	Cath B : **Catherine-de-Barnes**	Dorr : **Dorridge**
Bilb : **Bilbrook**	Cats : **Catshill**	Dray B : **Drayton Bassett**
Bils : **Bilston**	C'wich : **Chadwich**	Dud : **Dudley**
Birm : **Birmingham**	Chase : **Chasetown**	Earls : **Earlswood**
Birm A : **Birmingham International Airport**	Chel W : **Chelmsley Wood**	Edg : **Edgbaston**

Locality Abbreviations

Erd : **Erdington**
Ess : **Essington**
E'shll : **Ettingshall**
F'stne : **Featherstone**
Fen E : **Fen End**
Foot : **Footherley**
F'bri : **Fordbridge**
F'hses : **Fordhouses**
Forh : **Forhill**
Four O : **Four Oaks**
Fran : **Frankley**
Gorn : **Gornalwood**
Gt Barr : **Great Barr**
Gt Wyr : **Great Wyrley**
Hag : **Hagley**
Hale : **Halesowen**
Hall G : **Hall Green**
Hamm : **Hammerwich**
H Ard : **Hampton in Arden**
Hand : **Handsworth**
Harb : **Harborne**
Head H : **Headley Heath**
Hilt : **Hilton**
Himl : **Himley**
Hints : **Hints**
Hock : **Hockley**
H'ley H : **Hockley Heath**
Hodg H : **Hodge Hill**
H'wd : **Hollywood**
Hopw : **Hopwood**
Hunn : **Hunnington**
I'ley : **Iverley**
K Hth : **King's Heath**
K'hrst : **Kingshurst**
K Nor : **King's Norton**
K'sdng : **Kingstanding**
K'wfrd : **Kingswinford**
Kinv : **Kinver**
Kitts G : **Kitt's Green**
Know : **Knowle**
Lea M : **Lea Marston**
Lick : **Lickey**
Lit As : **Little Aston**
Lit H : **Little Hay**
Lit P : **Little Packington**
Lit Wyr : **Little Wyrley**
Longb : **Longbridge**
Lwr G : **Lower Gornal**
Lwr P : **Lower Penn**
Loz : **Lozells**

Lutley : **Lutley**
L Ash : **Lydiate Ash**
Lye : **Lye**
Lynn : **Lynn**
Maj G : **Major's Green**
Marlb : **Marlbrook**
Mars G : **Marston Green**
Mer : **Meriden**
Midd : **Middleton**
Min : **Minworth**
M'path : **Monkspath**
Mose : **Moseley**
Mox : **Moxley**
Muck C : **Muckley Corner**
Nat E C : **National Exhibition Centre**
Nech : **Nechells**
Neth : **Netherton**
New O : **New Oscott**
N'fld : **Northfield**
Nort C : **Norton Canes**
Oaken : **Oaken**
O'bry : **Oldbury**
Old H : **Old Hill**
Olton : **Olton**
Oxl : **Oxley**
Patt : **Pattingham**
Pedm : **Pedmore**
Pels : **Pelsall**
Pend : **Pendeford**
Penn : **Penn**
P'ntt : **Pensnett**
P Barr : **Perry Barr**
Pert : **Perton**
Quar B : **Quarry Bank**
Quin : **Quinton**
Redn : **Rednal**
Roms : **Romsley**
R'ley : **Roughley**
Row R : **Rowley Regis**
Rub : **Rubery**
Rus : **Rushall**
Salt : **Saltley**
Sed : **Sedgley**
Seis : **Seisdon**
S Oak : **Selly Oak**
S End : **Shard End**
Share : **Shareshill**
Sheld : **Sheldon**
S'fld : **Shelfield**
Shen W : **Shenstone Woodend**

Shir : **Shirley**
Small H : **Small Heath**
Smeth : **Smethwick**
Sol : **Solihull**
S'brk : **Sparkbrook**
S'hll : **Sparkhill**
Stech : **Stechford**
Stir : **Stirchley**
Ston : **Stonnall**
Stourb : **Stourbridge**
Stourt : **Stourton**
S'tly : **Streetly**
S Cold : **Sutton Coldfield**
Swind : **Swindon**
Tett : **Tettenhall**
Tid G : **Tidbury Green**
Tip : **Tipton**
Tiv : **Tividale**
Tres : **Trescott**
Try : **Trysull**
Tys : **Tyseley**
Up Gor : **Upper Gornal**
W Hth : **Wall Heath**
Walm : **Walmley**
Wals : **Walsall**
Wals W : **Walsall Wood**
W End : **Ward End**
Wat O : **Water Orton**
W'bry : **Wednesbury**
Wed : **Wednesfield**
W'frd : **Weeford**
W Cas : **Weoley Castle**
W Brom : **West Bromwich**
Wild : **Wildmoor**
W'hall : **Willenhall**
Win G : **Winson Green**
Wis : **Wishaw**
Witt : **Witton**
Woll : **Wollaston**
W'cte : **Wollescote**
Wolv : **Wolverhampton**
Wom : **Wombourne**
Word : **Wordsley**
Wrot P : **Wrottesley Park**
W Grn : **Wylde Green**
Wyt : **Wythall**
Yard : **Yardley**
Yard W : **Yardley Wood**

3B Business Village B21: Hand 2H 99

A

A1 Trad. Est. B66: Smeth 2F 99
Aaron Manby Ct. DY4: Tip 5H 61
Abacus Bldg. B12: Birm 2A 118
Abberley Cl. B63: Hale 3H 127
Abberley Ind. Cen. B66: Smeth 4H 99
Abberley Rd. B68: O'bry 3H 113
  DY3: Lwr G 3G 75
Abberley St. B66: Smeth 4H 99
  DY2: Dud 1E 95
Abberton Cl. B63: Hale 2C 128
Abberton Ct. *B23: Erd* *5C 84*
  (off Dunlin Cl.)
Abberton Gro. B90: M'path 2F 165
Abbess Gro. B25: Yard 2C 120
Abbey Cl. B71: W Brom 2A 80
Abbey Ct. B68: O'bry 5H 97
Abbey Cres. B63: Crad 1F 127
  B68: O'bry 3B 114
Abbeydale Rd. B31: N'fld 5E 145
Abbey Dr. WS3: Pels 2E 21
Abbeyfield Rd. B23: Erd 6D 68
  WV10: Bush 3A 16
Abbey Gdns. B67: Smeth 2C 114
Abbey Mans. B24: Erd 1H 85

Abbey Rd. B17: Harb 6H 115
  B23: Erd 5D 84
  B63: Crad 1E 127
  B67: Smeth 2B 114
  DY2: Dud 3F 95
  DY3: Gorn 4G 75
Abbey Sq. WS3: Blox 5E 19
Abbey St. B18: Hock 4C 100
  DY3: Gorn 4G 75
Abbey St. Nth. B18: Hock 4C 100
Abbots Cl. B93: Know 2C 166
  WS4: Rus 3G 33
Abbotsford Av. B43: Gt Barr 3B 66
Abbotsford Dr. DY1: Dud 2A 94
Abbotsford Rd. B11: S'brk 5B 118
Abbots Rd. B14: K Hth 6G 133
Abbots Way B18: Hock 3D 100
  WV3: Wolv 2C 42
Abbott Rd. B63: Hale 5E 127
Abbotts M. DY5: Brie H 2H 109
Abbotts Pl. WS3: Blox 6B 20
Abbotts Rd. B24: Erd 6F 85
Abbotts St. WS3: Blox 5B 20
Abdon Av. B29: S Cas 6F 131
Aberdeen St. B18: Win G 5A 100
Aberford Cl. WV12: W'hall 5D 30
Abigails Cl. B26: Sheld 4F 121
Abingdon Cl. WV1: Wolv 1D 44
Abingdon Rd. B23: Erd 6B 68
  DY2: Neth 6F 95
  WS3: Blox 5F 19
  WV1: Wolv 1D 44

Abingdon Way B35: Cas V 4E 87
  WS3: Blox 5F 19
Ablewell St. WS1: Wals 2D 48
Ablow St. WV2: Wolv 6A 170 (3G 43)
Abney Dr. WV14: Cose 4B 60
Abney Gro. B44: K'sdng 3B 68
Aboyne Cl. B5: Edg 5F 117
Ab Row B4: Birm 2H 5 (6H 101)
Acacia Av. B37: K'hrst 3B 106
  WS5: Wals 1E 65
Acacia Cl. B37: K'hrst 3B 106
  B69: Tiv 5B 78
  DY2: Dud 4C 76
Acacia Cres. WV8: Bilb 3H 13
Acacia Dr. WV14: Cose 6C 60
Acacia Rd. B30: B'vlle 5A 132
Acacia Ter. B12: Bal H 6A 118
Academy, The
  B13: Mose 3A 134
Accord M. WS10: Darl 4D 46
Ace Bus. Pk. B33: Kitts G 1H 121
Acfold Rd. B20: Hand 2A 82
Acheson Rd. B28: Hall G 5F 149
  B90: Hall G, Shir 5F 149
Achilles Cl. WS6: Gt Wyr 4F 7
  (not continuous)
Ackers, The (Activity Cen.) 5D 118
Ackleton Gdns. WV3: Wolv 4D 42
Ackleton Gro. B29: W Cas 5D 130
ACOCKS GREEN 2A 136
Acocks Green Bowl 2H 135
Acocks Green Station (Rail) 1A 136

Acorn Cl. B27: A Grn 6H 119
  B30: B'ville 5A 132
  B70: W Brom 4H 79
  WS6: Gt Wyr 4G 7
Acorn Ct. B45: Redn 2B 158
Acorn Gdns. B30: Stir 5C 132
Acorn Gro. B1: Birm 6D 100
  DY8: Word 2C 108
  WV8: Cod 5E 13
Acorn Rd. B62: B'hth 3C 112
  WV11: Wed 6A 18
Acorn St. WV13: W'hall 1C 46
Acre Ri. WV12: W'hall 4B 30
Acres, The WV3: Wolv 2A 42
Acres Rd. DY5: Quar B 3H 109
Acton Dr. DY3: Lwr G 4F 75
Acton Gro. B44: K'sdng 2A 68
  WV14: Bils 1D 60
Adam Ct. B63: Hale 1H 127
Adams Brook Dr. B32: Bart G 4H 129
Adams Cl. B66: Smeth 2B 98
  DY4: Tip 4H 61
Adam's Hill B32: Bart G 4H 129
Adams Rd. WS8: Bwnhls 2C 22
  WV3: Wolv 4A 42
Adams St. B7: Birm 4H 101
  B70: W Brom 4H 79
  WS2: Wals 1B 48
Ada Rd. B9: Birm 1B 118
  B25: Yard 5H 119
  B66: Smeth 6F 99
Ada Wrighton Cl. WV12: W'hall 2C 30
Addenbrooke Ct. B64: Old H 3H 111
Addenbrooke Dr. B73: W Grn 3H 69
Addenbrooke Pl. WS10: Darl 4D 46
Addenbrooke Rd. B67: Smeth 6D 98
Addenbrooke St. WS3: Blox 2A 32
  WS10: Darl 3D 46
Addenbrook Way DY4: Tip 5D 62
Adderley Gdns. B8: Salt 4D 102
           (not continuous)
Adderley Pk. Cl. B8: Salt 5E 103
Adderley Park Station (Rail) 6D 102
Adderley Rd. B8: Salt 6C 102
Adderley Rd. Sth. B8: Salt 6C 102
Adderley St. B9: Birm 2A 118
Adderley Trad. Est. B8: Salt 5C 102
Addington Way WV4: Tiv 5D 78
Addison Cl. WS10: W'bry 3C 64
Addison Cft. DY3: Lwr G 2E 75
Addison Gro. WV11: Wed 6D 16
Addison Pl. B46: Wat O 4D 88
  WV14: Bils 4A 46
Addison Rd. B7: Nech 1C 102
  B14: K Hth 6G 133
  DY5: Brie H 1F 109
  WS10: W'bry 3C 64
  WV3: Wolv 3D 42
Addison St. WS10: W'bry 3F 63
Addison Ter. WS10: W'bry 3F 63
Adelaide Av. B70: W Brom 6G 63
Adelaide St. B12: Birm 3H 117
  DY5: Brie H 6H 93
Adelaide Twr. B34: S End 4G 105
        (off Packington Av.)
Adelphi Ct. DY5: Brie H 1H 109
       (off The Promenade)
Adey Rd. WV11: Wed 1H 29
Adkins La. B67: Smeth 2D 114
Admington Rd. B33: Sheld 3G 121
Admiral Pl. B13: Mose 1H 133
Admirals Way B65: Row R 1B 112
Adrian Boult Hall 4C 4 (1F 117)
Adrian Ct. B24: Erd 1H 85
Adrian Cft. B13: Mose 4C 134
Adria Rd. B11: S'hll 1B 134
Adshead Rd. DY2: Dud 2E 95
Adstone Gro. B31: N'fld 6D 144
Advent Gdns. B70: W Brom 4H 79
         (off Brook St.)
Adwalton Rd. WV6: Pert 6F 25
Agenoria Dr. DY8: Stourb 6D 108
Ainsdale Cl. DY8: Stourb 3D 124

Ainsdale Gdns. B24: Erd 2A 86
  B63: Hale 3F 127
Ainsworth Rd. B31: N'fld 5H 145
  WV10: Bush 2A 16
Aintree Gro. B34: S End 3A 106
Aintree Rd. WV10: F'hses 3H 15
Aintree Way DY1: Dud 4A 76
Aire Cft. B31: N'fld 6F 145
Airfield Dr. WS9: A'rdge 6A 34
Air Ministry Cotts. B35: Cas V 5D 86
Airport Way B26: Birm A 1E 139
Ajax Cl. WS6: Gt Wyr 4F 7
Akrill Cl. B70: W Brom 2H 79
Akrill Cott. Homes, The
  B70: W Brom 2H 79
Alameda Gdns. WV6: Tett 3D 26
Alamein Rd. WV13: W'hall 2G 45
Alasdair Ho. B17: Harb 6F 115
Albany Ct. B62: Quin 4G 113
       (off Binswood Rd.)
Albany Cres. WV14: Bils 5E 45
Albany Gdns. B91: Sol 3A 152
Albany Gro. DY6: K'wfrd 2C 92
  WV11: Ess 6C 18
Albany Ho. B34: S End 2F 105
Albany Rd. B17: Harb 5G 115
  WV1: Wolv 1F 43
Albemarle Rd. DY8: Stourb 3D 124
Albermarle Rd. DY6: K'wfrd 4E 93
Albert Av. B12: Bal H 5A 118
Albert Clarke Dr. WV12: W'hall 2C 30
Albert Cl. WV8: Cod 3E 13
Albert Dr. B63: Hale 3H 127
  DY3: Swind 5E 73
Albert Ho. WS10: Darl 5C 46
        (off Factory St.)
Albert Rd. B6: Aston 1F 101
  B14: K Hth 6G 133
  B17: Harb 6F 115
  B21: Hand 6A 82
  B23: Erd 4D 84
  B33: Stech 1B 120
  B63: Hale 3H 127
  B68: O'bry 3A 114
  WV6: Wolv 6D 26
Albert Smith Pl. B65: Row R 5A 96
Albert St. B4: Birm 4F 5 (1G 117)
  B5: Birm 3G 5 (6H 101)
  B69: O'bry 1G 97
  B70: W Brom 6A 80
  DY4: Tip 5H 61
  DY5: P'ntt 2H 93
  DY6: W Hth 1H 91
  DY8: Stourb 6D 108
  DY9: Lye 6A 110
  WS2: Wals 1C 48
  WS10: W'bry 3F 63
Albert St. E. B69: O'bry 2H 97
Albert Wlk. B17: Harb 6G 115
Albion Av. WV13: W'hall 1C 46
Albion Bus. Pk. B66: Smeth 1C 98
Albion Fld. Dr. B71: W Brom 3B 80
Albion Ho. B70: W Brom 5A 80
Albion Ind. Est. B70: W Brom 5G 79
Albion Ind. Est. Rd. B70: W Brom . . .5F 79
Albion Pde. DY6: W Hth 1H 91
Albion Rd. B11: S'brk 6D 118
  B21: Hand 6H 81
  B70: W Brom 5F 79
        (not continuous)
  B71: W Brom 1F 99
  WS8: Bwnhls 5A 10
  WV13: W'hall 1B 46
Albion Rdbt. B70: W Brom 3F 79
Albion St. B1: Birm 2A 4 (6D 100)
  B69: O'bry 6E 79
  DY4: Tip 2H 77
  DY5: Brie H 6H 93
  DY6: W Hth 6H 73
  WV1: Wolv 3D 170 (1H 43)
  WV13: W'hall 1C 46
  WV14: Bils 5G 45
Albion Ter. B46: Wat O 4D 88
       (off St Pauls Ct.)

Alborn Cres. B38: K Nor 1H 159
Albright Ho. B69: O'bry 5E 97
       (off Kempsey Cl.)
Albrighton Ho. B20: Hand 4B 82
Albrighton Rd. B63: Hale 2G 127
  WV7: Alb 5A 12
Albright Rd. B68: O'bry 5B 98
Albutts Rd. WS8: Bwnhls 2F 9
  WS11: Bwnhls 2F 9
Alcester Dr. B73: New O 2D 68
  WV13: W'hall 2F 45
Alcester Gdns. B14: K Hth 6G 133
ALCESTER LANES END 2G 147
Alcester Rd. B13: Mose 3G 133
  B47: H'wd 6A 148
  B47: H'wd, Wyt 6H 161
Alcester Rd. Sth. B14: K Hth 6G 133
        (Addison Rd.)
  B14: K Hth 5H 147
        (Maypole La.)
Alcester St. B12: Birm 6H 5 (3H 117)
Alcombe Gro. B33: Stech 1C 120
Alcott Cl. B93: Dorr 6G 167
Alcott Gro. B33: Kitts G 6H 105
Alcott La. B37: Mars G 3B 122
Alcove, The WS3: Blox 5B 20
Aldbourne Way B38: K Nor 2H 159
Aldbury Rd. B14: K Hth 5A 148
Aldeburgh Cl. WS3: Blox 4G 19
Aldeford Dr. DY5: Brie H 3H 109
Alderbrook Cl. DY3: Sed 4F 59
Alderbrook Rd. B91: Sol 4D 150
Alder Cl. B47: H'wd 3B 162
  B76: Walm 6C 70
Alder Coppice DY3: Sed 3G 59
Alder Cres. WS5: Wals 1F 65
Alder Dale WV3: Wolv 2C 42
Alderdale Av. DY3: Sed 2G 59
Alderdale Cres. B92: Sol 6A 138
Alder Dr. B37: Chel W 2D 122
Alderflat Pl. B7: Birm 4C 102
Alderford Cl. WV8: Pend 1D 26
Alder Gro. B62: Quin 5E 113
Alderham Cl. B91: Sol 3H 151
Alderhithe Gro. B74: Lit As 6B 36
Alder La. B30: B'vile 1G 145
  CV7: Bal C 4H 169
Alderlea Cl. DY8: Stourb 3E 125
Alderley Cres. WS3: Wals 4C 32
Alderman Bowen Leisure Cen. 6G 103
Alderminster Rd. B91: Sol 6F 151
Aldermore Dr. B75: S Cold 5D 54
Alderney Gdns. B38: K Nor 6H 145
Alderpark Rd. B91: Sol 4D 150
Alderpits Rd. B34: S End 2H 105
       (not continuous)
Alder Rd. B12: Bal H 1A 134
  DY6: K'wfrd 4D 92
  WS10: W'bry 5G 47
Alders, The B62: Roms 3A 142
Aldersea Dr. B6: Aston 2H 101
Aldershaw Rd. B26: Yard 6C 120
Aldershaws B90: Dic H 4G 163
Aldersley Av. WV6: Tett 2C 26
Aldersley Cl. WV6: Tett 2D 26
Aldersley High School Sports Cen. . .6B 14
Aldersley Leisure Village 3D 26
Aldersley Rd. WV6: Tett 4C 26
Aldersley Stadium 3D 26
Aldersmead Rd. B31: N'fld 5G 145
Alderson Rd. B8: Salt 5F 103
Alderton Cl. B91: Sol 6F 151
Alderton Dr. WV3: Wolv 3C 42
Alder Way B74: S'tly 3G 51
Alderwood Pl. B91: Sol 4F 151
Alderwood Pct. DY3: Sed 4G 59
Alderwood Ri. DY3: Up Gor 2H 75
Aldgate Dr. DY5: Brie H 4G 109
Aldgate Gro. B19: Birm 4F 101
Aldis Cl. B28: Hall G 4E 135
  WS2: Wals 4G 47
Aldis Rd. WS2: Wals 4G 47
ALDRIDGE 3D 34

Aldridge By-Pass WS9: A'rdge 4D 34
Aldridge Cl. B68: O'bry 5A 98
 DY8: Word 3C 108
Aldridge Rd. B44: Gt Barr, P Barr 3E 67
 B68: O'bry 3H 113
 B74: Lit As 4H 35
 B74: S'tly 2F 51
 WS4: Wals 6G 33
 WS9: A'rdge 4H 35
Aldridge Sailing Club 1A 34
Aldridge St. WS10: Darl 4D 46
Aldridge Youth Theatre 3D 34
Aldwych Cl. WS9: A'rdge 1D 34
Aldwyck Dr. WV3: Wolv 3G 41
Aldwyn Av. B13: Mose 3H 133
Alexander Gdns. B42: P Barr 4F 83
Alexander Hill DY5: Quar B 3B 110
Alexander Ind. Pk.
 WV14: Bils 1E 61
Alexander Rd. B27: A Grn 1H 135
 B67: Smeth 1C 114
 WS2: Wals 1F 47
 WV8: Bilb 4A 14
Alexander Ter. B67: Smeth 3D 98
Alexander Way B8: Salt 6F 103
Alexandra Av. B21: Hand 2H 99
Alexandra Ct. DY3: Gorn 4G 75
 (off Redhall Rd.)
Alexandra Cres. B71: W Brom 5C 64
Alexandra Ho. B27: A Grn 3B 136
Alexandra Ind. Est. DY4: Tip 1A 78
Alexandra Pl. DY1: Dud 3D 76
 WV14: Bils 5F 45
Alexandra Rd. B5: Edg 5G 117
 B21: Hand 2H 99
 B30: Stir 1C 146
 B63: Hale 2H 127
 DY4: Tip 2H 77
 WS1: Wals 4C 48
 WS10: Darl 5E 47
 WV4: Penn 6E 43
Alexandra St. DY1: Dud 6D 76
 WV3: Wolv 2F 43
Alexandra Theatre 5D 4 (1F 117)
Alexandra Way B69: Tiv 5A 78
 WS9: A'rdge 4D 34
Alford Cl. B45: Redn 2A 158
Alfreda Av. B47: H'wd 1H 161
Alfred Gunn Ho. B68: O'bry 5H 97
Alfred Knight Way
 B15: Birm 3E 117
Alfred Rd. B11: S'hll 6B 118
 B21: Hand 1A 100
Alfred Squire Rd. WV11: Wed 4E 29
Alfred St. B6: Aston 1B 102
 B12: Bal H 6B 118
 B14: K Hth 6H 133
 B66: Smeth 2G 99
 B70: W Brom 4B 80
 WS3: Blox 6H 19
 WS10: Darl 6C 46
Alfryth Ct. B15: Edg 3E 117
 (off Lee Cres.)
Algernon Rd. B16: Edg 5H 99
Alice St. WV14: Bils 5F 45
Alice Wlk. WV14: Bils 6F 45
Alison Cl. DY4: Tip 3A 62
Alison Dr. DY8: Stourb 3D 124
Alison Rd. B62: Hale 2F 129
Allan Cl. B66: Smeth 4F 99
All Angels Wlk. B68: O'bry 5H 97
Allbut St. B64: Crad H 2F 111
Allcock St. B9: Birm 1A 118
 DY4: Tip 5C 62
Allcroft Rd. B11: Tys 3F 135
Allenby Cl. DY6: K'wfrd 4E 93
Allen Cl. B43: Gt Barr 6A 66
Allendale Gro. B43: Gt Barr 5A 66
Allendale Rd. B25: Yard 4H 119
 B76: Walm 5C 70
Allen Dr. B70: W Brom 6D 80
 WS10: Darl 5C 46
Allen Ho. B43: Gt Barr 6A 66

Allen Rd. DY4: Tip 4H 61
 WS10: W'bry 6F 47
 WV6: Wolv 6D 26
Allens Av. B18: Hock 3B 100
 B71: W Brom 6G 63
Allen's Cl. WV12: W'hall 4B 30
Allens Cft. Rd. B14: K Hth 2D 146
Allens Farm Rd. B31: N'fld 4B 144
Allen's La. WS3: Pels 5D 20
Allen's Rd. B18: Hock 3B 100
Allen St. B70: W Brom 4H 79
Allerdale Rd. WS8: Clay 6A 10
Allerton Ct. B71: W Brom 4A 64
Allerton La. B71: W Brom 5A 64
Allerton Rd. B25: Yard 4H 119
Allesley Cl. B74: S Cold 5A 54
Allesley St. B6: Aston 4G 101
Alleston Rd. WV10: Bush 5H 15
Alleston Wlk. WV10: Bush 5H 15
Alley, The DY3: Lwr G 4F 75
Alleyne Gro. B24: Erd 5G 85
Alleyne Rd. B24: Erd 6G 85
Allingham Gro. B43: Gt Barr 1G 67
Allington Cl. WS5: Wals 3H 49
Allison St. B5: Birm 5G 5 (1H 117)
Allman Rd. B24: Erd 3H 85
Allmyn Dr. B74: S'tly 5A 52
ALL SAINTS 4C 100
All Saints Dr. B74: Four O 1F 53
All Saints Ind. Est. B18: Hock 4C 100
All Saints Rd. B14: K Hth 1G 147
 B18: Hock 4D 100
 WS10: Darl 5E 47
 WV2: Wolv 6C 170 (3H 43)
All Saints St. B18: Hock 4C 100
All Saints Way B71: W Brom 3B 80
Allsops Cl. B65: Row R 5H 95
Allwell Dr. B14: K Hth 5H 147
Allwood Gdns. B32: Bart G 3G 129
Alma Av. DY4: Tip 6A 62
Alma Cres. B7: Birm 5B 102
Alma Ind. Est. WS10: Darl 5C 46
Alma Pas. B17: Harb 5H 115
Alma Pl. B12: Bal H 6B 118
 DY2: Dud 6E 77
Alma St. B19: Hock 3G 101
 B63: Crad 6E 111
 B66: Smeth 3G 99
 WS2: Wals 5B 32
 WS10: Darl 5C 46
 WS10: W'bry 2H 63
 WV10: Wolv 6B 28
 WV13: W'hall 1B 46
Alma Way B19: Loz 2F 101
Alma Works WS10: Darl 6D 46
Almond Av. WS2: Wals 5E 31
 WS5: Wals 1E 65
Almond Cl. B29: W Cas 1E 145
 WS3: Pels 5D 20
Almond Cft. B42: Gt Barr 1B 82
Almond Gro. WV6: Wolv 5G 27
Almond Rd. DY6: K'wfrd 1C 92
Alms Ho's. WS1: Wals 3B 48
 WV4: Penn 2D 58
Alnwick Ho. B23: Erd 1F 85
Alnwick Rd. WS3: Blox 3H 19
Alperton Dr. DY9: W'cte 3A 126
Alpha Cl. B12: Bal H 5G 117
Alpha Twr. B1: Birm 5B 4 (1E 117)
Alpha Way WS6: Gt Wyr 5G 7
Alpine Dr. DY2: Neth 5D 94
Alpine Way WV3: Wolv 1A 42
Alport Cft. B9: Birm 1B 118
Alston Cl. B74: Four O 1G 53
 B91: Sol 1H 151
Alston Gro. B9: Bord G 6H 103
Alston Ho. B69: O'bry 3D 96
Alston Rd. B9: Bord G 6H 103
 B69: O'bry 2E 97
 B91: Sol 1H 151
Alston St. B16: Birm 1C 116
Althorpe Dr. B93: Dorr 6H 165

Alton Av. WV12: W'hall 5B 30
Alton Cl. WV10: Bush 4A 16
Alton Gro. B71: W Brom 6C 64
 DY2: Dud 6G 77
Alton Rd. B29: S Oak 2B 132
Alum Dr. B9: Bord G 6G 103
Alumhurst Av. B8: W End 5G 103
ALUM ROCK 6H 103
Alum Rock Rd. B8: Salt, W End 4D 102
Alumwell Cl. WS2: Wals 2H 47
Alumwell Rd. WS2: Wals 2H 47
Alvaston Cl. WS3: Blox 4A 20
Alvechurch Highway B60: L Ash 6C 156
Alvechurch Rd. B31: Longb 1F 159
 B63: Hale 3H 127
Alverley Cl. DY6: K'wfrd 1H 91
Alverstoke Cl. WV9: Pend 5E 15
Alveston Gro. B9: Bord G 1H 119
 B93: Know 2D 166
Alveston Rd. B47: H'wd 2A 162
Alvin Cl. B62: B'hth 2F 113
Alvington Cl. WV12: W'hall 5D 30
Alvis Wlk. B36: Cas B 6B 88
Alwen St. DY8: Word 1D 108
Alwin Rd. B65: Row R 1B 112
Alwold Cl. B29: W Cas 3D 130
Alwold Rd. B29: W Cas, S Oak 3D 130
Alwyn Cl. WS6: Gt Wyr 2F 7
Alwynn Wlk. B23: Erd 4B 84
Amal Way B6: Witt 5H 83
Amanda Av. WV4: Penn 1D 58
Amanda Dr. B26: Yard 2E 121
Amazon Lofts B1: Birm 6D 100
 (off Tenby St.)
Ambassador Rd. B26: Birm A 1E 139
Ambell Cl. B65: Row R 4H 95
Amber Ct. B23: Erd 6F 69
Amber Dr. B69: O'bry 4G 97
Ambergate Cl. WS3: Blox 4A 20
Ambergate Dr. DY6: W Hth 1A 92
Amberley Ct. B29: S Oak 5A 132
Amberley Grn. B43: Gt Barr 1A 82
Amberley Gro. B6: Witt 4A 84
Amberley Rd. B92: Olton 1D 136
Amberley Way B74: S'tly 2G 51
Amber Way B62: Hale 5B 112
Amberwood Cl. WS2: Wals 6D 30
AMBLECOTE 4C 108
Amblecote Av. B44: Gt Barr 3G 67
Amblecote Rd. DY5: Brie H 4G 109
Ambleside B32: Bart G 4A 130
Ambleside Cl. WV14: Bils 2G 61
Ambleside Dr. DY5: Brie H 3G 109
Ambleside Gro. WV12: W'hall 6B 18
Ambleside Way DY6: K'wfrd 3B 92
Ambrose Cl. WV13: W'hall 1G 45
Ambrose Cres. DY6: K'wfrd 1B 92
Ambury Way B43: Gt Barr 5H 65
AMC Cinema 2C 116
Amelas Cl. DY5: Brie H 2E 109
Amersham Cl. B32: Quin 6C 114
Amesbury Rd. B13: Mose 2G 133
Ames Rd. WS10: Darl 4C 46
Amethyst Ct. B92: Olton 4D 136
AMF Bowling
 Wolverhampton, Birmingham Rd.
 ....6C 170 (3H 43)
 Wolverhampton, Bushbury La.
 ....3G 27
Amherst Av. B20: Hand 4C 82
Amington Cl. B75: R'ley 5B 38
Amington Rd. B25: Yard 5H 119
 B90: Shir 1G 163
Amiss Gdns. B10: Small H 3C 118
Amity Cl. B66: Smeth 4F 99
Amos Av. WV11: Wed 2D 28
Amos La. WV11: Wed 2E 29
Amos M. B73: Bold 4G 69
Amos Rd. DY9: W'cte 3B 126
Amphion Ct. DY4: Tip 1B 78
Amphlett Cft. DY4: Tip 3A 78
Amphletts Cl. DY2: Neth 6G 95
Ampleforth Dr. WV13: W'hall 3B 46
Ampton Rd. B15: Edg 4D 116

Amroth Cl.—Arley Ho.

Amroth Cl. B45: Redn 2H **157**
Amwell Gro. B14: K Hth 4H **147**
Anchorage Rd. B23: Erd 4D **84**
B74: S Cold 5H **53**
Anchor Brook Ind. Pk.
WS9: A'rdge 2B **34**
Anchor Cl. B16: Edg 2A **116**
Anchor Cres. B18: Win G 4B **100**
Anchor Dr. DY4: Tip 4A **78**
Anchor Hill DY5: Brie H 2G **109**
Anchor La. B91: Sol 1H **151**
WV14: Cose 3D **60**
(not continuous)
Anchor Mdw. WS9: A'rdge 3C **34**
Anchor Pde. WS9: A'rdge 3D **34**
Anchor Rd. WS9: A'rdge 3D **34**
WV14: Cose 3E **61**
Andersleigh Dr. WV14: Cose 5C **60**
Anderson Cres. B43: Gt Barr 2A **66**
Anderson Gdns. DY4: Tip 3A **78**
Anderson Rd. B23: Erd 1E **85**
B67: Smeth 2E **115**
DY4: Tip 2A **78**
Anders Sq. WV6: Pert 5E **25**
Anderton Cl. B74: S Cold 4G **53**
Anderton Ct. B13: Mose 3A **134**
Anderton Pk. Rd. B13: Mose 2A **134**
Anderton Rd. B11: S'brk 5B **118**
Anderton St. B1: Birm 6D **100**
Andover Cres. DY6: K'wfrd 5D **92**
Andover St. B5: Birm 4H **5** (1H **117**)
Andrew Cl. WV12: W'hall 3D **30**
Andrew Ct. B76: Walm 2D **70**
Andrew Dr. WV12: W'hall 3D **30**
Andrew Gdns. B21: Hand 5A **82**
Andrew Rd. B63: Hale 2A **128**
B71: W Brom 3D **64**
DY4: Tip 4A **62**
Andrews Cl. DY5: Quar B 3A **110**
Andrews Rd. WS9: Wals W 3D **22**
Andyfreight Bus. Pk. DY9: Lye 6C **110**
Anerley Gro. B44: Gt Barr 1H **67**
Anerley Rd. B44: Gt Barr 1H **67**
Angela Av. B65: Row R 5D **96**
Angela Pl. WV14: Bils 5F **45**
Angelica Cl. WS5: Wals 2E **65**
Angelina St. B12: Birm 3H **117**
Angel Pas. DY8: Stourb 6E **109**
Angel St. DY1: Dud 1D **94**
WV13: W'hall 1A **46**
Anglesey Av. B36: Cas B 2D **106**
Anglesey Cl. WS7: Chase 1A **10**
Anglesey Cres. WS8: Bwnhls 3B **10**
Anglesey Rd. WS8: Bwnhls 3B **10**
Anglesey St. B19: Loz 2E **101**
Anglian Rd. WS9: A'rdge 3H **33**
Anglo African Ind. Pk.
B69: O'bry 5E **79**
Angus Cl. B71: W Brom 1A **80**
Anita Av. DY4: Tip 5A **78**
Anita Cft. B23: Erd 5D **84**
Ankadine Rd. DY8: Amb 5F **109**
Ankerdine Ct. B63: Hale 2A **128**
Ankermoor Cl. B34: S End 3F **105**
Annan Av. WV10: Bush 2A **28**
Ann Cft. B26: Sheld 1H **137**
Anne Cl. B70: W Brom 4E **79**
Anne Ct. B76: Walm 2E **71**
Anne Gro. DY4: Tip 4B **62**
Anne Rd. B66: Smeth 2G **99**
DY5: Quar B 2C **110**
WV4: Penn 5F **43**
Ann Rd. B47: Wyt 6A **162**
Annscroft B38: K Nor 5H **145**
Ann St. WV13: W'hall 6B **30**
Ansbro Cl. B18: Win G 4B **100**
Ansculf Rd. DY5: Brie H 2F **109**
Ansell Rd. B11: S'brk 5C **118**
B24: Erd 6F **85**
Ansley Way B92: Sol 6H **137**
Anslow Gdns. WV11: Wed 6H **17**
Anslow Rd. B23: Erd 2C **84**
Anson Cl. WS6: Gt Wyr 4F **7**
WV6: Pert 4E **25**
Anson Ct. B70: W Brom 6F **63**
Anson Gro. B27: A Grn 3B **136**
Anson Rd. B70: W Brom 1E **79**
WS2: Wals 1E **47**
WS6: Gt Wyr 4F **7**
Anstey Cft. B37: F'bri 5C **106**
Anstey Gro. B27: A Grn 4H **135**
Anstey Rd. B44: K'sdng 1G **83**
Anston Junc. WS2: Wals 2E **47**
Anston Way WV11: Wed 2F **29**
Anstree Cl. WS6: C Hay 4D **6**
Anstruther Rd. B15: Edg 4H **115**
Anthony Rd. B8: Salt 6E **103**
Anton Dr. B76: Walm 1E **87**
Antony Rd. B90: Shir 6H **149**
Antringham Gdns. B15: Edg 3H **115**
Antrobus Rd. B21: Hand 6A **82**
B73: Bold 4E **69**
Anvil Cres. WV14: Cose 3E **61**
Anvil Dr. B69: O'bry 3E **97**
Anvil Wlk. B70: W Brom 3F **79**
Apex Bus. Pk. WS11: Nort C 1D **8**
Apex Ind. Pk. DY4: Tip 5D **62**
Apex Rd. WS8: Bwnhls 6G **9**
Apley Rd. DY8: Woll 4C **108**
Apollo Cft. B24: Erd 4B **86**
Apollo Rd. B68: O'bry 3A **98**
DY9: W'cte 6C **110**
Apollo Way B20: Hand 6F **83**
B66: Smeth 4G **99**
Apperley Way B63: Crad 4D **110**
Appian Cl. B14: K Hth 2G **147**
Appian Way B90: Ches G 5B **164**
Appleby Cl. B14: K Hth 2F **147**
Appleby Gdns. WV11: Ess 5C **18**
Appleby Gro. B90: M'path 3F **165**
Applecross B74: Four O 2F **53**
Appledore Cl. WS6: Gt Wyr 2G **7**
Appledore Ct. WS3: Blox 1H **31**
Appledore Rd. WS5: Wals 3H **49**
Appledore Ter. WS5: Wals 3H **49**
Appledorne Gdns. B34: S End 3F **105**
Applesham Cl. B11: S'brk 5D **118**
Appleton Av. B43: Gt Barr 5H **65**
DY8: Stourb 3E **125**
Appleton Cl. B30: B'vlle 5A **132**
Appleton Cres. WV4: Penn 6E **43**
Apple Tree Cl. B23: Erd 3B **84**
Appletree Cl. B31: Longb 6D **144**
B91: Cath B 2D **152**
Appletree Gro. WS9: A'rdge 5D **34**
WV6: Wolv 4G **27**
Applewood Gro. B64: Old H 3H **111**
April Cft. B13: Mose 2B **134**
Apse Cl. WV5: Wom 6F **57**
Apsley Cl. B68: O'bry 4G **113**
Apsley Cft. B38: K Nor 5D **146**
Apsley Gro. B24: Erd 5G **85**
B93: Dorr 6G **167**
Apsley Ho. B64: Old H 1H **111**
Apsley Rd. B68: O'bry 4G **113**
Aqueduct Rd. B90: Shir 5E **149**
Aragon Dr. B73: S Cold 5G **53**
Arbor Ct. B71: W Brom 1C **80**
Arboretum Rd. WS1: Wals 1D **48**
Arbor Ga. WS9: Wals W 3D **22**
Arbor Way B37: Chel W 2E **123**
Arbour Dr. WV14: Bils 1H **61**
Arbourtree Ct. WV5: Wom 6H **57**
Arbury Dr. DY8: Word 6B **92**
Arbury Hall Rd. B90: Shir 1B **164**
Arbury Wlk. B76: Min 2H **87**
Arcade B31: N'fld 3E **145**
Arcade, The DY3: Up Gor 2A **76**
WS1: Wals 2C **48**
Arcadia *B70: W Brom* *4A **80***
(off W. Bromwich Ringway)
Arcadian Shop. Cen.
B5: Birm 6E **5** (2G **117**)
Arcal St. DY3: Sed 6A **60**
Arch, The B9: Birm 1A **118**
Archer Cl. B68: O'bry 4H **97**
WS10: W'bry 2E **63**
Archer Ct. DY9: W'cte 3A **126**
Archer Gdns. B64: Crad H 2E **111**
Archer Rd. B14: Yard W 3C **148**
WS3: Blox 3C **32**
Archers Cl. B23: Erd 5D **68**
(not continuous)
Archer Way B65: B'hth 2D **112**
Archery Rd. CV7: Mer 4H **141**
Arches, The B10: Small H 3B **118**
Arch Hill St. DY2: Neth 4E **95**
Archibald Rd. B19: Loz 1E **101**
Archway, The WS4: Wals 6D **32**
Arcot Rd. B28: Hall G 3F **135**
Ardath Rd. B38: K Nor 5C **146**
Ardav Rd. B70: W Brom 5F **63**
Ardedale B90: Shir 1A **164**
Arden Bldgs. B93: Dorr 6B **166**
Arden Bus. Pk. B45: Fran 6G **143**
Arden Cl. CV7: Bal C 2H **169**
CV7: Mer 4H **141**
DY8: Woll 4C **108**
DY8: Word 6A **92**
Ardencote Rd. B13: Mose 6A **134**
Arden Ct. B24: Erd 4H **85**
B42: P Barr 3F **83**
B92: H Ard 6A **140**
DY3: Lwr G *4H **75***
(off Chiltern Cl.)
Arden Cft. B46: Col 6H **89**
B92: Sol 1G **137**
Arden Dr. B26: Yard 4D **120**
B73: W Grn 5H **69**
B75: S Cold 6F **55**
(not continuous)
B93: Dorr 6G **167**
Arden Gro. B16: Edg 2C **116**
B19: Loz 1E **101**
B69: O'bry 4G **97**
Arden Ho. B92: H Ard 1B **154**
Ardenlea Ct. B91: Sol 2G **151**
Ardenleigh Way B24: Erd 5G **85**
Arden Oak Rd. B26: Sheld 6H **121**
Arden Pl. WV14: Bils 1B **62**
Arden Rd. B6: Aston 1F **101**
B8: Salt 6C **102**
B27: A Grn 1H **135**
B45: Fran 6G **143**
B47: H'wd 3A **162**
B67: Smeth 5E **99**
B93: Dorr 6G **167**
Arden Va. Rd. B93: Know 2D **166**
Arderne Dr. B37: F'bri 2C **122**
Ardgowan Gro. WV4: E'shll 6B **44**
Ardingley Wlk. DY5: Brie H 4F **109**
Ardley Cl. DY2: Dud 1F **95**
Ardley Rd. B14: K Hth 2A **148**
Arena B40: Nat E C 2G **139**
Arena Theatre **2C 170 (1G 43)**
Arena Wlk. B1: Birm 5A **4**
Aretha Cl. DY6: K'wfrd 3E **93**
Argil Cl. WV11: Wed 1F **29**
Argus Cl. B76: Walm 2D **70**
Argyle Cl. DY8: Word 2C **108**
WS4: Wals 6F **33**
Argyle Rd. WS4: Wals 6F **33**
WV2: Wolv 5F **43**
Argyle St. B7: Nech 1C **102**
Argyll Ho. *WV1: Wolv* *5G **27***
(off Lomas St.)
Arkle Cft. B36: Hodg H 1A **104**
B65: Row R 3H **95**
Arkley Gro. B28: Hall G 6H **135**
Arkley Rd. B28: Hall G 6H **135**
Arkwright Rd. B32: Quin 6A **114**
WS2: Wals 4H **31**
Arlen Dr. B43: Gt Barr 4H **65**
Arlescote Cl. B75: Four O 1A **54**
Arlescote Rd. B92: Sol 3G **137**
Arless Way B17: Harb 2E **131**
Arleston Way B90: Shir 1C **164**
Arley Cl. B69: O'bry 4D **96**
Arley Ct. DY2: Neth 3E **95**
Arley Dr. DY8: Stourb 2C **124**
Arley Gro. WV4: Penn 6B **42**
Arley Ho. B26: Yard 2E **121**

Arley Rd.—Ashwood Ct.

Arley Rd. B8: Salt 4D **102**
B29: S Oak 2B **132**
B91: Sol 3E **151**
Arley Vs. *B18: Win G* *5H* ***99***
(off Cape St.)
Arlidge Cl. WV14: Bils 1F **61**
Arlington Cl. DY6: K'wfrd 5B **92**
Arlington Ct. DY8: Stourb 1F **125**
Arlington Gro. B14: K Hth 5B **148**
Arlington Ho. *B15: Edg* *4E* ***117***
(off Summer Rd.)
Arlington Rd. B14: K Hth 5B **148**
B71: W Brom 1B **80**
Armada Cl. B23: Erd 6D **84**
Armoury Rd. B11: Small H 5D **118**
Armoury Trad. Est.
B11: Small H 5D **118**
Armside Cl. WS3: Pels 3F **21**
Armstead Rd. WV9: Pend 4D **14**
Armstrong Cl. DY8: Amb 4F **109**
Armstrong Dr. B36: Cas B 6B **88**
WS2: Wals 5G **31**
WV6: Wolv 4E **27**
Armstrong Way WV13: W'hall 3B **46**
Arnhem Cl. WV11: Wed 1D **28**
Arnhem Rd. WV13: W'hall 3G **45**
Arnhem Way DY4: Tip 2C **78**
Arnold Cl. WS2: Wals 6F **31**
Arnold Gro. B30: K Nor 3H **145**
B90: Shir 3H **149**
Arnold Rd. B90: Shir 3H **149**
Arnside Ct. B23: Erd 3B **84**
Arnwood Cl. WS2: Wals 1F **47**
Arosa Dr. B17: Harb 2F **131**
Arps Rd. WV8: Cod 4F **13**
Arran Cl. B43: Gt Barr 2A **66**
Arran Rd. B34: Hodg H 3D **104**
Arran Way B36: Cas B 2C **106**
Arras Rd. DY2: Dud 5G **77**
Arrow Cl. B93: Know 3C **166**
Arrowfield Grn. B38: K Nor 2H **159**
Arrow Ind. Est. WV12: W'hall 3C **30**
Arrow Rd. WS3: Blox 3C **32**
Arrow Wlk. B38: K Nor 6D **146**
Arsenal St. B9: Bord G 2C **118**
Arter St. B12: Bal H 5H **117**
Arthur Gunby Cl. B75: S Cold 4D **54**
Arthur Harris Cl. B66: Smeth 6G **99**
Arthur Pl. B1: Birm 3A **4** (6D **100**)
Arthur Rd. B15: Edg 5D **116**
B21: Hand 1B **100**
B24: Erd 3H **85**
B25: Yard 5H **119**
DY4: Tip 1A **78**
Arthur St. B10: Small H 2B **118**
B70: W Brom 6B **80**
WS2: Wals 4H **47**
WV2: Wolv 5H **43**
WV14: Bils 5F **45**
Arthur Terry Sports Cen., The **6G 37**
Artillery St. B9: Birm 1B **118**
Arton Cft. B24: Erd 5F **85**
Arundel Av. WS10: W'bry 2F **63**
Arundel Ct. *B29: W Cas* *6G* ***131***
(off Abdon Av.)
Arundel Cres. B92: Olton 4E **137**
Arundel Dr. B69: Tiv 1A **96**
Arundel Gro. WV6: Pert 6F **25**
Arundel Ho. B23: Erd 1F **85**
Arundel Pl. B11: S'brk 5A **118**
Arundel Rd. B14: K Hth 6A **148**
DY8: Word 1A **108**
WV10: Oxl 5F **15**
WV12: W'hall 2C **30**
Arundel St. WS1: Wals 4C **48**
(not continuous)
Arun Way B76: Walm 4E **71**
Asbury Ct. B43: Gt Barr 5G **65**
Asbury Rd. CV7: Bal C 4H **169**
WS10: W'bry 3C **64**
Asbury Wlk. B43: Gt Barr 4G **65**
Ascot Cl. B16: Birm 1B **116**
B69: O'bry 3E **97**
Ascot Ct. B29: W Cas 6G **131**
Ascot Dr. DY1: Dud 5B **76**
WV4: Penn 1E **59**
Ascote La. B90: Dic H 4G **163**
Ascot Gdns. DY8: Word 1B **108**
Ascot Rd. B13: Mose 3H **133**
Ascot Wlk. B69: O'bry 3E **97**
Ash Av. B12: Bal H 6A **118**
Ashborough Dr. B91: Sol 2G **165**
Ashbourne Gro. B6: Aston 1G **101**
Ashbourne Ridge B63: Crad 6F **111**
Ashbourne Rd. B16: Edg 6H **99**
WS3: Blox 4A **20**
WV1: Wolv 6C **28**
WV4: E'shll 2A **60**
Ashbourne Way B90: Shir 1C **164**
Ash Bri. Ct. B45: Redn 3H **157**
Ashbrook Cres. B91: Sol 1G **165**
Ashbrook Dr. B45: Redn 1H **157**
Ashbrook Gro. B30: Stir 5D **132**
Ashbrook Rd. B30: Stir 5E **133**
Ashburn Gro. WV13: W'hall 1C **46**
Ashburton Rd. B14: K Hth 2F **147**
Ashbury Covert B30: K Nor 4E **147**
Ashby Cl. B8: W End 3A **104**
Ashby Ct. B91: Sol 6G **151**
Ash Cl. WV8: Bilb 4G **13**
Ashcombe Av. B20: Hand 4A **82**
Ashcombe Gdns. B24: Erd 4B **86**
Ashcott Cl. B38: K Nor 5H **145**
Ash Ct. B66: Smeth 1A **98**
DY8: Stourb 1E **125**
Ash Cres. B37: K'hrst 3B **106**
DY6: K'wfrd 3C **92**
Ashcroft B15: Edg 6A **116**
B66: Smeth 4G **99**
Ashcroft Gro. B20: Hand 5F **83**
Ashdale Cl. DY6: K'wfrd 1B **92**
Ashdale Dr. B14: K Hth 6B **148**
Ashdale Gro. B26: Yard 3E **121**
Ashdene Cl. B73: S Cold 2G **69**
Ashdene Gdns. DY8: Word 1A **108**
Ashdown Cl. B13: Mose 4A **134**
B45: Fran 5G **143**
Ashdown Dr. DY8: Word 6C **92**
Ash Dr. B31: Longb 6A **144**
B71: W Brom 1A **80**
Ashen Cl. DY3: Sed 2G **59**
Ashenden Ri. WV3: Wolv 2G **41**
Ashenhurst Rd. DY1: Dud 2A **94**
Ashenhurst Wlk. DY1: Dud 1C **94**
Ashes Rd. B69: O'bry 5F **97**
Ashfern Dr. B76: Walm 6D **70**
Ashfield Av. B14: K Hth 4G **133**
Ashfield Cl. WS3: Wals 5D **32**
Ashfield Ct. B30: K Nor 3A **146**
Ashfield Cres. DY2: Neth 6E **95**
DY9: W'cte 2B **126**
Ashfield Gdns. B14: K Hth 4H **133**
Ashfield Gro. B63: Hale 3G **127**
WV10: F'hses 4G **15**
Ashfield Ho. B28: Hall G 4E **149**
Ashfield Rd. B14: K Hth 4H **133**
WV3: Wolv 1B **42**
WV10: F'hses 4G **15**
WV14: Bils 3A **62**
Ashford Cl. B24: Erd 3B **86**
Ashford Dr. B76: Walm 2D **86**
DY3: Sed 6A **60**
Ashford Twr. B12: Birm 3A **118**
Ash Furlong Cl. CV7: Bal C 3H **169**
Ashfurlong Cres. B75: S Cold 4C **54**
Ash Grn. DY1: Dud 2C **76**
Ash Gro. B9: Birm 1B **118**
B12: Bal H 6B **118**
B31: N'fld 3E **145**
DY3: Gorn 5G **75**
DY9: W'cte 2H **125**
Ashgrove Ho. *B45: Rub* *2E* ***157***
(off Callowbrook La.)
Ashgrove Rd. B44: Gt Barr 3E **67**
Ash Hill WV3: Wolv 2B **42**
Ashill Rd. B45: Redn 2H **157**
Ashland St. WV3: Wolv 2F **43**
(not continuous)
Ash La. WS6: Gt Wyr 2G **7**
Ashlawn Cres. B91: Sol 2B **150**
Ashleigh Dr. B20: Hand 5D **82**
Ashleigh Gro. B13: Mose 4B **134**
Ashleigh Hgts. B91: Sol 2E **151**
Ashleigh Rd. B69: Tiv 1C **96**
B91: Sol 3F **151**
Ashley Cl. B15: Edg 4E **117**
DY6: K'wfrd 5A **92**
DY8: Stourb 3B **124**
Ashley Gdns. B8: Salt 5D **102**
WV8: Cod 3F **13**
Ashley Mt. WV6: Tett 4B **26**
Ashley Rd. B23: Erd 4E **85**
B66: Smeth 5G **99**
WS3: Blox 6F **19**
WV4: Penn 6C **42**
Ashley St. WV14: Bils 5G **45**
Ashley Ter. B29: S Oak 4A **132**
Ashley Way CV7: Bal C 2H **169**
Ashmall WS7: Hamm 1F **11**
Ashmead Dr. B45: Coft H 5A **158**
Ashmead Gro. B24: Erd 5G **85**
Ashmead Ri. B45: Coft H 5A **158**
Ash M. B27: A Grn 6A **120**
Ashmole Rd. B70: W Brom 6F **63**
ASHMOOR LAKE **5B 30**
Ashmore Av. WV11: Wed 1A **30**
Ashmore Ind. Est. WS2: Wals 6C **32**
Ashmore Lake Ind. Est.
WV12: W'hall 5B **30**
Ashmore Lake Rd. WV12: W'hall 5B **30**
Ashmore Lake Way WV12: W'hall 5B **30**
ASHMORE PARK **1H 29**
Ashmore Rd. B30: K Nor 2B **146**
Ashmores Ind. Est. DY1: Dud 4G **77**
Ashold Farm Rd. B24: Erd 5B **86**
Asholme Cl. B36: Hodg H 2A **104**
Ashorne Cl. B28: Hall G 6H **135**
Ashover Gro. *B18: Win G* *5A* ***100***
(off Heath Grn. Rd.)
Ashover Rd. B44: Gt Barr 2F **67**
Ash Rd. B8: Salt 5D **102**
DY1: Dud 4D **76**
DY4: Tip 3G **77**
WS10: W'bry 6F **47**
Ash St. B64: Old H 1H **111**
WS3: Blox 6B **20**
WV3: Wolv 2E **43**
WV14: Bils 2G **61**
Ashtead Cl. B76: Walm 1F **87**
Ashted Cir. B7: Birm 1H **5** (5A **102**)
Ashted Lock B7: Birm 1H **5** (5H **101**)
Ashted Wlk. B7: Birm 5B **102**
Ash Ter. B69: Tiv 6B **78**
Ashton Cft. B91: Sol 6E **151**
Ashtoncroft B16: Birm 1C **116**
Ashton Dr. WS4: S'fld 4G **21**
Ashton Pk. Dr. DY5: Brie H 2G **109**
Ashton Rd. B25: Yard 4H **119**
Ashtree Cl. DY5: Brie H 3E **109**
Ash Tree Dr. B26: Yard 4B **120**
Ashtree Dr. DY8: Stourb 2E **125**
Ashtree Gro. WV14: Bils 2B **62**
Ash Tree Rd. B30: Stir 1C **146**
Ashtree Rd. B64: Old H 1H **111**
B69: Tiv 6C **78**
WS3: Pels 4E **21**
Ashurst Rd. B76: Walm 1D **86**
Ashville Av. B34: Hodg H 2D **104**
Ashville Dr. B63: Hale 6A **112**
Ash Wlk. B76: Walm 3D **70**
Ashwater Dr. B14: K Hth 5F **147**
Ash Way B23: Erd 5C **68**
Ashway B11: S'hll 6B **118**
Ashwell Dr. B90: Shir 3B **150**
Ashwells Gro. WV9: Pend 5E **15**
Ashwin Rd. B21: Hand 2B **100**
ASHWOOD **4E 91**
Ashwood Av. DY8: Word 1A **108**
Ashwood Cl. B69: O'bry 5F **97**
B74: S'tly 3G **51**
Ashwood Ct. B13: Mose 2A **134**
B34: Hodg H 4B **104**

Ashwood Dr. B37: Chel W 6F **107**
Ashwood Gro. WV4: Penn 6E **43**
Ashwood Lwr. La. DY6: K'wfrd 4E **91**
   DY7: Stourt 4E **91**
Ashworth Rd. B42: Gt Barr 4D **66**
Askew Bri. Rd. DY3: Gorn 4F **75**
Askew Cl. DY3: Up Gor 2A **76**
Aspbury Cft. B36: Cas B 6H **87**
Aspen Cl. B27: A Grn 3H **135**
   B76: Walm 3D **70**
Aspen Dr. B37: Chel W 3E **123**
Aspen Gdns. B20: Hand 6D **82**
Aspen Gro. B9: Bord G 6G **103**
   B47: Wyt 4B **162**
   WV12: W'hall 2E **31**
Aspen Ho. B91: Sol 5D **150**
Aspen Way WV3: Wolv 2E **43**
Asquith Dr. B69: Tiv 5C **78**
Asquith Rd. B8: W End 4H **103**
Asra Cl. B66: Smeth 1E **99**
Asra Ho. B66: Smeth 1E **99**
            (off Oxford Rd.)
Astbury Av. B67: Smeth 6D **98**
Astbury Cl. WS3: Blox 3G **19**
   WV1: Wolv 2C **44**
Aster Wlk. WV9: Pend 4E **15**
Aster Way WS5: Wals 2E **65**
Astle Dr. B69: O'bry 6E **79**
Astley Av. B62: Quin 5F **113**
Astley Cl. DY4: Tip 1D **78**
Astley Cres. B62: Quin 6F **113**
Astley Pl. WV2: Wolv 5H **43**
Astley Rd. B21: Hand 6H **81**
Astley Wlk. B90: Shir 2H **149**
ASTON 2H **101**
Aston Bri. Rd. B6: Aston 4H **101**
Aston Brook Grn. B6: Aston 4H **101**
Aston Brook St. B6: Aston 3H **101**
           (not continuous)
Aston Brook St. E. B6: Aston 4H **101**
Aston Bury B15: Edg 4H **115**
Aston Chu. Rd. B7: Nech 2C **102**
   B8: Salt .2C **102**
Aston Chu. Trad. Est. B7: Nech 3D **102**
Aston Cl. WV14: Bils 1B **62**
Aston Ct. B23: Erd 5C **84**
   B71: W Brom 4B **64**
Aston Cross Bus. Pk. B6: Aston 3A **102**
Aston Events Cen. 1A **102**
Aston Expressway B6: Aston 4H **101**
Aston Hall .1H **101**
Aston Hall Rd. B6: Aston 1A **102**
           (not continuous)
Aston La. B6: Aston 5F **83**
   B20: Hand 5F **83**
Aston Mnr. Cl. B20: Hand 5G **83**
Aston Manor Transport Mus. 6H **83**
Aston Newton Pool & Fitness Cen. . .3G **101**
Aston Rd. B6: Aston, Birm 4H **101**
   B69: Tiv 6A **78**
   DY2: Dud 1D **94**
   WV13: W'hall 1G **45**
Aston Rd. Nth. B6: Aston 3H **101**
Aston Science Pk. B7: Birm . . .1H **5** (5H **101**)
Aston's Cl. DY5: Brie H 4A **110**
Aston Seedbed Cen. B7: Nech 3A **102**
Aston's Fold DY5: Brie H 4A **110**
Aston Station (Rail) 1B **102**
Aston St. B4: Birm 2F **5** (5H **101**)
           (not continuous)
   DY4: Tip .6C **62**
   WV3: Wolv 3E **43**
Aston Students Guild 1G **5**
Aston Triangle, The
   B4: Birm 2G **5** (6H **101**)
Aston University 1G **5** (5H **101**)
Aston Villa FC 6H **83**
Astor Dr. B13: Mose 4C **134**
Astoria Cl. WV12: W'hall 6D **18**
Astoria Gdns. WV12: W'hall 6D **18**
Astor Rd. B74: S'tly 2A **52**
   DY6: K'wfrd 4D **92**
Athelney Ct. WS3: Pels 4E **21**
Athelstan Gro. WV6: Pert 4F **25**

Atherstone Cl. B90: Shir 5E **149**
Atherstone Rd. WV1: Wolv 1D **44**
Athlone Rd. WS5: Wals 3G **49**
Athol Cl. B32: Bart G 5B **130**
Athole St. B12: Birm 4A **118**
Atlantic Ct. WV13: W'hall 2A **46**
            (off Cheapside)
Atlantic Rd. B44: Gt Barr 5H **67**
Atlantic Way WS10: W'bry 4E **63**
Atlas Cft. WV10: Oxl 3G **27**
Atlas Est. B6: Witt 5A **84**
   B11: Tys 6G **119**
Atlas Gro. B70: W Brom 4F **79**
Atlas Trad. Est. WV14: Bils 3H **61**
Atlas Way B1: Birm 5A **4**
Attenborough Cl. B19: Hock 4F **101**
Attingham Dr. B43: Gt Barr 3H **65**
   DY1: Dud 5D **76**
Attleboro La. B46: Wat O 5C **88**
Attlee Cl. B69: Tiv 5D **78**
Attlee Cres. WV14: Bils 3G **61**
Attlee Rd. WS2: Wals 5E **31**
Attwell Pk. WV3: Wolv 4B **42**
Attwell Rd. DY4: Tip 4H **61**
Attwood Cl. B8: Salt 3E **103**
Attwood Gdns. WV4: E'shll 6A **44**
Attwood St. B63: Hale 6H **111**
   DY9: Lye .6B **110**
Aubrey Rd. B10: Small H 3D **118**
   B32: Harb 4C **114**
Auchinleck Ho. B15: Birm 2D **116**
           (off Broad St.)
Auchinleck Sq. B15: Birm 2D **116**
      (off Islington Row Middleway)
Auckland Dr. B36: Cas B 1B **106**
Auckland Ho. B32: Quin 1D **130**
Auckland Rd. B11: S'brk 4A **118**
   B67: Smeth 3C **98**
   DY6: K'wfrd 5C **92**
Auden Cl. WV6: Pert 5F **25**
Audleigh Ho. B15: Birm 3E **117**
         (off Bell Barn Rd.)
Audlem Wlk. WV10: Wolv 4C **28**
Audley Rd. B33: Stech 5C **104**
AUDNAM 2D **108**
Audnam DY8: Word 2D **108**
Augusta Rd. B13: Mose 1G **133**
   B27: A Grn 6A **120**
Augusta Rd. E. B13: Mose 1H **133**
Augusta St. B18: Birm 1A **4** (5E **101**)
Augustine Gro. B18: Hock 3B **100**
   B74: Four O 4F **37**
Augustus Cl. B46: Col 6H **89**
Augustus Ct. B15: Edg 3B **116**
Augustus Rd. B15: Edg 3H **115**
Augustus St. WS2: Wals 2B **48**
Aulton Rd. B75: R'ley 6C **38**
Ault St. B70: W Brom 6B **80**
Austcliff Dr. B91: Sol 1G **165**
Austen Pl. B15: Edg 3D **116**
Austen Wlk. B71: W Brom 2B **80**
Austin Cl. B27: A Grn 1B **136**
   B31: N'fld 5E **145**
   DY1: Dud .5B **76**
Austin Ct. B1: Birm 4A **4** (1D **116**)
Austin Cft. B36: Cas B 6A **88**
Austin Ho. WS4: Wals 6D **32**
Austin Ri. B31: Longb 2D **158**
Austin Rd. B21: Hand 6G **81**
Austin St. B35: Cas V 3F **87**
   WV6: Wolv 5F **27**
AUSTIN VILLAGE 6D **144**
Austin Way B42: P Barr 2C **82**
Austrey Cl. B93: Know 3C **166**
Austrey Gro. B29: W Cas 5E **131**
Austrey Rd. DY6: K'wfrd 4E **93**
Austy Cl. B36: Hodg H 1C **104**
Automotive Components Pk.
   WS10: W'bry 2C **62**
Autumn Berry Gro. DY3: Sed 1A **76**
Autumn Cl. WS4: S'fld 6G **21**
Autumn Dr. DY3: Lwr G 3H **75**
   WS4: S'fld 5F **21**
Autumn Gro. B19: Hock 3E **101**

Autumn Ho. B37: K'hrst 4D **106**
Avalon Cl. B24: Erd 3H **85**
Avebury Gro. B30: Stir 6E **133**
Avebury Rd. B30: Stir 5E **133**
Ave Maria Cl. B64: Old H 2G **111**
Avenbury Dr. B91: Sol 3A **152**
Avenue, The B27: A Grn 1B **136**
   B45: Rub 2E **157**
   B65: Row R 6A **96**
   B76: Walm 4C **70**
   WV3: Wolv 3H **41**
   WV4: Penn 1C **58**
   WV10: F'stne 1D **16**
   WV10: Wolv 4B **28**
Avenue Cl. B7: Nech 3A **102**
   B93: Dorr 6C **166**
Avenue Rd. B6: Aston 3H **101**
   B7: Nech 3A **102**
   B14: K Hth 5F **133**
   B21: Hand 5H **81**
   B23: Erd .3F **85**
   B65: B'hth, Row R 2D **112**
   B93: Dorr 6C **166**
   DY2: Dud 3B **94**
   WS10: Darl 5D **46**
   WV3: Wolv 1C **42**
   WV14: Cose 5E **61**
Averill Rd. B26: Yard 2E **121**
Avern Cl. DY4: Tip 1B **78**
Aversley Rd. B38: K Nor 6H **145**
Avery Cft. B35: Cas V 5D **86**
Avery Dell Ind. Est. B30: K Nor 2D **146**
Avery Dr. B27: A Grn 1A **136**
Avery Ho. B16: Edg 2C **116**
Avery Myers Cl. B68: O'bry 4H **97**
Avery Rd. B66: Smeth 3H **99**
   B73: New O 3C **68**
Aviary Cl. B71: W Brom 1A **80**
Aviemore Cres. B43: Gt Barr 1D **66**
Avington Cl. DY3: Sed 6H **59**
Avion Cen. WV6: Wolv 5E **27**
Avion Cl. WS1: Wals 4D **48**
Avoca Cl. B12: Birm 3A **118**
Avocet Cl. B33: Stech 6C **104**
Avon Cl. B14: K Hth 6F **147**
   DY5. P'ntt .2F **93**
   WV6: Pert 6F **25**
Avon Ct. B73: S Cold 6H **53**
Avon Cres. WS3: Pels 6E **21**
Avoncroft Ho. B37: Chel W 1C **122**
Avondale Cl. DY6: K'wfrd 1C **92**
Avondale Ct. B31: N'fld 6C **144**
Avondale Rd. B11: S'hll 1C **134**
   WV6: Wolv 6D **26**
Avon Dr. B13: Mose 3B **134**
   B36: Cas B 1B **106**
   WV13: W'hall 1C **46**
Avon Gro. WS5: Wals 2E **65**
Avon Ho. B15: Birm 3F **117**
Avon M. DY8: Word 6H **91**
Avon Rd. B63: Crad 6D **110**
   B90: Shir 6B **150**
   DY8: Stourb 2D **124**
   WS3: Blox 6C **20**
Avon St. B11: S'hll 6D **118**
Avon Way B47: Wyt 6G **161**
Avro Way B35: Cas V 5F **87**
Awbridge Rd. DY2: Neth 6E **95**
Awefields Cres. B67: Smeth 5B **98**
Awlmakers Gro. WS3: Blox 2A **32**
Axcess 10 Bus. Pk. WS10: Wals 2E **47**
Axletree Way WS10: W'bry 5G **47**
Ayala Cft. B36: Hodg H 6C **86**
Aylesbury Cres. B44: K'sdng 5H **67**
Aylesbury Rd. B31: Longb 1D **158**
Aylesford Cl. DY3: Sed 3G **59**
Aylesford Dr. B37: Mars G 4C **122**
   B74: Four O 4E **37**
Aylesford Rd. B21: Hand 6H **81**
Aylesmore Cl. B32: Bart G 4A **130**
   B92: Olton 5C **136**
Aynsley Ct. B90: Shir 5A **150**
Ayre Rd. B24: Erd 3H **85**
Ayres Cl. B34: S End 3A **106**

Ayrshire Cl. B36: Hodg H 1B 104
Ayrton Cl. WV6: Pert 5G 25
Azalea Cl. WV8: Bilb 4H 13
Azalea Gro. B9: Bord G 1F 119
Aziz Isaac Cl. B68: O'bry 3H 97

B

Babington Rd. B21: Hand 2A 100
Bablake Cft. B92: Olton 4E 137
Babors Fld. WV14: Cose 2C 60
Babworth Cl. WV9: Pend 5E 15
Baccabox La. B47: H'wd 2G 161
Bacchus Rd. B18: Hock 3B 100
  B21: Hand 2B 100
Bache St. B70: W Brom 6A 80
Bach Mill Dr. B28: Hall G 4D 148
Backhouse La. WV11: Wed 5E 29
Back La. B64: Crad H 2D 110
  B90: Dic H 4G 163
  WS9: A'rdge 2H 35
  WS14: Foot 1E 37
Back Rd. B30: K Nor 5B 146
  B38: K Nor 5B 146
  DY6: K'wfrd 2B 92
Back to Backs 2G 117
                        (off Hurst St.)
BACONS END 5D 106
Bacons End B37: K'hrst 4D 106
Baddesley Rd. B92: Olton 3C 136
Bader Rd. WS2: Wals 1F 47
  WV6: Pert 6E 25
Bader Wlk. B35: Cas V 5D 86
Badger Cl. B90: Ches G 5B 164
Badger Ct. WV10: Wolv 5H 27
Badger Dr. WV10: Wolv 5H 27
Badgers Bank Rd. B74: Four O 4F 37
Badgers Cl. WS3: Pels 2E 21
Badgers Cft. B62: Hale 4B 112
Badger St. DY3: Up Gor 2A 76
  DY9: Lye 5A 110
Badgers Way B34: Stech 4E 105
Badminton Cl. DY1: Dud 4B 76
Badon Covert B14: K Hth 5F 147
Badsey Cl. B31: N'fld 3G 145
Badsey Rd. B69: O'bry 4D 96
Baggeridge Cl. DY3: Sed 5E 59
Baggeridge Country Pk. 1C 74
Baggeridge Country Pk. Vis. Cen. ..6D 58
Baggott St. WV2: Wolv 4G 43
Baginton Cl. B91: Sol 2F 151
Baginton Rd. B35: Cas V 3E 87
Bagley Ind. Pk. DY2: Neth 5F 95
Bagley's Rd. DY5: Brie H 5G 109
Bagley St. DY9: Lye 6G 109
Bagnall Cl. B25: Yard 5B 120
Bagnall Rd. WV14: Bils 6E 45
Bagnall St. B70: W Brom 5C 80
                        (Beeches Rd.)
  B70: W Brom 6D 62
                          (Shaw St.)
  DY4: Tip 6D 62
                        (Chimney Rd.)
  DY4: Tip 4C 62
                        (Newman Rd.)
  WS3: Blox 3A 32
Bagnall Wlk. DY5: Brie H 2H 109
Bagnell Rd. B13: Mose 6H 133
Bagot St. B4: Birm 5G 101
Bagridge Cl. WV3: Wolv 3H 41
Bagridge Rd. WV3: Wolv 3H 41
Bagshawe Cft. B23: Erd 6D 68
Bagshaw Rd. B33: Stech 6C 104
Bailey Rd. WV14: Bils 4D 44
Baileys Ct. B65: Row R 6B 96
Bailey St. B70: W Brom 3G 79
  WV1: Wolv 1A 44
Bainbridge Rd. B66: Smeth 6G 99
Bakeman Ho. B25: Yard 5B 120
                      (off The Tivoli)
Baker Av. WV14: Cose 3B 60
Baker Ho. Gro. B43: Gt Barr 6H 65
Baker Rd. WV14: Bils 2G 61

Bakers Gdns. WV8: Cod 3E 13
Bakers La. B73: S'tly 6A 52
  B74: S'tly 6H 51
  WS9: A'rdge 3D 34
Baker St. B10: Small H 2D 118
  B11: S'hll 1C 134
  B21: Hand 1B 100
  B70: W Brom 4H 79
  DY4: Tip 3G 77
                    (not continuous)
Bakers Way WV8: Cod 3E 13
Bakewell Cl. WS3: Blox 4A 20
Balaams Wood Dr. B31: Longb 6H 143
Balaclava Rd. B14: K Hth 5G 133
Balcaskie Cl. B15: Edg 4A 116
Balden Rd. B32: Harb 4C 114
Bald's La. DY9: Lye 6B 110
Baldmoor Lake Rd. B23: Erd 6F 69
Baldwin Cl. B69: Tiv 5D 78
Baldwin Ho. B19: Hock 3G 101
Baldwin Rd. B30: K Nor 5C 146
Baldwins Ho. DY5: Quar B 3B 110
                   (off Maughan St.)
Baldwins La. B28: Hall G 3E 149
Baldwin St. B66: Smeth 3F 99
  WV14: Bils 1H 61
Baldwin Way DY3: Swind 5E 73
Balfour Ct. B74: Four O 6G 37
  WV6: Wolv 5D 26
                    (off Balfour Cres.)
Balfour Cres. WV6: Wolv 5D 26
Balfour Dr. B69: Tiv 5C 78
Balfour Ho. B16: Edg 2B 116
Balfour Rd. DY6: K'wfrd 1B 92
Balfour St. B12: Bal H 5G 117
Balham Gro. B44: K'sdng 3A 68
Balholm B62: Hale 6D 112
Balking Cl. WV14: Cose 2D 60
Ballarat Wlk. DY8: Stourb 6D 108
Ballard Cres. DY2: Neth 4F 95
Ballard Rd. DY2: Neth 4F 95
Ballard Wlk. B37: K'hrst 3C 106
Ballfields DY4: Tip 2D 78
Ball Ho. WS3: Blox 1H 31
                  (off Somerfield Rd.)
Balliol Bus. Pk. WV9: Pend 4B 14
Balliol Ho. B37: F'bri 1B 122
Ball La. WV10: Cov H 1G 15
BALLS HILL 5G 63
Balls Hill WS1: Wals 1D 48
Balls St. WS1: Wals 2D 48
Balmain Cres. WV11: Wed 1D 28
Balmoral Cl. B62: Hale 4B 112
  WS4: Rus 2H 33
Balmoral Ct. B1: Birm 3A 4
Balmoral Dr. WV5: Wom 4G 57
  WV12: W'hall 2B 30
Balmoral Rd. B23: Erd 2F 85
  B32: Bart G 6G 129
  B36: Cas B 2C 106
  B74: Four O 4F 37
  DY8: Word 6A 92
  WV4: Penn 6E 43
Balmoral Vw. DY1: Dud 5A 76
Balmoral Way B65: Row R 5D 96
  WS2: Wals 5G 31
BALSALL 4H 169
BALSALL COMMON 3H 169
BALSALL HEATH 6H 117
Balsall Heath Rd. B5: Edg 4F 117
  B12: Bal H 4G 117
BALSALL STREET 3G 169
Balsall St. CV7: Bal C 4B 168
Balsall St. E. CV7: Bal C 3G 169
Baltimore Rd. B42: P Barr 1C 82
Balvenie Way DY1: Dud 4B 76
Bamber Cl. WV3: Wolv 3C 42
Bamford Cl. WS3: Blox 4A 20
Bamford Ho. WS3: Blox 4A 20
Bamford Rd. WS3: Blox 4A 20
  WV3: Wolv 3E 43
Bampfylde Pl. B42: Gt Barr 6E 67
Bamville Rd. B8: W End 4G 103

Banbery Dr. WV5: Wom 3F 73
Banbrook Cl. B92: Sol 5H 137
Banbury Cl. DY3: Sed 1A 76
Banbury Cft. B37: F'bri 1B 122
Banbury Ho. B33: Kitts G 1A 122
Banbury St. B5: Birm 3G 5 (6H 101)
Bancroft Cl. WV14: Cose 6D 60
Bandywood Cres. B44: Gt Barr 2H 67
Bandywood Rd. B44: Gt Barr 1G 67
Banfield Av. WS10: Darl 4C 46
Banfield Rd. WS10: Darl 1C 62
Banford Av. B8: W End 5G 103
Banford Rd. B8: W End 5G 103
Bangham Pit Rd. B31: N'fld 1C 144
Bangley La. B78: Hints 3H 39
Bangor Ho. B37: F'bri 5D 106
Bangor Rd. B9: Bord G 1D 118
Bankdale Rd. B8: W End 5H 103
Bankes Rd. B10: Small H 2E 119
Bank Farm Cl. DY9: Pedm 4G 125
Bankfield Rd. DY4: Tip 5C 62
  WV14: Bils 6F 45
                    (not continuous)
Banklands Rd. DY2: Dud 3G 95
Bank Rd. DY2: Neth 3F 95
  DY3: Gorn 4G 75
                    (not continuous)
Bankside B13: Mose 3D 134
  B43: Gt Barr 6A 66
  WV5: Wom 6F 57
Bankside Cres. B74: S'tly 4H 51
Bankside Way WS9: A'rdge 5D 22
Banks St. WV13: W'hall 1A 46
Bank St. B14: K Hth 5G 133
  B64: Crad H 2E 111
  B71: W Brom 1A 80
  DY5: Brie H 6H 93
  DY9: Lye 6B 110
  WS1: Wals 2D 48
  WV10: Wolv 4A 28
  WV14: Bils 2G 61
  WV14: Cose 5D 60
Bankwell St. DY5: Brie H 5G 93
Banner La. B92: Bars 6B 154
Bannerlea Rd. B37: K'hrst 4B 106
Bannerley Rd. B33: Sheld 2G 121
Banners Ct. B73: S'tly 2B 68
BANNERS GATE 1B 68
Banners Ga. Rd. B73: S'tly 2B 68
Banners Gro. B23: Erd 1G 85
Banner's La. B63: Crad 5F 111
Banner's Rd. B63: Crad 5F 111
Banners Wlk. B44: K'sdng 3B 68
Bannington Ct. WV12: W'hall 5D 30
Bannister Rd. WS10: W'bry 3D 62
Bannister St. B64: Crad H 2F 111
Banstead Cl. WV2: Wolv 4A 44
Bantams Cl. B33: Kitts G 1G 121
Bantock Av. WV3: Wolv 3D 42
Bantock Ct. WV3: Wolv 3C 42
Bantock Gdns. WV3: Wolv 2C 42
Bantock House Mus. 2D 42
Bantocks, The B70: W Brom 1G 79
Bantock Way B17: Harb 6H 115
Banton Cl. B23: Erd 5D 68
Bantry Cl. B26: Sheld 1G 137
BAPTIST END 3E 95
Baptist End Rd. DY2: Dud, Neth ...4E 95
Barbara Rd. B28: Hall G 3E 149
Barbel Dr. WV10: Wolv 5C 28
Barberry Ho. B38: K Nor 6B 146
Barbers La. B92: Cath B 1E 153
Barbourne Cl. B91: Sol 2F 165
Barbrook Dr. DY5: Brie H 4F 109
Barcheston Rd. B29: W Cas 4E 131
  B93: Know 4C 166
Barclay Cl. WV3: Wolv 1E 43
Barclay Rd. B67: Smeth 2C 114
Barcroft WV13: W'hall 6B 30
Bardenholme Gdns. DY9: W'cte 2H 125
Bardfield Cl. B42: Gt Barr 5B 66
Bardon Dr. B90: Shir 5A 150
Bard St. B11: S'hll 6C 118
Bardwell Cl. WV8: Pend 1D 26

Barford Cl. B76: Walm 1D 70
  WS10: Darl 3C 46
Barford Cres. B38: K Nor 5E 147
Barford Ho. B5: Birm 4G 117
Barford Rd. B16: Birm 5A 100
  B90: Shir .5B 150
Barford St. B5: Birm 3G 117
Bargate Dr. WV6: Wolv 5E 27
Bargehouse Wlk. B38: K Nor 2A 160
Bargery Rd. WV11: Wed 6A 18
Barham Cl. B90: M'path 4E 165
Barker Rd. B74: S Cold 4H 53
Barker St. B19: Loz 2D 100
  B68: O'bry 3A 98
Bark Piece B32: Bart G 2A 130
Barlands Cft. B34: S End 3F 105
Barle Gro. B36: Cas B 2B 106
Barley Cl. DY3: Sed 6B 60
  WS9: A'rdge 1G 51
  WV8: Pend 6C 14
Barleycorn Dr. B16: Edg 5H 99
Barley Cft. WV6: Pert 6D 24
Barleyfield Ho. WS1: Wals *3C 48*
                 (off Bath St.)
Barleyfield Ri. DY6: W Hth 1G 91
Barleyfield Row WS1: Wals 3C 48
Barlow Cl. B45: Fran 5E 143
  B68: O'bry 6G 97
Barlow Dr. B70: W Brom 6D 80
Barlow Rd. WS10: W'bry 6G 47
Barlow's Rd. B15: Edg 6H 115
Barmouth Cl. WV12: W'hall 3C 30
Barnabas Rd. B23: Erd 3F 85
Barnaby Sq. WV10: Bush 3B 16
Barnard Cl. B37: Chel W 2F 123
Barnardo's Cen. B7: Birm 4A 102
Barnard Pl. WV2: Wolv 5A 44
Barnard Rd. B75: S Cold 4C 54
  WV11: Wed 6H 17
Barn Av. DY3: Sed 6G 59
Barnbrook Rd. B93: Know 2C 166
Barn Cl. B30: Stir 1D 146
  B63: Hale .3G 127
  B64: Crad H 5G 111
  DY9: Lye 1G 125
Barn Cft. B32: Bart G 4C 130
Barncroft WS6: Gt Wyr 2G 7
  WS7: Chase 1C 10
Barncroft Rd. B69: Tiv 1A 96
Barncroft St. B70: W Brom 5G 63
Barnes Cl. B37: F'bri 1A 122
Barnes Hill B29: W Cas 3D 130
Barnesmeadow Pl. WV14: Cose 5D 60
Barnesville Cl. B10: Small H 3G 119
Barnet Rd. B23: Erd 2D 84
Barnett Cl. DY6: K'wfrd 5B 92
  WV14: Bils 1F 61
Barnett Gro. DY6: K'wfrd 5B 92
Barnett La. DY6: K'wfrd 4B 92
  DY8: Word 4B 92
Barnett Rd. WV13: W'hall 2G 45
Barnetts La. WS8: Bwnhls 5B 10
Barnett St. B69: Tiv 5A 78
  DY4: Tip 3A 78
  DY8: Word 6B 92
Barney Cl. DY4: Tip 4H 77
Barn Farm Cl. WV14: Bils 4A 46
Barnfield Dr. B92: Sol 1A 152
Barnfield Gro. B20: Hand 2A 82
Barnfield Rd. B62: B'hth 4D 112
  DY4: Tip 6G 61
  WV1: Wolv 1C 44
Barnfield Trad. Est. DY4: Tip 6G 61
Barnford Cl. B10: Small H 2C 118
Barnford Cres. B68: O'bry 6H 97
Barnfordhill Cl. B68: O'bry 5H 97
Barn Grn. WV3: Wolv 4D 42
BARN HILL 4C 162
Barn Ho. B8: W End 5B 104
Barnhurst La. WV8: Bilb, Pend 4B 14
Barn La. B13: Mose 6A 134
  B21: Hand 2A 100
  B92: Olton 1C 136
Barn Mdw. B25: Yard 2B 120

Barnmoor Ri. B91: Sol 6G 137
Barn Owl Dr. WS3: Pels 3D 20
Barn Owl Wlk. DY5: Brie H 5G 109
Barnpark Covert B14: K Hth 5E 147
Barn Piece B32: Quin 1H 129
Barnsbury Av. B72: W Grn 1A 86
Barns Cl. WS9: Wals W 3B 22
Barns Cft. B74: Lit As 5B 36
Barnsdale Cres. B31: N'fld 3C 144
Barns La. WS4: A'rdge 2H 33
  WS4: Ras .2G 33
  WS9: A'rdge 2H 33
Barnsley Rd. B17: Edg 2E 115
Barnstaple Rd. B66: Smeth 4F 99
Barn St. B5: Birm 5H 5 (1H 117)
Barnswood Cl. B63: Crad 6E 111
Barnt Grn. Rd. B45: Coft H 5A 158
Barnt Green Sailing Club 6E 159
Barnwood Rd. B32: Quin 1D 130
  WV8: Pend 6C 14
Barons Cl. B17: Harb 5E 115
Barons Ct. B92: Sol 1G 137
Barons Ct. Trad. Est. WS9: Wals W . . .5A 22
Barrack Cl. B75: S Cold 5E 55
Barrack La. B63: Crad 5D 110
Barracks Cl. WS3: Blox 1C 32
Barracks La. WS3: Blox 1B 32
  WS8: Bwnhls 4E 11
  WS9: Bwnhls 4E 11
Barracks Pl. WS3: Blox 1C 32
Barrack St. B7: Birm 5A 102
  B70: W Brom 5G 63
Barra Cft. B35: Cas V 3F 87
Barrar Cl. DY8: Amb 3C 108
Barratts Cft. DY5: P'ntt 6G 75
Barratts Ho. B14: K Hth 5G 147
Barratts Rd. B38: K Nor 6C 146
BARR COMMON 6D 34
Barr Comn. Cl. WS9: A'rdge 6D 34
Barr Comn. Rd. WS9: A'rdge 6D 34
Barretts La. CV7: Bal C 6H 169
Berrett St. B66: Smeth 5G 99
Barrhill Cl. B43: Gt Barr 3A 66
Barrington Cl. WS5: Wals 2E 65
  WV10: Oxl 6G 15
Barrington Rd. B45: Rub 2E 157
  B92: Olton 3C 136
Barr Lakes La. WS9: A'rdge 4A 50
Barron Rd. B31: N'fld 4F 145
Barrow Cl. WS9: Bwnhls 3B 22
Barrow Hill Rd. DY5: P'ntt 6G 75
Barrow Ho. B16: Edg 2B 116
            (off Meyrick Wlk.)
Barrows La. B26: Sheld, Yard 3C 120
           (not continuous)
Barrows Rd. B11: S'brk 5C 118
Barrow Wlk. B5: Birm 4G 117
           (not continuous)
Barrs Cres. B64: Crad H 3H 111
Barrs Rd. B64: Crad H 4G 111
Barrs St. B68: O'bry 5G 97
Barr St. B19: Hock 4E 101
           (not continuous)
  DY3: Lwr G 4G 75
Barry Jackson Twr. B6: Aston 2H 101
Barry Rd. WS5: Wals 4G 49
Barsham Cl. B5: Edg 5G 117
Barsham Dr. DY5: Brie H 3G 109
BARSTON 6A 154
Barston La. B91: Sol 5D 152
           (not continuous)
  B92: Bars, H Ard 4E 153
  CV7: Bal C 6D 154
Barston Rd. B68: O'bry 4A 98
Bartholomew Row B5: Birm . . .3G 5 (6H 101)
Bartholomew St. B5: Birm 4G 5 (1H 117)
Bartic Av. DY6: K'wfrd 5D 92
Bartleet Rd. B67: Smeth 4B 98
Bartlett Cl. DY4: Tip 4B 62
Bartley Cl. B92: Olton 3D 136
Bartley Cres. B31: N'fld 2B 144
Bartley Dr. B31: N'fld 3C 144
BARTLEY GREEN 4B 130
Bartley Green Leisure Cen. 4A 130

Bartley Ho. B32: Bart G 5B 130
Bartley Woods B32: Bart G 3H 129
Barton Cft. B28: Hall G 3F 149
Barton Dr. B93: Know 6D 166
Barton La. DY6: W Hth 1A 92
Barton Lodge Rd. B28: Hall G 3E 149
Barton Pas. B3: Birm 4C 4
Barton Rd. WV4: E'shll 1B 60
Bartons Bank B6: Aston 2G 101
Barton St. B70: W Brom 5H 79
Bar Wlk. WS9: A'rdge 6E 23
Barwell Cl. B93: Dorr 5A 166
Barwell Ct. B9: Birm 1B 118
Barwell Rd. B9: Birm 1B 118
Barwick St. B3: Birm 3D 4 (6F 101)
Basalt Cl. WS2: Wals 5G 31
Basil Gro. B31: N'fld 3C 144
Basil Rd. B31: N'fld 3C 144
Baslow Cl. B33: Stech 5C 104
  WS3: Blox 4H 19
Baslow Rd. WS3: Blox 4H 19
Bason's La. B68: O'bry 4A 98
Bassano Rd. B65: B'hth 2C 112
Bassenthwaite Ct. DY6: K'wfrd 3B 92
Bassett Cl. B76: Walm 1C 70
  WV4: Penn 5A 42
  WV12: W'hall 5D 30
Bassett Cft. B10: Small H 3B 118
Bassett Rd. B63: Crad 5C 110
  WS10: W'bry 2A 64
          (not continuous)
Bassetts Gro. B37: K'hrst 4B 106
BASSETT'S POLE 1F 55
Bassnage Rd. B63: Hale 3G 127
Batch Cft. WV14: Bils 6F 45
Batchcroft WS10: Darl 3D 46
Batchelor Cl. DY8: Amb 3D 108
Bateman Dr. B73: W Grn 3H 69
Bateman Rd. B46: Col 6H 89
BATEMAN'S GRFFN 3G 161
Batemans La. B47: H'wd, Wyt 4G 161
Bates Cl. B76: Walm 6F 71
Bates Gro. WV10: Wolv 4C 28
Bate St. WS2: Wals 6C 32
  WV4: E'shll 2A 60
Bath Av. WV1: Wolv 2A 170 (1F 43)
Bath Ct. B15: Birm 2E 117
  B29: W Cas 6F 131
Batheaston Cl. B38: K Nor 2H 159
Bath Mdw. B63: Crad 6G 111
Bath Pas. B5: Birm 6E 5 (2G 117)
Bath Rd. DY4: Tip 2A 78
  DY5: Quar B 1C 110
  DY8: Stourb 6D 108
  WS1: Wals 3C 48
  WV1: Wolv 1F 43
Bath Row B15: Birm 2E 117
  B69: O'bry 1D 96
Bath St. B4: Birm 1E 5 (5G 101)
  DY2: Dud .1E 95
  DY3: Sed 4A 60
  WS1: Wals 2C 48
  WV1: Wolv 2A 44
  WV13: W'hall 2B 46
  WV14: Bils 1F 43
Bath Wlk. B12: Bal H 6G 117
Batmans Hill Rd. DY4: Tip 3G 61
  WV14: Bils 3G 61
Batson Ri. DY5: Brie H 3E 109
Battenhall Rd. B17: Harb 6E 115
Battery Retail Pk. B29: S Oak 3A 132
Battery Way B11: Tys 1E 135
Battlefield Hill WV5: Wom 6A 58
Battlefield La. WV5: Wom 1H 73
Bavaro Gdns. DY5: Quar B 1C 110
Baverstock Rd. B14: K Hth 5G 147
Baxterley Grn. B76: Walm 4D 70
  B91: Sol 3B 150
Baxter Rd. DY5: Brie H 1G 109
Baxters Grn. B90: Shir 1G 163
Baxters Rd. B90: Shir 1H 163
Bay Av. WV14: Bils 1H 61

Bayer St. WV14: Cose 5E 61
Bayford Av. B26: Sheld 1G 137
   B31: Longb 3C 158
Bayley Cres. WS10: Darl 3C 46
Bayley Ho. WS8: Bwnhls 1B 22
Bayleys La. DY4: Tip 5C 62
Bayley Twr. B36: Hodg H 1C 104
Baylie Ct. DY8: Stourb 6D 108
                (off Green St.)
Baylie St. DY8: Stourb 1D 124
Baylis Av. WV11: Wed 1H 29
Bayston Av. WV3: Wolv 3C 42
Bayston Rd. B14: K Hth 3G 147
Bayswater Rd. B20: Hand 6F 83
   DY3: Lwr G 4H 75
Bay Tree Cl. B38: K Nor 1H 159
Baytree Cl. WS3: Blox 5G 19
Baytree Rd. WS3: Blox 5G 19
Baywell Cl. B90: M'path 2E 165
Beach Av. B12: Bal H 6B 118
   WV5: Cose 2B 60
Beach Brook Cl. B11: S'hll 6B 118
Beachburn Way B20: Hand 4C 82
Beach Cl. B31: N'fld 6G 145
Beachcroft Rd. DY6: W Hth 6A 74
Beach Dr. B63: Hale 6A 112
Beach Rd. B11: S'hll 6B 118
   WV14: Bils 4F 45
Beach St. B63: Hale 6A 112
Beach Trade Cen. B12: Bal H 6B 118
Beachwood Av. DY6: W Hth 6A 74
Beacon Cl. B43: Gt Barr 4B 66
   B45: Rub 3G 157
   B66: Smeth 2E 99
Beacon Ct. B43: Gt Barr 4B 66
   B74: S'tly 3H 51
Beacon Dr. WS1: Wals 3E 49
Beacon Hgts. WS9: A'rdge 5D 50
Beacon Hill B6: Aston 1G 101
   B45: Rub 4F 157
   WS9: A'rdge 2E 51
Beacon Ho. B45: Rub 2E 157
        (off Callowbrook La.)
Beacon La. B45: Lick 6D 156
   B60: L Ash 6D 156
   DY3: Sed 4A 60
Beacon M. B43: Gt Barr 4B 66
Beacon Pas. DY3: Sed 5H 59
             (off High St.)
Beacon Ri. DY3: Sed 4A 60
   DY9: W'cte 1H 125
   WS9: A'rdge 6D 34
Beacon Rd. B43: Gt Barr 3D 50
   B44: K'sdng 1A 68
   B73: Bold 4G 69
   WS5: Wals 6H 49
   WS9: A'rdge 3D 50
   WV12: W'hall 1C 30
Beaconsfield Av. WV4: E'shll 5H 43
Beaconsfield Ct. WS1: Wals 3F 49
Beaconsfield Cres. B12: Bal H 6G 117
Beaconsfield Dr. WV4: E'shll 5H 43
Beaconsfield Rd. B12: Bal H 1G 133
   B74: S Cold 4H 53
Beaconsfield St. B71: W Brom 2A 80
Beacon St. WS1: Wals 2E 49
   WV14: Cose 4B 60
Beacon Trad. Est. WS9: A'rdge 3C 34
Beacon Vw. B45: Rub 3F 157
   WS2: Wals 1F 47
        (not continuous)
Beacon Vw. Dr. B74: S'tly 6H 51
Beaconview Ho. B71: W Brom 4D 64
Beacon Vw. Rd. B71: W Brom 3C 64
Beacon Way B43: Gt Barr 4F 65
   WS9: Wals W 4C 22
Beakes Rd. B67: Smeth 6D 98
Beaks Farm Gdns. B16: Edg 1H 115
Beaks Hill Rd. B38: K Nor 6A 146
Beak St. B1: Birm 5D 4 (1F 117)

Beale Cl. B35: Cas V 5E 87
Beale Ho. B16: Edg 2B 116
Beales St. B6: Aston 1B 102
Beale St. DY8: Stourb 6D 108
Bealeys Av. WV11: Wed 1E 29
Bealeys Cl. WS3: Blox 4G 19
Bealeys Fold WV11: Wed 4F 29
        (off Nicholls Fold)
Bealeys La. WS3: Blox 4G 19
Beaminster Rd. B91: Sol 3E 151
Beamish La. WV8: Cod W 2A 12
Beamont Cl. DY4: Tip 1G 77
Bean Cft. B32: Bart G 2A 130
Bean Dr. DY4: Tip 1F 77
Bean Rd. DY2: Dud 1F 95
   DY4: Tip 1E 77
Bean Rd. Ind. Est. DY4: Tip 1E 77
Beardmore Rd. B72: W Grn 5A 70
Bearing Way WV11: Wed 6G 29
Bearley Cft. B90: Shir 1A 164
Bearmore Rd. B64: Old H 2G 111
Bearnett Dr. WV4: Penn 3A 58
Bearnett La. WV4: Lwr P 4H 57
   WV5: Wom 4H 57
BEAR WOOD 2E 115
BEARWOOD 1F 115
Bearwood Ho. B66: Smeth 5E 99
Bearwood Rd. B66: Smeth 2E 115
Bearwood Shop. Cen. B66: Smeth 2E 115
Beasley Gro. B43: Gt Barr 4D 66
Beaton Cl. WV13: W'hall 1G 45
Beaton Rd. B74: Four O 6G 37
Beatrice St. WS3: Blox 3A 32
Beatrice Wlk. B69: Tiv 5A 78
Beatty Ho. DY4: Tip 5A 62
Beaubrook Gdns. DY8: Word 6C 92
Beauchamp Av. B20: Hand 2B 82
Beauchamp Cl. B76: Walm 6F 71
Beauchamp Rd. B13: Mose 2B 148
   B91: Sol 2F 151
Beaudesert Cl. B47: H'wd 3A 162
Beaudesert Rd. B20: Hand 1D 100
   B47: H'wd 3A 162
Beaufort Av. B34: Hodg H 3B 104
Beaufort Pk. B36: Hodg H 4B 104
Beaufort Rd. B16: Edg 2B 116
   B23: Erd 5E 85
Beaufort Way WS9: A'rdge 5D 34
Beaulieu Av. DY6: K'wfrd 5D 92
Beaumaris Cl. DY1: Dud 4B 76
Beaumont Cl. WS6: Gt Wyr 3F 7
Beaumont Dr. B17: Harb 1F 131
   DY5: Brie H 4F 109
Beaumont Gdns. B18: Hock 3B 100
Beaumont Gro. B91: Sol 2D 150
Beaumont Pk. B30: K Nor 3B 146
Beaumont Rd. B30: B'vlle 1A 146
   B62: B'hth 3E 113
   WS6: Gt Wyr 3F 7
   WS10: W'bry 1F 63
Beaumont Way WS11: Nort C 1E 9
Beausale Dr. B93: Know 2D 166
Beau Rd. WV13: W'hall 3H 45
Beauty Bank B64: Crad H 3A 112
Beauty Bank Cres. DY8: Stourb 5C 108
Beaver Cl. WV11: Wed 4H 29
Bebington Cl. WV8: Pend 1D 26
Beccles Dr. WV13: W'hall 3H 45
Beckbury Av. WV4: Penn 6A 42
Beckbury Rd. B29: W Cas 4E 131
Beck Cl. B66: Smeth 5E 99
Beckenham Av. B44: K'sdng 4A 68
Beckensall Cl. DY1: Dud 6D 76
Becket Cl. B74: Four O 3F 37
Beckett St. WV14: Bils 5G 45
Beckfield Cl. B14: K Hth 5G 147
   WS4: S'fld 1G 33
Beckford Cft. B93: Dorr 6B 166
Beckman Rd. DY9: Pedm 3G 125
Beckminster Rd. WV3: Wolv 4D 42
Beconsfield Dr. B93: Dorr 6G 167
Becton Gro. B42: Gt Barr 6F 67
Bedcote Pl. DY8: Stourb 6F 109
Beddoe Cl. DY4: Tip 2D 78

Beddow Av. WV14: Cose 6E 61
Beddows Rd. WS3: Wals 4C 32
Bedford Dr. B75: S Cold 5C 54
Bedford Ho. B36: Cas B 3D 106
   WV1: Wolv 4D 44
        (off Lomas St.)
Bedford Rd. B11: S'brk 2A 118
   B71: W Brom 6H 63
   B75: S Cold 5C 54
Bedford St. DY4: Tip 2B 78
   WV1: Wolv 4D 44
Bedford Ter. B19: Loz 1F 101
Bedlam Wood Rd. B31: Longb 6A 144
Bedworth Cft. DY4: Tip 3B 78
Bedworth Gro. B9: Bord G 1H 119
Beebee Rd. WS10: W'bry 5F 47
Beecham Cl. WS9: A'rdge 1C 34
Beech Av. B12: Bal H 6A 118
   B32: Quin 4B 114
   B37: Chel W 2D 122
   B62: B'hth 3C 112
Beech Cl. B75: Four O 5G 37
   DY3: Sed 4A 60
   WV10: Oxl 1F 27
Beech Ct. B8: Salt 4E 103
   B30: K Nor 3A 146
   B43: Gt Barr 4H 65
   B45: Redn 2B 158
   B66: Smeth 1A 98
   B73: Bold 5F 69
   B91: Sol 2H 151
   DY8: Stourb 1F 125
   WS1: Wals 3E 49
   WS6: Gt Wyr 1F 7
Beech Cres. DY4: Tip 5C 62
   WS10: W'bry 6F 47
Beechcroft B15: Edg 4C 116
Beechcroft Av. B28: Hall G 1G 149
Beechcroft Ct. B74: Four O 2G 53
Beechcroft Cres. B74: S'tly 2F 51
Beechcroft Est. B63: Crad 5E 111
Beechcroft Pl. WV10: Oxl 2G 27
Beechcroft Rd. B36: Cas B 1F 105
   B64: Old H 2G 111
Beechdale B68: O'bry 4H 113
Beechdale Av. B44: Gt Barr 3G 67
Beech Dene Gro. B23: Erd 2E 85
Beecher Pl. B63: Crad 6F 111
Beecher Rd. B63: Crad 6F 111
Beecher Rd. E. B63: Crad 6F 111
Beecher St. B63: Crad 6E 111
Beeches, The B15: Edg 3E 117
   B70: W Brom 5C 80
   B74: Four O 5D 36
   WV1: Wolv 6E 27
Beeches Av. B27: A Grn 1A 136
Beeches Cl. B45: Rub 2D 156
   DY6: K'wfrd 4B 92
Beeches Ct. B45: Redn 2H 157
Beeches Dr. B24: Erd 2A 86
Beeches Farm Dr. B31: Longb 2E 159
Beeches Pl. WS3: Blox 2B 32
Beeches Rd. B42: Gt Barr 6D 66
        (not continuous)
   B65: B'hth 2B 112
   B68: O'bry 6A 98
   B70: W Brom 4C 80
        (not continuous)
   WS3: Blox 3B 32
Beeches Rd. Pas. B70: W Brom 5C 80
Beeches Vw. Av. B63: Crad 1E 127
Beeches Wlk. B73: S Cold 2H 69
Beeches Way B31: Longb 2E 159
Beechey Cl. B43: Gt Barr 6F 51
Beech Farm Cft. B31: N'fld 4E 145
Beechfield Av. B11: S'brk 5B 118
Beechfield Cl. B62: B'hth 3C 112
Beechfield Gro. WV14: Cose 6D 60
Beechfield Rd. B11: S'brk 5B 118
   B67: Smeth 5D 98
Beech Gdns. WV8: Cod 5F 13
Beech Ga. B74: Lit As 4B 36
Beechglade B20: Hand 3B 82

Beech Grn. DY1: Dud 2C 76
Beech Gro. B14: K Hth 2A 148
Beech Hill Rd. B72: W Grn 6A 70
Beech Ho. B31: N'fld 4F 145
(off Church Rd.)
B91: Sol 5D 150
Beechhouse La. WV5: Seis 5A 56
Beech Hurst B38: K Nor 1A 160
Beech Hurst Gdns. WV5: Seis ..3A 56
BEECH LANES 4D 114
Beech M. B64: Old H 1G 111
Beechmore Rd. B26: Sheld 6D 120
Beechmount Dr. B23: Erd 1G 85
Beechnut Cl. B91: Sol 2H 151
Beechnut La. B91: Sol 3A 152
(not continuous)
Beech Rd. B23: Erd 6F 69
B30: B'vlle 6A 132
B47: H'wd 3B 162
B69: Tiv 1A 96
DY1: Dud 3E 77
DY6: K'wfrd 4C 92
DY8: Stourb 2C 124
WS10: W'bry 6F 47
WV10: Oxl 1F 27
WV13: W'hall 1G 45
Beech St. WV14: Cose 5E 61
Beech Tree Av. WV11: Wed 1E 29
Booch Tree Cl. DY6: K'wfrd 1C 92
Beechtree Rd. WS9: Wals W 5B 22
Beech Wlk. B38: K Nor 1B 160
Beech Way B66: Smeth 4F 99
Beechwood B20: Hand 4A 82
Beechwood Av. WV11: Wed 1D 28
Beechwood Cl. B90: Ches G ...5C 164
WS3: Blox 4H 19
Beechwood Ct. B30: K Nor 4E 147
WV6: Tett 6A 26
Beechwood Cft. B74: Lit As 4D 36
Beechwood Dr. WV6: Tett 1G 41
Beechwood Pk. Rd. B91: Sol ...1C 150
Beechwood Rd. B14: K Hth ...2H 147
B43: Gt Barr 4B 66
B67: Smeth 3C 114
B70: W Brom 4H 79
DY2: Dud 6G 77
Beehive La. B76: Curd 1E 89
Beehive Wlk. DY4: Tip 2G 77
Bee La. WV10. F'hses 4H 15
Beeston Cl. B6: Aston 2A 102
DY5: Brie H 3H 109
Beeton Rd. B18: Win G 3A 100
Beet St. B65: B'hth 2C 112
Beever Rd. DY4: Tip 6D 62
Beggars Bush La. WV5: Wom ...2H 73
Beighton Cl. B74: Four O 3F 37
Beilby Rd. B30: Stir 1D 146
Belbroughton Rd. B63: Hale ...3H 127
DY8: Stourb 2C 124
Belcher's La. B8: W End 1G 119
B9: Bord G 1G 119
Beldray Pk. WV14: Bils 5G 45
Beldray Rd. WV14: Bils 5G 45
Belfont Trad. Est. B62: Hale ..1C 128
Belfry, The WV6: Pert 5D 24
Belfry Cl. WS3: Blox 4G 19
Belfry Dr. DY8: Woll 5C 108
Belgrade Rd. WV10: Oxl 6F 15
Belgrave Ct. DY6: K'wfrd 5D 92
Belgrave Interchange B5: Birm ..4F 117
Belgrave Middleway B5: Birm ..4G 117
B12: Birm 4G 117
Belgrave Rd. B62: B'hth 3D 112
Belgrave Ter. B21: Hand 2C 100
Belgrave Wlk. WS2: Wals 6H 31
Belgravia Cl. B5: Edg 4G 117
Belgravia Cl. Walkway B5: Edg ..4G 117
Belgravia Ct. B37: K'hrst 4G 106
Belgrove Cl. B15: Edg 5A 116
Belinda Cl. WV13: W'hall 6H 29
Bellamy Cl. B90: Shir 6B 150
Bellamy Farm Rd. B90: Shir ..6B 150
Bellamy La. WV11: Wed 2E 29
Bell Av. WV13: W'hall 1A 46

Bell Barn Rd. B15: Birm 3E 117
(not continuous)
Bell Barn Shop. Cen. B15: Birm ..3E 117
Bell Cl. B9: Bord G 6E 103
B36: Cas B 3D 106
WS10: Darl 4D 46
Bell Ct. B31: N'fld 2D 144
Bellcroft B16: Birm 1D 116
Bell Dr. B8: Salt 6F 103
WS5: Wals 6E 49
Bellefield Av. B18: Win G 5A 100
Bellefield Rd. B18: Win G 5A 100
Belle Isle DY5: Brie H 6G 93
Bellemere Rd. B92: H Ard 2B 154
Bellencroft Gdns. WV3: Wolv ..4A 42
Bell End B65: Row R 6C 96
Bellevale B63: Hale 6G 111
Belle Vue DY8: Word 1A 108
Bellevue B5: Edg 4F 117
WV14: Cose 3G 61
Bellevue Av. B16: Edg 5H 99
Belle Vue Dr. B62: Hale 5D 112
Belle Vue Gdns. B65: Row R ...6C 96
Belle Vue Rd. B65: Row R 1C 112
DY5: Quar B 2C 110
Bellevue Rd. B26: Sheld 4F 121
WV14: Bils 3A 62
Bellevue St. WV14: Cose 3B 60
Belle Vue Ter. B92: H Ard 1A 154
Belle Wlk. B13: Mose 3B 134
Bellfield B31: N'fld 3D 144
Bellfield Ho. B14: K Hth 6F 147
(off Thornham Way)
Bell Flwer Dr. WS5: Wals 2D 64
Bell Fold B68: O'bry 3A 98
BELL GREEN 3D 160
Bell Grn. La. B38: Head H ...4D 160
Bell Heather Rd. WS8: Clay ..1H 21
Bell Heath Way B32: Bart G ..3G 129
Bell Hill B31: N'fld 2E 145
Bell Holloway B31: N'fld 2D 144
Bellington Cft. B90: M'path ...3E 165
Bell Inn Shop. Cen., The
B31: N'fld 3E 145
Bellis St. B16: Edg 2B 116
Bell La. B31: N'fld 3E 145
(not continuous)
B33: Kitts G 2A 122
WS3: Blox 5G 19
WS5: Wals 1D 64
Bellman Cl. WS10: Darl 4D 46
Bell Mdw. DY9: Pedm 5F 125
Bell Mdw. Way B14: K Hth ...5G 147
(not continuous)
Bell Pl. WV2: Wolv 6B 170 (3G 43)
Bell Rd. DY2: Neth 4E 95
WS5: Wals 5H 49
WV5: Try 4C 56
Bells Farm Cl. B14: K Hth ...5E 147
Bellsize Cl. WS11: Nort C 1D 8
Bells La. B14: K Hth 5D 146
DY8: Word 2B 108
Bells Moor Rd. B70: W Brom ..1G 79
Bell St. B70: W Brom 5B 80
DY4: Tip 2G 77
DY5: Brie H 1H 109
DY5: P'ntt 2H 93
(Belmont Rd.)
DY5: P'ntt 2H 93
(Hartland St.)
DY8: Stourb 6D 108
WS10: Darl 4D 46
WV1: Wolv 4B 170 (2G 43)
WV14: Bils 5E 45
WV14: Cose 3E 61
Bell St. Sth. DY5: Brie H 1H 109
Bell Wlk. B37: F'bri 2B 122
Bell Wharf Pl. WS5: Wals ...5G 49
Bellwood Rd. B31: N'fld 3D 144
Belmont Cl. DY4: Tip 1H 77
WS9: A'rdge 3C 34
WS11: Cann 1G 7
Belmont Covert B31: N'fld ...2F 145
Belmont Cres. B31: N'fld 1F 145

Belmont Gdns. WV14: Bils 1A 62
Belmont Pas. B9: Birm 1A 118
Belmont Rd. B21: Hand 1G 99
B45: Rub 3G 157
B66: Smeth 1E 115
DY5: P'ntt 3H 93
DY9: W'cte 6A 110
WV4: Penn 6E 43
Belmont Rd. E. B21: Hand ...1G 99
Belmont Row B4: Birm ...2H 5 (6A 102)
Belmont St. WV14: Bils 1A 62
Belper, The DY1: Dud 6D 76
Belper Ent. Pk. B70: W Brom ..3F 79
Belper Rd. B70: W Brom 4F 79
WS3: Blox 4A 20
Belper Row DY2: Neth 5G 95
Belstone Cl. B14: K Hth 1F 147
Belton Av. WV11: Wed 6D 16
Belton Gro. B45: Redn 1A 158
Belvedere Av. WV4: Penn 6F 43
Belvedere Cl. DY6: K'wfrd 5D 92
WS7: Chase 1B 10
Belvedere Gdns. WV6: Tett ...2C 26
Belvedere Rd. B24: Erd 5G 85
Belvide Gdns. WV8: Cod 3F 13
Belvide Gro. B29: W Cas 5F 131
Belvidere Gdns. B11: S'hll ...1C 134
Belvidere Rd. WS1: Wals 3D 48
Belvoir Cl. DY1: Dud 5A 76
Belwell Dr. B74: Four O 1G 53
Belwell La. B74: Four O 1G 53
Belwell Pl. B74: Four O 1G 53
Bembridge Cl. WV12: W'hall ..1B 30
Bembridge Rd. B33: Yard 6E 105
Benacre Dr. B5: Birm 4H 5 (1H 117)
Benbeck Gro. DY4: Tip 2E 77
Bencroft WV8: Bilb 3H 13
Bendall Rd. B44: K'sdng 3B 68
Benedon Rd. B26: Sheld 4E 121
Benmore Av. B5: Edg 5F 117
Bennett Av. DY1: Dud 1D 76
Bennett Rd. B74: Four O 6D 37
Bennett's Hill B2: Birm ...4D 4 (1F 117)
DY2: Dud 1G 95
Bennett's La. WV6: Patt, Tres ...3A 40
Bennett's Rd. B8: Salt 3D 102
Bennett St. B19: Loz 1F 101
Ben Nevis Way DY8: Amb 5E 109
Bennitt Cl. B70: W Brom 6A 80
Benson Av. WV4: Penn 6G 43
Benson Cl. WV6: Pert 4E 25
Benson Ind. Est. B18: Hock ..3B 100
Benson Rd. B14: K Hth 6B 148
B18: Hock 3B 100
Bent Av. B32: Quin 5B 114
Bentham Ct. B31: N'fld 2D 144
BENTLEY 6F 31
Bentley Bridge Leisure Pk. ...5D 28
Bentley Bri. Way WV11: Wed ..5D 28
Bentley Cl. B76: Walm 5D 70
Bentley Dr. WS2: Wals 1H 47
WV8: Cod 3F 13
Bentley Farm Cl. B93: Ben H ..5A 166
Bentley Gro. B29: W Cas 5D 130
BENTLEY HEATH 4B 166
Bentley Heath Cotts. B93: Know ..4B 166
Bentley La. WS2: Wals 5G 31
WV12: W'hall 4D 30
Bentley La. Ind. Pk. WS2: Wals ..6G 31
Bentley Mill Cl. WS2: Wals ...2F 47
Bentley Mill La. WS2: Wals ...2F 47
Bentley Mill Way WS2: Wals ..2F 47
Bentley New Dr. WS2: Wals ..6H 31
Bentley Pl. WS2: Wals 5A 32
Bentley Rd. B36: Cas B 2H 105
WV10: Bush 5A 16
Bentley Rd. Nth. WS2: Wals ..2E 47
Bentley Rd. Sth. WS2: Wals ...3D 46
Bentmead Gro. B38: K Nor ...6C 146
Benton Av. B11: S'hll 5C 118
Benton Cl. WV12: W'hall 5D 30
Benton Cres. WS3: Blox 5B 20
Benton Rd. B11: S'brk 5C 118
Bentons La. WS6: Gt Wyr 4G 7

Bentons Mill Cft. B7: Nech 1C **102**
Bent St. DY5: Brie H 5H **93**
Ben Willetts Wlk. B65: B'hth 2C **112**
Benyon Cen., The WS2: Wals 2G **31**
Beoley Cl. B72: W Grn 4A **70**
Beoley Gro. B45: Rub 2F **157**
Berberry Cl. B30: B'vlle 1H **145**
Berchelai Av. B31: N'fld 1C **144**
Beresford Cres. B70: W Brom 4H **79**
Beresford Dr. B73: Bold 4G **69**
Beresford Rd. B69: O'bry 2A **98**
  WS3: Blox .1C **32**
Berets, The B75: S Cold 5D **54**
Bericote Cft. B27: A Grn 2B **136**
Berkeley Cl. WV6: Pert 6F **25**
Berkeley Dr. DY6: K'wfrd 2A **92**
Berkeley M. B25: Yard 4G **119**
Berkeley Pct. B14: K Hth 5H **147**
Berkeley Rd. B25: Yard 4G **119**
  B90: Shir 4F **149**
Berkeley Rd. E. B25: Yard 4H **119**
Berkeley St. WS2: Wals 4H **47**
Berkley Cl. WS2: Wals 6F **31**
Berkley Ct. B1: Birm 6A **4**
Berkley Cres. B13: Mose 4C **134**
Berkley Ho. B23: Erd 1F **85**
Berkley St. B1: Birm 5A **4** (1E **117**)
Berkshire, The WS3: Blox 4G **19**
Berkshire Cl. B71: W Brom 6H **63**
Berkshire Cres. WS10: W'bry 1A **64**
Berkswell Cl. B74: Four O 5E **37**
  B91: Sol 5F **137**
  DY1: Dud 4A **76**
Berkswell Hall CV7: Berk 4H **155**
Berkswell Rd. B24: Erd 3H **85**
Bermuda Cl. DY1: Dud 1D **76**
Bernard Pl. B18: Hock 4B **100**
Bernard Rd. B17: Edg 1F **115**
  B68: O'bry .1A **114**
  DY4: Tip 6B **62**
Bernard St. B71: W Brom 3A **80**
  WS1: Wals .3E **49**
Berners St. B19: Loz 2F **101**
Bernhard Dr. B21: Hand 1A **100**
Bernwall Cl. DY8: Stourb 1D **124**
Berrandale Rd. B36: Hodg H 1D **104**
Berrington Dr. WV14: Cose 5D **60**
Berrington Wlk. B5: Birm 4G **117**
Berrow Cott. Homes B93: Know 3E **167**
Berrow Dr. B15: Edg 4A **116**
Berrowside Rd. B34: S End 3A **106**
Berry Av. WS10: Darl 6B **46**
Berrybush Gdns. DY3: Sed 6A **60**
Berry Cl. B19: Hock 3F **101**
Berry Cres. WS5: Wals 1G **65**
Berry Dr. B66: Smeth 3E **99**
  WS9: A'rdge 4A **34**
Berryfield Rd. B26: Sheld 5H **121**
Berryfields WS9: A'rdge 4A **34**
  WS9: Ston .2G **23**
Berryfields Rd. B76: Walm 2D **70**
Berry Hall La. B91: Cath B, Sol 3C **152**
Berrymound Vw. B47: H'wd 2C **162**
Berry Rd. B8: Salt 4E **103**
  DY1: Dud 2E **77**
Berry St. B18: Hock 3B **100**
  WV1: Wolv 3C **170** (1H **43**)
Bertha Rd. B11: S'brk 6D **118**
Bertram Cl. DY4: Tip 4C **62**
Bertram Rd. B10: Small H 2D **118**
  B67: Smeth .3C **98**
Berwick Gro. B31: N'fld 4B **144**
  B43: Gt Barr 1D **66**
Berwicks La. B37: Chel W 2D **122**
  (not continuous)
Berwood Farm Rd. B72: W Grn 1A **86**
Berwood Gdns. B24: Erd 2A **86**
Berwood Gro. B92: Olton 4F **137**
Berwood La. B24: Erd 4C **86**
Berwood Pk. B35: Cas V 5E **87**
Berwood Rd. B72: W Grn 1B **86**
Berwyn Gro. WS6: C Hay 2F **7**
Besant Gro. B27: A Grn 4G **135**
Besbury Cl. B93: Dorr 6F **167**

BESCOT 5A **48**
Bescot Cres. WS1: Wals 5B **48**
Bescot Cft. B42: Gt Barr 1D **82**
Bescot Dr. WS2: Wals 5H **47**
Bescot Ind. Est. WS10: W'bry 1D **62**
Bescot Rd. WS2: Wals 5H **47**
Bescot Stadium 5B **48**
Bescot Stadium Station (Rail) 6B **48**
Bescot St. WS1: Wals 4B **48**
Besford Gro. B31: N'fld 4B **144**
  B90: M'path 3F **165**
Besom Way WS6: C Hay 3C **6**
Bessborough Rd. B25: Yard 3B **120**
Best Rd. WV14: Bils 4F **45**
Best St. B64: Old H 1H **111**
Beswick Gro. B33: Kitts G 5E **105**
Beta Gro. B14: Yard W 3C **148**
Bethesda Gdns. B63: Crad 4E **111**
Betjeman Pl. WV10: Bush 6C **16**
Betley Gro. B33: Stech 4E **105**
Betony Cl. WS5: Wals 2E **65**
Betsham Cl. B44: K'sdng 4B **68**
Bettany Glade WV10: Bush 3A **16**
Betteridge Dr. B76: Walm 1C **70**
Betton Rd. B14: K Hth 2G **147**
Bett Rd. B20: Hand 4B **82**
Betty's La. WS11: Nort C 1D **8**
Beulah Ct. B63: Hale 1A **128**
Bevan Av. WV4: E'shll 1A **60**
Bevan Cl. WS4: S'fld 6G **21**
  WV14: Bils .5H **45**
Bevan Ind. Est. DY5: Brie H 1E **109**
Bevan Rd. DY4: Tip 3B **78**
  DY5: Brie H .1E **109**
Bevan Way B66: Smeth 1D **98**
Beverley Cl. B72: W Grn 6A **70**
  CV7: Bal C 5H **169**
Beverley Ct. Rd. B32: Quin 5A **114**
Beverley Cres. WV4: E'shll 1B **60**
Beverley Cft. B23: Erd 6D **84**
Beverley Dr. DY6: K'wfrd 2A **92**
Beverley Rd. B26: Sheld 6F **121**
Beverley Rd. B45: Rub 2G **157**
  B71: W Brom 4B **64**
Beverston Rd. DY4: Tip 3B **62**
  WV6: Pert 5G **25**
Bevington Rd. B6: Aston 6H **83**
Bevin Rd. WS2: Wals 6E **31**
Bevis Gro. B44: Gt Barr 2H **67**
Bewdley Av. B12: Bal H 5A **118**
Bewdley Dr. WV1: Wolv 1D **44**
Bewdley Ho. B26: Yard 1E **121**
Bewdley Rd. B30: Stir 5D **132**
Bewdley Vs. B18: Win G 5H **99**
  (off Cape St.)
Bewlay Cl. DY5: Brie H 4F **109**
Bewley Rd. WV12: W'hall 5D **30**
Bewlys Av. B20: Hand 3A **82**
Bexley Gro. B71: W Brom 6C **64**
Bexley Rd. B44: K'sdng 5B **68**
Bhylls Cres. WV3: Wolv 4A **42**
Bhylls La. WV3: Wolv 3H **41**
Bibby's Grn. WV10: Bush 3B **16**
Bibsworth Av. B13: Mose 5D **134**
Bibury Rd. B28: Hall G 6E **135**
Bicester Sq. B35: Cas V 3F **87**
BICKENHILL .4F **139**
Bickenhill Grn. Ct. B92: Bick 4F **139**
Bickenhill La. B37: Mars G 5E **123**
  (not continuous)
  B92: Cath B .1E **153**
Bickenhill Pk. Rd. B92: Olton 4B **136**
Bickenhill Parkway B40: Nat E C 5F **123**
Bickenhill Rd. B37: Mars G 4C **122**
Bickenhill Trad. Est. B40: Mars G 6F **123**
Bickford Rd. B6: Witt 6A **84**
  WV10: Wolv 4B **28**
Bickington Rd. B32: Bart G 4B **130**
Bickley Av. B11: S'brk 5C **118**
  B74: Four O .4E **37**
Bickley Gro. B26: Sheld 6F **121**
Bickley Rd. WS4: Rus 2G **33**
  WV14: Bils .4A **46**
Bicknell Cft. B14: K Hth 5G **147**

Bickon Dr. DY5: Quar B 3B **110**
Bickton Cl. B24: Erd 1A **86**
Biddings La. WV14: Cose 3D **60**
Biddlestone Gro. WS5: Wals 1G **65**
Biddlestone Pl. WS10: Darl 4B **46**
Biddulph Ct. B73: S Cold 3G **69**
Bideford Dr. B29: S Oak 4G **131**
Bideford Rd. B66: Smeth 4F **99**
Bidford Cl. B90: Shir 5B **150**
Bidford Rd. B31: N'fld 4C **144**
Bierton Rd. B25: Yard 3A **120**
Biggin Cl. B35: Cas V 4E **87**
  WV6: Pert 4E **25**
Big Peg, The B18: Birm 1A **4** (5E **101**)
Bigwood Dr. B32: Bart G 4B **130**
  B75: S Cold .5E **55**
Bilberry Cres. B76: Walm 2C **70**
Bilberry Dr. B45: Rub 3G **157**
Bilberry Rd. B14: K Hth 1E **147**
Bilboe Rd. WV14: Bils 2H **61**
BILBROOK 3H **13**
Bilbrook Ct. WV8: Bilb 4H **13**
Bilbrook Gro. B29: W Cas 3D **130**
  WV8: Bilb 4H **13**
Bilbrook Ho. WV8: Bilb 4H **13**
Bilbrook Rd. WV8: Bilb, Cod 3G **13**
  (not continuous)
Bilbrook Station (Rail) 5H **13**
Bilhay La. B70: W Brom 2G **79**
Bilhay St. B70: W Brom 2G **79**
Billau Rd. WV14: Cose 3F **61**
BILLESLEY 1C **148**
Billesley Indoor Tennis Cen. 6B **134**
Billesley La. B13: Mose 5H **133**
Billingham Cl. B91: Sol 1F **165**
Billingsley Rd. B26: Yard 3E **121**
Bills La. B90: Shir 6F **149**
Billsmore Grn. B92: Sol 6G **137**
Bills St. WS10: Darl 4E **47**
Billy Buns La. WV5: Wom 5G **57**
Billy Wright Cl. WV4: Penn 5C **42**
Bilport La. WS10: W'bry 5F **63**
BILSTON 6G **45**
Bilston Central Ind. Est. WV14: Bils . .6G **45**
Bilston Central Stop (MM) 6F **45**
Bilston Craft Gallery & Mus. 5G **45**
Bilston Ind. Est. WV14: Bils 6A **46**
Bilston Key Ind. Est. WV14: Bils 6H **45**
Bilston Leisure Cen. 5F **45**
Bilston Rd. DY4: Tip 3B **62**
  WS10: W'bry 2D **62**
  WV2: E'shll, Wolv 4D **170** (2A **44**)
  WV13: W'hall 4A **46**
Bilston St. DY3: Sed 5H **59**
  WS10: Darl .5D **46**
  (not continuous)
  WV1: Wolv 4C **170** (2H **43**)
  WV13: W'hall 2A **46**
Bilston St. Island
  WV1: Wolv 4D **170** (2H **43**)
Bilton Grange Rd. B26: Yard 4D **120**
Bilton Ind. Est. B38: K Nor 1A **160**
Binbrook Rd. WV12: W'hall 5D **30**
Bincomb Av. B26: Sheld 5F **121**
Binfield St. DY4: Tip 3A **78**
Bingley Av. B8: W End 5H **103**
Bingley Ent. Cen. WV3: Wolv 3E **43**
  (off Norfolk Rd.)
Bingley St. WV3: Wolv 3E **43**
Binley Cl. B25: Yard 5B **120**
  B90: Shir 1G **163**
Binstead Rd. B44: K'sdng 3A **68**
Binswood Rd. B62: Quin 4G **113**
Binton Cft. B13: Mose 5H **133**
Binton Rd. B90: Shir 6F **149**
Birbeck Ho. B36: Cas B 3D **106**
Birbeck Pl. DY5: P'ntt 3F **93**
Birchall St. B12: Birm 2H **117**
Birch Av. B31: Longb 6A **144**
  DY5: Quar B 1C **110**
  WS8: Bwnhls 5A **10**
Birch Cl. B17: Harb 6H **115**
  B30: B'vlle .1H **145**
  B76: Walm .3D **70**

Birch Coppice DY5: Quar B 2C **110**
   (not continuous)
  WV5: Wom 1E **73**
Birchcoppice Gdns. WV12: W'hall . . .5E **31**
Birch Ct. B30: K Nor 3A **146**
  B66: Smeth 1B **98**
  WS4: Wals *5E* **33**
   (off Lichfield Rd.)
  WV1: Wolv *5E* **27**
   (off Boscobel Cres.)
Birch Cres. B69: Tiv 6A **78**
Birch Cft. B24: Erd 2B **86**
  B37: Chel W 2E **123**
  WS9: A'rdge 1E **35**
Birchcroft B66: Smeth 4G **99**
Birch Cft. Rd. B75: S Cold 4B **54**
Birchdale Av. B23: Erd 3E **85**
Birchdale Rd. B23: Erd 2D **84**
Birch Dr. B62: B'hth 3E **113**
  B74: Lit As 4D **36**
  B75: S Cold 4D **54**
  DY8: Stourb 5C **108**
Birches Av. WV8: Bilb 6A **14**
Birches Barn Av. WV3: Wolv 4D **42**
Birches Barn Rd. WV3: Wolv 3D **42**
Birches Cl. B13: Mose 4H **133**
BIRCHES GREEN 5G **85**
Birches Grn. Rd. B24: Erd 5H **85**
Birches Pk. Rd. WV8: Cod 5G **13**
Birches Ri. WV13: W'hall 2H **45**
Birches Rd. WV8: Bilb 5G **13**
BIRCHFIELD 5E **83**
Birchfield Av. WV6: Tett 3H **25**
Birchfield Cl. B63: Hale 3G **127**
Birchfield Cres. DY9: W'cte 2B **126**
Birchfield Gdns. B6: Aston 1F **101**
  WS5: Wals 1G **65**
Birchfield La. B69: O'bry 5E **97**
   (not continuous)
Birchfield Rd. B19: Loz 1F **101**
  B20: Hand 6F **83**
  DY9: W'cte 2B **126**
Birchfields Rd. WV12: W'hall 4A **30**
Birchfield Twr. B20: Hand 6F **83**
Birchfield Way WS5: Wals 1F **65**
Birch Ga. DY9: W'cte 1B **126**
Birchglade WV3: Wolv 2B **42**
Birch Gro. B68: O'bry 4B **114**
  CV7: Bal C 1H **169**
Birch Hill Av. WV5: Wom 2F **73**
Birch Hollow B15: Edg 5B **116**
  B68: O'bry 4B **114**
Birchill Pl. WV5: Wom 2F **73**
BIRCHILLS 1A **48**
Birchills Canal Mus. 5A **32**
Birchills Ho. Ind. Est. WS2: Wals . . .5A **32**
Birchills St. WS2: Wals 6A **32**
Birch La. B68: O'bry 4B **114**
  WS4: S'fld 6G **21**
  WS9: A'rdge 6F **23**
Birchley Ho. B69: O'bry 3D **96**
Birchley Ind. Est. B69: O'bry 4E **97**
Birchley Pk. Av. B69: O'bry 3E **97**
Birchley Ri. B92: Olton 6D **120**
Birchmoor Cl. B28: Hall G 6H **135**
Birchover Rd. WS2: Wals 5G **31**
Birch Rd. B6: Witt 5A **84**
  B45: Rub 3E **157**
  B68: O'bry 3B **114**
  DY3: Sed 4B **60**
  WV11: Wed 6H **17**
Birch Rd. E. B6: Witt 5B **84**
Birch St. B68: O'bry 3A **98**
  DY4: Tip 2H **77**
  WS2: Wals 6B **32**
  WV1: Wolv 2A **170** (1G **43**)
Birch Ter. DY2: Neth 5E **95**
Birchtree Gdns. DY5: Quar B 2C **110**
Birch Tree Gro. B91: Sol 3C **150**
Birchtree Hollow WV12: W'hall 4D **30**
Birchtrees B24: Erd 3B **86**
Birchtrees Cft. B26: Yard 6B **120**

Birchtrees Dr. B33: Kitts G 1H **121**
Birch Wlk. B68: O'bry 4B **114**
Birchwood Cl. WV11: Ess 4A **18**
Birchwood Cres. B12: Bal H 1B **134**
Birchwood Rd. B12: Bal H 1A **134**
  WV4: Penn 6E **43**
Birchwoods B32: Bart G 3H **129**
Birchwood Wlk. DY6: K'wfrd 1C **92**
Birchy Cl. B90: Dic H 3F **163**
Birchy Leasowes La. B90: Dic H 4E **163**
Birdbrook Rd. B44: Gt Barr 4G **67**
Birdcage Wlk. B38: K Nor 5B **146**
  DY2: Dud 6F **77**
Bird End B71: W Brom 5D **64**
Birdie Cl. B38: K Nor 6H **145**
Birdlip Gro. B32: Quin 5A **114**
Birds Mdw. DY5: P'ntt 2F **93**
Bird St. DY3: Lwr G 4G **75**
Birdwell Cft. B13: Mose 6B **134**
Birkdale Av. B29: S Oak 4B **132**
Birkdale Cl. DY8: Stourb 4D **124**
  WV1: Wolv 1C **44**
Birkdale Dr. B69: Tiv 2A **96**
Birkdale Gro. B29: S Oak 5C **132**
Birkdale Rd. WS3: Blox 4G **19**
Birkenshaw Rd. B44: Gt Barr 5G **67**
Birley Gro. B63: Hale 1G **127**
BIRMINGHAM 4E **5** (1F **117**)
Birmingham Alexander Sports Stadium
  . . . . .1E **83**
Birmingham Botanical Gdns. 4D **116**
Birmingham Bus. Est. B37: Mars G . .3G **123**
Birmingham City FC 2C **118**
Birmingham Crematorium
  B42: P Barr 2E **83**
Birmingham Hippodrome Theatre
  . . . . .6D **4** (2G **117**)
BIRMINGHAM INTERNATIONAL AIRPORT
  . . . . .1E **139**
Birmingham International Station (Rail)
  . . . . .1F **139**
Birmingham Mus. & Art Gallery
  . . . . .3C **4** (1F **117**)
Birmingham Mus. of Transport, The
  . . . . .6G **161**
Birmingham Nature Cen. 1E **133**
Birmingham New Rd. DY1: Dud 6A **44**
  DY4: Tip 6A **44**
  WV4: E'shll 6A **44**
  WV14: Cose 6A **44**
Birmingham One Bus. Pk.
  B1: Birm 6D **100**
Birmingham Railway Mus. 6F **119**
Birmingham Repertory Theatre
  . . . . .4B **4** (1E **117**)
Birmingham Rd. B31: Hopw 1F **155**
  B36: Cas B 1E **105**
  B37: K'hrst 4D **106**
  B43: Gt Barr 5G **49**
  B45: Rub 5C **156**
  B46: Col 4E **107**
  B46: Wat O 5B **88**
  B48: Hopw 4F **159**
  B61: L Ash, Rub 5C **156**
   (not continuous)
  B63: Hale 2B **128**
  B65: Row R 1C **112**
  B69: O'bry 2H **97**
  B70: W Brom 6C **80**
  B71: W Brom 6E **81**
  B72: S Cold, W Grn 6H **69**
  CV7: Mer 2D **140**
  DY1: Dud 5G **77**
  DY9: Hag 6G **125**
  WS1: Wals 2D **48**
  WS5: Wals 4F **49**
   (Lake Av.)
  WS5: Wals 1D **64**
   (Wellington Rd.)
  WS9: A'rdge 4C **34**
  WS14: Shen W 2G **37**
  WV2: Wolv 5C **170** (2H **43**)
Birmingham Sports Cen. 5H **117**
Birmingham Squash Rackets Cen. . . .1H **115**

Birmingham St. B63: Hale 2B **128**
  B69: O'bry 2G **97**
  DY2: Dud 6F **77**
  DY8: Stourb 6E **109**
  DY9: Stourb 6E **109**
  WS1: Wals 2D **48**
  WS10: Darl 5E **47**
  WV13: W'hall 1B **46**
Birmingham Town Hall 4C **4** (1F **117**)
Birnham Cl. DY4: Tip 2F **77**
Birstall Way B38: K Nor 1G **159**
Bisell Way DY5: Brie H 4H **109**
Bishbury Cl. B15: Edg 3A **116**
Bishop Asbury Cottage Mus. 5G **65**
Bishop Asbury Cres. B43: Gt Barr . . .5G **65**
Bishop Cl. B45: Fran 6E **143**
  DY2: Dud 1G **95**
Bishop Rd. WS10: W'bry 3A **64**
Bishop Ryder Ho. B4: Birm 2G **5**
Bishops Cl. B66: Smeth 5G **99**
Bishop's Ct. B31: N'fld 4F **145**
  B37: Mars G 3G **123**
Bishops Ga. B31: N'fld 5E **145**
Bishopsgate St. B15: Birm . . .6A **4** (2D **116**)
Bishops Mdw. B75: R'ley 6C **38**
Bishops Rd. B73: S Cold 2H **69**
Bishop St. B5: Birm 3G **117**
Bishops Wlk. B64: Crad H 5A **112**
Bishops Way B74: Four O 3F **37**
Bishopton Cl. B90: Shir 6A **150**
Bishopton Rd. B67: Smeth 2D **114**
Bishton Gro. DY2: Neth 5F **95**
Bisley Gro. B24: Erd 5G **85**
Bismillah Bldg. B19: Birm 1C **4** (5F **101**)
Bissell Cl. B28: Hall G 1F **149**
Bissell Dr. WS10: W'bry 2D **64**
Bissell St. B5: Birm 3G **117**
  B32: Quin 1C **130**
  WV14: Bils 6H **45**
Bi-Tec Ind. Pk. WV1: Wolv 2C **44**
Biton Cl. B17: Harb 6F **115**
Bittell Cl. B31: Longb 2D **158**
  WV10: Bush 3A **16**
Bittell Ct. B31: Longb 2D **158**
Bittell Farm Rd. B48: Hopw 6F **159**
Bitterne Dr. WV6: Wolv 5E **27**
Bittern Wlk. DY5: Brie H 5G **109**
Blackacre Rd. DY2: Dud 1F **95**
Blackberry Av. B9: Bord G 6G **103**
Blackberry Cl. DY1: Dud 1A **94**
Blackberry La. B63: Hale 3A **128**
  B65: Row R 4H **95**
  B74: Four O 4E **37**
  WS9: Wals W 3D **22**
Blackbird Cft. B36: Cas B 2C **106**
Blackbrook Cl. DY2: Dud 6C **94**
Blackbrook Rd. DY2: Dud, Neth 4C **94**
Blackbrook Valley Ind. Est.
  DY2: Dud 4C **94**
Blackbrook Way WV10: Bush 3A **16**
Blackburn Av. WV6: Tett 2C **26**
Blackburne Rd. B28: Hall G 1F **149**
Blackbushe Cl. B17: Harb 4D **114**
Blackcat Cl. B37: F'bri 6C **106**
Black Country Ho. B69: O'bry 2F **97**
Black Country Mus. 3F **77**
Black Country New Rd.
  B70: W Brom 1D **78**
  DY4: Tip 1D **78**
  WS10: Darl, W'bry 1B **62**
  WS10: Tip, W'bry 2D **62**
  WV14: Bils 5A **46**
Black Country Route WS2: Wals 4B **46**
  WV13: W'hall 4B **46**
  WV14: Cose, Bils 2D **60**
Blackdown Cl. B45: Fran 5G **143**
Blackdown Rd. B93: Know 3D **166**
Blackett Ct. B73: S Cold 2A **70**
Blackfirs La. B37: Mars G 4E **123**
Blackford Cl. B63: Hale 3F **127**
Blackford Rd. B11: S'hll 1C **134**
  B90: Shir 2A **164**
Blackford St. B18: Win G 4A **100**
Blackhalve La. WV11: Wed, Ess 1D **28**

Blackham Dr. B73: Bold 6G 69
Blackham Rd. WV11: Wed 1H 29
Black Haynes Rd. B29: W Cas 1E 145
BLACKHEATH .2C 112
Blackheath Mkt. B65: B'hth 2D 112
Blackheath Trad. Est. B65: Row R 1E 113
Black Horse La. WS10: Darl 6D 46
BLACK LAKE 1H 79
Black Lake B70: W Brom 1G 79
Black Lake Ind. Est. B70: W Brom 1H 79
Black Lake Stop (MM) 1G 79
Blacklea Cl. B25: Yard 2B 120
Black Mill DY1: Dud 3F 77
Blackmoor Cft. B33: Kitts G 1H 121
Blackpit La. WV4: Lwr P 2E 57
Blackrock Rd. B23: Erd 1B 84
Blackroot Cl. WS7: Hamm 1F 11
Blackroot Rd. B23: Erd 1B 84
Blackroot Ho. B73: New O 3C 68
(off Welshmans Rd.)
Blackroot Rd. B74: S Cold 4G 53
Blacksmith Dr. B75: R'ley 6C 38
Blacksmith Way B70: W Brom 5A 80
Blackthorn Cl. B30: B'vlle 1G 145
Blackthorne Av. WS7: Chase 1B 10
Blackthorne Cl. B91: Sol 3C 150
DY1: Dud .3B 76
Blackthorne Rd. B67: Smeth 5B 98
DY1: Dud .3B 76
WS5: Wals .6D 48
Blackthorn Rd. B30: B'vlle 1G 145
B36: Cas B 1G 105
DY8: Word 2D 108
Blackwater Cl. DY5: P'ntt 3E 93
Blackwell Rd. B72: W Grn 4B 70
Blackwood Av. WV11: Wed 1D 28
Blackwood Dr. B74: S'tly 3G 51
Blackwood Rd. B74: S'tly 2G 51
Blades Ho. B71: W Brom 5E 65
Blades Rd. B70: W Brom 3D 78
Blaenwern Dr. B63: Crad 4D 110
Blagdon Rd. B63: Hale 5A 112
Blair Gro. B37: Chel W 2F 123
Blakedon Rd. WS10: W'bry 2E 63
Blakedown Rd. B63: Hale 4G 127
Blakedown Way B69: O'bry 5E 97
Blake Hall Cl. DY5: Brie H 4G 109
Blake Ho. WS2: Wals 3A 48
(off St Johns Rd.)
Blakeland Rd. B44: K'sdng 1G 83
Blakeland St. B9: Bord G 1F 119
Blake La. B9: Bord G 1F 119
BLAKELEY 2G 73
Blakeley Av. WV6: Tett 2D 26
Blakeley Hall Gdns. B69: O'bry 2H 97
Blakeley Hall Rd. B69: O'bry 2H 97
Blakeley Heath Dr. WV5: Wom 2G 73
Blakeley Ri. WV6: Tett 2D 26
Blakeley Wlk. DY2: Neth 5E 95
Blakeley Wood Rd. DY4: Tip 5C 62
Blakemere Av. B25: Yard 3C 120
Blakemere Ho. B16: Birm 1C 116
(off Graston Cl.)
Blakemore Cl. B32: Bart G 2D 130
Blakemore Dr. B75: S Cold 5D 54
Blakemore Rd. B70: W Brom 5G 79
WS9: Wals W 4C 22
Blakenall Cl. WS3: Blox 1B 32
BLAKENALL HEATH 1B 32
Blakenall Heath WS3: Blox 1B 32
Blakenall La. WS3: Blox 2A 32
Blakenall Row WS3: Blox 1B 32
Blakeney Av. B17: Harb 4E 115
DY8: Woll .5B 108
Blakeney Cl. DY3: Sed 5G 59
Blakenhale Rd. B33: Sheld 2F 121
BLAKENHALL 4G 43
Blakenhall Gdns. WV2: Wolv 4G 43
Blakenhall Ind. Est.
WV2: Wolv 4F 43
Blake Pl. B9: Bord G 1F 119
Blakesley Cl. B76: Walm 2D 86
Blakesley Rd. B25: Yard 2B 120
Blakesley Hall Mus. 2C 120

Blakesley M. B25: Yard 3B 120
B33: Stech 1C 120
Blakesley Rd. B25: Yard 2A 120
Blakesley Way B33: Stech 1B 120
Blake St. B74: Four O 3E 37
Blake Street Station (Rail) 3F 37
Blakewood Cl. B34: S End 4G 105
Blandford Av. B36: Cas B 6A 88
Blandford Dr. DY8: Word 6C 92
Blandford Rd. B32: Quin 6C 114
Blanefield WV8: Pend 5C 14
Blanning Ct. B93: Dorr 5A 166
Blay Av. WS2: Wals 1H 47
Blaydon Av. B75: R'ley 1C 54
Blaydon Ct. B17: Harb 1H 131
(off Metchley La.)
Blaydon Rd. WV9: Pend 5E 15
Blaythorn Av. B92: Olton 2E 137
Blaze Hill Rd. DY6: W Hth 1G 91
Blaze Pk. DY6: W Hth 1H 91
Bleak Hill Rd. B23: Erd 3C 84
Bleakhouse Rd. B68: O'bry 2A 114
Bleak St. B67: Smeth 3D 98
Blenheim Cl. WS4: Rus 2H 33
Blenheim Ct. B44: Gt Barr 5H 67
B91: Sol .3G 151
Blenheim Dr. B43: Gt Barr 5H 65
WS10: W'bry 6E 47
Blenheim Rd. B13: Mose 4H 133
B90: Shir .5B 150
DY6: K'wfrd 3D 92
WS11: Nort C 1F 9
WV12: W'hall 3B 30
Blenheim Way B35: Cas V 5F 87
B44: Gt Barr 5H 67
DY1: Dud .5A 76
Bletchley Rd. B24: Erd 3C 86
Blewitt Cl. B36: Cas B 5H 87
Blewitt St. DY5: P'ntt 3G 93
Blews St. B6: Birm 4G 101
Blithe Cl. DY8: Amb 3E 109
Blithfield Dr. DY5: Brie H 4F 109
Blithfield Gro. B24: Erd 2A 86
Blithfield Rd. WS8: Bwnhls 3F 9
Blockall WS10: Darl 4D 46
Blockall Cl. WS10: Darl 5C 46
BLOOMFIELD 6G 61
Bloomfield Cl. WV5: Wom 1D 72
Bloomfield Dr. WV12: W'hall 6D 18
Bloomfield Pk. DY4: Tip 1F 77
Bloomfield Pk. Trad. Est. DY4: Tip 1F 77
Bloomfield Rd. B13: Mose 2B 134
DY4: Tip 1G 77
Bloomfield St. Nth. B63: Hale 6H 111
Bloomfield St. W. B63: Hale 1H 127
Bloomfield Ter. DY4: Tip 1F 77
Bloomsbury Gro. B14: K Hth 6E 133
Bloomsbury St. B7: Nech 4B 102
WV2: Wolv 5A 170 (3G 43)
Bloomsbury Wlk. B7: Nech 4B 102
Bloor Mill Cl. WV13: W'hall 2H 45
Blossom Av. B29: S Oak 3B 132
BLOSSOMFIELD 5D 150
Blossomfield Cl. B38: K Nor 1H 159
DY6: K'wfrd 1C 92
Blossomfield Club 1E 165
Blossomfield Ct. B38: K Nor 1H 159
Blossomfield Gdns. B91: Sol 3E 151
Blossomfield Rd. B91: Sol 6C 150
Blossom Gro. B36: Hodg H 1C 104
B64: Old H 2H 111
(off Cherry Dr.)
Blossom Hill B24: Erd 3G 85
Blossom Rd. B24: Erd 3G 85
Blossom's Fold WV1: Wolv . .3B 170 (1G 43)
Blossomville Way B27: A Grn 1H 135
Blounts Rd. B23: Erd 2C 84
BLOWER'S GREEN 2D 94
Blowers Grn. Cres. DY2: Dud 2D 94
Blowers Grn. Pl. DY2: Dud 2D 94
Blower's Grn. Rd. DY2: Dud 2D 94
Bloxcidge St. B68: O'bry 5H 97
BLOXWICH 6H 19
Bloxwich Bus. Pk. WS2: Wals 2G 31

Bloxwich La. WS2: Wals 5G 31
Bloxwich Library Theatre 6H 19
Bloxwich North Station (Rail) 4F 19
Bloxwich Rd. WS2: Wals 4B 32
WS3: Blox 2A 32
Bloxwich Rd. Nth. WV12: W'hall 3D 30
Bloxwich Rd. Sth. WV13: W'hall 6A 30
Bloxwich Station (Rail) 6G 19
Bloxwich Swimming Baths & Leisure Cen.
. . . . .1A 32
Blucher St. B1: Birm 6C 4 (2F 117)
Blue Ball La. B63: Crad 5E 111
Blue Bell Cl. DY8: Word 1A 108
Bluebell Cres. WV11: Wed 4F 29
Bluebell Cft. B23: Erd 6C 68
B31: N'fld 3D 144
Bluebell Dr. B37: Chel W 1F 123
Bluebell La. WS6: Gt Wyr 4G 7
Bluebell Rd. B64: Old H 6G 95
DY1: Dud .4D 76
WS9: Wals W 4D 22
Bluebellwood Cl. B76: Walm 2E 71
Blue Bird Pk. B62: Hunn 5A 128
Bluebird Trad. Est. WV10: Wolv 4A 28
Blue Cedar Dr. B74: S'tly 5H 51
Blue Cedars DY8: Woll 5A 108
Blue Lake Rd. B93: Dorr 6H 167
Blue La. E. WS2: Wals 6B 32
Blue La. W. WS2: Wals 1B 48
Blue Rock Pl. B69: Tiv 2C 96
Blue Stone Wlk. B65: Row R 3C 96
Blundell Rd. B11: S'hll 6D 118
Bluntington Cl. B92: Olton 6D 136
Blythe Av. CV7: Bal C 6H 169
Blythe Ct. B46: Col 2H 107
B73: S Cold 6H 53
Blythefield Av. B43: Gt Barr 3G 65
Blythe Gdns. WV8: Cod 3F 13
Blythe Ga. B90: Bly P 6D 164
Blythe Gro. B44: Gt Barr 2H 67
Blythe Rd. B46: Col 2H 107
BLYTHE VALLEY PARK 6D 164
Blythe Valley Parkway B90: Bly P 5D 164
Blythe Way B91: Sol 4A 152
Blythewood Cl. B91: Sol 6B 152
Blythsford Rd. B28: Hall G 3F 149
Blythswood Rd. B11: Tys 1G 135
Blyton Cl. B16: Birm 6B 100
Board School Gdns. DY3: Up Gor 1A 76
Boar Hound Cl. B18: Hock 5C 100
Boat La. WS14: Muck C 4H 11
Boatmans La.
WS9: A'rdge, Wals W 5A 22
Boatmans Reach B14: K Hth 3E 147
Bobbin Cl. WS6: Gt Wyr 4F 7
Bobbington Way DY2: Neth 4F 95
Bob's Coppice Wlk. DY5: Quar B 4B 110
Boddis Ind. Pk. B64: Old H 1H 111
Bodenham Rd. B31: N'fld 5C 144
B68: O'bry 3H 113
Boden Rd. B28: Hall G 6F 135
Bodens La. WS9: A'rdge 4C 50
Bodiam Ct. WV6: Pert 6G 25
Bodicote Gro. B75: R'ley 1C 54
Bodington Rd. B75: Four O 6H 37
Bodmin Cl. WS5: Wals 4H 49
Bodmin Ct. DY5: Brie H 1H 109
Bodmin Gro. B7: Birm 4B 102
Bodmin Ri. WS5: Wals 4H 49
Bodmin Rd. DY2: Neth 1F 111
Bognop Rd. WV11: Ess 3E 17
BOLDMERE 5F 69
Boldmere Cl. B73: Bold 6G 69
Boldmere Ct. B43: Gt Barr 6A 66
(off South Vw.)
Boldmere Dr. B73: Bold 5G 69
Boldmere Gdns. B73: Bold 5F 69
Boldmere Rd. B73: Bold 3F 69
Boldmere Ter. B29: S Oak 4A 132
Boleyn Cl. WS6: C Hay 3D 6
Boleyn Rd. B45: Fran 6D 142
Bolney Rd. B32: Quin 6C 114
Bolton Ct. DY4: Tip 5C 62
Bolton Ind. Cen. B19: Hock 3D 100

Bolton Rd. B10: Small H 3B 118
  WV11: Wed 4E 29
Bolton St. B9: Birm 1B 118
Bolton Way WS3: Blox 4F 19
Bomers Fld. B45: Redn 2A 158
Bond, The B5: Birm 1A 118
Bond Dr. B35: Cas V 4E 87
Bondfield Rd. B13: Mose 1B 148
Bond Sq. B18: Hock 5C 100
Bond St. B19: Birm 1C 4 (5F 101)
  B30: Stir 6C 132
  B65: Row R 6E 97
  B70: W Brom 5A 80
  WV2: Wolv 5B 170 (2G 43)
  WV14: Cose 5C 60
Bone Mill La. WV1: Wolv 5H 27
Bonham Gro. B25: Yard 2R 120
Boningale Way B93: Dorr 6H 165
Bonner Dr. B76: Walm 2D 86
Bonner Gro. WS9: A'rdge 4B 34
Bonneville Cl. DY4: Tip 1F 77
Bonnington Way B43: Gt Barr 1F 67
Bonny Stile La. WV11: Wed 3D 28
Bonsall Rd. B23: Erd 1G 85
Bonville Gdns. WV10: Bush 3A 16
Booth Cl. DY6: K'wfrd 3E 93
  WS3: Blox 1B 32
Booth Ct. DY5: Brie H 1H 109
Booth Ho. WS4: Wals 6D 32
Booth Rd. WS10: W'bry 3A 64
Booth's Farm Rd. B42: Gt Barr 6C 66
Booth's La. B42: Gt Barr 4D 66
  (not continuous)
Booth St. B21: Hand 2G 99
  B66: Hand, Smeth 2G 99
  WS3: Blox 1A 32
  WS10: Darl 3D 46
Bordeaux Cl. DY1: Dud 4A 76
Borden Cl. WV8: Pend 1D 26
BORDESLEY 1B 118
Bordesley Cir. D10: Small H 2R 118
Bordesley Cl. B9: Bord G 1G 119
BORDESLEY GREEN 1E 119
Bordesley Grn. B9: Bord G 1D 118
Bordesley Grn. E. B9: Bord G 1H 119
  B33: Stech 1C 120
Bordesley Grn. Rd. B8: Salt 1D 118
  B9: Bord G 1D 118
Bordesley Grn. Trad. Est.
  B9: Bord G 1E 119
Bordesley Middleway B10: Small H .3A 118
  B11: S'brk 3A 118
Bordesley Station (Rail) 2A 118
Bordesley St. B5: Birm 4G 5 (1H 117)
Bordesley Trad. Est. B8: Salt 6D 102
Borneo St. WS4: Wals 5D 32
Borough Cres. B69: O'bry 1E 97
  DY8: Stourb 6C 108
Borrowdale Cl. DY5: Brie H 4F 109
Borrowdale Gro. B31: N'fld 4B 144
Borrowdale Rd. B31: N'fld 4A 144
Borrow St. WV13: W'hall 6A 30
Borwick Av. B70: W Brom 4G 79
Bosbury Ter. B30: Stir 6D 132
Boscobel Av. DY4: Tip 3H 77
Boscobel Cl. DY1: Dud 4B 76
Boscobel Cres. WV1: Wolv 5G 27
Boscobel Rd. B43: Gt Barr 3H 65
  B90: Ches G 4B 164
  WS1: Wals 3F 49
Boscombe Av. B11: S'brk 5C 118
Boscombe Rd. B11: Tys 1E 135
Boscote Cft. B31: N'fld 6E 131
Bosmere Ct. B31: N'fld 1A 144
Boss Dr. DY2: Dud 2E 95
Bossgate Cl. WV5: Wom 3G 73
Boston Gro. B44: K'sdng 5B 68
Bosty La. WS9: A'rdge 4G 33
Boswell Cl. WS10: Darl 6D 46
  WS10: W'bry 4C 62
Boswell Rd. B44: K'sdng 1H 83
  B74: S Cold 5A 54
  WV14: Bils 4H 45
Bosworth Cl. DY3: Sed 1B 76

Bosworth Ct. B26: Sheld 6E 121
Bosworth Dr. B37: Chel W, F'bri ...1B 122
Bosworth Rd. B26: Yard 1C 136
Botany Dr. DY3: Up Gor 2H 75
Botany Rd. WS5: Wals 6D 48
Botany Wlk. B16: Birm 1C 116
Botha Rd. B9: Bord G 6C 103
Botteley Rd. B70: W Brom 1G 79
Botterham La. DY3: Swind 4E 73
Bottetourt Rd. B29: W Cas 2E 131
  (not continuous)
Botteville Rd. B27: A Grn 3A 136
Bott La. DY9: Lye 5H 109
  WS1: Wals 2D 48
BOUCHALL 5F 109
Boughton Rd. B25: Yard 4A 120
Boulevard, The B73: W Grn 5H 69
  DY5: Brie H 1A 110
Boultbee Rd. B72: W Grn 6A 70
Boulton Ho. B70: W Brom 6B 80
Boulton Ind. Cen. B18: Hock 4D 100
Boulton Middleway B18: Birm 4D 100
  B19: Birm 4D 100
Boulton Retreat B21: Hand 2A 100
Boulton Rd. B21: Hand 2A 100
  B66: Smeth 3H 99
  B70: W Brom 6B 80
  B91: Sol 6G 137
Boulton Sq. B70: W Brom 6B 80
Boulton Wlk. B23: Erd 3B 84
Boundary Av. B65: Row R 1E 113
Boundary Cl. WV13: W'hall 2E 45
Boundary Ct. B37: F'bri 1A 122
Boundary Cres. DY3: Lwr G 4G 75
Boundary Dr. B13: Mose 3F 133
Boundary Hill DY3: Lwr G 4G 75
Boundary Ho. B5: Edg 6E 117
  B47: Wyt 6G 161
Boundary Ind. Est. WV10: F'hses ..2G 15
Boundary La. B90: Dic H 3G 163
Boundary Pl. B21: Hand 6G 81
Boundary Rd. B23: Erd 3E 85
  B74: S'tly 4H 51
  WS9: Wals W 4B 22
Boundary Way WV4: Penn 6A 42
  WV6: Tett 1F 41
Bourlay Cl. B45: Fran 5E 143
Bourn Av. B31: N'fld 2C 144
BOURNBROOK 3B 132
Bournbrook Ct. B5: S Oak 2C 132
Bournbrook Rd. B29: S Oak 2C 132
Bourne Av. B62: Quin 1F 129
  DY4: Tip 6C 62
Bournebrook Cl. DY2: Neth 4E 95
Bournebrook Cres. B62: Quin 1G 129
Bourne Cl. B13: Mose 1D 148
  B91: Sol 1A 152
Bourne Grn. B32: Quin 5C 114
Bourne Hill Cl. DY2: Neth 6G 95
Bourne Rd. B6: Aston 2B 102
Bournes Cl. B63: Hale 2H 127
Bournes Cres. B63: Hale 1G 127
Bournes Hill B63: Hale 1G 127
Bourne St. DY2: Dud 6F 77
  DY3: Sed 6C 60
  WV14: Cose 6C 60
Bourne Wlk. WS9: A'rdge 6F 35
Bourne Wlk. B65: Row R 4H 95
Bourne Way Gdns. B29: S Oak 5C 132
Bourn Mill Dr. B6: Aston 3G 101
BOURNVILLE 6A 132
Bournville La. B30: B'ville, Stir 6H 131
Bournville Station (Rail) 6C 132
Bourton Cl. WS5: Wals 2E 65
Bourton Cft. B92: Olton 5D 136
Bourton Rd. B92: Olton 5D 136
Bovey Cft. B76: Walm 6E 71
Bovingdon Rd. B35: Cas V 4E 87
Bowater Av. B33: Stech 2B 120
Bowater Ho. B19: Birm 4F 101
  (off Aldgate Gro.)
  B70: W Brom 5A 80
Bowater St. B70: W Brom 4A 80
Bowbrook Av. B90: M'path 4E 165

Bowcroft Gro. B24: Erd 1A 86
Bowden Rd. B67: Smeth 3C 98
Bowdler Rd. WV2: Wolv ...6D 170 (3H 43)
Bowen Av. WV4: E'shll 2C 60
Bowen-Cooke Av. WV6: Pert 3E 25
Bowen Ct. B13: Mose 2B 134
Bowen Rd. WV4: E'shll 6A 44
Bowercourt Cl. B91: Sol 6F 151
Bower La. DY5: Quar B 3B 110
Bowes Rd. B45: Rub 2E 157
Bowker St. WV13: W'hall 2E 45
Bowlas Av. B74: Four O 3H 53
BOWLING GREEN 6F 95
Bowling Grn., The B76: Walm 1D 70
Bowling Grn. Cl. B23: Erd 6E 69
  WS10: Darl 4D 46
Bowling Grn. Dr. B67: Smeth 1C 114
Bowling Grn. La. B20: Hand 1C 100
Bowling Grn. Rd. DY2: Neth 6F 95
  DY8: Stourb 6C 108
Bowlplex
  Birmingham 2C 116
  Dudley 4G 77
Bowman Rd. B42: Gt Barr 4D 66
Bowmans Ri. WV1: Wolv 6C 28
Bowness Gro. WV12: W'hall 6B 18
Bowood Cres. B31: N'fld 5F 145
Bowood Dr. WV6: Tett 3B 26
Bowood End B76: Walm 2C 70
Bowshot Cl. B36: Cas B 6H 87
Bowstoke Rd. B43: Gt Barr 5G 65
Bow St. B1: Birm 6D 4 (2F 117)
  WV13: W'hall 2B 46
  WV14: Bils 5G 45
Bowyer Rd. B8: Salt 5E 103
Bowyer St. B10: Small H 2A 118
Boxhill Cl. B6: Aston 3H 101
Box Rd. B37: Chel W 3E 123
Box St. WS1: Wals 2D 48
Box Trees Rd. B93: Dorr 6H 165
Boyd Gro. B27: A Grn 3A 136
Boydon Cl. WV2: E'chll 5C 44
Boyleston Rd. B28: Hall G 1G 149
Boyne Rd. B26: Sheld 4E 121
Boyton Gro. B44: Gt Barr 2H 67
Brabazon Gro. B35: Cas V 4D 86
Brabham Cres. B74: S'tly 5H 51
Bracadale Av. B24: Erd 3G 85
Bracebridge Cl. CV7: Bal C 3H 169
Bracebridge Ct. B17: Harb 6H 115
Bracebridge Rd. B24: Erd 6F 85
  B74: Four O 3F 53
Bracebridge St. B6: Aston 3G 101
Braceby Av. B13: Mose 6C 134
Brace St. WS1: Wals 3C 48
  (not continuous)
Brackenbury Rd. B44: K'sdng 5B 68
Bracken Cl. WV8: Pend 6C 14
Bracken Cft. B37: Chel W 6E 107
Brackendale Dr. WS5: Wals 2F 65
Brackendale Shop. Cen.
  WV12: W'hall 5D 30
Brackendale Way DY9: W'cte 1H 125
Bracken Dr. B75: S Cold 6E 55
Brackenfield Rd. B44: Gt Barr 3G 67
  B63: Hale 2C 127
Brackenfield Vw. DY1: Dud 1H 93
Bracken Pk. Gdns. DY8: Word 1D 108
Bracken Rd. B24: Erd 5A 86
Bracken Way B38: K Nor 2H 159
  B74: S'tly 3H 51
Brackenwood WS5: Wals 6H 49
Brackenwood Dr. WV11: Wed 4H 29
Brackley Av. B20: Hand 6E 83
Brackleys Way B92: Olton 3D 136
Bracknell Cl. B31: N'fld 3G 145
Bradbeer Ho. B16: Edg 2C 116
Bradburne Way B7: Birm 4A 102
Bradburn Rd. WV11: Wed 1D 28
Bradbury Cl. WS8: Bwnhls 2B 22
Bradbury Rd. B92: Olton 4D 136
Braden Rd. WV4: Penn 2B 58
Brades Cl. B63: Crad 4D 110
Brades Ri. B69: O'bry 1D 96

Brades Rd. B69: O'bry 6E **79**
BRADES VILLAGE 1D **96**
Bradewell Rd. B36: Cas B 6H **87**
Bradfield Ho. B26: Sheld 5A **122**
Bradfield Rd. B42: Gt Barr 6F **67**
Bradford Cl. B43: Gt Barr 6B **66**
Bradford Ct. B12: Birm 3A **118**
Bradford La. WS1: Wals 2C **48**
Bradford Mall WS1: Wals 2C **48**
Bradford Pl. B11: S'brk 5A **118**
     B70: W Brom 1C **98**
     WS1: Wals 2C **48**
Bradford Rd. B36: Cas B 1E **105**
     DY2: Dud 3B **94**
     WS8: Bwnhls 5A **10**
Bradford St. B5: Birm 6G **5** (2H **117**)
     B12: Birm 6G **5** (2H **117**)
     WS1: Wals 2C **48**
Bradgate Cl. WV12: W'hall 3C **30**
Bradgate Dr. B74: Four O 4E **37**
Bradgate Pl. B12: Bal H 6A **118**
BRADLEY .2G **61**
Bradley Cft. CV7: Bal C 3H **169**
Bradley La. WV14: Bils 2H **61**
Bradleymore Rd. DY5: Brie H 6H **93**
Bradley Rd. B34: S End 3H **105**
     DY8: Stourb 5D **108**
     WV2: Wolv 4A **44**
Bradleys Cl. B64: Crad H 4G **111**
Bradley's La. DY4: Tip 5F **61**
     WV14: Cose 5F **61**
Bradley St. DY4: Tip 5H **77**
     DY5: P'ntt 2F **93**
     WV14: Bils 1H **61**
BRADMORE 3C **42**
Bradmore Cl. B91: Sol 1E **165**
Bradmore Gro. B29: W Cas 5E **131**
Bradmore Rd. WV3: Wolv 3D **42**
Bradnock Cl. B13: Mose 6C **134**
BRADNOCK'S MARSH 4E **155**
Bradnocks Marsh Bus. Cen.
     B92: H Ard 4E **155**
Bradnocks Marsh La. B92: H Ard 6D **154**
Bradshaw Av. B38: K Nor 6H **145**
     WS10: Darl 6B **46**
Bradshaw Cl. B15: Birm 3E **117**
     DY4: Tip 4A **78**
Bradshawe Cl. B28: Hall G 4D **148**
Bradshaw St. WV1: Wolv 1A **44**
Bradstock Rd. B30: K Nor 3E **147**
Bradwell Cft. B75: R'ley 6C **38**
Braemar Av. DY8: Word 2A **108**
Braemar Cl. DY3: Sed 4G **59**
     WV12: W'hall 3B **30**
Braemar Dr. B23: Erd 2B **84**
Braemar Rd. B73: S Cold 3F **69**
     B92: Olton 4C **136**
     WS11: Nort C 1E **9**
Braeside Cft. B37: Chel W 1F **123**
Braeside Way WS3: Pels 4D **20**
Bragg Rd. B20: Hand 5F **83**
Braggs Farm La. B90: Dic H, Shir . . .5F **163**
Braid Cl. B38: K Nor 6H **145**
Brailes Cl. B92: Sol 6A **138**
Brailes Dr. B76: Walm 2D **70**
Brailes Gro. B9: Bord G 2H **119**
Brailsford Cl. WV11: Wed 1G **29**
Brailsford Dr. B15: Birm 6A **116**
     B66: Smeth 4E **99**
Braithwaite Dr. DY6: K'wfrd 3B **92**
Braithwaite Rd. B11: S'brk 4A **118**
Bramah Way DY4: Tip 1C **78**
Bramber Dr. WV5: Wom 1F **73**
Bramber Ho. B31: Longb 1D **158**
Bramber Way DY8: Stourb 3D **124**
Bramble Cl. B6: Aston 2G **101**
     B31: N'fld 1D **144**
     B46: Col 2H **107**
     B64: Old H 5H **95**
     WS8: Clay 2A **22**
     WV12: W'hall 2C **30**
Bramble Dell B9: Bord G 6G **103**
Bramble Dr. B26: Sheld 5E **121**
Bramble Grn. DY1: Dud 2B **76**

Brambles, The B76: Walm 5E **71**
     DY9: W'cte 2H **125**
Brambleside DY8: Word 2D **108**
Bramblewood WV5: Wom 6G **57**
Bramblewood Dr. WV3: Wolv 3C **42**
Bramblewoods B34: S End 4G **105**
Brambling Wlk. B15: Edg 4E **117**
     DY5: Brie H 5G **109**
Bramcote Dr. B91: Sol 6G **137**
Bramcote Ri. B75: S Cold 4A **54**
Bramcote Rd. B32: Quin 6A **114**
     (not continuous)
Bramdean Wlk. WV4: Penn 5A **42**
Bramerton Cl. WV11: Wed 3C **28**
Bramford Dr. DY1: Dud 1D **76**
Bramley Cl. B43: Gt Barr 2F **67**
     WS5: Wals 3H **49**
Bramley Cft. B90: Shir 5A **150**
Bramley Dr. B20: Hand 4D **82**
     B47: H'wd 3B **162**
Bramley M. Ct. B27: A Grn 6A **120**
Bramley Rd. B27: A Grn 6A **120**
     WS5: Wals 1F **65**
Brampton Av. B28: Hall G 1G **149**
Brampton Cres. B90: Shir 1H **149**
Bramshall Dr. B93: Dorr 6A **166**
Bramshaw Cl. B14: K Hth 5H **147**
Bramshill Cl. B15: Edg 3D **116**
Bramstead Av. WV6: Tett 1H **41**
Bramwell Dr. WS6: C Hay 4D **6**
Branchal Rd. WS9: A'rdge 6E **23**
Branch Rd. B38: K Nor 1A **160**
BRANDHALL 3H **113**
Brandhall Ct. B68: O'bry 1G **113**
Brandhall La. B68: O'bry 2H **113**
Brandhall Rd. B68: O'bry 1H **113**
Brandon Cl. B70: W Brom 5G **79**
     DY3: Sed 6A **60**
     WS9: A'rdge 6H **35**
Brandon Ct. B31: N'fld 6F **145**
Brandon Gro. B31: Longb 2D **158**
Brandon Pk. WV3: Wolv 4C **42**
Brandon Pas. B16: Birm 6A **100**
Brandon Pl. B34: S End 2H **105**
Brandon Rd. B28: Hall G 3E **135**
     B62: B'hth 2E **113**
     B91: Sol 6G **137**
Brandon Thomas Ct. B6: Aston 1B **102**
Brandon Way B70: W Brom 4G **79**
     DY5: Quar B 3A **110**
Brandon Way Ind. Est. B70: W Brom . . .4F **79**
Brandwood Cres. B30: K Nor 4F **147**
BRANDWOOD END 3E **147**
Brandwood Gro. B14: K Hth 2F **147**
Brandwood Ho. B14: K Hth 6F **133**
Brandwood Pk. Rd. B14: K Hth 2D **146**
Brandwood Rd. B14: K Hth 3F **147**
Branfield Cl. WV14: Cose 5C **60**
Branksome Av. B21: Hand 1B **100**
Branscombe Cl. B14: K Hth 2F **147**
Bransdale Cl. WV6: Wolv 4E **27**
Bransdale Rd. WS8: Clay 6A **10**
Bransford Ri. B91: Cath B 2D **152**
Bransford Twr. B12: Birm 3H **117**
Branston Ct. B18: Birm 4E **101**
Branston St. B18: Birm 4E **101**
Branthill Rd. B25: Yard 3A **120**
Branthill Cft. B91: Sol 6F **151**
Brantley Av. WV3: Wolv 2A **42**
Brantley Rd. B6: Witt 5A **84**
Branton Hill La. WS9: A'rdge 4E **35**
Brassie Cl. B38: K Nor 6H **145**
Brassington Av. B73: S Cold 1H **69**
Brasshouse La. B66: Smeth 3D **98**
BRATCH, THE 6E **57**
Bratch Cl. DY2: Neth 6E **95**
Bratch Comn. Rd. WV5: Wom 6E **57**
Bratch Hollow WV5: Wom 5G **57**
Bratch La. WV5: Wom 5F **57**
Bratch Pk. WV5: Wom 5F **57**
Bratt St. B70: W Brom 3A **80**
Braunston Cl. B76: Walm 3E **71**
Brawnes Hurst B26: Yard 2E **121**
Brayford Av. DY5: Brie H 4F **109**

Bray Ho. WV11: Wed 4E **29**
Braymoor Rd. B33: Kitts G 2A **122**
Brays Rd. B26: Sheld 5E **121**
Bray St. WV13: W'hall 1B **46**
Bream Cl. B37: Chel W 1E **123**
     WV10: Wolv 5D **28**
Breamore Cres. DY1: Dud 4B **76**
Brean Av. B26: Yard 6D **120**
Brearley Cl. B19: Birm 4G **101**
Brearley St. B19: Birm 4F **101**
     B21: Hand 1H **99**
Breaside Wlk. B37: Chel W 6E **107**
Brecknock Rd. B71: W Brom 1G **79**
Brecon Dr. DY8: Amb 5F **109**
Brecon Rd. B20: Hand 1D **100**
Brecon Twr. B16: Birm 1C **116**
Bredon Av. DY9: Lye 6G **109**
Bredon Ct. B63: Hale 2A **128**
Bredon Cft. B18: Hock 4C **100**
Bredon Rd. B69: O'bry 4D **96**
     DY8: Amb 5E **109**
Breech Cl. B74: S'tly 4G **51**
Breeden Dr. B76: Curd 1D **88**
Breedon Rd. B30: K Nor 2C **146**
Breedon Ter. B18: Hock 4C **100**
     (off Brookfield Rd.)
Breedon Way WS4: S'fld 6G **21**
Breener Ind. Est. DY5: Brie H 2F **109**
Breen Rydding Dr. WV14: Cose 4D **60**
Brelades Cl. DY1: Dud 5A **76**
Brennand Cl. B68: O'bry 3H **113**
Brennand Rd. B68: O'bry 2H **113**
Brentford Rd. B14: K Hth 2A **148**
     B91: Sol 4C **150**
Brentmill Cl. WV10: Bush 3B **16**
Brentnall Dr. B75: Four O 6H **37**
Brenton Rd. WV4: Penn 2D **58**
Brent Rd. B30: Stir 5F **133**
Brentwood Cl. B91: Sol 4C **150**
Brentwood Gro. B44: Gt Barr 5G **67**
Brenwood Cl. DY6: K'wfrd 2H **91**
Brereton Cl. DY2: Dud 1G **95**
Brereton Rd. WV12: W'hall 2C **30**
Bretby Cl. B93: Ben H 4B **166**
Bretby Gro. B23: Erd 1G **85**
Bretshall Cl. B90: M'path 4D **164**
Brett Dr. B32: Bart G 5A **130**
Brettell La. DY5: Brie H 3D **108**
     DY8: Amb 3D **108**
Brettell St. DY2: Dud 1D **94**
Bretton Gdns. WV10: Wolv 3B **28**
Bretton Rd. B27: A Grn 3B **136**
Brett St. B71: W Brom 2H **79**
Brevitt Rd. WV2: Wolv 5H **43**
Brewer's Dr. WS3: Pels 6E **21**
Brewers Ter. WS3: Pels 5E **21**
Brewer St. WS2: Wals 5C **32**
Brewery St. B6: Birm 4G **101**
     B21: Hand 1H **99**
     B67: Smeth 3D **98**
     DY2: Dud 6G **77**
     DY4: Tip 3H **77**
Brewins Way DY5: Brie H 5B **94**
Brewster St. DY2: Neth 4E **95**
Breydon Gro. WV13: W'hall 3H **45**
Brian Rd. B67: Smeth 3C **98**
Briar Av. B74: S'tly 2A **52**
Briarbeck WS4: S'fld 1G **33**
Briar Cl. B24: Erd 3G **85**
Briar Coppice B90: Ches G 5B **164**
Briar Ct. DY5: Brie H 1H **109**
     (off Hill St.)
Briarfield Rd. B11: Tys 2G **135**
Briarley B71: W Brom 4D **64**
Briar Rd. DY1: Dud 2B **76**
Briars, The B23: Erd 1D **84**
     WS9: A'rdge 2C **34**
Briars Cl. DY5: Brie H 5G **93**
Briarwood Cl. B90: Ches G 5B **164**
     WV2: E'shll 4C **44**
Brickbridge La. WV5: Wom 2E **73**
Brickfield Rd. B25: Yard 5H **119**
Brickheath Rd. WV1: Wolv 6C **28**
Brickhill Dr. B37: F'bri 1C **122**

Brickhouse La. B70: W Brom 1E 79
Brickhouse La. Sth. DY4: Tip 1D 78
Brickhouse Rd. B65: Row R 5A 96
Brickiln Ct. DY5: Brie H 1H 109
Brickiln St. WS8: Bwnhls 6B 10
Brick Kiln La. B44: Gt Barr 1G 83
    B47: Wyt 6G 161
    B91: Sol 1D 164
    DY3: Gorn 4E 75
Brick Kiln St. DY4: Tip 1G 77
    DY5: Brie H 4A 94
    DY5: Quar B 3C 110
Brickkiln St. WV13: W'hall 2H 45
Brick St. DY3: Sed 5H 59
Brickyard Cl. CV7: Bal C 5H 169
Brickyard Rd. WS9: A'rdge 6B 22
Briddsland Rd. B33: Kitts G 1A 122
Brides Wlk. B38: K Nor 2A 160
Bridge, The WS1: Wals 2C 48
Bridge Av. DY4: Tip 6C 62
    WS6: C Hay 1E 7
Bridgeburn Rd. B31: N'fld 5C 130
Bridge Cl. B11: S'hll 2B 134
    WS8: Clay 1A 22
Bridge Ct. B64: Old H 3H 111
                              (off Edgewood Cl.)
Bridge Cft. B12: Bal H 5G 117
Bridgefield Wlk. B65: Row R 4H 95
Bridgefoot Wlk. WV8: Pend 6D 14
Bridgeford Rd. B34: S End 3F 105
Bridgehead Wlk. B76: Walm 6D 70
Bridge Ind. Est. B91: Sol 6G 137
Bridgelands Way B20: Hand 6F 83
Bridgeman Cft. B36: Cas B 1G 105
Bridgeman St. WS2: Wals 2B 48
Bridgemary Cl. WV10: Bush 3B 16
Bridge Mdw. Dr. B93: Know 4B 166
Bridgemeadow Ho. B36: Hodg H 1C 104
Bridgend Cft. DY5: P'ntt 3F 93
Bridgenorth Ho. B33: Yard 2F 121
Bridge Piece B31: N'fld 5F 145
Bridge Rd. B8: Salt 5E 103
    DY4: Tip 1C 78
    WS4: S'fld 6F 21
Bridges Cres. WS11: Nort C 1D 8
Bridgeside Cl. WS8: Bwnhls 1B 22
Bridges Rd. WS11: Nort C 1D 8
Bridge St. B1: Birm 5B 4 (1E 117)
    B63: Crad 4E 111
    B69: O'bry 2G 97
    B70: W Brom 3H 79
    DY8: Word 2C 108
    WS1: Wals 1C 48
    WS8: Clay 1A 22
    WS10: W'bry 4F 63
    WV10: Wolv 5A 16
    WV13: W'hall 2H 45
    WV14: Bils 6G 45
    WV14: Cose 5E 61
Bridge St. Ind. Est. WS10: W'bry 4F 63
Bridge St. Nth. B66: Smeth 3F 99
Bridge St. Sth. B66: Smeth 3F 99
Bridge St. W. B19: Hock 4F 101
Bridge Trad. Cen., The
    B64: Crad H 3F 111
Bridge Trad. Est., The B66: Smeth 3F 99
Bridge Wlk. B27: A Grn 2B 136
Bridgewater Av. B69: O'bry 5G 97
Bridgewater St. B29: S Oak 4H 131
Bridgewater Cres. DY2: Dud 6G 77
Bridgewater Dr. WV5: Wom 6F 57
    WV14: Cose 3E 61
Bridge Way WS8: Clay 1A 22
Bridgnorth Av. WV5: Wom 3F 73
Bridgnorth Gro. WV12: W'hall 3B 30
Bridgnorth Rd. DY3: Himl 4H 73
    DY3: Swind 2A 72
    DY7: Stourt 4A 108
                              (not continuous)
    DY8: Woll 4A 108
    WV5: Wom 3F 73
    WV6: Pert, Tett, Tres 5A 40
Bridgwater Cl. WS9: Wals W 4B 22
Bridle Gro. B71: W Brom 5D 64

Bridle La. B74: S'tly 4G 51
    WS9: A'rdge 5E 51
Bridle Mead B38: K Nor 1H 159
Bridle Path, The B28: Hall G 2G 149
    B90: Shir 2H 149
Bridle Rd. DY8: Woll 5B 108
Bridlewood B74: S'tly 3H 51
Bridport Ho. B31: N'fld 6C 130
BRIERLEY HILL 1H 109
Brierley Hill Baths 1H 109
Brierley Hill Rd. DY5: Brie H 1E 109
    DY8: Word 1C 108
Brierley La. WV14: Bils, Cose 3G 61
Brierley Trad. Est., The DY5: Brie H . .6G 93
Brier Mill Rd. B63: Hale 2C 128
Briery Cl. B64: Crad H 4H 111
Briery Rd. B63: Hale 2G 127
Briffen Ho. B16: Birm 1D 116
Brigadoon Gdns. DY9: Pedm 3G 125
Brigfield Cres. B13: Mose 2B 148
Brigfield Rd. B13: Mose 2B 148
Brighton Cl. WS2: Wals 6B 32
Brighton Pl. WV3: Wolv 1E 43
Brighton Rd. B12: Bal H 6H 117
Bright Rd. B68: O'bry 4H 97
Brightstone Cl. WV10: Bush 3B 16
Brightstone Rd. B45: Fran 5H 143
Bright St. DY8: Woll 5B 108
    WS10: Darl 6D 46
    WV1: Wolv 6F 27
Brightwell Cres. B93: Dorr 6A 166
Brimfield Pl. WV6: Wolv 5D 26
                              (off Newbridge St.)
Brindle Cl. B26: Yard 6C 120
Brindle Ct. B23: Erd 4B 84
Brindlefields Way DY4: Tip 5A 78
Brindle Rd. WS5: Wals 1G 65
Brindley Av. WV11: Wed 6A 18
Brindley Cl. DY8: Word 2C 108
    WS2: Wals 4F 31
    WV5: Wom 1D 72
Brindley Ct. DY4: Tip 2G 77
Brindley Dr. B1: Birm 4B 4 (1E 117)
Brindley Pl. B1: Birm 5A 4 (1D 116)
Brindley Point B16: Birm 1D 116
Brindley Rd. B71: W Brom 5G 63
Brindley Way B66: Smeth 4G 99
Brineton Gro. B29: W Cas 4E 131
Brineton Ind. Est. WS2: Wals 2A 48
Brineton St. WS2: Wals 2A 48
Bringewood Gro. B32: Bart G 5H 129
Brinklow Cft. B34: S End 2H 105
Brinklow Rd. B29: W Cas 3D 130
Brinklow Twr. B12: Birm 4H 117
Brinley Way DY6: K'wfrd 3A 92
Brinsford Rd. WV10: F'hses 4G 15
Brinsley Cl. B91: Sol 5F 151
Brinsley Rd. B26: Sheld 3F 121
Brisbane Ct. B67: Smeth 4C 98
Briseley Cl. DY5: Brie H 3G 109
Bristam Cl. B69: O'bry 3E 97
BRISTNALL FIELDS 1H 113
Bristnall Hall Cres. B68: O'bry 6A 98
Bristnall Hall La. B68: O'bry 6A 98
Bristnall Hall Rd. B68: O'bry 1H 113
Bristol Ct. B29: W Cas 6G 131
Bristol Rd. B5: S Oak, Edg, Bal H 5H 131
    B23: Erd 4E 85
    B29: S Oak 5H 131
    DY2: Neth 1F 111
Bristol Rd. Sth. B31: Longb, N'fld 1B 158
    B45: Redn 4G 143
Bristol St. B5: Birm 6D 4 (3F 117)
Briston Cl. DY5: Brie H 3G 109
Britannia Gdns. B65: Row R 6C 96
Britannia Grn. DY3: Up Gor 2A 76
Britannia M. B65: Row R 6C 96
Britannia Pk. WS10: W'bry 2D 62
Britannia Rd. B65: Row R 1C 112
    WS1: Wals 6B 48
    WV14: Bils 2H 61
Britannia St. B69: Tiv 5C 78
Britannic Gdns. B13: Mose 3F 133

Britannic Pk. B13: Mose 3F 133
Britford Cl. B14: K Hth 4H 147
Brittan Cl. B34: S End 3A 106
Britton Dr. B72: W Grn 5A 70
Britwell Rd. B73: W Grn 3G 69
Brixfield Way B90: Dic H 4G 163
Brixham Rd. B16: Edg 5H 99
Broadacres B31: N'fld 1C 144
Broadcott Ind. Est. B64: Old H 2A 112
Broad Cft. DY4: Tip 1C 78
Broadfern Rd. B93: Know 1D 166
Broadfield Cl. B71: W Brom 4D 64
    DY6: K'wfrd 4B 92
Broadfield House Glass Mus. 4A 92
Broadfields Rd. B23: Erd 6H 69
Broadfield Wlk. B16: Birm 2D 116
Broad Gauge Way WV10: Wolv 1A 44
Broadheath Dr. WS4: S'fld 1H 33
Broadhidley Dr. B32: Bart G 4H 129
Broadlands WV10: F'hses 2H 15
Broadlands Dr. DY5: Brie H 4A 94
Broad La. B14: K Hth 3F 147
    WS3: Blox 4F 19
    WS4: S'fld 6G 21
    WV3: Wolv 3C 42
    WV11: Ess 1C 18
Broad La. Gdns. WS3: Blox 5G 19
Broad La. Nth. WV12: W'hall 3B 30
Broad Lanes WV14: Bils 2E 61
Broad La. Sth. WV11: Wed 4H 29
Broadmeadow DY6: K'wfrd 1C 92
    WS9: A'rdge 1D 34
Broadmeadow Cl. B30: K Nor 4D 146
Broad Mdw. Grn. WV14: Bils 4E 45
Broadmeadow Ho. B32: Bart G 5B 130
Broad Mdw. La. B30: K Nor 4D 146
Broadmeadow La. WS6: Gt Wyr 3G 7
Broadmeadows Cl. WV12: W'hall 1E 31
Broadmeadows Rd. WV12: W'hall 1E 31
Broadmoor Av. B67: Smeth 1B 114
    B68: O'bry 1B 114
Broadmoor Cl. WV14: Bils 1E 61
Broadmoor Rd. WV14: Bils 5E 61
Broadoaks B76: Walm 5E 71
Broad Oaks Rd. B91: Sol 1D 150
Broad Rd. B27: A Grn 2H 135
Broadstone Av. B63: Crad 1D 126
    WS3: Blox 3B 32
Broadstone Cl. WV4: Penn 6H 43
Broadstone Rd. B26: Yard 1D 120
Broad St. B1: Birm 2D 116
    B15: Birm 6A 4 (2D 116)
    B69: O'bry 4G 97
    DY5: P'ntt 3G 93
    DY6: K'wfrd 4B 92
    WV1: Wolv 2C 170 (1H 43)
    WV14: Bils 5E 45
    WV14: Cose 5E 61
Broad St. Junc. WV1: Wolv . .2D 170 (1H 43)
Broadwalk B31: Birm 6A 4 (2E 117)
Broadwalk Retail Pk. WS1: Wals 5B 48
Broadwaters Av. WS10: Darl 1C 62
Broadwaters Rd. WS10: Darl 1C 62
Broad Way WS4: S'fld 5G 21
Broadway B68: O'bry 2A 114
    B90: Shir 3G 149
    WS1: Wals 5D 48
    WV3: Wolv 2A 42
    WV8: Cod 4E 13
    WV10: Bush 5A 16
Broadway, The B20: Hand 5F 83
    B71: W Brom 6G 63
    DY1: Dud 4C 76
    DY8: Stourb 3B 124
                              (not continuous)
    WV5: Wom 2G 73
Broadway Av. B9: Bord G 1G 119
    B63: Hale 3A 128
Broadway Community Leisure Cen. 5G 83
Broadway Cft. B26: Sheld 5E 121
    B68: O'bry 2A 114
Broadway Gdns. WV10: Bush 5A 16
Broadway Nth. WS1: Wals 1D 48
Broadway Plaza B16: Birm 2C 116

Broadway W. WS1: Wals 5A 48
Broadwell Ind. Pk. B69: O'bry 6F 79
Broadwell Rd. B69: O'bry 1G 97
  B92: Olton 3E 137
Broadwyn Trad. Est. B64: Old H 2A 112
Broadyates Gro. B25: Yard 5A 120
Broadyates Rd. B25: Yard 5A 120
Brobury Cft. B91: Shir 3B 150
Brochan Way B31: N'fld 1C 144
Broches, The WS11: Nort C 1F 9
Brock Cl. B45: Redn 6G 143
Brockeridge Cl. WV12: W'hall 6C 18
Brockfield Ho. WV10: Wolv 5B 28
Brockhall Gro. B37: K'hrst 4B 106
Brockhill La. B48: A'chu 6D 160
Brockhurst Cres. WS5: Wals 6C 48
Brockhurst Dr. B28: Hall G 2G 149
  WV6: Wolv 5E 27
Brockhurst Ho. WS2: Wals 6B 32
Brockhurst La. B75: Can 3E 39
Brockhurst Pl. WS5: Wals 6D 48
Brockhurst Rd. B36: Hodg H 3A 104
  B75: R'ley 2B 54
Brockhurst St. WS1: Wals 5C 48
Brockley Cl. DY5: Brie H 6H 93
Brockley Gro. B13: Mose 4E 133
Brockley Pl. B7: Nech 2C 102
BROCKMOOR 5G 93
Brockmoor Cl. DY9: Pedm 3G 125
Brockmoor Ind. Est. DY5: Brie H 6E 93
Brock Rd. DY4: Tip 3C 78
Brockton Rd. B29: W Cas 4E 131
Brockwell Gro. B44: Gt Barr 1G 67
Brockwell Rd. B44: Gt Barr 1G 67
Brockworth Rd. B14: K Hth 5E 147
Brocton Cl. WS3: Blox 1G 31
  WV14: Cose 2D 60
Brogden Cl. B71: W Brom 5D 64
Bromfield Cl. B6: Aston 2G 101
Bromfield Ct. WV6: Tett 1H 41
Bromfield Cres. WS10: W'bry 1A 64
Bromfield Rd. WS10: W'bry 2A 64
BROMFORD 1A 104
Bromford Cl. B20: Hand 6C 82
  B23: Erd .2E 85
Bromford Ct. B31: N'fld 6F 145
Bromford Cres. B24: Erd 5G 85
Bromford Dale WV1: Wolv 6E 27
  WV6: Wolv 6E 27
Bromford Dell B31: N'fld 3G 145
Bromford Dr. B36: Hodg H 1H 103
Bromford Gdns. B15: Edg 3G 115
Bromford Ga. B24: Erd 1G 103
Bromford Hill B20: Hand 4E 83
Bromford Ho. B73: Bold 3F 69
Bromford La. B8: W End 3H 103
  B24: Erd .5G 85
  B70: W Brom 6G 79
Bromford Mere B92: Olton 5C 136
Bromford Mills Ind. Est. B24: Erd 6G 85
Bromford Pk. B69: O'bry 1G 97
Bromford Pk. Ho. B13: Mose 3B 134
                    (off Wake Grn. Pk.)

Bromford Pk. Ind. Est.
  B70: W Brom 6G 79
Bromford Ri. WV3: Wolv 3F 43
Bromford Rd. B8: W End 5G 85
  B36: Hodg H 2H 103
  B69: O'bry 1G 97
  B70: W Brom 1G 97
  DY2: Dud 3C 94
Bromford Rd. Ind. Est. B69: O'bry . . .6G 79
Bromford Wlk. B43: Gt Barr 4B 66
BROMLEY 4F 93
Bromley DY5: P'ntt 4F 93
Bromley Gdns. WV8: Cod 3G 13
Bromley La. DY6: K'wfrd 5C 92
Bromley Pl. WV4: Penn 6E 43
Bromley St. B9: Birm 2A 118
  DY9: Lye .5B 110
  WV2: Wolv 4G 43
Brompton Dr. DY5: Brie H 4F 109
Brompton Lawns WV6: Tett 6G 25
Brompton Pool Rd. B28: Hall G 4E 149

Brompton Rd. B44: Gt Barr 1G 67
Bromsgrove Rd. B62: Hunn, Roms . . .4A 142
  B63: Hale 2C 128
  DY9: Hag 6G 125
Bromsgrove St. B5: Birm 6E 5 (2G 117)
  B63: Hale 1C 128
Bromwich Ct. B13: Mose 1B 148
Bromwich Ct. B46: Col 5G 89
Bromwich Dr. B75: S Cold 4A 54
Bromwich La. DY9: Pedm 6F 125
Bromwich Wlk. B9: Bord G 6G 103
Bromwynd Cl. WV2: Wolv 5F 43
Bromyard Av. B76: Walm 5E 71
Bromyard Rd. B11: S'hll 2E 135
Bronte Cl. B90: Shir 6B 150
Bronte Ct. B90: Shir 6B 150
Bronte Farm Rd. B90: Shir 6B 150
Bronte Rd. WV2: E'shll 5B 44
Bronwen Rd. WV14: Cose 6E 61
Brookbank Av. B34: S End 3H 105
Brookbank Gdns. DY3: Gorn 5F 75
Brookbank Rd. DY3: Gorn 5F 75
Brook Cl. B33: Stech 5C 104
  B90: Shir .6F 149
  WS9: Wals W 4C 22
Brook Cres. DY6: W Hth 2A 92
  DY9: W'cte 2B 126
Brook Cft. B26: Sheld 4F 121
  B37: Mars G 4D 122
Brookdale DY3: Lwr G 4G 75
Brookdale Cl. B45: Redn 6G 143
Brookdale Dr. WV4: Penn 5C 42
Brook Dr. B32: Bart G 4B 130
Brook End WS7: Chase 1C 10
Brookend Dr. B45: Rub 1F 157
Brookes Cl. B69: Tiv 1B 96
Brookes Ho. WS1: Wals 2D 48
                    (off Paddock La.)
Brooke St. DY2: Dud 1E 95
Brook Farm Wlk. B37: Chel W 6F 107
Brookfield Cl. WS9: A'rdge 6C 22
Brookfield Rd. B18: Hock 4C 100
  B30: K Nor 4F 147
  WS9: A'rdge 6C 22
  WV8: Bilb 4H 13
BROOKFIELDS 5D 100
Brookfields Rd. B68: O'bry 5A 98
Brookfield Ter. B18: Hock 4C 100
Brookfield Way B92: Olton 6B 136
  DY4: Tip .1A 78
Brook Grn. La. B92: Bars 6A 154
Brook Gro. WV8: Bilb 4H 13
Brookhill Cl. WV12: W'hall 6C 18
Brookhill Rd. B8: W End 5G 103
Brookhill Way WV12: W'hall 6D 18
Brook Holloway DY9: W'cte 1B 126
Brookhouse Cl. WV10: F'stne 1D 16
Brook Ho. La. WV10: F'stne 1A 16
Brookhouse Rd. WS5: Wals 4F 49
Brookhurst La. B90: Dic H 3H 163
Brookhus Farm Rd. B76: Walm 5E 71
Brooking Cl. B43: Gt Barr 1F 67
Brookland Gro. WS9: Wals W 5B 22
Brookland Rd. WS9: Wals W 4B 22
Brooklands DY3: Swind 6E 73
  DY8: Word 2D 108
  WS5: Wals 2F 65
Brooklands Av. WS6: Gt Wyr 1F 7
Brooklands Cl. B28: Hall G 4F 135
Brooklands Dr. B14: K Hth 2G 147
Brooklands Pde. WV1: Wolv 2C 44
Brooklands Rd. B28: Hall G 4F 135
Brooklands Way B37: Mars G 3D 122
Brook La. B13: Mose 5A 134
  B32: Harb 6D 114
  B64: Old H 1G 111
  B92: Olton 5B 136
  WS6: Gt Wyr 2G 7
  WS9: Wals W 4B 22
Brooklea Gro. B38: K Nor 6C 146
Brooklyn Av. B6: Aston 2H 101
Brooklyn Gro. DY6: W Hth 1H 91
  WV14: Cose 5F 61
Brooklyn Rd. WS7: Chase 1C 10

Brookmans Av. B32: Quin 1B 130
Brook Mdw. Ct. B28: Hall G 1D 148
Brook Mdw. Rd. B34: S End 3E 105
  WS4: S'fld 1H 33
Brook Mdws. WV8: Bilb 3H 13
Brookpiece Ho. B14: K Hth 5G 147
                    (off Milston Cl.)
Brook Rd. B15: Edg 4A 116
  B45: Rub 2E 157
  B68: O'bry 1G 113
  DY8: Stourb 2F 125
  WS6: C Hay 1E 7
  WV5: Wom 1F 73
  WV13: W'hall 2G 45
Brooksbank Dr. B64: Old H 5H 95
Brooksby Gro. B93: Dorr 6H 167
Brooks Cft. B35: Cas V 5E 87
Brookside B31: N'fld 2D 144
  B43: Gt Barr 6H 65
  B90: Ches G 6B 164
  DY3: Gorn 5H 75
  WS10: W'bry 2H 63
Brookside Av. B13: Mose 6B 134
Brookside Cl. B23: Erd 6C 68
  B63: Hale 2F 127
  WV5: Wom 1E 73
Brookside Ind. Est. WS10: W'bry 2H 63
Brookside Way DY6: W Hth 2H 91
Brooks Rd. B72: W Grn 5A 70
Brook St. B3: Birm 2B 4 (6E 101)
  B66: Smeth 3F 99
  B70: W Brom 4H 79
  DY3: Gorn 4G 75
  DY3: Sed 6C 60
  DY4: Tip .1G 77
  DY5: Quar B 3C 110
  DY6: W Hth 6H 73
  DY8: Stourb 6C 108
  DY8: Word 2D 108
  DY9: Lye .6B 110
  WS2: Wals 2B 48
  WV14: Bils 6G 45
Brook St. Bus. Cen. DY4: Tip 1G 77
Brook Ter. WV14: Bils 6G 45
Brookthorpe Dr. WV12: W'hall 6C 30
Brookvale Gro. B92: Olton 4B 136
Brookvale M. B29: S Oak 3D 132
Brookvale Pk. Rd. B23: Erd 2B 84
Brookvale Rd. B6: Witt 5A 84
  B23: Erd .5A 84
  B92: Olton 4B 136
Brookvale Trad. Est. B6: Witt 4A 84
Brookview B67: Smeth 6D 98
Brook Vw. Cl. B19: Hock 3E 101
Brook Wlk. B32: Bart G 3B 130
Brookwillow Rd. B63: Hale 4F 127
Brookwood Av. B28: Hall G 2D 148
Broomcroft Rd. B37: K'hrst 4B 106
Broomdene Av. B34: S End 2E 105
Broom Dr. B14: K Hth 3G 147
Broome Av. B43: Gt Barr 6G 65
Broome Cl. B63: Hale 2A 128
Broome Ct. B36: Cas B 1G 105
Broome Gdns. B75: S Cold 6A 54
Broomehill Cl. DY5: Brie H 4G 109
Broome Rd. WV10: Bush 2A 28
Broomfield B67: Smeth 4D 98
Broomfield Rd. B23: Erd 5D 84
Broomfields Av. B91: Sol 2H 151
Broomfields Cl. B91: Sol 2H 151
Broomfields Farm Rd. B91: Sol 2H 151
Broomhall Av. WV11: Wed 3F 29
Broom Hall Cres. B27: A Grn 6H 135
Broom Hall Gro. B27: A Grn 5A 136
Broomhill Cl. B43: Gt Barr 5H 65
Broomhill La. B43: Gt Barr 5H 65
Broomhill Rd. B23: Erd 6B 68
                    (not continuous)
Broom Ho. B71: W Brom 4D 64
Broomhurst B15: Edg 3A 116
Broomie Cl. B75: S Cold 6B 54
Broom La. B90: Dic H 3G 163
Broomlea Cl. B74: S'tly 3G 51

Broom Rd. DY1: Dud 2C 76
  WS5: Wals 2F 65
Broom St. B12: Birm 3A 118
Broomy Cl. B34: Stech 4E 105
Broseley Av. B31: Longb 1F 159
Brosil Av. B20: Hand 4A 82
Brougham St. B19: Loz 2D 100
  (not continuous)
Brough Cl. B7: Nech 3B 102
  WV4: E'shll 2B 60
Broughton Ct. WV6: Pert 6G 25
Broughton Cres. B31: Longb 1B 158
Broughton Rd. B20: Hand 1C 100
  DY9: W'cte 2H 125
  WV3: Wolv 2A 42
Brownfield Rd. B34: S End 3G 105
BROWNHILLS 6B 10
Brownhills Bus. Pk. WS8: Bwnhls . .2B 22
BROWNHILLS COMMON 5A 10
Brownhills Rd. WS8: Wals W 2B 22
  WS11: Nort C 1E 9
BROWNHILLS WEST 3G 9
Brownhills West Station
  Chasewater Railway 2G 9
Browning Cl. WV12: W'hall 2E 31
Browning Cres. WV10: F'hses 5G 15
Browning Gro. WV6: Pert 5E 25
Browning Rd. DY3: Lwr G 3E 75
Browning St. B16: Birm 1D 116
Browning Twr. B31: N'fld 4G 145
Brownley Rd. B90: Shir 2B 164
Brown Lion St. DY4: Tip 6G 61
Brown Rd. WS10: Darl 4C 46
Brown's Coppice Av. B91: Sol 2B 150
Browns Cl. B13: Mose 3B 134
Brown's Dr. B73: Bold 5F 69
Brownsea Cl. B45: Fran 6E 143
Brownsea Dr. B1: Birm 6C 4 (2F 117)
BROWN'S GREEN 4B 82
Browns Grn. B20: Hand 4B 82
Brownshore La. WV11: Ess 3A 18
Browns La. B93: Know 3A 166
Brownsover Cl. B36: Cas B 6F 87
Brown St. WV2: Wolv 4H 43
Brownswall Est. DY3: Sed 6F 59
Brownswall Rd. DY3: Sed 6F 59
Broxwood Pk. WV6: Tett 6H 25
Brueton Av. B91: Sol 4H 151
Brueton Dr. B24: Erd 4G 85
Brueton Rd. WV14: Bils 4A 46
Bruford Rd. WV3: Wolv 3E 43
Brunel Cl. B12: Bal H 6A 118
Brunel Ct. WS10: Darl 5F 47
  WV5: Wom 6G 57
  WV14: Cose 5G 61
Brunel Dr. DY4: Tip 4G 61
Brunel Gro. WV6: Pert 3E 25
Brunel Rd. B69: O'bry 3D 96
Brunel St. B2: Birm 5C 4 (1F 117)
Brunel Wlk. WS10: Darl 5F 47
Brunel Way WV2: E'shll 4C 44
Brunslow Cl. WV10: Oxl 6G 15
  WV13: W'hall 2C 46
Brunswick Arc. B1: Birm 1D 116
  (off Brunswick St.)
Brunswick Ct. WS10: W'bry 2A 64
Brunswick Gdns. B21: Hand 6B 82
  WS10: W'bry 1H 63
Brunswick Ga. DY8: Stourb 4E 125
Brunswick Ho. B34: S End 2E 105
  B37: Mars G 3B 122
Brunswick Pk. Rd. WS10: W'bry 2G 63
Brunswick Rd. B12: Bal H 6A 118
  B21: Hand 6B 82
Brunswick Sq. B1: Birm 5A 4 (1D 116)
Brunswick St. B1: Birm 5A 4 (1D 116)
  WS2: Wals 4A 48
Brunswick Ter. WS10: W'bry 2F 63
Brunton Rd. B10: Small H 4F 119
Brushfield Rd. B42: Gt Barr 5F 67
Brutus Dr. B46: Col 6G 89
Bryan Av. WV4: Penn 1B 58
Bryan Budd Cl. B65: Row R 5B 96

Bryan Rd. WS2: Wals 5A 48
Bryanston Cl. B91: Sol 6D 136
Bryanston Rd. B91: Sol 6D 136
Bryant St. B18: Win G 4A 100
Bryce Rd. DY5: P'ntt 4E 93
  (not continuous)
Bryher Wlk. B45: Fran 6E 143
Brylan Cft. B44: K'sdng 1H 83
Brymill Ind. Est. DY4: Tip 6G 61
Bryn Arden Rd. B26: Yard 6C 120
Bryndale Av. B14: K Hth 4G 147
Brynmawr Rd. WV14: Cose 2C 60
Brynside Cl. B14: K Hth 5F 147
Bryony Cft. B23: Erd 6B 68
Bryony Gdns. WS10: Darl 4D 46
Bryony Rd. B29: W Cas 6F 131
BSA Bus. Pk. B11: Small H 5D 118
Buchanan Av. WS4: Wals 6E 33
Buchanan Cl. WS4: Wals 6E 33
Buchanan Rd. WS4: Wals 6E 33
Buckbury Cl. DY9: Pedm 4H 125
Buckbury Cft. B90: M'path 3F 165
Buckingham Cl. WS10: W'bry 1A 64
Buckingham Dr. WV12: W'hall 2B 30
Buckingham Gro. DY6: K'wrd 2A 92
Buckingham Ho. B31: Longb 1D 158
Buckingham M. B73: W Grn 2G 69
Buckingham Ri. DY1: Dud 5A 76
Buckingham Rd. B36: Cas B 2B 106
  B65: Row R 5D 96
  WV4: Penn 1E 59
Buckingham St. B19: Birm 5F 101
BUCKLAND END 2C 104
Buckland End B34: S End 3E 105
Buckland Ho. B15: Edg 4E 117
  (off Summer Rd.)
Bucklands End La. B34: Hodg H 3D 104
Buckle Cl. WS1: Wals 3D 48
Buckley Ct. B13: K Hth 5H 133
Buckley Rd. WV4: Penn 6B 42
Bucklow Wlk. B33: Stech 5C 104
Buckminster Dr. B93: Dorr 5A 166
Bucknall Cl. B13: Mose 3B 134
Bucknall Cres. B32: Bart G 5G 129
Bucknall Rd. WV11: Wed 6B 18
Bucknell Cl. B91: Sol 2G 151
BUCKPOOL 1D 108
Buckridge Cl. B38: K Nor 2B 158
Buckridge La. B90: Dic H 4G 163
  (not continuous)
Buck St. B5: Birm 3G 5 (6H 101)
Buckton Cl. B75: R'ley 1C 54
Budbrooke Gro. B34: S End 3A 106
Budden Rd. WV14: Cose 6F 61
Bude Rd. WS5: Wals 4H 49
Buffery Rd. DY2: Dud 2F 95
Bufferys Cl. B91: Sol 1F 165
Buildwas Cl. WS3: Blox 5F 19
Bulford Cl. B14: K Hth 5H 147
Bulger Rd. WV14: Bils 4E 45
Bullace Cft. B15: Edg 2H 131
Buller St. WV4: E'shll 6A 44
Bullfields Cl. B65: Row R 4H 95
Bullfinch Cl. DY1: Dud 1A 94
Bullivents Cl. B93: Ben H 4B 166
Bull La. B70: W Brom 4G 79
  WS10: Mox 2B 62
  WV5: Wom 5G 57
  WV14: Bils 2B 62
Bull Mdw. La. WV5: Wom 5G 57
Bullock's Row WS1: Wals 2D 48
Bullock St. B7: Birm 4A 102
  B70: W Brom 1B 98
Bullows Rd. WS8: Bwnhls 1G 21
Bull Ring B63: Hale 2B 128
  DY3: Sed 5H 59
  WV13: W'hall 6A 30
Bullring Shop. Cen.
  B5: Birm 5F 5 (1G 117)
Bull Ring Trad. Est.
  B12: Birm 6H 5 (2H 117)
Bull's La. B76: Walm 2F 71
  (not continuous)

Bull St. B4: Birm 3E 5 (6G 101)
  B17: Harb 5H 115
  B70: W Brom 4B 80
  DY1: Dud 1C 94
  DY3: Gorn 5G 75
  DY5: Brie H 2F 109
  (Goldencross Way)
  DY5: Brie H 1E 109
  (Hawbush Rd.)
  WS10: Darl 5E 47
Bull St. Trad. Est. DY5: Brie H 1F 109
Bulrush Cl. WS8: Bwnhls 6A 10
Bulwell Cl. B6: Aston 2A 102
Bulwer St. WV10: Wolv 6H 27
BUMBLE HOLE 4G 95
Bumblehole Mdws. WV5: Wom 6F 57
Bumble Hole Nature Reserve 4G 95
Bunbury Gdns. B30: K Nor 3G 145
Bunbury Rd. B31: N'fld 3F 145
Bundle Hill B63: Hale 2A 128
Bungalows, The B70: W Brom 1F 79
BUNKER'S HILL 4G 45
Bunkers Hill La. WV14: Bils 3G 45
Bunn's La. DY2: Dud 6H 77
Burbage Cl. WV10: Wolv 3B 28
Burberry Ct. DY4: Tip 5A 62
Burberry Gro. CV7: Bal C 3G 169
Burbidge Rd. B9: Bord G 6D 102
Burbury St. B19: Loz 2E 101
Burbury St. Sth. B19: Hock 3E 101
Burcombe Twr. B23: Erd 1H 85
Burcot Av. WV1: Wolv 1C 44
Burcot Ct. B74: Four O 1F 53
Burcote Rd. B24: Erd 4B 86
Burcot Wlk. WV1: Wolv 1C 44
Burdock Cl. WS5: Wals 2E 65
Burdock Ho. B38: K Nor 6B 146
Burdock Rd. B29: W Cas 1E 145
Burdons Cl. B34: Stech 4E 105
Bure Gro. WV13: W'hall 1D 46
Burfield Rd. B63: Crad 5E 111
Burford Cl. B92: Olton 2E 137
  WS5: Wals 2E 65
Burford Ct. B13: Mose 3B 134
Burford Pk. Rd. B38: K Nor 1A 160
Burford Rd. B44: K'sdng 6H 67
  B47: H'wd 3H 161
Burgess Cft. B92: Sol 6B 138
Burghley Dr. B71: W Brom 3D 64
Burghley Wlk. DY5: Brie H 3F 109
Burgh Way WS2: Wals 4G 31
Burhill Way B37: F'bri 4D 106
Burke Av. B13: Mose 4D 134
Burkitt Dr. DY4: Tip 5C 62
Burland Av. WV6: Tett 2C 26
Burleigh Cl. CV7: Bal C 2H 169
  WV12: W'hall 3B 30
Burleigh Cft. WS7: Chase 1C 10
Burleigh Rd. WV3: Wolv 4E 43
Burleigh St. WS1: Wals 3D 48
Burleton Rd. B33: Kitts G 1A 122
Burley Cl. B90: Shir 5F 149
Burley Way B38: K Nor 1G 159
Burlington Arc. B2: Birm 4D 4
Burlington Av. B70: W Brom 6C 80
Burlington M. B10: Small H 2F 119
Burlington Pas. B2: Birm 4D 4
Burlington Rd. B10: Small H 2E 119
  B70: W Brom 6C 80
Burlington St. B6: Aston 3G 101
Burlish Av. B92: Olton 4D 136
Burman Cl. B90: Shir 5G 149
Burman Dr. B46: Col 4H 107
Burman Rd. B90: Shir 5F 149
Burmarsh Wlk. WV8: Pend 1D 26
Burmese Way B65: Row R 3H 95
Burnaston Cres. B90: M'path 3G 165
Burnaston Rd. B28: Hall G 4E 135
Burnbank Gro. B24: Erd 3H 85
Burn Cl. B66: Smeth 5E 99
Burncross Way WV10: Wolv 3B 28
Burnell Gdns. WV3: Wolv 3C 42
Burnel Rd. B29: W Cas 3E 131
Burnett Ho. B69: O'bry 4D 96

Burnett Rd.—Camberley Rd.

Burnett Rd. B74: Lit As 1B 52
Burney La. B8: W End 4A 104
Burnfields Way WS9: A'rdge 2C 34
Burnham Av. B25: Yard 5A 120
WV10: Oxl 1F 27
Burnham Cl. DY6: K'wfrd 5D 92
Burnham Ct. B23: Erd 5C 84
DY5: Brie H 1H 109
(off Hill St.)
Burnham Mdw. B28: Hall G 1G 149
Burnham Rd. B44: Gt Barr 6G 67
Burnhill Gro. B29: W Cas 5E 131
Burnlea Gro. B31: N'fld 6G 145
Burnsall Cl. B37: F'bri 1B 122
WV9: Pend 4E 15
Burns Av. DY4: Tip 5A 62
WV10: F'hses 5H 15
Burns Cl. DY8: Amb 3E 109
Burns Dr. WS10: W'bry 4G 63
Burns Gro. DY3: Lwr G 3E 75
Burnside Ct. B73: W Grn 4G 69
Burnside Gdns. WS5: Wals 5H 49
Burnside Way B31: Longb 2D 158
Burns Pl. WS10: Mox 6A 46
Burns Rd. WS10: Mox 6A 46
Burnthurst Cres. B90: M'path 2E 165
Burnt Oak Dr. DY8: Stourb 6F 109
BURNT TREE 5H 77
Burnt Tree DY4: Tip 5H 77
BURNTWOOD JUNC. 2B 10
Burntwood Rd. WS7: Hamm 1F 11
Burrelton Way B43: Gt Barr 5H 65
Burrington Rd. B32: Bart G 5G 129
Burrowes St. WS2: Wals 6B 32
Burrow Hill Cl. B36: Cas B 1G 105
Burrows Ho. *WS2: Wals 6B 32*
(off Burrowes St.)
Burrows Rd. DY6: K'wfrd 5D 92
Bursledon Wlk. WV1: Wolv 3E 45
Burslem Cl. WS3: Blox 3G 19
Bursnips Rd. WV11: Ess 5B 18
Burton Av. WS4: Rus 1F 33
Burton Cres. WV10: Wolv 6A 28
Burton Farm Rd. WS4: Wals 6F 33
Burton Gro. B64: Old H 3G 111
Burton Rd. DY1: Dud 3B 76
WV10: Wolv 6A 28
Burton Rd. E. DY1: Dud 3B 76
Burton Wood Dr. B20: Hand 5F 83
Buryfield Rd. B91: Sol 1E 151
Bury Hill Rd. B69: O'bry 2D 96
Bury Mound Ct. B90: Shir 5C 148
Bush Av. B66: Smeth 4G 99
BUSHBURY 6A 16
Bushbury Ct. WV10: Bush 5A 16
Bushbury Crematorium WV10: Bush 4B 16
Bushbury Cft. B37: Chel W 6E 107
Bushbury La. WV10: Oxl, Bush 3G 27
Bushbury Rd. B33: Stech 4E 105
WV10: Wolv 3C 28
Bushbury Swimming Pool 6A 16
Bushell Dr. B91: Sol 3H 151
Bushey Cl. B74: S'tly 1H 51
Bushey Flds. Rd. DY1: Dud 1A 94
Bush Gro. B21: Hand 6G 81
WS3: Pels 5E 21
Bushley Cft. B91: Sol 1F 165
Bushman Way B34: S End 4A 106
Bushmore Rd. B28: Hall G 1G 149
Bush Rd. DY2: Neth 1E 111
DY4: Tip 3G 77
Bush St. WS10: Darl 4D 46
Bushway Cl. DY5: Brie H 1E 109
Bushwood Ct. B15: Edg 3E 117
B29: S Oak 4F 131
Bushwood Dr. B93: Dorr 6C 166
Bushwood Rd. B29: S Oak 4F 131
(not continuous)
Business Cen., The B11: Tys 5F 119
Bustleholme Av. B71: W Brom 4D 64
Bustleholme Cres. B71: W Brom 4C 64
Bustleholme La. B71: W Brom 4C 64
(not continuous)
Butchers La. B63: Crad 4E 111
Butchers Rd. B92: H Ard 1A 154
BUTCROFT 5E 47
Butcroft Gdns. WS10: Darl 5E 47
Bute Cl. B45: Fran 6E 143
WV12: W'hall 3B 30
Butler Lane Station (Rail) 6G 37
Butler Rd. B92: Olton 2D 136
Butlers Cl. B20: Hand 4C 82
B23: Erd 4D 68
Butlers La. B74: Four O 6F 37
B75: Four O 6G 37
Butlers Pct. WS1: Wals 1C 48
Butler's Rd. B20: Hand 4C 82
Butler St. B70: W Brom 3G 79
Butlin St. B7: Nech 2C 102
Buttercup Cl. WS5: Wals 2E 65
Butterfield Cl. WV6: Pert 6D 24
Butterfield Ct. DY1: Dud 5C 76
Butterfield Rd. DY5: P'ntt 2F 93
Butterfly Way B64: Old H 2H 111
Buttermere Cl. DY5: Brie H 4F 109
WV6: Tett 1B 26
Buttermere Ct. WV6: Pert 5F 25
Buttermere Dr. B32: Bart G 2D 130
WV11: Ess 5A 18
Buttermere Gro. WV12: W'hall 6B 18
Butter Wlk. B38: K Nor 1G 159
Butterworth Cl. WV14: Cose 4C 60
Buttery Rd. B67: Smeth 3C 98
Buttons Farm Rd. WV4: Penn 2B 58
Buttress Way B66: Smeth 3E 99
Butts, The WS4: Wals 6D 32
Butts Cl. WS11: Nort C 1C 8
Butts La. WS11: Nort C 1C 8
Butts Rd. WS4: Wals 6D 32
WV4: Penn 1D 58
Butts St. WS4: Wals 6D 32
Butts Way WS11: Nort C 1C 8
Buxton Cl. WS3: Blox 4A 20
Buxton Rd. B23: Erd 1B 84
B73: W Grn 4G 69
DY2: Dud 3B 94
WS3: Blox 4A 20
Byeways WS3: Blox 4A 20
Byfield Cl. B33: Kitts G 3A 122
Byfield Pas. B9: Bord G 1E 119
Byfield Vw. DY3: Sed 6A 60
Byfleet Cl. WV14: Cose 2C 60
Byford Way B37: Mars G 3D 122
Byland Way WS3: Blox 5F 19
By-Pass Link B91: Sol 4A 152
Byrchen Moor Gdns. DY5: P'ntt 2F 93
Byrne Rd. WV2: Wolv 4H 43
Byron Av. B23: Erd 4B 84
Byron Cl. B10: Small H 4D 118
Byron Ct. B74: Four O 4G 37
B93: Know 3C 166
Byron Cres. DY1: Dud 2D 76
Byron Cft. B74: Four O 3F 37
DY3: Lwr G 2E 75
Byron Gdns. B71: W Brom 2H 79
Byron Ho. B63: Crad 6D 110
Byron Rd. B10: Small H 4D 118
WV10: Bush 1C 28
WV12: W'hall 2E 31
Byron St. B71: W Brom 1H 79
DY5: P'ntt 2H 93
Bywater Ho. *WS1: Wals 2D 48*
(off Paddock La.)

C

Caban Cl. B31: N'fld 2C 144
Cable Dr. WS2: Wals 4A 32
Cable St. WV2: Wolv 3A 44
Cabot Gro. WV6: Pert 5E 25
Cadbury Dr. B35: Cas V 6E 87
Cadbury Ho. *B19: Birm 4F 101*
(off Gt. Hampton Row)
Cadbury Rd. B13: Mose 1B 134
Cadbury Way B17: Harb 6F 115
Cadbury World 6B 132
Caddick Cres. B71: W Brom 6B 64
Caddick Rd. B42: Gt Barr 4D 66
Caddick St. WV14: Cose 5C 60
(not continuous)
Cadet Dr. B90: Shir 4G 149
Cadgwith Gdns. WV14: Bils 3A 62
Cadine Gdns. B13: Mose 4E 133
Cadleigh Gdns. B17: Harb 2G 131
Cadle Rd. WV10: Bush 2A 28
Cadman Cres. WV10: Wolv 3C 28
Cadman's La. WS3: Blox 1B 20
WS6: Gt Wyr 5A 8
Cadnam Cl. B17: Harb 2G 131
WV13: W'hall 3B 46
Caernarvon Cl. WV12: W'hall 2C 30
Caernarvon Way DY1: Dud 5A 76
Caesar Way B46: Col 6H 89
Cahill Av. WV10: Wolv 5C 28
Cairn Dr. WS2: Wals 1F 47
Cairns St. WS2: Wals 6A 32
Caister Dr. WV13: W'hall 3H 45
Cakemore La. B68: O'bry 1F 113
Cakemore Rd. B65: Row R 1E 113
Cala Dr. B15: Edg 4D 116
Calcot Dr. WV6: Tett 2C 26
Calcutt Way B90: Dic H 3G 163
(not continuous)
Caldecote Gro. B9: Bord G 1A 120
Caldeford Av. B90: M'path 2E 165
Calder Av. WS1: Wals 1E 49
Calder Dr. B76: Walm 5D 70
Calderfields Cl. WS4: Wals 6E 33
Calder Gro. B20: Hand 5B 82
Calder Ri. DY3: Sed 1B 76
Calder Twr. B20: Hand 6F 83
CALDMORE 3C 48
Caldmore Grn. WS1: Wals 3C 48
Caldmore Rd. WS1: Wals 2C 48
Caldwell Ct. B91: Sol 2G 151
Caldwell Gro. B91: Sol 2G 151
Caldwell Ho. B70: W Brom 5A 80
Caldwell Rd. B9: Bord G 6H 103
Caldwell St. B71: W Brom 5B 64
Caldy Wlk. B45: Fran 6F 143
Caledonia DY5: Quar B 4H 109
Caledonian Cl. WS5: Wals 2G 65
Caledonia Rd. WV2: Wolv 3H 43
(not continuous)
Caledonia St. WV14: Bils 5G 45
Caledon Pl. WS2: Wals 4A 48
Caledon St. WS2: Wals 4A 48
(not continuous)
Calewood Rd. DY5: Quar B 4H 109
CALIFORNIA 2E 131
California Ho. *B32: Bart G 3C 130*
(off Millmead Rd.)
California Rd. B69: Tiv 1B 96
California Way B32: Bart G 2D 130
Callaghan Dr. B69: Tiv 4C 78
Callcott Dr. DY5: Quar B 4H 109
Callear Rd. WS10: W'bry 4D 62
Calley Cl. DY4: Tip 4H 77
Callow Bri. Rd. B45: Rub 2F 157
Callowbrook La. B45: Rub 1F 157
Calshot Rd. B42: Gt Barr 4B 66
Calstock Rd. WV12: W'hall 5D 30
Calthorpe Cl. WS5: Wals 5A 50
Calthorpe Mans. B15: Edg 2D 116
Calthorpe Rd. B15: Edg 3C 116
B20: Hand 5E 83
WS5: Wals 5H 49
Calver Cres. WV11: Wed 4H 29
Calver Gro. B44: Gt Barr 2F 67
Calverley Rd. B38: K Nor 6H 145
Calverton Gro. B43: Gt Barr 5A 66
Calverton Wlk. WV6: Wolv 4F 27
Calves Cft. WV13: W'hall 6A 30
Calvin Cl. WV5: Wom 2F 73
WV10: F'hses 4H 15
Camberley B71: W Brom 4D 64
Camberley Cres. WV4: E'shll 3A 60
Camberley Dr. WV4: Penn 1E 59
Camberley Gro. B23: Erd 1E 85
Camberley Ri. B71: W Brom 4D 64
Camberley Rd. DY6: K'wfrd 6D 92

Camborne Cl. B6: Aston 2G 101
Camborne Cl. WS5: Wals 4H 49
Camborne Rd. WS5: Wals 4H 49
Cambourne Rd. B65: Row R 6C 96
Cambrai Dr. B28: Hall G 5E 135
Cambria Cl. B90: Maj G 2E 163
Cambridge Av. B73: W Grn 5H 69
  B91: Sol 4C 150
Cambridge Cl. WS9: A'rdge 1C 34
Cambridge Cres. B15: Edg 4E 117
Cambridge Dr. B37: Mars G 3B 122
Cambridge Rd. B13: Mose 4H 133
  B66: Smeth .2E 99
                  (not continuous)
  DY2: Dud 2C 94
Cambridge St. B1: Birm 4A 4 (1E 117)
  B70: W Brom 5H 79
  WS1: Wals .4C 48
  WV10: Wolv 5H 27
Cambridge Twr. B1: Birm 4A 4 (6E 101)
Cambridge Way B27: A Grn 1B 136
Camden Cl. B36: Cas B 1E 105
  WS5: Wals .2F 65
Camden Dr. B1: Birm 2A 4 (6D 100)
Camden St. B1: Birm 5C 100
  B18: Hock 2A 4 (5C 100)
  WS1: Wals .3B 48
  WS9: Wals W 3A 22
Camden Way DY6: K'wfrd 6B 74
  WV9: Pend .4D 14
Camelia Gdns. DY8: Word 1C 108
Camelot Way B10: Small H 3C 118
Cameo Dr. DY8: Amb 3D 108
Cameronian Cft. B36: Hodg H 1A 104
Cameron Rd. WS4: Wals 6E 33
Camford Gro. B14: K Hth 4H 147
Cam Gdns. DY5: P'ntt 3F 93
Camino Rd. B32: Bart G 2D 130
Camomile Cl. WS5: Wals 2E 65
Campbell Cl. WS4: Wals 6E 33
Campbells Grn. B26: Sheld 1F 137
Campbell St. DY5: Brie H 5G 93
Campden Grn. B92: Olton 2E 137
Camp Hill B12: Birm 3A 118
  DY8: Word 2C 108
Camp Hill Cir. B11: S'brk 3A 118
Camp Hill Ind. Est. B12: Birm 4A 118
Camphill La. WS10: W'bry 3F 63
Camphill Pct. WS10: W'bry 3F 63
Campians Av. WS6: C Hay 3D 6
Campion Cl. B38: K Nor 1B 160
  WS5: Wals .2E 65
  WV5: Wom .1E 73
Campion Ct. DY4: Tip 2F 77
Campion Dr. WV10: F'stne 1C 16
Campion Gdns. B24: Erd 1A 86
Campion Gro. B63: Hale 2F 127
Campion Ho. B38: K Nor 1A 160
  WV10: Wolv 5B 28
Campion Way B90: Dic H 4G 163
Camp La. B21: Hand 6F 81
  B38: K Nor 4B 146
Camplea Cft. B37: F'bri 1C 122
Camplin Cres. B20: Hand 2A 82
Camp Rd. B75: R'ley 2H 37
  WS14: Lit H 2H 37
Camp St. B9: Bord G 2C 118
  WS10: W'bry 3F 63
  WV1: Wolv 1B 170 (6G 27)
Campville Cres. B71: W Brom 4C 64
Campville Gro. B37: K'hrst 4B 106
Campwood Cl. B30: B'vlle 5A 132
Camrose Cft. B12: Bal H 6H 117
  B34: S End .3F 105
Camrose Gdns. WV9: Pend 4E 15
Camrose Twr. B7: Nech 3B 102
Canal Cotts. DY2: Neth 6D 94
Canal La. B24: Erd 6G 85
Canal Side B30: K Nor 4C 146
  B48: Hopw 6G 159
  B69: O'bry .2F 97
  DY2: Neth .5G 95
Canalside Cl. WS3: Blox 6D 20
  WS10: W'bry 3C 64

Canal Side Dr. B38: K Nor 6C 146
Canalside Ind. Est. DY5: Brie H 2G 109
Canal St. B69: O'bry 2F 97
  DY4: Tip 3F 77
  DY5: Brie H .4A 94
  DY8: Amb .5D 108
  WS2: Wals .1B 48
  WV14: Cose 5E 61
Canal Vw. Ind. Est. DY5: Brie H 2F 109
Canary Gro. B19: Loz 1E 101
Canberra Gdns. B34: S End 3A 106
Canberra Rd. WS5: Wals 6G 49
Canberra Way B12: Birm 3A 118
Canford Cl. B12: Birm 4H 117
Canford Cres. WV8: Cod 4E 13
Canning Cl. WS5: Wals 5H 49
Canning Gdns. B18: Win G 5A 100
Canning Rd. WS5: Wals 5H 49
Cannock Rd.
  WV10: Bush, F'stne, Share 2D 16
  WV10: Bush, Wolv 5H 27
  WV12: W'hall 2C 30
Cannon Bus. Pk. WV14: Cose 4E 61
Cannon Dr. WV14: Cose 3E 61
Cannon Hill Gro. B12: Bal H 6G 117
Cannon Hill Pl. B12: Bal H 6G 117
Cannon Hill Rd. B12: Bal H 6F 117
Cannon Raceway 4E 61
Cannon Rd. WV5: Wom 1G 73
Cannon St. B2: Birm 4D 4 (1G 117)
  WS2: Wals .5C 32
  WV13: W'hall 1B 46
Cannon St. Nth. WS2: Wals 5C 32
Canterbury Av. WV13: W'hall 1D 46
Canterbury Cl. B23: Erd 5D 84
  B65: Row R 5E 97
  B71: W Brom 5C 64
  WS3: Pels .3E 21
Canterbury Dr. B37: Mars G 4C 122
  WV6: Pert .5D 24
Canterbury Rd. B20: Hand 6F 83
  B71: W Brom 5C 64
  WV4: Penn .6C 42
Canterbury Twr. B1: Birm 6D 100
               (off St Marks St.)
Cantlow Ho. B12: Birm 4H 117
Cantlow Rd. B13: Mose 1A 148
Canton La. B46: Col 2H 89
Canute Cl. WS1: Wals 4D 48
Canvey Cl. B45: Fran 6E 143
CANWELL 4E 39
Canwell Av. B37: K'hrst 4B 106
Canwell Dr. B75: Can 4E 39
Canwell Gdns. WV14: Bils 1E 61
Capcroft Rd. B13: Mose 1A 148
Cape Cl. WS8: Bwnhls 1C 22
Cape Hill B66: Smeth 5F 99
Cape Hill Retail Cen. B66: Smeth 5F 99
Capener Rd. B43: Gt Barr 3C 66
Capern Gro. B32: Harb 6D 114
Cape St. B18: Win G 5H 99
  B70: W Brom 3E 79
Capethorn Rd. B66: Smeth 6E 99
Capilano Rd. B23: Erd 6C 68
Capponfield Cl. WV14: Cose 2D 60
Capstone Av. B18: Hock 5C 100
  WV10: Oxl .1F 27
Captain's Cl. WV3: Wolv 1B 42
Carcroft Rd. B25: Yard 3B 120
Cardale St. B65: B'hth 1D 112
Carden Cl. B70: W Brom 3F 79
Carder Cres. WV14: Bils 1F 61
Carder Dr. DY5: Brie H 1G 109
Cardiff Gro. B37: Mars G 2C 122
Cardiff St. WV3: Wolv 3F 43
Cardigan Cl. B71: W Brom 6A 64
Cardigan Dr. WV12: W'hall 3B 30
Cardigan St. B4: Birm 2H 5 (6H 101)
Cardinal Cl. B17: Edg 1E 115
Cardington Av. B42: Gt Barr 4D 66
Cardoness Pl. DY1: Dud 5B 76
Careless Grn. DY9: Lye, W'cte 1B 126
Careynon Ct. WS3: Blox 1H 31

Carhampton Rd. B75: S Cold 5E 55
Carillon Gdns. B65: Row R 6C 96
Carisbrooke Av. B37: Chel W 1E 123
Carisbrooke Cl. WS10: W'bry 3C 64
Carisbrooke Cres. WS10: W'bry 2C 64
Carisbrooke Dr. B62: Hale 1D 128
Carisbrooke Gdns. WV10: Bush 4A 16
Carisbrooke Ho. B31: Longb 1D 158
Carisbrooke Rd. B17: Edg 2F 115
  WS10: W'bry 3B 64
  WV6: Pert .6G 25
  WV10: Bush 4A 16
Carless Av. B17: Harb 4F 115
Carless St. WS1: Wals 3C 48
Carlisle St. B18: Win G 4A 100
Carlson Pk. B17: Harb 6F 115
Carl St. WS2: Wals 4B 32
Carlton Av. B21: Hand 6A 82
  B74: S'tly 1H 51
  DY9: W'cte 2A 126
  WV11: Wed 2C 28
  WV14: Bils .4H 45
Carlton Cl. B75: S Cold 4B 54
  DY1: Dud 1E 77
Carlton Cft. B74: S'tly 1A 52
Carlton M. B36: Cas B 1H 105
Carlton M. Flats B36: Cas B 1H 105
Carlton Rd. B9: Small H 2D 118
  B66: Smeth .1E 99
  WV3: Wolv .4E 43
Carlyle Bus. Pk. B70: W Brom 2F 79
Carlyle Gro. WV10: Bush 1C 28
Carlyle Rd. B16: Edg 2A 116
  B19: Loz 1E 101
  B65: Row R 1C 112
  WV10: Bush 1C 28
Carmel Gro. B32: Bart G 4H 129
Carmodale Av. B42: P Barr 1D 82
Carnegie Av. DY4: Tip 3A 78
Carnegie Dr. WS10: W'bry 2G 63
Carnegie Rd. B65: Row R 1B 112
Carnford Rd. B26: Sheld 5F 121
Carnforth Cl. DY6: K'wtrd 2H 91
Carnoustie Cl. B75: S Cold 3A 54
  WS3: Blox .4G 19
Carnwath Rd. D73: Ncw O 3E 69
Carol Cres. B63: Hale 6H 111
  WV11: Wed 3G 29
Carol Gdns. DY8: Amb 3D 108
Caroline Pl. B13: Mose 2H 133
Caroline Rd. B13: Mose 1H 133
Caroline St. B3: Birm 1B 4 (5E 101)
  B70: W Brom 5H 79
  DY2: Dud 6G 77
Carpathian, The B18: Birm 1A 4
Carpathian Ct. B18: Birm 5E 101
Carpenter Glade B63: Crad 6F 111
Carpenter Pl. B12: Bal H 5A 118
Carpenter Rd. B15: Edg 4C 116
Carpenters Ct. B12: Birm 5A 118
              (off Vaughton St.)
Carpenter's Rd. B19: Loz 2E 101
Carriageway Wlk. B30: K Nor 4F 147
Carrick Cl. WS3: Pels 2E 21
Carriers Cl. WS2: Wals 2F 47
Carriers Fold WV5: Wom 6H 57
Carrington Rd. WS10: W'bry 3B 64
CARROWAY HEAD 5G 39
Carroway Head Hill B75: Bass P, Can . . .6F 39
Carrs La. B4: Birm 4F 5 (1G 117)
Carshalton Gro. WV2: Wolv 4A 44
Carshalton Rd. B44: K'sdng 3A 68
  WS4: Wals .4E 33
Cartbridge La. WS4: Wals 4E 33
Cartbridge La. Sth. WS4: Wals 5E 33
Cartbridge Wlk. WS3: Wals 3E 33
Carter Av. WV8: Bilb 4H 13
Carter Rd. B43: Gt Barr 3B 66
  WV6: Wolv .4F 27
Carters Cl. B37: Mars G 4C 122
  B76: Walm .2D 70
Cartersfield La. WS9: Ston 1F 23
Carters Grn. B70: W Brom 3H 79

Carter's Hurst B33: Sheld 2F 121
Carter's La. B62: Quin 6F 113
Cartland Rd. B11: S'brk 4C 118
  B14: K Hth 5D 132
  B30: Stir 5D 132
Cartmel Ct. B23: Erd 3B 84
Cartway, The WV6: Pert 5D 24
Cartwright Gdns. B69: Tiv 5C 78
Cartwright Ho. WS3: Blox 6H 19
Cartwright Rd. B75: R'ley 6A 38
Cartwright St. WV2: Wolv 6C 170 (3H 43)
Carver Ct. B24: Erd 1A 86
  DY4: Tip .4A 62
Carver Gdns. DY8: Stourb 3C 124
Carver St. B1: Birm 5D 100
Casern Vw. B75: S Cold 5E 55
Casewell Rd. DY6: W Hth 1A 92
Casey Av. B23: Erd 5D 68
Cash-Joynson Av. WS10: Darl 3C 46
Caslon Cres. DY8: Stourb 1B 124
Caslon Rd. B63: Crad 5E 111
Caslow Flats B63: Crad 1E 127
Cassandra Cl. DY5: P'ntt 6G 75
Cassowary Rd. B20: Hand 4B 82
Castello Dr. B36: Cas B 6H 87
Castillo Ct. B14: K Hth 2A 148
Castings, The WV14: Cose 3F 61
Castle, The DY8: Stourb 2F 125
Castlebridge Gdns. WV11: Wed 2H 29
Castlebridge Rd. WV11: Wed 3H 29
CASTLE BROMWICH 1F 105
Castle Bromwich Bus. Pk.
  B35: Cas V 6D 86
Castle Bromwich Hall
  B36: Cas B 1E 105
Castle Cl. B64: Old H 2B 112
  B92: Olton 4F 137
  WS8: Bwnhls 3B 10
Castle Ct. B34: S End 2A 106
  DY1: Dud 5G 77
Castle Cres. B36: Cas B 1G 105
CASTLECROFT 2G 41
Castle Cft. B68: O'bry 3B 114
Castlecroft WS11: Nort C 1C 8
Castlecroft Av. WV3: Wolv 3G 41
Castlecroft Gdns. WV3: Wolv 3A 42
Castlecroft La. WV3: Wolv 3F 41
Castle Cft. Rd. WV14: Bils 4G 45
Castlecroft Rd. WV3: Wolv 3F 41
                      (not continuous)
Castle Dr. B46: Col 4H 107
  WV12: W'hall 4B 30
Castleford Gro. B11: S'hll 1C 134
Castleford Rd. B11: S'hll 1C 134
Castlefort Rd. WS9: Wals W 4C 22
Castlegate Dr. DY1: Dud 5G 77
Castlegate Island DY1: Dud 5G 77
Castlegate Way DY1: Dud 5G 77
Castle Gro. DY8: Stourb 2F 125
Castle Hgts. B64: Old H 3B 112
                      (off Granville Rd.)
Castle Hill DY1: Dud 5F 77
Castlehill Rd. WS9: Wals W 4D 22
Castlehills Dr. B36: Cas B 1E 105
Castle Ho. B33: Yard 2F 121
Castle La. B92: Olton 4D 136
Castlemill DY4: Tip 5H 77
Castle Mill Rd. DY1: Dud 3E 77
Castle Rd. B29: W Cas 3E 131
  B30: K Nor 3B 146
  DY4: Tip .3F 77
  WS9: Wals W 5C 22
Castle Rd. E. B68: O'bry 3B 114
Castle Rd. W. B68: O'bry 3A 114
Castle Sq. B29: W Cas 4E 131
Castle St. B70: W Brom 5G 63
  DY1: Dud 6F 77
  DY3: Sed 5H 59
  DY4: Tip .2G 77
  WS8: Bwnhls 3B 10
  WS10: Darl 3D 46
                      (not continuous)
  WV1: Wolv 3C 170 (1H 43)
  WV14: Cose 5E 61

Castleton Rd. B42: Gt Barr 6F 67
  WS3: Blox 4A 20
Castleton St. DY2: Neth 4E 95
CASTLE VALE 4F 87
Castle Va. Ind. Est. B76: Min 2E 87
Castle Va. Shop. Cen. B35: Cas V 4D 86
Castle Vw. DY1: Dud 5D 76
Castle Vw. Cl. WS10: Mox 1A 62
Castle Vw. Ent. Pk. B35: Cas V 4G 87
Castle Vw. Ind. Est. DY4: Tip 4H 77
Castle Vw. Rd. WV14: Bils 1A 62
Castle Vw. Ter. WV14: Cose 5D 60
Castle Yd. WV1: Wolv 3C 170 (1H 43)
Caswell Rd. DY3: Sed 5G 59
Catalpa Gro. B74: S'tly 4H 51
Cat & Kittens La. WV10: F'stne 1A 16
Cater Dr. B76: Walm 3D 70
Caterham Dr. DY6: K'wfrd 6D 92
Catesby Dr. DY6: K'wfrd 1B 92
Catesby Ho. B37: K'hrst 4B 106
Catesby Pk. B38: K Nor 4A 146
Catesby Rd. B90: Shir 6H 149
Cateswell Rd. B11: Tys 3F 135
  B28: Hall G 4F 135
Cathcart Rd. DY8: Stourb 6C 108
Cathedral Cl. DY4: Tip 2G 77
Cathel Dr. B42: Gt Barr 6C 66
Catherine Ct. B24: Erd 3A 86
CATHERINE-DE-BARNES 2D 152
Catherine de Barnes La.
  B92: Bick, Cath B 1E 153
Catherine Dr. B73: S Cold 5G 53
Catherine Rd. WV14: Cose 4C 60
Catherines Cl. B91: Cath B 3D 152
Catherine St. B6: Aston 2A 102
Catherton Cl. DY4: Tip 3C 62
Catholic La. DY3: Sed 1G 75
Catisfield Cres. WV8: Pend 6D 14
Cat La. B34: S End 2F 105
Caton Gro. B28: Hall G 6G 135
Cato St. B7: Birm 5B 102
Cato St. Nth. B7: Nech 4C 102
CATSHILL .6C 10
Catshill Rd. WS8: Bwnhls 6C 10
Cattell Dr. B75: S Cold 6F 55
Cattell Rd. B9: Bord G 2C 118
Cattells Gro. B7: Nech 3C 102
Cattermole Gro. B43: Gt Barr 2E 67
Cattock Hurst Dr. B72: W Grn 6B 70
Causeway B65: Row R 1C 112
Causeway, The B25: Yard 4B 120
CAUSEWAY GREEN 6F 97
Causeway Grn. Rd. B68: O'bry 6F 97
Causeway Rd. WV14: Cose 5F 61
Causey Farm Rd. B63: Hale 5E 127
Cavalier Cir. WV10: Bush 3A 16
Cavalier Dr. B63: Hale 2A 128
Cavandale Av. B44: Gt Barr 4G 67
Cavell Cl. WS2: Wals 1B 48
Cavell Rd. DY2: Dud 6H 77
Cavendish Cl. B38: K Nor 6D 146
  DY6: K'wfrd 5B 92
Cavendish Ct. B17: Harb 3F 115
  B93: Dorr 6C 166
Cavendish Gdns. WS2: Wals 5G 31
  WV1: Wolv 2E 45
Cavendish Rd. B16: Edg 6H 99
  B62: Hale 1F 129
  WS2: Wals 4G 31
  WV1: Wolv 2D 44
Cavendish Way WS9: A'rdge 4D 34
Caversham Pl. B73: S Cold 1H 69
Caversham Rd. B44: K'sdng 3A 68
Cawdon Gro. B93: Dorr 6G 167
Cawdor Cres. B16: Edg 2B 116
Cawney Hill DY2: Dud 1G 95
Caxton Ga. B2: Birm 4E 5
Caxton Ga. Shop. Cen. B2: Birm 1G 117
Caxton Gro. B44: K'sdng 4C 68
Caynham Rd. B32: Bart G 5H 129
Cayton Gro. B23: Erd 1F 85
Cearl Ct. B27: A Grn 3A 136
Cecil Dr. B69: Tiv 5D 78

Cecil Rd. B24: Erd 4F 85
  B29: S Oak 4E 133
Cecil St. B19: Birm 5G 101
  DY8: Stourb 6D 108
  WS4: Wals 6D 32
Cedar Av. B36: Cas B 1G 105
  WS8: Bwnhls 5C 10
  WV14: Cose 6D 60
Cedar Bri. Cft. B74: Four O 3H 53
Cedar Cl. B30: B'vlle 1A 146
  B68: O'bry 3A 114
  DY8: Stourb 3B 124
  WS5: Wals 1F 65
Cedar Dr. B24: Erd 2A 86
  B31: Longb 2F 159
  B74: S'tly 2G 51
Cedar Gro. WS6: Gt Wyr 1H 7
  WV3: Wolv 4D 42
  WV8: Bilb 4H 13
  WV14: Bils 4H 45
Cedar Ho. B36: Hodg H 1D 104
  B91: Sol .6D 150
Cedarhurst B32: Harb 6E 115
  B91: Sol .4G 151
Cedar Pk. Rd. WV12: W'hall 6C 18
Cedar Rd. B30: B'vlle 1A 146
  DY1: Dud .4D 76
                      (not continuous)
  DY4: Tip .2F 77
  WS10: W'bry 3G 63
  WV13: W'hall 1G 45
Cedars, The B25: Yard 2C 120
  B93: Know 5C 166
  WV6: Tett 4B 26
  WV6: Wolv 6D 26
Cedars Av. B27: A Grn 1A 136
  DY6: K'wfrd 5B 92
  WV5: Wom 2G 73
Cedar Tree B23: Erd 5E 85
Cedar Wlk. B37: Chel W 1D 122
          (off Chelmsley Wood Shop. Cen.)
Cedar Way B31: Longb 6D 144
  WV11: Wed 2E 29
Cedarwood B74: Four O 3H 53
Cedarwood Cft. B42: Gt Barr 5B 66
Cedarwood Dr. CV7: Bal C 3H 169
Cedarwood Rd. DY3: Up Gor 2H 75
Celandine Cl. DY6: K'wfrd 5A 92
Celandine Rd. DY1: Dud 3C 76
Celandines, The WV5: Wom 1E 73
Celbury Way B43: Gt Barr 5H 65
Celts Cl. B65: Row R 5C 96
Cemetery La. B18: Birm 4D 100
Cemetery Rd. B66: Smeth 3A 98
  B67: Smeth 5D 98
  B68: O'bry 3A 98
  B75: S Cold 5B 54
  DY9: Lye 6H 109
  WS10: Darl 3F 47
  WV13: W'hall 6A 30
Cemetery St. WS6: C Hay 3C 6
  WV14: Bils 5E 45
Cemetery Way WS3: Blox 6H 19
Centenary Cl. B31: N'fld 6E 145
Centenary Dr. B21: Hand 6A 82
Centenary Plaza B1: Birm . . .5B 4 (1E 117)
Centenary Sq. B1: Birm 4B 4 (1E 117)
Centenary Way B1: Birm 2F 117
                      (off Blucher St.)
  B1: Birm .4B 4
                      (off Queensway)
  B2: Birm .5E 5
                      (off New St.)
Central Arc. WV1: Wolv 3B 170 (1G 43)
Central Av. B31: Longb 1G 158
  B64: Crad H 4E 111
  B65: Row R 1C 112
  DY4: Tip .6H 61
  DY9: W'cte 2A 126
  WV14: Bils 4G 45
Central Baths 2A 170 (1F 43)
Central Blvd. B90: Bly P 6D 164
Central Bus. Pk. B33: Kitts G 2H 121
Central Cl. WS3: Blox 6G 19

Central Dr. DY3: Gorn 5G **75**
WS3: Blox 1F **31**
WV14: Cose 6E **61**
Central Gro. B27: A Grn 3A **136**
Central Links Ind. Est. B7: Nech . . .3B **102**
Central Pk. Dr. B18: Win G 4B **100**
Central Pk. Ind. Est. DY2: Neth 6G **95**
Central Sq. B1: Birm 5A **4**
B23: Erd 3G **85**
Central Trad. Est. DY6: K'wfrd 6D **74**
WV2: Wolv 4A **44**
Central Way DY5: Brie H 6A **94**
Centre City B5: Birm 6D **4**
Centre La. B63: Hale 2B **128**
Centreway, The B14: Yard W 3D **148**
Centurion Cl. B46: Col 6H **89**
Century Dr. WV13: W'hall 3A **46**
Century Ho. B69: O'bry 3D **96**
Century Ind. Est. B44. Gt Barr 2G **67**
Century M. B64: Old H 1H **111**
Century Pk. B9: Bord G 1C **118**
B37: Mars G 5E **123**
Century Rd. B69: O'bry 1G **97**
Century Twr. B5: Edg 6E **117**
Ceolmund Cres. B37: Chel W 6D **106**
Chaceley Gro. B23: Erd 6D **68**
Chadbrook Crest B15: Edg 4A **116**
Chadbury Cft. B91: Sol 1F **165**
Chadbury Rd. B63: Hale 2C **128**
Chaddersley Cl. B45: Rub 6F **143**
Chaddesley Ct. DY1: Dud 6D **76**
Chaddesley Dr. DY9: Pedm 4F **125**
Chaddesley Rd. B31: N'fld 5H **145**
B63: Hale 3H **127**
Chadley Cl. B91: Sol 1E **151**
Chad Rd. B15: Edg 3B **116**
WV14: Cose 6C **60**
Chadshunt Cl. B36: Cas B 5H **87**
Chadsmoor Ter. B7: Nech 3B **102**
Chad Sq. B15: Edg 4A **116**
Chadstone Cl. B90: M'path 4F **165**
CHAD VALLEY 4A **116**
Chad Valley Cl. B17: Harb 5H **115**
Chadwell Dr. B90: Shir 1H **149**
Chadwell Gdns. WV8: Cod 3F **13**
Chadwick La. B61: C'wich 2A **156**
Chadwick Av. B45: Redn 3H **157**
Chadwick Cl. WV4: Penn 5A **42**
Chadwick Ct. B43: Gt Barr 3A **66**
Chadwick Ho. B45: Rub 2C **157**
Chadwick La. B93: Know 6A **168**
Chadwick Rd. B75: S Cold 6D **54**
Chadworth Av. B93: Dorr 5A **166**
Chaffcombe Rd. B26: Sheld 5G **121**
Chaffinch Cl. DY3: Sed 3G **59**
Chaffinch Dr. B36: Cas B 2D **106**
Chaffinch Rd. DY9: W'cte 2H **125**
Chainmakers Cl. WV14: Cose 3F **61**
Chain Wlk. B19: Loz 1F **101**
Chalcot Gro. B20: Hand 2A **82**
Chaldon Cl. WV9: Pend 6E **15**
Chale Gro. B14: K Hth 4A **148**
Chalfont Pl. DY9: W'cte 3A **126**
Chalfont Rd. B20: Hand 5D **82**
Chalford Rd. B23: Erd 5C **68**
Chalford Way B90: Shir 6A **150**
Chalgrove Av. B38: K Nor 6A **146**
Chalgrove Cres. B91: Sol 6F **151**
Challenge Way WV10: Wolv 4A **28**
Challenor Av. WV13: W'hall 1F **45**
Chalybeate Cl. B45: Fran 6F **143**
Chamberlain Clock 1A **4** (5D **100**)
Chamberlain Cl. B69: Tiv 5D **78**
Chamberlain Ct. B14: K Hth 4G **133**
B18: Birm 5E **101**
Chamberlain Cres. B90: Shir 5G **149**
Chamberlain Hall B15: Edg 5C **116**
Chamberlain Ho. B16: Edg 2C **116**
(off Skipton Rd.)
Chamberlain Rd. B13: Mose 1H **147**
Chamberlains La. WV4: Penn 2C **58**
Chamberlain Sq. B3: Birm 4C **4** (1F **117**)
(not continuous)

Chamberlain Wlk. B66: Smeth 4F **99**
Chance Cft. B68: O'bry 3H **113**
Chancel Ind. Est. DY6: K'wfrd 1C **92**
WS10: Darl 6D **46**
WV1: Wolv 2C **44**
WV13: W'hall 1B **46**
Chancellors Cl. B15: Edg 3A **116**
Chancel Way B6: Witt 2H **83**
B62: Hale 5C **112**
Chancery Way DY5: Quar B 1B **110**
Chandler Dr. WV4: Penn 2B **58**
Chandler Ho. B69: O'bry 5D **96**
WV9: Pend 6E **15**
Chandlers Cl. B18: Win G 4B **100**
WV9: Pend 6E **15**
Chandlers Keep WS8: Bwnhls 1B **22**
Chandos Av. B13: Mose 2H **133**
Chandos Rd. B12: Birm 3A **118**
Channon Dr. DY5: Brie H 3H **109**
Chanston Av. B14: K Hth 3G **147**
Chanterelle Gdns. WV4: Penn 1E **59**
Chantrey Cres. B43: Gt Barr 1F **67**
WV14: Bils 4H **45**
Chantry Av. WS3: Blox 1A **32**
Chantry Cl. B47: H'wd 2A **162**
Chantry Dr. B62: Quin 5G **113**
Chantry Heath Cres. B93: Know 1E **167**
Chantry Rd. B13: Mose 1G **133**
B21: Hand 1B **100**
DY7: Stourt 4A **108**
Chapel Ash WV3: Wolv 1F **43**
Chapel Ash Island
WV1: Wolv 3A **170** (1F **43**)
Chapel Av. WS8: Bwnhls 3A **10**
Chapel Cl. B64: Old H 3B **112**
WV5: Wom 2F **73**
Chapel Ct. DY5: Brie H 1H **109**
(off The Promenade)
DY5: P'ntt 2G **93**
(off Chapel St.)
Chapel Dr. B47: Wyt 6H **161**
CV7: Bal C 1H **169**
WS8: Bwnhls 3A **10**
Chapelfield M. B45: Rub 3F **157**
DY8: Stourb 1E **125**
Chapelfield Rd. B45: Redn 2G **157**
Chapel Flds. Rd. B92: Olton 3D **136**
Chapel Grn. WV13: W'hall 1A **46**
Chapel Ho. La. B63: Crad 5E **111**
Chapelhouse Rd. B37: F'bri 1B **122**
Chapel Ho. St. B12: Birm 6H **5** (2H **117**)
Chapel La. B29: S Oak 3A **132**
B43: Gt Barr 2A **66**
B47: Wyt 6G **161**
DY3: Swind 3C **72**
WV8: Cod 4E **13**
Chapel Pas. B69: O'bry 5G **97**
Chapel Sq. WS6: C Hay 2D **6**
Chapel St. B21: Hand 2H **99**
B63: Hale 2A **128**
B70: W Brom 2H **79**
DY2: Neth 5F **95**
DY4: Tip 2G **77**
(not continuous)
DY5: P'ntt 2G **93**
DY5: Quar B 3B **110**
DY6: W Hth 1H **91**
DY8: Stourb 1E **125**
DY8: Word 6B **92**
DY9: Lye 6A **110**
WS3: Blox 1B **32**
WS3: Pels 4D **20**
WS8: Bwnhls 3A **10**
WS11: Nort C 1C **8**
WV2: Wolv 4H **43**
WV5: Wom 2F **73**
(not continuous)
WV14: Bils 6H **45**
Chapel Vw. B67: Smeth 5D **98**
Chapel Wlk. B30: K Nor 4C **146**
DY3: Gorn 5G **75**
Chapelwood Gro. B42: P Barr 2F **83**
Chapman Rd. B10: Small H 3C **118**
CHAPMAN'S HILL 6B **142**
Chapman's Hill B62: Roms 6B **142**

Chapmans Pas. B1: Birm 6C **4** (2F **117**)
Chapman St. B70: W Brom 4H **79**
Chapter Ho. B70: W Brom 2G **79**
Chapter Pl. B68: O'bry 4H **113**
Charfield Cl. B30: B'ville 6H **131**
Charingworth Rd. B92: Sol 3G **137**
Charity Bick Way B70: W Brom 5A **80**
Charlbury Av. B37: F'bri 1B **122**
Charlbury Cres. B26: Yard 3D **120**
Charlbury Twr. B5: Birm 3G **117**
(off Southacre Av.)
Charlecote Cft. B90: Shir 1A **164**
Charlecote Dr. B23: Erd 6E **69**
DY1: Dud 4A **76**
Charlecote Gdns. B73: Bold 5G **69**
Charlecote Ri. WV13: W'hall 3H **45**
Charlecott Cl. B13: Mose 6D **134**
CHARLEMONT 5C **64**
Charlemont Av. B71: W Brom 5C **64**
Charlemont Cl. WS5: Wals 5G **49**
Charlemont Cres. B71: W Brom 5C **64**
Charlemont Gdns. WS5: Wals 5G **49**
Charlemont Rd. B71: W Brom 5C **64**
WS5: Wals 5F **49**
Charles Av. B65: Row R 5C **96**
WV4: Penn 6F **43**
WV11: Ess 3H **17**
Charles Cl. B8: Salt 5D **102**
WS6: C Hay 4D **6**
Charles Ct. B13: Mose 3B **134**
B76: Walm 2D **70**
(off Berryfields Rd.)
Charles Cres. WS3: Pels 2E **21**
Charlesdale Dr. WS9: A'rdge 5D **34**
Charles Dr. B7: Nech 3B **102**
Charles Edward Rd. B26: Yard 5B **120**
Charles Foster St. WS10: Darl 5C **46**
Charles Henry St. B12: Birm 3H **117**
Charles Holland St. WV13: W'hall 1B **46**
Charles Lanes Trust Ho's.
B28: Hall G 5G **135**
Charles Pearson Ct. B66: Smeth 4F **99**
(off Mill Dr.)
Charles Rd. B6: Aston 6A **84**
B9: Small H 1E **119**
B10: Small H 3E **119**
B20: Hand 6E **83**
B63: Hale 1H **127**
B91: Sol 5C **150**
DY4: Tip 1A **78**
DY5: Quar B 2C **110**
DY8: Stourb 1C **124**
Charles St. B66: Smeth 2G **99**
B70: W Brom 2E **79**
WS2: Wals 1B **48**
WV13: W'hall 6C **30**
Charles St. Ind. Est.
B70: W Brom 2E **79**
Charles Wlk. B65: Row R 4C **96**
Charles Wesley Ct. WV3: Wolv 4E **43**
(off Claremont Rd.)
Charlesworth Av. B90: M'path 3F **165**
Charleville Rd. B19: Hock 2D **100**
Charlotte Cl. B69: Tiv 5A **78**
Charlotte Gdns. B66: Smeth 4F **99**
Charlotte Rd. B15: Edg 4E **117**
B30: Stir 1C **146**
WS10: W'bry 4C **62**
Charlotte St. B3: Birm 3B **4** (6E **101**)
DY1: Dud 1D **94**
WS1: Wals 1E **49**
Charlton Dr. B64: Crad H 4F **111**
Charlton Pl. B8: Salt 4D **102**
Charlton Rd. B44: K'sdng 6A **68**
Charlton St. DY1: Dud 6D **76**
DY5: Brie H 6E **93**
Charminster Av. B25: Yard 3B **120**
Charnley Dr. B75: R'ley 1C **54**
Charnwood Av. DY3: Sed 3H **59**
Charnwood Bus. Pk. WV14: Bils 6E **45**
Charnwood Cl. B45: Fran 4H **143**
DY5: Brie H 4F **109**
WV14: Bils 2B **62**
Charnwood Ct. DY9: W'cte 3A **126**

Charnwood Rd. B42: Gt Barr 6B **66**
WS5: Wals 1E **65**
Charter Cl. WS11: Nort C 1C **8**
Charter Cres. B64: Old H 3B **112**
Charterfield Dr. DY6: K'wfrd 1B **92**
Charterfield Shop. Cen.
DY6: K'wfrd 1C **92**
Charterhouse Dr. B91: Sol 6F **151**
Charter Rd. DY4: Tip 4C **62**
Charters Av. WV8: Bilb 6H **13**
Charters Cl DY4: Tip 2G **77**
Charter St. DY5: Brie H 4A **94**
Chartist Rd. B8: Salt 3D **102**
Chartley Cl. B93: Dorr 6A **166**
WV6: Pert 5F **25**
Chartley Rd. B23: Erd 6D **84**
B71: W Brom 1B **80**
Chartway, The WS3: Pels 3E **21**
Chartwell Cl. DY1: Dud 1D **76**
Chartwell Dr. B74: Four O 5D **36**
B90: Ches G 4B **164**
WV5: Wom 2F **73**
WV10: Bush 6A **16**
Chase, The B76: Walm 6B **70**
WV6: Wolv 3F **27**
Chase Av. WS6: C Hay 2F **7**
Chase Gro. B24: Erd 1B **86**
Chase Link, The WS8: Bwnhls 4C **10**
Chasepool Rd. DY3: Swind 2C **90**
Chase Rd. DY3: Gorn 6F **75**
DY5: P'ntt 6F **75**
WS3: Blox 1G **31**
WS8: Bwnhls 4C **10**
Chase Sailing Club, The 1H **9**
Chasetown Leisure Cen. 1A **10**
Chase Vw. WV4: E'shll 3A **60**
Chasewater Country Pk. 1G **9**
Chasewater Outdoor Education Cen. 1H **9**
Chasewater Railway
Brownhills West Station 2G **9**
Chasewater Railway Heritage Cen. 2H **9**
Chasewater Sports Cen. 2G **9**
Chassieur Wlk. B46: Col 1H **107**
Chater Dr. B76: Walm 4E **71**
Chatham Rd. B23: N'fld 4E **145**
Chatsworth Av. B43: Gt Barr 4G **65**
Chatsworth Cl. B72: W Grn 6B **70**
B90: Ches G 4B **164**
WV12: W'hall 4B **30**
Chatsworth Cres. WS4: Rus 2H **33**
Chatsworth Gro. WV6: Tett 2G **25**
Chatsworth M. DY8: Word 6H **91**
Chatsworth Rd. B62: Hale 4A **112**
Chatsworth Way B15: Birm 3E **117**
Chattaway Dr. CV7: Bal C 3H **169**
Chattaway St. B7: Nech 2C **102**
CHATTLE HILL 5F **89**
Chattle Hill B46: Col 5G **89**
Chattock Av. B91: Sol 3A **152**
Chattock Cl. B36: Hodg H 2C **104**
Chatwell Gro. B29: S Oak 3F **131**
Chatwin Pl. WV14: Bils 2G **61**
Chatwin St. B66: Smeth 2D **98**
Chatwins Wharf St. DY4: Tip 2H **77**
Chaucer Av. DY3: Lwr G 2E **75**
DY4: Tip .5B **62**
WV12: W'hall 1E **31**
Chaucer Cl. B23: Erd 4B **84**
DY8: Amb 3E **109**
WV14: Cose 5F **61**
Chaucer Gro. B27: A Grn 3H **135**
Chaucer Ho. B63: Crad 6D **110**
Chaucer Rd. WS3: Blox 1C **32**
Chauson Gro. B91: Sol 1E **165**
Chavasse Rd. B72: S Cold 2A **70**
CHAWN HILL .2G **125**
Chawn Hill DY9: Pedm 2G **125**
Chawn Hill Cl. DY9: Pedm 2G **125**
Chawn Pk. Dr. DY9: Pedm 2G **125**
Chaynes Gro. B33: Kitts G 6H **105**
Cheadle Dr. B23: Erd 5D **68**
Cheam Gdns. WV6: Tett 1C **26**
Cheapside B5: Birm 6G **5** (2H **117**)
B12: Birm 2H **117**

Cheapside WV1: Wolv 3B **170** (1G **43**)
WV13: W'hall 2A **46**
Cheapside Ind. Est. B12: Birm 2H **117**
Cheatham St. B7: Nech 3C **102**
Checketts St. WS2: Wals 1A **48**
Checkley Cl. B90: Shir 3G **149**
Checkley Cft. B76: Walm 5D **70**
Cheddar Rd. B12: Bal H 5G **117**
Chedworth Cl. B29: W Cas 6F **131**
Chedworth Ct. B29: S Oak 5A **132**
Cheedon Cl. B93: Dorr 6F **167**
Chelford Cres. DY6: K'wfrd 6E **93**
Chells Gro. B13: Mose 2B **148**
Chelmar Cl. B36: Cas B 1B **106**
Chelmar Dr. DY5: P'ntt 3E **93**
Chelmarsh Av. WV3: Wolv 2G **41**
Chelmorton Rd. B42: Gt Barr 6F **67**
Chelmscote Rd. B92: Olton 4D **136**
Chelmsley Av. B46: Col 3H **107**
Chelmsley Circ. B37: Chel W 1D **122**
Chelmsley Gro. B33: Kitts G 6A **106**
Chelmsley La. B37: Mars G 3B **122**
(not continuous)
Chelmsley Rd. B37: Chel W, F'bri 6B **106**
CHELMSLEY WOOD 1D **122**
Chelmsley Wood Ind. Est.
B37: F'bri 5D **106**
Chelmsley Wood Shop. Cen.
B37: Chel W 1D **122**
Chelsea B37: K'hrst 4B **106**
(off Chilvers Gro.)
Chelsea Cl. B32: Quin 1D **130**
Chelsea Ct. B29: W Cas 6F **131**
Chelsea Dr. B74: Four O 5F **37**
Chelsea Way DY6: K'wfrd 3B **92**
Chelston Dr. WV6: Wolv 5C **26**
Chelston Rd. B31: N'fld 5C **144**
Cheltenham Cl. WV6: Wolv 3F **27**
Cheltenham Dr. B36: Hodg H 1B **104**
DY6: K'wfrd 3H **91**
Cheltenham M. B74: Four O 2G **53**
Chelthorn Way B91: Sol 5G **151**
Cheltondale B90: Shir 1A **164**
Cheltondale Rd. B91: Sol 1D **150**
Chelveston Cres. B91: Sol 6F **151**
Chelwood Gdns. WV14: Bils 6D **44**
Chelworth Rd. B38: K Nor 5D **146**
Chem Rd. WV14: Bils 6E **45**
Cheniston Rd. WV12: W'hall 3C **30**
Chepstow Cl. WV6: Pert 5F **25**
Chepstow Gro. B45: Redn 3H **157**
Chepstow Rd. WS3: Blox 6F **19**
WV10: F'hses 2H **15**
Chepstow Vs. B12: Bal H 6B **118**
Chepstow Way WS3: Blox 6F **19**
Chequer St. WV3: Wolv 5E **43**
Chequerfield Dr. WV3: Wolv 5E **43**
Chequers Av. WV5: Wom 4G **57**
Cherhill Covert B14: K Hth 5E **147**
Cherington Rd. B29: S Oak 5C **132**
Cherish Ho. B12: Birm 3A **118**
Cheriton Gro. WV6: Pert 6E **25**
Cheriton Wlk. B23: Erd 4B **84**
Cherrington Cl. B31: N'fld 6C **130**
Cherrington Dr. WS6: Gt Wyr 1F **7**
Cherrington Gdns. DY9: Pedm 6G **125**
WV6: Tett 1H **41**
Cherrington Way B91: Sol 6F **151**
Cherry Brook WS11: Nort C 2D **8**
Cherry Cres. B24: Erd 4F **85**
Cherrydale Ct. DY1: Dud 5B **76**
Cherry Dr. B9: Birm 2B **118**
B64: Old H 2H **111**
Cherry Gdns. B73: W Grn 6H **69**
(off Emscote Dr.)
Cherry Grn. DY1: Dud 3B **76**
Cherry Gro. B66: Smeth 4G **99**
(off Rosedale Av.)
DY8: Stourb 1C **124**
WV11: Wed 2E **29**
Cherry Hill Wlk. DY1: Dud 1C **94**
Cherry La. B73: Bold 6G **69**
DY3: Himl 4A **74**
WS10: W'bry 3G **63**

Cherry Lea B34: S End 3F **105**
CHERRY ORCHARD 2H **111**
Cherry Orchard B64: Old H 2H **111**
WV8: Cod .3F **13**
Cherry Orchard Av. B63: Hale 6H **111**
Cherry Orchard Cres. B63: Hale 5H **111**
Cherry Orchard Rd. B20: Hand 2B **82**
Cherry Rd. DY4: Tip 6H **61**
Cherry St. B2: Birm 4E **5** (1G **117**)
B63: Hale 6H **111**
DY8: Stourb 1C **124**
WV3: Wolv 2F **43**
Cherry Tree Av. WS5: Wals 1E **65**
Cherry Tree Ct. B30: K Nor 2B **146**
DY9: W'cte 2A **126**
Cherry Tree Crt. B27: A Grn 6A **120**
Cherry Tree Gdns. WV8: Bilb 4H **13**
Cherry Tree La. B63: Hale 4F **127**
WV8: Bilb .4H **13**
Cherry Tree Rd. DY6: K'wfrd 1C **92**
WS11: Nort C 1F **9**
Cherry Wlk. B47: H'wd 4B **162**
Cherrywood Cl. WV14: Cose 4E **61**
Cherrywood Ct. B92: Olton 3E **137**
Cherrywood Cres. B91: Sol 1G **165**
Cherrywood Grn. WV14: Bils 3F **45**
Cherrywood Ind. Est. B9: Bord G 6D **102**
Cherrywood Rd. B9: Bord G 1D **118**
B74: S'tly 2F **51**
Cherrywood Way B74: Lit As 4D **36**
Chervil Cl. B42: Gt Barr 6E **67**
Chervil Ri. WV10: Wolv 6B **28**
Cherwell Ct. B73: S Cold 6H **53**
Cherwell Dr. B36: Cas B 1B **106**
WS8: Bwnhls 3G **9**
Cherwell Gdns. B6: Aston 1F **101**
Cheshire Av. B90: Shir 4G **149**
Cheshire Cl. DY8: Woll 3B **108**
Cheshire Ct. B34: S End 2F **105**
Cheshire Gro. WV6: Pert 5E **25**
Cheshire Rd. B6: Witt 5A **84**
B67: Smeth 5E **99**
WS2: Wals 1F **47**
Cheslyn Dr. WS6: C Hay 2D **6**
Cheslyn Gro. B14: K Hth 4A **148**
CHESLYN HAY .3D **6**
Cheslyn Hay Leisure Cen. 2C **6**
Chessetts Gro. B13: Mose 1A **148**
Chester Av. WV6: Tett 2D **26**
Chester Cl. B37: F'bri 1C **122**
WV13: W'hall 1D **46**
Chester Ct. B29: W Cas 6F **131**
(off Abdon Av.)
B37: Chel W 1F **123**
(off Hedingham Gro.)
Chesterfield Cl. B31: N'fld 5F **145**
Chesterfield Ct. B30: K Nor 3A **146**
WS9: Wals W 3B **22**
Chester Gdns. B73: New O 4E **69**
Chestergate Cft. B24: Erd 3B **86**
Chester Hayes Ct. B24: Erd 2A **86**
Chester House 3E **167**
Chester Pl. WS2: Wals 2H **47**
Chester Ri. B68: O'bry 3H **113**
CHESTER ROAD 6H **69**
Chester Rd. B23: Erd 4D **68**
B24: Erd .2A **86**
B35: Cas V 2A **86**
B36: Cas B 1E **105**
B37: Chel W, F'bri 4D **106**
B46: Col .4H **123**
B64: Crad H 3E **111**
B71: W Brom 4H **63**
B73: New O, Bold 4D **68**
B74: S'tly 1H **51**
CV7: Lit P 1B **140**
DY2: Neth 1F **111**
WS8: Bwnhls, Wals W 1C **22**
WS9: A'rdge, Wals W 1C **22**
Chester Rd. Nth. B73: S'tly, New O 6A **52**
WS8: Bwnhls 4H **9**
Chester Road Station (Rail) 6G **69**
Chester St. B6: Aston 4H **101**
WV6: Wolv 5F **27**

Chester St. Wharf—Church Rd.

Chester St. Wharf B6: Aston 4H **101**
Chesterton Av. B12: Bal H 6B **118**
Chesterton Cl. B91: Sol 2C **150**
Chesterton Rd. B12: Bal H 6A **118**
WV10: Bush 1C **28**
Chesterwood B47: H'wd 3A **162**
WS9: A'rdge 1H **51**
Chesterwood Gdns. B20: Hand 5F **83**
Chesterwood Rd. B13: Mose 1H **147**
Chestnut Av. DY1: Dud 4E **77**
DY4: Tip 6H **61**
Chestnut Cl. B27: A Grn 1A **136**
B74: S'tly 6A **36**
B92: Olton 5B **136**
DY8: Stourb 3B **124**
WV8: Cod 5F **13**
Chestnut Ct. B36: Cas B 2A **106**
Chestnut Dr. B24: Erd 3A **86**
B36: Cas B 1E **105**
B45: Coft H 5B **158**
WS4: S'fld 6F **21**
WS6: C Hay 2D **6**
WS6: Gt Wyr 2F **7**
WV5: Wom 2G **73**
Chestnut Gro. B17: Harb 6H **115**
B46: Col 2H **107**
DY6: K'wfrd 2D **92**
WV11: Wed 2E **29**
Chestnut Ho. B37: Chel W 1D **122**
Chestnut Pl. B14: K Hth 5H **133**
WS3: Blox 3B **32**
Chestnut Rd. B13: Mose 1A **134**
B68: O'bry 4A **114**
WS3: Blox 3C **32**
WS10: W'bry 4G **63**
Chestnuts Av. B26: Sheld 4F **121**
Chestnut Wlk. *B37: Chel W 1D 122*
(off Chelmsley Wood Shop. Cen.)
Chestnut Way WV3: Wolv 3B **42**
Chestom Rd. WV14: Bils 5D **44**
Chestom Rd. Ind. Est. WV14: Bils 5D **44**
Cheston Ind. Est. B7: Nech 3A **102**
Cheston Rd. B7: Nech 3A **102**
Cheswell Cl. WV6: Tett 1H **41**
Cheswick Cl. WV13: W'hall 3H **45**
CHESWICK GREEN 5B **164**
Cheswick Way B90: Ches G 5B **164**
Cheswood Dr. B76: Walm 1F **87**
Chetland Cft. B92: Sol 6B **138**
Chettle Rd. WV14: Bils 2H **61**
Chetton Grn. WV10: F'hses 4F **15**
Chetwood Cl. WV6: Wolv 4E **27**
Chetwynd Cl. WS2: Wals 6C **30**
Chetwynd Rd. B8: W End 4H **103**
WV2: Wolv 5F **43**
Cheveley Av. B45: Redn 2H **157**
Chevening Cl. DY3: Sed 6A **60**
Cheveridge Cl. B91: Sol 5F **151**
Cheverton Rd. B31: N'fld 3C **144**
Cheviot Rd. DY8: Amb 5E **109**
WV2: E'shll 4B **44**
Cheviot Way B63: Hale 2F **127**
Cheylesmore Cl. B73: S Cold 1H **69**
Cheyne Ct. *B17: Harb 6H 115*
(off Greenfield Rd.)
Cheyne Gdns. B28: Hall G 4E **149**
Cheyne Pl. B17: Harb 6H **115**
Cheyne Wlk. DY5: Brie H 4G **109**
Cheyne Way B17: Harb 6H **115**
Cheyney Cl. WV6: Wolv 4E **27**
Chichester Av. DY2: Neth 5F **95**
Chichester Ct. B73: S Cold 6H **53**
Chichester Dr. B32: Quin 6G **113**
Chichester Gro. B37: Chel W 2C **122**
(not continuous)
Chigwell Cl. B35: Cas V 4E **87**
Chilcote Cl. B28: Hall G 3F **149**
Childs Av. WV14: Cose 3C **60**
Childs Oak Cl. CV7: Bal C 3G **169**
Chilgrove Gdns. WV6: Tett 4A **26**
Chilham Dr. B37: Chel W 1E **123**
Chillenden Ct. *WV13: W'hall 1C 46*
(off Mill St.)
Chillinghome Rd. B36: Hodg H 1B **104**
Chillington Cl. WS6: Gt Wyr 4F **7**
Chillington Dr. DY1: Dud 4B **76**
WV8: Cod 3F **13**
Chillington Flds. WV1: Wolv 2C **44**
Chillington La. WV8: Cod 2D **12**
Chillington Pl. WV14: Bils 6E **45**
Chillington Rd. DY4: Tip 4C **62**
Chillington St. WV1: Wolv 3B **44**
Chillington Wlk. B65: Row R 6C **96**
Chillington Works Ind. Est.
WV1: Wolv 2B **44**
Chiltern Cl. B63: Hale 3E **127**
DY3: Lwr G 4H **75**
WS6: C Hay 4D **6**
Chiltern Dr. WV13: W'hall 2F **45**
Chiltern Rd. DY8: Amb 5F **109**
Chilterns, The B69: O'bry 4E **97**
Chilton Ct. *B23: Erd 5C 84*
(off Park App.)
Chilton Rd. B14: Yard W 3D **148**
Chilvers Gro. B37: K'hrst 4B **106**
Chilwell Cl. B91: Sol 6F **151**
Chilwell Cft. B19: Hock 4G **101**
Chilworth Av. WV11: Wed 2H **29**
Chilworth Cl. B6: Aston 3H **101**
Chimes Cl. B33: Kitts G 2A **122**
Chimney Rd. DY4: Tip 6D **62**
Chingford Cl. DY8: Word 5A **92**
Chingford Rd. B44: K'sdng 5A **68**
Chinley Gro. B44: K'sdng 4C **68**
Chinn Brook Rd. B13: Mose 2B **148**
Chip Cl. B38: K Nor 5H **145**
Chipperfield Rd. B36: Hodg H 1C **104**
Chipstead Rd. B23: Erd 6D **68**
Chipstone Cl. B91: Sol 1G **165**
Chirbury Gro. B31: Longb 6F **145**
Chirton Gro. B14: K Hth 1F **147**
Chiseldon Cft. B14: K Hth 4A **148**
Chisholm Gro. B27: A Grn 5A **136**
Chiswell Rd. B18: Win G 5A **100**
Chiswick Ct. B23: Erd 5E **85**
Chiswick Ho. *B15: Birm 3E 117*
(off Bell Barn Rd.)
Chiswick Wlk. B37: Chel W 1F **123**
Chivenor Ho. B35: Cas V 5E **87**
Chivington Cl. B90: M'path 3F **165**
Chorley Av. B34: Hodg H 3D **104**
Chorley Gdns. WV14: Bils 6D **44**
Christchurch Cl. B15: Edg 3A **116**
Christ Chu. Gro. WS1: Wals 4E **49**
Christina Ct. B71: W Brom 3B **80**
Christine Cl. DY4: Tip 3C **62**
Christopher Ct. *B23: Erd 5D 68*
(off Marshmount Way)
Christopher Rd. B29: S Oak 3G **131**
B62: Hale 2E **129**
WV2: Wolv 3A **44**
Christopher Taylor Ct. B30: B'vlle 2A **146**
Chubb St. WV1: Wolv 2D **170** (1H **43**)
CHUCKERY, THE 2E **49**
Chuckery Rd. WS1: Wals 2E **49**
Chudleigh Gro. B43: Gt Barr 5H **65**
Chudleigh Rd. B23: Erd 3E **85**
Churchacre B23: Erd 5C **68**
Church Av. B13: Mose 2H **133**
B20: Hand 1E **101**
B46: Wat O 4D **88**
DY8: Amb 4E **109**
CHURCHBRIDGE 1G **7**
Churchbridge B69: O'bry 4F **97**
(not continuous)
Churchbridge Ind. Est. *B69: O'bry 4F 97*
(off Churchbridge)
Church Cl. B37: K'hrst 3C **106**
B47: Wyt 6A **162**
Church Ct. B64: Old H 2G **111**
Church Cres. WV11: Ess 4H **17**
Church Cft. B63: Hale 1A **128**
Churchcroft B17: Harb 1F **131**
Church Cross Vw. DY1: Dud 1H **93**
Church Dale Rd. B44: Gt Barr 2F **67**
Churchdown Ct. *B23: Erd 5C 84*
(off Dunlin Ct.)
Church Dr. B30: Stir 6D **132**
CHURCHFIELD 1B **80**
Churchfield Av. DY4: Tip 5H **61**
Churchfield Cl. B7: Nech 3C **102**
Churchfield Rd. WV10: Oxl 1F **27**
Churchfields Rd. WS10: W'bry 1F **63**
Churchfield St. DY2: Dud 1E **95**
Church Gdns. B67: Smeth 5E **99**
Church Grn. B20: Hand 5B **82**
WV14: Bils 3E **45**
Church Gro. B13: Mose 2C **148**
B20: Hand 6D **82**
CHURCH HILL 2F **63**
Church Hill B31: N'fld 4F **145**
(not continuous)
B32: Fran 2G **143**
B46: Col 2H **107**
B72: S Cold 6A **54**
DY5: Brie H 1H **109**
WS1: Wals 2D **48**
WS10: W'bry 2F **63**
(Ethelfleda Ter.)
WS10: W'bry 2F **63**
(Walsall St.)
WV4: Penn 2C **58**
WV8: Cod 2F **13**
Church Hill Cl. B91: Sol 5G **151**
Church Hill Ct. WS10: W'bry 2F **63**
Church Hill Dr. WV6: Tett 4C **26**
Church Hill Rd. B20: Hand 6D **82**
B91: Sol 4G **151**
WV6: Tett 3B **26**
Church Hill St. B67: Smeth 3D **98**
Church Ho. WS2: Wals 4A **48**
Church Ho. Dr. B72: S Cold 6A **54**
Churchill Cl. B69: Tiv 5C **78**
Churchill Dr. B65: Row R 1B **112**
DY8: Amb 4E **109**
Churchill Gdns. DY3: Sed 6G **59**
Churchill Pde. B75: S Cold 6E **55**
Churchill Pl. B33: Sheld 2F **121**
Churchill Rd. B9: Bord G 6F **103**
B63: Hale 3H **127**
B73: New O 2D **68**
B75: S Cold 6E **55**
WS2: Wals 1D **46**
Churchill Shop. Pct., The DY2: Dud 6F **77**
Churchill Wlk. DY4: Tip 5A **62**
Church La. B6: Aston 1A **102**
B20: Hand 5B **82**
B33: Stech 6D **104**
B63: Hale 1B **128**
B71: W Brom 1H **79**
B76: Curd 1D **88**
B92: Bick 4F **139**
WS7: Hamm 2F **11**
WS9: Ston 3G **23**
WV2: Wolv 5A **170** (2G **43**)
WV5: Seis, Try 3A **56**
WV8: Cod 3F **13**
Church La. Ind. Est. B71: W Brom 1A **80**
Church M. DY4: Tip 6H **61**
Church Moat Way WS3: Blox 1H **31**
Churchover Cl. B76: Walm 1B **86**
Church Pl. WS3: Blox 1B **32**
Church Rd. B6: Aston 2B **102**
B13: Mose 2A **134**
B15: Edg 4C **116**
B24: Erd 3F **85**
B25: Yard 4B **120**
B26: Sheld 6F **121**
B31: N'fld 3E **145**
B33: Yard 3C **120**
B42: P Barr 2F **83**
B63: Crad 5E **111**
B65: Row R 6C **96**
B67: Smeth 5D **98**
B73: Bold 5F **69**
B73: S Cold 2H **69**
B90: Shir 5H **149**
DY2: Neth 4D **94**
DY3: Swind 4D **72**
DY8: Stourb 2F **125**
DY8: Word 1B **108**
DY9: Lye 6A **110**

Church Rd. WS3: Pels 4E 21
  WS8: Bwnhls 6B 10
    (not continuous)
  WS9: Ston 4G 23
  WS11: Nort C 1C 8
  WV3: Wolv 4C 42
  WV5: Wom 6H 57
  WV6: Pert 5E 25
  WV6: Tett 6H 25
    (School Rd.)
  WV6: Tett 4C 26
    (The Rock)
  WV8: Cod 3F 13
    (not continuous)
  WV10: Oxl 6G 15
  WV12: W'hall 3D 30
  WV14: Cose 4F 61
Churchside Way WS9: A'rdge 5D 22
Church Sq. B69: O'bry 2G 97
Church St. B3: Birm 3D 4 (6F 101)
  B19: Loz 2E 101
  B35: Cas V 3F 87
  B62: B'hth 2D 112
  B64: Old H 2G 111
  B69: O'bry 1G 97
  B70: W Brom 3A 80
  DY2: Dud 1E 95
  DY3: Lwr G 4H 75
  DY4: Tip .5A 78
  DY5: Brie H 2G 109
  DY5: P'ntt 2H 93
  DY5: Quar B 2B 110
  DY8: Stourb 6E 109
  WS1: Wals 2D 48
  WS3: Blox 1H 31
  WS7: Chase 1A 10
  WS8: Clay 1A 22
  WS10: Darl 4D 46
    (Bell St.)
  WS10: Darl 1B 62
    (Black Country New Rd.)
  WV2: Wolv 5A 170 (2G 43)
  WV10: Wolv 5C 28
  WV11: Wed 4E 29
  WV13: W'hall 1B 46
    (not continuous)
  WV14: Bils 6F 45
Church Ter. B33: Yard 2C 120
  B75: Four O 6H 37
Church Va. B20: Hand 6D 82
  B71: W Brom 1B 80
  WS11: Nort C 1C 8
Church Va. M. B71: W Brom 2B 80
Church Vw. B11: S'brk 5D 118
  WS9: A'rdge 4D 34
  WS9: Wals W 4B 22
Church Vw. Cl. WS3: Blox 1A 32
Church Vw. Dr. B64: Old H 2H 111
Church Wlk. B8: W End 3G 103
  B46: Col 3H 107
  B65: Row R 5C 96
  WV3: Wolv 4D 42
  WV6: Tett 4C 26
  WV13: W'hall 2B 46
Churchward Cl. DY8: Amb 5F 109
Churchward Gro. WV5: Wom 6G 57
Church Way WS4: S'fld 5F 21
Churchwell Ct. B63: Hale 2B 128
Churchwell Gdns. B71: W Brom 1B 80
Churchyard Rd. DY4: Tip 2B 78
Churnet Gro. WV6: Pert 5F 25
Churn Hill Rd. WS9: A'rdge 5C 34
Churns Hill La. DY3: Himl 4H 73
Churston Cl. WS3: Blox 4G 19
Churton House (The Crystal Glass Cen.)
  . . . . .3C 108
Churwell Ct. WV5: Wom 1G 73
Cider Av. DY5: Quar B 3A 110
    (not continuous)
Cinder Bank DY2: Neth 2D 94
Cinder Bank Island DY2: Dud 2D 94
CINDER HILL 4B 60
Cinder Rd. DY3: Gorn 6F 75
Cinder Way WS10: W'bry 2E 63

Cineworld Cinema
  Birmingham 2D 116
  Great Park 1G 157
  Solihull 4G 151
  Wednesfield 5D 28
Cinquefoil Leasow DY4: Tip 1C 78
Circle, The B17: Harb 4G 115
Circuit Cl. WV13: W'hall 6B 30
Circular Rd. B27: A Grn 3A 136
Circus Av. B37: Chel W 1E 123
City, The DY4: Tip 4A 78
City Arc. B2: Birm 4E 5
    (off Corporation St.)
City Est. B64: Crad H 3F 111
City Ga. B24: Erd 6E 85
City Hgts. B4: Birm 1D 4
City Plaza B2: Birm 4E 5
City Rd. B16: Edg 2F 115
  B17: Edg 2F 115
  B69: Tiv 2B 96
City Trad. Est. B16: Birm 6C 100
City Vw. B8: Salt 5D 102
  B23: Erd .4E 85
City Wlk. B5: Birm 6E 5 (2G 117)
Claerwen Gro. B31: N'fld 2C 144
Claines Rd. B31: N'fld 3G 145
  B63: Crad 6F 111
Claire Cl. B26: Sheld 4G 121
Clairvaux Gdns. B92: Olton 2B 150
Clandon Cl. B14: K Hth 5E 147
Clanfield Av. WV11: Wed 1H 29
Clapgate Gdns. WV14: Cose 2C 60
Clap Ga. Gro. WV5: Wom 1E 73
Clapgate La. B32: Bart G 3G 129
Clapgate Rd. WV5: Wom 6E 57
Clapton Gro. B44: K'sdng 4B 68
Clare Av. WV11: Wed 6H 17
Clare Ct. B90: Shir 5D 148
Clare Cres. WV14: Cose 3B 60
Clare Dr. B15: Edg 3B 116
Clare Ho. B36: Cas B 2C 106
Clarel Av. B8: Salt 6C 102
Claremont Ct. B64: Old H 2G 111
Claremont M. WV3: Wolv 4E 43
Claremont Pl. B18: Hock 4B 100
Claremont Rd. B11: S'brk 4B 118
  B18: Hock 3D 100
  B66: Smeth 5F 99
  DY3: Sed .5A 60
  WV3: Wolv 4E 43
Claremont St. B64: Old H 2G 111
  WV14: Bils 5E 45
Claremont Way B63: Hale 2B 128
Clarence Av. B21: Hand 1G 99
Clarence Ct. B68: O'bry 1A 114
Clarence Gdns. B74: Four O 1F 53
Clarence M. B17: Harb 5H 115
Clarence Rd. B11: S'hll 1C 134
  B13: K Hth 4A 134
  B17: Harb 5H 115
  B21: Hand 1G 99
  B23: Erd .4D 84
  B74: Four O 4E 37
  DY2: Dud 3F 95
  WV1: Wolv 2A 170 (1G 43)
  WV14: Bils 4G 45
Clarence St. DY3: Up Gor 1A 76
  WV1: Wolv 3A 170 (1G 43)
Clarenden Pl. B17: Harb 6G 115
Clarendon Dr. DY4: Tip 4D 62
Clarendon Pl. B62: Quin 4F 113
  WS3: Pels 3D 20
Clarendon Rd. B16: Edg 2A 116
  B67: Smeth 5D 98
  B75: R'ley 6A 38
  WS4: S'fld 5G 21
Clarendon St. WS3: Blox 6H 19
  WV3: Wolv 1E 43
Clarendon Way B91: Sol 4G 151
Clare Rd. WS3: Wals 3E 33
  WV10: Bush 2A 28
Clarewell Av. B91: Sol 1F 165
Clarke Ho. WS3: Blox 6H 19

Clarkes Gro. DY4: Tip 1C 78
Clarke's La. B71: W Brom 6A 64
  WV13: W'hall 6C 30
Clark Rd. WV3: Wolv 1D 42
Clarksland Cl. B37: Mars G 3C 122
Clarks La. B90: Dic H 3G 163
Clarkson Pl. DY5: Quar B 5A 110
Clarkson Rd. WS10: W'bry 1G 63
Clark St. B16: Birm 1B 116
  DY8: Stourb 6C 108
Clarry Dr. B74: Four O 3F 53
Clary Gro. WS5: Wals 2E 65
CLATTERBATCH 6F 109
Claughton Rd. DY2: Dud 6F 77
Claughton Rd. Nth. DY2: Dud 6F 77
Clausen Cl. B43: Gt Barr 1G 67
Clavedon Cl. B31: N'fld 6C 130
Claverdon Cl. B91: Sol 4C 150
  WS8: Bwnhls 5C 10
Claverdon Dr. B43: Gt Barr 5H 65
  B74: Lit As 5B 36
Claverdon Gdns. B27: A Grn 6H 119
Claverdon Ho. B13: Mose 6A 134
Claverley Cl. DY1: Dud 6D 76
Claverley Dr. WV4: Penn 6B 42
Claybrook St. B5: Birm 6E 5 (2G 117)
Claycroft Pl. DY9: Lye 6A 110
Claycroft Ter. DY1: Dud 1D 76
Claydon Gro. B14: K Hth 4A 148
Claydon Rd. DY6: W Hth 6A 74
Clay Dr. B32: Quin 6G 113
CLAYHANGER 1A 22
Clayhanger La. WS8: Bwnhls, Clay . . .6H 9
Clayhanger Rd. WS8: Bwnhls 1B 22
Clay La. B26: Yard 6C 120
  B69: O'bry 5G 97
Clay Pit La. B90: Dic H 4G 163
    (not continuous)
Claypit La. B70: W Brom 4G 79
Clayton Cl. WV2: Wolv 4G 43
Clayton Dr. B36: Cas B 1G 105
Clayton Gdns. B45: Lick 6G 157
Clayton Ho. B16: Edg 2B 116
Clayton Rd. B8: Salt 4D 102
  WV14: Cose 6D 60
Clayton Wlk. B35: Cas V 5E 87
Clear Vw. DY6: K'wfrd 3H 91
Clearwell Gdns. DY1: Dud 4A 76
Clee Hill Dr. WV3: Wolv 2G 41
Clee Hill Rd. DY3: Lwr G 3G 75
Clee Rd. B31: Longb 1E 159
  B68: O'bry 5A 98
  DY2: Dud .2C 94
  DY8: Amb 5E 109
Cleeve Dr. B74: Four O 3F 37
Cleeve Ho. B24: Erd 5G 85
Cleeve Rd. B14: Yard W 3C 148
  WS3: Blox 4F 19
Cleeve Way WS3: Blox 5F 19
Clee Vw. Mdw. DY3: Sed 3H 59
Clee Vw. Rd. WV5: Wom 2E 73
Clematis Dr. WV9: Pend 4D 14
Clem Attlee Ct. WV14: Wolv 3E 45
Clement Pl. WV14: Bils 4F 45
Clement Rd. B62: B'hth 2D 112
  WV14: Bils 4F 45
Clements Cl. B69: O'bry 5F 97
Clements Rd. B25: Yard 3B 120
Clement St. B1: Birm 3A 4 (6D 100)
  WS2: Wals 2B 48
Clemson St. WV13: W'hall 1A 46
Clent Cl. DY1: Dud 6D 76
Clent Hill Dr. B65: Row R 4A 96
Clent Ho. B63: Hale 3A 128
Clent Rd. B21: Hand 6H 81
  B45: Rub .1E 157
  B68: O'bry 3A 114
  DY8: Amb 5E 109
Clent Vw. B66: Smeth 6F 99
Clent Vw. Rd. B32: Bart G 4G 129
  B63: Crad 1E 127
  DY8: Stourb 2A 124
    (not continuous)

Clent Vs. B12: Bal H 1B 134
Clent Way B32: Bart G 5G 129
Cleobury La. B90: Tid G 4F 163
  B94: Earls 4F 163
Cleton St. DY4: Tip 4B 78
Cleton St. Bus. Pk.
  DY4: Tip 4B 78
Clevedon Av. B36: Cas B 1A 106
Clevedon Rd. B12: Bal H 5G 117
Cleveland Cl. WV11: Wed 6H 17
  WV13: W'hall 2F 45
Cleveland Ct. B13: Mose 3B 134
Cleveland Rd. WV2: Wolv . .5D 170 (2H 43)
Cleveland St. DY1: Dud 6D 76
  DY8: Stourb 1C 124
  WV1: Wolv 4B 170 (2G 43)
Cleveland Twr. B1: Birm 6D 4
Cleves Cres. WS6: C Hay 4D 6
Cleves Dr. B45: Rub 2E 157
Cleves Rd. B45: Rub 1E 157
Clewley Dr. WV9: Pend 4E 15
Clewley Gro. B32: Quin 6H 113
Clews Cl. WS1: Wals 4C 48
Clewshaw La. B38: Head H 5D 160
Cley Cl. B5: Edg 5F 117
Cliff, The DY8: Stourb 5E 109
Cliff Dr. DY4: Tip 5D 62
Cliffe Dr. B33: Kitts G 6G 105
Clifford Cl. DY4: Tip 6C 62
Clifford Rd. B67: Smeth 2D 114
  B70: W Brom 5G 79
  B93: Ben H 5B 166
Clifford St. B19: Loz 2F 101
  DY1: Dud .1D 94
  WV6: Wolv 6E 27
Clifford Wlk. B19: Loz 2F 101
Cliff Rock Rd. B45: Redn 6F 157
Clift Cl. WV12: W'hall 3C 30
Clifton Av. WS8: Bwnhls 6H 9
  WS9: A'rdge 1E 35
Clifton Cl. D6: Acton 2H 101
  B69: O'bry 5G 97
Clifton Cres. B91: Sol 6C 150
Clifton Dr. B73: S Cold 5H 53
Clifton Gdns. WV8: Bilb 4A 14
Clifton Grn. B28: Hall G 2G 149
Clifton Ho. B12: Bal H 6A 118
Clifton La. B71: W Brom 5C 64
Clifton Rd. B6: Aston 2H 101
  B12: Bal H 6H 117
  B36: Cas B 1A 106
  B62: B'hth 3D 112
  B67: Smeth 5D 98
  B73: S Cold 1G 69
  WV6: Tett .4B 26
Clifton Rd. Ind. Est. B12: Bal H 6H 117
                                        (off Clifton Rd.)
Clifton St. B64: Old H 2H 111
  DY8: Stourb 1C 124
  WV3: Wolv 1F 43
  WV14: Cose 4B 60
Clifton Ter. B23: Erd 3F 85
Clinic Dr. DY9: Lye 6A 110
Clinton Gro. B90: Shir 6C 150
Clinton Rd. B46: Col 3H 107
  B90: Shir .1B 164
  WV14: Bils 4A 46
Clinton St. B18: Win G 4A 100
Clipper Vw. B16: Edg 2A 116
Clipston Rd. B8: Salt 5F 103
Clissold Cl. B12: Birm 4G 117
Clissold Pas. B18: Hock 5C 100
Clissold St. B18: Hock 5C 100
Clive Cl. B75: R'ley 1B 54
Cliveden Av. B42: P Barr 3E 83
  WS9: A'rdge 6D 22
Cliveden Coppice B74: Four O 2F 53
Clivedon Way B62: Hale 4A 112
Cleveland St. B19: Birm 1E 5 (5G 101)
Clive Pl. B19: Birm 1D 4 (5H 101)
Clive Rd. B32: Quin 4B 114
  CV7: Bal C 6H 169
Clive St. B71: W Brom 2A 80
Clockfields Dr. DY5: Brie H 2E 109

Clock La. B92: Bick 3F 139
Clockmill Av. WS3: Pels 4C 20
Clockmill Pl. WS3: Pels 4D 20
Clockmill Rd. WS3: Pels 4C 20
Clodeshall Rd. B8: Salt 5E 103
Cloister Dr. B62: Hale 2D 128
Cloisters, The WS4: Wals 6D 32
Clonmel Rd. B30: Stir 1C 146
Clopton Cres. B37: F'bri 5D 106
Clopton Rd. B33: Sheld 3G 121
Close, The B17: Harb 4D 114
  B29: S Oak 5H 131
  B47: H'wd 4A 162
  B62: Hunn 6A 128
  B63: Crad 5F 111
  B92: Olton 5D 136
  DY3: Lwr G 3G 75
  DY3: Swind 5E 73
  WS10: W'bry 2E 63
Close La. B32: Bart G 3F 129
Clothier Gdns. WV13: W'hall 6A 30
Clothier St. WV13: W'hall 6A 30
Cloudbridge Dr. B92: Sol 6B 138
Cloudsley Gro. B92: Olton 2D 136
Clover Av. B37: Chel W 1F 123
Clover Ct. B38: K Nor 5H 145
Cloverdale WV6: Pert 5D 24
Clover Dr. B32: Bart G 3A 130
Clover Hill WS5: Wals 3A 50
Clover La. DY6: W Hth 2G 91
Clover Lea Sq. B8: W End 3G 103
Clover Ley WV10: Wolv 6B 28
Clover Piece DY4: Tip 1C 78
Clover Ridge WS6: C Hay 2C 6
Clover Rd. B29: W Cas 6E 131
Club La. WV10: Cov H 1G 15
Club Row DY3: Up Gor 2A 76
Club Vw. B38: K Nor 5H 145
Clunbury Cft. B34: S End 4F 105
Clunbury Rd. B31: Longb 1E 159
Clun Cl. B69: Tiv 6H 77
Clun Rd. B31: N'fld 1D 144
Clyde Av. B62: B'hth 3E 113
Clyde Ct. B73: S Cold 6H 53
Clyde M. DY5: P'ntt 3F 93
Clyde Rd. B93: Dorr 6H 167
Clydesdale B26: Sheld 6E 121
Clydesdale Rd. B32: Quin 5H 113
  DY2: Neth .6E 95
  WS8: Clay 1A 22
Clydesdale Twr. B1: Birm 6D 4
Clyde St. B12: Birm 2A 118
  B64: Old H 2G 111
Clyde Twr. B19: Loz 1F 101
C M T Ind. Est. B69: O'bry 1G 97
COALBOURNBROOK 3D 108
Coalbourn La. DY8: Amb 4D 108
Coalbourn Way DY5: Brie H 6E 93
Coalheath La. WS4: S'fld 1G 33
Coalmeadow Cl. WS3: Blox 4F 19
COAL POOL 3D 32
Coalpool La. WS3: Wals 3D 32
Coalpool Pl. WS3: Wals 3D 32
Coalport Rd. WV1: Wolv 2C 44
Coalway Av. B26: Sheld 1G 137
  WV3: Penn 5E 43
Coalway Gdns. WV3: Wolv 5B 42
Coalway Rd. WS3: Blox 1G 31
  WV3: Penn 5B 42
Coatsgate Wlk. WV8: Pend 6D 14
Cobbles, The B72: W Grn 6A 70
Cobble Wlk. B18: Hock 4C 100
Cobbs Wlk. B65: Row R 4H 95
Cobden Cl. DY4: Tip 5H 61
  WS10: Darl 5F 47
Cobden Gdns. B12: Bal H 5G 117
Cobden St. DY8: Woll 5B 108
  WS1: Wals 4B 48
  WS10: Darl 5F 47
Cobham Bus. Cen. B9: Bord G 1D 118
Cobham Cl. B35: Cas V 4D 86
Cobham Ct. M. DY9: Hag 6H 125
Cobham Rd. B9: Bord G 1D 118
  B63: Hale .1B 128

Cobham Rd. DY8: Stourb 3E 125
  WS10: W'bry 3C 64
Cob La. B30: B'vle 6G 131
Cobs Fld. B30: B'vlle 1G 145
Coburg Cft. DY4: Tip 1C 78
Coburn Dr. B75: R'ley 1B 54
Cochrane Cl. DY4: Tip 1C 78
  DY9: Pedm 5G 125
Cochrane Rd. DY2: Dud 3A 94
COCK GREEN 5B 96
Cock Hill La. B45: Redn, Rub 6F 143
Cockley Wharf Ind. Est. DY5: Brie H . .5F 93
Cockshed La. B62: B'hth 3C 112
Cockshut Hill B26: Yard 3E 121
Cockshutt La. WV2: Wolv 4H 43
Cocksmead Cft. B14: K Hth 2F 147
Cocksmoor Ho. B14: K Hth 6F 133
Cocks Moors Woods Leisure Cen. . . .3H 147
Cockthorpe Cl. B17: Harb 4D 114
Cocton Cl. WV6: Pert 4E 25
CODSALL 3F 13
Codsall Coppice Nature Reserve . . .3G 111
Codsall Gdns. WV8: Cod 3E 13
Codsall Ho. WV8: Cod 3E 13
Codsall Leisure Cen. 3G 13
Codsall Rd. B64: Crad H 3G 111
  WV6: Tett .6A 14
  WV8: Tett .6A 14
Codsall Station (Rail) 4E 13
CODSALL WOOD 1B 12
Codsall Wood Rd. WV8: Cod, Cod W . .1B 12
Cofield Rd. B73: Bold 4F 69
Cofton Chu. La. B45: Coft H 6A 158
Cofton Ct. B45: Redn 2B 158
COFTON COMMON 1F 159
Cofton Ct. B45: Redn 2B 158
Cofton Gro. B31: Longb 3C 158
COFTON HACKETT 6A 158
Cofton Lake Rd. B45: Coft H 6A 158
Cofton Rd. B31: Longb 2E 159
Cokeland Pl. B64: Crad H 3F 111
Colaton Cl. WV10: Wolv 5A 28
Colbourne Ct. B33: Stech 6B 104
Colbourne Rd. DY4: Tip 3A 78
Coldbath Rd. B13: Mosc 5B 134
Coldridge Cl. WV8: Pend 6D 14
Coldstream Dr. DY8: Word 6C 92
Coldstream Rd. B76: Walm 5C 70
Coldstream Way B6: Witt 5G 83
                                        (not continuous)
Cole Bank Rd. B13: Mose 5D 134
  B28: Hall G 5E 135
Colebourne Rd. B13: Mose 6C 134
Colebridge Cres. B46: Col 1H 107
Colebrook Cft. B90: Shir 5F 149
Colebrook Rd. B11: S'hll 6D 118
  B90: Shir .5E 149
COLE END 1H 107
Coleford Cl. DY8: Word 1A 108
Coleford Dr. B37: F'bri 1C 122
Cole Grn. B90: Shir 6E 149
COLEHALL .4E 105
Cole Hall La. B33: Stech 5E 105
  B34: S End, Stech 3E 105
                                        (not continuous)
Cole Holloway B31: N'fld 5C 130
Colehurst Cft. B90: M'path 3D 164
Coleman Rd. WS10: W'bry 6G 47
Coleman St. WV6: Wolv 5D 26
Colemeadow Rd. B13: Mose 2B 148
  B46: Col 2H 107
Colenso Rd. B16: Edg 5H 99
Coleraine Rd. B42: Gt Barr 1C 82
Coleridge Cl. WS3: Pels 2E 21
  WV12: W'hall 2E 31
Coleridge Dr. WV6: Pert 5E 25
Coleridge Pas. B4: Birm 2F 5 (6G 101)
Coleridge Ri. DY3: Lwr G 3E 75
Coleridge Rd. B43: Gt Barr 6A 66
Colesbourne Av. B14: K Hth 5E 147
Colesbourne Rd. B92: Olton 2E 137
Coles Cres. B71: W Brom 6H 63
Colesden Wlk. WV4: Penn 5A 42
Coleshaven B46: Col 3H 107
COLESHILL .2H 107

COLESHILL HEATH 2E 123
Coleshill Heath Rd.
  B37: Mars G, Chel W 4E 123
  B46: Col 4E 123
Coleshill Ind. Est. B46: Col 5G 89
  (not continuous)
Coleshill Leisure Cen. 3H 107
Coleshill Rd. B36: Hodg H 3B 104
  B37: Mars G 4C 122
  B46: Wat O 4D 88
  B75: S Cold 6A 54
  B76: Curd 1D 88
  (not continuous)
Coleshill Station (Rail) 5H 89
Coleshill St. B4: Birm 2G 5 (6H 101)
  B72: S Cold 6A 54
Coleshill Trad. Est. B46: Col 6H 89
Coleside Av. B13: Mose 6D 134
Coles La. B71: W Brom 6G 63
  B72: S Cold 1A 70
Cole St. DY2: Neth 6G 95
Cole Valley Rd. B28: Hall G 1D 148
Coleview Cres. B33: Kitts G 6A 106
Coleville Rd. B76: Walm 1F 87
Coley's La. B31: N'fld 5E 145
Colgreave Av. B11: Mose 3D 134
Colindale Rd. B44: K'sdng 2A 68
Colinwood Cl. WS6: Gt Wyr 4F 7
Collector Rd. B36: Cas B 6F 87
  B37: F'bri 6C 88
Colleen Av. B30: K Nor 4D 146
College Cl. WS10: W'bry 3G 63
College Ct. WV6: Tett 5B 26
College Dr. B20: Hand 5B 82
College Farm Dr. B23: Erd 5D 68
College Ga. B8: Salt 5E 103
College Gro. B20: Hand 2D 100
College High Community Leisure Cen., The
  . . . . .1B 84
College Hill B73: S Cold 1H 69
College Rd. B8: Salt 6E 103
  B13: Mose 3C 134
  B20: Hand 5A 82
  B32: Quin 5G 113
  B44: P Barr, K'sdng 2G 83
  B73: New O 2G 83
  DY8: Stourb 1E 125
  WV6: Tett 5B 26
College St. B18: Hock 5C 100
College Vw. WV6: Tett 6B 26
College Wlk. B29: S Oak 5H 131
Collets Brook B75: Bass P 1F 55
Collett Cl. DY8: Amb 5E 109
Collett Rd. WV6: Pert 4E 25
Colletts Gro. B37: K'hrst 4B 106
Colley Av. WV10: Bush 1B 28
Colley Ga. B63: Crad 5E 111
Colley La. B63: Crad 4E 111
Colley Orchard B63: Crad 5E 111
Colley St. B70: W Brom 3B 80
Collier Cl. WS6: C Hay 3D 6
  WS8: Bwnhls 6G 9
Collier's Cl. WV12: W'hall 3B 30
Colliers Fold DY5: P'ntt 4F 93
Colliery Dr. WS3: Blox 4F 19
Colliery Rd. B71: W Brom 6E 81
  WV1: Wolv 1B 44
Collindale Ct. DY6: K'wfrd 6B 74
Collingbourne Av. B36: Hodg H 2B 104
Collingdon Av. B26: Sheld 5G 121
Collings Ho. B16: Edg 2C 116
Colling Wlk. B37: K'hrst 3C 106
Collingwood Cen., The B43: Gt Barr . . .2F 67
Collingwood Dr. B43: Gt Barr 1F 67
Collingwood Rd. B30: K Nor 4F 147
  WV10: Bush 5A 16
Collins Cl. B32: Quin 6G 113
Collins Rd. WS8: Bwnhls 2C 22
  WS10: W'bry 2A 64
Collins St. B70: W Brom 4E 79
  WS1: Wals 4C 48
Collis St. DY8: Amb 3D 108
Collister Cl. B90: Shir 3H 149
Colly Cft. B37: K'hrst 4B 106

Collycroft Pl. B27: A Grn 6H 119
Colman Av. WV11: Wed 3H 29
Colman Cres. B68: O'bry 1A 114
Colman Hill B63: Crad 6F 111
Colman Hill Av. B63: Crad 5F 111
Colmers Farm Leisure Cen. 1H 157
Colmers Wlk. B31: Longb 6B 144
Colmore Av. B14: K Hth 6F 133
Colmore Cir. Queensway
  B4: Birm 3E 5 (6G 101)
Colmore Cres. B13: Mose 4B 134
Colmore Dr. B75: S Cold 6E 55
Colmore Flats B19: Birm 1D 4 (5F 101)
Colmore Ga. B3: Birm 3E 5
Colmore Rd. B14: K Hth 6F 133
Colmore Row B3: Birm 4C 4 (1F 117)
Colmore Sq. B4: Birm 2E 5 (6G 101)
Coln Cl. B31: N'fld 1D 144
Colonial Ind. Pk. B64: Crad H 4F 111
Colonial Rd. B9: Bord G 6F 103
Colshaw Rd. DY8: Stourb 1C 124
Colston Rd. B24: Erd 5H 85
Colsyll Gdns. DY1: Dud 1D 94
Colt Cl. B74: S'tly 4G 51
Coltham Rd. WV12: W'hall 3C 30
Coltishall Cl. B35: Cas V 5D 86
COLTON HILLS 1E 59
Colton Hills Sports Cen. 1F 59
Coltsfoot Cl. WV11: Wed 4G 29
Coltsfoot Vw. WS6: C Hay 3E 7
Columbia Cl. B5: Edg 5F 117
Columbine Cl. WS5: Wals 2E 65
Columbus Av. DY5: Brie H 6B 94
Colville Cl. DY4: Tip 5D 62
Colville Rd. B12: Bal H 6B 118
Colville Wlk. B12: Bal H 6B 118
Colwall Rd. DY3: Lwr G 3H 75
Colwall Wlk. B27: A Grn 1B 136
Colworth Rd. B31: N'fld 3C 144
Colyns Gro. B33: Stech 4D 104
Comber Cft. B13: Mose 5D 134
Comber Dr. DY5: P'ntt 3F 93
Comberford Ct. WS10: W'bry 3G 63
Comberford Dr. WS10: W'bry 6B 48
Comberton Rd. B26: Sheld 4F 121
Combine Cl. B75: R'ley 5B 38
Combrook Grn. B34: S End 3H 105
Comet Rd. B26: Birm A 1E 139
Commercial Rd. WS2: Wals 2G 31
  WV1: Wolv 2A 44
Commercial St. B1: Birm 6B 4 (2E 117)
Commissary Rd. B26: Birm A 2C 138
Commonfield Cft. B8: Salt 4D 102
Common La. B8: Salt 3F 103
  B26: Sheld 6E 121
COMMON SIDE 3E 9
Commonside DY5: P'ntt 3G 93
  WS3: Pels 5E 21
  WS8: Bwnhls 1C 22
Communication Row B15: Birm 2E 117
Community Leisure Cen. 3E 79
COMPTON 1A 42
Compton Cl. B91: Sol 3B 150
Compton Ct. B74: Four O 6F 37
  DY2: Neth 3E 95
  WV3: Wolv 1D 42
Compton Cft. B37: Chel W 2F 123
Compton Dr. B74: S'tly 4G 51
  DY2: Dud 1H 95
  DY6: K'wfrd 4B 92
Compton Grange B64: Crad H 3E 111
Compton Gro. B63: Crad 1E 127
  DY6: K'wfrd 4B 92
Compton Hill Dr. WV3: Wolv 1B 42
Compton Ho. B33: Yard 2F 121
Compton Pk. WV3: Wolv 1C 42
Compton Pk. Recreation Cen. 6C 26
Compton Rd. B24: Erd 6E 85
  B62: Quin 6F 113
  B64: Crad H 2E 111
  DY9: Pedm 4H 125
  WV3: Wolv 1C 42
Compton Rd. W. WV3: Wolv 1A 42

Comsey Rd. B43: Gt Barr 2D 66
Comwall Cl. WS3: Blox 3A 32
  (not continuous)
Conchar Cl. B72: W Grn 3A 70
Conchar Rd. B72: W Grn 3A 70
Concorde Dr. B35: Cas V 5D 86
Concorde Rd. B26: Birm A 1E 139
Condover Cl. WS2: Wals 6D 30
Condover Rd. B31: Longb 1F 159
Conduit Rd. WS11: Nort C 1E 9
Coneybury Wlk. B76: Min 2H 87
Coneyford Rd. B34: S End 3G 105
  (not continuous)
Coneygree Community Cen. 3H 77
Coneygree Ind. Est. DY4: Tip 4H 77
Coney Grn. DY8: Stourb 6F 109
Coney Grn. Dr. B31: Longb 1D 158
Coney Grn. Ho. B31: Longb 1D 158
Coneygree Rd. DY4: Tip 5H 77
Congreve Pas. B3: Birm 4C 4 (1F 117)
Conifer Cl. DY5: Brie H 3G 109
Conifer Ct. B13: Mose 3G 133
Conifer Dr. B21: Hand 2A 100
  B31: N'fld 4F 145
Conifer Paddock B62: B'hth 3E 113
Conifer Rd. B74: S'tly 3G 51
Conington Gro. B17: Harb 6E 115
Coniston Av. B92: Olton 1D 136
Coniston Cl. B28: Hall G 6F 135
Coniston Cres. B43: Gt Barr 6B 66
Coniston Dr. DY6: K'wfrd 2H 91
Coniston Ho. B17: Harb 6H 115
  B69: O'bry 4D 96
Coniston Rd. B23: Erd 2D 84
  B74: S'tly 6H 35
  WV6: Tett 1B 26
Conker La. B93: Dorr 5A 166
Connaught Av. WS10: W'bry 2A 64
Connaught Cl. WS5: Wals 5E 49
Connaught Dr. WV5: Wom 4G 57
Connaught Gdns. B5: Edg 5G 117
Connaught Ho. WV1: Wolv 1E 43
Connaught Rd. WV1: Wolv 1E 43
  WV14: Bils 4H 45
Connops Way DY9: Lye 6A 110
Connor Rd. B71: W Brom 5C 64
Conolly Dr. B45: Redn 6H 143
Conrad Cl. B11: S'brk 4A 118
Consort Cres. DY5: P'ntt 3G 93
Consort Dr. WS10: Darl 3D 46
Consort Rd. B30: K Nor 4C 146
Constable Cl. B43: Gt Barr 2F 67
Constables, The B68: O'bry 1H 113
Constance Av. B70: W Brom 6B 80
Constance Rd. B5: Edg 6F 117
Constantine La. B46: Col 6H 89
Constantine Way WV14: Bils 3A 62
Constitution Hill B19: Birm 1C 4 (5F 101)
  DY2: Dud 1E 95
Constitution Hill E. DY2: Dud 1F 95
Containerbase B44: P Barr 2G 83
Convent Cl. WV2: Wolv 5C 170 (2H 43)
Conway Av. B32: Quin 5H 113
  B68: O'bry 1H 113
  B71: W Brom 4H 63
Conway Cl. B90: Shir 6B 150
  DY1: Dud 1E 77
  DY6: K'wfrd 5D 92
Conway Cres. WV12: W'hall 2C 30
Conway Dr. B65: Row R 1B 112
Conway Gro. B43: Gt Barr 6H 65
Conway Ho. WS3: Blox 3B 32
Conway Rd. B11: S'brk 5C 118
  B37: F'bri 6D 106
  B90: Shir 6B 150
  WV6: Pert 6F 25
Conwy Cl. WS2: Wals 5G 31
Conybere St. B12: Birm 4G 117
Conyworth Cl. B27: A Grn 1B 136
Cook Av. DY2: Dud 2F 95
Cook Cl. B93: Know 3E 167
  WV6: Pert 5E 25
Cookes Cft. B31: N'fld 5F 145
Cookesley Cl. B43: Gt Barr 1F 67

Cookley Cl. B63: Hale 3H 127
Cookley Way B69: O'bry 4E 97
Cooknell Dr. DY8: Word 1C 108
Cook Rd. WS3: Blox 5B 20
Cooksey La. B44: Gt Barr 1G 67
Cooksey Rd. B10: Small H 3B 118
(not continuous)
Cook's La. B37: K'hrst 6B 106
Cookspiece Wlk. B33: Stech 6D 104
Cook St. B7: Nech 2C 102
WS10: Darl 5F 47
WV2: Wolv 4G 43
Coombe Cft. WV9: Pend 4E 15
Coombe Hill B64: Old H 3B 112
Coombe Pk. B74: Four O 4F 53
Coombe Rd. B20: Hand 6G 83
B90: Shir .5A 150
Coombes La. B31: Longb 3D 158
COOMBESWOOD 3D 112
Coombs Rd. B62: Hale 5B 112
Coombswood Bus. Pk.
B62: B'hth .3B 112
Coombswood Way B62: B'hth 4B 112
Cooper Av. DY5: Brie H 1E 109
Cooper Cl. B70: W Brom 5C 80
COOPER'S BANK 6G 75
Cooper's Bank Rd. DY3: Gorn 6G 75
DY5: P'ntt .6G 75
Cooper's La. B67: Smeth 4D 98
Coopers Rd. B20: Hand 4C 82
Cooper St. B70: W Brom 4B 80
WV2: Wolv 3B 44
Copeley Hill B23: Erd 6C 84
Copes Cres. WV10: Wolv 3C 28
Copeshill Ct. B75: S Cold 1C 70
Cope St. B18: Hock 6C 100
WS3: Blox 3A 32
WS10: Darl 5E 47
Cophall Cl. DY4: Tip 2D 78
Cophams Cl. B92: Sol 3G 137
Coplow Cl. CV7: Bal C 3G 169
Coplow St. B16: Birm 6B 100
Coplow St. B16: Birm 6B 100
Coplow Ter. B16: Birm 6B 100
(off Coplow St.)
Copnor Gro. B26: Yard 5C 120
Coppenhall Gro. B33: Kitts G 6E 105
Copperbeech Cl. B32: Harb 6D 114
Copper Beech Dr. DY6: K'wfrd 6B 74
WV5: Wom 1H 73
Copperbeech Dr. B12: Bal H 6A 118
Copperbeech Gdns. B20: Hand 5B 82
Copperfield Ct. B90: Dic H 4G 163
Coppice, The B20: Hand 5C 82
B31: Longb 5A 144
B42: P Barr 4G 83
DY4: Tip 4C 62
WV12: W'hall 3C 30
Coppice Ash Cft. B19: Loz 1F 101
Coppice Av. DY9: W'cte 2B 126
Coppice Cl. B24: Erd 4F 85
B45: Rub 2F 157
B90: Ches G 5A 164
B91: Sol 6E 137
DY3: Sed .6F 59
DY5: Quar B 2B 110
WS6: C Hay 1D 6
WS7: Hamm 2H 11
WS8: Bwnhls 5G 9
WS9: A'rdge 6B 22
WV6: Tett .3H 25
WV12: W'hall 3C 30
Coppice Oak B13: Mose 2A 134
Coppice Ri. DY5: Quar B 1C 110

Coppice Rd. B13: Mose 2A 134
B64: Crad H 4G 111
B92: Sol 6A 138
WS9: Wals W 3B 22
WV3: Wolv 3B 42
WV14: Cose 5C 60
Coppice Side WS8: Bwnhls 5H 9
Coppice Side Ind. Est. WS8: Bwnhls . .6G 9
Coppice St. B70: W Brom 3G 79
DY4: Tip 3F 77
(Canal St.)
DY4: Tip 1G 77
(Furnace Pde.)
Coppice Vw. Rd. B73: S'tly 1A 68
Coppice Wlk. B90: Ches G 5A 164
Coppice Way B37: Chel W 1D 122
(off Chelmsley Wood Shop. Cen.)
Copplestone Cl. B34: S End 3F 105
Coppy Hall Gro. WS9: A'rdge 6D 22
Coppy Nook La. WS7: Hamm 1D 10
Copse, The B13: Mose 3B 134
B74: Four O 2F 53
Copse Cl. B31: N'fld 5E 145
Copse Cres. WS3: Pels 3E 21
Copse Rd. DY2: Neth 6F 95
Copson Cl. B70: W Brom 4G 79
Copstone Dr. B93: Dorr 6B 166
Copston Gro. B29: W Cas 5F 131
Copthall Rd. B21: Hand 5G 81
COPT HEATH 6C 152
Copt Heath Cft. B93: Know 1D 166
Copt Heath Dr. B93: Know 2C 166
Copt Heath Golf Course 1C 166
Copt Heath Wharf B91: Sol 5D 152
Copthorne Av. WS7: Chase 1B 10
Copthorne Rd. B44: Gt Barr 2G 67
WV3: Wolv 4E 43
Coralin Cl. B37: Chel W 1D 122
Corbett Cres. DY8: Amb 4E 109
Corbett Rd. B47: H'wd 2A 162
DY5: Brie H 2H 109
Corbetts Cl. B92: H Ard 6R 140
Corbett St. B66: Smeth 5F 99
Corbridge Av. B44: Gt Barr 4H 67
Corbridge Rd. B73: S Cold 3F 69
Corbyn Rd. B9: Bord G 6H 103
DY1: Dud .1B 94
Corbyn's Cl. DY5: P'ntt 2F 93
Corbyn's Hall La. DY5: P'ntt 2F 93
Corbyn's Hall Rd. DY5: P'ntt 2F 93
Cordley St. B70: W Brom 3H 79
Corfe Cl. B32: Harb 6D 114
WV6: Pert .6F 25
Corfe Dr. B69: Tiv 1A 96
Corfe Rd. WV14: Cose 5C 60
Corfton Dr. WV6: Tett 5A 26
Coriander Cl. B45: Fran 6H 143
Corinne Cl. B45: Redn 3G 157
Corinne Cft. B37: K'hrst 5C 106
Corisande Rd. B29: S Oak 3G 131
Corley Av. B31: N'fld 4F 145
Corley Cl. B90: Shir 6E 149
Cornbow Cen. B63: Hale 2B 128
Cornbrook Rd. B29: W Cas 6D 130
Cornbury Gro. B91: Shir 3B 150
Corncrake Cl. B72: S Cold 3B 70
Corncrake Dr. B36: Cas B 1C 106
Corncrake Rd. DY3: Lwr G 4A 76
Cornel Cl. B37: Chel W 3E 123
Cornerstone B13: Mose 2H 133
Cornerstone Country Club
B31: N'fld .2F 145
Cornerway B38: K Nor 2B 160
CORNETS END 1H 155
Cornets End La. CV7: Mer 5E 141
Cornfield WV8: Pend 6C 14
Cornfield Cl. DY6: W Hth 1G 91
Cornfield Cft. B37: Chel W 6F 107
B76: Walm 2D 70
Cornfield Pl. B65: Row R 5H 95
(off Allsops Cl.)
Cornfield Rd. B31: N'fld 3F 145
B65: Row R 5H 95
B76: Walm 4D 70

Cornflower Cl. WV10: F'stne 1C 16
Cornflower Cres. DY2: Dud 1H 95
Cornflower Rd. WS8: Clay 1H 21
Corngreaves, The B34: S End 3G 105
Corngreaves Rd. B64: Crad H 2F 111
Corngreaves Trad. Est. B64: Crad H . .4F 111
Corngreaves Wlk. B64: Crad H 4G 111
Corn Hill WS5: Wals 3A 50
WV10: Wolv 3D 170 (1H 43)
Cornhill Gro. B30: Stir 1E 147
Corn Mill Cl. B32: Bart G 4C 130
B76: Walm 4D 70
WS1: Wals 4B 48
Cornmill Gro. WV6: Pert 6D 24
Cornovian Cl. WV6: Pert 4E 25
Corns Gro. WV5: Wom 2F 73
Corns Ho. WS10: Darl 5E 47
(off Birmingham St.)
Corns St. WS10: Darl 6E 47
Cornwall Av. B68: O'bry 3H 113
Cornwall Cl. DY6: K'wfrd 1B 92
WS9: A'rdge 6C 22
WS10: W'bry 2B 64
Cornwall Ga. WV12: W'hall 4B 30
Cornwall Ho. B90: Bly P 6D 164
Cornwallis Rd. B70: W Brom 6B 79
Cornwall Pl. WS2: Wals 6E 31
Cornwall Rd. B20: Hand 5B 82
B45: Fran .6E 143
B66: Smeth 2F 99
DY8: Woll .3B 108
WS5: Wals 4F 49
WV6: Tett .5A 26
Cornwall Rd. Ind. Est. B66: Smeth . . .2F 99
Cornwall St. B3: Birm 3C 4 (6F 101)
Cornwall Twr. B18: Hock 4D 100
Cornwell Cl. DY4: Tip 2A 78
Cornwood La. B90: Dic H 4G 163
Cornyx La. B91: Sol 1H 151
Coronation Av. WV13: W'hall 1D 46
Coronation Rd. B8: Salt 3F 103
B29: S Oak 3B 132
B43: Gt Barr 1A 66
DY4: Tip 5A 62
WS4: S'fld .5F 21
WS9: Wals W 4C 22
WS10: W'bry 2A 64
WV10: Wolv 4C 28
WV14: Bils 6E 45
Corporation Rd. DY2: Dud 5G 77
Corporation Sq. B4: Birm . .3F 5 (6G 101)
Corporation St. B2: Birm 4E 5 (1G 117)
(not continuous)
B4: Birm 1F 5 (5H 101)
WS1: Wals 3C 48
WS10: W'bry 3G 63
WV1: Wolv 3A 170 (1G 43)
Corporation St. W. WS1: Wals 3B 48
Corrie Cft. B26: Sheld 4F 121
B32: Bart G 5H 129
Currin Gro. DY6: W Hth 1A 92
Corron Hill B63: Hale 1B 128
(off Cobham Rd.)
Corsers Ct. WV6: Pert 5E 25
Corser St. DY1: Dud 5B 76
DY8: Stourb 2E 125
WV1: Wolv 2B 44
Corsican Cl. WV12: W'hall 2E 31
Corvedale Rd. B29: W Cas 1E 145
Corve Gdns. WV6: Tett 4C 26
Corve Vw. DY3: Sed 4G 59
Corville Gdns. B26: Sheld 1G 137
Corville Rd. B62: Quin 5F 113
Corwen Cft. B31: N'fld 1C 144
Cory Cft. DY4: Tip 2A 78
COSELEY 4F 61
Coseley Baths 4F 61
Coseley Hall WV14: Cose 5E 61
Coseley Leisure Cen. 4D 60
Coseley Rd. WV14: Bils 6E 45
Coseley Station (Rail) 4E 61
Cosford Cl. WV6: Pert 4E 25
Cosford Cres. B35: Cas V 4E 87
Cosford Dr. DY2: Neth 5G 95

Cosgrove Wlk. WV8: Pend 6D 14
Cossington Rd. B23: Erd 6D 68
Costock Cl. B37: Mars G 3D 122
Cotford Rd. B14: K Hth 5A 148
Cotheridge Cl. B90: M'path 3G 165
Cot La. DY6: K'wfrd 4A 92
Cotleigh Gro. B43: Gt Barr 2G 67
Cotman Cl. B43: Gt Barr 2E 67
Coton Gro. B90: Shir 5E 149
Coton La. B23: Erd 3F 85
Coton Rd. B20: Hand 6F 43
Cotsdale Rd. WV4: Penn 2C 58
Cotsford B91: Sol 4E 151
Cotswold Av. WS6: Gt Wyr 2F 7
Cotswold Cl. B45: Fran 5H 143
   B69: O'bry 4E 97
   WS9: A'rdge 6E 23
Cotswold Ct. WV2: Penn 5F 43
                    (off Goldthorn Hill)
Cotswold Cft. B63: Hale 4E 127
Cotswold Gro. WV12: W'hall 6B 18
Cotswold Rd. DY8: Amb 5F 109
   WV2: E'shll 4B 44
Cottage Cl. WV11: Wed 3E 29
                    (not continuous)
Cottage Gdns. B45: Rub 4F 157
Cottage La. B76: Min 1H 87
   WV10: F'hses 4H 15
Cottage M. WS9: A'rdge 5G 35
Cottage St. DY5: Brie H 6H 93
   DY6: K'wfrd 2B 92
Cottage Vw. WV8: Bilb 3H 13
Cottage Wlk. B70: W Brom 5B 80
COTTERIDGE 3B 146
Cotteridge Rd. B30: K Nor 3C 146
Cotterills Av. B8: W End 5A 104
Cotterills La. B8: W End 5H 103
Cotterills Rd. DY4: Tip 6B 62
Cottesbrook Rd. B27: A Grn 1B 136
Cottesfield Cl. B8: W End 5H 103
Cottesmore Cl. B71: W Brom 5D 64
Cottesmore Ho. B20: Hand 5B 82
Cottle Cl. WS2: Wals 6F 31
Cotton La. B13: Mose 3H 133
Cottrells Cl. B14: Yard W 3C 148
Cottrells M. B46: Wat O 5D 88
Cottrell St. B71: W Brom 3B 80
Cottsmeadow Dr. B8: W End 5A 104
COTWALL END 6G 59
Cotwall End Countryside Cen. 1G 75
Cotwall End Rd. DY3: Lwr G, Sed 3F 75
Cotwall End Valley Local Nature Reserve
   . . . . .3F 75
Cotysmore Rd. B75: S Cold 5B 54
Couchman Rd. B8: Salt 5E 103
Coulter Gro. WV6: Pert 5D 24
Council Cres. WV12: W'hall 5C 30
Counterfield Dr. B65: Row R 4H 95
Countess Dr. WS4: Rus 2H 33
Countess St. WS1: Wals 4B 48
Country Pk. Vw. B76: Walm 4D 70
COUNTY BRIDGE 1D 46
County Cl. B30: Stir 1D 146
   B32: Bart G 2A 130
County La. DY8: I'ley 5B 124
   WV8: Alb 2A 12
County Pk. Av. B62: Hale 2C 128
Court, The B93: Know 4B 168
Courtenay Gdns. B43: Gt Barr 3A 66
Courtenay Rd. B44: Gt Barr 6G 67
Court Farm Rd. B23: Erd 1E 85
Court Farm Way B29: W Cas 6D 130
Courtland Rd. DY6: K'wfrd 1C 92
Courtlands, The WV6: Wolv 5C 26
Courtlands Cl. B5: Edg 5E 117
Court La. B23: Erd 5E 69
Court Oak Gro. B32: Harb 5D 114
Court Oak Rd. B17: Harb 5C 114
   B32: Harb 5C 114
Court Pde. WS9: A'rdge 3D 34
Court Pas. DY1: Dud 6E 77
Court Rd. B11: S'hll 1C 134
   B12: Bal H 5G 117

Court Rd. WV4: E'shll 2C 60
   WV6: Wolv 5D 26
Court St. B64: Old H 2H 111
   DY8: Stourb 6E 109
Court Way WS2: Wals 1C 48
Courtway Av. B14: K Hth 6B 148
Courtway Ho. B29: S Oak 4F 131
Court Yd., The B70: W Brom 4G 79
Courtyard, The B46: Col 5H 89
   B91: Sol 3G 151
Cousins St. WV2: Wolv 4H 43
Coveley Gro. B18: Hock 4C 100
Coven Cl. WS3: Pels 2E 21
Coven Gro. B29: S Oak 3F 131
COVEN HEATH 1H 15
Coven La. WV9: Coven 2D 14
Coven St. WV10: Wolv 5H 27
Coventry Rd. B10: Small H 2A 118
   B25: Yard 4G 119
   B26: Yard, Sheld 5C 120
   B46: Col 6H 107
   B92: Bick 2C 138
Coventry St. B5: Birm 5G 5 (1H 117)
   DY8: Stourb 6E 109
   WV1: Wolv 1C 44
Cover Cft. B76: Walm 4E 71
Coverdale Rd. B92: Olton 1E 137
Covert, The WV8: Pend 6C 14
Covert La. DY8: Stourb 4B 124
Cowles Cft. B25: Yard 2C 120
Cowley Cl. B36: Cas B 6B 88
Cowley Dr. B27: A Grn 1B 136
   DY1: Dud 5B 76
Cowley Gro. B11: Tys 6E 119
Cowley Rd. B11: Tys 6E 119
Cowper Cl. WV12: W'hall 2E 31
Cowslip Cl. B29: W Cas 6E 131
   B38: K Nor 1B 160
Cowslip Wlk. DY5: Brie H 5G 109
Coxcroft Av. DY5: Quar B 3B 110
Coxmoor Cl. WS3: Blox 4F 19
Cox Rd. WV14: Cose 4G 61
Cox's La. B64: Old H 1H 111
Cox St. B3: Birm 1C 4 (5F 101)
   WV10: Wolv 3G 27
Coxwell Gdns. B16: Birm 1B 116
Coyne Cl. DY4: Tip 2F 77
Coyne Rd. B70: W Brom 5H 79
Crabbe St. DY9: Lye 6B 110
Crab La. DY6: K'wfrd 5E 93
   WV12: W'hall 6D 18
Crabmill Cl. B38: K Nor 2A 160
   B93: Know 2E 167
Crabmill La. B38: Head H 2E 161
Crabourne Rd. DY2: Neth 1D 110
Crabtree Cl. B31: N'fld 5G 145
   B71: W Brom 5D 64
   DY9: Hag 6F 125
Crabtree Dr. B37: F'bri 1B 122
Crab Tree Ho. B33: Stech 6C 104
Crabtree Rd. B18: Hock 4C 100
   WS1: Wals 1E 49
Crackley Way DY2: Dud 3C 94
Craddock Rd. B67: Smeth 3C 98
Craddock St. WV6: Wolv 5E 27
CRADLEY 4E 111
Cradley Cft. B21: Hand 4G 81
Cradley Flds. B63: Crad 6E 111
Cradley Forge DY5: Quar B 3C 110
CRADLEY HEATH 2G 111
Cradley Heath Factory Cen.
   B64: Crad H 3E 111
Cradley Heath Station (Rail) 3D 110
Cradley Leisure Cen. 4D 110
Cradley Mill DY5: Quar B 4B 110
Cradley Pk. Rd. DY2: Neth 1E 111
Cradley Rd. B64: Crad H 3E 111
   DY2: Neth 5F 95
Cradock Rd. B8: Salt 4E 103
Craig Cft. B37: Chel W 1F 123
Crail Gro. B43: Gt Barr 1D 66
Cramlington Rd. B42: Gt Barr 5C 66
Cramp Hill WS10: Darl 5D 46
Cranbourne Av. WV4: E'shll 2A 60

Cranbourne Cl. B45: Fran 5G 143
Cranbourne Gro. B44: K'sdng 5A 68
Cranbourne Pl. B71: W Brom 3B 80
Cranbourne Rd. B44: K'sdng 5A 68
   DY8: Stourb 1E 125
Cranbrook Ct. WV13: W'hall 1C 46
                    (off Mill St.)
Cranbrook Gro. WV6: Pert 6F 25
Cranbrook Rd. B21: Hand 6G 81
Cranby St. B8: Salt 4C 102
Craneberry Rd. B37: F'bri 1A 122
Cranebrook Hill B78: Hints 4H 39
Cranebrook La. WS14: Hilt, Lynn 1H 23
Crane Cl. WS1: Wals 6E 33
Crane Dr. WS7: Chase 1C 10
Crane Hollow WV5: Wom 2E 73
Cranehouse Rd.
   B44: K'sdng 3B 68
Cranemoor Cl. B7: Nech 3C 102
Crane Rd. WV14: Bils 2H 61
Cranesbill Rd. B29: W Cas 1E 145
Cranes Pk. Rd. B26: Sheld 6G 121
Crane Ter. WV6: Tett 4C 26
Cranfield Gro. B26: Yard 3D 120
Cranfield Pl. WS5: Wals 1D 64
Cranford Gro. B91: Sol 6F 151
Cranford Rd. WV3: Wolv 3A 42
Cranford St. B66: Smeth 4G 99
Cranford Way B66: Smeth 4G 99
Cranham Dr. DY6: K'wfrd 4C 92
Cranhill Cl. B92: Olton 4F 137
Crankhall La. B71: W Brom 2H 63
   WS10: W'bry 2H 63
Cranleigh Cl. WS9: A'rdge 4D 34
   WV12: W'hall 6C 18
Cranleigh Ho. B23: Erd 1F 85
Cranleigh Pl. B44: P Barr 2G 83
Cranley Dr. WV8: Cod 3F 13
Cranmer Av. WV12: W'hall 2D 30
Cranmer Cl. WS6: C Hay 4D 6
Cranmere Av. WV6: Tett 3G 25
Cranmere Ct. WV6: Tett 3G 25
Cranmer Gro. B74: Four O 3F 37
Cranmoor Cres. B63: Hale 6A 112
Cranmore Av. B21: Hand 2H 99
   B90: Shir 1C 164
Cranmore Blvd. B90: Shir 1B 164
Cranmore Cl. DY4: Tip 5A 62
Cranmore Dr. B90: Shir 1C 164
Cranmore Rd. B36: Cas B 6H 87
   B90: Shir 1B 164
   WV3: Wolv 6D 26
Cransley Gro. B91: Sol 6E 151
Crantock Cl. WV11: Ess 6C 18
Crantock Rd. B42: P Barr 3E 83
Cranwell Grn. WV5: Wom 2F 73
Cranwell Rd. B24: Erd 4B 86
Cranwell Way B35: Cas V 4E 87
Crathorne Av. WV10: Oxl 6G 15
Crauford Ct. DY8: Stourb 2E 125
Crauford St. DY8: Stourb 2E 125
Craven Hgts. B92: H Ard 6A 140
Craven St. WV2: E'shll 5B 44
Crawford Av. B67: Smeth 4D 98
   WS10: Darl 4C 46
   WV4: E'shll 2B 60
Crawford Rd. B76: Walm 5D 70
   WV3: Wolv 1E 43
Crawford St. B8: Salt 5C 102
Crawley Wlk. B64: Crad H 2F 111
Crawshaws Rd. B36: Cas B 6G 87
Crayford Rd. B44: K'sdng 4A 68
Craythorne Av. B20: Hand 2A 82
Crecy Cl. B76: Walm 1C 70
Credenda Rd. B70: W Brom 6G 79
Credon Gro. B15: Edg 1B 132
Creed Way B70: W Brom 3H 79
Cregoe St. B15: Birm 2E 117
Cremore Av. B8: Salt 4E 103
Cremorne Rd. B75: Four O 1H 53
Cremorne Wlk. B75: Four O 1H 53
Crendon Rd. B65: Row R 3A 96
Crescent, The B18: Hock 3D 100
   B37: Mars G 3G 123

Crescent, The B43: Gt Barr 4C 66
    (Handsworth Dr.)
  B43: Gt Barr 2F 67
    (King's Rd.)
  B46: Wat O 4D 88
  B64: Crad H 4A 112
  B65: Row R 1B 112
  B90: Shir 3G 149
  B91: Sol 3F 151
  B92: H Ard 6B 140
  DY1: Dud 3G 77
  DY9: Lye 1G 125
  WS1: Wals 3E 49
  WS6: Gt Wyr 3G 7
  WS10: W'bry 1G 63
  WV6: Tett 6H 25
  WV13: W'hall 2C 46
  WV14: Bils 5F 45
Crescent Arc. B91: Sol 4G 151
    (off Touchwood Shop. Cen.)
Crescent Av. B18: Hock 3D 100
  DY5: Brie H 1G 109
Crescent Ind. Pk. DY2: Dud 2D 94
Crescent Rd. DY2: Neth 4D 94
  WS10: Darl 5D 46
  WV13: W'hall 1C 46
Crescent Studios B18: Hock 3D 100
Crescent Theatre 1D 116
Crescent, The Stop (MM) 5F 45
Crescent Twr. B1: Birm 4A 4
Cressage Av. B31: N'fld 6E 145
Cressett Av. DY5: Brie H 5F 93
Cressett La. DY5: Brie H 5G 93
Cressington Dr. B74: Four O 2G 53
Cresswell Ct. WV9: Pend 4E 15
Cresswell Cres. WS3: Blox 5F 19
Cresswell Gro. B24: Erd 3B 86
Cressy Cl. B14: K Hth 3D 146
Crest, The B31: Longb 2F 159
Crest Vw. B14: K Hth 3B 148
  B74: S'tly 3H 51
Crestwood Dr. B44: Gt Barr 6G 67
Crestwood Glen WV6: Tett 2C 26
Creswell Rd. B28: Hall G 6H 135
Creswick Gro. B45: Redn 2A 158
Crew Dr. DY4: Tip 5A 78
Crew Rd. WS10: W'bry 1G 63
Creynolds Cl. B90: Ches G 6B 164
Creynolds La. B90: Ches G 6B 164
Cricket Cl. WS5: Wals 4F 49
Cricketers Mdw. B64: Crad H 4G 111
Cricket Mdw. DY3: Up Gor 2A 76
  WV10: F'hses 3H 15
Cricket St. B70: W Brom 6F 63
Crick La. B20: Hand 1C 100
Cricklewood Dr. B62: Hale 2D 128
Crimmond Ri. B63: Hale 6G 111
Crimscote Cl. B90: M'path 3D 164
Cripps Rd. WS2: Wals 6E 31
Criterion Works WV13: W'hall 3A 46
Cricketts Av. B21: Hand 2H 99
Crockett's La. B66: Smeth 4A 99
Cricketts Rd. B21: Hand 2G 99
Crockett St. DY1: Dud 5C 76
Crockford Dr. B75: Four O 6H 37
Crockford Rd. B71: W Brom 4A 64
Crockington La. WV5: Seis, Try 3A 56
Crocus Cres. WV9: Pend 4E 15
Croft, The B31: N'fld 4F 145
  DY2: Dud 3B 94
  DY3: Sed 4A 60
  WS5: Wals 3A 50
  WS6: C Hay 3E 7
  WV5: Wom 2D 72
  WV12: W'hall 3D 30
Croft Apartments WV13: W'hall 1A 46
    (off Croft St.)
Croft Cl. B25: Yard 3C 120
Croft Ct. B36: Cas B 1F 105
Croft Cres. WS8: Bwnhls 6H 9
Croft Down Rd. B92: Sol 1H 137
Croftdown Rd. B17: Harb 5D 114
Crofters Cl. DY8: Stourb 1F 125
Crofters Ct. B15: Edg 5A 116

Crofters La. B75: R'ley 6C 38
Crofters Wlk. WV8: Pend 6C 14
Croft Ho. WS1: Wals 2D 48
    (off Paddock La.)
Croft Ind. Est. B37: Chel W 1F 123
  WV13: W'hall 1A 46
Croft La. WV10: Bush 2C 28
Croftleigh Gdns. B91: Sol 5C 150
Crofton Gdns. B36: Hodg H 1D 104
Croft Pde. WS9: A'rdge 3D 34
Croft Rd. B26: Yard 3C 120
Crofts, The B76: Walm 6E 71
Croft St. WS2: Wals 6B 32
  WV13: W'hall 1A 46
    (not continuous)
Croftway, The B20: Hand 1A 82
Croftwood Rd. DY9: W'cte 1H 125
Cromane Sq. B43: Gt Barr 6A 66
Cromdale Dr. B63: Hale 2F 127
Cromer Gdns. WV6: Wolv 4D 26
Crome Rd. B43: Gt Barr 2F 67
Cromer Rd. B12: Bal H 6H 117
Crompton Av. B20: Hand 6E 83
Crompton Cl. WS2: Wals 4G 31
Crompton Ct. WV8: Bilb 3H 13
Crompton Rd. B7: Nech 1C 102
  B20: Hand 6E 83
  B45: Fran 6D 142
  DY4: Tip 3A 78
Cromwell Cl. B65: Row R 4H 95
  WS2: Wals 5E 31
Cromwell Ct. WS6: Gt Wyr 4G 7
Cromwell Dr. DY2: Dud 1H 95
Cromwell La. B31: N'fld 5B 130
Cromwell Rd. WV10: Bush 4A 16
Cromwell St. B7: Nech 4B 102
  B71: W Brom 3A 80
  DY2: Dud 1G 95
Crondal Pl. B15: Edg 4D 116
CRONEHILLS, THE 4A 80
Cronehills Linkway B70: W Brom 3B 80
Cronehills St. B70: W Brom 3B 80
Crooked Ho. La. DY3: Gorn, Himl 5D 74
Crookham Cl. B17: Harb 4D 114
Crookhay La. B71: W Brom 5G 63
Crook La. WS9: A'rdge 4C 50
Croome Cl. B11: S'hll 2B 134
Cropredy Rd. B31: Longb 1E 159
Cropthorne Dr. B47: H'wd 2B 162
Cropthorne Rd. B90: Shir 4A 150
Crosbie Rd. B17: Harb 5F 115
Crosby Cl. B1: Birm 6D 100
  WV6: Wolv 4D 26
Cross, The DY6: K'wfrd 3B 92
Cross Cl. B64: Old H 1H 111
Cross Farm Mnr. B17: Harb 1H 131
    (off Cross Farm Rd.)
Cross Farm Rd. B17: Harb 1G 131
Cross Farms La. B45: Rub 6F 143
Crossfield Rd. B33: Kitts G 5F 105
Crossgate Rd. DY2: Dud 3B 94
Cross Ho. WV2: Wolv 4G 43
    (off Blakenhall Gdns.)
Crossing, The B69: O'bry 1G 97
    (off Broadwell Rd.)
Crossings Ind. Est., The WS3: Blox 1H 31
    (off Fryer's Rd.)
Crosskey Cl. B33: Kitts G 1A 122
Crossland Cres. WV6: Tett 3D 26
Cross La. B43: Gt Barr 4A 66
  DY3: Sed 5H 59
  WS14: Foot 1E 37
Crossley St. DY2: Neth 5F 95
Cross Pl. DY3: Sed 4A 60
Cross Quays Bus. Pk. B69: Tiv 5B 78
    (off Hallbridge Way)
Cross St. B21: Hand 1G 99
  B63: Hale 2A 128
  B65: B'hth 2C 112
  B66: Smeth 3E 99
  B68: O'bry 5G 97
  DY1: Dud 6D 76
  DY6: K'wfrd 3B 92
  DY6: W Hth 1H 91

Cross St. DY8: Stourb 6C
  DY8: Word 6E
  WS3: Pels 6E
  WS6: C Hay 3D
  WS10: Darl 4D 46
  WS10: W'bry 2E 63
  WV1: Wolv 2B 44
  WV13: W'hall 2A 46
  WV14: Bils 3G 61
    (not continuous)
Cross St. Nth. WV1: Wolv 5H 27
Cross St. Sth. WV2: Wolv 4G 43
Cross Wlk. B69: Tiv 1C 96
Cross Walks Rd. DY9: Lye 6A 110
Crossway La. B44: K'sdng 1H 83
Crossways Ct. B44: K'sdng 6B 68
Crossways Grn. B44: K'sdng 6B 68
Crossways Shop. Cen. WV10: Wolv 6C 28
Crosswells Rd. B68: O'bry 4H 97
Crosswell Way WV14: Bils 6G 45
Crowberry Cl. WS8: Clay 1H 21
Crowesbridge M. WV14: Cose 5D 60
Crowhurst Rd. B31: Longb 2C 158
Crowland Av. WV6: Pert 5E 25
Crowle Dr. DY9: Lye 6G 109
Crown Av. B20: Hand 5F 83
Crown Cen., The DY8: Stourb 6E 109
Crown Cl. B65: Row R 5D 96
  DY3: Sed 4H 59
Crown Ct. B74: Four O 6E 37
  WS10: Darl 3C 46
Crown La. B74: Four O 6E 37
  DY8: I'ley 6A 124
  DY8: Stourb 6D 108
Crownmeadow Dr. DY4: Tip 6D 62
Crownoakes Dr. DY8: Word 1C 108
Crown Rd. B9: Bord G 1D 118
  B30: K Nor 3C 146
Crown St. WV1: Wolv 5H 27
Crown Wlk. DY4: Tip 5A 78
Crown Wharf Shop. Pk. WS2: Wals 1B 48
Crows Nest Cl. B76: Walm 2D 70
Crowther Gdns. B63: Crad 4E 111
Crowther Gro. WV6: Wolv 5D 26
Crowther Rd. B23: Erd 2C 84
  WV6: Wolv 5C 26
Crowther St. WV10: Wolv 5A 28
Croxall Way B66: Smeth 4F 99
Croxdene Av. WS3: Blox 6F 19
    (not continuous)
Croxley Gdns. WV13: W'hall 3H 45
Croxstalls Av. WS3: Blox 1G 31
Croxstalls Cl. WS3: Blox 6G 19
Croxstalls Pl. WS3: Blox 1G 31
Croxstalls Rd. WS3: Blox 6G 19
Croxton Gro. B33: Stech 5E 105
Croyde Av. B42: Gt Barr 6C 66
Croydon Ct. B29: W Cas 6G 131
    (off Abdon Av.)
Croydon Rd. B24: Erd 6F 85
  B29: S Oak 2B 132
Croy Dr. B35: Cas V 3F 87
Crucible, The WV14: Cose 3E 61
Crusader Cl. B69: O'bry 4E 97
Crychan Cl. B45: Fran 5H 143
Cryersoak Cl. B90: M'path 2F 165
Crystal Av. DY8: Word 2D 108
Crystal Dr. B66: Smeth 1A 98
Crystal Ho. B66: Smeth 3F 99
Crystal Leisure Cen. 6D 108
Cubley Rd. B28: Hall G 4E 135
Cuckoo Cl. B33: Stech 5D 104
Cuckoo Rd. B6: Aston 1C 102
  B7: Nech 1C 102
Cuin Rd. B66: Smeth 4G 99
Cuin Wlk. B66: Smeth 4G 99
    (off Cuin Rd.)
Culey Gro. B33: Kitts G 1H 121
Culey Wlk. B37: Chel W 1F 123
Culford Dr. B32: Bart G 5A 130
Culham Cl. B27: A Grn 3B 136
Cullwick St. WV1: Wolv 4C 44
Culmington Rd. B31: Longb 1D 158
Culmore Cl. WV12: W'hall 5D 30

...re Rd. B62: B'hth 2E 113
...erhouse Dr. DY5: Brie H 2E 109
...verley Cres. B93: Know 3B 166
...vert Way B66: Smeth 2B 98
...ulwell Ind. Est. WV10: Wolv 6A 28
Culwell St. WV10: Wolv . . .1D 170 (6H 27)
Culwell Trad. Est. WV10: Wolv 5B 28
Cumberford Av. B33: Kitts G 2A 122
Cumberland Av. B5: Birm 4G 117
Cumberland Cl. DY6: K'wfrd 5C 92
Cumberland Ho. WV1: Wolv 5G 27
(off Lomas St.)
Cumberland Rd. B68: O'bry 4H 113
B71: W Brom 1B 80
WV13: W'hall 1D 46
WV14: Bils 4F 45
Cumberland St. B1: Birm . . .5A 4 (1D 116)
Cumberland Wlk. B75: S Cold 6F 55
Cumbrian Cft. B63: Hale 3F 127
Cumbria Way B8: Salt 3D 102
Cunningham Rd. WS2: Wals 1E 47
WV6: Pert 5E 25
Cupfields Av. DY4: Tip 5B 62
Cupfields Cres. DY4: Tip 6C 62
Curbar Rd. B42: Gt Barr 1E 83
Curdale Rd. B32: Bart G 5H 129
CURDWORTH 1D 88
Curlew Dr. WS8: Bwnhls 6A 10
Curlews Cl. B23: Erd 5C 68
Curral Rd. B65: Row R 6B 96
Curtin Dr. WS10: Mox 1B 62
Curtis Cl. B66: Smeth 5G 99
Curzon Circ. B4: Birm 6A 102
Curzon St. B4: Birm 3H 5 (6H 101)
WV2: Wolv 4H 43
Cushman Av. WV5: Wom 6E 57
Custard Factory, The
B9: Birm 6H 5 (2H 117)
Cuthbert Rd. B18: Win G 5A 100
Cutlass Ct. B1: Birm 6A 4 (2E 117)
Cutlers Rough Cl. B31: N'fld 2D 144
Cutler St. B66: Smeth 3F 99
Cutsdean Cl. B31: N'fld 1D 144
Cutshill Cl. B36: Cas B 1G 105
Cutting, The WS4: Wals 6D 32
Cuttle Pool La. B93: Know 5H 167
Cutworth Cl. B76: Walm 2E 71
Cwerne Dr. DY3: Gorn 4G 75
Cygnet Cl. WV6: Tett 1A 42
Cygnet Ct. WV5: Wom 2F 73
Cygnet Dr. WS8: Bwnhls 6A 10
Cygnet Gro. B23: Erd 1A 84
Cygnet La. DY5: P'ntt 2G 93
Cygnet Rd. B70: W Brom 2G 79
Cygnus Bus. Pk. Ind. Cen.
B70: W Brom 1F 79
Cygnus Way B70: W Brom 2F 79
Cypress Av. DY3: Up Gor 2H 75
Cypress Gdns. B74: S Cold 4G 53
DY6: K'wfrd 5A 92
WS5: Wals 1G 65
Cypress Gro. B31: Longb 6C 144
Cypress Rd. DY2: Dud 6H 77
WS5: Wals 1G 65
Cypress Sq. B27: A Grn 6A 120
Cypress Way B31: Longb 1D 158
Cyprus Cl. B29: W Cas 6E 131
Cyprus St. B69: O'bry 1G 97
(not continuous)
WV2: Wolv 5G 43
Cyril Rd. B10: Small H 3C 118

D

Dacer Cl. B30: Stir 2D 146
Dace Rd. WV10: Wolv 5D 28
Dadford Vw. DY5: Brie H 1F 109
Dad's La. B13: Mose 4E 133
Daffodil Cl. DY3: Sed 6A 60
Daffodil Pl. WS5: Wals 3H 49
Daffodil Rd. WS5: Wals 3H 49
Daffodil Way B31: Longb 1C 158
Dagger La. B71: W Brom 3C 80

Dagnall Rd. B27: A Grn 2B 136
Dahlia Cl. WV1: Wolv 2E 45
Daimer Cl. B36: Cas B 6B 88
Daimler Rd. B14: Yard W 4D 148
Dainton Gro. B32: Bart G 4A 130
Dairy Cl. DY4: Tip 2B 78
Dairy Ct. B68: O'bry 4B 114
DAISY BANK 3H 49
Daisy Bank Cl. WS3: S'fld 5F 21
Daisy Bank Cres. WS5: Wals 3H 49
Daisy Dr. B23: Erd 2A 84
Daisy Farm Rd. B14: K Hth 5B 148
Daisy Mdw. DY4: Tip 1C 78
Daisy Rd. B16: Edg 1B 116
Daisy St. WV14: Cose 3F 61
Daisy Wlk. WV9: Pend 4E 15
Dakota Apartments B16: Birm 1D 116
(off Grosvenor St. W.)
Dalbeg Cl. WV8: Pend 1C 26
Dalbury Rd. B28: Hall G 2E 149
Dalby Rd. WS3: Wals 3D 32
Dale Cl. B43: Gt Barr 4H 65
B66: Smeth 6E 99
DY4: Tip 2D 78
Dalecote Av. B92: Sol 5A 138
Dale End B4: Birm 4F 5 (1G 117)
WS10: Darl 5D 46
(not continuous)
Dale Mdw. Cl. CV7: Bal C 3H 169
Dale Rd. B29: S Oak 2A 132
B62: B'hth 4E 113
DY8: Stourb 3D 124
Dales Cl. WV6: Wolv 3F 27
Dales La. WS9: A'rdge 4G 33
Dalesman Cl. DY6: K'wfrd 2H 91
Dale St. B66: Smeth 6E 99
WS1: Wals 4B 48
(not continuous)
WS10: W'bry 2E 63
WV3: Wolv 2F 43
WV14: Bils 6H 45
Dale Ter. B69: Tiv 1C 96
Daleview Rd. B14: Yard W 3C 148
Dale Wlk. B25: Yard 4H 119
Dalewood Cft. B26: Sheld 5D 120
Dalewood Rd. B37: K'hrst 4B 106
Daley Cl. B1: Birm 6D 100
Daley Rd. WV14: Bils 3H 61
Dalkeith Rd. B73: New O 3D 68
Dalkeith St. WS2: Wals 6A 32
Dallas Rd. B23: Erd 3C 84
Dallimore Cl. B92: Olton 2D 136
Dalloway Cl. B5: Edg 5F 117
Dalston Cl. DY2: Dud 3F 95
Dalston Rd. B27: A Grn 1A 136
Dalton Ct. B23: Erd 4B 84
WV5: Wom 6E 57
Dalton Pl. B92: Olton 3F 137
Dalton Rd. WS2: Wals 6G 31
Dalton St. B4: Birm 3F 5 (6G 101)
WV3: Wolv 3F 43
Dalton Twr. B4: Birm 1G 5
Dalton Way B4: Birm 3E 5 (6G 101)
Dalvine Rd. DY2: Neth 1D 110
Dalwood Cl. WV14: Cose 6D 60
Damar Cft. B14: K Hth 3F 147
Damian Cl. B67: Smeth 4D 98
Dam Mill Cl. WV8: Bilb 6A 14
Damson Cl. WV12: W'hall 3A 30
Damson La. B91: Sol 1A 152
B92: Sol 2A 152
Damson Pk. 4B 138
Damson Parkway B91: Sol 2A 152
B92: Sol 2B 138
Damson Wharf DY4: Tip 4A 78
Danbury Cl. B76: Walm 3E 71
Danbury Gdns. WV10: F'hses 5G 15
Danbury Rd. B90: Shir 5H 149
Danby Gro. B24: Erd 5H 85
Dando Rd. DY2: Dud 1F 95
Dandy Bank Rd. DY6: P'ntt 1E 93
Dandy's Wlk. WS1: Wals 2D 48
Dane Gro. B13: Mose 5F 133
Danehill Wlk. WV8: Pend 1D 26

Danesbury Cres. B44: K'sdng 5A 68
Danes Cl. WV11: Ess 3H 17
Danescourt Rd. WV6: Tett 3A 26
Danesmoor Rd. B25: Yard 4B 120
Daneswood Dr. WS9: Wals W 4B 22
Dane Ter. B65: Row R 4C 96
Daneways Cl. B74: S'tly 3A 52
Danford Cl. DY8: Stourb 1E 125
Danford Gdns. B10: Small H 3C 118
Danford La. B91: Sol 4C 150
Danford Rd. B47: H'wd 3H 161
Danford Way B43: Gt Barr 5H 65
Dangerfield Ho. B70: W Brom 6C 80
Dangerfield La. WS10: Darl 6C 46
Daniels La. WS9: A'rdge 5E 35
Daniels Rd. B9: Bord G 1G 119
Danks St. DY4: Tip 5A 78
Danzey Grn. Rd. B36: Cas B 6F 87
Danzey Gro. B14: K Hth 4E 147
Darby Cl. WV14: Cose 3C 60
DARBY END 5G 95
Darby End Rd. DY2: Neth 5G 95
Darby Ho. WS2: Wals 4A 48
(off Caledon St.)
Darby Rd. B68: O'bry 4A 98
WS10: W'bry 2H 63
Darby's Hill Rd. B69: Tiv 1A 96
Darby St. B65: B'hth 2C 112
Darbys Way DY4: Tip 2B 78
Darell Cft. B76: Walm 2C 70
Daren Cl. B36: Cas B 1B 106
Dare Rd. B23: Erd 3E 85
Darfield Wlk. B12: Birm 3H 117
Darges La. WS6: Gt Wyr 1F 7
Darkhouse La. WV14: Cose 3E 61
Darkies, The B31: N'fld 4F 145
(not continuous)
Dark La. B38: Head H 2E 161
B47: H'wd 2E 161
B62: Roms 3A 142
WS6: Gt Wyr 4A 8
DARLASTON 4D 46
WS10: Darl 4E 47
DARLASTON GREEN 3D 46
Darlaston La. WV14: Bils 4A 46
Darlaston Rd. WS2: Wals 4F 47
WS10: Darl, W'bry 6D 46
Darlaston Rd. Ind. Est. WS10: Darl 6D 46
Darlaston Row CV7: Mer 4H 141
Darlaston Swimming Pool 4E 47
Darley Av. B34: Hodg H 3D 104
Darleydale Av. B44: Gt Barr 4G 67
Darley Dr. WV6: Wolv 4F 27
Darley Ho. B69: O'bry 3D 96
Darley Mead Ct. B91: Sol 3A 152
Darley Way B74: S'tly 4A 52
Darlington St. WS10: Darl 1D 62
WV1: Wolv 3A 170 (1G 43)
WV3: Wolv 1F 43
Darnel Cft. B10: Small H 2B 118
Darnel Hurst Rd. B75: R'ley 6A 38
Darnford Cl. B28: Hall G 2G 149
B72: W Grn 6B 70
Darnick Rd. B73: New O 2D 68
Darnley Rd. B16: Birm 1C 116
Darris Rd. B29: S Oak 5C 132
Dartford Rd. WS3: Blox 6F 19
Dartmoor Cl. B45: Fran 5G 143
Dartmouth Av. B8: Word 5B 92
WS3: Wals 4C 32
WV13: W'hall 1A 46
Dartmouth Cir. B6: Birm 4H 101
Dartmouth Cl. WS3: Wals 4C 32
Dartmouth Cres. WV14: Bils 4A 46
Dartmouth Dr. WS9: A'rdge 4B 34
Dartmouth Ho. WS3: Wals 3D 32
(off Ryecroft Pl.)
Dartmouth Middleway B6: Birm 4H 101
B7: Birm 1H 5 (4H 101)
Dartmouth Pl. WS3: Wals 3D 32
Dartmouth Rd. B29: S Oak 3B 132
B66: Smeth 1D 98
Dartmouth Sq. B70: W Brom 5B 80

Dartmouth St. B70: W Brom 4H 79
 WV2: Wolv 6D **170** (3H **43**)
  (not continuous)
Dartmouth Street Stop (MM) 4H 79
Dart St. B9: Birm 2B 118
Darvel Rd. WV12: W'hall 5D 30
Darwall St. WS1: Wals 1C 48
Darwin Ct. WV6: Pert 5E 25
Darwin Ho. B13: Mose 3B 134
 B37: Chel W 2E 123
Darwin Pl. WS2: Wals 3H 31
Darwin Rd. WS2: Wals 4H 31
Darwin St. B12: Birm 3H 117
  (not continuous)
Dassett Gro. B9: Bord G 1A 120
Dassett Rd. B93: Ben H 5B 166
Dauntsey Covert B14: K Hth 5F 147
Davena Dr. B29: W Cas 3C 130
Davena Gro. WV14: Cose 2F 61
Davenport Dr. B35: Cas V 4G 87
Davenport Rd. WV6: Tett 4H 25
 WV11: Wed 3G 29
Daventry Gro. B32: Quin 5A 114
Davey Rd. B20: Hand 6G 83
 B70: W Brom 2G 79
David Harman Dr. B71: W Brom 6D 64
David Lloyd Leisure
 Birmingham 2F 67
 Solihull, Cranmore Blvd. 2C 164
 Solihull, Highlands Rd. 3C 164
David Peacock Cl. DY4: Tip 2A 78
David Rd. B20: Hand 5D 82
 DY4: Tip 6A 62
Davids, The B31: N'fld 1G 145
Davies Av. WV14: Cose 2F 61
Davies Ho. B69: O'bry 2G 97
 WS3: Blox 5H 19
Davis Av. DY4: Tip 3G 77
Davis Gro. B25: Yard 5B 120
Davison Rd. B67: Smeth 6D 98
Davis Rd. WV12: W'hall 1D 30
Davy Rd. WS2: Wals 4G 31
Dawberry Cl. B14: K Hth 2F 147
Dawberry Flds. Rd. B14: K Hth 2E 147
Dawberry Rd. B14: K Hth 2E 147
DAW END 3G 33
Daw End WS4: Rus 3G 33
Daw End La. WS4: Rus 2F 33
Dawes Av. B70: W Brom 6A 80
Dawes La. WS8: Bwnhls 4C 10
Dawley Brook Rd. DY6: K'wfrd 2B 92
Dawley Cl. WS2: Wals 4H 47
Dawley Cres. B37: Mars G 2D 122
Dawley Rd. DY6: W Hth 1A 92
Dawley Trad. Est. DY6: K'wfrd 1B 92
Dawlish Rd. B29: S Oak 2B 132
 B66: Smeth 4F 99
 DY1: Dud 1D 76
Dawn Dr. DY4: Tip 3C 62
Dawney Dr. B75: Four O 5G 37
Dawn Rd. B31: N'fld 1C 144
Dawson Av. WV14: Cose 3C 60
Dawson Ct. B24: Erd 4F 85
Dawson Rd. B21: Hand 1A 100
Dawson Sq. WV14: Bils 6E 45
Dawson St. B66: Smeth 6E 99
 WS3: Blox 1B 32
Day Av. WV11: Wed 2G 29
Day Ho. DY4: Tip 5C 62
DAYHOUSE BANK 6B 142
Dayhouse Bank B62: Roms 6B 142
Daylesford Rd. B92: Olton 2E 137
Day St. WS3: Wals 6C 32
Deakin Av. WS8: Bwnhls 4B 10
Deakin Rd. B24: Erd 4F 85
 B75: S Cold 4C 54
Deakins Rd. B25: Yard 4H 119
Deal Dr. B69: Tiv 6A 78
Deal Gro. B31: N'fld 3E 145
Deanbrook Cl. B90: M'path 3E 165
Dean Cl. B44: K'sdng 5B 68
 B72: W Grn 6H 69
 DY8: Amb 5F 109

Dean Ct. DY5: Brie H 1H **109**
  (off The Promenade)
 WV6: Pert 3E 25
Deanery Row WV1: Wolv 1B **170** (6G **27**)
Dean Rd. B23: Erd 2F 85
 WS4: Rus 2G 33
 WV5: Wom 2F 73
Deansbank Cen. WS1: Wals 3B 48
Deansfield Rd. WV1: Wolv 1C 44
Deans La. WV13: W'hall 1F 45
Deans Pl. WS3: Wals 3D 32
Dean's Rd. WV1: Wolv 6C 28
Dean St. B5: Birm 6F 5 (2G **117**)
 DY3: Sed 5H 59
Dearman Rd. B11: S'brk 4B 118
Dearmont Rd. B31: Longb 2C 158
Dearne Ct. DY3: Sed 1C 76
Debden Cl. B93: Dorr 6F 167
Debenham Cres. B25: Yard 2B 120
Debenham Rd. B25: Yard 2B 120
Deblen Dr. B16: Edg 2H 115
Deborah Cl. WV2: Penn 5G 43
Dee Gro. B38: K Nor 1A 160
Deelands Rd. B45: Rub 1F 157
Deeley Cl. B15: Edg 4E 117
 B64: Crad H 4G 111
Deeley Dr. DY4: Tip 1C 78
Deeley Pl. WS3: Blox 1H 31
Deeley St. DY5: Quar B 2A 110
 WS3: Blox 1H 31
Deepdale Av. B26: Sheld 1F 137
Deepdale La. DY3: Lwr G 4A 76
Deepdales WV5: Wom 1E 73
DEEPFIELDS 3D 60
Deeplow Cl. B72: S Cold 1A 70
Deepmoor Rd. B33: Yard 6D 104
Deepmore Av. WS2: Wals 6H 31
Deepwood Cl. WS4: S'fld 1F 33
Deepwood Gro. B32: Bart G 5H 129
Deer Cl. WS3: Blox 6A 20
Deerham Cl. B23: Erd 6D 68
Deerhurst Ct. B91: Sol 3H 151
Deerhurst Rd. B20: Hand 2E 82
Dee Rd. WS3: Blox 6C 20
Deer Pk. Way B91: Sol 6G 151
Deer Wlk. WV8: Pend 5D 14
Dee Wlk. B36: Cas B 1C 106
  (not continuous)
Defford Av. WS4: S'fld 6G 21
Defford Dr. B68: O'bry 5H 97
De Havilland Dr. B35: Cas V 5E 87
Deighton Rd. WS5: Wals 1F 65
Delamere Cl. B36: Cas B 6H 87
Delamere Dr. WS5: Wals 2G 65
Delamere Rd. B28: Hall G 6F 135
 WV12: W'hall 2C 30
Delancey Keep B75: S Cold 6E 55
Delhurst Rd. B44: Gt Barr 4F 67
 WV4: E'shll 2A 60
Delingpole Wlk. B64: Old H 3G 111
Delius Ho. B16: Birm 1D 116
Dell, The B31: N'fld 1B 144
 B36: Cas B 6B 88
 B74: Four O 3G 53
 B92: Olton 4E 137
 DY8: Woll 5C 108
Della Dr. B32: Bart G 5B 130
Dell Farm Cl. B93: Know 3D 166
Dellows Cl. B38: K Nor 2H 159
Dell Rd. B30: K Nor 2C 146
 DY5: P'ntt 4F 93
Dell Stadium, The 4F 93
Delmore Way B76: Walm 1F 87
Delph Dr. DY5: Quar B 4A 110
Delphinium Cl. B9: Bord G 6F 103
Delph La. DY5: Brie H 3H 109
Delph Rd. DY5: Brie H 2G 109
Delph Rd. Ind. Est. DY5: Brie H 2G 109
Delrene Rd. B28: Hall G 4F 149
 B90: Shir 4F 149
DELVES, THE 6D 48
Delves Cres. WS5: Wals 6E 49
Delves Grn. Rd. WS5: Wals 5E 49
Delves Rd. WS1: Wals 4D 48

Delville Cl. WS10: W'bry . . . . .1F 6.
Delville Rd. WS10: W'bry 1F 63
Delville Ter. WS10: W'bry 1F 63
De Marnham Cl. B70: W Brom 6C 80
De Montfort Ho. B37: K'hrst 4B 106
De Montfort M. B46: Col 3H 107
De Moram Gro. B92: Sol 6B 138
Demuth Way B69: O'bry 4F 97
Denaby Gro. B14: Yard W 3D 148
Denbigh Cl. DY1: Dud 5B 76
Denbigh Ct. B29: W Cas 6G **131**
  (off Tugford Rd.)
Denbigh Cres. B71: W Brom 1H 79
Denbigh Dr. B71: W Brom 6G 63
 WS10: W'bry 1B 64
Denbigh Rd. DY4: Tip 2C 78
Denbigh St. B9: Bord G 1D 118
Denby Cl. B7: Birm 4B 102
Denby Cft. B90: M'path 3F 165
Dencer Cl. B45: Rub 1F 157
Dencil Cl. B63: Crad 6F 111
Dene Av. DY6: K'wfrd 5A 92
Dene Ct. Rd. B92: Olton 4D 136
Dene Cft. WS3: Blox 6G 19
Denegate Cl. B76: Walm 1F 87
Dene Hollow B13: Mose 1C 148
Dene Rd. DY8: Stourb 2D 124
 WV4: Lwr P 1F 57
Denewood Av. B20: Hand 5C 82
Denford Gro. B14: K Hth 2F 147
Dengate Dr. CV7: Bal C 2H 169
Denham Ct. B23: Erd 5E 84
  (off Park App.)
Denham Gdns. WV3: Wolv 3H 41
Denham Rd. B27: A Grn 6H 119
Denholme Gro. B14: K Hth 4A 148
Denholm Rd. B73: New O 2D 68
Denise Dr. B17: Harb 1G 131
 B37: K'hrst 5B 106
 WV14: Cose 5D 60
Denleigh Rd. DY6: K'wfrd 5D 92
Denmark Cl. WV6: Wolv 5E 27
Denmead Dr. WV11: Wed 1H 29
Denmore Gdns. WV1: Wolv 1D 44
Dennfield Dr. WS6: C Hay 2C 6
Dennis Hall Rd. DY8: Amb 3D 108
Dennis Hall Rd. DY8: Amb 3E 109
Dennis Rd. B12: Bal H 1B 134
  (not continuous)
Dennis St. DY8: Amb 3D 108
Denshaw Rd. B14: K Hth 1F 147
Denstone Gdns. WV10: Bush 4A 16
Denton Cft. B93: Dorr 6H 165
Denton Gro. B33: Stech 1B 120
 B43: Gt Barr 6H 65
Denton Rd. DY9: W'cte 1C 126
Denver Rd. B14: K Hth 5A 148
Denville Cl. WV14: Bils 4G 45
Denville Cres. B9: Bord G 6H 103
Derby Av. WV6: Tett 2C 26
Derby Dr. B37: Chel W 1D 122
Derby St. B9: Birm 1A 118
 WS2: Wals 5B 32
Dereham Cl. B8: Salt 5D 102
Dereham Wlk. WV14: Bils 3G 61
Dereton Cl. DY1: Dud 1A 94
DERITEND 6H 5 (2A **118**)
Derron Av. B26: Yard 6C 120
Derry Cl. B17: Harb 2E 131
Derrydown Cl. B23: Erd 4E 85
Derrydown Rd. B42: P Barr 2D 82
Derry St. DY5: Brie H 1H 109
 WV2: Wolv 3H 43
Derwent Cl. B74: S'tly 1H 51
 DY5: P'ntt 3F 93
 WV13: W'hall 1C 46
Derwent Ct. B73: S Cold 6H 53
Derwent Gro. B30: Stir 5E 133
Derwent Ho. B17: Harb 6H 115
 B69: O'bry 4D 96
Derwent Rd. B30: Stir 5E 133
 WV6: Tett 1B 26
Desford Av. B42: Gt Barr 6E 67
Dettonford Rd. B32: Bart G 5H 129

evereux Cl. B36: Cas B 1G 105
evereux Rd. B70: W Brom 6C 80
B75: Four O 2A 54
Devey Dr. DY4: Tip 1D 78
Devil's Elbow La. WV11: Wed 2G 29
Devine Cft. DY4: Tip 2A 78
Devitts Cl. B90: M'path 2D 164
Devon Cl. B20: Hand 5B 82
Devon Ct. B29: W Cas 6F 131
(off Holdgate Rd.)
Devon Cres. B71: W Brom 1A 80
DY2: Dud 2B 94
WS9: A'rdge 6C 22
Devon Rd. B45: Fran 5E 143
B67: Smeth 4C 114
DY8: Woll 4C 108
WS10: W'bry 1A 64
WV1: Wolv 6F 27
WV13: W'hall 1D 46
Devonshire Av. B18: Hock 3B 100
Devonshire Ct. B74: Four O 1F 53
Devonshire Dr. B71: W Brom 4C 80
Devonshire Rd. B20: Hand 5B 82
B67: Smeth 3C 98
Devonshire St. B18: Hock 3B 100
Devon St. B7: Birm 5C 102
Devon Way B31: Longb 1C 158
Devoran Cl. WV6: Wolv 5F 27
Dewberry Dr. WS5: Wals 2E 65
Dewberry Rd. DY8: Word 2D 108
Dewhurst Cft. B33: Kitts G 6F 105
Dewsbury Cl. DY8: Word 6C 92
Dewsbury Dr. WV4: Penn 2E 59
Dewsbury Gro. B42: P Barr 2E 83
Deykin Av. B6: Witt 5A 84
Deyncourt Rd. WV10: Wolv 2C 28
Dial Cl. B14: K Hth 5G 147
Dial La. B70: W Brom 1F 79
DY8: Amb 3C 108
Diamond Pk. Dr. DY8: Word 2C 108
Diana Cl. WS9: Wals W 4D 22
Diana Way B45: Fran 5F 143
Diane Cl. DY4: Tip 3B 62
Dibble Cl. WV12: W'hall 4D 30
Dibble Rd. B67: Smeth 3D 98
Dibdale Ct. DY3: Lwr G 4H 75
(off Yorkdale Cl.)
Dibdale Rd. DY1: Dud 4B 76
Dibdale Rd. W. DY1: Dud 4A 76
Dibdale St. DY1: Dud 5B 76
Dice Pleck B31: N'fld 5G 145
Dickens Cl. DY3: Lwr G 2F 75
DICKENS HEATH 4F 163
Dickens Heath Rd.
B90: Dic H, Tid G 5E 163
Dickens Rd. WV10: Bush 1C 28
WV14: Cose 3F 61
Dickinson Av. WV10: Bush 1A 28
Dickinson Dr. B76: Walm 1C 70
WS2: Wals 5A 48
Dickinson Rd. WV5: Wom 3G 73
Dick Sheppard Av. DY4: Tip 5B 62
Diddington Av. B28: Hall G 2G 149
Diddington La. B92: Bick, H Ard 5C 140
Didgley Gro. B37: K'hrst 4C 106
DIGBETH 6H 5 (2H 117)
Digbeth B5: Birm 5F 5 (1G 117)
WS1: Wals 2C 48
Digby Ct. B27: A Grn 2A 136
Digby Cres. B46: Wat O 4D 88
Digby Dr. B37: Mars G 5D 122
Digby Ho. B37: K'hrst 5B 106
Digby Rd. B46: Col 3H 107
B73: S Cold 2G 69
DY6: K'wfrd 1B 92
Digby Wlk. B33: Sheld 3G 121
Dilke Rd. WS9: A'rdge 4B 34
Dilliars Wlk. B70: W Brom 2G 79
Dillington Ho. B37: Chel W 1D 122
Dilloway's La. WV13: W'hall 2G 45
Dimmingsdale Bank B32: Quin 1A 130
Dimmingsdale Rd. WV4: Lwr P 6E 41
Dimminsdale WV13: W'hall 2A 46
Dimmocks Av. WV14: Cose 5F 61

Dimmock St. WV4: E'shll 6A 44
Dimsdale Gro. B31: N'fld 4C 144
Dimsdale Rd. B31: N'fld 4B 144
Dingle, The B29: S Oak 3A 132
B69: O'bry 1D 96
B90: Ches G 4B 164
WV3: Wolv 2B 42
Dingle Av. B64: Crad H 3G 111
Dingle Cl. B30: B'vlle 6H 131
DY2: Dud 2G 95
Dingle Ct. B69: O'bry 1E 97
(off Dingle St.)
B91: Sol 6D 150
Dingle Hollow B69: O'bry 1D 96
WV13: W'hall 5A 30
Dingle Mdw. Ct. B69: O'bry 1E 97
Dingle Rd. DY2: Dud 2G 95
DY6: K'wfrd 5E 93
DY9: Pedm 3F 125
WS8: Clay 1A 22
WV5: Wom 1F 73
Dingle Vw. DY3: Sed 1G 75
Dingley Rd. WS10: W'bry 6G 47
Dinham Gdns. DY1: Dud 4A 76
Dinmore Av. B31: N'fld 3F 145
Dinsdale Wlk. WV6: Wolv 4E 27
Dippons Dr. WV6: Tett 6G 25
Dippons La. WV6: Pert 3E 25
WV6: Tett 3F 25
Dippons Mill Cl. WV6: Tett 6G 25
Direct 2 Ind. Pk. B69: O'bry 6E 79
Dirtyfoot La. WV4: Lwr P 6G 41
Discovery Cl. DY4: Tip 2C 78
Ditch, The WS1: Wals 2D 48
Ditton Gro. B31: Longb 3D 158
Dixon Cl. B35: Cas V 5E 87
DY4: Tip 1C 78
Dixon Ct. B10: Small H 3B 118
Dixon Ho. B16: Edg 2C 116
Dixon Rd. B10: Small H 3B 118
DIXON'S GREEN 1G 95
Dixon's Grn. Ct. DY2: Dud 1F 95
(off Dixon's Grn. Rd.)
Dixon's Grn. Rd. DY2: Dud 1F 95
Dixon St. WV2: E'shll 5A 44
Dobbins Oak Rd. DY9: W'cte 4H 125
Dobbs Mill Cl. B29: S Oak 3D 132
Dobbs St. WV2: Wolv 6B 170 (3G 43)
Dock, The DY9: Lye 6B 110
Dockar Rd. B31: N'fld 5C 144
Dockers Cl. CV7: Bal C 5H 169
Dock La. DY1: Dud 6D 76
Dock La. Ind. Est. DY1: Dud 6D 76
(off Dock La.)
Dock Mdw. Dr. WV4: E'shll 1C 60
Dock Rd. DY8: Word 1D 108
Doctors Hill DY9: Pedm 2G 125
Doctors La. DY6: K'wfrd 4F 91
Doctor's Piece WV13: W'hall 1B 46
Doddington Gro. B32: Bart G 5H 129
Dodford Cl. B45: Rub 2F 157
DOE BANK 3H 53
Doe Bank Ct. B74: Four O 3H 53
Doe Bank La. B43: Gt Barr 5E 51
WS9: A'rdge 5E 51
Doe Bank Rd. DY4: Tip 4C 62
Dogge La. Cft. B27: A Grn 3H 135
Dog Kennel La. B68: O'bry 4A 98
B90: Shir 2A 164
WS1: Wals 1D 48
Dogkennel La. B63: Hale 2B 128
Dogpool La. B30: Stir 4D 132
Doidge Rd. B23: Erd 4D 84
Dollery Dr. B5: Edg 6E 117
Dollis Gro. B44: Gt Barr 2H 67
Dollman St. B7: Birm 6B 102
Dolman Rd. B6: Aston 1G 101
Dolobran Rd. B11: S'brk 4B 118
Dolphin Cl. WS3: Blox 6D 20
Dolphin La. WV12: W'hall 2D 30
(off Huntington Rd.)

Dolphin Ho. WS3: Blox 1D 32
Dolphin La. B27: A Grn 4H 135
(not continuous)
Dolphin Rd. B11: S'hll 6D 118
Dolton Way DY4: Tip 1G 77
Dominic Dr. B30: K Nor 3H 145
Doncaster Way B36: Hodg H 1A 104
Don Cl. B15: Edg 3H 115
Donegal Rd. B74: S'tly 6H 51
Donibristle Cft. B35: Cas V 3E 87
Donnington Cl. DY1: Dud 5B 76
Donnington Ho. B33: Yard 1F 121
Donovan Dr. B73: S Cold 5G 53
Dooley Cl. WV13: W'hall 1G 45
Dora Herbert Ct. B12: Bal H 6G 117
Doran Cl. B63: Hale 4F 127
Doranda Way B71: W Brom 6D 80
Doranda Way Ind. Pk.
B71: W Brom 6D 80
Dora Rd. B10: Small H 3E 119
B21: Hand 2A 100
B70: W Brom 6A 80
Dora St. WS2: Wals 4H 47
Dorchester Cl. WV12: W'hall 1C 30
Dorchester Ct. B91: Sol 3E 151
Dorchester Dr. B17: Harb 1F 131
Dorchester Rd. B91: Sol 3E 151
DY9: W'cte 3H 125
WV12: W'hall 1C 30
Dordale Cl. B31: Longb 6A 144
Dordon Cl. B90: Shir 6E 149
Doreen Gro. B24: Erd 5G 85
Doris Rd. B9: Bord G 1D 118
B11: S'hll 1B 134
B46: Col 1H 107
Dorking Ct. B29: W Cas 6G 131
(off Abdon Av.)
Dorlcote Rd. B8: Salt 5G 103
Dormie Cl. B38: K Nor 6H 145
Dormington Rd. B44: Gt Barr 2G 67
Dormston Cl. B91: Sol 2G 165
Dormston Dr. B29: W Cas 3D 130
DY3: Sed 5A 60
Dormston Sports & Art Cen. 5A 60
Dormston Trad. Est. DY1: Dud 3A 76
Dormy Dr. B31: Longb 2E 159
Dorncliffe Av. B33: Sheld 4H 121
Dornie Dr. B38: K Nor 6B 146
Dornton Rd. B30: Stir 5E 133
Dorothy Adams Cl. B64: Old H 3G 111
Dorothy Gdns. B20: Hand 5C 82
Dorothy Rd. B11: Tys 6H 119
B67: Smeth 6E 99
Dorothy St. WS1: Wals 4B 48
DORRIDGE 6B 166
Dorridge Cft. B93: Dorr 6G 167
Dorridge Rd. B93: Dorr 6H 167
Dorridge Station (Rail) 6G 167
Dorrington Grn. B42: P Barr 2C 82
Dorrington Rd. B42: P Barr 1C 82
Dorset Cl. B45: Fran 5F 143
Dorset Cotts. B30: Stir 1C 146
Dorset Ct. B29: W Cas 6F 131
(off Abdon Av.)
Dorset Dr. WS9: A'rdge 6C 22
Dorset Rd. B8: Salt 3D 102
B17: Edg 6F 99
DY8: Woll 4B 108
Dorset Twr. B18: Hock 5D 100
Dorsett Pl. WS3: Blox 2A 32
Dorsett Rd. WS10: Darl 5C 46
WS10: W'bry 3B 64
Dorsett Rd. Ter. WS10: Darl 5C 46
Dorsheath Gdns. B23: Erd 3F 85
Dorsington Rd. B27: A Grn 4B 136
Dorstone Covert B14: K Hth 5E 147
Dorville Cl. B38: K Nor 1H 159
Douay Rd. B24: Erd 1H 85
Double Row DY2: Neth 5G 95
Doughty St. DY4: Tip 2C 78
Douglas Av. B36: Hodg H 3B 104
B68: O'bry 4B 98
Douglas Davies Cl. WV12: W'hall . . .5C 30
Douglas Pl. WV10: Oxl 3G 27

Douglas Rd.—Duke St.

Douglas Rd. B21: Hand 1A **100**
B27: A Grn 1H **135**
B47: H'wd 2A **162**
B62: B'hth 2E **113**
B68: O'bry 5B **98**
B72: S Cold 2A **70**
DY2: Dud 1F **95**
WV14: Cose 5F **61**
Doulton Cl. B32: Quin 2D **130**
Doulton Dr. B66: Smeth 3E **99**
Doulton Rd. B64: Old H 6H **95**
B65: Row R 6H **95**
Doulton Trad. Est. B65: Row R 5H **95**
Dovebridge Cl. B76: Walm 1D **70**
Dove Cl. B25: Yard 3C **120**
WS1: Wals 2E **49**
WS10: W'bry 1G **63**
Dovecote Cl. B91: Sol 5F **137**
DY4: Tip .2C **78**
WV6: Tett 5A **26**
Dovecotes, The B75: Four O 6H **37**
Dovedale Av. B90: Shir 6H **149**
WS3: Pels 2E **21**
WV12: W'hall 4A **30**
Dovedale Ct. B29: W Cas 6G **131**
B46: Wat O 4C **88**
WV4: E'shll 3B **60**
Dovedale Dr. B28: Hall G 1F **149**
Dovedale Rd. B23: Erd 5C **68**
DY6: K'wfrd 1C **92**
WV4: E'shll 2A **60**
Dove Dr. DY8: Amb 3E **109**
Dove Gdns. B38: K Nor 5D **146**
Dove Hollow WS6: Gt Wyr 4F **7**
Dove Ho. Ct. B91: Sol 6D **136**
Dovehouse La. B91: Sol 6D **136**
Dovehouse Pool Rd. B6: Aston 1G **101**
Dover Cl. B32: Bart G 6G **129**
Dover Ct. *B29: W Cas 6G* ***131***
(off Abdon Av.)
Dovercourt Rd. B26: Sheld 6G **121**
Doverdale Cl. B63: Crad 6F **111**
Dover Ho. *WS3: Blox 2A* ***32***
(off Providence Cl.)
Dove Ridge DY8: Amb 4E **109**
Doveridge Cl. B91: Sol 6C **136**
Doveridge Pl. WS1: Wals 3D **48**
Doveridge Rd. B28: Hall G 2E **149**
Doversley Rd. B14: K Hth 2E **147**
Dover St. B18: Hock 3C **100**
WV14: Bils 5F **45**
Dove Way B36: Cas B 1B **106**
Dovey Dr. B76: Walm 6E **71**
Dovey Gro. B65: Row R 1B **112**
Dovey Rd. B13: Mose 3D **134**
B69: Tiv 1D **96**
Dovey Twr. B7: Birm 5A **102**
Dowar Rd. B45: Redn 2A **158**
Dowells Cl. B13: Mose 3H **133**
Dowells Gdns. DY8: Word 6B **92**
Doweries, The B45: Rub 1F **157**
Dower Rd. B75: Four O 2H **53**
Dowles Cl. B29: W Cas 1F **145**
Downcroft Av. B38: K Nor 5A **146**
Downend Cl. WV10: Bush 3B **16**
Downes Ct. DY4: Tip 2G **77**
Downey Cl. B11: S'brk 4B **118**
Downfield Cl. WS3: Blox 3G **19**
Downfield Dr. DY3: Sed 1A **76**
Downham Cl. WS5: Wals 2A **50**
Downham Pl. WV3: Wolv 3D **42**
Downham Wood WS5: Wals 3A **50**
Downie Rd. WV8: Bilb 4A **14**
Downing Cl. B65: B'hth 2C **112**
B93: Know 5C **166**
WV11: Wed 2A **30**
Downing Ho. B37: Chel W 2D **122**
Downing St. B63: Hale 6A **112**
B66: Smeth 2F **99**
Downing St. Ind. Est. B66: Smeth 2G **99**
Downland Cl. B38: K Nor 6B **146**
Downs, The WS9: A'rdge 1G **51**
WV10: Oxl 3G **27**
Downsfield Rd. B26: Sheld 4F **121**
Downside Rd. B24: Erd 6E **85**
Downs Rd. WV13: W'hall 3C **46**
Downton Cres. B33: Kitts G 6A **106**
Dowry Ho. *B45: Rub 1F* ***157***
(off Rubery La. Sth.)
Dowty Way WV9: Pend 4E **15**
Drainage Board Cotts. *B24: Erd 6F* ***85***
(off Saltley Cotts.)
Drake Cl. WS3: Blox 6H **19**
Drake Cft. B37: Chel W 6F **107**
Drake Rd. B23: Erd 4B **84**
B66: Smeth 2C **98**
WS3: Blox 6H **19**
Drakes Cl. B47: H'wd 4H **161**
DRAKES CROSS **4A 162**
Drakes Cross Pde. B47: H'wd 4A **162**
Drakes Grn. WV14: Bils 2H **61**
Drakes Hill Cl. DY8: Stourb 1A **124**
Drake St. B71: W Brom 2A **80**
Drancy Av. WV12: W'hall 3D **30**
(not continuous)
Drawbridge Rd. B90: Maj G 1E **163**
Draycote Cl. B92: Sol 6H **137**
Draycott Av. B23: Erd 3D **84**
Draycott Cl. WV4: Penn 6A **42**
Draycott Dr. B31: N'fld 6C **130**
Draycott Rd. B66: Smeth 2C **98**
Drayman Cl. WS1: Wals 3D **48**
Drayton Cl. B75: Four O 6H **37**
Drayton Rd. B14: K Hth 5G **133**
B66: Smeth 2E **115**
B90: Shir .1C **164**
Drayton St. WS2: Wals 1H **47**
WV2: Wolv 6B **170** (3G **43**)
Drayton St. E. WS2: Wals 1A **48**
Dreadnought Rd. DY5: P'ntt 2F **93**
Dreamwell Ind. Est. B11: Tys 5G **119**
Dreel, The B15: Edg 4A **116**
Dreghorn Rd. B36: Hodg H 1C **104**
Drem Cft. B35: Cas V 5E **87**
Dresden Cl. WV4: E'shll 1C **60**
Drew Cres. DY9: W'cte 3H **125**
Drew Rd. DY9: W'cte 2H **125**
Drew's Holloway B63: Crad 6F **111**
Drew's Holloway Sth. B63: Crad 6F **111**
Drews Ho. *B14: K Hth 6F* ***147***
(off Netheravon Cl.)
Drews La. B8: W End 3G **103**
Drews Mdw. Cl. B14: K Hth 5E **147**
DRIFFOLD **1G 69**
Driffold B73: S Cold 1H **69**
Driffold Vs. B73: S Cold 2H **69**
Driftwood Cl. B38: K Nor 2H **159**
Drive, The B20: Hand 5C **82**
B23: Erd .5E **85**
B48: Hopw 6F **159**
B63: Crad 6F **111**
B63: Hale 2A **128**
DY5: Brie H 4G **93**
WS3: Blox 5C **20**
WS4: S'fld 6G **21**
WV6: Tett .4A **26**
WV8: Cod .4F **13**
Drive Flds. WV4: Lwr P 5H **41**
Droicon Trad. Est. B65: Row R 4C **96**
Droveway, The WV8: Pend 5C **14**
WV9: Pend 5C **14**
Droxford Wlk. WV8: Pend 6C **14**
Druid Pk. Rd. WV12: W'hall 6C **18**
Druids Av. B65: Row R 5D **96**
WS9: A'rdge 6E **23**
DRUID'S HEATH **6D 22**
Druids La. B14: K Hth 5E **147**
Druids Wlk. WS9: Wals W 4C **22**
Drummond Cl. WV11: Wed 5A **18**
Drummond Gro. B43: Gt Barr 2E **67**
Drummond Rd. B9: Bord G 1F **119**
DY9: W'cte 6B **110**
Drummond St. WV1: Wolv . . .1A **170** (6G **27**)
Drummond Way B37: Chel W 1E **123**
Drury La. B91: Sol 4G **151**
(not continuous)
DY8: Stourb 6E **109**
WV8: Cod .3F **13**
Drybrook Cl. B38: K Nor 1A **160**
Drybrooks Cl. CV7: Bal C 3H **169**
Dryden Cl. DY4: Tip 6A **62**
WV12: W'hall 1E **31**
Dryden Gro. B27: A Grn 3H **135**
Dryden Pl. WS3: Blox 2C **32**
Dryden Rd. WS3: Blox 2C **32**
WV10: Bush 6B **16**
Drylea Gro. B36: Hodg H 2D **104**
Dubarry Av. DY6: K'wfrd 2A **92**
Duchess Pde. B70: W Brom 4B **80**
Duchess Pl. B16: Edg 2C **116**
Duchess Rd. B16: Edg 2C **116**
WS1: Wals 6B **48**
Duckhouse Rd. WV11: Wed 2F **29**
Duck La. WV8: Bilb 5H **13**
WV14: Bils 6G **45**
Duddeston Dr. B8: Salt 5D **102**
Duddeston Mnr. Rd. B7: Birm 5A **102**
Duddeston Mill Rd. B7: Birm 5B **102**
B8: Birm, Salt 5B **102**
Duddeston Mill Trad. Est. B8: Salt 5C **102**
Duddeston Station (Rail) **5B 102**
Dudding Rd. WV4: Penn 6H **43**
Dudhill Rd. B65: Row R 6A **96**
Dudhill Wlk. B65: Row R 6H **95**
DUDLEY **6E 77**
Dudley Castle 5F **77**
Dudley Central Trad. Est. DY2: Dud 1E **95**
Dudley Cl. B65: Row R 3A **96**
Dudley Cres. WV11: Wed 3G **29**
DUDLEY FIELDS **5G 93**
Dudley Gro. B18: Win G 5A **100**
Dudley Innovation Cen. DY6: P'ntt 2D **92**
Dudley Leisure Cen. 6D **76**
Dudley Mus. & Art Gallery 6E **77**
Dudley Pk. Rd. B27: A Grn 2A **136**
DUDLEY PORT **3B 78**
Dudley Port DY4: Tip 4A **78**
Dudley Port Station (Rail) **3B 78**
Dudley Rd. B18: Win G 5H **99**
B63: Hale 5B **112**
B65: Row R 3H **95**
B69: O'bry 6E **79**
DY3: Himl 4A **74**
DY3: Sed .6A **60**
DY4: Tip 2F **77**
DY5: Brie H 6H **93**
DY6: K'wfrd 2D **92**
DY6: W Hth 1A **92**
DY9: Lye .5A **110**
WV2: Wolv 6C **170** (3H **43**)
Dudley Rd. E. B69: O'bry, Tiv 5C **78**
Dudley Rd. W. B69: Tiv 5A **78**
DY4: Tip 5A **78**
Dudley Row DY2: Dud 6F **77**
DUDLEY'S FIELDS **1G 31**
Dudley Southern By-Pass DY2: Dud . . .2C **94**
Dudley St. B5: Birm 5E **5** (1G **117**)
B70: W Brom 2F **79**
DY3: Sed .5H **59**
WS1: Wals 2C **48**
WS10: W'bry 3E **63**
WV1: Wolv 3B **170** (1G **43**)
WV14: Bils 6F **45**
(not continuous)
Dudley Wlk. WV4: Penn 6G **43**
Dudley Wood Av. DY2: Neth 1E **111**
Dudley Wood Rd. DY2: Neth 2E **111**
Dudley Zoo .5F **77**
Dudmaston Way DY1: Dud 4A **76**
Dudnill Gro. B32: Bart G 5G **129**
Duffield Cl. WV8: Pend 6D **14**
Dufton Rd. B32: Quin 6C **114**
Dugdale Cres. B75: Four O 6A **38**
Dugdale Ho. B71: W Brom 5E **65**
Dugdale St. B18: Win G 5H **99**
Dukes Rd. B30: K Nor 3C **146**
Duke St. B65: Row R 1B **112**
B70: W Brom 3H **79**
B72: S Cold 1H **69**
DY3: Up Gor 2H **75**
DY8: Stourb 5E **109**
WV1: Wolv 2A **44**

Duke St. WV3: Wolv 4E **43**
  WV11: Wed 4F **29**
Dulvern Gro. B14: K Hth 2F **147**
Dulverton Rd. B6: Witt 6A **84**
Dulwich Gro. B44: K'sdng 5B **68**
Dulwich Rd. B44: K'sdng 5A **68**
Dumbleberry Av. DY3: Sed 6G **59**
Dumblederry La. WS9: A'rdge 1A **34**
Dunard Rd. B90: Shir 4F **149**
Dunbar Cl. B32: Bart G 4B **130**
Dunbar Gro. B43: Gt Barr 1D **66**
Duncalfe Dr. B75: Four O 6H **37**
Duncan Edwards Cl. DY1: Dud 1C **94**
Duncan Ho. B73: W Grn 4H **69**
Duncan St. WV2: Wolv 4G **43**
Dunchurch Cl. CV7: Bal C 2H **169**
Dunchurch Cres. B73: New O 2C **68**
Dunchurch Dr. B31: N'fld 6C **130**
Dunchurch Ho. B5: Birm 3G **117**
Duncombe Grn. B46: Col 2H **107**
Duncombe Gro. B17: Harb 4D **114**
Duncombe St. DY8: Woll 5B **108**
Duncroft Rd. B26: Yard 3D **120**
Duncroft Wlk. DY1: Dud 1D **76**
Duncumb Rd. B75: S Cold 6E **55**
Dundalk La. WS6: C Hay 3D **6**
Dundas Av. DY2: Dud 1H **95**
Dunedin Ho. B32: Quin 1D **130**
Dunedin Rd. B44: Gt Barr 2G **67**
Dunham Cft. B93: Dorr 6H **165**
Dunkirk Av. B70: W Brom 3D **78**
Dunkley St. WV1: Wolv 1A **170** (6G **27**)
Dunley Ct. B23: Erd 5C **84**
                (off Dunlin Cl.)
Dunley Cft. B90: M'path 3D **164**
Dunlin Cl. B23: Erd 5C **84**
  DY6: K'wfrd 3E **93**
Dunlin Dr. WV10: F'stne 1C **16**
Dunlop Way B35: Cas V 6C **86**
Dunnerdale Rd. WS8: Clay 1H **21**
Dunnigan Rd. B32: Bart G 2D **130**
DUNN'S BANK 4B **110**
Dunn's Bank DY5: Quar B 4B **110**
                (Lynval Rd.)
  DY5: Quar B 4C **110**
            (Saltbrook Rd.)
Dunsfold Cl. WV14: Cose 2C **60**
Dunsfold Cft. B6: Aston 3H **101**
Dunsford Cl. DY5: Brie H 4F **109**
Dunsford Rd. B66: Smeth 1E **115**
Dunsink Rd. B6: Aston 6H **83**
Dunslade Cres. DY5: Quar B 3B **110**
Dunslade Rd. B23: Erd 6E **69**
Dunsley Dr. DY8: Word 6C **92**
Dunsley Gro. WV4: Penn 1E **59**
Dunsley Rd. DY8: Woll 1A **124**
Dunsmore Dr. DY5: Quar B 3B **110**
Dunsmore Gro. B91: Sol 6D **136**
Dunsmore Rd. B28: Hall G 3E **135**
Dunstall Av. WV6: Wolv 4G **27**
Dunstall Gro. B29: W Cas 5D **130**
DUNSTALL HILL 4F **27**
Dunstall Hill WV6: Wolv 4G **27**
Dunstall Hill Trad. Est. WV6: Wolv . . .4G **27**
Dunstall La. WV6: Wolv 4E **27**
Dunstall Pk. 3E **27**
Dunstall Pk. WV6: Wolv 3F **27**
Dunstall Rd. R63: Hale 2F **127**
  WV6: Wolv 5F **27**
Dunstan Cft. B90: Shir 1A **164**
Dunster Cl. B30: K Nor 3D **146**
Dunster Gro. WV6: Pert 6F **25**
Dunster Rd. B37: Chel W 6E **107**
Dunston Cl. DY6: K'wfrd 2B **92**
  WS6: Gt Wyr 5E **7**
Dunton Cl. B75: Four O 5G **37**
Dunton Hall Rd. B90: Shir 1G **163**
Dunton Rd. B37: K'hrst 5B **106**
Dunton Trad. Est. B7: Nech 2D **102**
Dunvegan Rd. B24: Erd 3G **85**
Durant Cl. B45: Fran 5D **142**
Durban Rd. B66: Smeth 5G **99**
D'Urberville Cl. WV2: E'shll 5B **44**
           (off D'Urberville Rd.)

D'Urberville Rd. WV2: E'shll 4B **44**
           (not continuous)
Durberville Rd. Ind. Est.
  WV2: E'shll 4B **44**
Durham Av. WV13: W'hall 6C **30**
Durham Ct. B29: W Cas 6G **131**
           (off Abdon Av.)
Durham Cft. B37: Chel W 1D **122**
Durham Dr. B71: W Brom 6B **64**
Durham Ho. WV1: Wolv 5G **27**
           (off Lomas St.)
Durham Pl. WS2: Wals 2H **47**
Durham Rd. B11: S'hll 1B **134**
  B65: Row R 5E **97**
  DY2: Neth 1F **111**
  DY8: Woll 3B **108**
  WS2: Wals 3H **47**
  WS10: W'bry 1B **64**
Durham Twr. B1: Birm 6D **100**
Durley Dean Rd. B29: S Oak 3G **131**
Durley Dr. B73: New O 2C **68**
Durley Rd. B25: Yard 5A **120**
Durlston Gro. B28: Hall G 5G **135**
Durnford Cft. B14: K Hth 6G **147**
Dursley Cl. B92: Olton 5F **137**
  WV12: W'hall 5D **30**
Dutton's La. B75: R'ley 5C **38**
Duxford Rd. B42: Gt Barr 5D **66**
Dwellings La. B32: Quin 6H **113**
Dyas Av. B42: Gt Barr 6B **66**
Dyas Rd. B44: Gt Barr 4F **67**
  B47: H'wd 2A **162**
Dyce Cl. B35: Cas V 3E **87**
Dymoke St. B12: Birm 3H **117**
Dynes Wlk. B67: Smeth 4E **99**
Dyott Rd. B13: Mose 4A **134**
Dyson Cl. WS2: Wals 6F **31**
Dyson Gdns. B8: Salt 4E **103**

E

Eachelhurst Rd. B24: Erd 3C **86**
  B76: Walm 3C **86**
Eachus Rd. WV14: Cose 5F **61**
EACHWAY 3F **157**
Eachway B45: Rub 3F **157**
Eachway Farm Cl. B45: Redn 3G **157**
Eachway La. B45: Redn 3G **157**
Eadgar Ct. B43: Gt Barr 6H **65**
Eagle Cl. B65: Row R 5H **95**
  DY1: Dud 1B **94**
  WS6: C Hay 3D **6**
Eagle Ct. WV3: Wolv 5E **43**
Eagle Ct. Bus. Pk.
  B26: Sheld 1A **138**
Eagle Cft. B14: K Hth 5G **147**
Eagle Gdns. B24: Erd 5G **85**
Eagle Gro. B36: Cas B 1C **106**
Eagle Ind. Est. DY4: Tip 6E **63**
Eagle La. DY4: Tip 1D **78**
Eagle St. DY4: Tip 1C **78**
  WV2: Wolv 3A **44**
  WV3: Wolv 4E **43**
Eagle Trad. Est. B63: Hale 1A **128**
Ealing Gro. B44: K'sdng 4A **68**
Eanwulf Ct. B15: Edg 3E **117**
Earlsbury Gdns. B20: Hand 6F **83**
Earls Ct. Rd. B17: Harb 5E **115**
Earls Ferry Gdns. B32: Bart G 6H **129**
Earlsmead Rd. B21: Hand 1G **99**
Earls Rd. WS4: Rus 2G **33**
Earlston Way B43: Gt Barr 5H **65**
Earl St. B70: W Brom 3H **79**
  DY6: K'wfrd 5B **92**
  WS1: Wals 4B **48**
  WV14: Bils 6F **45**
  WV14: Cose 5F **61**
Earls Way B63: Hale 1B **128**
Earlswood Ct. B20: Hand 5C **82**
Earlswood Cres. WV9: Pend 4E **15**
Earlswood Dr. B74: S Cold 4A **54**
Earlswood Ho. B5: Birm 4G **117**
           (off Barrow Wlk.)

Earlswood Rd. B30: K Nor 4F **147**
  B93: Dorr 6F **167**
  DY6: K'wfrd 1C **92**
Easby Way B8: Salt 4E **103**
  WS3: Blox 5F **19**
Easenhall Cl. B93: Know 5C **166**
Easmore Cl. B14: K Hth 5F **147**
Eastacre WV13: W'hall 2A **46**
East Av. B69: Tiv 2C **96**
  WV11: Wed 3E **29**
Eastbourne Av. B34: Hodg H 3B **104**
Eastbourne St. WS4: Wals 6D **32**
Eastbrook Cl. B76: Walm 1B **70**
Eastbury Dri B92: Olton 2E **137**
Eastbury Dr. B92: Olton 2E **137**
E. Car Pk. Rd. B40: Nat E C 1H **139**
EASTCOTE 4H **153**
Eastcote Cl. B90: Shir 4B **150**
Eastcote La. B92: H Ard 4H **153**
Eastcote Rd. B27: A Grn 4G **135**
  WV10: Wolv 4B **28**
East Cft. Rd. WV4: Penn 1A **58**
Eastdean Cl. B23: Erd 1D **84**
East Dr. B5: Edg 1E **133**
Eastern Av. DY5: Brie H 1F **109**
Eastern Cl. WS10: Mox 2C **62**
Eastern Rd. B29: S Oak· 2D **132**
  B73: W Grn 4H **69**
Easterton Cft. B14: K Hth 5G **147**
Eastfield Cl. WS9: A'rdge 3C **34**
Eastfield Dr. B92: Sol 5A **138**
Eastfield Gro. WV1: Wolv 1B **44**
Eastfield Retreat WV1: Wolv 1B **44**
Eastfield Rd. B8: W End 5A **104**
  B9: Bord G 5A **104**
  DY4: Tip .5A **62**
  WV1: Wolv 1B **44**
East Ga. B16: Edg 6A **100**
East Grn. WV4: Penn 5B **42**
East Rd. B13: Mose 1C **148**
East Holme B9: Bord G 1C **118**
Easthope Rd. B33: Stech 5E **105**
Eastlake Cl. B43: Gt Barr 2F **67**
Eastlands Rd. B13: Mose 4A **134**
Eastleigh DY3: Sed 5G **59**
Eastleigh Cft. B76: Walm 6E **71**
Eastleigh Dr. B62: Roms 3A **142**
Eastleigh Gro. B25: Yard 3B **120**
East Meadway B33: Kitts G 1H **121**
East M. B44: Gt Barr 3F **67**
Eastmoor Cl. B74: S'tly 1B **52**
Eastney Cres. WV8: Pend 1C **26**
Easton Gdns. WV11: Wed 4H **29**
Easton Gro. B27: A Grn 4A **136**
  B47: H'wd 2B **162**
East Pk. Trad. Est. WV1: Wolv 3B **44**
East Pk. Way WV1: Wolv 2D **44**
East Pathway B17: Harb 5G **115**
East Ri. B75: S Cold 5B **54**
East Rd. B24: Erd 5B **86**
  DY4: Tip .5B **62**
  WV10: B'frd, F'stne 1C **16**
East St. DY2: Dud 1G **95**
  DY3: Gorn 4H **75**
  DY5: Quar B 3C **110**
  WS1: Wals 4D **48**
  WV1: Wolv 2A **44**
East Vw. Rd. B72: S Cold 2B **70**
Eastville B31: N'fld 4F **145**
Eastward Glen WV8: Bilb 6A **14**
East Way B17: Harb 5G **115**
Eastway B40: Nat E C 2H **139**
  B92: Bick 2H **139**
Eastwood Rd. B12: Bal H 6F **117**
  B43: Gt Barr 5A **66**
  DY2: Dud 3G **95**
Eatesbrook Rd. B33: Kitts G 6G **105**
Eathorpe Cl. B34: S End 3H **105**
Eaton Av. B70: W Brom 3G **79**
Eaton Cl. B74: S Cold 4H **53**
Eaton Cres. DY3: Gorn 4F **75**
Eaton Pl. DY6: K'wfrd 4C **92**
Eaton Ri. WV12: W'hall 3B **30**

Eaton Wood B24: Erd 4B 86
Eaton Wood Dr. B26: Yard 6B 120
Eaves Ct. Dr. DY3: Sed 4G 59
Eaves Grn. Gdns. B27: A Grn 6H 119
Ebenezer St. B70: W Brom 1F 79
WV14: Cose 5D 60
Ebley Rd. B20: Hand 3C 82
Ebmore Dr. B14: K Hth 5F 147
Ebrington Av. B92: Sol 2F 137
Ebrington Cl. B14: K Hth 3F 147
Ebrington Rd. B71: W Brom 1B 80
Ebrook Rd. B72: S Cold 1A 70
EBSTREE 1C 56
Ebstree Mdw. WV5: Seis 3A 56
Ebstree Rd. WV4: Try 3A 56
WV5: Seis, Try 3A 56
Ebury Rd. B30: K Nor 3D 146
Eccleshall Av. WV10: Oxl 1F 27
Eccleston Cl. B75: S Cold 6D 54
Ecclestone Rd. WV11: Wed 1A 30
Echo Way WV4: E'shll 1C 60
Eckersall Rd. B38: K Nor 4A 146
Eckington Wlk. B38: K Nor 2A 160
Eclipse Ind. Est. DY4: Tip 2G 77
Edale Cl. DY6: K'wfrd 2H 91
WV4: E'shll 2A 60
Edale Rd. B42: Gt Barr 6E 67
Eddish Rd. B33: Kitts G 6F 105
Eddison Rd. B46: Col 3G 89
Edelweiss Cl. WS5: Wals 2F 65
Edenbridge Rd. B28: Hall G 5G 135
Edenbridge Vw. DY1: Dud 4A 76
Eden Cl. B31: Longb 1C 158
B69: Tiv .5D 78
Edencroft B15: Edg 3E 117
Edendale Rd. B26: Sheld 5F 121
Eden Gdns. B65: Row R 1B 112
DY3: Sed 5A 60
Eden Gro. B37: Chel W 2F 123
B71: W Brom 2B 80
Edenhall Rd. B32: Quin 5H 113
Eden Ho. DY8: Stourb 6E 109
Edenhurst Rd. B31: Longb 3D 158
Eden Pl. B3: Birm 4C 4 (1F 117)
Eden Rd. B92: Sol 2H 137
Edensor Cl. WV10: Wolv 5A 28
EDGBASTON 6C 116
Edgbaston .6F 117
Edgbaston Archery & Lawn Tennis Society
. . . . .4B 116
Edgbaston Pk. Rd. B15: Edg 6C 116
Edgbaston Priory Club 5E 117
Edgbaston Rd. B5: Edg 6F 117
B12: Bal H 1G 133
B66: Smeth 5E 99
Edgbaston Rd. E. B12: Bal H 6H 117
Edgbaston Shop. Cen. B16: Edg 3C 116
Edgbaston St. B5: Birm 6E 5 (2G 117)
Edgcombe Rd. B28: Hall G 4F 135
Edge Hill Av. WV10: Bush 5C 16
WV6: Pert 6E 25
Edge Hill Dr. DY3: Sed 3G 59
Edgehill Rd. B31: Longb 1E 159
Edgemond Av. B24: Erd 3D 86
Edge St. WV14: Cose 5F 61
Edgewood Rd. B64: Old H 3H 111
Edgewood Rd. B38: K Nor 2A 160
B45: Redn 2H 157
Edgeworth Cl. WV12: W'hall 5C 30
Edgware Rd. B23: Erd 2D 84
Edinburgh Av. WS2: Wals 6E 31
Edinburgh Ct. B24: Erd 3B 86
Edinburgh Cres. DY8: Word 2A 108
Edinburgh Dr. WS4: Rus 2H 33
WV12: W'hall 3B 30
Edinburgh La. WS2: Wals 5G 31
Edinburgh Rd. B68: O'bry 3H 113
DY2: Dud 3F 95
WS5: Wals 3F 49
WV14: Bils 2H 61
Edison Ct. WV12: W'hall 2D 30
(off Huntington Rd.)
Edison Gro. B32: Quin 6B 114

Edison Rd. WS2: Wals 4G 31
Edison Wlk. WS2: Wals 4H 31
Edith Pope Ho. B42: Gt Barr 5F 67
Edith Rd. B66: Smeth 6F 99
Edith St. B70: W Brom 4H 79
Edmonds Cl. B33: Kitts G 1F 121
Edmonds Ct. B10: Small H 4D 118
B26: Yard 4D 120
Edmonds Rd. B68: O'bry 1A 114
Edmonton Av. B44: K'sdng 4B 68
Edmonton Ho. B5: Edg 4F 117
Edmoor Cl. WV12: W'hall 3C 30
Edmund Rd. B8: Salt 5D 102
DY3: Up Gor 1A 76
Edmund St. B3: Birm 3C 4 (6F 101)
Ednam Cl. B71: W Brom 5D 64
Ednam Gro. WV5: Wom 6G 57
Ednam Rd. DY1: Dud 6E 77
WV4: Penn 5G 43
Edsome Way B36: Hodg H 1D 104
Edstone Cl. B30: K Nor 4F 147
B93: Dorr 5B 166
Edstone M. B36: Hodg H 1D 104
Edward Av. WS9: A'rdge 2C 34
Edward Cl. WV14: Bils 2G 61
Edward Ct. B16: Edg 2G 115
B76: Walm 2D 70
WS1: Wals 3E 49
Edward Fisher Dr. DY4: Tip 2A 78
Edwardian Cl. B90: Shir 2B 150
Edward Rd. B5: Edg 5F 117
B12: Bal H 5F 117
B14: K Hth 6H 147
B46: Wat O 4E 89
B63: Hale 1H 127
B67: Smeth 5D 98
B68: O'bry 3A 114
DY4: Tip 6A 62
WV6: Pert 4E 25
Edwards Rd. B24: Erd 2G 85
B75: R'ley 6B 38
DY2: Neth 5E 95
Edward St. B1: Birm 4A 4 (1D 116)
B68: O'bry 5G 97
B70: W Brom 4A 80
DY1: Dud 6D 76
WS2: Wals 6H 31
WS10: Darl 5E 47
WV4: E'shll 5B 44
Edwin Phillips Dr.
B71: W Brom 5H 63
Edwin Rd. B30: Stir 6D 132
Edwinstowe Cl. DY5: Quar B 1C 110
Eel St. B69: O'bry 2F 97
Effingham Rd. B13: Mose 1C 148
Egbert Cl. B6: Aston 1B 102
Egelwin Cl. WV6: Pert 4E 25
Egerton Rd. B24: Erd 4B 86
B74: S'tly 2H 51
WV10: Bush 4A 16
EGG HILL 4H 143
Egghill La. B31: N'fld 3G 143
B32: Fran 3G 143
B45: Fran 3G 143
Eggington Rd. DY8: Woll 4B 108
Egginton Rd. B28: Hall G 2E 149
Egmont Gdns. WV11: Wed 3H 29
Eileen Gdns. B37: K'hrst 5B 106
Eileen Rd. B11: S'hll 2B 134
Elan Cl. DY3: Lwr G 4H 75
Elan Rd. B31: Longb 5A 144
DY3: Sed 5G 59
Elbow St. B64: Old H 1H 111
Elbury Cft. B93: Know 4B 166
Elcock Dr. B42: P Barr 2F 83
Eldalade Way WS10: W'bry 3B 64
Elderberry Cl. DY8: Stourb 2A 124
WS5: Wals 2D 64
Elderfield B33: Sheld 3F 121
Elderfield Rd. B30: K Nor 4D 146
Elder Gro. WV5: Wom 1F 73
Eldersfield Gro. B91: Sol 2F 165
Elderside Cl. WS8: Bwnhls 5B 10
Elder Way B23: Erd 5E 85

Eldon Ct. WS1: Wals 2D 48
(off Eldon St.)
Eldon Dr. B76: Walm 6C 70
Eldon Rd. B16: Edg 2B 116
B62: Quin 2G 129
Eldon St. WS1: Wals 2D 48
WS10: Darl 4D 46
Eldridge Cl. WV9: Pend 5D 14
Eleanor Rd. WV14: Bils 5F 45
Electra Pk. B6: Witt 6B 84
Electric Av. B6: Witt 6B 84
Elford Cl. B14: K Hth 2G 147
B73: S'tly 1A 52
Elford Gro. B37: Mars G 2D 122
WV14: Bils 1E 61
Elford Rd. B17: Harb 2F 131
B71: W Brom 4C 64
Elgar Ct. B15: Edg 4C 116
Elgar Cres. DY5: P'ntt 2H 93
Elgar Ho. B16: Birm 1D 116
Elgin Cl. DY3: Sed 4A 60
DY8: Amb 4E 109
Elgin Ct. WV6: Pert 5E 25
Elgin Rd. WS3: Blox 3G 19
Eligin Gro. B25: Yard 4A 120
Eliot Cft. WV14: Cose 3F 61
Eliot St. B7: Nech 1C 102
Elisabeth Ct. B74: Four O 6H 37
Elizabeth Av. WS10: W'bry 2A 64
WV4: Penn 6F 43
WV14: Bils 2H 61
Elizabeth Ct. B17: Harb 1H 131
(off Metchley La.)
Elizabeth Cres. B68: O'bry 1B 114
Elizabeth Gro. B90: Shir 5A 150
DY2: Dud 2H 95
Elizabeth Ho. B76: Walm 2D 70
DY9: Lye 6H 109
WS5: Wals 4H 49
Elizabeth M. B69: Tiv 5A 78
Elizabeth Prout Gdns. B65: B'hth 2B 112
Elizabeth Rd. B13: Mose 3E 133
B33: Stech 6A 104
B63: Hale 2H 127
B70: W Brom 3D 78
B73: New O 1C 68
WS5: Wals 4F 49
Elizabeth Wlk. DY4: Tip 4A 62
Elkington Cft. B90: M'path 4E 165
Elkington St. B6: Aston 4G 101
Elkstone Cl. B92: Olton 2F 137
Elkstone Covert B14: K Hth 5E 147
Elland Gro. B27: A Grn 3A 136
Ellards Dr. WV11: Wed 4H 29
Ellen St. B18: Hock 5C 100
(not continuous)
Ellenvale Cl. WV14: Cose 5C 60
Ellerby Gro. B24: Erd 3C 86
Ellerside Gro. B31: N'fld 5D 144
Ellerslie Cl. DY5: Quar B 3H 109
Ellerslie Rd. B13: Mose 6C 134
Ellerton Rd. B44: K'sdng 4B 68
Ellerton Wlk. WV10: Wolv 4B 28
Ellesborough Rd. B17: Harb 3F 115
Ellesmere Rd. B8: Salt 5D 102
Ellice Dr. B36: Cas B 2D 106
Elliott Gdns. B45: Redn 4A 158
Elliott Rd. B29: S Oak 4A 132
Elliotts La. WV8: Cod 4G 13
Elliotts Rd. DY4: Tip 2G 77
Elliott Way B6: Witt 3G 83
Elliot Way B6: Witt 4H 83
Ellis Av. DY5: Brie H 1E 109
Ellison St. B70: W Brom 6A 80
Ellis St. B1: Birm 6C 4 (2F 117)
Elliston Av. B44: Gt Barr 5G 67
Ellowes Rd. DY3: Lwr G 3G 75
Elm Av. B12: Bal H 6A 118
WS10: W'bry 1F 63
WV11: Wed 1D 28
WV14: Bils 5F 45
Elmay Rd. B26: Sheld 4E 121
Elm Bank B13: Mose 2A 134
Elmbank Gro. B20: Hand 2A 82

Elmbank Rd. WS5: Wals 1G 65
Elmbridge Cl. B63: Crad 6F 111
Elmbridge Dr. B90: M'path 3F 165
Elmbridge Rd. B44: K'sdng 1G 83
Elmbridge Way B31: N'fld 5H 145
. . . . . DY3: Sed 1A 76
Elm Cl. DY3: Gorn 5F 75
. . . . . DY8: Stourb 3B 124
Elm Ct. B13: Mose 1H 133
. . . . . B66: Smeth 1A 98
. . . . . WS1: Wals 3E 49
Elm Cres. DY4: Tip 1H 77
Elm Cft. B68: O'bry 4A 114
Elmcroft B66: Smeth 4G 99
Elmcroft Av. B32: Bart G 4G 129
Elmcroft Gdns. WV10: Bush 4A 16
Elmcroft Rd. B26: Yard 4D 120
Elmdale B62: Quin 4G 113
Elmdale Cres. B31: N'fld 2C 144
Elmdale Dr. WS9: A'rdge 1E 35
Elmdale Gro. B31: N'fld 3C 144
Elmdale Rd. WV4: Penn 6E 43
. . . . . WV14: Cose 6C 60
ELMDON 3B 138
Elmdon Cl. B92: Sol 3H 137
. . . . . WV10: Oxl 6E 15
Elmdon Coppice B92: Sol 6B 138
Elmdon Ct. B29: W Cas 6G 131
. . . . (off Abdon Av.)
. . . . . B37: Mars G 4C 122
ELMDON HEATH 1A 152
Elmdon La. B26: Birm A 2C 138
. . . . . B37: Mars G 4B 122
Elmdon Pk. 3A 138
Elmdon Pk. Rd. B92: Sol 3H 137
Elmdon Rd. B27: A Grn 1B 136
. . . . . B29: S Oak 3C 132
. . . . . B37: Mars G 4C 122
. . . . . WV10: Oxl 6E 15
Elmdon Trad. Est. B37: Mars G 6E 123
Elm Dr. B31: Longb 6A 144
. . . . . B43: Gt Barr 4H 65
. . . . . B62: B'hth 2E 113
Elm Farm Av. B33: Mars G 4B 122
Elm Farm Rd. WV2: Wolv 4H 43
Elmfield Av. B24: Erd 3D 86
Elmfield Cres. B13: Mose 3H 133
Elmfield Rd. B36: Cas B 2A 106
Elmfield Vw. DY1: Dud 4C 76
Elm Grn. DY1: Dud 2C 76
Elm Gro. B37: K'hrst 3B 106
. . . . . CV7: Bal C 6H 169
. . . . . WV8: Bilb 4G 13
Elmhurst Av. B65: Row R 6C 96
Elmhurst Dr. DY6: K'wfrd 5D 92
. . . . . WS7: Chase 1C 10
Elmhurst Rd. B21: Hand 6A 82
Elmley Cl. WV14: Cose 6D 60
Elmley Gro. B30: K Nor 5D 146
. . . . . WV6: Pert 6F 25
Elm Lodge B92: H Ard 6A 140
Elmore Cl. B37: F'bri 5C 106
Elmore Grn. Cl. WS3: Blox 1H 31
Elmore Grn. Rd. WS3: Blox 6G 19
Elmore Rd. B33: Kitts G 6E 105
Elmore Row WS3: Blox 6H 19
Elm Rd. B30: B'vlle 5B 132
. . . . . B76: Walm 3D 70
. . . . . DY1: Dud 3E 77
. . . . . DY6: K'wfrd 3C 92
. . . . . WS3: Blox 3B 32
. . . . . WS11: Nort C 1F 9
Elms, The B16: Birm 6B 100
Elms Cl. B38: K Nor 1G 159
. . . . . B91: Sol 2H 151
Elmsdale WV6: Tett 1G 41
Elmsdale Ct. WS1: Wals 3D 48
Elms Rd. B15: Edg 1B 132
. . . . . B72: S Cold 2A 70
Elmstead Av. B33: Sheld 4H 121
Elmstead Cl. WS5: Wals 2A 50
Elmstead Twr. B5: Birm 4G 117
. . . . (off Berrington Wlk.)
Elmstead Wood WS5: Wals 2A 50

Elmstone Cl. DY1: Dud 3B 76
Elm St. WV3: Wolv 2E 43
. . . . . WV13: W'hall 1C 46
Elm Ter. B69: Tiv 6A 78
Elm Tree Cl. WV5: Wom 2F 73
Elm Tree Gro. B63: Crad 5F 111
Elm Tree Ri. B92: H Ard 1A 154
Elm Tree Rd. B17: Harb 5E 115
. . . . . B30: Stir 1C 146
Elmtree Rd. B74: S'tly 3F 51
Elm Tree Way B64: Old H 2H 111
Elmwood Av. WV11: Ess 4A 18
Elmwood Cl. B5: Edg 5F 117
. . . . . CV7: Bal C 6H 169
Elmwood Ct. B73: S'tly 6A 52
Elmwood Gdns. B20: Hand 5D 82
Elmwood Gro. B47: H'wd 3A 162
Elmwood Ri. DY3: Sed 4F 59
Elmwood Rd. B24: Erd 5A 86
. . . . . B74: S'tly 6A 52
. . . . . DY8: Word 6A 92
Elmwoods B32: Bart G 3H 129
Elphinstone End B24: Erd 1A 86
Elsma Rd. B68: O'bry 3A 114
Elston Hall La. WV10: Bush 6H 15
Elstree Rd. B23: Erd 2D 84
Elswick Gro. B44: K'sdng 5B 68
Elswick Rd. B44: K'sdng 4B 68
Elsworth Gro. B25: Yard 5A 120
Elsworth Rd. B31: N'fld 5H 145
Eltham Gro. B44: K'sdng 4B 68
Elton Cl. WV10: Bush 3A 16
Elton Cft. B93: Dorr 5B 166
Elton Gro. B27: A Grn 3G 135
Eltonia Cft. B26: Sheld 5F 121
Elva Cft. B36: Cas B 6B 88
Elvaston Way B90: Dic H 4F 163
Elvers Grn. La. B93: Know 3G 167
Elvetham Rd. B15: Edg 4E 117
Elvetham Rd. Nth. B15: Birm 3E 117
Elviron Dr. WV6: Tett 4H 25
Elwell Cres. DY1: Dud 1B 76
Elwells Cl. WV14: Cose 2C 60
Elwell St. B70: W Brom 2F 79
. . . . . WS10: W'bry 2H 63
Elwyn Rd. B73: S Cold 2G 69
Ely Cl. B37: Chel W 1D 122
. . . . . B65: Row R 5E 97
Ely Cres. B71: W Brom 6H 63
Ely Gro. B32: Quin 1D 130
Ely Pl. WS2: Wals 2H 47
Ely Rd. WS2: Wals 2H 47
Emay Cl. B70: W Brom 5F 63
Embankment, The DY5: Brie H 6A 94
Embassy Dr. B15: Edg 3C 116
. . . . . B69: O'bry 1E 97
Embassy Rd. B69: O'bry 1E 97
Embleton Gro. B34: Hodg H 3E 105
Emerald Ct. B8: W End 4A 104
. . . . . B92: Olton 4D 136
Emerson Cl. DY3: Lwr G 3E 75
Emerson Gro. WV10: Bush 1B 28
Emerson Rd. B17: Harb 5G 115
. . . . . WV10: Bush 6B 16
Emery Cl. B23: Erd 6D 84
. . . . . WS1: Wals 3D 48
Emery Ho. B23: Erd 1C 84
Emery St. WS1: Wals 3D 48
Emily Gdns. B16: Birm 6B 100
Emily Rd. B26: Yard 5B 120
Emily St. B12: Birm 3H 117
. . . . . B70: W Brom 5H 79
Emmanuel Rd. B73: W Grn 6H 69
Emmeline St. B9: Birm 2B 118
Empire Cl. WS9: A'rdge 1B 34
Empire Ind. Pk. WS9: A'rdge 1B 34
Empress Way WS10: Darl 3D 46
Emscote Dr. B73: W Grn 6H 69
Emscote Grn. B91: Sol 5C 150
Emscote Rd. B6: Aston 6H 83
Emsworth Cres. WV9: Pend 5E 15
Emsworth Gro. B14: K Hth 1F 147
Enderby Cl. B93: Ben H 5B 166

Enderby Dr. WV4: Penn 1D 58
Enderley Cl. WS3: Blox 4H 19
Enderley Dr. WS3: Blox 4H 19
End Hall Rd. WV6: Tett 6G 25
Endhill Rd. B44: K'sdng 1A 68
Endicott Rd. B6: Aston 6H 83
Endmoor Gro. B23: Erd 1D 84
Endsleigh Gro. B28: Hall G 5G 135
Endwood Cl. B20: Hand 5C 82
Endwood Ct. Rd. B20: Hand 5C 82
Endwood Dr. B74: Lit As 5C 36
. . . . . B91: Sol 5D 150
Energy Way B10: Small H 5F 119
. . . . (not continuous)
Enfield Cl. B23: Erd 1F 85
Enfield Ct. B29: W Cas 6G 131
. . . . (off Abdon Av.)
Enfield Rd. B15: Edg 3D 116
. . . . . B65: Row R 6D 96
Enford Cl. B34: S End 3H 105
Engine La. DY9: Lye 5H 109
. . . . . WS8: Bwnhls 5F 9
. . . . . WS10: Mox 1A 62
Engine St. B66: Smeth 3F 99
. . . . . B69: O'bry 3G 97
Englestede Cl. B20: Hand 4B 82
Englewood Dr. B28: Hall G 5G 135
Ennerdale Cl. WS8: Clay 6A 10
Ennerdale Dr. B63: Hale 3F 127
. . . . . WV6: Pert 5F 25
Ennerdale Rd. B43: Gt Barr 1B 82
. . . . . WV6: Tett 1B 26
Ennersdale Bungs. B46: Col 6H 89
Ennersdale Cl. B46: Col 6H 89
Ennersdale Rd. B46: Col 6H 89
Ensall Dr. DY8: Word 2C 108
Ensbury Cl. WV12: W'hall 5D 30
Ensdale Row WV13: W'hall 2A 46
Ensdon Gro. B44: K'sdng 4B 68
Ensford Cl. B74: Four O 4E 37
Enstone Rd. B23: Erd 6G 69
. . . . . DY1: Dud 1B 94
Enterprise Dr. B74: S'tly 4G 51
. . . . . DY9: Lye 5C 110
Enterprise Gro. WS3: Pels 2F 21
Enterprise Ho. B23: Erd 2G 85
Enterprise Trad. Est. DY5: Brie H 6B 94
Enterprise Way B7: Birm 5H 101
Enville Cl. B37: Mars G 2D 122
. . . . . WS3: Blox 4G 19
Enville Comn. Rd. DY3: Stourt 5A 90
. . . . . DY7: Stourt 5A 90
Enville Gro. B11: S'brk 6D 118
Enville Pl. DY8: Stourb 6D 108
. . . . (off Short St.)
Enville Rd. DY3: Lwr G 3H 75
. . . . . DY6: W Hth 1G 91
. . . . . WV4: Penn 1A 58
Enville St. DY8: Stourb 6D 108
Epping Cl. B45: Fran 5H 143
. . . . . WS3: Wals 3D 32
Epping Gro. B44: K'sdng 6A 68
Epsom Cl. WV6: Pert 5F 25
Epsom Ct. B29: W Cas 6G 131
Epsom Gro. B44: K'sdng 5B 68
Epwell Gro. B44: K'sdng 1H 83
Epwell Rd. B44: K'sdng 1H 83
Epworth Ct. DY5: P'ntt 4F 93
Equipoint B25: Yard 4B 120
Erasmus Rd. B11: S'brk 4A 118
Ercall Cl. B23: Erd 1A 84
ERDINGTON 3G 85
Erdington Court Sports Club 5F 69
Erdington Fire Station B24: Erd 2G 85
. . . . (off Orphange Rd.)
Erdington Hall Rd. B24: Erd 5E 85
Erdington Ind. Pk. B24: Erd 3D 86
Erdington Rd. WS9: A'rdge 5D 34
Erdington Station (Rail) 2F 85
Erdington Swimming Pool & Turkish Suite
. . . . .3G 85
Erica Cl. B29: W Cas 5E 131
Erica Rd. WS5: Wals 2F 65
Ermington Cres. B36: Hodg H 1C 104

Ermington Rd. WV4: Penn 6H 43
Ernest Clarke Cl. WV12: W'hall 5C 30
Ernest Rd. B12: Bal H 1B 134
  B67: Smeth 3C 98
  DY2: Dud 6H 77
Ernest St. B1: Birm 6C 4 (2F 117)
Ernsford Cl. B93: Dorr 6G 167
Erskine St. B7: Birm 5B 102
Esher Rd. B44: Gt Barr 1H 67
  B71: W Brom 1B 80
Eskdale Cl. WV1: Wolv 1C 44
Eskdale Wlk. DY5: Brie H 3F 109
Esme Rd. B11: S'hll 1B 134
Esmond Cl. B30: B'vlle 2H 145
Esporta Health & Fitness
  Birmingham 2C 116
  Wolverhampton 5H 43
Essendon Gro. B8: W End 5H 103
Essendon Rd. B8: W End 5H 103
Essendon Wlk. B8: W End 5H 103
Essex Av. B71: W Brom 6A 64
  DY6: K'wfrd 4H 91
  WS10: W'bry 1A 64
Essex Ct. B29: W Cas 6G 131
Essex Gdns. DY8: Woll 4B 108
Essex Ho. WV1: Wolv 5G 27
  (off Lomas St.)
Essex Rd. B75: R'ley 2B 54
  DY2: Dud 3C 94
Essex St. B5: Birm 6D 4 (2F 117)
  WS2: Wals 4C 32
ESSINGTON .4A 18
Essington Cl. DY8: Word 2C 108
Essington Ho. B8: W End 4G 103
Essington Ind. Est. WV11: Ess 3H 17
Essington St. B16: Birm 2D 116
Essington Way WV1: Wolv 2D 44
Este Rd. B26: Yard 3E 121
Estone Wlk. B6: Aston 2H 101
Estria Rd. B15: Edg 4D 116
Estridge La. WS6: Gt Wyr 3G 7
Ethelfleda Ter. WS10: W'bry 2F 63
Ethelred Cl. B74: Four O 6G 37
Ethel Rd. B17: Harb 6H 115
Ethel St. B2: Birm 4D 4 (1F 117)
  B67: Smeth 1D 114
  B68: O'bry 5G 97
Etheridge Rd. WV14: Bils 4E 45
Eton Cl. DY3: Sed 6B 60
Eton Ct. B74: Four O 1F 53
  (off Vesey Cl.)
Eton Dr. DY8: Stourb 2E 125
Eton Rd. B12: Bal H 1B 134
Etruria Way WV14: Bils 4G 45
Etta Gro. B44: Gt Barr 1H 67
ETTINGSHALL 6C 44
ETTINGSHALL PARK 1A 60
Ettingshall Pk. Farm La. WV4: E'shll 1A 60
Ettingshall Rd. WV2: E'shll 4C 44
  WV14: Cose 3C 60
Ettington Cl. D03: Dorr 6F 167
Ettington Rd. B6: Aston 1G 101
Ettymore Cl. DY3: Sed 5H 59
Ettymore Rd. DY3: Sed 5H 59
Ettymore Rd. W. DY3: Sed 5G 59
Etwall Rd. B28: Hall G 2E 149
Euan Cl. B17: Harb 3G 115
Euro Bus. Pk. B69: O'bry 6D 78
Euro Ct. B13: Mose 3B 134
Europa Av. B70: W Brom 5D 80
  (not continuous)
European Bus. Pk. B69: O'bry 2E 97
Euroway Pk. B69: O'bry 1A 98
Evans Cl. DY4: Tip 2E 77
Evans Gdns. B29: S Oak 4H 131
Evans Pl. WV14: Bils 4G 45
Evans St. WV6: Wolv 5E 27
  WV13: W'hall 2F 45
  WV14: Cose 4B 60
Eva Rd. B18: Win G 3H 99
  B68: O'bry 6A 98
Evason Ct. B6: Aston 6G 83
EVE HILL 5D 76
Eve La. DY1: Dud 2B 76

Evelyn Cft. B73: Bold 5G 69
Evelyn Rd. B11: S'hll 1C 134
Evenlode Cl. B92: Olton 2F 137
Evenlode Gro. WV13: W'hall 2D 46
Evenlode Rd. B92: Olton 2E 137
Everest Rd. B20: Hand 4C 82
  WS2: Wals 6F 31
Evergreen Cl. WV14: Cose 5D 60
Everit Dr. B93: Know 3C 166
Eversley Dale B24: Erd 5G 85
Eversley Gro. DY3: Sed 3G 59
  WV11: Wed 3E 29
Eversley Rd. B9: Small H 2D 118
  (not continuous)
Evers St. DY5: Quar B 3C 110
Everton Rd. B8: W End 5A 104
Eves Cft. B32: Bart G 4A 130
Evesham Cres. WS3: Blox 4F 19
Evesham Ri. DY2: Neth 6F 95
Eveson Rd. DY8: Stourb 3B 124
Evolution DY8: Amb 3D 108
Ewart Rd. WS2: Wals 6E 31
Ewell Rd. B24: Erd 3H 85
Ewhurst Av. B29: S Oak 4B 132
  (Heeley Rd.)
  B29: S Oak 5C 132
  (Umberslade Rd.)
Ewhurst Cl. WV13: W'hall 3H 45
Exbury Cl. WV9: Pend 5D 14
Excelsior Gro. WS3: Pels 2F 21
Exchange, The WS3: Blox 6H 19
Exchange St. DY5: Brie H 5H 93
  WV1: Wolv 3B 170 (1G 43)
Exe Cft. B31: Longb 1F 159
Exeter Dr. B37: Mars G 3B 122
Exeter Pas. B1: Birm 2F 117
Exeter Pl. WS2: Wals 2I 47
Exeter Rd. B29: S Oak 3B 132
  B66: Smeth 4F 99
  DY2: Neth 1F 111
Exeter St. B1: Birm 6D 4 (2F 117)
Exford Cl. DY5: Brie H 4F 109
Exhall Cl. B91: Sol 5C 150
Exhall Ct. B23: Erd 5C 84
Exhibition Way B40: Nat E C 1F 139
Exmoor Grn. WV11: Wed 2E 29
Exon Cl. DY4: Tip 1H 77
Expressway, The B70: W Brom 3H 79
Exton Cl. WV11: Wed 1H 29
Exton Gdns. B66: Smeth 3H 99
  (off Foundry La.)
Exton Way B8: Salt 4D 102
Eyland Gro. WS1: Wals 1D 48
Eymore Cl. B29: W Cas 1F 145
Eyre St. B18: Hock 6C 100
Eyston Av. DY4: Tip 5D 62
Eyton Cft. B12: Birm 4H 117
Ezekiel La. WV12: W'hall 3C 30

F

Fabian Cl. B45: Fran 5F 143
Fabian Cres. B90: Shir 6H 149
Facet Rd. B38: K Nor 5C 146
Factory Est. B44: P Barr 1G 83
Factory Rd. B18: Hock 3B 100
  DY4: Tip .1G 77
Factory St. WS10: Darl 5C 46
Fairbourne Av. B44: Gt Barr 3G 67
  B65: Row R 5E 97
Fairbourn Twr. B23: Erd 1G 85
Fairburn Cres. WS3: Pels 2F 21
Faircroft Av. B76: Walm 1D 86
Faircroft Rd. B36: Cas B 6H 87
Fairdene Way B43: Gt Barr 5H 65
Fairfax Dr. B31: Longb 1F 159
Fairfax Rd. B31: Longb 1E 159
  B75: S Cold 6D 54
  WV10: Bush 5H 15
Fairfield Dr. B62: B'hth 2E 113
  WS3: Pels 3F 21
  WV8: Cod .3E 13
Fairfield Gro. B62: B'hth 2E 113

Fairfield Mt. WS1: Wals 3D 48
Fairfield Pk. Ind. Est. B62: B'hth 2E 113
Fairfield Pk. Rd. B62: B'hth 2E 113
Fairfield Ri. CV7: Mer 4H 141
  DY8: Woll 6A 108
Fairfield Rd. B14: K Hth 5G 133
  B62: B'hth 2E 113
  B63: Hale 3A 128
  DY2: Dud .2F 95
  DY8: Word 1D 108
Fairford Cl. B91: Shir 2B 150
Fairford Gdns. DY8: Word 6C 92
Fairford Rd. B44: K'sdng 1H 83
Fairgreen Gdns. DY5: P'ntt 4G 93
Fairgreen Way B29: S Oak 4B 132
  B74: S'tly .2A 52
Fairground Way WS1: Wals 3B 48
Fairhaven Cft. B62: B'hth 2E 113
Fairhills DY3: Sed 5H 59
Fairhill Way B11: S'brk 4B 118
Fairholme Rd. B36: Hodg H 2H 103
Fairlawn B15: Edg 4C 116
Fairlawn Cl. WV12: W'hall 6C 18
Fairlawn Dr. DY6: K'wfrd 5B 92
Fairlawns B26: Yard 2E 121
  B76: Walm 5E 71
Fairlawn Way WV12: W'hall 6C 18
Fairlie Cres. B38: K Nor 6H 145
Fairmead Ri. B38: K Nor 6A 146
Fairmile Rd. B63: Hale 5H 111
Fairoak Dr. WV6: Tett 6H 25
Fair Oaks Dr. WS6: Gt Wyr 5G 7
Fairview Av. B42: Gt Barr 1D 82
Fairview Cl. WS6: C Hay 3D 6
  WV11: Wed 3D 28
Fairview Ct. WS2: Wals 1D 46
Fairview Cres. DY6: K'wfrd 1D 92
  WV11: Wed 2D 28
Fairview Gro. WV11: Wed 2D 28
Fairview Ind. Est. B76: Curd 1D 88
Fairview Rd. DY1: Dud 4C 76
  WV4: Penn 1A 58
  WV11: Wed 2D 28
Fairway B31: N'fld 5C 144
  WS4: S'fld .6H 21
Fairway, The B38: K Nor 5H 145
Fairway Av. B69: Tiv 1A 96
Fairway Dr. B45: Rub 3F 157
Fairway Grn. WV14: Bils 4F 45
Fairway Rd. B68: O'bry 1F 113
Fairways, The B76: Walm 1D 86
Fairways Av. DY8: Stourb 3C 124
Fairways Cl. DY8: Stourb 3C 124
Fairyfield Av. B43: Gt Barr 4H 65
Fairyfield Ct. B43: Gt Barr 4H 65
Fakenham Cft. B17: Harb 4D 114
Falcon Cl. WS6: C Hay 3C 6
Falcon Cres. WV14: Cose 3B 60
Falcondale Rd. WV12: W'hall 6C 18
Falconhurst Rd. B29: S Oak 3G 131
FALCON LODGE 6F 55
Falcon Lodge Cres. B75: S Cold 6D 54
Falcon Pl. B69: Tiv 2C 96
Falcon Ri. DY8: Woll 5A 108
Falcon Rd. B68: O'bry 1F 113
Falcons, The B75: S Cold 6F 55
Falcon Vw. B30: K Nor 3C 146
Falcon Way DY1: Dud 6B 76
Falfield Cl. B65: Row R 3D 96
Falfield Gro. B31: Longb 2C 158
Falkland Cft. B30: Stir 1D 146
Falklands Cl. DY3: Swind 5E 73
Falkland Way B36: Cas B 4D 106
Falkwood Gro. B93: Know 3B 166
Fallindale Rd. B26: Sheld 5F 121
FALLINGS HEATH 5F 47
Fallings Heath Cl. WS10: Darl 4F 47
FALLINGS PARK 4B 28
Fallings Pk. Ind. Est. WV10: Wolv 4B 28
Fallow Fld. B74: Lit As 6B 36
Fallowfield B15: Edg 3A 116
  WV6: Pert .5D 24
  WV8: Pend 5C 14
Fallowfield Av. B28: Hall G 2F 149

Fallow Fld. Rd. B65: Row R 6A 96
Fallowfield Rd. B63: Hale 2F 127
  B92: Sol .3G 137
  WS5: Wals 3A 50
Fallows Ho. B19: Hock 4G 101
Fallows Rd. B11: S'brk 5C 118
Fallow Wlk. B32: Bart G 3G 129
Falmouth Rd. B34: Hodg H 4C 104
  WS5: Wals 4H 49
Falstaff Av. B47: H'wd 3A 162
Falstaff Cl. B76: Walm 6F 71
Falstaff Ct. B75: S Cold 6G 55
Falstaff Rd. B90: Shir 5H 149
Falstone Rd. B73: New O 3D 68
Fancott Rd. B31: N'fld 2E 145
Fancourt Av. WV4: Penn 1B 58
Fane Rd. WV11: Wed 4A 18
Fanshawe Rd. B27: A Grn 4A 136
Fanum Ho. B63: Hale 2B 128
Faraday Av. B32: Quin 6B 114
  B46: Col .2H 89
  B76: Curd 2G 89
Faraday Ct. B32: Quin 6B 114
Faraday Ho. B15: Birm 3E 117
Faraday Rd. WS2: Wals 3H 31
Faraday Wharf B7: Birm 5H 101
Farbrook Way WV12: W'hall 3B 30
Farclose Ho. B15: Edg 4E 117
Farcroft Av. B21: Hand 1H 99
Farcroft Gro. B21: Hand 6H 81
Farcroft Rd. B21: Hand 6H 81
Fareham Cres. WV4: Penn 5A 42
Farfield Cl. B31: N'fld 5F 145
Far High Dr. DY4: Tip 2B 78
Far Highfield B76: Walm 1B 70
Farhill Cl. B71: W Brom 5D 64
Farlands Dr. DY8: Stourb 2E 125
Farlands Gro. B43: Gt Barr 6B 66
Farlands Rd. DY8: Stourb 2E 125
Farleigh Dr. WV3: Wolv 3G 41
Farleigh Rd. WV6: Pert 6G 25
Farley Cen. B70: W Brom 5B 80
Farley La. B62: Roms 5A 142
Farley Rd. B23: Erd 3B 84
Farley St. DY4: Tip 2D 78
Farlow Cft. B37: Mars G 3B 122
Farlow Rd. B31: N'fld 4G 145
Farmacre B9: Birm 1B 118
Farm Av. B68: O'bry 6G 97
Farmbridge Cl. WS2: Wals 6D 30
Farmbridge Rd. WS2: Wals 6D 30
Farmbridge Way WS2: Wals 6D 30
Farmbrook Av. WV10: F'hses 4H 15
Farm Cl. B92: Sol 3G 137
  DY3: Sed .6F 59
  WV8: Bilb 5H 13
Farmcote Rd. B33: Stech 5E 105
Farmcroft Rd. DY9: W'cte 2A 126
Farmdale Gro. B45: Redn 3G 157
Farm End Cl. B71: W Brom 4D 64
Farmer Rd. B10: Small H 4G 119
Farmers Cl. B76: Walm 1C 70
Farmers Ct. B63: Hale 1H 127
Farmers Fold WV1: Wolv 3B 170
Farmers Wlk. B21: Hand 2H 99
Farmer Way DY4: Tip 4B 62
Farm Ho. La. B75: R'ley 6C 38
Farm Ho. Way B43: Gt Barr 1A 66
Farmhouse Way B90: M'path 2F 165
  WV12: W'hall 4E 31
Farmoor Gro. B34: S End 3A 106
Farmoor Way WV10: Bush 3A 16
Farm Rd. B11: S'brk 4B 118
  B65: Row R 5A 96
  B67: Smeth 6C 98
  B68: O'bry 6G 97
  DY2: Neth 6C 94
  DY4: Tip .6C 62
  DY5: Quar B 2A 110
  WV3: Wolv 3A 42
Farmside Cl. DY9: W'cte 2B 126
Farmside Grn. WV9: Pend 5D 14

Farmstead Cl. B75: R'ley 6B 38
  WS1: Wals 6C 48
Farmstead Rd. B92: Sol 3G 137
Farm St. B19: Hock 3E 101
  B70: W Brom 6A 80
  WS2: Wals 5C 32
Farnborough Ct. B75: Four O 1H 53
Farnborough Dr. B90: M'path 3D 164
Farnborough Rd. B35: Cas V 5E 87
Farnbury Cft. B38: K Nor 5B 146
Farn Cl. B33: Stech 6D 104
Farncote Dr. B74: Four O 6F 37
Farndale Av. WV6: Wolv 4D 26
Farndale Cl. DY5: Brie H 5F 109
Farndon Av. B37: Mars G 4D 122
Farndon Rd. B8: Salt 5F 103
Farndon Way B23: Erd 5D 68
Farnham Cl. B43: Gt Barr 5B 66
Farnham Rd. B21: Hand 5H 81
Farnhurst Rd. B36: Hodg H 2H 103
Farnol Rd. B26: Yard 3D 120
Farnworth Gro. B36: Cas B 6A 88
Farquhar Rd. B13: Mose 2H 133
  B15: Edg 5B 116
Farquhar Rd. E. B15: Edg 5B 116
Farran Way B43: Gt Barr 6A 66
Farren Rd. B31: Longb 6B 144
Farrier Cl. B76: Walm 5D 70
Farrier Rd. B43: Gt Barr 2F 67
Farriers, The B26: Sheld 6F 121
Farriers Mill WS3: Pels 3C 20
Farrier Way DY6: W Hth 2G 91
Farringdon Ho. WS2: Wals 6B 32
                    (off Green La.)
Farringdon St. WS2: Wals 1B 48
Farrington Rd. B23: Erd 2B 84
  WV4: E'shll 2H 59
Farrow Rd. B44: Gt Barr 2G 67
Farthing Cl. B1: Birm 2A 4
Farthing La. B72: S Cold 1H 69
  B76: Curd 1E 89
Farthing Pools Cl. B72: S Cold 1A 70
Farthings, The B17: Harb 5H 115
Farthings La. DY2: Dud 2C 94
Farvale Rd. B76: Min 1G 87
Far Vw. WS9: A'rdge 5D 22
Farway Gdns. WV8: Cod 5F 13
Far Wood Rd. B31: N'fld 5C 130
Fashoda Rd. B29: S Oak 4D 132
Fastlea Rd. B32: Bart G 4B 130
Fastmoor Oval B33: Kitts G 2A 122
Fast Pits Rd. B25: Yard 3H 119
Fatherless Barn Cres. B63: Crad 1E 127
Faulkland Cres. WV1: Wolv . . .1C 170 (6H 27)
Faulkner Cl. DY8: Stourb 1D 124
Faulkner Rd. B92: Olton 4F 137
Faulkners Farm Dr. B23: Erd 1B 84
Faulknor Dr. DY5: P'ntt 2F 93
Faversham Cl. WS2: Wals 6D 30
  WV8: Pend 1C 26
Fawdry Cl. B73: S Cold 6H 53
Fawdry St. B9: Birm 1A 118
  B66: Smeth 4G 99
  WV1: Wolv 6F 27
Fawley Cl. WV13: W'hall 3H 45
Fawley Gro. B14: K Hth 2D 146
Fazeley St. B5: Birm 4G 5 (1H 117)
Fazeley St. Ind. Est.
  B5: Birm 4H 5 (1A 118)
Fearon Pl. B66: Smeth 4E 99
FEATHERSTONE 1D 16
Featherstone Cl. B90: Shir 5B 150
Featherstone Cres. B90: Shir 5B 150
Featherstone Rd. B14: K Hth 1G 147
Featherston Rd. B74: S'tly 1A 52
FEIASHILL 6B 56
Feiashill Cl. WV5: Try 6B 56
Feiashill Rd. WV5: Try 5B 56
Felbrigg Cl. DY5: Brie H 3G 109
Feldings, The B24: Erd 3A 86
Feldon La. B62: B'hth 4E 113
Felgate Cl. B90: M'path 1E 165
Fellbrook Cl. B33: Stech 5D 104
Fell Gro. B21: Hand 5G 81

Fellmeadow Rd. B33: Yard 1E 121
Fellmeadow Way DY3: Sed 1A 76
Fellows Av. DY6: W Hth 1A 92
Fellows La. B17: Harb 5E 115
Fellows Pk. Gdns. WS2: Wals 5H 47
Fellows Rd. WV14: Bils 4F 45
Fellows St. WV2: Wolv 3G 43
Felsted Way B7: Birm 5A 102
Felstone Rd. B44: Gt Barr 4G 67
Feltham Cl. B33: Kitts G 2A 122
Felton Cft. B33: Kitts G 6E 105
Felton Gro. B91: Sol 6F 151
Fenbourne Cl. WS4: S'fld 1G 33
Fenchurch Cl. WS2: Wals 5B 32
Fencote Av. B37: F'bri 5C 106
FEN END 6F 169
Fen End Rd. CV8: Fen E 6E 169
Fen End Rd. W. B93: Know 4B 168
  CV8: Fen E 5A 168
Fenmere Cl. WV4: Penn 6H 43
Fennel Cl. WS6: C Hay 2D 6
Fennel Cft. B34: S End 2F 105
Fennel Rd. DY5: Brie H 4G 109
Fennis Cl. B93: Dorr 6B 166
Fenn Ri. DY8: Word 6A 92
  WV12: W'hall 3B 30
Fens Cres. DY5: Brie H 4G 93
Fens Pool Av. DY5: Brie H 4H 93
Fensway, The B34: Stech 4E 105
Fenter Cl. B13: Mose 6H 117
Fentham Cl. B92: H Ard 1B 154
Fentham Ct. B92: Olton 5D 136
Fentham Grn. B92: H Ard 6A 140
Fentham Rd. B6: Aston 1F 101
  B23: Erd .4D 84
  B92: H Ard 1A 154
Fenton Rd. B27: A Grn 6H 119
  B47: H'wd 2A 162
Fenton St. B66: Smeth 2C 98
  DY5: Brie H 6H 93
Fenton Way B27: A Grn 1H 135
Fereday Rd. WS9: Wals W 4D 22
Fereday's Cft. DY3: Sed 6H 59
Fereday St. DY4: Tip 5H 61
Ferguson Dr. DY4: Tip 1B 78
Ferguson Rd. B68: O'bry 4B 98
Ferguson St. WV11: Wed 6A 18
Fern Av. DY4: Tip 6H 61
Fernbank Cl. B63: Hale 3F 127
Fernbank Cres. WS5: Wals 1G 65
Fernbank Rd. B8: W End 5G 103
Ferncliffe Rd. B17: Harb 1F 131
Fern Cl. WS4: S'fld 6G 21
  WV14: Cose 5D 60
Ferndale Av. B43: Gt Barr 6B 66
Ferndale Ct. B17: Harb 1H 131
               (off Metchley La.)
Ferndale Cres. B12: Birm 3A 118
  B46: Col .4H 107
Ferndale M. B46: Col 4H 107
Ferndale Pk. DY9: Pedm 5F 125
Ferndale Rd. B28: Hall G 5F 135
  B46: Col .4H 107
  B68: O'bry 2F 113
  B74: S'tly 3H 51
  CV7: Bal C 3F 169
  WV11: Ess 4B 18
Ferndene Rd. B11: Tys 2F 135
Ferndown Av. DY3: Sed 6G 59
Ferndown Cl. B26: Yard 2E 121
  WS3: Blox 3H 19
Ferndown Gdns. WV11: Wed 4H 29
Ferndown Rd. B91: Sol 1F 151
Fern Dr. WS6: Gt Wyr 1G 7
Fernfail Ct. B23: Erd 2E 85
Fernhill Ct. B23: Erd 5C 84
Fernhill Gro. B44: Gt Barr 2H 67
Fernhill La. CV7: Bal C 5F 169
  CV8: Fen E 5E 169
Fernhill Rd. B92: Olton 3C 136
Fernhurst Dr. DY5: P'ntt 2F 93
Fernhurst Rd. B8: Salt 6G 103
Fernleigh Ct. B91: Sol 2G 151
Fernleigh Gdns. DY8: Word 6A 92

Fernleigh Rd. WS4: Wals 6F 33
Fernley Av. B29: S Oak 3D 132
Fernley Rd. B11: S'hll 1C 134
Fern Leys WV3: Wolv 2B 42
Fern Rd. B24: Erd 3G 85
DY1: Dud 3E 77
WV3: Wolv 3F 43
Fernside Gdns. B13: Mose 2B 134
Fernside Rd. WV13: W'hall 6F 29
Fernwood Cl. B73: Bold 4E 69
Fernwood Cft. B14: K Hth 1G 147
DY4: Tip 3H 77
Fernwood Rd. B73: Bold 5E 69
Fernwoods B32: Bart G 3H 129
Ferrers Cl. B75: R'ley 1B 54
Ferrie Gro. WS8: Bwnhls 6A 10
Ferris Gro. B27: A Grn 4G 135
Festival Av. WS10: Darl 1C 62
Festival Ct. DY2: Neth 4E 95
Festival Way WV6: Wolv 4F 27
Fibbersley WV11: Wed 5H 29
WV13: W'hall 5H 29
Fibbersley Bank WV13: W'hall 5H 29
Fiddlers Grn. B92: H Ard 6A 140
Field Av. B31: N'fld 2D 144
Field Cl. B26: Sheld 5E 121
DY8: Word 1E 109
WS3: Blox 1A 32
WS4: S'fld 5F 21
Field Cott. Dr. DY8: Stourb 2F 125
Field Ct. WS4: S'fld 5F 21
Fieldfare WS7: Hamm 1F 11
Fieldfare Cl. B64: Old H 5H 95
Fieldfare Cft. B36: Cas B 1C 106
Fieldfare Rd. DY9: W'cte 1H 125
Fieldgate Trad. Est.
    WS1: Wals 2D 48
Field Head Pl. WV6: Tett 5H 25
Fieldhead Rd. B11: Tys 2G 135
Fieldhouse Rd. B25: Yard 3A 120
WV4: E'shll 1A 60
Fielding La B91. Sol 1F 165
    (not continuous)
Field La. B32: Bart G 5G 129
B91: Sol 1C 162
DY8: Stourb 2E 125
WS4: S'fld 5F 21
WS6: Gt Wyr 2F 7
Field Maple Rd. B74: S'tly 5H 51
Field M. DY2: Neth 6G 95
Fieldon Cl. B90: Shir 4A 150
Field Rd. DY2: Dud 6G 77
DY4: Tip 5H 61
WS3: Blox 1A 32
Field Rd. Ind. Est. WS3: Blox 1A 32
Fields, The WS10: Darl 3H 13
Fieldside Wlk. WV14: Bils 3F 45
Fieldstone Vw. DY3: Lwr G 3H 75
Field St. WV10: Wolv 6A 28
WV13: W'hall 1A 46
WV14: Bils 2G 61
Fieldview Cl. WV14: Cose 3G 61
Field Vw. Dr. B65: Row R 6F 97
Field Wlk. WS9: A'rdge 2D 34
Fieldways Cl. B47: H'wd 2A 162
Fifield Gro. B33: Yard 6D 104
Fifth Av. B9: Bord G 1F 119
DY5: Brie H 6B 94
WV10: Bush 2H 27
Filey Rd. WV10: Oxl 5F 15
Fillingham Cl. B37: Chel W 2F 123
Fillongley Rd. CV7: Mer 4H 141
Filton Cft. B35: Cas V 3E 87
Fimbrell Cl. DY5: Brie H 3E 109
Finbury Cl. B92: Olton 4D 136
Finchall Cft. B92: Sol 6A 138
Fincham Cl. WV9: Pend 4E 15
Finch Cl. B65: Row R 5H 95
Finch Cft. CV7: Bal C 2H 169
Finchdene Gro. WV3: Wolv 2B 42
Finch Dr. B74: S'tly 6A 52
Finches End B34: S End 4G 105
Finchfield Cl. DY8: Stourb 1A 124
Finchfield Gdns. WV3: Wolv 2C 42

Finchfield Hill WV3: Wolv 1A 42
    (not continuous)
Finchfield La. WV3: Wolv 3A 42
Finchfield Rd. WV3: Wolv 2C 42
Finchfield Rd. W. WV3: Wolv 2B 42
Finch Ho. DY4: Tip 2G 77
    (off Chapel St.)
Finchley Av. B19: Loz 1E 101
Finchley Cl. DY3: Lwr G 5H 75
Finchley Rd. B44: K'sdng 3B 68
Finchmead Rd. B33: Kitts G 2A 122
Finchpath Rd. B70: W Brom 1G 79
Finch Rd. B19: Loz 1E 101
Findlay Rd. B14: K Hth 4G 133
Findon Rd. B8: W End 3H 103
Finford Cft. CV7: Bal C 3H 169
Fingerpost Dr. WS3: Pels 2E 21
Finlarigg Dr. B15: Edg 5B 116
Finmere Rd. B28: Hall G 5F 135
Finmere Way B90: Shir 4B 150
Finnemore Rd. B9: Bord G 1G 119
Finneywell Cl. WV14: Cose 2D 60
Finsbury Dr. DY5: Brie H 4G 109
Finsbury Gro. B23: Erd 1D 84
Finstall Cl. B7: Birm 5A 102
B72: W Grn 4A 70
Finwood Cl. B92: Sol 5A 138
Fir Av. B12: Bal H 6A 118
Firbank Cl. B30: B'vlle 6A 132
Firbank Way WS3: Pels 5D 20
Firbarn Cl. B76: Walm 2B 70
Firbeck Gro. B44: K'sdng 4A 68
Firbeck Rd. B44: K'sdng 4A 68
Fir Cft. DY5: Brie H 3G 109
Fircroft B31: N'fld 5D 130
B91: Sol 1D 150
WV14: Bils 2A 62
Fircroft Ho. B37: Chel W 1C 122
Firecrest Cl. B23: Erd 6B 68
Fire Sta. Rd. B26: Birm A 6C 122
Fir Gro. B14: K Hth 2H 147
DY8: Woll 5A 108
WV3: Wolv 2E 43
Firhill Cft. B14: K Hth 5F 147
Firmstone Ct. DY8: Woll 4C 108
Firmstone St. DY8: Woll 4C 108
Firs, The B11: S'brk 5C 118
CV7: Mer 4H 141
Firsbrook Cl. WV6: Wolv 4D 26
Firsbrook Ho. WV6: Wolv 4E 27
Firsby Rd. B32: Quin 6C 114
Firs Cl. B67: Smeth 4E 99
Firs Dr. B90: Shir 6G 149
Firs Farm Dr. B36: Hodg H 1D 104
Firsholm Cl. B73: Bold 6G 69
Firs La. B67: Smeth 4E 99
Firs Rd. DY6: K'wfrd 3C 92
Firs St. DY2: Dud 6F 77
First Av. B6: Witt 5H 83
B9: Bord G 2E 119
B29: S Oak 2D 132
B76: Min 2E 87
DY6: P'ntt 6E 75
WS8: Bwnhls 5C 10
WV10: Bush 3A 28
First Exhibition Av. B40: Nat E C 1F 139
First Mdw. Piece B32: Quin 1C 130
Fir St. DY3: Sed 6D 58
Firsvale Rd. WV11: Wed 4H 29
Firsway WV6: Tett 1G 41
Firswood Rd. B33: Sheld 2G 121
Firth Dr. B14: Yard W 2B 148
B62: B'hth 3E 113
Firth Pk. Cres. B62: B'hth 3E 113
Firtree Cl. B44: Gt Barr 6G 67
Fir Tree Dr. DY3: Sed 6A 60
WS5: Wals 1F 65
Fir Tree Gro. B73: Bold 4F 69
Fir Tree Rd. WV3: Wolv 3B 42
Fir Tree Rd. B24: Erd 4H 85
Fisher Cl. B45: Fran 5E 143
Fisher Rd. B69: O'bry 2A 98
WS3: Blox 5F 19

Fishers Dr. B90: Dic H 4F 163
Fisher St. DY2: Dud 6F 77
DY4: Tip 4A 78
    (Dudley Port)
DY4: Tip 2D 78
    (Great Bridge)
DY5: Brie H 1F 109
WV3: Wolv 3F 43
WV13: W'hall 1C 46
FISHLEY .4A 20
Fishley Cl. WS3: Blox 3A 20
Fishley La. WS3: Blox, Lit Wyr 4B 20
Fishpool Cl. B36: Hodg H 1A 104
Fistral Gdns. WV3: Wolv 4D 42
Fithern Cl. DY3: Up Gor 2A 76
Fitness First
    Birmingham 5D 132
    Brierley Hill 6A 94
    Smethwick 2E 115
    Solihull 2F 137
    Sutton Coldfield 1H 53
    Walsall Wood 3C 22
    Wednesbury 3D 62
    Wolverhampton 6C 170
        (in AMF Bowling)
Fitters Mill Cl. B5: Edg 5G 117
Fitton Av. DY6: K'wfrd 4E 93
Fitzgerald Pl. DY5: Brie H 5F 109
Fitzguy Cl. B70: W Brom 6C 80
Fitzmaurice Rd. WV11: Wed 2H 29
Fitz Roy Av. B17: Harb 4D 114
Fitzroy Rd. B31: N'fld 4A 144
Five Flds. Rd. WV12: W'hall 4A 30
Five Oaks Rd. WV13: W'hall 3G 45
FIVE WAYS 3E 117
Five Ways B15: Birm 2D 116
B33: Stech 1B 120
DY3: Lwr G 4H 75
DY5: Brie H 1H 109
WV1: Wolv 5G 27
WV3: Penn 4A 42
Five Ways Cl. DY3: Lwr G 4H 75
Five Ways Shop. Cen. B15: Birm 2D 116
Five Ways Station (Rail) 3D 116
Flackwell Rd. B23: Erd 6E 69
Fladbury Cl. DY2: Neth 6F 95
Fladbury Cres. B29: S Oak 4H 131
Fladbury Gdns. B19: Hand 1E 101
Fladbury Pl. B19: Loz 2E 101
Flamborough Cl. B34: Hodg H 2E 105
Flamborough Way WV14: Cose 6D 60
Flanders Dr. DY6: K'wfrd 1B 92
Flash La. WV4: Lwr P 3E 57
Flash Rd. B69: O'bry 2G 97
Flatlea B31: N'fld 3D 144
Flatts, The WS10: Darl 4E 47
Flavell Av. WV14: Cose 4F 61
Flavell Cl. B32: Bart G 4H 129
Flavells La. B25: Yard 3A 120
DY3: Gorn 5F 76
Flavell St. DY1: Dud 1D 76
Flax Cl. B47: H'wd 4A 162
Flax Gdns. B38: K Nor 1B 160
Flaxhall St. WS2: Wals 3H 47
Flaxley Cl. B33: Stech 6D 104
Flaxley Parkway B33: Stech 5C 104
Flaxley Rd. B33: Kitts G, Stech 5B 104
Flaxton Gro. B33: Kitts G 5E 105
Flaxton Wlk. WV6: Wolv 4E 27
Flecknoe Cl. B36: Cas B 6G 87
Fledburgh Dr. B76: Walm 1B 70
Fleet St. B3: Birm 3B 4 (6E 101)
WV14: Bils 6F 45
Fleetwood Gro. B26: Yard 2E 121
Fleetwood Ho. B13: Mose 1H 133
Fleming Pl. WS2: Wals 3G 31
Fleming Rd. B32: Quin 6B 114
WS2: Wals 3G 31
    (not continuous)
Flemmynge Cl. WV8: Cod 3E 13
Fletcher Gro. B93: Know 5C 166
Fletcher Rd. WV12: W'hall 6D 18
Fletcher's La. WV13: W'hall 1C 46
Fletcher St. DY9: Lye 6B 110

Fletchers Wlk. B3: Birm 4B **4** (1E **117**)
Fletton Gro. B14: K Hth 4A **148**
Flinkford Cl. WS5: Wals 5H **49**
Flint Grn. Rd. B27: A Grn 2H **135**
Flintham Cl. B27: A Grn 2C **136**
Flint Ho. *WV1: Wolv* *5G* **27**
⁣ (off Lomas St.)
Flintway, The B33: Stech 5C **104**
Floodgate St. B5: Birm 6H **5** (2H **117**)
Flood St. DY2: Dud 1F **95**
Flood St. Island DY2: Dud 1F **95**
Flora Rd. B25: Yard 4H **119**
Florence Av. B11: S'hll 5C **118**
⁣ B73: W Grn 6H **69**
⁣ WV4: E'shll 1B **60**
Florence Bldgs. B29: S Oak 3B **132**
Florence Dr. B73: W Grn 6H **69**
Florence Gro. B18: Win G 5A **100**
⁣ B71: W Brom 4C **64**
Florence Rd. B14: K Hth 5H **133**
⁣ B21: Hand 1H **99**
⁣ B27: A Grn 1B **136**
⁣ B66: Smeth 5F **99**
⁣ B69: O'bry 2D **96**
⁣ B70: W Brom 6C **80**
⁣ B73: W Grn 6H **69**
⁣ DY4: Tip 6A **62**
⁣ WV8: Bilb 4A **14**
Florence St. B1: Birm 6C **4** (2F **117**)
⁣ WS1: Wals 2E **49**
Florian Gro. WS10: Darl 4E **47**
Florida Way DY6: K'wfrd 3E **93**
Flowerdale Cl. WV14: Cose 5D **60**
Floyd Gro. CV7: Bal C 5H **169**
Floyds La. WS4: Rus 3G **33**
Floyer Rd. B10: Small H 2E **119**
Flyford Cft. B29: W Cas 3D **130**
Foden Rd. B42: Gt Barr 5C **66**
Foel Gro. B31: N'fld 1C **144**
Foinavon Cl. B65: Row R 3H **95**
Fold, The B38: K Nor 6C **146**
⁣ WS10: Darl 5D **46**
⁣ WV4: Penn 1D **58**
⁣ WV5: Seis 3A **56**
⁣ WV8: Oaken 5D **12**
Fold St. WV1: Wolv 4A **170** (2G **43**)
Foldyard Cl. B76: Walm 5E **71**
Foley Av. WV6: Tett 6A **26**
Foley Chu. Cl. B74: S'tly 1A **52**
Foley Ct. B74: S'tly 2H **51**
Foley Dr. WV6: Tett 6A **26**
Foley Gro. WV5: Wom 2E **73**
Foley Ho. B68: O'bry 3H **113**
Foley Rd. B8: W End 4H **103**
⁣ DY9: Pedm 3F **125**
Foley Rd. E. B74: S'tly 2H **51**
Foley Rd. W. B74: S'tly 2F **51**
Foley St. WS10: W'bry 2G **63**
Foley Wood Cl. B74: S'tly 2G **51**
Foliot Flds. B25: Yard 3B **120**
Folkes Rd. DY9: Lye 5C **110**
Folkestone Cft. B36: Hodg H 1C **104**
Folliott Rd. B33: Kitts G 6E **105**
Follyhouse Cl. WS1: Wals 4D **48**
Follyhouse La. WS1: Wals 4D **48**
Fontley Cl. B26: Yard 2D **120**
Fontwell Rd. WV10: F'hses 3H **15**
Footherley La. WS14: Foot, Shen W . .1F **37**
FORDBRIDGE 6C **106**
Fordbridge Rd. B37: K'hrst 5B **106**
Ford Brook La. WS3: S'fld 5F **21**
Fordbrough, The B74: Four O 2G **53**
Forder Gro. B14: K Hth 5A **148**
Forde Way Gdns. B38: K Nor 2H **159**
Fordfield Rd. B33: Kitts G 5G **105**
Fordham Gro. WV9: Pend 4E **15**
Fordhouse La. B30: Stir 1D **146**
Fordhouse Rd. WV10: Bush 6H **15**
Fordhouse Rd. Ind. Est.
⁣ WV10: Bush 1H **27**
FORDHOUSES 5E **15**
Fordraught La. B62: Roms 3B **142**
Fordrift, The B37: Mars G 6C **122**
Fordrough B25: Yard 4F **119**

Fordrough, The B31: N'fld 6F **145**
⁣ B90: Maj G 1B **162**
Fordrough Av. B9: Bord G 6E **103**
Fordrough La. B9: Bord G 6E **103**
Fords Rd. B90: Maj G 2E **163**
Ford St. B18: Hock 4D **100**
⁣ B67: Smeth 3D **98**
⁣ WS2: Wals 4A **48**
Fordwater Rd. B74: S'tly 5H **51**
Foredraft Cl. B32: Bart G 3A **130**
Foredraft St. B63: Crad 6F **111**
Foredrove La. B92: Sol 1A **152**
Foreland Way WV3: Blox 2B **32**
Forest Cl. B66: Smeth 2C **98**
⁣ B74: S'tly 4G **51**
Forest Ct. B13: Mose 2A **134**
⁣ B93: Dorr 6B **166**
⁣ WV12: W'hall 1C **30**
Forest Dale B45: Redn 3H **157**
Forest Dr. B17: Harb 5H **115**
⁣ B64: Old H 1H **111**
Foresters Way B75: R'ley 6C **38**
Forest Ga. WV12: W'hall 1D **30**
Forest Glade WS6: C Hay 3F **7**
Forest Hill Rd. B26: Sheld 6G **121**
Forest La. WS2: Wals 4B **32**
Forest of Mercia Innovation Cen., The
⁣ 2H **9**
Forest Pk. B76: Walm 1C **70**
Forest Pl. WS3: Wals 3C **32**
Fore St. B2: Birm 4E **5** (1G **117**)
Forest Rd. B13: Mose 2A **134**
⁣ B25: Yard 5A **120**
⁣ B68: O'bry 4A **114**
⁣ B93: Dorr 6C **166**
⁣ DY1: Dud 3F **77**
Forest Way B47: H'wd 3B **162**
⁣ WS6: Gt Wyr 4G **7**
Forfar Wlk. B38: K Nor 5H **145**
Forge, The B63: Crad 3D **110**
Forge Cl. WS7: Hamm 1F **11**
⁣ WV8: Pend 6C **14**
Forge Cft. B76: Walm 1F **87**
Forge La. B62: Hale 6C **112**
⁣ B64: Crad H 3D **110**
⁣ B71: W Brom 6E **65**
⁣ B74: Foot, Lit As 3C **36**
⁣ B76: Min, Walm 1F **87**
⁣ (not continuous)
⁣ DY6: W Hth 1G **91**
⁣ WS9: A'rdge 4C **34**
⁣ (Birmingham Rd.)
⁣ WS9: A'rdge 2H **35**
⁣ (Mill La.)
⁣ WS14: Foot 1B **36**
Forge Leys WV5: Wom 1E **73**
Forge Mill Nature Reserve 6F **65**
Forge Rd. DY8: Stourb 5D **108**
⁣ (not continuous)
⁣ WS3: Pels 2D **20**
⁣ WS10: Darl 5C **46**
⁣ WV12: W'hall 5C **30**
Forgers Wlk. B42: Gt Barr 5D **66**
Forge St. WS10: Darl 1E **63**
Forge Trad. Est. B62: Hale 6C **112**
Forge Valley Way WV5: Wom 1E **73**
Forge Way B69: O'bry 3E **97**
FORHILL 5C **160**
Forhill Mnr. B38: Forh 6B **160**
Forman's Rd. B11: S'hll 2D **134**
Forman Trad. Est. B11: S'hll 2D **134**
Formby Av. WV6: Pert 5D **24**
Formby Way WS3: Blox 4G **19**
Forrell Gro. B31: Longb 2F **159**
Forrest Av. WV11: Ess 3A **18**
Forrester St. WS2: Wals 1A **48**
Forrester St. Pct. WS2: Wals 1A **48**
Forster St. B7: Birm 6A **102**
⁣ B67: Smeth 2C **98**
Forsythia Cl. B31: N'fld 5D **130**
Forsythia Gro. WV8: Bilb 4G **13**
Fort Cen., The 5F **87**
Fort Cres. WS9: Wals W 4C **22**
Fort Dunlop B24: Erd 6B **86**

Forth Dr. B37: F'bri 5D **106**
Forth Gro. B38: K Nor 1A **160**
Forth Way B62: B'hth 3E **113**
Fort Ind. Est., The B35: Cas V 6C **86**
Fortnum Cl. B33: Kitts G 1H **121**
Forton Cl. WV6: Tett 1H **41**
Fort Parkway B24: Erd 1H **103**
⁣ B35: Cas V 1H **103**
Fort Shop. Pk., The B24: Erd 6H **85**
Forum B40: Nat E C 2G **139**
Forward Rd. B26: Birm A 2C **138**
Fosbrooke Rd. B10: Small H 3G **119**
Fosseway Dr. B23: Erd 5E **69**
Fossil Dr. B45: Redn 2G **157**
Foster Av. WV14: Cose 4D **60**
Foster Gdns. B18: Hock 3B **100**
Foster Grn. WV6: Pert 6E **25**
Foster Pl. DY8: Woll 5C **108**
Foster Rd. WV10: Bush 3A **28**
Foster St. DY8: Stourb 6E **109**
⁣ WS3: Blox 1B **32**
⁣ WS10: Darl 4D **46**
Foster St. E. DY8: Stourb 6E **109**
Foster Way B5: Edg 6E **117**
⁣ (not continuous)
Fotherley Brook Rd. WS9: A'rdge . . .4H **35**
Foundry La. B66: Smeth 2G **99**
⁣ WS3: Pels 4C **20**
Foundry Rd. B18: Win G 4A **100**
⁣ DY6: W Hth 1H **91**
Foundry St. DY4: Tip 5G **61**
⁣ DY6: W Hth 1A **92**
⁣ WV14: Bils 1A **62**
⁣ WV14: Cose 4E **61**
Fountain Arc. DY1: Dud 6E **77**
Fountain Cl. B31: Longb 3C **158**
Fountain Ct. B4: Birm 2E **5**
⁣ B66: Smeth 5E **99**
Fountain Ho. B63: Hale 2B **128**
Fountain La. B69: O'bry 6F **79**
⁣ DY4: Tip 5F **61**
⁣ WV14: Cose 5F **61**
Fountain Rd. B17: Edg 2F **115**
Fountains Rd. WS3: Blox 5E **19**
Fountains Way WS3: Blox 5E **19**
Four Acres B32: Quin 1A **130**
Four Ashes Rd. B93: Ben H, Dorr . . .6H **165**
Four Crosses Rd. WS4: S'fld 6G **21**
Four Dwellings Leisure Cen. 1H **129**
Fourlands Av. B72: W Grn 6B **70**
Fourlands Rd. B31: N'fld 1C **144**
FOUR OAKS 6G **37**
Four Oaks Comn. Rd. B74: Four O . . .6E **37**
Four Oaks Ct. B74: Four O 2H **53**
FOUR OAKS PARK 3G **53**
Four Oaks Rd. B74: Four O 1G **53**
Four Oaks Station (Rail) 3H **53**
Four Stones Cl. B91: Sol 6E **151**
Four Stones Gro. B5: Edg 5G **117**
Fourth Av. B9: Bord G 1F **119**
⁣ B29: S Oak 2E **133**
⁣ WS8: Bwnhls 4C **10**
⁣ (not continuous)
⁣ WV10: Bush 3A **28**
Fourways B64: Crad H 2F **111**
Four Winds Rd. DY2: Dud 3G **95**
Fowey Cl. B76: Walm 6E **71**
Fowey Rd. B34: Hodg H 3D **104**
Fowgay Dr. B91: Sol 6D **150**
Fowler Cl. B66: Smeth 1E **99**
⁣ WV6: Pert 3E **25**
Fowler Rd. B75: S Cold 6E **55**
Fowler St. B7: Nech 4B **102**
⁣ WV2: Wolv 5G **43**
Fowlmere Rd. B42: Gt Barr 5D **66**
Fox & Goose Shop. Cen. B8: W End . .4A **104**
Foxbury Dr. B93: Dorr 6C **166**
Fox Cl. B75: S Cold 4D **54**
FOXCOTE .2C **126**
Foxcote Av. B21: Hand 2A **100**
Foxcote Cl. B90: Shir 1B **164**
Foxcote Dr. B90: Shir 1B **164**
Foxcote La. B63: Crad 2D **126**
Fox Covert DY8: Stourb 6D **108**

Fox Cres. B11: S'hll 1D **134**
Foxcroft Cl. WS7: Burn 1C **10**
Foxdale Dr. DY5: Brie H 6F **93**
Foxdale Gro. B33: Kitts G 1G **121**
Foxes Mdw. B30: K Nor 3B **146**
  B76: Walm 5E **71**
Foxes Ridge B64: Crad H 3G **111**
Foxes Way CV7: Bal C 3H **169**
Foxfield B31: N'fld 3D **144**
Foxfield Dr. DY8: Stourb 2E **125**
Fox Foot Dr. DY5: Brie H 5G **93**
Foxford Cl. B36: Cas B 6H **87**
  B72: W Grn 6B **70**
Foxglove Cl. B27: A Grn 4H **135**
  WS3: Pels 2E **21**
  WV11: Wed 4G **29**
Foxglove Cres. B37: K'hrst 6A **106**
Foxglove Rd. DY1: Dud 3B **76**
Foxglove Way B21: Hand 2H **99**
  B23: Erd 6B **68**
Fox Grn. Cres. B27: A Grn 4G **135**
Fox Gro. B27: A Grn 3G **135**
Fox Hill B29: S Oak 5G **131**
Fox Hill Cl. B29: S Oak 5G **131**
Fox Hill Rd. B75: R'ley 1C **54**
  (not continuous)
Foxhills Pk. DY2: Neth 5E **95**
Foxhills Rd. DY8: Word 2B **108**
  WV4: Penn 2A **58**
Foxhollies Dr. B63: Hale 1G **127**
Fox Hollies Leisure Cen. 4G **135**
Fox Hollies Rd. B27: A Grn 2H **135**
  B28: A Grn, Hall G 6F **135**
  B76: Walm 5D **70**
  (not continuous)
Fox Hollow WV6: Tett 1A **42**
Fox Hollow Cl. B45: Redn 2A **158**
Foxhope Cl. B38: K Nor 5E **147**
Foxhunt Rd. B63: Hale 3G **127**
Foxland Av. B45: Redn 2A **158**
  WS6: Gt Wyr 2G **7**
Foxland Cl. B37: Chel W 1F **123**
  B90: Ches G 5B **164**
Foxlands Av. WV4: Penn 2B **58**
Foxlands Cros. WV4: Pcnn 2A **58**
Foxlands Dr. B72: W Grn 6B **70**
  DY3: Up Gor 2H **75**
  WV4: Penn 2A **58**
Foxlea Rd. B63: Hale 4F **127**
Foxley Dr. B91: Cath B 2D **152**
Foxmeadow Cl. DY3: Sed 6A **60**
Fox Mill Est. B11: S'hll 2D **134**
Foxoak Ent. Cen. *B64: Crad H* 2F **111**
  (off Foxoak St.)
Foxoak St. B64: Crad H 3E **111**
Fox's La. WV1: Wolv 5G **27**
Fox St. B5: Birm 3G **5** (6H **101**)
  DY1: Dud 1E **77**
Foxton Rd. B8: Salt 4F **103**
Fox Wlk. WC9: Wals W 4D **22**
Foxwell Gro. B9: Bord G 6A **104**
Foxwell Rd. B9: Bord G 6H **103**
Foxwood Av. B43: Gt Barr 3D **66**
Foxwood Gro. B37: K'hrst 4B **106**
Foxyards Rd. DY4: Tip 2F **77**
Foyle Rd. B38: K Nor 6A **146**
Fozdar Cres. WV14: Cose 4D **60**
Fradley Cl. B30: K Nor 3H **145**
Framefield Dr. B91: Sol 1A **152**
Framlingham Gro. WV6: Pert 6G **25**
Frampton Cl. B30: B'vlle 6H **131**
  B37: Chel W 6F **107**
Frampton Way B43: Gt Barr 1F **67**
Frances Dr. WS3: Blox 5H **19**
Frances Rd. B19: Loz 1E **101**
  B23: Erd 4D **84**
  B30: K Nor 2C **146**
Franchise Gdns. WS10: W'bry 5F **47**
Franchise St. B42: P Barr 5G **83**
  WS10: W'bry 6E **47**
Francis Cl. B74: S'tly 3H **51**
  DY6: K'wfrd 1B **92**
Francis Rd. B16: Edg 2C **116**
  B25: Yard 5G **119**

Francis Rd. B27: A Grn 6B **120**
  B33: Stech 1B **120**
  B67: Smeth 4B **98**
  DY8: Woll 6A **108**
Francis Sharp Ho. WS3: Blox 5G **19**
Francis St. B7: Birm 5A **102**
  B70: W Brom 6B **80**
  WV1: Wolv 5G **27**
Francis Wlk. B31: Longb 2E **159**
Francis Ward Cl. B71: W Brom 5G **63**
Frankburn Rd. B74: S'tly 3G **51**
Frank Fisher Way B70: W Brom 5A **80**
Frankfort St. B19: Hock 3F **101**
Frankholmes Dr. B90: M'path 3D **164**
FRANKLEY 2H **143**
Frankley Av. B62: Quin 6F **113**
FRANKLEY BEECHES 3G **143**
Frankley Beeches Rd.
  B31: Longb, N'fld 5A **144**
Frankley Community Leisure Cen. . .6F **143**
FRANKLEY GREEN 2G **143**
Frankley Grn. B32: Fran 2D **142**
Frankley Grn. La. B32: Fran 2E **143**
FRANKLEY HILL 4F **143**
Frankley Hill La. B32: Fran 4F **143**
Frankley Hill Rd. B45: Fran 4F **143**
Frankley Ind. Pk. B45: Fran 5H **143**
Frankley La. B31: N'fld 1B **144**
  B32: Bart G, N'fld 1A **144**
Frankley Lodge Rd. B31: Fran 3B **144**
Frankley Rd. B68: O'bry 3H **113**
FRANKLEY SERVICE AREA 6F **129**
Frankley Ter. B17: Harb 6F **115**
Franklin Rd. B30: B'vlle 2A **146**
Franklin St. B18: Win G 4A **100**
Franklin Way B30: B'vlle 1B **146**
Franklyn Cl. WV6: Pert 4E **25**
Frank Rd. B67: Smeth 3C **98**
Frank St. B12: Birm 4H **117**
Franks Way B33: Stech 1C **120**
Frank Tommey Cl. B65: B'hth 2C **112**
Frankton Cl. B92: Sol 3F **137**
Frankton Gro. B9: Bord G 1H **119**
Fraser Rd. B11: S'brk 6D **118**
Fraser St. WV14: Bils 6G **45**
  (not continuous)
Frayne Av. DY6: K'wfrd 2A **92**
Freasley Cl. B90: Shir 5B **150**
Freasley Rd. B34: S End 3A **106**
Freda Ri. B69: Tiv 1D **96**
Freda Rd. B70: W Brom 6B **80**
Frederick Av. DY5: Brie H 6E **115**
Frederick Rd. B6: Aston 1G **101**
  B11: S'hll 1C **134**
  B15: Edg 3D **116**
  B23: Erd 5D **84**
  B29: S Oak 3H **131**
  B33: Stech 6B **104**
  B68: O'bry 4B **114**
  B73: W Grn 3G **69**
  WV11: Wed 4E **29**
Fredericks Cl. DY8: Stourb 1C **124**
Frederick St. B1: Birm 1A **4** (5E **101**)
  B70: W Brom 3A **80**
  WS2: Wals 1A **48**
  WV2: Wolv 6B **170** (3G **43**)
Frederick William St. WV13: W'hall . .1B **46**
Fred Smith Cl. WS10: W'bry 6H **47**
Freeland Gro. DY6: K'wfrd 5D **92**
Freeman Dr. B76: Walm 1D **70**
Freeman Pl. WV14: Bils 3G **45**
Freeman Rd. B7: Nech 3B **102**
  WS10: W'bry 2A **64**
Freeman St. B5: Birm 4F **5** (1G **117**)
  WV10: Wolv 1B **44**
Freemantle Dr. B34: S End 3A **106**
Freemount Sq. B43: Gt Barr 6A **66**
Free Port B26: Birm A 2B **138**
Freer Rd. B6: Aston 1F **101**
Freer St. WS1: Wals 1C **48**
Freeth Rd. WS8: Bwnhls 4C **10**
Freeth St. B16: Birm 1B **116**
  B69: O'bry 1F **97**
Freezeland St. WV14: Bils 5D **44**

Fremont Dr. DY1: Dud 4A **76**
French Rd. DY2: Dud 6G **77**
French Walls B66: Smeth 4G **99**
  WS6: C Hay 1E **7**
Frensham Cl. B37: Chel W 1E **123**
  WS6: C Hay 1E **7**
Frensham Way B17: Harb 5G **115**
Frenshaw Gro. B44: Gt Barr 5H **67**
Freshwater Dr. DY5: Brie H 3F **109**
Friardale Cl. WS10: W'bry 2B **64**
FRIAR PARK 3A **64**
Friar Pk. Farm WS10: W'bry 1B **64**
Friar Pk. Rd. WS10: W'bry 2A **64**
Friars Cl. DY8: Word 6A **92**
Friars Gorse DY7: Stourt 4A **108**
Friar St. WS10: W'bry 2H **63**
Friars Wlk. B37: Chel W 1F **123**
Friary Av. B90: M'path 3E **165**
Friary Gdns. B21: Hand 5H **81**
Friary Rd. B20: Hand 5A **82**
Friary La. B92: Cath B, H Ard 2E **153**
Friday Wharf B1: Birm 6A **4**
Friesland Dr. WV1: Wolv 6D **28**
Friezeland Rd. WS2: Wals 1H **47**
Friezland La. WS8: Bwnhls 2B **22**
Friezland Way WS8: Bwnhls 2C **22**
Frinton Gro. B21: Hand 2G **99**
Friston Av. B16: Birm 2D **116**
Frobisher Cl. WS6: Gt Wyr 4F **7**
Frobisher Rd. CV3: Cov 6J **145**
Frobisher Way B66: Smeth 2B **98**
Frodesley Rd. B26: Sheld 3F **121**
Froggatt Rd. WV14: Bils 4F **45**
Froggatts Ride B76: Walm 2D **70**
Frog Hall Cotts. DY7: I'ley 2A **124**
Frog La. CV7: Bal C 4G **169**
Frogmill Rd. B45: Fran 6H **143**
Frogmoor Ho. B25: Yard 4C **120**
Frogmore La. CV8: Fen E 6F **169**
Frome Cl. DY3: Lwr G 5H **75**
Frome Dr. WV11: Wed 4E **29**
Frome Way B14: K Hth 1E **147**
Frost St. WV2: E'shll 5C **44**
Fruxmere Cl. B91: Sol 1F **165**
Froyle Cl. WV6: Tett 4A **26**
Froysell St. WV13: W'hall 1B **46**
Fryer Rd. B31: Longb 2F **159**
Fryer's Cl. WS3: Blox 2H **31**
Fryer's Rd. WS2: Wals 3G **31**
  WS3: Blox 3G **31**
Fryer St. WV1: Wolv 2C **170** (1H **43**)
Fuchsia Dr. WV9: Pend 4D **14**
Fugelmere Cl. B17: Harb 4D **114**
Fulbrook Gro. B29: W Cas 5D **130**
Fulbrook Rd. DY1: Dud 6C **76**
Fulford Cl. B47: Wyt 4C **162**
Fulford Dr. B76: Min 2F **87**
Fulford Gro. B26: Sheld 5G **121**
Fulford Hall Rd. B90: Tid G 6D **162**
  B94: Earls 6D **162**
FULFORD HEATH 6D **162**
Fulham Rd. B11: S'hll 6B **118**
FULLBROOK 5D **48**
Fullbrook Cl. B90: M'path 4E **165**
Fullbrook Rd. WS5: Wals 6C **48**
Fullelove Rd. WS8: Bwnhls 6C **10**
Fullerton Cl. WV8: Pend 6C **14**
Fullwood Cres. DY2: Dud 3A **94**
Fullwoods End WV14: Cose 4E **61**
Fulmer Wlk. B18: Hock 6C **100**
Fulwell Gro. B44: K'sdng 6A **68**
Fulwell M. B37: Mars G 3D **122**
Fulwood Av. B62: B'hth 3F **113**
Furber Pl. DY6: K'wfrd 3D **92**
Furlong, The WS10: W'bry 6E **47**
Furlong La. B63: Crad 5E **111**
Furlong Mdw. B31: N'fld 5G **145**
Furlongs, The DY8: Stourb 2F **125**
  WV11: Wed 4D **28**
Furlongs Rd. DY3: Sed 1H **75**
Furlong Wlk. DY3: Lwr G 3H **75**
Furnace Cl. WV5: Wom 2E **73**
Furnace Coppice B63: Hale 5B **112**

Furnace Hill B63: Hale 5B 112
Furnace La. B63: Hale 6B 112
Furnace Pde. DY4: Tip 1G 77
Furnace Rd. DY2: Dud 1E 95
Furness Cl. WS3: Blox 4F 19
Furst St. WS8: Bwnhls 5C 10
Furzebank Way WV12: W'hall 5E 31
Furze Way WS5: Wals 3A 50

G

Gables, The B24: Erd 3B 86
　DY6: W Hth 1H 91
Gaddesby Rd. B14: K Hth 5H 133
Gadds Dr. B65: Row R 5D 96
Gadsby Av. WV11: Wed 2A 30
Gads Grn. DY2: Neth 4G 95
Gads Grn. Cres. DY2: Dud 3G 95
Gads La. B70: W Brom 5G 79
　DY1: Dud .6E 77
Gadwall Cft. B23: Erd 4B 84
Gaiety Ho. B66: Smeth 4E 99
　(off Regent St.)
Gail Cl. WS9: Wals W 3D 22
Gailey Cft. B44: Gt Barr 2G 67
Gail Pk. WV3: Wolv 4B 42
Gainford Cl. WV8: Pend 6D 14
Gainford Rd. B44: K'sdng 4C 68
Gainsborough Cres. B43: Gt Barr . . .1F 67
　B93: Know 3C 166
Gainsborough Dr. WV6: Pert 5F 25
Gainsborough Hill DY8: Stourb 2D 124
Gainsborough Pl. DY1: Dud 5A 76
Gainsborough Rd. B42: Gt Barr 1D 82
Gainsborough Trad. Est. DY9: Lye . .1G 125
Gainsford Dr. B62: Hale 5B 112
Gains La. WS3: Lit Wyr 3A 8
　WS11: Lit Wyr 3A 8
Gairloch Rd. WV12: W'hall 6B 18
Gaitskell Ter. B69: Tiv 5D 78
Gaitskell Way B66: Smeth 2D 98

Gala Bingo
　Aldridge 3D 34
　Darlaston 4F 47
　Dudley .5F 77
　Great Park 6H 143
　Harborne 6G 115
　Kings Heath 4G 133
　Stockland Green 2D 84
　Tower Hill 1D 82
　Tyburn .4C 86
　Walsall 2B 48
　Wednesfield 2H 29
　Wolverhampton 1H 27
　Yardley 5B 120
　(off The Swan Shop. Cen.)

Gala Casino
　Birmingham 5D 4 (1F 117)
Galahad Way WS10: W'bry 3G 63
Gala Leisure Cen. 4A 80
Galbraith Cl. WV14: Cose 5F 61
Galena Way B6: Aston 3G 101
Gale Wlk. B65: Row R 4H 95
Gallagher Ct. B13: Mose 3B 134
　(off Wake Grn. Pk.)
Gallery, The WV1: Wolv 4D 170 (2G 43)
Gallery Sq. WS2: Wals 1B 48
Galloway Av. B34: Hodg H 3D 104
Galton Cl. B24: Erd 3D 86
　DY4: Tip .1C 78
Galton Dr. B43: Gt Barr 4B 66
　DY2: Dud .3D 94
Galton Rd. B67: Smeth 1D 114
Galton Twr. B1: Birm 4A 4 (1E 117)
Gamesfield Grn. WV3: Wolv 2D 42
Gammage St. DY2: Dud 1D 94
Gandy Rd. WV12: W'hall 3A 30
Gannah's Farm Cl. B76: Walm 2D 70
GANNOW GREEN 6C 142
Gannow Grn. La. B45: Rub 6C 142
Gannow Mnr. Cres. B45: Fran 5E 143
Gannow Mnr. Gdns. B45: Fran 6F 143
Gannow Rd. B45: Rub 2E 157

Gannow Shop. Cen. B45: Fran 6E 143
Gannow Wlk. B45: Rub 2E 157
Ganton Rd. WS3: Blox 3G 19
Ganton Wlk. WV8: Pend 1D 26
Garden Cl. B8: W End 4G 103
　B45: Fran .5G 143
　B93: Know 3B 166
Garden Cres. WS3: Pels 4D 20
Garden Cft. WS9: A'rdge 2D 34
Gardeners Wlk. B91: Sol 4G 151
Gardeners Way WV5: Wom 3F 73
Garden Gro. B20: Hand 1A 82
Gardens, The B23: Erd 4E 85
　B72: W Grn 5H 69
Garden St. WS2: Wals 6C 32
Garden Wlk. DY2: Dud 6E 77
　DY3: Gorn .5G 75
　(not continuous)
　WV14: Bils 5H 45
Garfield Rd. B26: Sheld 3F 121
Garland Cres. B62: B'hth 3E 113
Garlands, The WV11: Wed 2E 29
Garland St. B9: Birm 6C 102
Garland Way B31: N'fld 2F 145
　(not continuous)
Garman Cl. B43: Gt Barr 3A 66
Garner Cl. WV14: Cose 2F 61
Garnet Av. B43: Gt Barr 1D 66
Garnet Cl. WS9: Ston 3G 23
Garnett Dr. B75: S Cold 5C 54
Garrard Gdns. B73: S Cold 6H 53
Garratt Cl. B68: O'bry 5A 98
Garratt's La. B64: Old H 1H 111
Garratt St. B71: W Brom 2H 79
　DY5: Brie H 4A 94
Garret Cl. DY6: K'wfrd 1B 92
GARRETT'S GREEN 3G 121
Garrett's Grn. Ind. Est. B33: Sheld . .2G 121
Garretts Grn. La. B26: Sheld 4D 120
　B33: Sheld 3F 121
Garretts Wlk. B14: K Hth 5G 147
Garrick Cl. DY1: Dud 4B 76
Garrick St. WV1: Wolv 4C 170 (2H 43)
Garrison Cir. B9: Birm 1A 118
Garrison Ct. B9: Birm 1B 118
　(off Barwell Rd.)
Garrison La. B9: Birm, Bord G 1B 118
Garrison St. B9: Birm 1B 118
Garston Way B43: Gt Barr 5H 65
Garth, The B14: Yard W 3D 148
Garway Gro. B25: Yard 5H 119
Garwood Rd. B26: Yard 1D 120
Gas St. B1: Birm 5A 4 (1E 117)
Gatacre St. DY3: Gorn 4H 75
Gatcombe Cl. WV10: Bush 3B 16
Gatcombe Rd. DY1: Dud 5A 76
Gatehouse Fold DY2: Dud 6F 77
　(off Birmingham St.)
Gatehouse Trad. Est. WS8: Bwnhls . .4D 10
Gate La. B73: Bold 3F 69
　B93: Dorr .5F 165
　B94: H'ley H 5F 165
Gateley Rd. B68: O'bry 4C 114
Gate St. B8: Salt 4D 102
　DY3: Sed .6A 60
　DY4: Tip 5A 78
Gatis St. WV6: Wolv 5E 27
Gatwick Rd. B35: Cas V 3G 87
Gauden Rd. DY9: W'cte 4H 125
Gavin Way B6: Witt 3H 83
Gawne La. B64: Old H 6H 95
Gaydon Cl. WV6: Pert 4E 25
Gaydon Gro. B29: S Oak 3E 131
Gaydon Pl. B73: S Cold 1H 69
Gaydon Rd. B92: Sol 2H 137
　WS9: A'rdge 5C 34
Gayfield Av. DY5: Brie H 2A 110
GAY HILL 2D 160
Gayhill La. B38: Head H 1D 160
Gayhurst Dr. B25: Yard 5A 120
Gayle Gro. B27: A Grn 5A 136
Gayton Rd. B71: W Brom 1B 80

Geach St. B19: Hock 3F 101
Geach Twr. B19: Birm 4F 101
　(off Uxbridge St.)
Gedney Cl. B90: Shir 4C 148
Geeson Cl. B35: Cas V 3F 87
Gee St. B19: Hock 3F 101
Gem Ho. B4: Birm 2G 5
Geneva Rd. DY4: Tip 2F 77
Genge Av. WV4: E'shll 1A 60
Genners App. B31: N'fld 5B 130
Genners La. B31: N'fld 6B 130
　B32: Bart G, N'fld 5A 130
Genthorn Cl. WV4: E'shll 1B 60
Gentian B74: Four O 5F 37
Gentian Cl. B31: N'fld 1D 144
Gentleshaw La. B91: Sol 5B 152
Geoffrey Cl. B76: Walm 6F 71
Geoffrey Pl. B11: S'hll 2C 134
Geoffrey Rd. B11: S'hll 2C 134
　B90: Shir .4F 149
George Arthur Rd. B8: Salt 5D 102
George Av. B65: Row R 1D 112
George Bird Cl. B66: Smeth 3E 99
George Cl. DY2: Dud 1G 95
George Frederick Rd.
　B73: S'tly .1A 68
George Henry Rd. DY4: Tip 6E 63
George Rd. B15: Edg 3D 116
　B23: Erd 3B 84
　B25: Yard .5G 119
　B29: S Oak 2A 132
　B43: Gt Barr 3B 66
　B46: Wat O 4E 89
　B63: Hale .1H 127
　B68: O'bry 1H 113
　B73: New O 4D 68
　B91: Sol 4G 151
　DY4: Tip 1F 77
　WV14: Cose 4F 61
George Rose Gdns. WS10: Darl 5C 46
George St. B3: Birm 3A 4 (6E 101)
　B12: Bal H 6G 117
　B19: Loz 2D 100
　B21: Hand .1G 99
　B70: W Brom 5B 80
　DY1: Dud .1D 76
　DY8: Word 2D 108
　WS1: Wals 2C 48
　WV2: E'shll 4C 44
　WV2: Wolv 5C 170 (2H 43)
　WV13: W'hall 5A 30
George St. W. B18: Hock 5C 100
Georgian Gdns. WS10: W'bry 2F 63
Georgina Av. WV14: Cose 2F 61
Geraldine Rd. B25: Yard 4H 119
Gerald Rd. DY8: Woll 4C 108
Geranium Gro. B9: Bord G 6F 103
Geranium Rd. DY2: Dud 1H 95
Gerardsfield Rd. B33: Kitts G 6H 105
Germander Dr. WS5: Wals 2F 65
Gerrard Cl. B19: Loz 2F 101
Gerrards Dr. B19: Loz 2F 101
Gerrard St. B19: Loz 2E 101
Gertrude Pl. B18: Hock 4C 100
Gervase Dr. DY1: Dud 4E 77
Geston Rd. DY1: Dud 1B 94
Gibbet Hill B69: Tiv 2A 96
Gibbet La. DY7: Kinv 1A 124
Gibbet Rd. B29: S Oak 4G 131
Gibbons Gro. WV6: Wolv 5D 26
Gibbons Hill Rd. DY3: Sed 3H 59
Gibbons Ind. Est. DY6: K'wfrd 2E 93
Gibbon's La. DY5: P'ntt 2E 93
Gibbons Rd. B75: Four O 6H 37
　WV6: Wolv 5D 26
Gibbs Hill Rd. B31: Longb 2F 159
Gibb Sq. B9: Birm 6H 5 (2A 118)
Gibbs Rd. DY9: Lye 6C 110
Gibbs St. WV6: Wolv 5E 27
Gibb St. B9: Birm 6H 5 (2H 117)
GIB HEATH .3B 100
Gibson Dr. B20: Hand 1D 100
　B66: Smeth 3E 99

Gibson Rd. B20: Hand 1D **100**
  WV6: Pert 6E **25**
Gideon Cl. B25: Yard 5B **120**
Gideons Cl. DY3: Up Gor 2H **75**
Giffard Rd. WV1: Wolv 4D **44**
  WV10: Bush 4A **16**
Gifford Ct. DY5: Brie H 1H **109**
                      (off Hill St.)
GIGGETTY 1E **73**
Giggetty La. WV5: Wom 1E **73**
Gigmill Way DY8: Stourb 1C **124**
Gilbanks Rd. DY8: Woll 4B **108**
Gilberry Cl. B93: Know 4C **166**
Gilbert Av. B69: Tiv 2B **96**
Gilbert Cl. WV11: Wed 2A **30**
Gilbert Ct. WS4: Wals 5E **33**
              (off Lichfield Rd.)
Gilbert Ent. Pk. WV12: W'hall 5B **30**
Gilbert La. WV5: Wom 6H **57**
Gilbert Rd. B66: Smeth 5F **99**
GILBERTSTONE 5D **120**
Gilbertstone Av. B26: Yard 6C **120**
Gilbert St. DY4: Tip 5H **77**
Gilbeys Cl. DY8: Word 2C **108**
Gilby Rd. B16: Birm 1C **116**
Gilchrist Dr. B15: Edg 3A **116**
Gildas Av. B38: K Nor 6C **146**
Giles Cl. B33: Stech 6C **104**
  B92: Sol 6B **138**
Giles Cl. Ho. B33: Stech 6C **104**
Giles Hill DY8: Stourb 5E **109**
Giles Rd. B68: O'bry 4H **97**
Gilldown Pl. B15: Edg 4D **116**
Gillespie Cft. B6: Aston 2H **101**
Gillhurst Rd. B17: Harb 4F **115**
Gillies Ct. B33: Stech 6B **104**
Gilling Gro. B34: Hodg H 3E **105**
Gillingham Cl. WS10: W'bry 6B **48**
Gillity Av. WS5: Wals 3F **49**
Gillity Cl. WS5: Wals 3F **49**
Gillity Ct. WS5: Wals 4H **49**
Gilliver Rd. B90: Shir 5H **149**
Gillman Cl. B26: Sheld 1H **137**
Gillott Cl. B91: Sol 4A **152**
Gillott Rd. B16: Edg 2G **115**
Gillows Cft. B90: M'path 2E **165**
Gillscroft Rd. B33: Kitts G 5E **105**
Gill St. B70: W Brom 6A **80**
  DY2: Neth 5G **95**
Gilmorton Cl. B17: Harb 4F **115**
  B91: Sol 6G **151**
Gilpin Cl. B8: W End 2A **104**
Gilpin Cres. WS3: Pels 3E **21**
Gilpins Cft. WS6: C Hay 4D **6**
GILSON .6F **89**
Gilson Dr. B46: Col 2F **107**
Gilson Rd. B46: Col 6F **89**
Gilson St. DY4: Tip 5C **62**
Gilson Way B37: K'hrst 4C **106**
Gilwell Rd. B34: S End 3A **106**
Gimble Wlk. B17: Harb 3E **115**
           (not continuous)
Gin Cridden DY9: Lye 5A **110**
Gipsy Cl. CV7: Bal C 4H **169**
Gipsy La. B23: Erd 2A **84**
  CV7: Bal C 4H **169**
  WV13: W'hall 2B **46**
Girton Ho. B36: Cas B 1B **106**
Gisborn Cl. B10: Small H 3B **118**
GK Davies Trad. Est. B63: Crad 5C **110**
Glade, The B26: Sheld 1H **137**
  B74: S'tly 2G **51**
  DY9: Lye 6A **110**
  WV8: Pend 6C **14**
Glades, The WS9: A'rdge 2D **34**
Gladeside Cl. WS4: S'fld 1H **33**
Gladstone Dr. B69: Tiv 5C **78**
  DY8: Woll 6B **108**
Gladstone Rd. DY6: K'wfrd 1B **92**
Gladstone Rd. B11: S'brk 5B **118**
  B23: Erd 4D **84**
  B26: Yard 4A **120**
  B93: Dorr 6H **167**
  DY8: Woll 5B **108**

Gladstone St. B6: Aston 1A **102**
  B71: W Brom 1A **80**
  WS2: Wals 5B **32**
  WS10: Darl 5E **47**
Gladys Rd. B25: Yard 4H **119**
  B67: Smeth 1D **114**
Gladys Ter. B67: Smeth 1D **114**
Glaisdale Gdns. WV6: Wolv 4E **27**
Glaisdale Rd. B28: Hall G 5G **135**
Glaisedale Gro. WV13: W'hall 1C **46**
Glaisher Dr. WV10: Wolv 3G **27**
Glamis Rd. WV12: W'hall 2B **30**
Glanville Dr. B75: Four O 5G **37**
Glasbury Cft. B38: K Nor 2A **160**
Glascote Cl. B90: Shir 3G **149**
Glascote Gro. B34: S End 2G **105**
Glaslyn Av. B65: Row R 1B **112**
Glassford Dr. WV6: Tett 3C **26**
Glasshouse Hill DY8: Stourb 2F **125**
Glastonbury Cres. WS3: Blox 5E **19**
Glastonbury Rd. B14: Yard W 3C **148**
  B71: W Brom 4B **64**
Glastonbury Way WS3: Blox 6E **19**
Glaston Dr. B91: Sol 6E **151**
Gleads Cft. B62: Quin 2G **129**
Gleaston Wlk. WV1: Wolv 3E **45**
Gleave Rd. B29: S Oak 4A **132**
Glebe Dr. B73: Bold 5F **69**
Glebe Farm Rd. B33: Stech 4E **105**
Glebe Flds. B76: Curd 1D **88**
Glebefields Rd. DY4: Tip 5A **62**
Glebeland Cl. B16: Birm 2D **116**
Glebe La. DY8: Stourb 1C **124**
Glebe Pl. WS10: Darl 5B **46**
Glebe Rd. B91: Sol 2H **151**
  WV13: W'hall 3H **45**
Glebe St. WS1: Wals 3C **48**
Glebe Way CV7: Bal C 2G **169**
Glenavon Rd. B14: K Hth 4H **147**
Glen Cl. WS4: Wals 6E **33**
Glencoe Rd. B16: Edg 5G **99**
Glen Ct. WV3: Wolv 1C **42**
  WV8: Cod 3G **13**
Glencroft Rd. B92: Sol 1H **137**
Glendale Cl. B63: Hale 1B **128**
  WV3: Wolv 3A **42**
Glendale Dr. B33: Stech 6D **104**
  WV5: Wom 1G **73**
Glendale Twr. B23: Erd 1H **85**
Glendene Cres. B38: K Nor 2G **159**
Glendene Dr. B43: Gt Barr 5H **65**
Glen Devon Cl. B45: Fran 5G **143**
Glendon Rd. B23: Erd 1D **84**
Glendon Way B93: Dorr 6H **165**
Glendower Rd. B42: P Barr 3E **83**
  WS9: A'rdge 6D **22**
Gleneagles Dr. B43: Gt Barr 2A **66**
  B69: Tiv 2A **96**
  B75: S Cold 4A **54**
Gleneagles Rd. B26: Yard 3E **121**
  WS3: Blox 4F **19**
  WV6: Pert 4D **24**
Glenelg Dr. DY8: Stourb 3F **125**
Glenelg M. WS5: Wals 6H **49**
Glenfern Rd. WV14: Cose 5C **60**
Glenfield WV8: Pend 5C **14**
Glenfield Cl. B76: Walm 2C **70**
  B91: Sol 1G **165**
Glenfield Gro. B29: S Oak 4C **132**
Glengarry Cl. B32: Bart G 6H **129**
Glengarry Gdns. WV3: Wolv 2D **42**
Glenhill Dr. B38: K Nor 1C **160**
Glenhurst Cl. WS2: Wals 6D **30**
Glenmead Rd. B44: Gt Barr 5F **67**
Glenmore Cl. WV3: Wolv 4C **42**
Glenmore Dr. B38: K Nor 5H **145**
Glen Pk. Rd. DY3: Gorn 5H **75**
Glenpark Rd. B8: Salt 4E **103**
Glen Ri. B13: Mose 1C **148**
Glen Rd. DY3: Up Gor 2H **75**
  DY8: Stourb 2D **124**
Glenroyde B38: K Nor 2A **160**
Glen Side B32: Bart G 3B **130**
Glenside Av. B92: Sol 2G **137**

Glenthorne Dr. WS6: C Hay 2E **7**
Glenthorne Rd. B24: Erd 5G **85**
Glentworth B76: Walm 3E **71**
Glentworth Gdns. WV6: Wolv 4F **27**
Glenville Dr. B23: Erd 2E **85**
Glenwood Cl. DY5: Quar B 3H **109**
Glenwood Dr. B90: Ches G 5B **164**
Glenwood Ri. WS9: Ston 4F **23**
Glenwood Rd. B38: K Nor 1H **159**
Globe St. WS10: W'bry 4F **63**
Gloucester Flats B65: Row R 5E **97**
Gloucester Ho. WV1: Wolv 5G **27**
              (off Lomas St.)
Gloucester Pl. WV13: W'hall 1D **46**
Gloucester Rd. DY2: Neth 1F **111**
  WS5: Wals 3F **49**
  WS10: W'bry 2A **64**
Gloucester St. B5: Birm 6E **5** (2G **117**)
  WV6: Wolv 5F **27**
Gloucester Way B37: Mars G 2C **122**
Glover Cl. B28: Hall G 1F **149**
Glover Rd. B75: S Cold 6D **54**
Glovers Cft. B37: F'bri 6B **106**
Glovers Fld. Dr. B7: Nech 2C **102**
Glover's Rd. B10: Small H 3C **118**
Glover St. B9: Birm 1A **118**
  B70: W Brom 6B **80**
Glovers Trust Homes B73: Bold 5F **69**
Glyme Dr. WV6: Tett 4C **26**
Glyn Av. WV14: Bils 2B **62**
Glyn Dr. WV14: Bils 2B **62**
Glyne Ct. B73: S Cold 6H **53**
Glyn Farm Rd. B32: Quin 6A **114**
Glynn Cres. B63: Crad 4D **110**
Glynne Av. DY6: K'wfrd 5B **92**
Glyn Rd. B32: Quin 5B **114**
Glynside Av. B32: Quin 5B **114**
Godrich Ho. B13: Mose 2A **134**
Goffs Cl. B32: Bart G 2D **130**
Goldborough Cl. WV14: Cose 2F **61**
Goldby Dr. WS10: W'bry 1E **63**
Gold Crest Cl. DY2: Neth 1F **111**
Goldcrest Cft. B36: Cas B 1C **106**
Goldencrest Dr. B69: O'bry 1E **97**
Golden Cft. B20: Hand 6B **82**
Golden End Dr. B93: Know 3F **167**
GOLDEN END 3F **167**
Golden Hillock Rd. B10: Small H 4D **118**
  B11: S'brk, Small H 6D **118**
  DY2: Neth 6E **95**
Goldfinch Cl. B30: B'vlle 5H **131**
Goldfinch Rd. DY9: W'cte 2G **125**
Goldicroft Rd. WS10: W'bry 1G **63**
Goldieslie Cl. B73: W Grn 3H **69**
Goldieslie Rd. B73: W Grn 3H **69**
GOLDS GREEN 6E **63**
Golds Hill Gdns. B21: Hand 2B **100**
Golds Hill Rd. B21: Hand 1B **100**
Golds Hill Way DY4: Tip 6D **62**
Goldsmith Rd. B14: K Hth 5H **133**
  WS3: Blox 2C **32**
Goldstar Way B33: Kitts G 1G **121**
Goldthorn Av. WV4: Penn 5F **43**
Goldthorn Cres. WV4: Penn 5E **43**
Goldthorne Av. B26: Sheld 1G **137**
GOLDTHORN HILL 6F **43**
Goldthorn Hill WV2: Penn 5E **43**
Goldthorn Hill Rd. WV2: Penn 5F **43**
GOLDTHORN PARK 1G **59**
Goldthorn Rd. WV2: Wolv 5F **43**
Goldthorn Ter. WV2: Wolv 4F **43**
Goldthorn Wlk. DY5: Brie H 3H **109**
Golf Club Dr. WS1: Wals 5E **49**
Golf La. WV14: Bils 4F **45**
Golson Cl. B75: S Cold 5D **54**
Gomeldon Av. B14: K Hth 4H **147**
Gomer St. WV13: W'hall 1A **46**
Gomer St. W. WV13: W'hall 1A **46**
Gonville Ho. B36: Cas B 1B **106**
Gooch Cl. DY8: Amb 5E **109**
Gooch St. B5: Birm 3G **117**
Gooch St. Nth. B5: Birm 2G **117**
Goodall Gro. B43: Gt Barr 6G **51**

Goodall St. WS1: Wals		2D **48**
Goodby Rd. B13: Mose		2F **133**
Goode Av. B18: Hock		4C **100**
Goode Cl. B68: O'bry		5A **98**
Goodeve Wlk. B75: S Cold		6F **55**
Goodison Gdns. B24: Erd		2G **85**
Goodleigh Av. B31: Longb		3C **158**
Goodman Cl. B28: Hall G		1F **149**
Goodman St. B1: Birm		6D **100**
Goodrest Av. B62: Quin		6F **113**
Goodrest Cft. B14: Yard W		3C **148**
Goodrest La. B38: Head H		3B **160**
		(not continuous)
Goodrich Av. WV6: Pert		6G **25**
Goodrich Covert B14: K Hth		5E **147**
Goodrick Way B7: Nech		3B **102**
Goodway Ho. *B4: Birm*		*1E **5***
		(off Shadwell St.)
Goodway Rd. B44: Gt Barr		5G **67**
B92: Sol		2A **138**
Goodwood Cl. B36: Hodg H		1B **104**
Goodwood Dr. B74: S'tly		4H **51**
Goodwyn Av. B68: O'bry		4B **114**
Goodyear Av. WV10: Bush		1A **28**
Goodyear Rd. B67: Smeth		1B **114**
Goosemoor La. B23: Erd		6E **69**
Gopsal St. B4: Birm		2H **5** (6A **102**)
Gorcott La. B90: Dic H		4G **163**
Gordon Av. B19: Loz		2F **101**
B71: W Brom		5A **64**
WV4: E'shll		2B **60**
Gordon Cl. B69: Tiv		5D **78**
Gordon Ct. B33: Stech		6B **104**
Gordon Cres. DY5: Brie H		4A **94**
Gordon Dr. DY1: Tip		1C **78**
Gordon Pl. WV14: Bils		6E **45**
Gordon Rd. B17: Harb		5H **115**
B19: Loz		1E **101**
Gordon St. *B9: Birm*		*1B **118***
		(off Garrison La.)
WS10: Darl		5D **46**
WV2: Wolv		6D **170** (3H **43**)
Gorey Cl. WV12: W'hall		1B **30**
Gorge Rd. DY3: Sed		5A **60**
WV14: Cose		5A **60**
Gorleston Gro. B14: K Hth		5B **148**
Gorleston Rd. B14: K Hth		5B **148**
GORNALWOOD		4G **75**
Gornal Wood Crematorium		
DY3: Gorn		5G **75**
Gorsebrook Rd. WV6: Wolv		4F **27**
WV10: Wolv		4G **27**
Gorse Cl. B29: W Cas		5E **131**
B37: F'bri		1B **122**
Gorse Farm Rd. B43: Gt Barr		5A **66**
Gorse Farm Wood Nature Reserve		5B **66**
Gorsefield Rd. B34: S End		4G **105**
Gorse La. WS5: Try		1A **72**
Gorsemoor Way WV11: Ess		4B **18**
Gorse Rd. DY1: Dud		3C **76**
WV11: Wed		1A **30**
Gorsey La. B46: Col		5A **162**
B47: Wyt		5A **162**
WS3: Lit Wyr		3B **8**
WS6: Gt Wyr		4F **7**
Gorsey Way B46: Col		5G **89**
WS9: A'rdge		4A **34**
Gorsly Piece B32: Quin		1A **130**
Gorstie Cft. B43: Gt Barr		5A **66**
Gorsty Av. DY5: Brie H		6G **93**
Gorsty Cl. B71: W Brom		5D **64**
Gorsty Hayes WV8: Cod		4F **13**
Gorsty Hill Rd. B65: B'hth		3B **112**
Gorsymead Gro. B31: Longb		5A **144**
Gorsy Rd. B32: Quin		1B **130**
Gorton Cft. CV7: Bal C		2H **169**
Gorway Cl. WS1: Wals		4D **48**
Gorway Gdns. WS1: Wals		4E **49**
Gorway Rd. WS1: Wals		4D **48**
GOSCOTE		5C **20**
Goscote Cl. WS3: Wals		2D **32**
Goscote Ind. Est. WS3: Blox		6C **20**
Goscote La. WS3: Blox, Wals		6C **20**
Goscote Lodge Cres. WS3: Wals		2E **33**

Goscote Pl. WS3: Wals		2E **33**
Goscote Rd. WS3: Pels		2D **20**
Gosford St. B12: Bal H		5H **117**
Gosford Wlk. B92: Olton		4F **137**
Gosmoor Ho. B26: Yard		4C **120**
Gospel End Rd. DY3: Sed		5E **59**
Gospel End St. DY3: Sed		6H **59**
GOSPEL END VILLAGE		5E **59**
Gospel Farm Rd. B27: A Grn		5H **135**
Gospel La. B27: A Grn		6A **136**
Gospel Oak Rd. DY4: Tip		4B **62**
Gosport Cl. WV1: Wolv		4D **44**
Goss, The DY5: Brie H		2H **109**
Goss Cft. B29: S Oak		4H **131**
Gossey La. B33: Kitts G		1G **121**
Gosta Grn. B4: Birm		1G **5** (5H **101**)
Gotham Rd. B26: Yard		5C **120**
GOTHERSLEY		6E **91**
Gothersley La. DY7: Stourt		6D **90**
Goths Cl. B65: Row R		5C **96**
Gough Av. WV11: Wed		1D **28**
Gough Dr. DY4: Tip		2C **78**
Gough Rd. B11: S'brk		6D **118**
B15: Edg		4E **117**
WV14: Cose		4E **61**
Gough St. B1: Birm		6C **4** (2F **117**)
WV1: Wolv		1A **44**
WV13: W'hall		6C **30**
Gould Firm La. WS9: A'rdge		3G **35**
Gowan Rd. B8: Salt		5E **103**
Gower Av. DY6: K'wfrd		5D **92**
Gower Ho. *B62: Quin*		*5F **113***
		(off Lockington Cft.)
Gower Rd. B62: Quin		5E **113**
DY3: Sed		5F **59**
Gower St. B19: Loz		2F **101**
WS2: Wals		4H **47**
WV2: Wolv		3A **44**
		(not continuous)
WV13: W'hall		1A **46**
Gozzard St. WV14: Bils		6G **45**
Gracechurch Cen. B72: S Cold		6H **53**
Gracemere Cres. B28: Hall G		4E **149**
Grace Rd. B11: S'brk		4C **118**
B69: Tiv		1C **96**
DY4: Tip		6A **62**
Gracewell Homes B13: Mose		4D **134**
Gracewell Rd. B13: Mose		4D **134**
Grafton Cl. B23: Erd		5C **84**
WV6: Wolv		5D **26**
Grafton Dr. WV13: W'hall		3F **45**
Grafton Gdns. DY3: Lwr G		4F **75**
Grafton Gro. B19: Loz		2E **101**
Grafton Pl. WV14: Bils		4G **45**
Grafton Rd. B11: S'brk		4B **118**
B21: Hand		6H **81**
B68: O'bry		2F **113**
B71: W Brom		3B **80**
B90: Shir		5C **148**
Graham Cl. DY4: Tip		4B **62**
Graham Cres. B45: Rub		2G **157**
Graham Rd. B8: Salt		5F **103**
B25: Yard		5A **120**
B62: B'hth		3C **112**
B71: W Brom		3B **80**
DY8: Word		5B **92**
Graham St. B1: Birm		2A **4** (6E **101**)
B19: Loz		2E **101**
Grainger Cl. DY4: Tip		1D **78**
Graingers La. B64: Crad H		3E **111**
Grainger St. DY2: Dud		2F **95**
Graiseley Ct. WV3: Wolv		5A **170**
Graiseley Hill WV2: Wolv		6A **170** (3G **43**)
Graiseley La. WV11: Wed		4D **28**
Graiseley Recreation Cen.		3G **43**
Graiseley Row WV2: Wolv		6A **170** (3G **43**)
Graiseley St. WV3: Wolv		5A **170** (1A **43**)
Graith Cl. B28: Hall G		4E **149**
Grammar School La. B63: Hale		1A **128**
Grampian Rd. DY8: Amb		5E **109**
Granada Ind. Est. B69: O'bry		2F **97**
Granary, The WS9: A'rdge		2D **34**
Granary Cl. DY6: W Hth		1G **91**
Granary La. B76: Walm		2D **70**

Granary Rd. WV8: Pend		6C **14**
Granbourne Rd. WS2: Wals		5D **30**
Granby Av. B33: Sheld		2G **121**
Granby Bus. Pk. B33: Sheld		2H **121**
Granby Cl. B92: Olton		4C **136**
Grandborough Dr. B91: Sol		6E **151**
Grand Cl. B66: Smeth		6F **99**
Grand Junc. Way WS1: Wals		5B **48**
Grand Theatre		3C **170** (1H **43**)
Grandys Cft. B37: F'bri		6B **106**
Grange, The B20: Hand		3B **82**
B62: Quin		5F **113**
WV5: Wom		6G **57**
Grange Av. B75: Four O		6A **38**
WS9: A'rdge		5C **22**
Grange Ct. DY1: Dud		6C **76**
DY9: Lye		2G **125**
WS2: Wals		1D **46**
WV3: Wolv		2F **43**
Grange Cres. B45: Rub		1E **157**
B63: Hale		2B **128**
WS4: S'fld		1F **33**
Grange Dr. B74: S'tly		1H **51**
GRANGE ESTATE		1G **125**
Grange Farm Dr. B38: K Nor		6H **145**
Grangefield Cl. WV8: Pend		6D **14**
Grange Hill B62: Hale		3C **128**
Grange Hill Rd. B38: K Nor		6A **146**
Grange La. B75: R'ley		6A **38**
DY6: K'wfrd		5D **92**
DY9: Lye		2G **125**
Grange Ri. B38: K Nor		2B **160**
Grange Rd. B6: Aston		1G **101**
B10: Small H		2D **118**
B14: K Hth		5F **133**
B24: Erd		2H **85**
B29: S Oak		2B **132**
B63: Hale		2B **128**
B64: Old H		2A **112**
B66: Smeth		6E **99**
B70: W Brom		4H **79**
B91: Sol		6C **136**
B93: Dorr		6F **167**
CV7: Bal C		2F **169**
DY1: Dud		6D **76**
DY9: Lye		1G **125**
WV2: Wolv		5F **43**
WV6: Tett		4A **26**
WV14: Cose		6D **60**
Grange, The (Sports and Social Club)		
		3C **128**
Grange St. DY1: Dud		6D **76**
WS1: Wals		4D **48**
Grange Wlk. B31: Longb		2G **159**
Grangewood B73: Bold		6G **69**
Grangewood Ct. B92: Olton		6C **136**
Granmore Ho. B90: Shir		6C **150**
Granshaw Cl. B38: K Nor		6B **146**
Grant Cl. B71: W Brom		2A **80**
DY6: K'wfrd		1B **92**
Grant Ct. B30: K Nor		2C **146**
Grantham Rd. B11: S'brk		4B **118**
B66: Smeth		6F **99**
Grantley Cres. DY6: K'wfrd		3A **92**
Grantley Dr. B37: F'bri		6D **106**
Granton Cl. B14: K Hth		2F **147**
Granton Rd. B14: K Hth		2F **147**
Grantown Gro. WS3: Blox		3G **19**
Grant St. B15: Birm		3F **117**
WS3: Blox		1H **31**
Granville Cl. WV2: Wolv		6D **170** (3H **43**)
Granville Ct. B15: Birm		6A **4** (2E **117**)
Granville Dr. DY6: K'wfrd		4D **92**
Granville Rd. B64: Old H		3B **112**
B93: Dorr		6H **167**
Granville Sq. B15: Birm		6A **4** (2E **117**)
Granville St. B1: Birm		6A **4** (2E **117**)
WV2: Wolv		6D **170** (3H **43**)
WV13: W'hall		6A **30**
Grasdene Gro. B17: Harb		1G **131**
Grasmere Av. B74: Lit As		1A **52**
WV6: Pert		6F **25**
Grasmere Cl. B43: Gt Barr		6B **66**
DY6: K'wfrd		2H **91**

Grasmere Cl. WV6: Tett 1C 26
  WV11: Wed 2E 29
Grasmere Ho. B69: O'bry 5D 96
Grasmere Rd. B21: Hand 2B 100
Grassington Dr. B37: F'bri 2B 122
Grassmere Ct. WS6: C Hay 2D 6
Grassmere Dr. DY8: Stourb 1D 124
Grassmoor Rd. B38: K Nor 5A 146
Grassy La. WV10: Wed 6D 16
Graston Cl. B16: Birm 1C 116
Gratham Cl. DY5: Brie H 4F 109
Grattidge Rd. B27: A Grn 3B 136
Gravel Bank B32: Bart G 2B 130
Gravel Hill WV5: Wom 1H 73
GRAVELLY HILL 5E 85
Gravelly Hill B23: Erd 6D 84
Gravelly Hill Nth. B23: Erd 5E 85
Gravelly Hill Station (Rail) 5E 85
Gravelly Ind. Pk. B24: Erd 1E 103
                    (Jarvis Way)
  B24: Erd 1F 103
                (Thompson Dr.)
Gravelly La. B23: Erd 2F 85
  WS9: Ston 5G 23
Gravity M. B68: O'bry 6A 98
Graydon Ct. B74: S Cold 4H 53
Grayfield Av. B13: Mose 2A 134
Grayland Cl. B27: A Grn 3H 135
Grayling Cl. WS10: Mox 2B 62
Grayling Rd. DY9: Lye 5G 109
Grayling Wlk. B37: Chel W 6E 107
  WV10: Wolv 5D 28
Grayshott Cl. B23: Erd 2E 85
Grays Rd. B17: Harb 5H 115
Gray St. B9: Birm 1B 118
Grayswood Pk. Rd. B32: Quin 5A 114
Grayswood Rd. B31: Longb 2D 158
Grazebrook Cft. B32: Bart G 5B 130
Grazebrook Ind. Pk. DY2: Dud 3D 94
Grazebrook Rd. DY2: Dud 2E 95
Grazewood Cl. WV12: W'hall 1B 30
Greadler St. WV12: W'hall 4C 30
Gt. Arthur St. B66: Smeth 2D 98
GREAT BARR .1A 66
Great Barr Leisure Cen 4F 67
Gt. Barr St. B9: Birm 1A 118
Gt. Brickkiln St. WV3: Wolv 5A 170 (2E 43)
GREAT BRIDGE 1E 79
Great Bridge DY4: Tip 2D 78
Gt. Bridge Ind. Est. DY4: Tip 6C 62
Gt. Bridge Rd. WV14: Bils 1A 62
Gt. Bridge St. B70: W Brom 2E 79
Gt. Bridge W. Ind. Cen. DY4: Tip 1D 78
Gt. Brook St. B7: Birm 1H 5 (5A 102)
Gt. Charles St. Queensway
  B3: Birm 3C 4 (6F 101)
Gt. Colmore St. B15: Birm 3F 117
Great Cornbow B63: Hale 2B 128
              (not continuous)
Gt. Croft Ho. WS10: Darl 5D 46
           (off Lawrence Way)
Gt. Farley Dr. B31: Longb 6A 144
Gt. Francis St. B7: Birm 5B 102
Gt. Hampton Row B19: Birm 5E 101
Gt. Hampton St. B18: Birm 4E 101
  WV1: Wolv 6F 27
              (not continuous)
Great Hill DY1: Dud 6D 76
Gt. King St. B19: Birm 4E 101
Gt. King St. Nth. B19: Hock 3E 101
Gt. Lister St. B7: Birm 5H 101
Great Meadow DY4: Tip 2B 78
Gt. Moor Rd. WV6: Patt 1A 40
Great Oaks B26: Sheld 6F 121
Greatorex Ct. B71: W Brom 5H 63
GREAT PARK .6H 143
Gt. Stone Rd. B31: N'fld 4E 145
Gt. Tindal St. B16: Birm 1C 116
Gt. Western Arc. B2: Birm 3E 5 (6G 101)
Gt. Western Cl. B18: Win G 3A 100
Gt. Western Ct. B27: A Grn 1A 136
Gt. Western Dr. B64: Old H 2A 112
Gt. Western Ind. Est. B18: Win G 3A 100

Gt. Western St. WS10: W'bry 3E 63
  WV1: Wolv 1C 170 (6H 27)
Gt. Western Way DY4: Tip 1D 78
Gt. Wood Rd. B10: Small H 2C 118
GREAT WYRLEY 2E 7
Greaves, The B76: Min 1B 88
Greaves Av. WS5: Wals 4G 49
Greaves Cl. WS5: Wals 3G 49
Greaves Cres. WV12: W'hall 1C 30
Greaves Rd. DY2: Neth 4F 95
Greaves Sq. B38: K Nor 6D 146
Grebe Cl. B23: Erd 4B 84
Greek Cathedral 3A 4 (6D 100)
Green, The B23: Erd 2G 85
  B31: Longb 5A 144
  B32: Quin 5G 113
  B36: Cas B 2F 105
  B38: K Nor 5B 146
  B68: O'bry 1H 113
  B72: W Grn 4B 70
  B91: Sol 2H 151
  CV7: Mer 4H 141
  DY8: Word 1B 108
  WS3: Blox 6H 19
              (not continuous)
  WS9: A'rdge 3D 34
              (not continuous)
  WS10: Darl 4D 46
  WV5: Try 5C 56
Greenacre Dr. WV8: Bilb 5H 13
Greenacre Rd. DY4: Tip 4A 62
Green Acres B27: A Grn 3H 135
  DY3: Sed 4F 59
  WV5: Wom 2F 73
Greenacres B32: Bart G 4C 130
  B76: Walm 5E 71
  WV6: Tett 4H 25
Greenacres Av. WV10: Bush 5D 16
Greenacres Cl. WS9: A'rdge 1G 51
Green Acres Rd. B38: K Nor 1H 159
Greenaleigh Rd. B14: Yard W 3D 148
Green Av. B28: Hall G 4E 135
Greenaway Cl. B43: Gt Barr 2E 67
Greenaway Ct. WV10: F'stne 1E 17
             (off the Avenue)
Green Bank Av. B28: Hall G 4E 135
Greenbank Gdns. DY8: Word 1C 108
Greenbank Rd. CV7: Bal C 3F 169
Green Barns La. WS14: Lit H 1H 37
Greenbush Dr. B63: Hale 6A 112
Green Cl. B47: Wyt 6A 162
Green Ct. B24: Erd 5E 85
  B28: Hall G 5F 135
Green Cft. B9: Bord G 6G 103
  WV14: Bils 5F 45
Greencroft B17: K'wfrd 5B 92
Green Dr. B32: Bart G 4A 130
  WV10: Oxl 2G 27
Greenend Rd. B13: Mose 3H 133
Greenfels Ri. DY2: Dud 1H 95
  CV7: Bal C 2G 169
  DY8: Stourb 6D 108
Greenfield Cres. B15: Edg 3C 116
Greenfield Cft. WV14: Cose 3F 61
Greenfield Ho. B26: Sheld 5H 121
Greenfield La. WV10: Bush, F'hses . . .2H 15
Greenfield Rd. B17: Harb 6G 115
  B43: Gt Barr 6G 65
  B67: Smeth 5C 98
Green Flds. WS9: A'rdge 2C 34
Greenfields Rd. DY6: K'wfrd 4B 92
  WS4: S'fld 5H 21
  WV5: Wom 2G 73
Greenfield Vw. DY3: Sed 6F 59
Greenfinch Rd. B36: Cas B 1C 106
  DY9: W'cte 2H 125
Greenford Ho. B23: Erd 1B 84
  B70: W Brom 6E 63
             (off Maria St.)
Greenford Rd. B14: K Hth 4B 148
Green Gables B74: S Cold 4H 53
Green Gables Dr. B47: H'wd 2A 162
Greenhill WV5: Wom 1H 73

Green Hill Av. B14: K Hth 4H 133
Greenhill Cl. WV12: W'hall 4B 30
  WV5: Wom 2H 73
Greenhill Dr. B29: S Oak 4G 131
Greenhill Gdns. B43: Gt Barr 3A 66
  B62: Hale 5D 112
  WV5: Wom 2H 73
Greenhill Rd. B13: Mose 4H 133
  B21: Hand 5H 81
  B62: B'hth 4D 112
  B72: W Grn 5H 69
  DY3: Up Gor 2A 76
Greenhill Wlk. WS1: Wals 3D 48
Green Hill Way B90: Shir 2H 149
Greenhill Way WS9: A'rdge 6D 22
Greenholm Rd. B44: Gt Barr 6G 67
Greening Dr. B15: Edg 4C 116
Greenland Av. B31: N'fld 5E 145
Greenland Cl. DY6: K'wfrd 1C 92
Greenland Ct. B8: Salt 3E 103
Greenland Ri. B92: Sol 6H 137
Greenland Rd. B29: S Oak 4D 132
Greenlands WV5: Wom 6F 57
Greenlands Rd. B37: Chel W 1D 122
Green La. B9: Small H 2C 118
  B21: Hand 1G 99
  B32: Quin 5A 114
  B36: Cas B 1H 105
  B38: K Nor 1A 160
  B43: Gt Barr 5H 65
  B46: Col 4H 107
      (Castle Dr., not continuous)
  B46: Col 1D 106
     (Collector Rd., not continuous)
  B46: Col 5F 107
            (Ryeclose Cft.)
  B62: B'hth 2D 112
  B90: Shir 6E 149
  CV7: Bal C 2H 169
  DY3: Up Gor 2B 76
  DY6: K'wfrd 2B 92
  DY9: Lye 6H 109
  WS2: Wals 3A 32
  WS3: Blox 2A 32
  WS3: Pels 3E 21
  WS4: S'fld 6G 21
  WS8: Hamm 3C 10
  WS9: A'rdge 4G 35
  WS9: Wals W 6G 21
  WV6: Tett 2C 26
Green La. Ind. Est. B9: Bord G 2E 119
GREEN LANES 4E 45
Green Lanes B73: W Grn 6H 69
  WV14: Bils 4E 45
Green La. Wlk. B38: K Nor 1B 160
Greenleas Gdns. B63: Hale 2C 128
Green Leigh B23: Erd 5F 69
Greenleighs DY3: Sed 2H 59
Greenly Rd. WV4: Penn, E'shll 6H 43
Green Man Entry DY1: Dud 6F 77
Green Mdw. WV11: Wed 4G 29
Green Mdw. Cl. WV5: Wom 2E 73
Green Mdw. Rd. B29: W Cas 6D 130
  WV12: W'hall 2B 30
Greenoak Cres. B30: Stir 5E 133
  WV14: Cose 6C 60
Green Oak Rd. WV8: Bilb 5H 13
Greenock Cres. WV4: E'shll 6A 44
Green Pk. Av. WV14: Bils 3E 45
Green Pk. Dr. WV14: Bils 3E 45
Green Pk. Rd. B31: N'fld 5C 144
  DY2: Dud 1H 95
Greenridge Rd. B20: Hand 2A 82
Green Rd. B13: Mose 4D 134
  B28: Hall G 4D 134
  DY2: Dud 2F 95
Green Rock La. WS3: Blox 6B 20
Greenroyde DY9: Pedm 4F 125
Greens, The WV6: Pert 6E 25
            (off Edge Hill Dr.)
Greensand WV14: Cose 3F 61
GREENSFORGE 3D 90
Greensforge La. DY7: Stourt 6E 91

Greens Health & Fitness Club
  Rednal 1H 157
Greenside B17: Harb 6G 115
  B90: Ches G 5B 164
Greenside Gdns. WS5: Wals 1F 65
Greenside Rd. B24: Erd 2A 86
Green Side Way WS5: Wals 1D 64
Greensill Av. DY4: Tip 5H 61
Greenslade Cft. B31: N'fld 5E 145
Greenslade Rd. B90: Shir 5C 148
  DY3: Sed 3F 59
  WS5: Wals 4G 49
Greensleeves B74: Four O 2F 53
Greenstead Rd. B13: Mose 4D 134
Green St. B12: Birm 6H 5 (2H 117)
  B67: Smeth 4D 98
  B69: O'bry 2G 97
  B70: W Brom 6C 80
  DY8: Stourb 6D 108
  WS2: Wals 6A 32
  WV14: Cose 5E 61
Greensway WV11: Wed 1D 28
Greenvale B31: N'fld 2D 144
Greenvale Av. B26: Sheld 5H 121
Green Wlk. B17: Harb 4D 114
Greenway B20: Hand 1B 82
  DY3: Sed 4A 60
  WS9: A'rdge 5D 22
Greenway, The B37: Mars G 5C 122
  B73: S'tly 2B 68
Greenway Av. DY8: Word 2C 108
Greenway Dr. B73: S'tly 2B 68
Greenway Gdns. B38: K Nor 2A 160
  DY3: Sed 4A 60
Greenway Rd. WV14: Bils 1G 61
Greenways B31: N'fld 5E 145
  B63: Crad 6E 111
  DY8: Word 2A 108
Greenway St. B9: Bord G 2C 118
Greenway Wlk. B33: Kitts G 2A 122
Green Wickets B14: K Hth 1H 147
Greenwood B25: Yard 3B 120
Greenwood Av. B27: A Grn 3G 135
  B65: Row R 6D 96
  B68: O'bry 4H 97
Greenwood Cl. B14: K Hth 2G 147
Greenwood Cotts. DY1: Dud 2C 76
             (off Maple Grn.)
Greenwood Pk. WS9: A'rdge 5E 23
Greenwood Pl. B44: K'sdng 4B 68
Greenwood Rd. B71: W Brom 5H 63
  WS9: A'rdge 5C 22
  WV10: Oxl 2F 27
Greenwoods, The DY8: Stourb 6C 108
Greenwood Sq. B37: Chel W 1D 122
    (off Chelmsley Wood Shop. Cen.)
Greenwood Way B37: Chel W 1D 122
    (off Chelmsley Wood Shop. Cen.)
GREET 6C 118
Greethurst Dr. B13: Mose 3C 134
GREETS GREEN 4F 79
Greets Grn. Ind. Est. B70: W Brom . . .3F 79
Greets Grn. Rd. B70: W Brom 4F 79
Greetville Cl. B34: Stech 4E 105
Gregg Ct. B12: Bal H 1H 133
Gregory Av. B29: W Cas 5D 130
Gregory Cl. WS10: W'bry 3F 63
Gregory Ct. WV11: Wed 4F 29
Gregory Dr. DY1: Dud 5C 76
Gregory Rd. DY8: Woll 6A 108
Gregston Ind. Est. B69: O'bry 2H 97
Grendon Dr. B73: New O 2D 68
Grendon Gdns. WV3: Penn 5B 42
Grendon Rd. B14: K Hth 4A 148
  B92: Olton 5D 136
Grenfell Ct. B72: W Grn 4H 69
Grenfell Dr. B15: Edg 3B 116
Grenfell Rd. WS3: Blox 4B 20
Grenville Cl. WS2: Wals 6D 30
Grenville Dr. B23: Erd 4B 84
  B66: Smeth 1B 98
Grenville Pl. B70: W Brom 4E 79
Grenville Rd. B90: Shir 5H 149
  DY1: Dud 6A 76

Gresham Rd. B28: Hall G 1F 149
  B68: O'bry 3A 98
Gresham Twr. B12: Birm 3H 117
Gresley Cl. B75: Four O 5G 37
Gresley Gro. B23: Erd 5C 84
Gressel La. B33: Kitts G 6G 105
Grestone Av. B20: Hand 3A 82
Greswolde Dr. B24: Erd 3H 85
Greswolde Pk. Rd.
  B27: A Grn 1H 135
Greswolde Rd. B11: S'hll 2C 134
  B91: Sol 1C 150
Greswold Gdns. B34: Stech 4E 105
Greswold St. B71: W Brom 2H 79
Gretton Cres. WS9: A'rdge 4A 34
Gretton Rd. B23: Erd 6D 68
  WS9: A'rdge 4B 34
Greville Dr. B15: Edg 5E 117
Grevis Cl. B13: Mose 1H 133
Grevis Rd. B25: Yard 2C 120
Greyfort Cres. B92: Olton 4D 136
Greyfriars Cl. B92: Olton 1B 150
Greyhound La. DY8: Stourb 3B 124
  WV4: Lwr P 6E 41
Greyhurst Cft. B91: Sol 1G 165
Grey Mill Cl. B90: M'path 3D 164
Greystoke Av. B36: Hodg H 2B 104
Greystoke Dr. DY6: K'wfrd 3B 92
Greystone Pas. DY1: Dud 6D 76
Greystone St. DY1: Dud 6E 77
Greytree Cres. B93: Dorr 6A 166
Grice St. B70: W Brom 1A 98
Griffin Cl. B31: N'fld 1F 145
Griffin Gdns. B17: Harb 1H 131
Griffin Ind. Est. B65: Row R 6F 97
Griffin La. B90: Dic H 4G 163
Griffin Rd. B23: Erd 2C 84
Griffin's Brook Cl. B30: B'vlle 6H 131
Griffin's Brook La. B30: B'vlle 1G 145
Griffin St. B70: W Brom 4B 80
  DY2: Neth 5E 95
  WV1: Wolv 2B 44
Griffiths Dr. WV5: Wom 2G 73
  WV11: Wed 1H 29
Griffiths Rd. B71: W Brom 4A 64
  DY1: Dud 1C 76
  WV12: W'hall 1D 30
Griffiths St. DY4: Tip 2G 77
Grigg Gro. B31: Longb 6C 144
Grimley Rd. B31: N'fld 5H 145
Grimpits La. B38: Head H 2C 160
Grimshaw Rd. B27: A Grn 4G 135
Grimstone St. WV10: Wolv . . .1D 170 (6H 27)
Grindleford Rd. B42: Gt Barr 6F 67
Gristhorpe Rd. B29: S Oak 4C 132
Grizedale Cl. B45: Fran 5H 143
Grocott Rd. WS10: Mox 1B 62
Grosmont Av. B12: Bal H 5A 118
Grosvenor Av. B20: Hand 5E 83
  B74: S'tly 2H 51
Grosvenor Cl. B75: R'ley 2A 54
  WV10: Bush 5H 15
Grosvenor Ct. B20: Hand 5E 83
  B38: K Nor 5B 146
  DY3: Lwr G 5H 75
  DY9: Pedm 4F 125
          (off Redlake Rd.)
  WV3: Wolv 5A 170
  WV11: Wed 4F 29
Grosvenor Cres. WV10: Bush 5H 15
Grosvenor Ho. B23: Erd 2G 85
Grosvenor Pk. WV4: Penn 6D 42
Grosvenor Rd. B6: Aston 1B 102
  B17: Harb 5E 115
  B20: Hand 5E 83
  B68: O'bry 6G 97
  B91: Sol 6D 150
  DY3: Lwr G 5H 75
  WV4: E'shll 2A 60
  WV10: Bush 5H 15
Grosvenor Rd. Sth. DY3: Gorn 5H 75
Grosvenor Shop. Cen. B31: N'fld 3E 145
Grosvenor Sq. B28: Hall G 2F 149

Grosvenor St. B5: Birm 3G 5 (6H 101)
  WV10: Wolv 6B 28
Grosvenor St. W. B16: Birm 2D 116
Grosvenor Ter. B15: Birm 2D 116
Grosvenor Way DY5: Quar B 4A 110
Grotto La. WV6: Tett 4C 26
Groucutt St. WV14: Cose 5E 61
Grounds Dr. B74: Four O 6F 37
Grounds Rd. B74: Four O 6F 37
Grout St. B70: W Brom 3E 79
Grove, The B8: Salt 5C 102
  B31: Longb 1F 159
  B43: Gt Barr 1A 66
  B45: Coft H 5B 158
  B46: Col 5H 107
  B65: Row R 1C 112
  B74: Lit As 4D 36
  B92: H Ard 4A 140
  DY5: Brie H 3G 109
  WS5: Wals 2F 65
  WV4: E'shll 6A 44
  WV11: Wed 3D 28
Grove Av. B13: Mose 3A 134
  B21: Hand 1B 100
  B27: A Grn 2H 135
  B29: S Oak 4A 132
  B63: Hale 2H 127
  B91: Sol 2G 151
Grove Cott. Rd. B9: Small H 1D 118
Grove Cotts. WS3: Blox 1H 31
Grove Ct. B42: Gt Barr 1B 82
Grove Cres. B70: W Brom 6C 80
  DY5: Brie H 4G 93
  WS3: Pels 4D 20
Grove Farm Dr. B75: S Cold 6D 54
Grovefield Cres. CV7: Bal C 1H 169
Grove Gdns. B20: Hand 5B 82
Grove Hill WS5: Wals 3A 50
Grove Hill Rd. B21: Hand 6B 82
Groveland Rd. DY4: Tip 4A 78
Grovelands Cres. WV10: F'hses 4H 15
Grove La. B17: Harb 1G 131
  B20: Hand 5B 82
  B21: Hand 1B 100
  B66: Smeth 4G 99
           (not continuous)
  WS3: Lit Wyr 4C 8
  WV6: Tett 1H 41
Groveley La. B31: Longb 3C 158
  B45: Coft H 5A 158
Grove M. B31: Longb 1F 159
Grove Pk. DY6: W Hth 1A 92
Grove Rd. B11: S'hll 2C 134
  B14: K Hth 6F 133
  B68: O'bry 2B 114
  B91: Sol 2G 151
  B93: Know 5C 166
  DY9: W'cte 1B 126
Groveside Way WS3: Pels 2E 21
Grove St. B66: Smeth 5H 99
  DY2: Dud 1G 95
  WV2: Wolv 6C 170 (3H 43)
  WV10: Wolv 6B 28
Grove Ter. WS1: Wals 2D 48
GROVE VALE 4H 65
Grove Va. Av. B43: Gt Barr 4G 65
Grove Vs. B64: Crad H 4F 111
Grove Way B74: S'tly 4H 51
Grovewood Dr. B38: K Nor 6A 146
Guardian Ct. B26: Yard 4D 120
  B31: N'fld 4B 144
  B91: Sol 4H 151
Guardian Ho. B68: O'bry 4A 114
Guardians Way B31: N'fld 5C 130
Guernsey Dr. B36: Cas B 3D 106
Guest Av. WV11: Wed 1E 29
Guest Gro. B19: Hock 3E 101
Guild Av. WS3: Blox 2B 32
Guild Cl. B16: Birm 1C 116
Guild Cft. B19: Hock 3F 101
Guildford Ct. B29: W Cas 6G 131
            (off Abdon Av.)
Guildford Cft. B37: Mars G 3B 122
Guildford Rd. B19: Hock 3F 101

Guildford St. B19: Loz 2F 101
Guildhall M., The WS1: Wals 2D 48
(off Goodall St.)
Guillemard Ct. B37: Chel W 2D 122
Guiting Rd. B29: W Cas 6E 131
Gullane Cl. B38: K Nor 6H 145
Gullswood Cl. B14: K Hth 5F 147
Gumbleberrys Cl. B8: W End 5A 104
Gun Barrel Ind. Cen. B64: Crad H 5H 111
Gunmakers Wlk. B19: Loz 2F 101
Gunner Gro. B75: S Cold 5E 55
Gunner La. B45: Rub 2D 156
Gunns Way B92: Olton 6B 136
Guns La. B70: W Brom 3H 79
Gunstock Cl. B74: S'tly 4G 51
GUNSTONE .1G 13
Gunstone La. WV8: Cod, Cod W 2F 13
(not continuous)
GUNS VILLAGE 3H 79
Guns Village Stop (MM) 3H 79
Gunter Rd. B24: Erd 4C 86
Gupta Trad. Est. B69: O'bry 6F 79
Gurnard Cl. WV12: W'hall 6B 18
Gurney Pl. WS2: Wals 4G 31
Gurney Rd. WS2: Wals 4G 31
Guthram Cl. B23: Erd 5E 69
Guthrie Cl. B19: Hock 3F 101
Guthrum Cl. WV6: Pert 4F 25
Guy Av. WV10: Bush 3H 27
Guys Cliffe Av. B76: Walm 4D 70
Guy's La. DY3: Gorn 5F 75
Guys Motors Ind. Pk. WV10: Wolv 4B 28
Gwalia Gro. B23: Erd 3F 85
Gwendoline Way WS9: Wals W 3D 22
GWS Ind. Est. WS10: W'bry 4D 62
Gypsy La. B46: Wat O 5F 89

H

Habberley Cft. B91: Sol 6F 151
Habberley Rd. B65: Row R 1D 112
Habitat Ct. B24: Erd 2A 86
B76: Walm 2D 70
Hackett Cl. WV14: Cose 4B 60
Hackett Ct. B69: O'bry 2G 97
(off Canal St.)
Hackett Dr. B66: Smeth 2B 98
Hackett Rd. B65: Row R 6E 97
Hackett St. DY4: Tip 6C 62
Hackford Rd. WV4: E'shll 1A 60
Hack St. B9: Birm 2A 118
Hackwood Ho. B69: O'bry 4D 96
Hackwood Rd. WS10: W'bry 3H 63
Hadcroft Grange DY9: W'cte 1H 125
Haddock Rd. WV14: Bils 4E 45
Haddon Cres. WV12: W'hall 2C 30
Haddon Cft. B63: Hale 4E 127
Haddon Rd. B42: Gt Barr 6F 67
Haddon Twr. B5: Birm 3F 117
Haden Arch Cl. B63: Hale 5A 112
Haden Cir. B12: Birm 4H 117
Haden Cl. B64: Crad H 4H 111
DY8: Word 1B 108
Haden Cres. WV11: Wed 3A 30
Haden Cross Dr. B64: Crad H 4A 112
Hadendale B64: Crad H 4A 112
Haden Hill .3H 111
Haden Hill WV3: Wolv 1E 43
Haden Hill Leisure Cen. 3H 111
Haden Hill Rd. B63: Hale 5A 112
Haden Pk. Rd. B64: Crad H 4G 111
Haden Rd. B64: Old H 1G 111
DY4: Tip .4A 62
Haden St. B12: Bal H 5H 117
Haden Wlk. B65: Row R 6C 96
Haden Way B12: Bal H 5H 117
Hadfield Cl. B24: Erd 4B 86
Hadfield Cft. B19: Birm 4E 101
Hadfield Way B37: F'bri 5C 106
Hadland Rd. B33: Sheld 2F 121
Hadleigh Cft. B76: Walm 1E 87
Hadley Cl. B47: Wyt 4A 162

Hadley Ct. B16: Edg 2H 115
Hadley Cft. B66: Smeth 2E 99
Hadley Pl. WV14: Bils 4E 45
WV14: Bils 4E 45
Hadley Rd. WS2: Wals 3F 31
Hadleys Cl. DY2: Neth 5G 95
Hadley Stadium 6E 99
Hadley St. B68: O'bry 5G 97
Hadley Way WS2: Wals 3F 31
Hadlow Cft. B33: Sheld 4H 121
Hadrian Dr. B46: Col 6H 89
Hadyn Gro. B26: Sheld 5F 121
Hadzor Rd. B68: O'bry 3B 114
Hafren Cl. B45: Fran 5H 143
Hafton Gro. B9: Small H 2D 118
Haggar St. WV2: Wolv 5G 43
HAGLEY 6G 125
Hagley C'way. DY9: Hag 6B 126
Hagley Cl. DY9: Hag 6G 125
Hagley Grange DY9: Hag 6F 125
Hagley Hall Gdns. DY9: Hag 6H 125
Hagley Hill DY9: Hag 6A 126
Hagley Mall B63: Hale 2B 128
Hagley Pk. Dr. B45: Redn 3G 157
Hagley Rd. B16: Edg 2F 115
B17: Edg 2F 115
B63: Hale 5E 127
DY8: Pedm, Stourb 1E 125
DY9: Pedm 4G 125
Hagley Rd. W. B17: Harb 4A 114
B32: Quin 5G 113
B62: Quin 5G 113
B68: Quin 5G 113
Hagley St. B63: Hale 2B 128
Hagley Vw. Rd. DY2: Dud 1E 95
Hagley Vs. B12: Bal H 1B 134
(off Taunton Rd.)
B12: S'hll 6B 118
(off Taunton Rd.)
Hagley Wood La. DY9: Hag 5D 126
Haig Cl. B75: S Cold 4A 54
Haig Rd. B13: Mose 6A 134
Haig Rd. DY2: Dud 6H 77
Haig St. B71: W Brom 2A 80
Hailes Pk. Cl. WV4: Wolv 5A 44
Hailsham Rd. B23: Erd 2F 85
Hailstone Cl. B65: Row R 4A 96
Haines Cl. DY4: Tip 3B 78
Haines St. B70: W Brom 5B 80
Hainfield Dr. B91: Sol 2A 152
Hainge Rd. B69: Tiv 5C 78
Hainult Cl. DY8: Word 5B 92
Halas Ind. Est. B62: Hale 6B 112
Halberton St. B71: W Brom 2A 80
Haldane Cl. B33: Yard 1F 121
Haldon Gro. B31: Longb 2C 158
Halecroft Av. WV11: Wed 4F 29
Hale Gro. B24: Erd 3B 86
Halesbury Ct. B63: Hale 3H 127
(off Ombersley Rd.)
Hales Cres. B67: Smeth 6C 98
Halescroft Sq. B31: N'fld 1C 144
Hales Gdns. B23: Erd 5C 68
Hales La. B67: Smeth 5C 98
Halesmere Way B63: Hale 2C 128
HALESOWEN 2B 128
Halesowen By-Pass
B62: Hale 2D 128
B62: Roms, Hale 4H 127
Halesowen Ind. Pk. B62: Hale 5B 112
(Coombs Rd.)
B62: Hale 5C 112
(Hereward Ri.)
Halesowen Leisure Cen. 2B 128
Halesowen Rd. B61: L Ash 6C 156
B62: Quin 5E 113
B64: Crad H 3H 111
B64: Old H 1G 111
DY2: Neth 4E 95
(Baptist End Rd.)
DY2: Neth 5F 95
(Cradley Rd.)
Halesowen St. B65: B'hth 3C 112
B69: O'bry 2F 97

Hales Rd. B63: Hale 2A 128
(Highfield La.)
B63: Hale 1A 128
(Islington)
WS10: W'bry 1G 63
Hales Way B69: O'bry 2F 97
Halesworth Rd. WV9: Pend 6D 14
Hale Trad. Est. DY4: Tip 2B 78
Halewood Gro. B28: Hall G 6G 135
Haley St. WV12: W'hall 4C 30
Halfcot Av. DY9: Pedm 2G 125
Halford Cres. WS3: Wals 4D 32
Halford Gro. B24: Erd 3C 86
Halford Rd. B91: Sol 1C 150
Halford's La. B66: Smeth 2E 99
B71: W Brom 2E 99
Halford's La. Ind. Est. B66: Smeth 1E 99
Halfords Pk. B66: Smeth 1E 99
Halfpenny Fld. Wlk. B35: Cas V 5E 87
Halfway Cl. B44: Gt Barr 1G 83
Halifax Ho. B5: Edg 4F 117
Halifax Rd. B90: Shir 4H 149
Haliscombe Gro. B6: Aston 1G 101
Halkett Glade B33: Stech 6B 104
Halladale B38: K Nor 6B 146
Hallam Cl. B71: W Brom 2C 80
Hallam Ct. B71: W Brom 2B 80
Hallam Cres. WV10: Wolv 3A 28
Hallam Dr. B71: W Brom 2C 80
Hallam St. B12: Bal H 6G 117
B71: W Brom 3B 80
Hall Arts Cen. 4F 95
Hallbridge Cl. WS3: Pels 5D 20
Hallbridge Way B69: Tiv 5B 78
Hallchurch Rd. DY2: Dud 2B 94
Hall Cres. B71: W Brom 1A 80
Hallcroft Cl. B72: W Grn 6A 70
Hallcroft Way B93: Know 3C 166
WS9: A'rdge 4E 35
Hall Dale Cl. B28: Hall G 2F 149
Hall Dr. B37: Mars G 4C 122
HALL END 1B 80
Hall End WS10: W'bry 2F 63
Hallens Dr. WS10: W'bry 2D 62
Hallett Dr. WV3: Wolv 5A 170 (2F 43)
Hallewell Rd. B16: Edg 6H 99
HALL GREEN
B28 . . . . .5F 135
B71 . . . . .4A 64
WV14 . . . . .3G 61
Hall Green Little Theatre 3G 135
Hall Grn. Rd. B71: W Brom 4A 64
Hall Green Stadium 4F 135
Hall Green Station (Rail) 4F 135
Hall Grn. St. WV14: Bils 2G 61
Hall Gro. WV14: Cose 5E 61
Hall Hays Rd. B34: S End 2A 106
Hall La. DY2: Neth 3E 95
DY4: Tip .5B 62
DY9: Hag 6H 125
WS3: Pels 4D 20
WS6: Gt Wyr 1F 7
WS7: Hamm 1F 11
(not continuous)
WS9: Wals W 3A 22
WS14: Muck C 3H 11
WV14: Cose 4B 60
Hall Mdw. DY9: Hag 6H 125
Hallmeadow Rd. CV7: Bal C 6H 155
Hallmoor Rd. B33: Kitts G 6F 105
Hall of Memory, The 4B 4 (1E 117)
Hallot Cl. B23: Erd 5D 68
Halloughton Rd. B74: S Cold 4G 53
Hall Pk. St. WV14: Bils 5D 44
Hall Rd. B8: Salt 5D 102
B20: Hand 1C 100
B36: Cas B 1E 105
B67: Smeth 5C 98
Hall Rd. Av. B20: Hand 1C 100
Hallstead Rd. B13: Mose 2B 148
Hall St. B18: Birm 1B 4 (5E 101)
B64: Old H 1H 111
B68: O'bry 4H 97
B70: W Brom 5A 80

Hall St. DY2: Dud 6F 77
— DY3: Sed 5H 59
— DY4: Tip 2G 77
— DY8: Stourb 2E 125
— WS2: Wals 6B 32
— WS10: Darl 4B 46
— WV11: Wed 4E 29
— WV13: W'hall 2B 46
— WV14: Bils 6G 45
Hall St. E. WS10: Darl 4C 46
Hall St. Sth. B70: W Brom 1B 98
Hallswelle Gro. B43: Gt Barr 1G 67
Hall Wlk. B46: Col 4G 107
(Birmingham Rd.)
— B46: Col 5H 107
(Stonebridge Rd.)
Hallwood Dr. B43: Gt Barr 4A 66
Halow Cl. B31: N'fld 5H 145
Halsbury Gro. B44: K'sdng 5B 68
Halstead Gro. B91: Sol 1E 165
Halton Rd. B73: New O, S Cold 2D 68
Halton St. DY2: Neth 4E 95
Hamar Way B37: Mars G 2D 122
Hamberley Ct. B18: Win G 5H 99
Hamble Cl. DY5: P'ntt 3E 93
Hamble Ct. B73: S Cold 6H 53
Hambledon Cl. WV9: Pend 5E 15
Hamble Gro. WV6: Pert 6E 25
Hamble Rd. B42: Gt Barr 4B 66
— WV4: Penn 5A 42
Hambleton Rd. B63: Hale 3F 127
Hambletts Rd. B70: W Brom 4G 79
Hambrook Cl. WV6: Wolv 4E 27
Hambury Dr. B14: K Hth 6F 133
Hamilton Av. B17: Harb 3E 115
— B62: Hale 2C 128
— DY8: Woll 5B 108
Hamilton Cl. DY3: Sed 6G 59
— DY8: Word 1A 108
Hamilton Ct. B13: Mose 1H 133
— B30: K Nor 3A 146
Hamilton Dr. B29: S Oak 5H 131
— B69: Tiv 5C 78
— DY8: Word 1A 108
Hamilton Gdns. WV10: Bush 4A 16
Hamilton Ho. B66: Smeth 4G 99
— WS3: Blox 6A 20
Hamilton Rd. B21: Hand 1H 99
— B67: Smeth 1C 114
— DY4: Tip 1C 78
Hamilton St. B68: O'bry 4H 113
— WS3: Blox 6A 20
Ham La. DY6: K'wfrd 6C 74
— DY9: Pedm 4G 125
Hamlet, The WS11: Nort C 1C 8
Hamlet Gdns. B28: Hall G 5F 135
Hamlet Rd. B28: Hall G 5F 135
Hammer Bank DY5: Quar B 3C 110
Hammersley Cl. B63: Crad 4D 110
HAMMERWICH 1F 11
Hammerwich Link WS7: Hamm 2H 11
Hammond Av. WV10: Bush 1A 28
Hammond Dr. B23: Erd 2F 85
Hammond Way DY8: Amb 4E 109
Hampden Cl. DY5: Quar B 3C 110
Hampden Retreat B12: Bal H 5G 117
Hampshire Ct. B29: W Cas 6F 131
Hampshire Dr. B15: Edg 3A 116
Hampshire Rd. B71: W Brom 5G 63
Hampson Cl. B11: S'brk 5B 118
Hampstead Glade B63: Hale 3C 128
Hampton Cl. B73: New O 3C 68
Hampton Cl. B15: Edg 3D 116
(off George Rd.)
— B71: W Brom 4A 64
— B92: H Ard 1B 154
— WV10: Bush 5D 16
Hampton Ct. Rd. B17: Harb 5D 114
Hampton Dr. B74: Four O 3H 53
Hampton Gdns. DY9: Pedm 2G 125
Hampton Grange CV7: Mer 4H 141
Hampton Gro. WS3: Pels 3D 20
HAMPTON IN ARDEN 1A 154
Hampton in Arden Station (Rail) 6B 140

Hampton La. B91: Cath B, Sol 3H 151
(not continuous)
— CV7: Mer 5E 141
Hampton Pl. WS10: Darl 3C 46
Hampton Rd. B6: Aston 6F 83
— B23: Erd 3D 84
— B93: Know 2E 167
— WV10: Oxl 6F 15
Hamptons, The B93: Know 3E 167
Hampton St. B19: Birm 1C 4 (5F 101)
— DY2: Neth 4E 95
— WV14: Cose 5D 60
Hampton Vw. WV10: Wolv 5B 28
Hampton Wlk. WV1: Wolv 3B 170
HAMS HALL 3H 89
Hams Hall Distribution Pk. B46: Col 2H 89
Hams La. B76: Lea M 2G 89
Hams Rd. B8: Salt 5D 102
HAMSTEAD 6B 66
Hamstead Cl. WV11: Wed 3F 29
Hamstead Hall Av. B20: Hand 2A 82
Hamstead Hall Rd. B20: Hand 3A 82
Hamstead Hill B20: Hand 4B 82
Hamstead Ho. B43: Gt Barr 6B 66
Hamstead Ind. Est. B42: P Barr 2C 82
Hamstead Rd B19: Hock 2D 100
Hamstead Rd. B20: Hand 6D 82
— B43: Gt Barr 5G 65
Hamstead Station (Rail) 1B 82
Hamstead Ter. WS10: W'bry 3G 63
Hanbury Cl. B75: S Cold 5D 54
Hanbury Ct. DY8: Stourb 1E 125
(off College Rd.)
Hanbury Cres. WV4: Penn 5C 42
Hanbury Cft. B27: A Grn 2C 136
Hanbury Dr. B69: O'bry 5E 97
Hanbury Hill DY8: Stourb 1E 125
Hanbury Pas. DY8: Stourb 6E 109
Hanbury Rd. B70: W Brom 4G 79
— B93: Dorr 5B 166
— WS8: Bwnhls 3A 10
Hanch Pl. WS1: Wals 3D 48
Hancock Rd. B8: Salt 5F 103
Hancox St. B68: O'bry 1H 113
Handley Gro. B31: Longb 5A 144
Handley St. WS10: W'bry 1G 63
HANDSWORTH 6A 82
Handsworth Booth Street Stop (MM) ...2G 99
Handsworth Cl. B21: Hand 2H 99
Handsworth Dr. B43: Gt Barr 2C 66
Handsworth Horticultural Institute 5A 82
(off Oxhill Rd.)
Handsworth Leisure Cen. 6B 82
Handsworth New Rd. B18: Win G 3A 100
HANDSWORTH WOOD 5C 82
Handsworth Wood Rd. B20: Hand 4B 82
Hangar Rd. B26: Birm A 2C 138
Hanging La. B31: N'fld 5C 144
Hangleton Dr. B11: S'brk 5D 118
Hanley Cl. B63: Hale 1G 127
Hanley St. B19: Birm 1E 5 (5F 101)
Hannafore Rd. B16: Edg 6H 99
Hannah Rd. WV14: Bils 2A 62
Hanney Hay Rd. WS7: Chase, Hamm 1C 10
— WS8: Hamm 1C 10
Hannon Rd. B14: K Hth 2G 147
Hanover Cl. B6: Aston 2G 101
Hanover Ct. WS2: Wals 2E 47
— WV6: Tett 5A 26
Hanover Dr. B24: Erd 1F 103
Hanover Rd. B65: Row R 5C 96
Hansell Dr. B93: Dorr 6F 167
Hansom Rd. B32: Quin 6A 114
Hanson Cl. B66: Smeth 2E 99
Hanson Gro. B92: Olton 6D 120
Hansons Bri. Rd. B24: Erd 2D 86
Hanwell Cl. B76: Walm 6F 71
Hanwood Cl. B12: Birm 3H 117
Harald Cl. WV6: Pert 4E 25
Harbeck Av. B44: Gt Barr 5H 67
Harbet Dr. B40: Nat E C 1G 139
Harbinger Rd. B38: K Nor 5D 146
HARBORNE 5F 115

Harborne Ct. B17: Harb 1G 131
Harborne Ho. B17: Harb 1E 131
Harborne La. B17: Harb, S Oak 2H 131
— B29: S Oak 3A 132
Harborne Pk. Rd. B17: Harb 6G 115
Harborne Pool & Fitness Cen. 6F 115
Harborne Rd. B15: Edg 5A 116
— B68: O'bry 2B 114
Harborough Ct. B74: Four O 1G 53
Harborough Dr. B36: Cas B 6H 87
— WS9: A'rdge 4C 34
Harborough Wlk. DY9: Pedm 3G 125
Harbours Hill B61: Wild 4A 156
Harbour Ter. WV3: Wolv 2E 43
Harbury Cl. B76: Walm 1F 87
Harbury Rd. B12: Bal H 6F 117
Harby Cl. B37: Mars G 3D 122
Harcourt Dr. B74: Four O 5F 37
— DY3: Gorn 5H 75
Harcourt Rd. B23: Erd 1E 85
— B64: Crad H 3H 111
— WS10: W'bry 1F 63
HARDEN 2C 32
Harden Cl. WS3: Blox 2C 32
Harden Ct. B31: N'fld 6C 144
Harden Gro. WS3: Blox 2C 32
Harden Keep B66: Smeth 5E 99
Harden Mnr. Ct. B63: Hale 2C 128
Harden Rd. WS3: Blox, Wals 2B 32
Harden Va. B63: Hale 6G 111
Harding St. WV14: Cose 3F 61
Hardon Rd. WV4: E'shll 6B 44
Hardware St. B70: W Brom 3B 80
HARDWICK 2G 51
Hardwick Ct. B74: S'tly 1H 51
— DY9: Lye 6H 109
Hardwick Dr. B62: Hale 4A 112
Hardwicke Wlk. B14: K Hth 5F 147
Hardwicke Way DY9: Lye 6H 109
Hardwick Rd. B74: S'tly 1H 51
— B92: Olton 1C 136
Hardy Ct. B13: Mose 1H 133
Hardy Rd. WS3: Blox 1C 32
— WS10: W'bry 2G 63
Hardy Sq. WV2: E'shll 5B 44
Harebell Cl. WS5: Wals 2E 65
Harebell Cres. DY1: Dud 3C 76
Harebell Gdns. B38: K Nor 1B 160
Harebell Wlk. B37: Chel W 1F 123
Hare Gro. B31: N'fld 4B 144
Haresfield B90: Dic H 4G 163
Hare St. WV14: Bils 6H 45
(not continuous)
Harewell Dr. B75: R'ley 2A 54
Harewood Av. B43: Gt Barr 3G 65
— WS10: W'bry 2A 64
Harewood Cl. B28: Hall G 2E 149
Harford St. B19: Birm 5E 101
— B71: W Brom 3A 80
Hargate La. B70: W Brom 3A 80
Hargrave Cl. B46: Wat O 4D 88
Hargrave Rd. B90: Shir 5C 148
Hargreave St. WV1: Wolv 4C 44
Hargreaves St. WV1: Wolv 4C 44
Harland Rd. B74: Four O 6G 37
Harlech Cl. B32: Bart G 6G 129
— B69: Tiv 6A 78
Harlech Ho. WS3: Blox 3A 32
(off Providence Cl.)
Harlech Rd. WV12: W'hall 3C 30
Harlech Twr. B23: Erd 1G 85
Harlech Way DY1: Dud 5B 76
Harlequin Dr. B13: Mose 3G 133
Harleston Rd. B44: Gt Barr 5H 67
Harley Cl. WS8: Bwnhls 1C 22
Harley Dr. WV14: Bils 1D 60
Harlow Gro. B28: Hall G 1G 149
Harlstones Cl. DY8: Amb 3E 109
Harlyn Cl. WV14: Bils 3A 62
Harman Rd. B72: W Grn 6H 69
Harmer St. B18: Hock 4C 100
Harman Rd. DY8: Woll 6A 108
Harmony Ho. B10: Small H 2C 118
Harnall Cl. B90: Shir 2C 164

Harness Cl. WS5: Wals 1D **64**
Harold Rd. B16: Edg 2B **116**
B67: Smeth 6C **98**
Harper Av. WV11: Wed 2E **29**
Harper Gro. DY4: Tip 1F **77**
Harper Rd. WV14: Bils 5F **45**
Harpers Rd. B14: K Hth 6A **148**
B31: N'fld 6E **145**
Harper St. WV13: W'hall 1A **46**
Harpur Cl. WS4: Wals 5E **33**
Harpur Rd. WS4: Wals 5E **33**
Harrier Rd. B27: A Grn 3B **136**
Harrier Way B42: P Barr 4F **83**
Harriet Cl. DY5: P'ntt 4F **93**
Harringay Dr. DY8: Stourb 2C **124**
Harringay Rd. B44: K'sdng 3H **67**
Harrington Cft. B71: W Brom 6D **64**
Harringworth Ct. WS4: S'fld 1G **33**
Harriots Hayes Rd. WV8: Cod W 1A **12**
Harris Cl. B18: Hock 3C **100**
Harris Dr. B42: Gt Barr 5C **66**
B66: Smeth 6F **99**
Harrison Cl. WS3: Blox 6A **20**
WS6: C Hay 4D **6**
Harrison Ct. DY8: Amb 2E **109**
Harrison Ho. B14: K Hth 4H **147**
Harrison Rd. B24: Erd 3F **85**
B74: Four O 4E **37**
DY8: Word 2E **109**
WS4: S'fld 5G **21**
Harrison's Fold DY2: Neth 4E **95**
Harrisons Grn. B15: Edg 5A **116**
Harrisons Pleck B13: Mose 2H **133**
Harrison's Rd. B15: Edg 5A **116**
Harrison St. WS3: Blox 6H **19**
Harrold Av. B65: Row R 6E **97**
Harrold Rd. B65: Row R 6E **97**
Harrold St. DY4: Tip 6C **62**
Harrop Way DY8: Amb 3C **108**
Harrowby Dr. DY4: Tip 3A **78**
Harrowby Pl. WV13: W'hall 2D **46**
WV14: Bils 1A **62**
Harrowby Rd. WV10: F'hses 4F **15**
WV14: Bils 1A **62**
Harrow Cl. DY9: Hag 6E **125**
Harrowfield Rd. B33: Stech 5C **104**
Harrow Rd. B29: S Oak 2B **132**
DY6: K'wfrd 6B **74**
Harrow St. WV1: Wolv 5F **27**
Harry Mitchell Leisure Cen. 4D **98**
Harry Perks St. WV13: W'hall 6A **30**
Harry Price Ho. B69: O'bry 4D **96**
Hart Dr. B73: Bold 5G **69**
Hartfield Cres. B27: A Grn 3G **135**
Hartfields Way B65: Row R 4H **95**
Hartford Cl. B17: Harb 4E **115**
Hartill Rd. WV4: Penn 2B **58**
Hartill St. WV13: W'hall 3B **46**
Hartington Cl. B93: Dorr 6A **166**
Hartington Rd. B19: Loz 1F **101**
Hartland Av. WV14: Cose 5C **60**
Hartland Rd. B31: Longb 3C **158**
B71: W Brom 5D **64**
DY4: Tip 2F **77**
Hartland St. DY5: P'ntt 2H **93**
Hartlebury Cl. B93: Dorr 6B **166**
Hartlebury Rd. B63: Hale 3H **127**
B69: O'bry 4D **96**
Hartledon Rd. B17: Harb 6F **115**
Hartley Dr. WS9: A'rdge 5D **34**
Hartley Gro. B44: K'sdng 2B **68**
Hartley Pl. B15: Edg 3B **116**
Hartley Rd. B44: K'sdng 2B **68**
Hartley St. WV3: Wolv 1E **43**
Harton Way B14: K Hth 2E **147**
Hartopp Rd. B8: Salt 5E **103**
B74: Four O 2F **53**
Hart Rd. B24: Erd 2G **85**
WV11: Wed 5F **29**
Hartsbourne Dr. B62: Hale 1D **128**
Harts Cl. B17: Harb 5H **115**
HARTS GREEN **6E 115**
Harts Grn. Rd. B17: Harb 6E **115**
HART'S HILL **4A 94**

Hartshill Cl. B34: S End 3E **105**
Hartshill Rd. B27: A Grn 3B **136**
B34: S End 3E **105**
Hartshorn St. WV14: Bils 6F **45**
Hartside Cl. B63: Hale 3F **127**
Harts Rd. B8: Salt 4E **103**
Hart St. WS1: Wals 3C **48**
Hartswell Dr. B13: Mose 1H **147**
Hartwell Cl. B91: Sol 6F **151**
Hartwell La. WS6: Gt Wyr 2G **7**
Hartwell Rd. B24: Erd 5H **85**
Hartwood Cres. WV4: Penn 6D **42**
Harvard Cl. DY1: Dud 4B **76**
Harvard Rd. B92: Olton 1F **137**
Harvest Cl. B30: Stir 1D **146**
DY3: Up Gor 2A **76**
Harvest Ct. B65: Row R 5A **96**
Harvesters Cl. WS9: A'rdge 1G **51**
Harvesters Rd. WV12: W'hall 4D **30**
Harvesters Wlk. WV8: Pend 6C **14**
Harvesters Way WV12: W'hall 4D **30**
Harvester Way DY6: W Hth 1G **91**
Harvest Flds. Way B75: R'ley 5B **38**
Harvest Gdns. B68: O'bry 5G **97**
Harvest Rd. B65: Row R 5A **96**
B67: Smeth 6B **98**
Harvest Wlk. B65: Row R 5A **96**
Harvey Ct. B33: Kitts G 6H **105**
Harvey Dr. B75: R'ley 1A **54**
Harvey M. B30: B'vlle 6A **132**
Harvey Rd. B26: Yard 4B **120**
WS2: Wals 4H **31**
Harvey's Ter. DY2: Neth 5F **95**
HARVILLS HAWTHORN **6F 63**
Harvills Hawthorn B70: W Brom 6F **63**
Harvine Wlk. DY8: Stourb 2C **124**
Harvington Dr. B90: M'path 3F **165**
Harvington Rd. B29: W Cas 5E **131**
B63: Hale 3H **127**
B68: O'bry 4G **113**
WV14: Cose 5D **60**
Harvington Wlk. B65: Row R 6C **96**
Harvington Way B76: Walm 5E **71**
Harwin Cl. WV6: Tett 2D **26**
Harwood Gro. B90: Shir 1A **164**
Harwood St. B70: W Brom 4H **79**
HASBURY **3G 127**
Hasbury Cl. B63: Hale 3G **127**
Hasbury Rd. B32: Bart G 5G **129**
Haseley Rd. B21: Hand 2A **100**
B91: Sol 1C **150**
Haselor Rd. B73: New O 4E **69**
Haselour Rd. B37: K'hrst 4B **106**
Haselwell Dr. B30: K Nor 4F **147**
Haskell St. WS1: Wals 4D **48**
Haslucks Cft. B90: Shir 4G **149**
HASLUCKS GREEN **6E 149**
Haslucks Grn. Rd. B90: Maj G, Shir . . .2E **163**
Hassop Rd. B42: Gt Barr 6F **67**
Hastings Ct. DY1: Dud 4B **76**
Hastings Rd. B23: Erd 6B **68**
Hostingwood Ind. Pk. B24: Erd 6H **85**
Haswell Rd. B63: Hale 2F **127**
Hatcham Rd. B44: K'sdng 3B **68**
Hatchett St. B19: Birm 4G **101**
Hatchford Av. B92: Sol 2G **137**
Hatchford Brook Rd. B92: Sol 2G **137**
Hatchford Ct. B92: Sol 2G **137**
Hatchford Wlk. B37: Chel W 2D **122**
Hatchford Way B26: Sheld 1A **138**
Hatch Heath Cl. WV5: Wom 6A **64**
Hateley Dr. WV4: E'shll 1A **60**
HATELEY HEATH **6A 64**
Hatfield Cl. B23: Erd 6D **68**
Hatfield Rd. B19: Loz 1F **101**
DY9: Lye 1G **125**
Hathaway Cl. CV7: Bal C 2H **169**
WV13: W'hall 5A **46**
Hathaway M. DY8: Word 6H **91**
Hathaway Rd. B75: Four O 5G **37**
B90: Shir 6H **149**
Hatherden Dr. B76: Walm 3E **71**
Hathersage Rd. B42: Gt Barr 6F **67**
Hatherton Gdns. WV10: Bush 5A **16**

Hatherton Gro. B29: W Cas 4D **130**
Hatherton Pl. WS9: A'rdge 2C **34**
Hatherton Rd. WS1: Wals 1C **48**
WV14: Bils 5H **45**
Hatherton St. WS1: Wals 1C **48**
WS4: Wals 6C **32**
WS6: C Hay 3C **6**
Hattersley Gro. B11: Tys 2G **135**
Hatton Cres. WV10: Wolv 2C **28**
Hatton Gdns. B42: Gt Barr 6D **66**
Hatton Rd. WV6: Wolv 6D **26**
Hattons Gro. WV8: Bilb 5H **13**
Hatton St. WV14: Bils 1G **61**
Haughton Rd. B20: Hand 6F **83**
Haunch La. B13: Mose 1H **147**
Haunchwood Dr. B76: Walm 6D **70**
Havacre La. WV14: Cose 3E **61**
Havelock Cl. WV3: Wolv 3D **42**
Havelock Rd. B8: Salt 4D **102**
B11: Tys 1E **135**
B20: Hand 6E **83**
Haven, The B14: Yard W 3D **148**
DY8: Word 1B **108**
WV2: Wolv 3G **43**
Haven Cvn. Pk. B92: Bick 3E **139**
Haven Cft. B43: Gt Barr 5H **65**
Haven Dr. B27: A Grn 2H **135**
Haverford Dr. B45: Redn 3H **157**
Havergal Wlk. B63: Crad 1D **126**
Haverhill Cl. WS3: Blox 4G **19**
Hawbridge Cl. B90: M'path 3F **165**
HAWBUSH **1E 109**
Hawbush Gdns. DY5: Brie H 2E **109**
Hawbush Rd. DY5: Brie H 2E **109**
WS3: Blox 3B **32**
Hawbush Urban Farm Vis. Cen. 2F **109**
Hawcroft Gro. B34: S End 3G **105**
Hawes Cl. WS1: Wals 5D **48**
Hawes La. B65: Row R 5B **96**
Hawes Rd. WS1: Wals 5D **48**
Haweswater Dr. DY6: K'wfrd 3B **92**
Hawfield Cl. B69: Tiv 2C **96**
Hawfield Gro. B72: W Grn 6A **70**
Hawfield Rd. B69: Tiv 2C **96**
Hawker Dr. B35: Cas V 5D **86**
Hawkesbury Rd. B90: Shir 6F **149**
Howkcs Cl. B30: Stir 5C **132**
Hawkesford Cl. B36: Cas B 1E **105**
B74: Four O 2H **53**
Hawkesford Rd. B33: Kitts G 6H **105**
Hawkeshaw Path B90: Bly P 5E **165**
(not continuous)
Hawkes La. B70: W Brom 6G **63**
HAWKESLEY **2A 160**
Hawkesley Cres. B31: Longb 6D **144**
Hawkesley Dr. B31: Longb 1D **158**
Hawkesley End B38: K Nor 2A **160**
Hawkesley Mill La. B31: N'fld 5D **144**
Hawkesley Rd. DY1: Dud 1B **94**
Hawkesley Sq. B38: K Nor 2A **160**
Hawkes St. B10: Small H 3D **118**
Hawkestone Cres. B70: W Brom 1F **79**
Hawkestone Rd. B29: W Cas 6E **131**
Hawkeswell Cl. B92: Olton 4C **136**
Hawkesyard Rd. B24: Erd 6E **85**
Hawkhurst Rd. B14: K Hth 5H **147**
Hawkinge Dr. B35: Cas V 4E **87**
Hawkins Cl. B5: Edg 5G **117**
Hawkins Cft. DY4: Tip 4A **78**
Hawkins Dr. WS11: Cann 1C **6**
Hawkins Pl. WV14: Bils 2H **61**
Hawkins St. B70: W Brom 5G **63**
Hawkley Cl. WV1: Wolv 1D **44**
Hawkley Rd. WV1: Wolv 1D **44**
Hawkmoor Gdns. B38: K Nor 1C **160**
Hawks Cl. WS6: C Hay 3D **6**
Hawksford Cres. WV10: Bush 2H **27**
Hawkshead Dr. B93: Know 3B **166**
Hawksmill Ind. Est. B9: Small H 2C **118**
Hawksmoor Dr. WV6: Pert 6D **24**
Hawkstone Ct. WV6: Pert 4D **24**
Hawkswell Av. WV5: Wom 2G **73**
Hawkswell Dr. DY6: K'wfrd 1B **92**
WV13: W'hall 2H **45**

Hawkswood Dr. CV7: Bal C 2H 169
    WS10: Mox 2B 62
Hawkswood Gro. B14: K Hth 4B 148
Hawksworth Cres. B37: Chel W 6F 107
Hawley Cl. WS4: Wals 5D 32
Hawley Ct. B43: Gt Barr 4A 66
Hawnby Gro. B76: Walm 3E 71
HAWNE 5G 111
Hawne Cl. B63: Hale 5G 111
Hawnelands, The B63: Hale 6H 111
Hawne La. B63: Hale 5G 111
Hawthorn Brook Way B23: Erd 5E 69
Hawthorn Cl. B9: Birm 2B 118
    B23: Erd .6F 69
Hawthorn Coppice B30: K Nor 3A 146
Hawthorn Cft. B68: O'bry 4B 114
Hawthornden Ct. B76: Walm 6B 70
Hawthorn Dr. B29: S Oak 4G 131
    B47: H'wd 3B 162
    CV7: Bal C 1H 169
Hawthorne Av. WS6: Gt Wyr 4G 7
Hawthorne Cft. B30: K Nor 2H 145
Hawthorne Gdns. B13: Mose 5B 134
Hawthorne Gro. DY3: Gorn 5H 75
Hawthorne Ho. WV10: Wolv 6B 28
Hawthorne La. WV8: Cod 5F 13
Hawthorne Rd. B15: Edg 4A 116
    B30: K Nor 3H 145
    B36: Cas B 2A 106
    B63: Hale 3G 127
    DY1: Dud 3E 77
    WS5: Wals 6D 48
    WS6: C Hay 1E 7
    WV2: Wolv 5H 43
    WV11: Ess 3A 18
    WV11: Wed 4H 29
    WV12: W'hall 2D 30
Hawthorn Gro. B19: Loz 1E 101
Hawthorn Pk. B20: Hand 4A 82
Hawthorn Pk. Dr. B20: Hand 4B 82
Hawthorn Pl. WS2: Wals 6E 31
Hawthorn Rd. B44: K'sdng 5H 67
    B72: W Grn 4A 70
    B74: S'tly 2A 52
    DY4: Tip .5A 62
    DY5: Quar B 3A 110
    WS4: S'fld 6F 21
    WS10: W'bry 1F 63
    WV1: Wolv 3D 44
Hawthorns, The 6F 81
Hawthorns, The B13: Mose 2H 133
    B68: O'bry 4B 114
Hawthorns Bus. Cen. B66: Smeth 1E 99
Hawthorns Ind. Est. B21: Hand 6F 81
Hawthorns Station, The (Rail & MM)
    . . . . .1F 99
Hawthorn Ter. WS10: W'bry 1F 63
Haxby Av. B34: Hodg H 3E 105
Haybarn, The B76: Walm 5E 71
Haybrook Dr. B11: Tys 1F 135
Haycock Pl. WS10: Darl 4C 46
Haycroft Av. B8: Salt 4E 103
Haycroft Dr. B74: Four O 5G 37
Haydn Sanders Sq. WS1: Wals 3C 48
Haydock Cl. B36: Hodg H 1A 104
    WV6: Wolv 3F 27
Haydon Cl. B93: Dorr 6G 167
Haydon Cft. B33: Kitts G 6E 105
Hayehouse Gro. B36: Hodg H 2C 104
HAYES, THE .5C 110
Hayes, The B31: Longb 2G 159
    DY9: Lye 6B 110
    WV12: W'hall 3B 30
Hayes Bus. Pk. DY9: Lye 5B 110
Hayes Cres. B68: O'bry 4B 98
Hayes Cft. B38: K Nor 2A 160
Hayes Dr. B24: Erd 2B 86
Hayes Gro. B24: Erd 1B 86
Hayes La. DY9: Lye 5C 110
Hayes Mdw. B72: W Grn 6B 70
Hayes Rd. B68: O'bry 4B 98
Hayes St. B70: W Brom 3G 79
Hayes Trad. Est., The DY9: Lye 5C 110
Hayes Vw. Dr. WS6: C Hay 1E 7

Hayfield Ct. B13: Mose 3B 134
Hayfield Gdns. B13: Mose 3C 134
Hayfield Rd. B13: Mose 3B 134
HAY GREEN .6H 109
Hay Grn. DY9: Lye 6H 109
Hay Grn. Cl. B30: B'vlle 1H 145
Hay Grn. La. B30: B'vlle 2G 145
Hay Gro. WS8: Bwnhls 5B 10
Hay Hall Rd. B11: Tys 6F 119
Hay Head Wood (Nature Reserve) . . .6A 34
Hay Hill WS5: Wals 3A 50
Hayland Rd. B23: Erd 1E 85
Hay La. B90: M'path 3D 164
Hayle Cl. B38: K Nor 5D 146
Hayley Ct. B24: Erd 1A 86
HAYLEY GREEN 4F 127
Hayley Grn. Rd. B32: Bart G 5H 129
Hayley Pk. Rd. B63: Hale 5E 127
Hayling Cl. B45: Fran 6F 143
Hayling Gro. WV2: Wolv 5F 43
Haylofts, The B63: Hale 4E 127
Haymarket, The WV8: Pend 6C 14
HAY MILLS 5H 119
Haynes La. WS5: Wals 1F 65
Hay Pk. B5: Edg 5F 117
Haypits Cl. B71: W Brom 6C 64
Hayrick Dr. DY6: W Hth 2G 91
Hay Rd. B25: Yard 4G 119
Hayseech B64: Crad H 4H 111
Hayseech Rd. B63: Hale 5H 111
Hays Kent Moat, The B26: Yard 2E 121
Haytor Av. B14: K Hth 2F 147
Haywain Cl. WV9: Pend 5E 15
Hayward Ind. Pk. WS9: A'rdge 2C 34
Hayward Rd. B75: S Cold 3A 54
Haywards Cl. B23: Erd 2E 85
    WS3: Pels 4D 20
Haywards Ind. Est. B35: Cas V 6F 87
Hayward St. WV14: Cose 5D 60
Hayway, The WS2: Wals 6G 31
Haywharf Rd. DY5: P'ntt 4F 93
Haywood Dr. B62: B'hth 3C 112
    WV6: Tett 5A 26
Haywood Rd. B33: Kitts G 1A 122
Haywood's Farm B71: W Brom 3D 64
Hazel Av. B73: New O 4C 68
    WS10: W'bry 1G 63
Hazelbank B38: K Nor 5A 146
Hazelbeach Rd. B8: Salt 4F 103
Hazelbeech Rd. B70: W Brom 5H 79
Hazel Cft. B31: N'fld 4E 145
    B37: Chel W 2D 122
Hazeldene Gro. B6: Aston 1G 101
Hazeldene Rd. B33: Sheld 4H 121
    B63: Hale 3G 127
Hazel Dr. B29: W Cas 6D 130
    B47: H'wd 4B 162
Hazel Gdns. B27: A Grn 1A 136
    WV8: Cod 3G 13
Hazelglen Gro. B18: Win G 5A 100
    (off Heath Grn. Rd.)
Hazel Gro. B70: W Brom 6A 80
    DY8: Stourb 2A 124
    WV5: Wom 6G 57
    WV11: Wed 2E 29
    WV14: Bils 4G 45
Hazelhurst Rd. B14: K Hth 1G 147
    B36: Cas B 2A 106
Hazel La. WS6: Gt Wyr 3H 7
Hazelmead Ct. B73: Bold 6G 69
Hazelmere Dr. WS7: Chase 1B 10
    WV3: Wolv 2G 41
Hazelmere Rd. B28: Hall G 4F 135
Hazeloak Rd. B90: Shir 6G 149
Hazel Rd. B45: Rub 3F 157
    DY1: Dud 5E 77
    DY4: Tip .4C 62
    DY6: K'wfrd 4C 92
    WV3: Wolv 4C 42
Hazelton Cl. B91: Sol 6F 151
Hazeltree Cft. B27: A Grn 3H 135
Hazeltree Gro. B93: Dorr 6A 166
Hazelville Gro. B28: Hall G 1G 149

Hazelville Rd. B28: Hall G 1G 149
Hazelwell Cres. B30: Stir 1D 146
Hazelwell Dr. B14: K Hth 1F 147
Hazelwell Fordrough B30: Stir 6D 132
Hazelwell La. B30: Stir 6C 132
Hazelwell Rd. B30: Stir 1C 146
Hazelwell St. B30: Stir 6C 132
Hazelwood Cl. WS6: C Hay 3D 6
Hazelwood Dr. WV11: Wed 4C 28
Hazelwood Gro. WV12: W'hall 4D 30
Hazelwood Rd. B27: A Grn 3H 135
    B74: S'tly 2F 51
    DY1: Dud 2B 76
Hazlemere Dr. B74: Four O 3G 53
Hazlitt Gro. B30: K Nor 3H 145
Headborough Wlk. WS9: A'rdge 6D 22
Headingley Rd. B21: Hand 5A 82
Headland Dr. B8: Salt 4D 102
Headland Rd. WV3: Wolv 2F 41
Headlands, The B74: Lit As 6C 36
Headley Cft. B38: K Nor 1H 159
HEADLEY HEATH 3E 161
Headley Heath La. B38: Head H 2D 160
Headley Ri. B90: Shir 5B 150
Headway Rd. WV10: F'hses 4G 15
Heale Cl. B63: Crad 4C 110
Heanor Cft. B6: Aston 1B 102
Heantum Cft. WV10: Wolv 4C 28
Heantum Ho. WV3: Wolv 4A 170
Heantum Mill Ct. WS10: W'bry 4D 62
Heantum Ri. WV1: Wolv 5G 27
Heartland M. B65: Row R 1B 112
Heartlands High Community Leisure Cen.
    . . . . .5A 102
Heartlands Parkway B7: Nech 4C 102
    B24: Erd .2E 103
Heartlands Pl. B8: Salt 5E 103
HEATH 1D 124
Heath Acres WS10: Darl 1C 62
Heath Bri. Cl. WS4: Rus 1E 33
Heathbrook Av. DY6: W Hth 2H 91
Heathcliff Rd. B11: Tys 1F 135
    DY2: Dud 2H 95
Heath Cl. B30: B'vlle 2H 145
    B75: S Cold 5D 54
    DY4: Tip .2B 78
    WS9: Ston 2G 23
Heathcote Av. B91: Sol 4C 150
Heathcote Ho. B17: Harb 6G 115
    (off Vivian Cl.)
Heathcote Rd. B30: K Nor 2C 146
Heath Ct. B12: Bal H 6H 117
Heath Cft. B31: Longb 2E 159
Heath Cft. Rd. B75: R'ley 2A 54
HEATH END 5E 21
Heather Av. WS5: Wals 1F 65
Heather Cl. B36: Cas B 1C 106
    WS3: Blox 1G 31
    WV11: Wed 4G 29
Heather Ct. Gdns. B74: Four O 3H 53
Heather Cft. B44: Gt Barr 4H 67
Heather Dale B13: Mose 3E 133
Heather Dr. B45: Rub 3F 157
Heather Gro. B91: Sol 1A 152
    WV12: W'hall 5E 31
Heather Ho. B38: K Nor 6B 146
Heatherleigh Rd. B36: Cas B 1B 106
Heather Rd. B10: Small H 4F 119
    B43: Gt Barr 5G 65
    B67: Smeth 3C 98
    DY1: Dud 3E 77
    WS3: Blox 1G 31
Heath Farm Rd. DY8: Stourb 3B 124
    WV8: Bilb 5H 13
Heathfield Av. B20: Hand 1D 100
Heathfield Cl. B64: Old H 1H 111
    B93: Know 4C 166
Heathfield Ct. B19: Loz 2D 100
Heathfield Dr. WS3: Blox 5H 19
Heathfield Gdns. DY8: Stourb 1D 124
Heathfield La. WS10: Darl 5C 46
Heathfield La. W. WS10: Darl 6B 46
Heathfield Rd. B14: K Hth 5G 133
    B19: Hand 1D 100

Heathfield Rd. B63: Hale 2G **127**
  B74: Four O 6F **37**
Heathfields WV8: Cod 6E **13**
Heath Gdns. B91: Sol 1H **151**
Heath Grn. DY1: Dud 2B **76**
Heathgreen Cl. B37: Chel W 6F **107**
Heath Grn. Gro. *B18: Win G* *5A 100*
  (off Heath Grn. Rd.)
Heath Grn. Rd. B18: Win G 5A **100**
Heath Gro. WV8: Bilb 4H **13**
Heath Hill Rd. WV6: Tett 2E **41**
Heath Ho. B14: K Hth 5H **147**
Heath Ho. Dr. WV5: Wom 2D **72**
Heath Ho. La. WV8: Cod 1E **25**
Heathland Av. B34: S End 2E **105**
Heathlands, The B65: B'hth 2C **112**
  DY8: Stourb 1F **125**
  WS2: Wals 6G **31**
  WV5: Wom 2D **72**
Heathlands Cl. DY6: K'wfrd 1C **92**
Heathlands Cres. B73: Bold 4F **69**
Heathlands Gro. B31: N'fld 6E **145**
Heathlands Rd. B73: Bold 3F **69**
Heath La. B71: W Brom 6B **64**
  DY8: Stourb 1E **125**
Heathleigh Rd. B38: K Nor 1G **159**
Heathmere Av. B25: Yard 3B **120**
Heathmere Dr. B37: F'bri 1B **122**
Heath Mill Cl. WV5: Wom 3D **72**
Heath Mill La. B9: Birm 6H **5** (2A **118**)
Heath Mill Rd. WV5: Wom 3D **72**
Heath Pk. WV10: Cov H 1G **15**
Heath Ri. B14: K Hth 6A **148**
Heath Rd. B30: B'vlle 2G **145**
  B47: H'wd 2A **162**
  B91: Sol 1H **151**
  DY2: Neth 1D **110**
  WS10: Darl 3E **47**
  WV12: W'hall 1C **30**
Heath Rd. Sth. B31: N'fld 3E **145**
Heathside Dr. B38: K Nor 6D **146**
  WS3: Pels 3E **21**
Heath St. B18: Win G 4H **99**
  B65: B'hth 2C **112**
  B66. Smeth 4H **99**
  DY8: Stourb 6D **108**
Heath St. Ind. Est. B66: Smeth 4H **99**
Heath St. Sth. B18: Win G 5B **100**
HEATH TOWN 5C **28**
Heath Town Leisure Cen. 5C **28**
Heath Trad. Pk. B66: Smeth 4H **99**
Heath Vw. WS10: Darl 6F **31**
Heath Way B34: Hodg H, S End 2D **104**
Heathway Cl. B34: S End 3E **105**
Heathy Farm Cl. B32: Bart G 4H **129**
Heathy Ri. B32: Bart G 3G **129**
Heaton Cl. WV10: Bush 2A **16**
Heaton Dr. B15: Edg 3A **116**
  B74: Four O 3F **53**
Heaton Rd. B91: Sol 1D **150**
Heaton St. B18: Hock 4D **100**
Hebden Gro. B28: Hall G 4E **149**
  WV12: W'hall 6B **18**
Heddon Pl. B7: Birm 6A **102**
Hedera Cl. WS5: Wals 2F **65**
Hedgefield Gro. B63: Crad 1E **127**
Hedgerow Dr. DY6: K'wfrd 6B **74**
Hedgerows, The B62: Roms 3A **142**
Hedgerow Wlk. WV8: Pend 6C **14**
Hedges, The WV5: Wom 1E **73**
Hedgetree Cft. B37: Chel W 1E **123**
Hedgings, The *B34: S End* *3F 105*
  (off Meadow Rd.)
Hedgley Gro. B33: Stech 5E **105**
Hedingham Gro. B37: Chel W 1F **123**
Hedley Cft. B35: Cas V 3F **87**
Hednesford Rd. WS8: Bwnhls 2G **9**
Heeley Rd. B29: S Oak 3A **132**
Hefford Dr. B66: Smeth 3E **99**
Heights, The B71: W Brom 4C **64**
Helena Pl. B66: Smeth 2A **98**
Helena St. B1: Birm 3A **4** (6E **101**)
Helenny Cl. WV11: Wed 4C **28**
Helford Cl. DY4: Tip 2F **77**

Hellaby Cl. B72: S Cold 1H **69**
Hellaby Ct. B73: Bold 6G **69**
Hellaby Ho. B74: Four O 6F **37**
Hellier Av. DY4: Tip 3B **78**
Hellier Dr. WV5: Wom 6E **57**
Hellier Rd. WV10: Bush 5A **16**
Hellier St. DY2: Dud 1E **95**
Helming Dr. WV1: Wolv 6D **28**
Helmsdale Way DY3: Sed 6C **60**
Helmsley Cl. DY5: Brie H 3G **109**
Helmsley Rd. WV11: Wed 1E **29**
Helmswood Dr. B37: Chel W 3E **123**
Helston Cl. DY8: Word 1A **108**
  WS5: Wals 4H **49**
Helstone Gro. B11: Tys 2G **135**
Helston Rd. WS5: Wals 4H **49**
Hembs Cres. B43: Gt Barr 5G **65**
Hemlingford Cft. B37: Mars G 4C **122**
Hemlingford Rd. B37: K'hrst 3A **106**
  B76: Walm 6E **71**
Hemmings Cl. DY8: Stourb 6D **108**
  WV10: Wolv 6A **28**
Hemmings St. WS10: Darl 3C **46**
Hemplands Rd. DY8: Stourb 6D **108**
Hempole La. DY4: Tip 6D **62**
Hemyock Rd. B29: W Cas 5F **131**
Henbury Dr. B37: Chel W 5F **107**
Henbury Rd. B27: A Grn 2B **136**
Henderson Ct. B68: O'bry 3H **113**
Henderson Wlk. DY4: Tip 5B **62**
Henderson Way B65: B'hth 2C **112**
Hendon Cl. DY3: Lwr G 5H **75**
  WV10: Bush 1A **28**
Hendon Rd. B11: S'hll 6B **118**
Heneage Pl. B7: Birm 5A **102**
Heneage St. B7: Birm 5A **102**
Heneage St. W. B7: Birm 1H **5** (5H **101**)
  (not continuous)
Henfield Cl. WV11: Wed 2F **29**
Hengham Rd. B26: Yard 2E **121**
Henley Cl. B73: W Grn 5H **69**
  DY4: Tip 2D **78**
  WS3: Blox 6C **20**
Henley Cres. B91: Sol 6F **137**
Henley Dr. B75: Four O 6G **37**
Henley Rd. WV10: Oxl 6F **15**
Henley St. B11: S'brk 4A **118**
Henley Vs. *B12: Bal H* *6B 118*
  (off Chesterton Rd.)
Henlow Cl. DY4: Tip 2F **77**
Henlow Rd. B14: K Hth 5H **147**
Hennalls, The B36: Hodg H 2D **104**
Henn Dr. DY4: Tip 5G **61**
Henne Dr. WV14: Cose 4E **61**
Henn St. DY4: Tip 5A **62**
Henrietta St. B19: Birm 1C **4** (5F **101**)
Henry Rd. B25: Yard 4A **120**
Henry St. WS2: Wals 2B **48**
Hensborough B90: Dic H 4G **163**
Hensel Dr. WV3: Wolv 3A **42**
Henshaw Gro. B25: Yard 4A **120**
Henshaw Rd. B10: Small H 3D **118**
Henstead St. B5: Birm 3F **117**
Henwood Cl. WV6: Tett 6A **26**
Henwood La. B91: Cath B 2D **152**
Henwood Rd. WV6: Tett 1A **42**
Hepburn Cl. WS9: A'rdge 5C **34**
Hepburn Edge B24: Erd 3H **85**
Hepworth Cl. WV6: Pert 5F **25**
Herald Ct. DY1: Dud 6E **77**
Herald Rd. B26: Birm A 1E **139**
Herbert Rd. B10: Small H 2C **118**
  B21: Hand 6B **82**
  B67: Smeth 2E **115**
  B91: Sol 4F **151**
  WS9: A'rdge 6C **22**
Herberts Pk. Rd. WS10: Darl 5B **46**
Herbert St. B70: W Brom 4B **80**
  WV1: Wolv 1C **170** (6H **27**)
  WV14: Bils 5D **44**
Herbhill Cl. WV4: Penn 1H **59**
Hereford Av. B12: Bal H 5A **118**
Hereford Cl. B45: Fran 5G **143**
  WS9: A'rdge 1C **34**

Hereford Ho. *WV1: Wolv* *6G 27*
  (off Oxley La.)
Hereford Pl. B71: W Brom 6H **63**
Hereford Rd. B68: O'bry 4H **113**
  DY2: Neth 6G **95**
Hereford St. WS2: Wals 5C **32**
Hereford Wlk. B37: Mars G 2B **122**
Hereward Ri. B62: Hale 6B **112**
Heritage, The *WS1: Wals* *3C 48*
  (off Sister Dora Gdns.)
Heritage Cl. B68: O'bry 5A **98**
Heritage Ct. B18: Birm 1A **4**
Heritage Way B33: Kitts G 6H **105**
  DY4: Tip 2B **78**
Hermes Ct. B74: Four O 6F **37**
Hermes Rd. B26: Birm A 1E **139**
Hermitage, The B91: Sol 1G **151**
Hermitage Dr. B76: Walm 2D **70**
Hermitage Rd. B15: Edg 2G **115**
  B23: Erd 4D **84**
  B91: Sol 2G **151**
Hermit St. DY3: Up Gor 2H **75**
Hermon Row B11: S'brk 6D **118**
Hernall Cft. B26: Sheld 4E **121**
Herne Cl. B18: Hock 5C **100**
Hernefield Rd. B34: S End 2E **105**
Hernehurst B32: Quin 6H **113**
Hern Rd. DY5: Brie H 5G **109**
Heron Cl. B90: Ches G 5B **164**
  WS8: Bwnhls 6A **10**
Heron Ct. *B73: W Grn* *6H 69*
  (off Florence Av.)
Herondale Cres. DY8: Stourb 1A **124**
Herondale Rd. B26: Sheld 5D **120**
  DY8: Stourb 1A **124**
Heronfield Dr. B31: Longb 3D **158**
Heronfield Way B91: Sol 2A **152**
Heron Ho. DY4: Tip 2G **77**
Heron Mill WS3: Pels 4C **20**
Heron Rd. B68: O'bry 1G **113**
Heronry, The WV6: Tett 1F **41**
Herons Way B29: S Oak 2G **131**
Heronswood Dr. DY5: Brie H 2H **109**
Heronswood Rd. B45: Redn 3H **157**
Heronville Dr. B70: W Brom 6G **63**
Heronville Ho. DY4: Tip 4B **78**
Heronville Rd. B70: W Brom 1F **79**
Heron Way B45: Rub 2F **157**
Herrick Rd. B8: Salt 4E **103**
Herrick St. WV3: Wolv 2F **43**
Herringshaw Cft. B76: Walm 2C **70**
Hertford St. B12: Bal H 6A **118**
Hertford Way B93: Know 5D **166**
Hervey Gro. B24: Erd 1B **86**
Hesket Av. B68: O'bry 2A **114**
Hesketh Cres. B23: Erd 2C **84**
Hessian Cl. WV14: Cose 3D **60**
Hestia Dr. B29: S Oak 5A **132**
Heston Av. B42: Gt Barr 5C **66**
Hever Av. R44: K'sdng 4A **68**
Hever Cl. DY1: Dud 4A **76**
Hewell Cl. B31: Longb 2D **158**
  DY6: K'wfrd 6B **74**
Hewitson Gdns. B67: Smeth 1D **114**
Hewitt St. WS10: Darl 5C **46**
Hexham Cft. B36: Hodg H 1A **104**
Hexham Way DY1: Dud 5B **76**
Hexton Cl. B90: Shir 5D **148**
Heybarnes Cir. B10: Small H 4F **119**
Heybarnes Rd. B10: Small H 4F **119**
Heycott Gro. B38: K Nor 5E **147**
Heydon Rd. DY5: P'ntt 4F **93**
Heyford Gro. B91: Sol 1G **165**
Heyford Way B35: Cas V 2F **87**
Heygate Way WS9: A'rdge 5D **22**
Heynesfield Rd. B33: Kitts G 6G **105**
Heythrop Gro. B13: Mose 5D **134**
Hickman Av. WV1: Wolv 2C **44**
Hickman Gdns. B16: Edg 2B **116**
Hickman Pl. WV14: Bils 5E **45**
Hickman Rd. B11: S'brk 5B **118**
  DY4: Tip 5H **61**
  DY5: Brie H 5G **93**
  WV14: Bils 6E **45**

Hickman's Av. B64: Old H 1G 111
Hickmans Cl. B62: Quin 5G 113
Hickman St. DY9: Lye 5G 109
Hickmerelands La. DY3: Sed 5H 59
Hickory Dr. B17: Edg 1E 115
Hidcote Av. B76: Walm 5E 71
Hidcote Gro. B33: Sheld 3G 121
     B37: Mars G 4C 122
Hidson Rd. B23: Erd 2C 84
Higgins Av. WV14: Cose 3F 61
Higgins La. B32: Quin 6A 114
Higgins Wlk. B66: Smeth 3F 99
Higgs Fld. Cres. B64: Old H 2B 112
Higgs Rd. WV11: Wed 6A 18
Highams Cl. B65: Row R 6B 96
Higham Way WV10: Wolv 3A 28
High Arcal Dr. DY3: Sed 6B 60
High Arcal Rd. DY3: Lwr G 4D 74
High Av. B64: Crad H 3H 111
High Beeches B43: Gt Barr 4H 65
HIGHBRIDGE 2E 21
Highbridge Rd. B73: Bold, W Grn 4F 69
     DY2: Neth 6C 94
High Brink Rd. B46: Col 2H 107
Highbrook Cl. WV9: Pend 5E 15
High Brow B17: Harb 4F 115
High Bullen WS10: W'bry 2F 63
Highbury Av. B21: Hand 1B 100
     B65: Row R 6D 96
Highbury Cl. B65: Row R 6D 96
Highbury Ct. B13: Mose 6G 133
Highbury Little Theatre 6G 69
Highbury Rd. B14: K Hth 5F 133
     B66: Smeth 2B 98
     B68: O'bry 4H 97
     B74: Four O 6C 36
High Clere B64: Crad H 4A 112
Highcrest Cl. B31: Longb 2E 159
High Cft. B43: Gt Barr 4G 65
     WS9: A'rdge 5D 22
Highcroft Av. DY8: Word 6A 92
Highcroft Cl. B92: Sol 3G 137
Highcroft Dr. B74: Four O 6E 37
Highcroft Rd. B23: Erd 4E 85
Highcroft Rd. B23: Erd 4E 85
Highcroft Vs. B23: Erd 3E 85
Highdown Cres. B90: M'path 3E 165
HIGH ERCAL 1G 109
High Ercal Av. DY5: Brie H 1G 109
High Farm Rd. B62: B'hth 3F 113
     B63: Hale 2G 127
Highfield CV7: Mer 4H 141
Highfield Av. WS4: S'fld 1G 33
     WV10: Bush 5C 16
Highfield Cl. B28: Hall G 2D 148
Highfield Ct. B73: W Grn 4H 69
Highfield Cres. B63: Crad 5F 111
     B65: B'hth 3B 112
     WV11: Wed 3D 28
Highfield Dr. B73: Bold 6F 69
Highfield La. B32: Quin 5H 113
     B63: Hale 2H 127
Highfield M. B63: Crad 5F 111
Highfield Pas. WS1: Wals 3C 48
Highfield Pl. B14: Yard W 2D 148
Highfield Rd. B8: Salt 5E 103
     B13: Mose 2B 134
     B14: Yard W 2D 148
     B15: Edg 3C 116
     B28: Hall G 2D 148
     B43: Gt Barr 6G 65
     B63: Crad 6F 111
     B65: B'hth 2B 112
     B67: Smeth 4D 98
     DY2: Dud 6G 77
     DY3: Sed 4H 59
     DY4: Tip 6A 62
     DY8: Word 1E 109
     WS3: Pels 3E 21
Highfield Rd. Nth. WS3: Pels 2D 20
HIGHFIELDS 1B 10
Highfields B23: Erd 3C 84
Highfields, The WV6: Tett 1G 41

Highfields Av. WV14: Bils 1G 61
Highfields Ct. WV4: Penn 5A 42
Highfields Dr. WV5: Wom 2G 73
     WV14: Cose 2F 61
Highfields Grange WS6: C Hay 4D 6
Highfields Pk. WS6: C Hay 4D 6
Highfields Rd. WS7: Chase 1B 10
     WV14: Bils, Cose 2E 61
Highfield Ter. B18: Hock 4C 100
Highfield Way WS9: A'rdge 5D 22
HIGHGATE 3H 117
Highgate B74: S'tly 2A 52
     DY3: Up Gor 2A 76
Highgate Av. WS1: Wals 3D 48
     WV4: Penn 5B 42
Highgate Bus. Cen. B12: Bal H 5B 118
Highgate Cl. B12: Birm 4H 117
     WS1: Wals 4D 48
Highgate Common Country Pk. 1A 90
Highgate Comn. E.
     DY3: Stourt, Swind 2A 90
     DY7: Stourt 1A 90
Highgate Dr. WS1: Wals 4D 48
Highgate Ho. B5: Birm 3G 117
     (off Southacre Av.)
Highgate Middleway B12: Birm 4H 117
Highgate Pl. B12: Birm 4A 118
Highgate Retail Est. B12: Birm 4A 118
Highgate Rd. B12: Bal H 5A 118
     DY2: Dud 3B 94
     WS1: Wals 3D 48
Highgate Sq. B12: Birm 4H 117
Highgate St. B12: Birm 4H 117
     B64: Old H 1H 111
     (not continuous)
Highgrove WV6: Tett 6A 26
Highgrove Cl. WV12: W'hall 2B 30
Highgrove Pl. DY1: Dud 5B 76
High Haden Cres.
     B64: Crad H, Old H 3A 112
High Haden Rd. B64: Crad H, Old H . . .3A 112
HIGH HEATH 3F 55
     B75 . . . . .3F 55
     WS4 .5G 21
High Heath Cl. B30: B'ville 2H 145
High Hill WV11: Ess 5A 18
High Holborn DY3: Sed 6H 59
High Ho. Dr. B45: Lick 6F 157
Highland Ho. B62: B'hth 3C 112
Highland M. WV14: Cose 4F 61
Highland Ridge B62: Quin 6E 113
Highland Rd. B23: Erd 2F 85
     B43: Gt Barr 2A 66
     B64: Old H 1G 111
     DY1: Dud 4C 76
     WS9: Wals W 4D 22
Highlands Ct. B90: Shir 1C 164
Highlands Ind. Est., The B90: Shir 1C 164
Highlands Rd. B90: Shir 1C 164
     WV3: Wolv 3B 42
High Leasowes B63: Hale 1A 128
High Mdw. Rd. B38: K Nor 5C 146
High Mdws. WV5: Wom 1G 73
     WV6: Tett 1A 42
Highmoor Cl. WV12: W'hall 2B 30
     WV14: Cose 2F 61
Highmoor Rd. B65: Row R 6B 96
Highmore Dr. B32: Bart G 5A 130
High Oak DY5: P'ntt 2G 93
Highover Dr. B75: Four O 5G 37
Highpark Av. DY8: Woll 6B 108
High Pk. Cl. B66: Smeth 4F 99
     DY3: Sed 4H 59
High Pk. Cres. DY3: Sed 4H 59
HIGH PARK ESTATE 6A 108
High Pk. Rd. B63: Crad 6E 111
High Pk. St. B7: Nech 3B 102
High Point B15: Edg 5A 116
High Ridge WS9: A'rdge 4B 34
High Ridge Cl. WS9: A'rdge 4A 34
     WS10: Mox 1A 62
High Rd. WV12: W'hall 4C 30
High St. B4: Birm 4E 5 (1G 117)
     B6: Aston 2G 101

High St. B8: Salt 4C 102
     B14: K Hth 5G 133
     B17: Harb 6G 115
     B23: Erd 3F 85
     B32: Quin 5G 113
     B35: Cas V 4F 87
     B46: Col 1H 107
     B63: Hale 1B 128
     B64: Crad H 3E 111
     B65: B'hth 2B 112
     B66: Smeth 3D 98
     B70: W Brom 3H 79
     (not continuous)
     B72: S Cold 5A 54
     B90: Shir 5C 148
     B91: Sol 3G 151
     B92: H Ard 1A 154
     B93: Know 3E 167
     DY1: Dud 1E 95
     DY3: Sed 4H 59
     DY3: Swind 5E 73
     DY4: Tip 5G 61
     (Bradley's La.)
     DY4: Tip 2G 77
     (Castle St.)
     DY5: Brie H 1H 109
     (Mill St.)
     DY5: Brie H 5F 93
     (School La.)
     DY5: P'ntt 2E 93
     DY5: Quar B 2B 110
     DY6: K'wfrd 3B 92
     DY6: W Hth 1H 91
     DY8: Stourb 6E 109
     DY8: Woll 5C 108
     DY8: Word 6C 92
     DY9: Lye 6A 110
     WS1: Wals 2C 48
     WS3: Blox 1H 31
     WS3: Pels 3E 21
     WS6: C Hay 3D 6
     WS7: Chase 1B 10
     (not continuous)
     WS8: Bwnhls 6B 10
     WS8: Clay 1A 22
     WS9: A'rdge 3D 34
     (not continuous)
     WS9: Wals W 4B 22
     WS10: Mox 1A 62
     WS11: Nort C 1F 9
     WV5: Wom 1H 73
     WV6: Tett 5B 26
     WV11: Wed 4E 29
     WV14: Bils 6F 45
High St. Amblecote DY8: Amb 3D 108
High St. Bordesley B12: Birm 2A 118
High St. Deritend B12: Birm . . .6H 5 (2H 117)
Highters Cl. B14: K Hth 5B 148
HIGHTER'S HEATH 5H 147
Highter's Heath La. B14: K Hth 6A 148
Highters Rd. B14: K Hth 4A 148
High Timbers B45: Fran 6F 143
High Twr. B7: Birm 4B 102
High Town B63: Crad 5E 111
Hightree Cl. B32: Bart G 4H 129
High Trees B20: Hand 4B 82
High Trees Rd. B93: Know 2C 166
High Vw. WV14: Cose 4B 60
Highview WS1: Wals 3D 48
     (off Highgate Rd.)
Highview Dr. DY6: K'wfrd 5D 92
Highview St. DY2: Dud 6G 77
Highwood Av. B92: Olton 4E 137
High Wood Cl. DY6: K'wfrd 3A 92
Highwood Cft. B38: K Nor 6H 145
Hiker Gro. B37: Chel W 1F 123
Hilary Cres. DY1: Dud 1D 76
Hilary Dr. B76: Walm 2E 71
     WS9: A'rdge 4C 34
     WV3: Wolv 4B 42
Hilary Gro. B31: N'fld 3D 144
Hilden Rd. B7: Birm 5A 102
Hilderic Cres. DY1: Dud 2B 94
Hilderstone Rd. B25: Yard 5A 120

Hildicks Cres. WS3: Wals 2D **32**
Hildicks Pl. WS3: Wals 2D **32**
HILL 5G **37**
Hill, The B32: Bart G 3C **130**
Hillaire Cl. B38: K Nor 5E **147**
Hillaries Rd. B23: Erd 5D **84**
Hillary Av. WS10: W'bry 2A **64**
Hillary Crest DY3: Up Gor 2A **76**
Hillary St. WS2: Wals 4A **48**
Hill Av. WV4: E'shll 2B **60**
Hill Bank DY9: Lye 6B **110**
Hillbank B69: Tiv 6D **78**
Hill Bank Dr. B33: Stech 5B **104**
Hill Bank Rd. B38: K Nor 5C **146**
   B63: Crad 5F **111**
Hillborough Rd. B27: A Grn 3C **136**
Hillbrook Gro. B33: Stech 6D **104**
Hillbrow Cres. B62: B'hth 3F **113**
Hillbury Dr. WV12: W'hall 1B **30**
Hill Cl. B31: N'fld 6F **145**
   DY3: Sed 4A **60**
Hillcrest DY3: Lwr G 3G **75**
Hillcrest Av. B43: Gt Barr 3A **66**
   B63: Crad 4D **110**
   DY5: Brie H 2G **109**
   WV10: Bush 6A **16**
Hillcrest Bus. Pk. DY2: Neth 2E **95**
Hillcrest Cl. DY2: Neth 4E **95**
Hillcrest Community Leisure Cen. 4D **94**
Hillcrest Gdns. WV12: W'hall 4D **30**
Hillcrest Gro. B44: K'sdng 6A **68**
Hillcrest Ind. Est. B64: Crad H 3F **111**
Hillcrest Ri. WS7: Burn 1D **10**
Hill Crest Rd. B13: Mose 3G **133**
Hillcrest Rd. B43: Gt Barr 3A **66**
   B62: Roms 3A **142**
   B72: W Grn 5A **70**
   DY2: Dud 6G **77**
Hillcroft Ho. B14: K Hth 5H **147**
Hill Cft. Rd. B14: K Hth 1E **147**
Hillcroft Rd. DY6: K'wfrd 2C **92**
Hillcross Wlk. B36: Hodg H 1D **104**
Hilldene Rd. DY6: K'wfrd 5A **92**
Hilldrop Gro. B17: Harb 2H **131**
Hilleys Cft. B37: F'bri 6B **106**
HILLFIELD 6F **151**
Hillfield M. B91: Sol 1F **165**
Hillfield Rd. B11: S'hll 2D **134**
   B91: Sol 5G **151**
Hillfields B67: Smeth 6B **98**
Hillfields Rd. DY5: Brie H 4F **109**
Hillfield Wlk. B65: Row R 4H **95**
Hill Gro. B20: Hand 5E **83**
Hillhampton Cl. B92: Sol 4G **137**
HILL HOOK 4E **37**
Hill Hook Nature Reserve 4F **37**
Hill Hook Rd. B74: Four O 4E **37**
Hill Ho. La. B33: Stech 6D **104**
   (not continuous)
Hillhurst Gro. B36: Cas B 6H **87**
Hillhurst Rd. B73: New O 2B **68**
Hilliards Cft. B42: Gt Barr 5C **66**
Hillingford Av. B43: Gt Barr 2E **67**
Hill La. B43: Gt Barr 3A **66**
   B75: Bass P 1F **55**
Hillman Dr. DY2: Dud 2G **95**
Hillman Gro. B36: Cas B 6A **88**
Hillmeads Dr. DY2: Dud 2G **95**
Hillmeads Rd. B38: K Nor 6C **146**
Hillmorton B74: Four O 6F **37**
Hillmorton Rd. B74: Four O 6F **37**
   B93: Know 4C **166**
Hillmount Cl. B28: Hall G 4F **135**
Hill Pk. WS9: Wals W 3C **22**
Hill Pas. B64: Old H 1G **111**
Hill Pl. WV11: Wed 6A **18**
Hill Rd. B69: Tiv 5A **78**
   WV13: W'hall 2F **45**
Hillside DY3: Lwr G 3G **75**
   WS8: Bwnhls 1C **22**
   WV5: Wom 6E **57**
Hillside Av. B63: Crad 5F **111**
   B65: B'hth 3B **112**
   DY5: Quar B 3C **110**

Hillside Cl. B32: Bart G 5G **129**
   WS8: Bwnhls 1C **22**
Hillside Ct. B43: Gt Barr 3H **65**
Hillside Cres. WS3: Pels 5D **20**
Hillside Cft. B92: Sol 1A **138**
Hillside Dr. B37: K'hrst 5B **106**
   B42: Gt Barr 1C **82**
   B74: S'tly 4H **51**
Hillside Gdns. B37: K'hrst 5B **106**
   WV1: Wolv 6C **28**
Hillside Ho. B45: Rub 1F **157**
Hillside Rd. B23: Erd 5D **84**
   B43: Gt Barr 3H **65**
   B74: Four O 5G **37**
   DY1: Dud 2C **76**
Hillside Wlk. WV1: Wolv 6C **28**
Hillstone Gdns. WV10: Bush 1B **28**
Hillstone Rd. B34: S End 4H **105**
Hill St. B2: Birm 1F **117**
   B5: Birm 4C **4** (1F **117**)
   B63: Hale 2A **128**
   B66: Smeth 3E **99**
   DY2: Neth 4D **94**
   DY3: Up Gor 2H **75**
   DY4: Tip .3H **77**
   DY5: Brie H 1H **109**
   DY5: Quar B 3C **110**
   DY8: Amb 3D **108**
   DY8: Stourb 1D **124**
   DY9: Lye 6B **110**
   WS1: Wals 2D **48**
   WS6: C Hay 3C **6**
   WS10: Darl 5E **47**
   WV11: Ess 4H **17**
   WV14: Bils 2G **61**
HILL TOP .6G **63**
Hill Top B70: W Brom 5G **63**
Hilltop DY9: W'cte 2A **126**
Hill Top Av. B62: B'hth 4E **113**
Hill Top Cl. B44: Gt Barr 1G **83**
Hill Top Dr. B36: Hodg H 2B **104**
Hill Top Ind. Est. B70: W Brom 1F **63**
   (Bilport La.)
   B70: W Brom 1A **114**
   (Pikehelve St.)
Hill Top Rd. B31: N'fld 4D **144**
   B68: O'bry 1A **114**
Hilltop Rd. DY2: Dud 1G **95**
Hill Top Wlk. WS9: A'rdge 6E **23**
Hillview WS9: A'rdge 5D **22**
Hillview Cl. B63: Hale 5G **111**
Hillview Rd. B45: Rub 1E **157**
Hill Village Rd. B75: Four O 4G **37**
Hillville Gdns. DY8: Stourb 2F **125**
HILL WOOD 5A **38**
Hillwood WS3: Pels 5D **20**
Hillwood Av. B90: M'path 3E **165**
Hillwood Cl. DY6: K'wfrd 5A **92**
Hillwood Comn. Rd. B75: Four O 5H **37**
Hillwood Rd. B31: N'fld 6C **130**
   B62: B'hth 4C **112**
   B75: Four O, R'ley 5H **37**
Hillyfields Rd. B23: Erd 3C **84**
Hilly Rd. WV14: Bils 3G **61**
Hilsea Cl. WV8: Pend 6D **14**
Hilston Av. B63: Hale 1H **127**
   WV4: Penn 1A **58**
HILTON 5H **11**
Hilton Av. B28: Hall G 3E **149**
Hilton Cl. WS3: Blox 5F **19**
Hilton Cross WV10: F'stne 2D **16**
Hilton Cross Bus. Pk.
   WV10: F'stne 2D **16**
Hilton Dr. B72: W Grn 5A **70**
Hilton La. WS6: Gt Wyr 3F **7**
   WV11: Ess 6A **6**
Hilton Main Ind. Est. WV11: F'stne 2E **17**
Hilton Pk. WV11: Ess 1G **17**
HILTON PARK SERVICE AREA 6A **6**
Hilton Pl. WV14: Bils 6H **45**
Hilton Rd. B69: Tiv 1C **96**
   WV4: E'shll 6B **44**
   WV10: F'stne 1D **16**
   WV12: W'hall 1C **30**

Hilton St. B70: W Brom 4G **79**
   WV10: Wolv 6A **28**
Hilton Trad. Est. WV4: E'shll 6B **44**
Hilton Way WV12: W'hall 1C **30**
Himbleton Cft. B90: M'path 2E **165**
HIMLEY 4H **73**
Himley Av. DY1: Dud 5B **76**
Himley By-Pass DY3: Himl 4G **73**
Himley Cl. B43: Gt Barr 3G **65**
   WV12: W'hall 4B **30**
Himley Cres. DY3: Lwr G . . . .
   (off Peak Dr.)
Himley Cres. WV4: Penn 6F **43**
Himley Gdns. WV4: Lwr G 3D **74**
Himley Gro. B45: Redn 3H **157**
Himley Hall & Pk. 3B **74**
Himley La. DY3: Himl, Swind 5E **73**
   (not continuous)
Himley Plantation 4G **73**
Himley Ri. B90: Ches G 5C **164**
Himley Rd. DY1: Dud 5G **75**
   DY3: Gorn 4D **74**
Himley St. DY1: Dud 6C **76**
Hinbrook Rd. DY1: Dud 6A **76**
Hinchliffe Av. WV14: Cose 3D **60**
Hinchwick Ct. B93: Dorr 6B **166**
Hinckes Rd. WV6: Tett 4A **26**
Hinckley St. B5: Birm 6D **4** (2F **117**)
Hincks St. WV2: E'shll 4C **44**
Hindhead Rd. B14: Yard W 3C **148**
Hindlip Cl. B63: Hale 3H **127**
Hindlow Cl. B7: Birm 5B **102**
Hindon Gro. B27: A Grn 6A **136**
Hindon Sq. B15: Edg 3B **116**
Hindon Wlk. B32: Bart G 3A **130**
Hingeston St. B18: Hock 5D **100**
Hingley Ct. B64: Old H 1G **111**
   (off Hill Pas.)
Hingley Cft. WS9: A'rdge 6H **35**
Hingley Ind. Pk. B64: Crad H 2E **111**
Hingley Rd. B63: Crad 5C **110**
Hingley St. B64: Crad H 2F **111**
HINKSFORD 1F **91**
Hinksford Gdns. DY3: Swind 5E **73**
Hinksford La. DY3: Swind 5E **73**
   DY6: K'wfrd 5E **73**
Hinksford Pk. Res. Mobile Homes
   DY6: K'wfrd 1E **91**
Hinsford Cl. DY6: K'wfrd 1C **92**
Hinstock Cl. WV4: Penn 1E **59**
Hinstock Rd. B20: Hand 6B **82**
Hintlesham Av. B15: Edg 6H **115**
Hinton Gro. WV11: Wed 4H **29**
Hintons Coppice B93: Know 3A **166**
Hipkins St. DY4: Tip 6G **61**
Hiplands Rd. B62: Hale 1F **129**
Hipsley Cl. B36: Cas B 6G **87**
Hipsmoor Cl. B37: K'hrst 6B **106**
Hirdemonsway B90: Dic H 4G **163**
Histons Dr. WV8: Cod 5F **13**
Ilistons Hill WV8: Cod 5F **13**
Hitchcock Cl. B67: Smeth 4B **98**
Hitches La. B15: Edg 4D **116**
Hitherside B90: Dic H 4H **163**
Hive Development Cen. B18: Hock 2C **100**
HMP Birmingham B18: Win G 4A **100**
Hobacre Cl. B45: Rub 1G **157**
Hobart Ct. B74: Four O 6G **37**
Hobart Cft. B7: Birm 5A **102**
Hobart Dr. WS5: Wals 5G **49**
Hobart Rd. DY4: Tip 4G **61**
Hobbis Ho. B38: K Nor 2G **159**
HOBBLE END 6H **7**
Hobble End La. WS6: Gt Wyr 1G **19**
Hobgate Cl. WV10: Wolv 5B **28**
Hobgate Rd. WV10: Wolv 5B **28**
Hob Grn. Rd. DY9: W'cte 3A **126**
Hobhouse Cl. B42: Gt Barr 6B **66**
Hob La. B92: Bars 3A **168**
Hobley St. WV13: W'hall 1C **46**
Hob Moor Cl. B9: Bord G 2G **119**
Hobmoor Cft. B25: Yard 4B **120**
Hob Moor Rd. B10: Small H 2F **119**
   B25: Yard 3A **120**

Hobnock Rd. WV11: Ess 3A 18
Hobs Hole La. WS9: A'rdge 2D 34
Hob's Mdw. B92: Olton 3E 137
Hobs Moat Rd. B92: Olton, Sol 3F 137
Hobson Cl. B18: Hock 4C 100
Hobson Rd. B29: S Oak 4D 132
Hobs Rd. WS10: W'bry 1G 63
HOCKLEY 4D 100
Hockley Brook Cl. B18: Hock 4C 100
Hockley Brook Trad. Est. B18: Hock ..3C 100
Hockley Cen. B18: Birm 1A 4
(off The Big Pen)
Hockley Cir. B19: Hock 3D 100
Hockley Cl. B19: Hock 3F 101
Hockley Flyover B18: Hock 3D 100
B19: Hock 3D 100
Hockley Hill B18: Birm 4D 100
Hockley Hill Ind. Est. B18: Hock ...4D 100
Hockley Ind. Est. B18: Hock 4D 100
Hockley La. DY2: Neth 6D 94
Hockley Pool Cl. B18: Hock 4D 100
Hockley Rd. B23: Erd 3D 84
WV14: Cose 6C 60
Hockley St. B18: Hock 5E 101
B19: Birm 5E 101
Hodder Gro. B71: W Brom 6D 64
HODGEHILL 3B 104
Hodge Hill Av. DY9: W'cte 2A 126
Hodge Hill Comn. B36: Hodg H ...2C 104
Hodgehill Cl. B36: Hodg H 2C 104
Hodge Hill Rd. B34: Hodg H 3C 104
Hodges Dr. B69: Tiv 6B 78
Hodgetts Cl. B67: Smeth 6B 98
Hodgetts Dr. B63: Hale 5F 127
Hodgkins Cl. WS8: Bwnhls 1C 22
Hodgkiss Cl. WS10: W'bry 1E 63
Hodgson Twr. B19: Hock 3F 101
Hodnell Cl. B36: Cas B 6G 87
Hodnet Cl. WV14: Bils 6D 44
Hodnet Dr. DY5: P'ntt 3G 93
Hodnet Gro. B5: Birm 3G 117
Hodson Av. WV13: W'hall 2C 46
Hodson Cl. WV11: Wed 1H 29
Hoff Beck Ct. B9: Birm 1B 118
Hogarth Cl. B43: Gt Barr 6F 51
WV13: W'hall 1G 45
Hogarth Ho. B15: Birm 3E 117
Hogg's La. B31: N'fld 3C 144
HOLBEACHE 6A 74
Holbeache La. DY6: K'wfrd 6A 74
Holbeache Rd. DY6: W Hth 1A 92
Holbeach Rd. B33: Yard 1F 121
Holbeche Rd. B75: S Cold 6F 55
B93: Know 2C 166
Holberg Gro. WV11: Wed 4H 29
Holborn Cen., The DY3: Sed 6H 59
Holborn Hill B6: Aston 1B 102
B7: Nech 1B 102
Holbrook Gro. B37: Mars G 2D 122
Holbrook Twr. B36: Hodg H 1B 104
Holbury Cl. WV9: Pend 5E 15
Holcroft Rd. B63: Crad 6E 111
DY6: W Hth 6A 74
DY9: Lye 1G 125
Holcroft St. DY4: Tip 5A 78
WV2: E'shll 4C 44
Holden Cl. B23: Erd 5F 85
Holden Cres. WS3: Wals 4C 32
Holden Cft. DY4: Tip 4A 78
Holden Pl. WS3: Wals 5C 32
Holden Rd. WS10: W'bry 3G 63
WV4: Penn 2B 58
Holdens, The B28: Hall G 1E 149
Holden Way B74: Four O 1H 53
B75: Four O 1H 53
Holder Rd. B11: S'brk 5C 118
B25: Yard 4A 120
Holders Gdns. B13: Mose 3E 133
Holders La. B13: Mose 3E 133
Holdford Rd. B6: Witt 5H 83
Holdgate Rd. B29: W Cas 6F 131
Hole Farm Rd. B31: N'fld 3G 145
Hole Farm Way B38: K Nor 2B 160

Hole La. B31: N'fld 1G 145
Holendene Way WV5: Wom 6E 57
Holford Av. WS2: Wals 5A 48
Holford Dr. B6: Witt 3G 83
B42: P Barr 3G 83
Holford Ind. Pk. B6: Witt 4H 83
Holford Way B6: Witt 3H 83
Holifast Rd. B72: W Grn 6H 69
Holland Av. B68: O'bry 5B 98
B93: Know 1D 166
Holland Ho. B19: Birm 4F 101
(off Gt. Hampton Row)
Holland Ind. Pk. WS10: Darl 3D 46
HOLLAND PARK 4A 10
Holland Rd. B43: Gt Barr 6H 65
B72: S Cold 2H 69
WV14: Bils 4G 45
Holland Rd. E. B6: Aston 3A 102
Holland Rd. W. B6: Aston 3H 101
Hollands Pl. WS3: Blox 6B 20
Hollands Rd. WS3: Blox 6B 20
Holland St. B3: Birm 3A 4 (6E 101)
B72: S Cold 1H 69
DY1: Dud 1D 94
DY4: Tip 6C 62
Hollands Way WS3: Pels 3D 20
Hollemeadow Av. WS3: Blox 2B 32
Holliars Gro. B37: K'hrst 4B 106
Holliday Pas. B1: Birm 6B 4 (2E 117)
Holliday Rd. B21: Hand 2B 100
B24: Erd 3G 85
Holliday St. B1: Birm 6A 4 (2E 117)
Holliday Wharf B1: Birm ...6B 4 (2E 117)
Hollie Lucas Rd. B13: Mose 6H 133
Hollies, The B6: Aston 1B 102
B16: Birm 2B 116
WV2: Wolv 6A 170 (3G 43)
WV5: Wom 6H 57
Hollies Cft. B5: Edg 6E 117
Hollies Dr. B62: Hale 5D 112
WS10: W'bry 2F 63
Hollies Ind. Est., The
WV2: Wolv 6A 170 (3G 43)
Hollies La. WV6: Patt 5A 24
Hollies Ri. B64: Crad H 3H 111
Hollies St. DY5: P'ntt 2H 93
Hollin Brow Cl. B93: Know 6D 166
Hollingberry La. B76: Walm 2D 70
Hollings Gro. B91: Sol 1F 165
Hollington Cres. B33: Stech 5E 105
Hollington Rd. WV1: Wolv 3D 44
Hollington Way B90: M'path 2G 165
Hollinwell Cl. WS3: Blox 4G 19
Hollister Dr. B32: Bart G 2D 130
Hollow, The B13: Mose 1G 133
Holloway B31: N'fld 1C 144
Holloway, The DY3: Swind 6D 72
DY8: Amb 4D 108
WV6: Tett 1A 42
Holloway Bank B70: W Brom 4F 63
WS10: W'bry 4F 63
Holloway Bank Trad. Est.
WS10: W'bry 4F 63
Holloway Cir. Queensway
B1: Birm 6D 4 (2F 117)
Holloway Ct. B63: Crad 6F 111
Holloway Dr. WV5: Wom 2E 73
HOLLOWAY END 5F 109
Holloway Head B1: Birm ...6C 4 (2F 117)
Holloway St. DY3: Lwr G, Up Gor ..3H 75
WV1: Wolv 4C 44
Holloway St. W. DY3: Lwr G 2H 75
Hollow Cft. B31: N'fld 4F 145
Hollowcroft Rd. WV12: W'hall ...1B 30
Hollowmeadow Ho. B36: Hodg H ..1B 104
Holly Av. B12: Bal H 6A 118
B29: S Oak 4D 132
HOLLY BANK 4C 22
Hollybank Av. WV11: Ess 4A 18
Hollybank Cl. WS3: Blox 5G 19
Hollybank Gro. B63: Hale 4F 127
Hollybank Rd. B13: Mose 4A 134
Hollyberry Av. B91: Sol 1E 165

Hollyberry Cl. B63: Hale 2A 128
Hollyberry Cft. B34: S End 3G 105
Hollybrow B29: W Cas 6E 131
Holly Bush Gro. B32: Quin 4B 114
Holly Bush La. WV10: Share 5A 6
(not continuous)
Hollybush La. DY8: Amb 4D 108
WV4: Penn 1B 58
WV8: Oaken 5D 12
Holly Bush Wlk. B64: Crad H 2F 111
Holly Cl. B76: Walm 3D 70
WV12: W'hall 3C 30
Hollycot Gdns. B12: Bal H 5H 117
Holly Ct. B23: Erd 2G 85
WS5: Wals 1E 65
Hollycroft Gdns. WV6: Tett 4H 25
Hollycroft Rd. B21: Hand 6H 81
Hollydale Rd. B24: Erd 4A 86
B65: Row R 6D 96
Holly Dell B38: K Nor 5D 146
Holly Dr. B27: A Grn 3H 135
B47: H'wd 2B 162
Hollyfaste Rd. B33: Sheld 2F 121
Hollyfield Av. B91: Sol 4C 150
Hollyfield Ct. B75: S Cold 6C 54
Hollyfield Cres. B75: S Cold ...1C 70
Hollyfield Dr. B75: S Cold 6C 54
Hollyfield Rd. B75: S Cold 6C 54
Hollyfield Rd. Sth. B76: Walm ..1D 70
Holly Gro. B19: Hand 1D 100
B29: S Oak 3B 132
(Heeley Rd.)
B29: S Oak 3B 132
(Tiverton Rd.)
B30: B'vlle 5B 132
DY8: Stourb 6D 108
WV3: Wolv 4D 42
Holly Hall Rd. DY2: Dud 3C 94
Hollyhedge Cl. B31: N'fld 1B 144
WS2: Wals 1A 48
Hollyhedge La. WS2: Wals 6A 32
Hollyhedge Rd. B71: W Brom 6C 64
Holly Hill B45: Fran 6F 143
WS6: Gt Wyr 5E 7
(off Holly La.)
Holly Hill Rd. B45: Fran 5G 143
Holly Hill Shop. Cen. B45: Fran ..6G 143
Hollyhock Rd. B27: A Grn 4F 135
DY2: Dud 6H 77
Hollyhurst B46: Wat O 4E 89
Hollyhurst Cvn. Pk. B62: Hunn ..1B 142
Hollyhurst Dr. DY8: Word 6B 92
Hollyhurst Gro. B26: Yard 5C 120
B90: Shir 1H 163
Hollyhurst Rd. B73: S'tly 2B 68
Holly La. B24: Erd 2H 85
B37: Mars G 3B 122
B66: Smeth 2C 98
B67: Smeth 4B 98
B75: Four O 6G 37
B76: Wis 2H 71
CV7: Bal C 4H 169
WS6: Gt Wyr 5E 7
WS9: A'rdge 1H 35
WS9: Wals W 3C 22
Holly Lodge Wlk. B37: F'bri 1B 122
Hollymoor Way B31: Longb 5A 144
Holly Mt. B16: Edg 2H 115
Hollymount B62: Quin 4G 113
Hollyoak Cft. B31: Longb 1F 159
Hollyoake Cl. B68: O'bry 1G 113
Hollyoak Gro. B91: Sol 6E 151
Hollyoak Rd. B74: S'tly 5H 51
Hollyoak St. B71: W Brom 3B 80
Holly Pk. Dr. B24: Erd 3H 85
Holly Pk. Ind. Est. B24: Erd ...5A 86
Hollypiece Ho. B27: A Grn 3G 135
Holly Pl. B6: Aston 1G 101
B29: S Oak 3D 132
Holly Rd. B16: Edg 2G 115
B20: Hand 1B 100
B30: K Nor 3C 146
B65: B'hth 2B 112
B68: O'bry 3A 114

Holly Rd. B71: W Brom 5C 64
  DY1: Dud 4C 76
  WS10: W'bry 6F 47
Holly St. B67: Smeth 4D 98
  DY1: Dud 3A 94
Holly Vw. WV11: Ess 4A 18
Hollywell Rd. B26: Sheld 5F 121
  B93: Know 4C 166
Hollywell St. WV14: Cose 4C 60
HOLLYWOOD 1A 162
Holly Wood B43: Gt Barr 4C 66
Hollywood Bowl
  Great Park 1H 157
Hollywood By-Pass B38: Head H 3G 161
  B47: Wyt 3G 161
Hollywood Cft. B42: Gt Barr 5B 66
Hollywood Dr. B47: H'wd 1A 162
Hollywood Gdns. B47: H'wd 1A 162
Hollywood La. B47: H'wd 1A 162
Hollywood Nature Reserve 4C 66
Holman Cl. WV13: W'hall 1G 45
Holman Rd. WV13: W'hall 1F 45
Holman Way WV13: W'hall 1G 45
Holmbridge Gro. WS4: S'fld 5G 21
Holme Mill WV10: F'hses 3H 15
Holmes, The WV10: F'hses 4H 15
Holmes Cl. B43: Gt Barr 6A 66
Holmes Dr. B45: Rub 3F 157
Holmesfield Rd. B42: Gt Barr 6E 67
Holmes Rd. WV12: W'hall 2D 30
Holme Way WS4: Rus 2F 33
Holmwood Rd. B10: Small H 2D 118
Holt Ct. Nth. B7: Birm 1H 5 (5H 101)
Holt Ct. Sth. B7: Birm 1H 5 (5H 101)
Holte Community Leisure Cen. 2F 101
Holto Dr. B75: R'ley 1B 54
Holte Rd. B6: Aston 6A 84
  B11: S'brk 6D 118
Holtes Wlk. B6: Aston 1B 102
Holt Rd. B62: B'hth 2E 113
Holtshill La. WS1: Wals 1D 48
Holt St. B7: Birm 1G 5 (5H 101)
Holy Farm Trekking Cen. 2G 129
Holyhead Community Leisure Cen. . . .1H 99
Holyhead Rd. B21: Hand 1C 62
  WS10: Darl 1C 62
  WS10: W'bry 2D 62
  WV8: Cod, Oaken 5B 12
Holyhead Rd. Ind. Est. WS10: W'bry . .2D 62
Holyhead Way B21: Hand 1H 99
Holyoak Cl. B6: Aston 6H 83
Holyrood Gro. B6: Aston 1G 101
Holy Well Cl. B16: Edg 1C 116
Holywell La. B45: Rub 3D 156
Home Cl. B28: Hall G 1F 149
Homecroft Rd. B25: Yard 3C 120
Homedene Rd. B31: N'fld 6C 130
Homefield Rd. WV8: Bilb 4H 13
Homelands B42: Gt Barr 6D 66
Homelands Pk. WV10: Cov H 1G 15
Homelea Rd. B25: Yard 3B 120
Homemead Gro. B45: Rub 2F 157
Home Mdw. Ho. B27: A Grn 3G 135
Home Peal Ho. B14: K Hth 1G 147
HOMER HILL 4D 110
Homer Hill Rd. B63: Crad 4E 111
Homer Rd. B75: R'ley 1A 54
  B91: Sol 4F 151
Homers Fold WV14: Bils 6F 45
Homer St. B12: Bal H 6H 117
Homerton Rd. B44: K'sdng 4B 68
Homestead Cl. DY3: Up Gor 2A 76
Homestead Dr. B75: R'ley 6A 38
Homestead Rd. B33: Sheld 2F 121
Home Twr. B7: Birm 4B 102
Homewood Cl. B76: Walm 2C 70
Honesty Cl. WS8: Clay 1H 21
Honeswode Cl. B20: Hand 1C 100
Honeyborne B75: S Cold 4B 54
Honeybourne Cl. B63: Hale 2A 128
Honeybourne Cres. WV5: Wom 2F 73
Honeybourne Rd. B33: Sheld 3G 121
  B63: Hale 2C 128
Honeybourne Way WV13: W'hall 1C 46

Honeycomb Way B31: N'fld 4C 144
Honeysuckle Av. DY6: K'wfrd 2C 92
Honeysuckle Cl. B32: Quin 6H 113
Honeysuckle Dr. WS5: Wals 2E 65
Honeysuckle Gro. B27: A Grn 6A 120
Honeysuckle Way WS6: Gt Wyr 1H 7
Honeytree Cl. DY6: K'wfrd 6D 92
Honiley Dr. B73: New O 3C 68
Honiley Rd. B33: Yard 1E 121
Honister Cl. DY5: Quar B 2B 110
Honiton Cl. B31: N'fld 3C 144
Honiton Cres. B31: N'fld 3C 144
Honiton Wlk. B66: Smeth 4F 99
Honiton Way WS9: A'rdge 4B 34
Honnington Ct. B29: W Cas 4D 130
Honor Av. WV4: Penn 6G 43
Hood Gro. B30: K Nor 3H 145
Hook Dr. B74: Four O 5F 37
Hooper St. B18: Win G 5B 100
Hoosen Cl. B62: Quin 5G 113
Hopedale Rd. B32: Quin 6A 114
Hope Pl. B29: S Oak 3B 132
Hope Rd. DY4: Tip 1C 78
Hope St. B5: Birm 3F 117
  B62: B'hth 3D 112
  B70: W Brom 5C 80
  DY2: Dud 1E 95
  DY8: Word 6B 92
  WS1: Wals 3C 48
Hope Ter. DY2: Neth 4E 95
Hopkins Cl. WS10: W'bry 2G 63
Hopkins Dr. B71: W Brom 6C 64
Hopkins St. DY4: Tip 5A 78
Hopstone Gdns. WV4: Penn 6D 42
Hopstone Rd. B29: W Cas 4E 131
Hopton Cl. DY4: Tip 3C 62
  WV6: Pert 6F 25
Hopton Cres. WV11: Wed 3G 29
Hopton Gdns. DY1: Dud 4C 76
Hopton Gro. B13: Mose 2C 148
Hopwas Gro. B37: K'hrst 4B 106
HOPWOOD 6G 159
Hopwood Cl. B63: Hale 3A 128
Hopwood Gro. B31: Longb 3C 158
Hopyard Cl. DY3: Gorn 4F 75
Hopyard Gdns. WV14: Cose 2D 60
Hopyard La. DY3: Gorn 5F 75
Hopyard Rd. WS2: Wals 1E 47
Horace Partridge Rd. WS10: Mox 6A 46
Horace St. WV14: Cose 5C 60
Horatio Dr. B13: Mose 1H 133
Hordern Cl. WV6: Wolv 4D 26
Hordern Cres. DY5: Quar B 3H 109
Hordern Gro. WV6: Wolv 4D 26
Hordern Pk. WV10: Cov H 1G 15
Hordern Rd. WV6: Wolv 4D 26
Hornbeam Cl. B29: W Cas 6F 131
Hornbeam Wlk. WV3: Wolv 2E 43
Hornbrook Gro. B92: Olton 6A 136
Hornby Gro. B14: Yard W 3C 148
Hornby Rd. WV4: Penn 1G 59
Horner Way B65: B'hth 2C 112
Horne Way B34: S End 4A 106
Horning Dr. WV14: Bils 2E 61
Hornsey Gro. B44: K'sdng 3A 68
Hornsey Rd. B44: K'sdng 3A 68
Hornton Cl. B74: Lit As 4D 36
Horrell Rd. B26: Sheld 4E 121
  B90: Shir 5F 149
Horsecroft Dr. B71: W Brom 5E 65
                  (off Tompstone Rd.)
Horse Fair B5: Birm 6D 4 (2F 117)
Horsehills Dr. WV3: Wolv 1C 42
Horselea Cft. B8: W End 5A 104
Horseley Flds. WV1: Wolv . . .3D 170 (1H 43)
HORSELEY HEATH 1C 78
Horseley Heath DY4: Tip 3B 78
Horseley Rd. DY4: Tip 3B 78
Horseshoe, The B68: O'bry 1A 114
Horseshoe Cl. WS2: Wals 4H 47
                 (off Wellington St.)
Horse Shoes La. B26: Sheld 6F 121
Horseshoe Wlk. DY4: Tip 2G 77
                 (off New Cross St.)

Horsfall Rd. B75: S Cold 6E 55
Horsham Av. DY8: Word 6A 92
Horsley Rd. B43: Gt Barr 1F 67
  B74: Lit As 1B 52
Horton Cl. DY3: Sed 5G 59
  WS10: Darl 4D 46
Horton Gro. B90: M'path 4E 165
Horton Pl. WS10: Darl 4D 46
Horton Sq. B12: Birm 4G 117
Horton St. B70: W Brom 5A 80
  DY4: Tip 2D 78
  WS10: Darl 4D 46
Hospital Dr. B15: Edg 1A 132
Hospital La. B69: Tiv 5B 78
  WS6: C Hay 2B 6
  WV14: Cose 6D 60
Hospital Rd. WS7: Burn 1C 10
Hospital St. B19: Birm, Hock . . .1D 4 (4F 101)
                 (not continuous)
  B23: Erd 3E 85
  WS2: Wals 5B 32
  WV2: Wolv 5D 170 (2H 43)
Hothersall Dr. B73: Bold 5F 69
Hotspur Rd. B44: K'sdng 4H 67
Hough Pl. WS2: Wals 4H 47
Hough Rd. B14: K Hth 1F 147
  WS2: Wals 4G 47
Houghton Ct. B28: Hall G 3D 148
Houghton St. B69: O'bry 3F 97
  B70: W Brom 1B 98
Hough Way WV11: Ess 4A 18
Houldey Rd. B31: N'fld 6F 145
Houliston Cl. WS10: W'bry 6H 47
Houndel Gro. WV5: Wom 6F 57
Houndsfield Cl. B47: H'wd 3C 162
Houndsfield Ct. B47: Wyt 4A 162
Houndsfield Gro. B47: Wyt 4A 162
                 (not continuous)
Houndsfield La. B47: H'wd 3C 162
  B47: Wyt 3C 162
  B90: Dic H 3C 162
Houndsfield M. B47: Wyt 4B 162
Houx, The B78: Amb 3C 108
Hove Rd. B27: A Grn 4A 136
Howard Ho. B92: H Ard 1B 154
Howard Rd. B14: K Hth 6F 133
  B20: Hand 5D 82
  B25: Yard 4A 120
  B43: Gt Barr 5G 65
  B92: Olton 2C 136
  WV11: Wed 1H 29
  WV14: Bils 2H 61
Howard Rd. E. B13: Mose 6H 133
Howard St. B19: Birm 1C 4 (5F 101)
  B70: W Brom 6F 63
  DY4: Tip 2B 78
  WV2: Wolv 6C 170 (3H 43)
Howard St. Ind. Est. B70: W Brom . . .6F 63
Howarth Way B6: Aston 2A 102
Howden Pl. B33: Stech 4E 105
Howdle's La. WS8: Bwnhls 3B 10
Howe Cres. WV12: W'hall 3C 30
Howell Rd. WV2: Wolv 4A 44
Howes Cft. B35: Cas V 5E 87
Howe St. B4: Birm 2H 5 (6H 101)
Howford Gro. B7: Birm 5B 102
Howland Cl. WV9: Pend 5D 14
Howley Av. B44: Gt Barr 4G 67
Howley Grange Rd. B62: Quin 6F 113
Howl Pl. DY4: Tip 2H 77
Hoylake Cl. WS3: Blox 4H 19
Hoylake Dr. B69: Tiv 2A 96
Hoylake Rd. WV6: Pert 4D 24
Hoyland Way B30: B'vlle 5A 132
HRS Ind. Pk. B33: Sheld 2G 121
Hub, The B69: O'bry 2G 97
Hubert Cft. B29: S Oak 3B 132
Hubert Rd. B29: S Oak 3B 132
Hubert St. B6: Aston 4H 101
Hucker Cl. WS2: Wals 4G 47
Hucker Rd. WS2: Wals 4G 47
Huddesford Dr. CV7: Bal C 1H 169
Huddlestone Cl. WV10: F'stne 1D 16
Huddleston Way B29: S Oak 4G 131

Huddocks Vw. WS3: Pels 2D 20
Hudson Av. B46: Col 3H 107
Hudson Gro. WV6: Pert 4E 25
Hudson Rd. B20: Hand 3B 82
　　DY4: Tip 3C 78
Hudson's Dr. B30: K Nor 3C 146
Hudswell Dr. DY5: Brie H 3H 109
Huggins Cl. CV7: Bal C 5H 169
Hughes Av. WV3: Wolv 3D 42
Hughes Pl. WV14: Bils 4F 45
Hughes Rd. WS10: Mox 6A 46
　　WV14: Bils 4F 45
Hugh Gaitskell Ct. WV14: Wolv 3E 45
Hugh Porter Way WV6: Tett 2D 26
Hugh Rd. B10: Small H 2E 119
　　B67: Smeth 4B 98
Hugh Vs. B10: Small H 2E 119
Hulbert Dr. DY2: Dud 3D 94
Hulbert Ind. Est. DY2: Dud 3D 94
Hulland Pl. DY5: Brie H 6G 93
Hullbrook Rd. B13: Mose 2C 148
Humara Ghar WS1: Wals 3C 48
Humber Av. B76: Walm 6E 71
Humber Gdns. B63: Crad 6E 111
Humber Gro. B36: Cas B 6B 88
Humber Rd. WV3: Wolv 2E 43
Humberstone Rd. B24: Erd 3C 86
Humber Twr. B7: Birm 5A 102
Hume St. B66: Smeth 5F 99
　　　　　　　　　　　　　　(not continuous)
Humpage Rd. B9: Bord G 1E 119
Humphrey Middlemore Dr.
　　B17: Harb 1H 131
Humphrey's Rd. WV10: Bush 2H 27
Humphrey St. DY3: Lwr G 4H 75
Humphries Cres. WV14: Bils 4H 61
Humphries Ho. WS8: Bwnhls 6B 10
Hundred Acre Rd. B74: S'tly 4H 51
Hungary Cl. DY9: Lye 6G 109
Hungary Hill DY9: Lye 6G 109
Hungerfield Rd. B36: Cas B 6G 87
Hungerford Rd. DY8: Stourb 3C 124
Hunningham Gro. B91: Sol 1F 165
HUNNINGTON 6B 128
Hunnington Cl. B32: Bart G 4G 129
Hunnington Cres. B63: Hale 3B 128
Hunscote Cl. B90: Shir 6F 149
Hunslet Cl. B32: Quin 1D 130
Hunslet Rd. B32: Quin 1D 130
Hunstanton Av. B17: Harb 4D 114
Hunstanton Cl. DY5: Brie H 4G 109
Hunter Ct. B5: Edg 6F 117
Hunter Cres. WS3: Blox 3D 32
Hunters Cl. WV14: Bils 4A 46
Hunters Ride DY7: Stourt 6H 91
Hunters Ri. B63: Hale 4F 127
Hunter's Rd. B19: Hock 2D 100
Hunter St. WV6: Wolv 5E 27
Hunter's Va. B19: Hock 3E 101
Hunters Wlk. B23: Erd 5C 68
Huntingdon Ho. B23: Erd 1B 84
Huntingdon Rd. B71: W Brom 1H 79
Huntington Rd. WV12: W'hall 2D 30
Huntingtree Rd. B63: Hale 1G 127
Huntlands Rd. B63: Hale 3G 127
Huntley Dr. B91: Sol 5F 151
Huntly Rd. B16: Edg 2C 116
Hunton Ct. B23: Erd 5E 85
　　　　　　　　　　　　(off Gravelly Hill Nth.)
Hunton Hill B23: Erd 4D 84
Hunton Rd. B23: Erd 4E 85
Hunt's La. WV12: W'hall 3D 30
Huntsman Cl. WV14: Cose 3F 61
Hunts Mill Dr. DY5: P'ntt 6G 75
Hunt's Rd. B30: Stir 6C 132
Hurdis Rd. B90: Shir 4G 149
Hurdlow Av. B18: Hock 4D 100
Hurley Cl. B72: W Grn 3A 70
　　WS5: Wals 5H 49
Hurley Gro. B37: K'hrst 4B 106
Hurley's Fold DY2: Neth 4D 94
Hurlingham Rd. B44: K'sdng 3A 68
Hurricane Pk. B24: Erd 1G 103
Hurricane Way B35: Cas V 5H 87

Hursey Dr. DY4: Tip 2A 78
Hurst, The B13: Mose 6C 134
　　B47: H'wd 3A 162
Hurstbourne Cres. WV1: Wolv 2D 44
Hurst Bus. Pk. DY5: Brie H 5C 94
Hurst Cl. B36: Cas B 2A 106
Hurstcroft Rd. B33: Kitts G 6F 105
HURST GREEN 2E 113
Hurst Grn. Rd. B62: B'hth 2E 113
　　B76: Min 1H 87
　　B93: Ben H 5B 166
Hurst Grn. Shop. Cen.
　　B62: B'hth 3F 113
HURST HILL .5C 60
Hurst Hill Ct. WV14: Cose 5C 60
　　　　　　　　　　　　　　(off Caddick St.)
　　WV14: Cose 5C 60
　　　　　　　　　　　　　　(Hartland Av.)
Hurst La. B34: S End 3H 105
　　DY4: Tip 2F 77
　　DY5: Brie H 6B 94
Hurst La. Nth. B36: Cas B 2A 106
Hurst Rd. B67: Smeth 6B 98
　　WV14: Cose 4G 60
Hurst St. B5: Birm 6E 5 (2G 117)
　　　　　　　　　　　　　　(not continuous)
Hurstway, The B23: Erd 5C 68
Hurstwood Rd. B23: Erd 5C 68
Huskison Cl. B69: Tiv 6B 78
Husphins La. WV8: Cod, Cod W 2A 12
Hussey Rd. WS8: Bwnhls 5A 10
Hutchings La. B90: Dic H 4G 163
Hut Hill La. WS6: Gt Wyr 1G 7
Hutton Av. B8: Salt 4D 102
Hutton Rd. B8: Salt 4D 102
　　B20: Hand 6D 82
Huxbey Dr. B92: Sol 5B 138
Huxley Cl. WV9: Pend 4E 15
Hyacinth Cl. WS5: Wals 2D 64
Hyatt Sq. DY5: Brie H 4G 109
Hyatts Wlk. B65: Row R 4H 95
Hyde, The DY9: W'cte 3H 125
Hyde Rd. WV11: Wed 3F 29
Hydes Rd. B71: W Brom 4A 64
　　WS10: W'bry 2G 63
Hyett Way WV14: Bils 3B 62
Hylda Rd. B20: Hand 6D 82
Hylstone Cres. WV11: Wed 3F 29
Hylton St. B18: Birm 4E 101
Hyperion Dr. WV4: Penn 2E 59
Hyperion Rd. B36: Hodg H 6C 86
　　DY7: Stourt 4A 108
Hyron Hall Rd. B27: A Grn 3A 136
Hyssop Cl. B7: Birm 4A 102
Hytall Rd. B90: Shir 5C 148
Hythe Gro. B25: Yard 3B 120

I

Ibberton Rd. B14: K Hth 4B 148
Ibis Gdns. DY6: K'wfrd 3E 93
Ibstock Rd. DY8: Stourb 1E 125
ICC & Symphony Hall 4A 4 (1E 117)
Icknield Cl. B74: S'tly 2A 52
Icknield Port Rd. B16: Birm 5A 100
Icknield Sq. B16: Birm 6C 100
Icknield St. B18: Birm, Hock 4D 100
　　　　　　　　　　　　　　(not continuous)
　　B38: Forh .6C 160
　　B38: Head H, K Nor 1C 160
Ida Rd. B70: W Brom 6B 80
　　WS2: Wals 2H 47
Idbury Rd. B44: K'sdng 6A 68
Ideal Works DY9: Lye 5C 110
Idmiston Cft. B14: K Hth 5H 147
Idonia Rd. WV6: Pert 4E 25
Ikon Gallery 5A 4 (1E 117)
Ilford Rd. B23: Erd 1D 84
Iliffe Way B17: Harb 1H 131
Ilkley Gro. B37: F'bri 1B 122
ILLEY 5E 129
Illeybrook Sq. B32: Bart G 3B 130
Illey Cl. B31: Longb 6H 143

Illey La. B32: Fran 5E 129
　　B62: Hunn, Hale 4C 128
Illshaw WV9: Pend 4F 15
Illshaw Heath Rd. B94: H'ley H 6B 164
Illshaw Path B90: Bly P 6D 164
Ilmington Dr. B73: New O 2C 68
Ilmington Rd. B29: W Cas 4D 130
Ilsham Gro. B31: Longb 3C 158
Ilsley Rd. B23: Erd 3E 85
IMAX Theatre 6H 101
Imex Bus. Pk. B9: Bord G 1D 118
　　B11: Tys 5F 119
　　B33: Stech 5C 104
　　DY4: Tip 4A 78
　　WV2: Wolv 4G 43
Imperial Ri. B46: Col 5G 89
Imperial Rd. B9: Bord G 1E 119
Impey Rd. B31: N'fld 6D 144
Impsley Cl. B36: Cas B 1F 105
Ince Rd. WS10: Darl 4C 46
Inchcape Av. B20: Hand 4C 82
Inchford Rd. B92: Sol 6A 138
Inchlaggan Rd. WV10: Wolv 3B 28
Infantry Pl. B75: S Cold 5E 55
Ingatestone Dr. DY8: Word 6A 92
Ingestre Cl. WS3: Blox 4F 19
Ingestre Dr. B43: Gt Barr 4H 65
Inge St. B5: Birm 6D 4 (2G 117)
Ingestre Rd. B28: Hall G 6F 135
　　WV10: Oxl 6G 15
Ingleby Gdns. WV6: Wolv 4D 26
Ingledew Cl. WS2: Wals 6D 30
Inglefield Rd. B33: Stech 6D 104
Inglemere Gro. B29: W Cas 6D 130
Inglenook Dr. B20: Hand 5D 82
Ingleside Vs. B11: S'hll 6C 118
　　　　　　　　　　　　　　(off Warwick Rd.)
Ingleton Rd. B8: W End 2G 103
Inglewood Av. WV3: Wolv 3D 42
Inglewood Cl. DY6: K'wfrd 4B 92
Inglewood Gro. B74: S'tly 1H 51
Inglewood Rd. B11: S'hll 6C 118
Ingoldsby Ct. B13: Mose 3B 134
Ingoldsby Rd. B31: N'fld 3G 145
Ingot Cl. WS2: Wals 3H 31
Ingram Dr. B43: Gt Barr 5G 65
Ingram Gro. B27: A Grn 3G 135
Ingram Pl. WS3: Blox 6B 20
Ingram Rd. WS3: Blox 6A 20
Inhedge, The DY1: Dud 6E 77
Inhedge St. DY3: Up Gor 2A 76
Inkberrow Cl. B69: O'bry 5E 97
Inkberrow Rd. B63: Hale 3H 127
Inkerman Gro. WV10: Wolv 1B 44
Inkerman Ho. B19: Hock 3G 101
　　　　　　　　　　　　(off Newtown Shop. Cen.)
Inkerman St. B7: Birm 6B 102
　　　　　　　　　　　　　　(not continuous)
　　WV10: Wolv 6B 28
Inland Rd. B24: Erd 5H 85
Innage, The B47: H'wd 4A 162
Innage Rd. B31: N'fld 3F 145
Innisfree Cl. B47: Wyt 5C 162
Innsworth Dr. B35: Cas V 3E 87
Inshaw Cl. B33: Stech 6C 104
Institute Rd. B14: K Hth 5H 133
Instone Rd. B63: Hale 2H 127
Instow Cl. WV12: W'hall 1B 30
Insull Av. B14: K Hth 6B 148
Intended St. B63: Crad 4E 111
International Ho. B37: Mars G 6F 123
International Sq. B37: Mars G 5E 123
Intown WS1: Wals 1D 48
Intown Row WS1: Wals 1D 48
Inverclyde Dr. WV4: E'shll 6B 44
Inverclyde Rd. B20: Hand 4C 82
Inverkip Wlk. WV4: E'shll 6B 44
　　　　　　　　　　　　　　(off Greenock Cres.)
Inverness Ho. WV1: Wolv 6G 27
　　　　　　　　　　　　　　(off Oxley La.)
Inverness Rd. B31: N'fld 4C 144
Inworth WV9: Pend 4F 15
Ionic Bus. Pk. DY1: Dud 5H 77

Ipsley Gro. B23: Erd 2A **84**
Ipstones Av. B33: Stech 5D **104**
Ipswich Cres. B42: Gt Barr 6D **66**
Ipswich Wlk. B37: Chel W 1D **122**
Ireland Grn. Rd. B70: W Brom 5H **79**
Ireton Rd. B20: Hand 3C **82**
WV10: Bush 4A **16**
Iris Cl. B29: W Cas 5F **131**
Iris Dr. B14: K Hth 3F **147**
Irnham Rd. B74: Four O 1G **53**
Iron Bri. Wlk. DY9: Pedm 5F **125**
Iron La. B33: Stech 5B **104**
Irvan Av. B70: W Brom 2F **79**
Irvine Cl. WS3: Blox 2H **31**
Irvine Rd. WS3: Blox 1H **31**
Irving Cl. DY3: Lwr G 3E **75**
Irving Rd. B92: Sol 1A **138**
WV14: Bils 4A **62**
Irving St. B1: Birm 2F **117**
Irwin Av. B45: Redn 3A **158**
Isaac Walton Pl. B70: W Brom 6E **63**
Isbourne Way B9: Birm 1B **118**
Isis Gro. B36: Cas B 1B **106**
WV13: W'hall 1C **46**
Island Rd. B21: Hand 6G **81**
Islington B63: Hale 1A **128**
Islington Row Middleway B15: Birm . .2D **116**
Ismere Rd. B24: Erd 5H **85**
Itchen Gro. WV6: Pert 6E **25**
Ithon Gro. B38: K Nor 1A **160**
Ivanhoe Rd. B43: Gt Barr 2D **66**
WV2: E'shll 5C **44**
Ivanhoe St. DY2: Dud 2C **94**
Ivatt Cl. WS4: Rus 2F **33**
IVERLEY 6B **124**
Iverley Rd. B63: Hale 1C **128**
Iverley Wlk. DY9: Pedm 3G **125**
Ivor Rd. B11: S'hll 1B **134**
Ivy Av. B12: Bal H 6A **118**
(Clifton Rd.)
B12. Bal H 6A **118**
(Runcorn Rd.)
Ivybridge Gro. B42: P Barr 4E **83**
Ivy Cft. WV9: Pend 4D **14**
Ivydale Av. B26: Sheld 6G **121**
Ivyfield Rd. B23: Erd 2B **84**
Ivy Gro. B18: Win G 5A **100**
(off Heath Grn. Rd.)
WS8: Wals W 3C **22**
Ivyhouse La. WV14: Cose 5D **60**
Ivy Ho. Rd. B69: O'bry 3D **96**
Ivyhouse Rd. B38: K Nor 1G **159**
Ivy Lodge Cl. B37: Mars G 4C **122**
Ivy Pl. B29: S Oak 3B **132**
Ivy Rd. B21: Hand 2C **100**
B30: Stir 1C **146**
B73: Bold 3F **69**
DY1: Dud 3C **76**
DY4: Tip 6H **61**
Ivy Way B90: Dic H 3G **163**
Izons Ind. Est. B70: W Brom 6F **79**
Izons La. B70: W Brom 6F **79**
Izons Rd. B70: W Brom 4A **80**

J

Jacamar Av. B33: Stech 5D **104**
Jacey Rd. B16: Edg 1H **115**
B90: Shir 3H **149**
Jack David Ho. DY4: Tip 2D **78**
Jackdaw Cl. DY3: Sed 3G **59**
Jackdaw Dr. B36: Cas B 1C **106**
Jack Hayward Way
WV1: Wolv 1B **170** (6G **27**)
Jack Holden Av. WV14: Cose 3C **60**
Jack Newell Ct. WV14: Cose 5E **61**
(off Castle St.)
Jack O'Watton Ind. Est. B46: Wat O . . .4F **89**
Jackson Av. B8: Salt 5F **103**
Jackson Cl. B11: S'brk 4B **118**
B68: O'bry 4H **97**
DY4: Tip 4B **62**

Jackson Cl. WS11: Nort C 1C **8**
WV10: F'stne 1C **16**
Jackson Ct. DY5: Quar B 2B **110**
Jackson Dr. B67: Smeth 4B **98**
Jackson Ho. B69: O'bry 2G **97**
Jackson Rd. B8: Salt 5F **103**
Jackson St. B68: O'bry 5A **98**
DY9: Lye 6A **110**
WV6: Wolv 5F **27**
Jackson Wlk. B35: Cas V 5E **87**
Jackson Way B32: Quin 6G **113**
Jacmar Cres. B67: Smeth 3C **98**
Jacobean La. B91: Sol 6C **152**
B93: Know 6C **152**
Jacob's Hall La. WS6: Gt Wyr 4G **7**
Jacoby Pl. B5: Edg 6E **117**
Jaffray Cres. B24: Erd 4F **85**
Jaffray Rd. B24: Erd 4F **85**
Jakeman Rd. B12: Bal H 6G **117**
Jamaica Row B5: Birm 6F **5** (2G **117**)
James Bri. Cl. WS2: Wals 4H **47**
James Brindley Wlk.
B1: Birm 4A **4** (1E **117**)
James Clift Ho. B69: O'bry 4D **96**
James Cl. B67: Smeth 4E **99**
WS10: Darl 5F **47**
James Ct. B13: Mose 3B **134**
B38: K Nor 5B **146**
James Dee Cl. DY5: Quar B 2C **110**
James Eaton Cl. B71: W Brom 2A **80**
James Ho. B17: Harb 6F **115**
(off Cadbury Way)
B19: Hock 3E **101**
(off Newtown Dr.)
James Lloyd Trust Flats B30: B'vlle . .2G **145**
James Memorial Homes B7: Nech 2C **102**
(off Stuart St.)
Jameson Rd. B6: Aston 1C **102**
Jameson St. WV6: Wolv 5F **27**
James Rd. B11: Tys 5F **119**
B43: Gt Barr 6A **66**
B46: Col 1H **107**
James Row B69: O'bry 1D **96**
James Samuel Pl. B12: Birm 4H **117**
James Scott Rd. B63: Crad 5C **110**
James St. B3: Birm 2B **4** (6E **101**)
WV13: W'hall 6A **30**
WV14: Bils 5G **45**
James Turner St. B18: Win G 3A **100**
James Watt Dr. B19: Hand 1D **100**
James Watt Ho. B66: Smeth 4F **99**
James Watt Ind. Pk. B66: Smeth 3G **99**
James Watt Queensway
B4: Birm 2F **5** (6G **101**)
James Watt St. B4: Birm 3F **5**
(off Dalton St.)
B71: W Brom 5H **63**
(not continuous)
Jane La. Cl. WS2: Wals 5F **31**
Janice Gro. B14: Yard W 3C **148**
Janine Av. WV11: Wed 2G **29**
Jaques Cl. B46: Wat O 5D **88**
Jardine Rd. B6: Aston 6H **83**
Jarratt Hall B29: S Oak 2A **132**
Jarvis Cres. B69: O'bry 5F **97**
Jarvis Rd. B23: Erd 1F **85**
Jarvis Way B24: Erd 1E **103**
J A S Ind. Pk. B65: Row R 5E **97**
Jasmin Cft. B14: K Hth 3G **147**
Jasmine Cl. WV9: Pend 4D **14**
Jasmine Gro. WV8: Bilb 4H **13**
Jasmine Rd. DY2: Dud 6H **77**
Jasmine Way WS10: Darl 4D **46**
Jason Rd. DY9: W'cte 1B **126**
Javelin Av. B35: Cas V 4F **87**
Javelin Pk. WS10: W'bry 3D **62**
Jayne Cl. B71: W Brom 4C **64**
WV11: Wed 2F **29**
Jay Rd. DY6: K'wfrd 1B **92**
Jay's Av. DY4: Tip 3B **78**
Jayshaw Av. B43: Gt Barr 4A **66**
Jeal Cl. B47: Wyt 6G **161**
Jean Dr. DY4: Tip 1D **78**
Jeavons Pl. WV14: Bils 6E **45**

Jedburgh Av. WV6: Pert 5E **25**
Jeddo St. WV2: Wolv 6A **170** (3G **43**)
Jeffcock Rd. WV3: Wolv 3D **42**
Jefferson Cl. B71: W Brom 5H **63**
Jefferson Pl. B71: W Brom 2B **80**
Jeffrey Av. WV4: E'shll 6B **44**
Jeffrey Rd. B65: Row R 6E **97**
Jeffries Ho. B69: O'bry 2G **97**
Jeffs Av. WV2: Wolv 6D **170** (3H **43**)
Jenkins Cl. WV14: Bils 6E **45**
Jenkinson Rd. WS10: W'bry 4D **62**
Jenkins St. B10: Small H 3C **118**
Jenks Av. WV10: Bush 1A **28**
Jenks Rd. WV5: Wom 2F **73**
Jennens Rd. B4: Birm 3G **5** (6H **101**)
B7: Birm 2H **5** (6H **101**)
Jenner Cl. WS2: Wals 3G **31**
Jenner Ho. WS2: Wals 3F **31**
Jenner Rd. WS2: Wals 3F **31**
Jenner St. WV2: Wolv 2B **44**
Jennifer Wlk. B25: Yard 3C **120**
Jennings St. B64: Old H 1H **111**
Jenny Cl. WV14: Bils 4G **61**
Jennyns Ct. WS10: W'bry 2F **63**
Jenny Walkers La. WV6: Pert 3D **40**
Jephcott Gro. B8: Salt 5G **103**
Jephcott Rd. B8: Salt 5G **103**
Jephson Dr. B26: Yard 4D **120**
Jeremiah Rd. WV10: Wolv 6B **28**
Jeremy Gro. B92: Sol 1F **137**
Jeremy Rd. WV4: Penn 6G **43**
Jerome Ct. B74: S'tly 2H **51**
Jerome K Jerome Birthplace Mus. 2C **48**
Jerome Retail Pk. WS1: Wals 2B **48**
Jerome Rd. B72: S Cold 1B **70**
WS2: Wals 2H **47**
Jerrard Cl. B75: S Cold 6A **54**
Jerrard Dr. B75: S Cold 6A **54**
Jerry's La. B23: Erd 6D **68**
Jersey Cft. B36: Cas B 3D **106**
Jersey Rd. B8: Salt 5D **102**
Jervis Cl. DY5: P'ntt 2G **93**
Jervis Ct. WS1: Wals 1D **48**
(off Dog Kennel La.)
Jervis Cres. B74: Four O 6D **36**
Jervis Pk. B74: Lit As 5C **36**
Jervis Ter. B21: Hand 1H **99**
Jervoise Dr. B31: N'fld 2F **145**
Jervoise La. B71: W Brom 4C **64**
Jervoise Rd. B29: W Cas 4D **130**
Jervoise St. B70: W Brom 3G **79**
Jesmond Gro. B24: Erd 3C **86**
Jessel Rd. WS2: Wals 1A **48**
Jessie Rd. WS9: A'rdge 6C **22**
Jesson Cl. WS1: Wals 4E **49**
Jesson Ct. WS1: Wals 3E **49**
Jesson Rd. B75: S Cold 6E **55**
DY3: Sed 1C **76**
WS1: Wals 3D **48**
Jesson St. B70: W Brom 5C **80**
Jevons Dr. DY4: Tip 2B **78**
Jevons Rd. B73: New O 2C **68**
Jevon St. WV14: Cose 5D **60**
(not continuous)
JEWELLERY QUARTER 1A **4** (5D **100**)
Jewellery Quarter Station (Rail & MM)
. . . . .5D **100**
Jew's La. DY3: Up Gor 3A **76**
Jiggin's La. B32: Bart G 5A **130**
Jill Av. B43: Gt Barr 5G **65**
Jillcot Rd. B92: Sol 2F **137**
Jinnah Cl. B12: Birm 3H **117**
Joan St. WV2: E'shll 5A **44**
Jockey Fld. DY3: Up Gor 1A **76**
Jockey La. WS10: W'bry 1G **63**
Jockey Rd. B73: Bold, New O, W Grn . .3D **68**
Joe Jones Ct. DY3: Sed 4A **60**
Joey's La. WV8: Bilb 3A **14**
John Bright Cl. DY4: Tip 5H **61**
John Bright St. B1: Birm 5D **4** (1F **117**)
John Corbett Dr. DY8: Amb 4E **109**
John F Kennedy Wlk. DY4: Tip 5A **62**
John Fletcher Cl. WS10: W'bry 1H **63**
John Harper St. WV13: W'hall 1B **46**

John Howell Dr. DY4: Tip 2A 78
John Kempe Way B12: Birm 4A 118
John Padden Cl. B65: Row R 2B 112
John Riley Dr. WV12: W'hall 1C 30
John Rd. B62: Hale 2F 129
Johns Gro. B43: Gt Barr 5G 65
Johns La. B69: Tiv 4C 78
   DY4: Tip .3B 78
   WS6: Gt Wyr 2F 7
John Smyth Ho. B1: Birm 3A 4 (6E 101)
Johnson Av. WV11: Wed 2H 29
Johnson Cl. B8: W End 3A 104
   B11: S'hll .6C 118
   WS10: Darl 6D 46
Johnson Dr. B35: Cas V 4D 86
Johnson Pl. WV14: Bils 4H 45
Johnson Rd. B23: Erd 2F 85
   WS10: Darl 6D 46
   WS10: W'bry 3A 64
   WV12: W'hall 2D 30
Johnson Row WV14: Cose 4B 60
Johnsons Bri. Rd. B71: W Brom 1A 80
Johnsons Gro. B68: O'bry 3A 114
Johnson St. B7: Nech 3C 102
   WV2: Wolv .4H 43
   WV14: Cose 4B 60
Johnstone St. B19: Loz 1F 101
Johnston St. B70: W Brom 6B 80
John St. B19: Loz 2D 100
   B65: B'hth .2C 112
   B69: O'bry .2G 97
   B70: W Brom 3H 79
                    (Guns La.)
   B70: W Brom 2F 79
                (Phoenix St.)
   DY5: Brie H 5H 93
   DY8: Word .2D 108
   WS2: Wals .6C 32
   WV2: E'shll .5C 44
   WV13: W'hall 2B 46
John St. Nth. B71: W Brom 2H 79
John Wensley Way WS10: W'bry 4G 63
John Wilmott Community Leisure Cen.
. . . . .1D 70
John Wooton Ho. WS10: Darl 5D 46
           (off Lawrence Way)
Joiners Cft. B92: Sol 5A 138
Joinings Bank B68: O'bry 5H 97
Jones Fld. Cres. WV1: Wolv 1C 44
Jones Ho. WS2: Wals 6B 32
Jones Rd. WV10: Oxl 3G 27
   WV12: W'hall 6D 18
Jones's La. WS6: Gt Wyr 4G 7
Jones Wood Cl. B76: Walm 6D 70
Jonfield Gdns. B43: Gt Barr 4B 66
Jonquil Cl. B23: Erd 6C 68
Jordan Cl. B66: Smeth 4F 99
   B75: Four O 2H 53
Jordan Ho. B36: Hodg H 1C 104
Jordan Leys DY4: Tip 2B 78
Jordan Pl. WV14: Bils 2G 61
Jordan Rd. B75: Four O 2H 53
Jordan Way WS9: A'rdge 6D 22
Joseph St. B69: O'bry 3F 97
Josiah Rd. B31: N'fld 5B 144
Jowett's La. B71: W Brom 5H 63
Joyberry Dr. DY8: Stourb 2D 124
Joynson St. WS10: Darl 6E 47
Jubilee Av. B71: W Brom 6H 63
Jubilee Bus. Pk. DY9: Lye 6C 110
Jubilee Cl. WS3: Wals 3C 32
   WS6: Gt Wyr 2F 7
Jubilee Ct. B27: A Grn 3A 136
   B31: N'fld 6F 145
Jubilee Gdns. B23: Erd 6B 68
Jubilee Rd. B45: Fran 5E 143
   DY4: Tip 6A 62
   WV14: Bils .1A 62
Jubilee St. B71: W Brom 6B 64
Jubilee Trad. Cen. B5: Birm 2G 117
Judge Cl. B69: O'bry 2G 97
Judge Rd. DY5: Quar B 4B 110
Julia Av. B24: Erd 3D 86
Julia Gdns. B71: W Brom 5D 64

Julian Cl. WS6: Gt Wyr 2G 7
   WV1: Wolv .1D 44
Julian Rd. WV1: Wolv 1D 44
Julie Cft. WV14: Bils 4G 61
Juliet Grn. WV10: Bush 2A 28
Juliet Rd. B62: Hale 2F 129
Julius Dr. B46: Col 6H 89
Junction 6 Ind. Pk. B6: Witt 6B 84
Junction Ind. Est. B66: Smeth 1D 98
Junction Rd. B21: Hand 1G 99
   DY8: Stourb 1F 125
   DY8: Word .3C 108
   DY9: Stourb 1F 125
   WV2: E'shll .4D 44
Junction St. B69: O'bry 6E 79
   DY2: Dud 1D 94
   WS1: Wals .3B 48
Junction St. Sth. B69: O'bry 4G 97
Junction Two Ind. Est. B69: O'bry 4F 97
           (off Demuth Way)
June Cft. B26: Sheld 6H 121
Juniper Cl. B27: A Grn 6H 119
   B76: Walm .2D 70
Juniper Dr. B76: Walm 6E 71
   WS5: Wals .1F 65
Juniper Ho. B20: Hand 4B 82
   B36: Hodg H 2D 104
Juniper Ri. B63: Crad 6E 111
Jupiter B16: Birm 2D 116
                (Ryland St.)
   B16: Birm 1D 116
      (Sherborne Wharf, not continuous)
Jury Rd. DY5: Quar B 4B 110
Jutland Rd. B13: Mose 6B 134

K

Kalum Dr. B70: W Brom 6G 63
Karen Way DY5: Brie H 3H 109
KATE'S HILL .6H 77
Katherine Ho. B17: Harb 6F 115
           (off Cadbury Way)
Katherine Rd. B67: Smeth 1D 114
Kathleen Rd. B25: Yard 4A 120
   B72: S Cold 1A 70
Katie Rd. B29: S Oak 4A 132
Katsura Cl. B74: S'tly 4H 51
Kayne Cl. DY6: K'wfrd 3A 92
Keanscott Dr. B68: O'bry 5A 98
Keasdon Gro. WV13: W'hall 6C 30
Keating Gdns. B75: Four O 5G 37
Keatley Av. B33: Kitts G 1A 122
Keats Av. B10: Small H 4D 118
Keats Cl. B74: Four O 3F 37
   DY3: Lwr G .2E 75
   DY8: Amb 3E 109
Keats Dr. WV14: Cose 3F 61
Keats Gro. B27: A Grn 4H 135
   WV10: Bush 1C 28
Keats Ho. B68: O'bry 5A 98
Keats Rd. WS3: Blox 2C 32
   WV10: Bush 5C 16
   WV12: W'hall 2E 31
Keble Gro. B26: Sheld 5F 121
   WS1: Wals .4E 49
Keble Ho. B37: F'bri 1C 122
Kedleston Cl. WS3: Blox 4G 19
Kedleston Ct. B28: Hall G 3F 149
Kedleston Rd. B28: Hall G 2F 149
Keegan Wlk. WS2: Wals 5F 31
Keel Dr. B13: Mose 4D 134
Keele Ho. B37: F'bri 5D 106
Keeley St. B9: Birm 1B 118
Keelinge St. DY4: Tip 2B 78
Keen St. B66: Smeth 5H 99
Keepers Cl. B18: Win G 4B 100
   B46: Col 5H 107
   DY6: W Hth .1H 91
   WS9: Wals W 4B 22
Keepers Ga. Cl. B74: S Cold 4A 54
Keepers Ho. B73: New O 3C 68
          (off Welshmans Hill)

Keepers La. WV6: Tett 5G 13
   WV8: Cod 5G 13
Keepers Rd. B74: Lit As 4C 36
Keeper's Ct. B9: Birm 1B 118
Kegworth Rd. B23: Erd 5C 84
Keir Hardie Wlk. B69: Tiv 5D 78
Keir Pl. DY8: Amb 3C 108
Keir Rd. WS10: W'bry 3A 64
Kelby Cl. B31: N'fld 3C 144
Kelby Rd. B31: N'fld 3D 144
Keldy Cl. WV6: Wolv 4D 26
Kelfield Av. B17: Harb 1F 131
Kelham Pl. B92: Olton 4F 137
Kelia Dr. B67: Smeth 3D 98
Kellett Rd. B7: Birm 5A 102
Kelling Cl. DY5: Brie H 3G 109
Kellington Cl. B8: W End 5F 103
Kellner Gdns. B69: O'bry 1G 97
Kelmarsh Dr. B91: Sol 6F 151
Kelmscott Rd. B17: Harb 4F 115
Kelsall Cl. WV1: Wolv 1D 44
Kelsall Cft. B1: Birm 6D 100
Kelsey Cl. B7: Birm 5B 102
Kelso Gdns. WV6: Pert 5D 24
Kelsull Cft. B37: F'bri 1C 122
Kelton Ct. B15: Edg 4C 116
Kelvedon Gro. B91: Sol 3G 151
Kelverdale Gro. B14: K Hth 3E 147
Kelverley Gro. B71: W Brom 4E 65
Kelvin Ho. DY1: Dud 5F 77
Kelvin Pl. WS2: Wals 3H 31
Kelvin Rd. B31: N'fld 6E 145
   WS2: Wals .3G 31
Kelvin Way B70: W Brom 6H 79
Kelvin Way Ind. Est.
   B70: W Brom 6H 79
Kelway Av. B43: Gt Barr 2D 66
Kelwood Dr. B63: Hale 6A 112
Kelynmead Rd. B33: Yard 1E 121
Kemberton Cl. WV3: Wolv 2A 42
Kemberton Rd. B29: S Oak 3E 131
   WV3: Wolv .2A 42
Kemble Cl. WV12: W'hall 6D 30
Kemble Cft. B5: Edg 4G 117
Kemble Dr. B35: Cas V 4E 87
Kemelstowe Cres. B63: Hale 5E 127
Kemerton Way B90: M'path 4D 164
Kempe Rd. B33: Kitts G 5E 105
Kempsey Cl. B63: Hale 1G 127
   B69: O'bry .5E 97
   B92: Olton .2E 137
Kempsey Covert B38: K Nor 2A 160
Kempsey Ho. B32: Bart G 5G 129
Kemps Grn. Rd. CV7: Bal C 3H 169
Kempson Av. B71: W Brom 2H 79
   B72: W Grn .4A 70
Kempson Rd. B36: Hodg H 1C 104
Kempsons Gro. WV14: Cose 2D 60
Kempthorne Av. WV10: Bush 6A 16
Kempthorne Gdns. WS3: Blox 5G 19
Kempthorne Rd. WV14: Bils 5H 45
Kempton Dr. WS6: Gt Wyr 3F 7
Kempton Pk. Rd. B36: Hodg H 1B 104
Kempton Way DY8: Stourb 2C 124
Kemsey Dr. WV14: Bils 2H 61
Kemshead Av. B31: Longb 1C 158
Kemsley Rd. B14: K Hth 5H 147
Kendal Av. B45: Redn 2H 157
   B46: Col 2H 107
Kendal Cl. WV6: Tett 3D 26
Kendal Ct. B23: Erd 4B 84
   B29: W Cas .6G 131
   WS9: Wals W 3B 22
Kendal Gro. B92: Sol 5B 138
Kendal Ho. B69: O'bry 5D 96
Kendall Ri. DY6: K'wfrd 4D 92
Kendal Ri. B68: O'bry 6H 97
   WV6: Tett 3D 26
Kendal Ri. Rd. B45: Redn 2H 157
Kendal Rd. B11: S'brk 4B 118
Kendal Twr. B17: Harb 6H 115
Kendrick Av. B34: S End 4A 106
Kendrick Cl. B92: Sol 1B 152
Kendrick Pl. WV14: Bils 1A 62

Kendrick Rd. B76: Walm 2D 86
  WV10: Bush 3A 28
  WV14: Bils 1A 62
Kendricks Rd. WS10: Darl 4F 47
Kendrick St. WS10: W'bry 2G 63
Keneggy M. B29: S Oak 3B 132
Kenelm Rd. B10: Small H 3E 119
  B68: O'bry 6G 97
  B73: S Cold 1H 69
  WV14: Cose 4E 61
Kenelm's Ct. B62: Roms 3A 142
Kenilworth Cl. B74: Four O 3G 53
  CV7: Bal C 3G 169
  DY4: Tip .3F 77
  DY8: Word 1B 108
Kenilworth Ct. B16: Edg 3B 116
  B24: Erd 5E 85
  DY1: Dud 1B 94
Kenilworth Cres. WS2: Wals 5G 31
  WV4: E'shll 1A 60
Kenilworth Ho. B13: Mose 1A 148
  WS3: Blox 3A 32
          (off Providence La.)
Kenilworth Rd. B20: Hand 6G 83
  B46: Col 2H 123
  B68: O'bry 3B 114
  B92: H Ard 1D 154
  B93: Know 3F 167
  CV7: Bal C 2E 155
  CV7: Mer 3C 140
  WV6: Pert 5F 25
Kenley Gro. B30: K Nor 4D 146
Kenley Way B91: Shir 3B 150
Kenmare Way WV11: Wed 5E 29
Kenmure Rd. B33: Sheld 4G 121
Kennedy Cl. B72: S Cold 1A 70
Kennedy Ct. DY8: Stourb 6D 108
Kennedy Cres. DY3: Lwr G 3H 75
  WS10: Darl 4C 46
Kennedy Cft. B26: Sheld 4E 121
Kennedy Gro. B30: Stir 1D 146
Kennedy Rd. WV10: Wolv 6H 27
Kennedy Twr. B4. Birm 2E 5
Kennerley Rd. B25: Yard 5B 120
Kennet Cl. WS8: Bwnhls 3G 9
Kennet Gro. B36: Cas B 1B 106
Kenneth Gro. B23: Erd 2A 84
Kennford Cl. B65: Row R 3C 96
Kennington Rd. WV10: Wolv 4B 28
Kenrick Cft. B35: Cas V 5E 87
Kenrick Ho. B70: W Brom 6C 80
Kenrick Park Stop (MM) 6C 80
Kenrick Way B70: W Brom 1B 98
  B71: W Brom 6D 80
Kensington Av. B12: Bal H 1A 134
Kensington Dr. B74: Four O 4F 37
Kensington Gdns. DY8: Word 2A 108
Kensington Rd. B29: S Oak 3C 132
  WV12: W'hall 3B 30
Kensington St. B19: Hock 3F 101
Kenswick Dr. B63: Hale 3A 128
Kent Av. WS2: Wals 6H 31
Kent Cl. B71: W Brom 6A 64
  WS2: Wals 4C 32
  WS9: A'rdge 6D 22
Kentish Rd. B21: Hand 1G 99
Kentmere Ter. B23: Erd 1H 85
Kenton Av. WV6: Wolv 5D 26
Kenton Wlk. B29: S Oak 3B 132
Kent Pl. DY2: Dud 3C 94
Kent Rd. B45: Fran 6F 143
  B62: Quin 5E 113
  DY8: Woll 4B 108
  WS2: Wals 6F 31
  WS10: W'bry 1A 64
  WV2: Wolv 4A 44
Kents Cl. B92: Olton 2D 136
Kents Ho. B33: Yard 1H 121
Kent St. B5: Birm 3G 117
  DY3: Up Gor 2A 76
  WS2: Wals 4C 32
Kent St. Nth. B18: Hock 4B 100
Kenward Cft. B17: Harb 4D 114
Kenway B47: H'wd 2A 162

Kenwick Rd. B17: Harb 1F 131
Kenwood Rd. B9: Bord G 6H 103
Kenyon Cl. DY8: Amb 4E 109
Kenyon St. B18: Birm 1B 4 (5E 101)
Kerby Rd. B23: Erd 3C 84
Kererwin Cl. B64: Old H 2A 112
Keresley Cl. B91: Sol 2G 151
Keresley Gro. B29: W Cas 3D 130
Kernthorpe Rd. B14: K Hth 3F 147
Kerr Dr. DY4: Tip 5G 61
Kerria Ct. B15: Birm 3F 117
Kerridge Cl. WV9: Pend 5E 15
Kerrison Ride B73: Bold 4F 69
Kerr La. B90: Dic H 3G 163
Kerry Cl. B31: N'fld 1D 144
  DY5: Brie H 5G 93
Kerry Ct. WS1: Wals 3E 49
Kersley Gdns. WV11: Wed 3H 29
Kerswell Dr. B90: M'path 4D 164
Kesterton Rd. B74: Four O 4E 37
Kesteven Cl. B15: Edg 5D 116
Kesteven Rd. B71: W Brom 6A 64
Keston Rd. B44: Gt Barr 1H 67
Kestrel Av. B25: Yard 3H 119
Kestrel Cl. B23: Erd 1D 84
  B35: Cas V 4F 87
Kestrel Dr. B74: Four O 4F 37
Kestrel Gro. B30: B'vlle 5H 131
  WV12: W'hall 1C 30
Kestrel Ho. DY4: Tip 2G 77
Kestrel Ri. WV6: Tett 2D 26
Kestrel Rd. B63: Crad 4D 110
  B68: O'bry 1F 113
  DY1: Dud 1B 94
Kestrel Way WS6: C Hay 3C 6
Keswick Dr. DY6: K'wfrd 3B 92
Keswick Gro. B74: S'tly 1H 51
Keswick Ho. B69: O'bry 5D 96
Keswick Rd. B92: Olton 1D 136
Ketley Cft. B12: Birm 4H 117
Ketley Flds. DY6: K'wfrd 4E 93
Ketley Hill Rd. DY1: Dud 1B 94
Ketley Rd. DY6: K'wfrd 3D 92
        (not continuous)
Kettlebrook Rd. B90: M'path 3F 165
Kettlehouse Rd. B44: Gt Barr 2H 67
Kettles Bank Rd. DY3: Gorn 5G 75
        (not continuous)
Kettles Wood Dr. B32: Bart G 3H 129
Kettlewell Way B37: F'bri 1B 122
Kotton Gro. B33: Shold 4H 121
Kew Cl. B37: K'hrst 6B 106
Kew Dr. DY1: Dud 5C 76
Kew Gdns. B33: Stech 2B 120
Kewstoke Cl. WV12: W'hall 6B 18
Kewstoke Cft. B31: N'fld 1C 144
Kewstoke Rd. WV12: W'hall 6B 18
Key Bus. Pk. B24: Erd 4C 86
Keyes Dr. DY6: K'wfrd 6B 74
Key Gdns. WV10: Wolv 5B 28
Key Hill B18: Birm 4D 100
Key Hill Cir. B18: Birm 4D 100
Key Hill Dr. B18: Birm 4D 100
Key Ind. Pk. WV13: W'hall 6F 29
Keynell Covert B30: K Nor 4E 147
Keynes Dr. WV14: Bils 5G 45
Keys Cres. B71: W Brom 1A 80
Keyse Rd. B75: S Cold 4D 54
Keysmith Cl. WV13: W'hall 2C 46
Keyte Cl. DY4: Tip 2A 78
Keyway, The WV13: W'hall 2H 45
Keyway Retail Pk.
  WV13: W'hall 3B 46
Keyworth Cl. DY4: Tip 2A 78
Khalsa Ind. Est. B66: Smeth 5H 99
Khyber Cl. WS10: Darl 4C 46
Kidd Cft. DY4: Tip 3C 62
Kidderminster Rd.
  DY6: K'wfrd, W Hth 6G 91
  DY7: I'ley 6A 124
  DY7: Stourt 6A 124
  DY9: Hag 6G 125
  DY10: I'ley 6A 124
Kielder Cl. WS5: Wals 2G 65

Kielder Gdns. DY9: Pedm 4F 125
Kier's Bri. Cl. DY4: Tip 4A 78
Kilburn Dr. DY6: K'wfrd 6C 74
Kilburn Gro. B44: Gt Barr 2H 67
Kilburn Pl. DY2: Dud 3F 95
Kilburn Rd. B44: Gt Barr 2H 67
Kilby Av. B16: Birm 1C 116
         (not continuous)
Kilbys Gro. B20: Hand 5B 82
Kilcote Rd. B90: Shir 5C 148
Kilmet Wlk. B67: Smeth 4E 99
Kilmore Cft. B36: Hodg H 6C 86
Kilmorie Rd. B27: A Grn 6A 120
Kiln Cft. B65: Row R 5A 96
Kiln La. B25: Yard 5H 119
  B90: Dic H 4G 163
Kilsby Gro. B91: Sol 1G 165
Kilvert Rd. WS10: W'bry 3H 63
Kimballs Wlk. B93: Know 3E 167
Kimberley Av. B8: Salt 4E 103
Kimberley Cl. B74: S'tly 6A 36
Kimberley Pl. WV14: Cose 6D 60
Kimberley Rd. B66: Smeth 2E 99
  B92: Olton 3E 137
Kimberley St. WV3: Wolv 2E 43
Kimberley Wlk. B76: Min 1H 87
Kimble Gro. B24: Erd 4B 86
Kimbley Ri. B71: W Brom 6G 63
Kimpton Cl. B14: K Hth 5G 147
Kimsan Cft. B74: S'tly 4A 52
Kinchford Cl. B91: Sol 1G 165
Kineton Cft. B32: Bart G 5B 130
Kineton Grn. Rd. B92: Olton 5B 136
Kineton Ho. B13: Mose 1A 148
Kineton Rd. B45: Rub 2E 157
  B73. New O 4E 69
Kinfare Dr. WV6: Tett 5H 25
Kinfare Ri. DY3: Up Gor 3A 76
King Charles Av. WS2: Wals 1E 47
King Charles Ct. B44: K'sdng 3B 68
King Charles Rd. B62: Quin 1F 129
King Edmund St. DY1: Dud 5D 76
         (not continuous)
King Edward VI Ho. B4: Birm 6H 101
         (off Aston Rd.)
King Edward Ct. B63: Hale 1A 128
King Edward Rd. B13: Mose 2H 133
King Edwards Cl. B20: Hand 1D 100
King Edwards Dr. B16: Birm 1D 100
King Edwards Gdns. B20: Hand 2D 100
King Edwards Rd. B1: Birm . . .4A 4 (1D 116)
         (Edward St.)
  B1: Birm 6H 101
       (Ladywood Middleway)
King Edward's Row WV2: Wolv 3G 43
King Edwards Sq. B73: S Cold 5A 54
King Edward St. WS10: Darl 5D 46
King Edwards Wharf B16: Birm 1D 116
Kingfield Rd. B90: Shir 5C 148
Kingfisher Cl. B26: Sheld 5F 121
  DY3: Sed 3G 59
  WS8: Bwnhls 6A 10
Kingfisher Dr. WV13: W'hall 1C 46
Kingfisher Dr. B36: Cas B 1C 106
  DY8: Stourb 1A 124
Kingfisher Gro. WV12: W'hall 1B 30
Kingfisher Ind. Est. B70: W Brom 3F 79
Kingfisher Rd. B23: Erd 6C 68
Kingfisher Vw. B34: Stech 4E 105
Kingfisher Way B30: B'vlle 5H 131
  DY4: Tip .2G 77
King George VI Av. WS1: Wals 3G 49
King George Cres. WS4: Rus 3F 33
King George Pl. WS4: Rus 3F 33
Kingham Cl. DY3: Gorn 5G 75
Kingham Covert B14: K Hth 5F 147
Kingholm Rd. B38. Tiv 5B 78
Kingsbridge Ho. B23: Erd 1B 84
Kingsbridge Rd. B32: Bart G 4B 130
Kingsbridge Wlk. B66: Smeth 4F 99
Kingsbrook Dr. B91: Sol 1F 165
Kingsbury Av. B24: Erd 4B 86
Kingsbury Bus. Pk. B76: Min 1A 88

Kingsbury Cl. B76: Min 2H 87
    WS4: Wals 5F 33
Kingsbury Leisure Cen. 5F 85
Kingsbury Pl. B24: Erd 3H 85
Kingsbury Rd. B24: Erd 5E 85
    B35: Cas V 5B 86
    B76: Curd, Min 2G 87
        (not continuous)
    DY4: Tip 5A 62
Kings Bus. Pk. B44: Gt Barr 2G 67
Kings Cinema 4B 80
Kingsclere Wlk. WV4: Penn 5A 42
Kingscliff Rd. B10: Small H 3G 119
King's Cl. B14: K Hth 1E 147
Kingscote Rd. B15: Edg 5H 115
    B93: Dorr 6F 167
Kings Ct. B1: Birm 6B 4 (2E 117)
    B3: Birm 1C 4 (5F 101)
    B37: Mars G 2G 123
    B75: Four O 6H 37
    DY4: Tip 3A 78
    WS10: W'bry 2E 63
Kings Cft. B26: Sheld 6E 121
    B36: Cas B 2B 106
Kingscroft Cl. B74: S'tly 4A 52
Kingscroft Rd. B74: S'tly 3A 52
Kingsdene Av. DY6: K'wfrd 5A 92
Kingsdown Av. B42: Gt Barr 1B 82
Kingsdown Rd. B31: N'fld 4D 130
Kingsey Rd. B66: Smeth 5G 99
Kingsfield Rd. B14: K Hth 5G 133
Kingsford Cl. B36: Cas B 6H 87
Kingsford Ct. B92: Olton 2F 137
Kingsford Nouveau DY6: K'wfrd 4E 93
Kings Gdns. B30: K Nor 3A 146
Kings Ga. B11: K Hth 5G 133
Kingsgate Ho. B37: Chel W 1C 122
Kings Grn. Av. B38: K Nor 5B 146
Kingshayes Rd. WS9: A'rdge 5D 22
KING'S HEATH 5G 133
KING'S HILL .6D 46
Kings Hill Bus. Pk. WS10: W'bry 1E 63
Kings Hill Cl. WS10: Darl 6E 47
Kingshill Dr. B38: K Nor 5B 146
Kings Hill Fld. WS10: Darl 6E 47
Kings Hill M. WS10: Darl 6D 46
KINGSHURST 4B 106
Kingshurst Ho. B37: K'hrst 4B 106
Kingshurst Rd. B31: N'fld 4E 145
    B90: Shir 6F 149
Kingshurst Way B37: K'hrst 5B 106
Kingsland Dr. B93: Dorr 6A 166
Kingsland Rd. B44: Gt Barr 1G 67
    WV1: Wolv 6F 27
Kingslea Rd. B91: Sol 5C 150
Kingsleigh Cft. B75: Four O 1H 53
Kingsleigh Dr. B36: Cas B 1E 105
Kingsleigh Rd. B20: Hand 5D 82
Kingsley Av. WV6: Tett 5H 25
Kingsley Bank Way B36: Sheld 4F 121
Kingsley Ct. B25: Yard 3C 120
Kingsley Gdns. WV8: Cod 4E 13
Kingsley Gro. DY3: Lwr G 2E 75
Kingsley Rd. B12: Bal H 5A 118
    B30: K Nor 3H 145
    DY6: K'wfrd 4H 91
Kingsley St. DY2: Neth 4E 95
    WS2: Wals 4H 47
Kingslow Av. WV4: Penn 5B 42
Kingsmere Cl. B24: Erd 5E 85
KINGS NORTON 5H 145
King's Norton Bus. Cen.
    B30: K Nor 3C 146
Kings Norton Community Leisure Cen.
                                                   . . . . .1B 160
Kings Norton Station (Rail) 3B 146
Kingsoak Gdns. DY2: Dud 2G 95
Kings Pde. B4: Birm 4F 5
Kingspiece Ho. B36: Hodg H 1C 104
Kings Rd. B11: Tys 6G 119
    B14: K Hth 1E 147
    B23: Erd 3C 84
    B25: Yard 6G 119
    B44: Gt Barr, K'sdng 2G 67

Kings Rd. B73: New O 3A 68
    DY3: Sed 5A 60
    WS4: Rus 2G 33
Kings Rd. Ind. Est. B11: Tys 5G 119
Kings Sq. B70: W Brom 4B 80
    WV14: Cose 5C 60
King's Standing Ancient Monument . . .1H 67
KINGSTANDING 5A 68
Kingstanding Cen., The B44: Gt Barr . .2H 67
Kingstanding Leisure Cen. 3A 68
Kingstanding Rd. B44: K'sdng 1H 83
Kingsthorpe Rd. B14: K Hth 4A 148
Kingston Ct. B29: W Cas 6F 131
    B74: S Cold 4H 53
Kingston Ind. Est. B9: Birm 2B 118
        (off Glover St.)
Kingston Rd. B9: Birm 2B 118
    B75: S Cold 5D 54
Kingston Row B1: Birm 4A 4 (1E 117)
Kingston Way DY6: K'wfrd 2A 92
King St. B11: S'brk 4A 118
    B63: Hale 1A 128
    B64: Old H 2H 111
    B66: Smeth 2F 99
    DY2: Dud 1E 95
    DY5: Quar B 3C 110
    DY8: Woll 5C 108
    DY9: Lye 1B 126
    WS1: Wals 4B 48
    WS7: Chase 1B 10
    WS9: Wals W 5B 22
    WS10: W'bry 2E 63
    WV1: Wolv 3B 170 (1G 43)
    WV13: W'hall 1B 46
    WV14: Bils 2G 61
    WV14: Cose 5C 60
King St. Pas. DY2: Dud 6E 77
    DY5: Quar B 3C 110
King St. Pct. WS10: Darl 5D 46
Kingsway B68: O'bry 4G 113
    DY8: Woll 3B 108
    WV10: Wolv 3C 28
    WV11: Ess 3A 18
Kingsway Av. DY4: Tip 5A 62
Kingsway Dr. B38: K Nor 5B 146
Kingsway Nth. WS9: A'rdge 3A 34
Kingsway Rd. WV10: Wolv 3C 28
Kingsway Sth. WS9: A'rdge 3A 34
Kingswear Av. WV6: Pert 6F 25
KINGSWINFORD 3B 92
Kingswinford Rd. DY1: Dud 2A 94
KING'S WOOD 1G 161
KINGSWOOD 5A 12
Kingswood Cl. B14: K Hth 4F 147
    B90: Shir 6B 150
Kingswood Cft. B7: Nech 2C 102
Kingswood Dr. B30: K Nor 4E 147
    B74: S'tly 1H 67
    WS6: Gt Wyr 1G 7
Kingswood Gdns. WV4: Penn 5D 42
Kingswood Ho. B14: K Hth 5G 147
Kingswood Rd. B13: Mose 1A 134
    B31: Longb 3D 158
    DY6: K'wfrd 5A 92
Kingswood Wlk. B31: Longb 2D 158
Kington Cl. WV12: W'hall 1B 30
Kington Gdns. B37: F'bri 2B 122
Kington Way B33: Stech 1B 120
King William St. DY8: Amb 3D 108
Kiniths Cres. B71: W Brom 2C 80
Kiniths Way B62: B'hth 2E 113
    B71: W Brom 3C 80
Kinlet Cl. WV3: Wolv 3G 41
Kinlet Gro. B31: N'fld 5G 145
Kinloch Dr. DY1: Dud 4B 76
Kinnerley St. WS1: Wals 2E 49
Kinnersley Cres. B69: O'bry 4D 96
Kinnerton Cres. B29: W Cas 3D 130
Kinross Cres. B43: Gt Barr 1D 66
Kinsey Gro. B14: K Hth 3H 147
Kinsham Dr. B91: Sol 1F 165
Kintore Cft. B32: Bart G 6H 129
Kintyre Cl. B45: Fran 6E 143

Kinvara Hgts. B5: Birm 6G 5 (2H 117)
Kinver Av. WV12: W'hall 4B 30
Kinver Cres. WS9: A'rdge 6E 23
Kinver Cft. B12: Bal H 4G 117
    B76: Walm 5E 71
Kinver Dr. DY9: Hag 6G 125
    WV4: Penn 6A 42
Kinver M. B37: Mars G 3C 122
Kinver Rd. B31: N'fld 5H 145
Kinver St. DY8: Word 2B 108
Kinwarton Cl. B25: Yard 5B 120
Kipling Av. WV14: Cose 4D 60
Kipling Cl. DY4: Tip 5A 62
Kipling Rd. B30: K Nor 3G 145
    DY3: Lwr G 2E 75
    WV10: F'hses 5H 15
    WV12: W'hall 2E 31
Kirby Cl. WV14: Bils 2G 61
Kirby Dr. DY1: Dud 4A 76
Kirby Rd. B18: Win G 3A 100
Kirkby Grn. B73: S Cold 2H 69
Kirkham Gdns. DY5: P'ntt 3G 93
Kirkham Gro. B33: Stech 5D 104
Kirkham Way DY4: Tip 2A 78
Kirklands Est. DY2: Dud 2E 95
Kirkside Gro. WS8: Bwnhls 6B 10
Kirkside M. WS8: Bwnhls 6B 10
Kirkstall Cl. WS3: Blox 5F 19
Kirkstall Cres. WS3: Blox 5F 19
Kirkstone Ct. DY5: Brie H 4F 109
Kirkstone Cres. B43: Gt Barr 1B 82
    WV5: Wom 1F 73
Kirkstone Way DY5: Brie H 4F 109
Kirkwall Rd. B32: Bart G 4B 130
Kirkwood Av. B23: Erd 6F 69
Kirmond Wlk. WV6: Wolv 4F 27
Kirstead Gdns. WV6: Tett 6H 25
Kirton Gro. B33: Stech 5E 105
    B91: Sol 6E 151
    WV6: Tett 4A 26
Kitchener Rd. B29: S Oak 4D 132
    DY2: Dud 6H 77
Kitchener St. B66: Smeth 3H 99
Kitchen La. WV11: Wed 6G 17
Kitebrook Cl. B90: M'path 2E 165
Kitegreen Cl. B37: Chel W 5F 107
Kitsland Rd. B34: S End 3A 106
Kitswell Gdns. B32: Bart G 5G 129
Kittermaster Rd. CV7: Mer 4H 141
Kittiwake Dr. DY5: Brie H 4G 109
Kittoe Rd. B74: Four O 6F 37
KITT'S GREEN 6G 105
Kitts Grn. B33: Kitts G 6F 105
Kitts Grn. Rd. B33: Kitts G 5E 105
Kitwell La. B32: Bart G 5G 129
Kitwood Dr. B92: Sol 6H 137
Kixley La. B93: Know 3E 167
Klaxon Ind. Est. B11: Tys 1F 135
Knarsdale Cl. DY5: Brie H 3G 109
Knaves Castle Av. WS8: Bwnhls 3B 10
Knebworth Cl. B44: Gt Barr 5G 67
Knightcote Dr. B91: Sol 1F 165
Knight Ct. B75: S Cold 6G 55
Knightley Rd. B91: Sol 5D 150
Knightlow Rd. B17: Harb 3E 115
Knighton Cl. B74: Four O 6F 37
Knighton Dr. B74: Four O 1F 53
Knighton Rd. B31: N'fld 3G 145
    B74: Four O 4D 36
    DY2: Neth 5F 95
Knights Av. WV6: Tett 3B 26
Knightsbridge Cl. B74: Four O 5F 37
Knightsbridge Ho. B37: K'hrst 4B 106
Knightsbridge La. WV12: W'hall 3C 30
Knightsbridge Rd. B92: Olton 4D 136
Knights Cl. B23: Erd 5E 85
    WV13: W'hall 1C 46
Knights Ct. WS11: Nort C 1E 9
Knights Cres. WV6: Tett 2C 26
Knightsfield Cl. B73: New O 2C 68
Knights Hill WS9: A'rdge 6D 34
Knight's Rd. B11: Tys 1G 135
Knightstowe Av. B18: Hock 5C 100
Knightswood Cl. B75: S Cold 4B 54

Knightwick Cres.—Langley Mill Junc.

Knightwick Cres. B23: Erd .2C **84**
Knipersley Rd. B73: Bold .1G **85**
Knoll, The B32: Bart G .4A **130**
DY6: K'wfrd .4C **92**
Knoll Cl. WS7: Chase .1C **10**
Knoll Cft. B90: Ches G .5B **164**
WS9: A'rdge .6E **23**
Knollcroft B16: Birm .1C **116**
Knott Ct. DY5: Brie H .1H **109**
Knottsall La. B68: O'bry .6H **97**
Knotts Farm Rd. DY6: K'wfrd .5E **93**
Knowlands Rd. B90: M'path .2E **165**
KNOWLE .**3E 167**
Knowle Cl. B45: Redn .2B **158**
KNOWLE GROVE .**6C 166**
Knowle Hill Rd. DY2: Neth .5D **94**
Knowle Rd. B11: S'hll .2D **134**
B65: Row R .5H **95**
B92: H Ard .6G **153**
Knowles Dr. B74: Four O .4G **53**
Knowles Rd. WV1: Wolv .2B **44**
Knowles St. WS10: W'bry .2G **63**
Knowle Wood Rd. B93: Dorr .6D **166**
Knox Rd. WV2: Wolv .5H **43**
Knoyle Ct. *DY8: Stourb .5D* ***108***
(off Scott's Rd.)
Knutsford St. B12: Bal H .5H **117**
Knutswood Cl. B13: Mose .6D **134**
Kohima Dr. DY8: Stourb .6C **108**
Kossuth Rd. WV14: Cose .4C **60**
Kyle Cl. WV10: Oxl .6F **15**
Kyles Way B32: Bart G .6H **129**
Kynaston Cres. WV8: Cod .5H **13**
Kynaston Ho. B71: W Brom .5A **64**
Kyngsford Rd. B33: Kitts G .6H **105**
Kyotts Lake Rd. B11: S'brk .4A **118**
Kyrwicks La. B11: S'brk .5A **118**
B12: Birm .5A **118**
Kyter La. B36: Cas B .1F **105**

L

Laburnum Av. B37: K'hrst .3B **106**
B67: Smeth .5C **98**
Laburnum Cl. B37: K'hrst .3B **106**
B47: H'wd .4A **162**
DY8: Woll .4C **108**
WS3: Pels .5E **21**
Laburnum Cotts. B21: Hand .1A **100**
Laburnum Cft. B69: Tiv .5B **78**
Laburnum Dr. B76: Walm .2E **71**
Laburnum Gro. B13: Mose .2H **133**
WS2: Wals .6F **31**
Laburnum Ho. B30: B'vlle .6B **132**
Laburnum Rd. B30: B'vlle .5B **132**
DY1: Dud .3D **76**
DY4: Tip .6H **61**
DY6: K'wfrd .3C **92**
WS5: Wals .1G **65**
WS9: Wals W .4C **22**
WS10: W'bry .1H **63**
WV1: Wolv .3D **44**
WV4: E'shll .2A **60**
Laburnum St. DY8: Woll .4C **108**
WV3: Wolv .2E **43**
Laburnum Trees *B47: H'wd .3A* ***162***
(off May Farm Cl.)
Laburnum Vs. B11: S'hll .6C **118**
Laburnum Way B31: Longb .6E **145**
Laceby Gro. B13: Mose .4D **134**
Ladbroke Dr. B76: Walm .3D **70**
Ladbroke Gro. B27: A Grn .5A **136**
Ladbrook Gro. DY3: Lwr G .4E **75**
Ladbrook Rd. B91: Sol .4G **151**
Ladbury Gro. WS5: Wals .1D **64**
Ladbury Rd. WS5: Wals .1E **65**
Ladeler Gro. B33: Kitts G .1A **122**
Ladies Wlk. DY3: Sed .5H **59**
Lady Bank B32: Bart G .6H **129**
Lady Bracknell M. B31: N'fld .3G **145**
Lady Byron La. B93: Know .2B **166**
Ladycroft B16: Birm .1C **116**
Lady Grey's Wlk. DY8: Stourb .1B **124**
Lady La. B90: Shir .6G **163**
B94: Earls .6G **163**
Ladymoor Rd. WV14: Bils .2E **61**
Ladypool Av. B11: S'brk .5B **118**
Ladypool Cl. B62: Hale .1C **128**
WS4: Wals .4E **33**
Ladypool Rd. B11: S'brk .5A **118**
B12: Bal H .1A **134**
Ladysmith Rd. B63: Crad .5E **111**
Ladywell Cl. WV5: Wom .5G **57**
Ladywell Wlk. B5: Birm .6E **5** (2G **117**)
LADYWOOD .**1D 116**
Ladywood Arts & Leisure Cen. .1B **116**
Ladywood Cir. *B16: Birm .1C* ***116***
(off Ladywood Middleway)
Ladywood Cl. DY5: Quar B .2B **110**
Ladywood Middleway B1: Birm .1C **116**
B16: Birm .1C **116**
Ladywood Rd. B16: Edg .2B **116**
B74: Four O .4G **53**
LA Fitness
Sutton Coldfield .**6G 69**
Laing Ho. B69: O'bry .4D **96**
Lake Av. WS5: Wals .4F **49**
Lake Cl. WS5: Wals .4G **49**
Lakedown Cl. B14: K Hth .6G **147**
Lakefield B31: N'fld .3D **144**
Lakefield Cl. B28: Hall G .6H **135**
Lakefield Rd. WV11: Wed .4G **29**
Lakehouse Ct. B23: Erd .5E **69**
Lakehouse Gro. B38: K Nor .4H **145**
Lakehouse Rd. B73: Bold .5E **69**
Laker Cl. DY8: Amb .4E **109**
Lakeside B74: Lit As .4B **36**
Lakeside Cen., The .**4C 146**
Lakeside Cl. WV13: W'hall .6G **29**
Lakeside Cl. DY5: Brie H .3F **109**
Lakeside Dr. B90: M'path .2D **164**
Lakeside Residences
B4: Birm .2F **5** (6H **101**)
Lakeside Rd. B70: W Brom .1G **79**
Lakeside Wlk. B23: Erd .3B **84**
Lakes Rd. B23: Erd .2A **84**
Lake St. DY3: Lwr G .4H **75**
Lake Vw. Cl. B30: B'vlle .2A **146**
Lakewood Dr. B45: Redn .6H **143**
Lakey La. B28: Hall G .5G **135**
Lambah Cl. WV14: Bils .4H **45**
Lamb Cl. B34: S End .4A **106**
Lamb Cres. WV5: Wom .1F **73**
Lambert Cl. B23: Erd .1D **84**
Lambert Ct. DY6: K'wfrd .1B **92**
Lambert End B70: W Brom .4H **79**
Lambert Fold DY2: Dud .1G **95**
Lambert Rd. WV10: Wolv .3B **28**
LAMBERT'S END .**4H 79**
Lambert St. B70: W Brom .4H **79**
Lambeth Cl. B37: F'bri .5D **106**
Lambeth Rd. B44: Gt Barr .2G **67**
WV14: Bils .4D **44**
Lambourn Cl. WS3: Blox .5A **20**
Lambourne Cl. WS6: Gt Wyr .2F **7**
Lambourne Gro. B37: F'bri .1B **122**
Lambourne Way DY5: Brie H .3F **109**
WS11: Nort C .1E **9**
Lambourn Rd. B23: Erd .3D **84**
WV13: W'hall .2D **46**
Lambscote Cl. B90: Shir .5C **148**
Lammas Cl. B92: Sol .4G **137**
Lammas Rd. DY8: Word .6A **92**
Lammermoor Av. B43: Gt Barr .3B **66**
Lamont Av. B32: Bart G .2D **130**
Lamorna Cl. WV3: Wolv .3H **41**
Lanark Cl. DY6: K'wfrd .4D **92**
Lanark Cft. B35: Cas V .4D **86**
Lancaster Av. B45: Rub .1G **157**
WS9: A'rdge .1D **34**
WS10: W'bry .2A **64**
Lancaster Cir. Queensway
B4: Birm .1F **5** (5G **101**)
Lancaster Cl. B30: B'vlle .1C **146**
Lancaster Dr. B35: Cas V .5F **87**
Lancaster Gdns. WV4: Penn .6C **42**
Lancaster Ho. B65: Row R .5E **97**
Lancaster Pl. WS3: Blox .5A **20**
Lancaster Rd. DY5: Brie H .1G **109**
Lancaster St. B4: Birm .1F **5** (5G **101**)
Lancelot Cl. B8: Salt .6E **103**
Lancelot Pl. B70: W Brom .3E **79**
Lanchester Rd. B38: K Nor .6C **146**
Lanchester Way B36: Cas B .6A **88**
Lander Cl. B45: Rub .3G **157**
Landgate Rd. B21: Hand .5G **81**
Land La. B37: Mars G .4C **122**
Landor Rd. B93: Know .3C **166**
Landor St. B8: Birm, Salt .6B **102**
Landport Rd. WV2: Wolv .3B **44**
Landrail Wlk. B36: Cas B .1C **106**
(not continuous)
Landrake Rd. DY6: K'wfrd .4D **92**
Landseer Gro. B43: Gt Barr .1F **67**
Landsgate DY8: Stourb .4E **125**
Landswood Cl. B44: K'sdng .4A **68**
Landswood Rd. B68: O'bry .5A **98**
LANDYWOOD .**3G 7**
Landywood Ent. Pk. WS6: Gt Wyr .5F **7**
Landywood Grn. WS6: C Hay .3E **7**
Landywood La. WS6: C Hay, Gt Wyr .3D **6**
Landywood Station (Rail) .**3F 7**
Lane Av. WS2: Wals .6H **31**
Lane Cl. WS2: Wals .6H **31**
Lane Ct. *WV1: Wolv .5G* ***27***
(off Boscobel Cres.)
Lane Cft. B76: Walm .5E **71**
LANE GREEN .**4H 13**
Lane Grn. Av. WV8: Bilb .6A **14**
Lane Grn. Ct. WV8: Bilb .4H **13**
Lane Grn. Rd. WV8: Bilb .4H **13**
Lane Grn. Shop. Pde. WV8: Bilb .4H **13**
LANE HEAD .**3C 30**
Lane Rd. WV4: E'shll .2C **60**
Lanes Cl. WV5: Wom .2E **73**
LANESFIELD .**1C 60**
Lanesfield Dr. WV4: E'shll .1C **60**
Lanesfield Ind. Est. WV4: E'shll .1C **60**
Laneside Av. B74: S'tly .4H **51**
Laneside Gdns. WS2: Wals .1H **47**
Lanes Shop. Cen., The B72: W Grn .6H **69**
Lane St. WV14: Bils, Cose .2F **61**
LANEY GREEN .**3A 6**
Langcomb Rd. B90: Shir .1G **163**
Langdale Cl. WS8: Clay .1A **22**
Langdale Cft. B21: Hand .2A **100**
Langdale Dr. WV14: Bils .4F **45**
Langdale Rd. B43: Gt Barr .6B **66**
Langdale Way DY9: W'cte .1H **125**
Langdon St. B9: Birm .1B **118**
Langdon Wlk. B26: Yard .1C **136**
Langfield Rd. B93: Know .2C **166**
Langford Av. B43: Gt Barr .5A **66**
Langford Cl. WS1: Wals .2E **49**
Langford Cft. B91: Sol .5G **151**
Langford Gro. B17: Harb .2G **131**
Langham Cl. B26: Sheld .4E **121**
Langham Grn. B74: S'tly .2H **51**
Langholme Dr. B44: K'sdng .4D **68**
Langland Dr. DY3: Sed .5G **59**
LANGLEY .**4G 97**
Langley Av. WV14: Cose .5E **61**
Langley Cl. WS9: Wals W .3C **22**
Langley Ct. B69: O'bry .4G **97**
WV4: Penn .5B **42**
Langley Cres. B68: O'bry .5H **97**
Langley Dr. B35: Cas V .6E **87**
Langley Gdns. B68: O'bry .5H **97**
WV3: Wolv .4B **42**
LANGLEY GREEN .**5H 97**
Langley Grn. Rd. B69: O'bry .5G **97**
Langley Green Station (Rail) .**4H 97**
Langley Gro. B10: Small H .3D **118**
Langley Hall Dr. B75: S Cold .6F **55**
Langley Hall Rd. B75: S Cold .6F **55**
B92: Olton .6A **136**
Langley Heath Dr. B76: Walm .2D **70**
Langley High St. B69: O'bry .4G **97**
LANGLEY MILL JUNC.
Falcon Lodge .**5H 55**
Littleworth End .**2G 55**

Langley Pk. Way B75: S Cold 5D 54
Langley Ri. B92: Sol 2A 138
Langley Rd. B10: Small H 3D 118
  B68: O'bry .5H 97
  WV4: Lwr P 6E 41
Langleys Rd. B29: S Oak 4A 132
Langley Swimming Cen. 5H 97
Langley Wlk. B15: Birm 2E 117
Langmead Cl. WS2: Wals 6D 30
Langsett Rd. WV10: Wolv 5A 28
Langstone Rd. B14: K Hth 5B 148
  DY1: Dud .6A 76
Langton Cl. B36: Cas B 3D 106
Langton Pl. WV14: Bils 5A 46
Langton Rd. B8: Salt 5E 103
Langtree Av. B91: Sol 6F 151
Langwood Ct. B36: Cas B 1F 105
Langworth Av. B27: A Grn 6A 120
Lannacombe Rd. B31: Longb 3C 158
Lansbury Av. WS10: Darl 1C 62
Lansbury Grn. B64: Old H 3B 112
Lansbury Rd. B64: Old H 3B 112
Lansbury Wlk. DY4: Tip 5A 62
Lansdale Av. B92: Sol 5B 138
Lansdowne Av. WV8: Cod 5E 13
Lansdowne Cl. DY2: Dud 3H 95
  WV14: Cose 6C 60
Lansdowne Ct. DY9: Pedm 4F 125
Lansdowne Rd. B21: Hand 2C 100
  B24: Erd 4F 85
  B62: B'hth 3F 113
  B63: Hale .3F 127
  WV1: Wolv 1A 170 (6F 27)
  WV14: Bils .4G 45
Lansdowne St. B18: Win G 5B 100
Lansdown Ho. B15: Birm 3F 117
Lansdown Pl. B18: Hock 4B 100
Lantern Rd. DY2: Neth 1E 111
LAPAL 1F 129
Lapal La. B62: Bart G 3F 129
Lapal La. Nth. B62: Hale 2E 129
Lapal La. Sth. B62: Hale 2E 129
Lapal Mnr. Ct. B32: Bart G 3F 129
Lapley Cl. WV1: Wolv 1D 44
Lappath Ho. B32: Bart G 5B 130
Lapper Av. WV4: E'shll 2B 60
Lapwing Cl. WS6: C Hay 4C 6
  WS8: Bwnhls 6A 10
Lapwing Cft. B23: Erd 6C 68
Lapwing Dr. B92: H Ard 6B 140
Lapwood Av. DY6: K'wfrd 3D 92
Lapworth Dr. B73: New O 2C 68
Lapworth Gro. B12: Bal H 5H 117
Lapworth Ho. B5: Birm 4G 117
Lapworth Mus. 2B 132
Lara Cl. B17: Harb 3F 115
Lara Gro. DY4: Tip 6A 78
Larch Av. B21: Hand 5H 81
Larch Cft. B37: Chel W 1D 122
  B69: Tiv 5B 78
Larch Dr. B31: Longb 6A 144
Larches La. WV3: Wolv 1E 43
Larches St. B11: S'brk 5A 118
Larchfield Cl. B20: Hand 4D 82
Larch Gdns. WV14: Bils 1H 61
Larch Gro. DY3: Sed 6A 60
Larch Ho. B20: Hand 4B 82
  B36: Hodg H 1D 104
Larchmere Dr. B28: Hall G 5F 135
  WV11: Ess .4B 18
Larch Rd. DY6: K'wfrd 3C 92
Larch Wlk. B25: Yard 3H 119
Larchwood Cres.
  B74: S'tly 3G 51
Larchwood Grn. WS5: Wals 1F 65
Larchwood Rd. WS5: Wals 1E 65
Larcombe Dr. WV4: Penn 6H 43
Large Av. WS10: Darl 1C 62
Lark Cl. B14: K Hth 5A 148
Larkfield Av. B36: Cas B 1F 105
Larkhill Rd. DY8: Stourb 1A 124
Larkhill Wlk. B14: K Hth 6F 147
Larkin Cl. WV10: Bush 6C 16
Lark Mdw. Dr. B37: K'hrst 6A 106

Larksfield B66: Smeth 5F 99
             (off Windmill La.)
Larksfield M. DY5: Brie H 4G 109
Larks Mill WS3: Pels 3C 20
Larkspur Av. WS7: Burn 1C 10
Larkspur Cft. B36: Hodg H 1B 104
Larkspur Dr. DY2: Dud 1H 95
Larkspur Way WS8: Clay 1H 21
Larkswood Dr. DY3: Sed 6H 59
  WV4: Penn .2A 58
Larne Rd. B26: Sheld 4E 121
Lashbrooke Ho. B45: Rub 2F 157
Latches Cl. WS10: Darl 5E 47
Latelow Rd. B33: Yard 1E 121
Latham Av. B43: Gt Barr 6A 66
Latham Cres. DY4: Tip 4A 78
Lath La. B66: Smeth 1B 98
Latham Gro. B33: Stech 4D 104
Latimer Gdns. B15: Edg 4F 117
Latimer Pl. B18: Win G 3A 100
Latimer St. WV13: W'hall 6B 30
Latymer Cl. B76: Walm 6E 71
Lauder Cl. DY3: Sed 4G 59
  WV13: W'hall 2F 45
Lauderdale Cl. WS8: Clay 1A 22
Lauderdale Gdns. WV10: Bush 4A 16
Laughton Cl. B31: Longb 2F 159
Launceston Cl. WS5: Wals 4H 49
Launceston Rd. WS5: Wals 4H 49
Launde, The B28: Hall G 4E 149
Laundry Rd. B66: Smeth 6G 99
Laureates Wlk. B74: Four O 2G 53
Laurel Av. B12: Bal H 6A 118
Laurel Cl. DY1: Dud 4C 76
Laurel Ct. B13: Mose 3H 133
Laurel Dr. B66: Smeth 1E 99
  B74: S'tly 3G 51
Laurel Gdns. B21: Hand 6A 82
  B27: A Grn .6A 120
Laurel Gro. B30: B'ville 1A 146
  WV3: Wolv .5C 42
  WV14: Bils .1A 62
Laurel La. B63: Hale 2B 128
Laurel Rd. B21: Hand 6A 82
  B30: K Nor 3C 146
  DY1: Dud 3B 76
  DY4: Tip 6H 61
  WS5: Wals .1F 65
Laurels, The B14: K Hth 4G 147
  B16: Birm .6B 100
           (off Marroway St.)
  B26: Sheld 6G 121
Laurels Cres. CV7: Bal C 6H 169
Laurel Ter. B6: Aston 6H 83
Laurence Cl. B31: N'fld 2F 145
Laurence Gro. WV6: Tett 2C 26
Lauriston Cl. DY1: Dud 4B 76
Lavender Cl. WS5: Wals 2D 64
  WV9: Pend .4D 14
Lavender Ct. B71: W Brom 6A 64
            (off Sussex Av.)
Lavender Gdns. B23: Erd 6B 68
Lavender Gro. WV3: Wals 4C 32
  WV14: Bils .5H 45
Lavender Hall La. CV7: Bal C 1H 169
Lavender Ho. B38: K Nor 1B 160
Lavender La. DY8: Stourb 2B 124
Lavender Rd. DY1: Dud 4D 76
Lavendon Rd. B42: P Barr 2D 82
Lavinia Rd. B62: Hale 2E 129
Law Cliff Rd. B42: Gt Barr 1D 82
Law Cl. B69: Tiv 5D 78
Lawden Rd. B10: Small H 3B 118
Lawford Cl. B7: Birm 6A 102
Lawford Gro. B5: Birm 3G 117
  B90: Shir .5D 148
Lawfred Av. WV11: Wed 4F 29
Lawley, The B63: Hale 4F 127
Lawley Cl. WS4: S'fld 6E 21
Lawley Middleway B4: Birm 5A 102
Lawley Rd. WV14: Bils 5D 44
Lawley St. B70: W Brom 4F 79
  DY1: Dud 6C 76
Lawn Av. DY8: Stourb 1C 124

Lawn La. WV9: Coven 2D 14
Lawnoaks Cl. WS8: Bwnhls 3H 9
Lawn Rd. WV2: E'shll 5B 44
Lawnsdale Cl. B46: Col 2H 107
Lawnsdown Rd. DY5: Quar B 4B 110
Lawnsfield Gro. B23: Erd 1D 84
Lawnside Grn. WV14: Bils 3F 45
Lawn St. DY8: Stourb 1C 124
LAWNS WOOD 6G 91
Lawnswood B76: Walm 5E 71
  DY7: Stourt 5G 91
Lawnswood Av. B90: Shir 4B 150
  DY8: Word .5A 92
  WS7: Chase 1B 10
  WV4: E'shll .1A 60
  WV6: Tett 1C 26
Lawnswood Dr. DY7: Stourt 6G 91
  WS9: Wals W 4C 22
Lawnswood Gro. B21: Hand 6G 81
Lawnswood Ri. WV6: Tett 1D 26
Lawnswood Rd. DY3: Up Gor 2H 75
  DY8: Word .6A 92
Lawnwood Rd. DY2: Neth 1D 110
Lawrence Av. WV10: Wolv 5C 28
  WV11: Wed .3H 29
Lawrence Ct. B68: O'bry 3H 113
Lawrence Dr. B76: Min 1H 87
Lawrence La. B64: Old H 2G 111
Lawrence St. DY9: Lye 5G 109
  WV13: W'hall 6A 30
Lawrence Twr. B4: Birm 2G 5
Lawrence Wlk. B43: Gt Barr 1F 67
Lawson Cl. WS9: A'rdge 5D 34
Lawson St. B4: Birm 1F 5 (5G 101)
Law St. B71: W Brom 2A 80
Lawnoaks Av. B29: S Oak 3D 132
Lawton Cl. B65: Row R 3D 96
Lawyers Wlk. WS1: Wals 2D 48
Laxey Rd. B16: Edg 6H 99
Laxford Cl. B12: Bal H 5G 117
Laxon Gro. B91: Sol 6G 137
Laxton Cl. DY6: K'wfrd 4E 93
Laxton Gro. B25: Yard 2B 120
Lazy Hill B38: K Nor 5D 146
  WS9: Ston 4F 23
Lazy Hill Rd. WS9: A'rdge 1D 34
Lea, The B33: Yard 1E 121
Lea Av. WS10: W'bry 4D 62
Lea Bank WV3: Wolv 1A 42
Lea Bank Rd. DY2: Neth 6D 94
Leabon Gro. B17: Harb 1G 131
Leabrook B26: Yard 3D 120
Leabrook Rd. DY4: Tip 4C 62
  WS10: W'bry 4C 62
Leabrook Rd. Nth. WS10: W'bry 4D 62
Leach Grn. La. B45: Redn 2G 157
Leach Heath La. B45: Rub 2F 157
Leacliffe Way WS9: A'rdge 6H 35
Leacote Dr. WV6: Tett 5A 26
Leacroft WV12: W'hall 2C 30
Leacroft Av. WV10: Bush 1A 28
Leacroft Cl. WS9: A'rdge 6D 22
Leacroft Gro. B71: W Brom 5H 63
Leacroft La. WS11: Cann 1F 7
Leacroft Rd. DY6: K'wfrd 1C 92
Leadbeater Ho. WS3: Blox 1H 31
       (off Somerfield Rd.)
Lea Dr. B26: Sheld 5E 121
LEA END 6B 160
Lea End La. B38: Forh 5G 159
  B48: Hopw 5G 159
Leafield Cres. B33: Stech 4E 105
Leafield Gdns. B62: B'hth 3D 112
Leafield Rd. B92: Sol 4F 137
Lea Ford Rd. B33: Kitts G 5G 105
Leaford Way DY6: K'wfrd 4D 92
Leafy Glade B74: S'tly 6A 36
Leafy Ri. DY3: Lwr G 3H 75
Lea Gdns. WV3: Wolv 3F 43
Lea Grn. Av. DY4: Tip 2E 77
Lea Grn. Dr. B47: Wyt 5C 162
Lea Grn. La. B47: Wyt 3C 162
Lea Hall Rd. B33: Yard 6E 105
Lea Hall Station (Rail) 1F 121

Leahill Cft. B37: F'bri 1B 122
Lea Hill Rd. B20: Hand 5E 83
Leaholme Gdns. DY9: Pedm 3F 125
Leahouse Gdns. B68: O'bry 6G 97
Lea Ho. Rd. B30: Stir 6C 132
Leahouse Rd. B68: O'bry 6G 97
Leahurst Cres. B17: Harb 1G 131
Lea La. WS6: Gt Wyr 2G 7
Lea Mnr. Dr. WV4: Penn 2C 58
Leam Cres. B92: Sol 4F 137
Lea M. B33: Yard 6E 105
Leamington Rd. B12: Bal H . . .6A 118
LEAMORE 4H 31
Leamore Cl. WS2: Wals 2G 31
Leamore Ent. Pk. WS2: Wals 3G 31
(Fryer's Rd.)
WS2: Wals 2G 31
(Willenhall La., not continuous)
Leamore Ind. Est. WS2: Wals . . .3H 31
Leamore La. WS2: Blox, Wals . . .2G 31
WS3: Blox 2G 31
Leamount Dr. B44: K'sdng 3C 68
Leander Cl. WS6: Gt Wyr 4F 7
Leander Gdns. B14: K Hth . . .2H 147
Leander Rd. DY9: W'cte 1B 126
Leandor Dr. B74: S'tly 4A 52
Lea Rd. B11: S'hll 1D 134
WV3: Wolv 6A 170 (4E 43)
Lear Rd. WV5: Wom 5H 57
Leasemaster Ho. B1: Birm 2A 4
Leason La. WV10: Bush 1C 28
Leasow, The WS9: A'rdge 4A 34
Leasow Dr. B15: Edg 2H 131
Leasowe Dr. WV6: Pert 5D 24
Leasowe Rd. B45: Rub 1F 157
DY4: Tip 3G 77
Leasowes Country Pk., The 1D 128
Leasowes Ct. B63: Hale 3A 128
Leasowes Dr. WV4: Penn 5B 42
Leasowes La. B62: Hale 6D 112
Leasowes Rd. B14: K Hth 4H 133
Leasowes Sports Cen. 5E 113
Leasows, The DY4: Tip 2C 78
Leatherhead Cl. B6: Aston 3H 101
Leather Mus., The 6C 32
Lea Va. Rd. DY8: Stourb 3D 124
Leavesden Gro. B26: Sheld . . .6E 121
Lea Vw. WS9: A'rdge 4A 34
WV12: W'hall 4A 30
Lea Village B33: Kitts G 1F 121
Lea Wlk. B45: Rub 1F 157
Lea Yield Cl. B30: Stir 6C 132
Lechlade Rd. B43: Gt Barr 5A 66
Leckie Rd. WS2: Wals 5C 32
Ledbury Cl. B16: Birm 1C 116
WS9: A'rdge 6E 23
Ledbury Ct. B29: W Cas 6G 131
(off Ruthall Cl.)
Ledbury Dr. WV1: Wolv 2D 44
Ledbury Ho. B33: Kitts G 1A 122
Ledbury Way B76: Walm 5E 71
Ledsam Gro. B32: Harb 5D 114
Ledsam St. B16: Birm 1C 116
Ledwell B90: Dic H 3G 163
LEE BANK 3E 117
Lee Bank Middleway B15: Birm . . .3E 117
Leebank Rd. B63: Hale 3G 127
Leech St. DY4: Tip 2C 78
Lee Ct. WS9: Wals W 4B 22
Lee Cres. B15: Edg 3E 117
Lee Gdns. B67: Smeth 4C 98
Lee Rd. B47: H'wd 2A 162
B64: Crad H 3H 111
Leeson Wlk. B17: Harb 1H 131
Lees Rd. WV14: Bils 2H 61
Lees St. B18: Hock 4B 100
Lees Ter. WV14: Bils 2H 61
Lee St. B70: W Brom 5G 63
Legge La. B1: Birm 2A 4 (6D 100)
WV14: Cose 3F 61
Legge St. B4: Birm 5H 101
B70: W Brom 4B 80
WV2: E'shll 5A 44
Legion Rd. B45: Rub 2E 157

Legs La. WV10: Bush 3A 16
Leicester Cl. B67: Smeth 2C 114
Leicester Pl. B71: W Brom 6A 64
Leicester Sq. WV6: Wolv 6E 27
Leicester St. WS1: Wals 1C 48
WV6: Wolv 5F 27
Leigham Dr. B17: Harb 4E 115
Leigh Cl. WS4: Wals 5E 33
Leigh Ct. B23: Erd 5C 84
WS4: Wals 6E 33
Leigh Rd. B8: Salt 3E 103
B75: S Cold 5F 55
WS4: Wals 6E 33
Leighs Cl. WS4: S'fld 6G 21
Leighs Rd. WS4: S'fld 6F 21
LEIGHSWOOD 1C 34
Leighswood Av. WS9: A'rdge . . .2C 34
Leighswood Ct. WS9: A'rdge . . .3D 34
Leighswood Gro. WS9: A'rdge . . .2C 34
Leighswood Ind. Est. WS9: A'rdge . .6B 22
(Brickyard Rd.)
WS9: A'rdge 2C 34
(Phoenix Dr.)
Leighswood Rd. WS9: A'rdge . . .2C 34
Leighton Cl. B43: Gt Barr 2E 67
DY1: Dud 5A 76
Leighton Rd. B13: Mose 3H 133
WV4: Penn 5D 42
WV14: Bils 1A 62
Leith Gro. B38: K Nor 1A 160
Lelant Gro. B17: Harb 6E 115
Lellow St. B71: W Brom 5H 63
Lemar Ind. Est. B30: Stir 4D 132
Le More B74: Four O 1G 53
Lemox Rd. B70: W Brom 5G 63
Lench Cl. B62: B'hth 2C 112
Lenches, The B69: O'bry 4E 97
(off Shelsley Av.)
Lench's Cl. B13: Mose 3H 133
Lenchs Grn. B5: Edg 4G 117
Lench St. B4: Birm 1F 5 (5G 101)
Lenchs Trust B32: Quin 5B 114
Lench's Trust Ho's. B12: Birm . . .4H 117
(Conybere St.)
B12: Birm 4H 117
(Ravenhurst St.)
B16: Birm 2C 116
(off Ladywood Middleway)
Len Davis Rd. WV12: W'hall . . .2B 30
Lennard Gdns. B66: Smeth 3H 99
Lennox Gdns. WV3: Wolv 3E 43
Lennox Gro. B73: Bold 6G 69
Lennox St. B19: Hock 3F 101
Lenton Cft. B26: Yard 1C 136
Lenwade Rd. B68: O'bry 3B 114
Leofric Ct. B15: Edg 3E 117
Leominster Ct. B45: Rub 1F 157
(off Deelands Rd.)
Leominster Ho. B33: Kitts G . . .1A 122
Leominster Rd. B11: S'hll 2E 135
Leominster Wlk. B45: Rub 1F 157
Leona Ind. Est. B62: B'hth 2D 112
Leonard Av. B19: Loz 1F 101
Leonard Gro. B19: Loz 1E 101
Leonard Rd. B19: Loz 1E 101
DY8: Woll 6A 108
Leopold Av. B20: Hand 2A 82
Leopold St. B12: Birm 3H 117
Lepid Gro. B29: S Oak 3H 131
Lerryn Cl. DY6: K'wfrd 4D 92
Lerwick Cl. DY6: K'wfrd 4D 92
Lesley Dr. DY6: K'wfrd 5C 92
Leslie Bentley Ho. B1: Birm 3A 4
Leslie Dr. DY4: Tip 4A 62
Leslie Ri. B69: Tiv 1C 96
Leslie Rd. B16: Edg 1B 116
B20: Hand 5F 83
B74: Lit As 1B 52
WV10: Wolv 4B 28
Lesscroft Cl. WV9: Pend 4E 15
Lester Gro. WS9: A'rdge 1G 51
Lester St. WV14: Bils 6H 45
Levante Gdns. B33: Stech 1B 120
Leve La. WV13: W'hall 1B 46

Level St. DY5: Brie H 6H 93
Leven Cft. B76: Walm 6E 71
Leven Dr. WV12: W'hall 6B 18
Levenwick Way DY6: K'wfrd 4E 93
Leverretts, The B21: Hand 5G 81
Lever St. WV2: Wolv 6C 170 (3H 43)
Leverton Ri. WV10: Oxl 3G 27
Leveson Av. WS6: C Hay 3E 7
Leveson Cl. DY2: Dud 1G 95
Leveson Ct. WV13: W'hall 1A 46
Leveson Cres. CV7: Bal C 6H 169
Leveson Dr. DY4: Tip 1G 77
Leveson Rd. WV11: Wed 1H 29
Leveson St. WV13: W'hall 1A 46
Leveson Wlk. DY2: Dud 1G 95
Levington Ct. WV6: Pert 5F 25
Levis's Trad. Est. B33: Stech . . .5B 104
Lewis Av. WV1: Wolv 6D 28
Lewis Cl. WV12: W'hall 4D 30
Lewis Gro. WV11: Wed 3F 29
Lewisham Ind. Est. B66: Smeth . . .2E 99
Lewisham Rd. B66: Smeth 2E 99
WV10: Oxl 5F 15
Lewisham St. B71: W Brom 3B 80
Lewis Rd. B30: Stir 6E 133
B68: O'bry 4H 113
DY9: Lye 6H 109
Lewis St. DY4: Tip 2D 78
WS2: Wals 5B 32
WV14: Bils 5G 45
Lewthorn Ri. WV4: Penn 1H 59
Lexington Grn. DY5: Brie H 4G 109
Leybourne Cres. WV9: Pend 5D 14
Leybourne Gro. B25: Yard 5H 119
Leybrook Rd. B45: Redn 1H 157
Leyburn Cl. WS2: Wals 5D 30
Leyburn Rd. B16: Edg 2C 116
Leycester Cl. B31: Longb 2E 159
Leycroft Av. B33: Kitts G 5H 105
Leydon Cft. B38: K Nor 5D 146
LEY HILL 2G 53
Ley Hill Farm Rd.
B31: N'fld 2C 144
Ley Hill Rd. B75: Four O 2A 54
Leylan Cft. B13: Mose 6C 134
Leyland Av. WV3: Wolv 2D 42
Leyland Cft. WS3: Pels 3D 20
Leyland Dr. DY2: Dud 1F 95
Leyman Cl. B14: Yard W 3C 148
Ley Ri. DY3: Sed 4G 59
Leys, The B31: N'fld 2F 145
WS10: Darl 5C 46
Leys Cl. DY9: Pedm 3G 125
Leys Cres. DY5: Brie H 6F 93
Leysdown Gro. B27: A Grn 5A 136
Leysdown Rd. B27: A Grn 5A 136
Leys Rd. DY5: Brie H 6E 93
Leys Wood Cft. B26: Sheld 5E 121
Leyton Cl. DY5: Brie H 3G 109
Leyton Gro. B44: K'sdng 4A 68
Leyton Rd. B21: Hand 1B 100
Libbards Ga. B91: Sol 1G 165
Libbards Way B91: Sol 1F 165
Liberty Ct. WS6: C Hay 2D 6
Liberty Pl. B16: Birm 1D 116
Library, Theatre and Solihull Arts Complex
. . . . .4G 151
Library Way B45: Rub 2F 157
Lich Av. WV11: Wed 2G 29
Lichen Gdns. B38: K Nor 2H 159
Lichfield Cl. WS6: Gt Wyr 4G 7
Lichfield Ct. B90: Shir 5D 148
WS4: Wals 5E 33
(off Lichfield Rd.)
Lichfield Pas. WV1: Wolv . . .2C 170 (1H 43)
Lichfield Rd. B6: Aston 2A 102
B46: Col, Wat O 3F 89
B74: Four O, S Cold 4F 37
B76: Curd, Wis 2F 89
WS3: Blox 5H 19
WS3: Pels 2E 21
WS4: Rus, S'fld, Wals 5E 33
WS8: Bwnhls 5B 10
WS9: Wals W, Bwnhls 4B 22

Lichfield Rd. WV11: Wed 4F 29
  WV12: W'hall 2A 30
Lichfield St. DY4: Tip 5H 61
  WS1: Wals .1D 48
  WS4: Wals .6D 32
  WV1: Wolv 3B 170 (1G 43)
  WV14: Bils .5F 45
Lich Gates WV1: Wolv 2B 170 (1G 43)
Lichwood Rd. WV11: Wed 2H 29
LICKEY 6G 157
Lickey Coppice B45: Coft H 5A 158
Lickey Hills Country Pk. 5G 157
Lickey Hills Vis. Cen. 6H 157
Lickey Rd. B45: Coft H 4H 157
  DY8: Amb .5F 109
Liddiard Ct. DY8: Woll 5C 108
Liddon Gro. B27: A Grn 5A 136
Liddon Rd. B27: A Grn 5A 136
LIFFORD 2D 146
Lifford Cl. B14: K Hth 2D 146
Lifford La. B30: K Nor 2C 146
Lifton Cft. DY6: K'wfrd 4D 92
Lightfields Wlk. B65: Row R 4A 96
Lighthorne Av. B16: Birm 1C 116
Lighthorne Rd. B91: Sol 1G 151
Lighthouse, The 2C 170
Lightning Way B31: Longb 2F 159
Lightwood Cl. B93: Know 1D 166
Lightwood Rd. DY1: Dud 4C 76
Lightwoods Hill B67: Smeth 3C 114
Lightwoods Rd. B67: Smeth 1E 115
  DY9: Pedm 4G 125
Lilac Av. B12: Bal H 6A 118
  B44: Gt Barr 6G 67
  B74: S'tly 3G 51
  DY4: Tip 6G 61
  WS5: Wals .1E 65
Lilac Dr. WV5: Wom 1F 73
Lilac Gro. WS2: Wals 6E 31
  WS10: W'bry 3G 63
Lilac La. WS6: Gt Wyr 5F 7
Lilac Rd. DY1: Dud 3D 76
  WV1: Wolv .3D 44
  WV12: W'hall 2E 31
Lilac Way B62: B'hth 3F 113
Lilian Gro. WV14: Bils 4G 61
Lilleshall Cres. WV2: Wolv 4H 43
Lilleshall Rd. B26: Sheld 4F 121
Lilley La. B31: Longb 1F 159
Lillington Cl. B75: S Cold 1E 71
Lillington Gro. B34: S End 4H 105
Lillington Rd. B90: Shir 1H 163
Lillycroft La. B38: Head H 2C 160
Lily Rd. B26: Yard 5B 120
Lily St. B71: W Brom 2A 80
Limberlost Cl. B20: Hand 4C 82
Limbrick Cl. B90: Shir 5F 149
Limbury Gro. B92: Sol 5B 138
Lime Av. B29: S Oak 3B 132
  WS2: Wals .6E 31
Lime Cl. B47: H'wd 4A 162
  B70: W Brom 3G 79
  DY4: Tip 2G 77
  WS2: Wals .6E 31
  WS6: Gt Wyr 1F 7
Lime Ct. B11: S'hll 1C 134
Lime Gro. B10: Small H 3D 118
  B12: Bal H .GH 117
  B19: Loz 1E 101
  B26: Yard 5B 120
  B37: Chel W 2D 122
  B66: Smeth .5F 99
              (Edith Rd.)
  B66: Smeth .5F 99
           (Windmill La.)
  B73: W Grn 6H 69
  WS4: Rus 3G 33
  WV14: Bils .4E 45
Limehurst Av. WV3: Wolv 3A 42
Limehurst Rd. WS4: Rus 4G 33
Lime Kiln Cl. B38: K Nor 2H 159
Limekiln La. B14: K Hth 3A 148
Lime Kiln Wlk. DY1: Dud 5F 77
Lime La. WS3: Lit Wyr 3D 8

Limepit La. DY1: Dud 4C 76
Lime Pitts Nature Reserve 4G 33
Limerick Cl. DY3: Gorn 5F 75
Lime Rd. DY3: Sed 4B 60
  WS10: W'bry 1F 63
Limes, The B11: S'brk 5C 118
  B16: Birm .6B 100
  B24: Erd 4F 85
  DY3: Himl 4H 73
  WS1: Wals .1E 49
  WS4: Rus 2H 33
Limes Av. B65: Row R 1C 112
  DY5: Brie H 4G 93
Limescroft Cl. WS4: Rus 2F 33
Limes Rd. DY1: Dud 4D 76
  WV6: Tett 5A 26
Lime St. WS1: Wals 2D 48
  WV3: Wolv .3E 43
  WV14: Cose 5C 60
Limes Vw. DY3: Sed 6H 59
Lime Ter. B6: Aston 6H 83
Lime Tree Av. WV6: Tett 6G 25
Lime Tree Gdns. WV8: Bilb 4H 13
Lime Tree Gro. B31: N'fld 5F 145
Lime Tree Rd. B8: Salt 3F 103
  B27: A Grn 6A 120
  WS5: Wals .1E 65
  WV8: Bilb 4H 13
Limetree Rd. B74: S'tly 3F 51
Lime Wlk. B38: K Nor 1A 160
Linacre Ho. B37: F'bri 1B 122
Linchmere Rd. B21: Hand 5G 81
Lincoln Av. WV13: W'hall 6D 30
Lincoln Cl. B27: A Grn 2C 136
Lincoln Ct. B29: W Cas 6G 131
           (off Tugford Rd.)
Lincoln Grn. WV10: Bush 5H 15
Lincoln Gro. B37: Mars G 2C 122
Lincoln Ho. WV10: Wolv 6A 28
Lincoln Rd. B27: A Grn 3B 136
  B67: Smeth 1C 114
  B71: W Brom 4B 64
  DY2: Neth .6F 95
  WS1: Wals .1E 49
Lincoln Rd. Nth. B27: A Grn 2C 136
Lincoln Rd. Wharf B92: Olton 3C 136
Lincoln St. B12: Bal H 6G 117
  WV10: Wolv 6A 28
Lincoln Twr. B16: Birm 2C 116
         (off Morville St.)
Lindale Av. B36: Hodg H 3A 104
Lindale Cres. DY5: Brie H 5F 109
Lindale Dr. WV5: Wom 1F 73
Linden Av. B43: Gt Barr 5H 65
  B62: B'hth .4E 113
  B69: Tiv 1D 96
Linden Cl. WS2: Wals 1D 46
  Dr. DY8: Stourb 2E 125
Linden La. WV12: W'hall 2E 31
Linden Lea WV3: Wolv 2B 42
Linden Rd. B30: B'vlle 5A 132
  B66: Smeth 1E 115
  DY1: Dud 4D 76
Linden Road Instruction Pool 6B 132
Lindens, The B32: Harb 4C 114
  WV6: Wolv .6C 26
Lindens Dr. B74: S'tly 6H 51
Linden Ter. B12: Bal H 6B 118
Lindenwood B73: S Cold 5H 53
Lindford Way B38: K Nor 5D 146
Lindley Av. DY4: Tip 4H 77
Lindon Cl. WS8: Bwnhls 1C 22
Lindon Dr. WS8: Bwnhls 6B 10
Lindon Rd. WS8: Bwnhls 2B 22
Lindon Vw. WS8: Bwnhls 2C 22
Lindrick Cl. WS3: Blox 4F 19
Lindridge Dr. B76: Min 1G 87
Lindridge Rd. B23: Erd 3B 84
  B75: S Cold 3D 54
  B90: Shir 6F 149
Lindrosa Rd. B74: S'tly 6H 35
Lindsay Rd. B42: Gt Barr 4D 66
Lindsey Av. B31: N'fld 3G 145

Lindsey Pl. DY5: Brie H 6G 93
Lindsey Rd. B71: W Brom 6A 64
Lindsworth App. B30: K Nor 4E 147
Lindsworth Cl. B30: K Nor 4F 147
Lindsworth Ct. B30: K Nor 4E 147
Lindsworth Rd. B30: K Nor 4D 146
Linfield Gdns. DY3: Sed 4G 59
Linford Gro. B25: Yard 2B 120
Linforth Dr. B74: S'tly 4A 52
Lingard Cl. B7: Nech 4B 102
Lingard Ho. B76: Walm 5D 70
Lingard Rd. B75: S Cold 6D 54
Lingfield Av. B44: Gt Barr 4G 67
  WV10: F'hses 2H 15
Lingfield Cl. WS6: Gt Wyr 3F 7
Lingfield Ct. B43: Gt Barr 6H 65
Lingfield Dr. WS6: Gt Wyr 3F 7
Lingfield Gdns. B34: S End 3F 105
Lingfield Grange B74: S'tly 2A 52
Lingfield Gro. WV6: Pert 5F 25
Lingfield Rd. WS11: Nort C 1E 9
Lingfield Way DY6: K'wfrd 4E 93
Lingham Cl. B92: Sol 6H 137
Ling Ho. WV10: Wolv 6B 28
Lingmoor Gro. WS9: A'rdge 2C 34
Linhope Dr. DY6: K'wfrd 4E 93
Link, The B27: A Grn 4G 135
Link One Ind. Pk. DY4: Tip 1E 79
Link Rd. B16: Edg 6A 100
  WS9: Wals W 4D 22
  WS5: Wom .6G 57
Links Av. WV6: Tett 2B 26
Links Cres. B68: O'bry 3H 113
Links Dr. B45: Rub 4G 157
  B91: Sol 1F 151
  DY8: Stourb 3C 124
Links Rd. B14: K Hth 6A 148
  B68: O'bry .3H 113
  WV4: Penn .2E 59
Links Side Way WS9: A'rdge 1E 35
Links Vw. B62: Hale 1D 128
  B74: S'tly 2B 52
Linkswood Cl. B13: Mose 4B 134
Linkwood Ind. Est. DY8: Woll 5C 108
Linley Cl. WS9: A'rdge 4A 34
Linley Dr. WV10: Bush 6A 16
Linley Gro. B14: K Hth 1E 147
  DY3: Gorn .5F 75
Linley Lodge Ind. Est. WS9: A'rdge . . .2A 34
Linley Rd. WS4: Rus 2H 33
Linley Wood Rd. WS9: A'rdge 4A 34
Linnet Cl. B30: B'vlle 5A 132
  B62: Hale 5B 112
          (Lodgefield Rd.)
  B62: Hale 4G 127
           (Manor Way)
Linnet Gro. B23: Erd 1B 84
  WV12: W'hall 1B 30
Linpole Wlk. B14: K Hth 5E 147
Linsey Rd. B92: Sol 3G 137
Linthouse La. WV11: Wed 1F 29
Lint Mdw. B47: H'wd 2B 162
Linton Av. B91: Sol 6E 151
Linton Cl. B63: Crad 6F 111
Linton Cft. WV14: Bils 6F 45
Linton Rd. B11: Tys 1G 135
  B43: Gt Barr 1E 67
  B64: Old H .6H 95
  WV4: Penn .6C 42
Linton Wlk. B23: Erd 4B 84
Linwood Ct. B23: Erd 4E 85
Linwood Rd. B21: Hand 1A 100
  B91: Sol 2B 150
  DY1: Dud 2D 76
Lionel St. B3: Birm 3B 4 (6E 101)
Lion Ind. Pk. WS9: A'rdge 1C 34
Lion Pas. DY8: Stourb 6D 108
Lion Rd. B64: Old H 2A 112
Lion's Den WS7: Hamm 3G 11
Lion St. DY8: Stourb 6D 108
Liskeard Rd. WS5: Wals 4H 49
Lisko Cl. DY5: Brie H 3E 109
Lismore Cl. B45: Fran 6E 143

Lismore Dr. B17: Harb 2E 131
Lissimore Dr. DY4: Tip 5A 78
    (not continuous)
Lissimore Ho. B70: W Brom 1C 98
    (off Maria St.)
Lisson Gro. B44: Gt Barr 1H 67
Listelow Cl. B36: Cas B 1F 105
Lister Cl. DY4: Tip 3A 78
    WS2: Wals 4H 31
Lister Rd. DY2: Dud 2E 95
    WS2: Wals 4H 31
Lister St. B7: Birm 1G 5 (5H 101)
    WV13: W'hall 2B 46
Listowel Rd. B14: K Hth 1F 147
Lisures Dr. B76: Walm 1B 70
Lit. Albert St. WS2: Wals 1C 48
Lit. Ann St. B5: Birm 5H 5 (1H 117)
LITTLE ASTON 4C 36
Lit. Aston Hall Dr. B74: Lit As 4A 36
Lit. Aston La. B74: Lit As 3C 36
Lit. Aston Pk. Rd. B74: Lit As 6A 36
Lit. Aston Rd. WS9: A'rdge 3D 34
Lit. Barr St. B9: Birm 1A 118
Little Birches WV3: Wolv 3D 42
LITTLE BLOXWICH 4B 20
Lit. Brick Kiln St.
    WV3: Wolv 5A 170 (2G 43)
LITTLE BROMWICH 1F 119
Lit. Bromwich Rd. B9: Bord G 2H 119
Lit. Broom St. B12: Birm 3A 118
Little Caldmore WS1: Wals 3C 48
Lit. Checkhill La. DY7: Stourt 5D 90
Lit. Clothier St. WV13: W'hall 6A 30
Lit. Clover Cl. B7: Nech 3C 102
Little Comn. WS3: Pels 3E 21
Little Cornbow B63: Hale 2B 128
Littlecote Cft. B14: K Hth 4A 148
Littlecote Dr. B23: Erd 6F 69
Lit. Cottage St. DY5: Brie H 1H 109
Little Cft. B43: Gt Barr 4G 65
Lit. Cross St. WS10: Darl 4C 46
Lit. Edward St. B9: Birm 1A 118
Lit. Fields Way B69: O'bry 2F 97
Lit. Francis Gro. B7: Birm 4B 102
Little Gorway WS1: Wals 4D 48
Lit. Green La. B9: Small H 2C 118
Lit. Green Lanes B73: W Grn 6H 69
Lit. Hall Rd. B7: Birm 5B 102
Lit. Hardwick Rd. WS9: A'rdge 1E 51
LITTLE HAY 1H 37
Lit. Hay La. WS14: Lit H, W'frd 2H 37
Lit. Heath Cft. B34: S End 2F 105
Little Hill WS10: W'bry 2F 63
Lit. Hill Gro. B38: K Nor 6C 146
Lit. Hill Ho. B24: Erd 1B 86
Lit. Hill Way B32: Bart G 3B 130
Lit. Johnsons La. WS9: A'rdge 2D 50
Lit. John St. DY5: Brie H 5H 93
Little La. B71: W Brom 2B 80
    WV12: W'hall 2D 30
Lit. Lawns WS8: Wals W 3C 22
LITTLE LONDON 6A 30
Little London WS1: Wals 4C 48
Lit. London Ho. WS1: Wals 4D 48
Littlemead Av. B31: N'fld 6G 145
Lit. Meadow Cft. B31: N'fld 3D 144
Lit. Meadow Wlk. B33: Stech 6C 104
Littlemead Rd. B90: Maj G 1E 163
Lit. Moor Hill B67: Smeth 4D 98
Lit. Newport St. WS1: Wals 2C 48
    (off Newport St.)
Lit. Oaks Rd. B6: Aston 1G 101
Littleover Av. B28: Hall G 1F 149
Little Park B32: Quin 1H 129
Lit. Park St. WV1: Wolv 3D 170 (1H 43)
Lit. Pitts Cl. B24: Erd 2B 86
Lit. Potter St. DY5: Brie H 1H 109
Lit. Pountney St.
    WV2: Wolv 6B 170 (3G 43)
Lit. Shadwell St. B4: Birm . . .1E 5 (5G 101)
Littleshaw Cft. B47: Wyt 5C 162
Littleshaw La. B47: Wyt 5C 162

Little's La. WV1: Wolv 1C 170 (6H 27)
    (not continuous)
Lit. Station St. WS2: Wals 1C 48
Little St. DY2: Dud 6F 77
LITTLE SUTTON 1A 54
Lit. Sutton La. B75: R'ley, S Cold 4A 54
Lit. Sutton Rd. B75: R'ley 1A 54
Littleton Cl. B76: Walm 3E 71
Littleton Cft. B91: Sol 1G 165
Littleton Rd. WV12: W'hall 2C 30
Littleton St. E. WS1: Wals 1D 48
Littleton St. W. WS2: Wals 1C 48
LITTLEWOOD 1E 7
Littlewood Cl. B91: Sol 1F 165
Littlewood La. WS6: C Hay 1E 7
    (not continuous)
Littlewood Rd. WS6: C Hay 1E 7
Lit. Wood St. WV13: W'hall 1A 46
Littleworth Av. DY1: Dud 1D 76
LITTLEWORTH END 3G 55
Littleworth Gro. B76: Walm 1D 70
LITTLE WYRLEY 5C 8
Liveridge Cl. B93: Know 3B 166
Liverpool Cft. B37: Mars G 3B 122
Liverpool St. B9: Birm 1A 118
Livery St. B3: Birm 1C 4 (5F 101)
    (not continuous)
Livingstone Av. WV6: Pert 4E 25
Livingstone Rd. B14: K Hth 1G 147
    B20: Hand 6E 83
    B70: W Brom 6H 79
    WS3: Blox 5C 20
    WV14: Bils 6D 44
LivingWell Health Club
    Birmingham 1D 116
    Sutton Coldfield 5A 4 (3D 68)
Lizafield Ct. B66: Smeth 2C 98
Lloyd Dr. WV4: Penn 3A 58
Lloyd Hill WV4: Penn 2A 58
Lloyd Ho. B19: Hock 3E 101
    (off Newtown Dr.)
Lloyd Rd. B20: Hand 3C 82
    WV6: Tett 4B 26
Lloyd Sq. B15: Edg 3B 116
Lloyds Rd. B62: B'hth 1A 112
Lloyd St. B10: Small H 3D 118
    B71: W Brom 3C 80
    DY2: Dud 1F 95
    WS10: W'bry 2E 63
    WV6: Wolv 5D 26
Locarno Rd. DY4: Tip 2H 77
Lochalsh Gro. WV12: W'hall 6B 18
Lochranza Cft. B43: Gt Barr 3A 66
Lock Dr. B33: Stech 6B 104
Locke Pl. B7: Birm 6A 102
Locket Cl. WS2: Wals 6B 31
Lockfield Cl. DY8: Word 2D 108
Lockhart Dr. B75: R'ley 2A 54
Locking Cft. B35: Cas V 4F 87
Lockington Cft. B62: Quin 5F 113
Lock Keepers Cl. WS11: Nort C 1D 8
Luckley Cl. WV10: Wolv 5B 28
Lock Mus. .2A 46
Lock Side DY4: Tip 2G 77
Lockside WS9: A'rdge 2B 34
    WV5: Wom 6E 57
Lockside Cl. DY5: Brie H 2H 109
Locksmith Cl. WV13: W'hall 1B 46
Lock St. WV1: Wolv 1D 170 (6H 27)
    (not continuous)
Locks Vw. DY8: Word 2C 108
Lockton Rd. B30: Stir 5E 133
Lockwood Rd. B31: N'fld 3D 144
LODE HEATH 2H 151
Lode La. B91: Sol 3F 151
    B92: Olton, Sol 4A 138
Lode Mill Ct. B92: Olton 5F 137
Lodge Cl. B62: Hale 2C 128
    WS5: Wals 5H 49
Lodge Cres. DY2: Neth 5C 94
Lodge Cft. B93: Know 3D 166
Lodge Dr. B26: Yard 3D 120
Lodge Farm Cl. B76: Walm 2D 70
Lodgefield Rd. B62: Hale 5B 112

Lodge Forge Rd. B64: Crad H 4E 111
Lodge Forge Trad. Est. B64: Crad H . . .4E 111
Lodge Gro. B31: N'fld 2C 144
    WS9: A'rdge 4C 34
LODGE HILL 3G 131
Lodge Hill Crematorium B29: S Oak . . .4F 131
Lodge Hill Rd. B29: S Oak 4H 131
Lodge La. DY6: K'wfrd 3G 91
    WS11: Cann 1C 6
Lodge Pool Cl. B44: Gt Barr 1G 83
Lodge Rd. B6: Aston 1G 101
    B18: Hock 4D 100
    B18: Hock, Win G 4A 100
    B67: Smeth 2C 98
    B70: W Brom 4H 79
    B93: Know 3D 166
    WS4: S'fld 6F 21
    WS5: Wals 6H 49
    (not continuous)
    WS10: Darl 6D 46
    WV10: Oxl 1F 27
    WV14: Bils 1H 61
Lodge St. B69: O'bry 2G 97
    WV12: W'hall 4C 30
Lodge Ter. B17: Harb 6G 115
Lodge Vw. WS6: C Hay 2C 6
Loeless Rd. B33: Kitts G 6E 105
Lofthouse Cres. B31: N'fld 4D 144
Lofthouse Gro. B31: N'fld 4D 144
Lofthouse Rd. B20: Hand 4A 82
Loftus Cl. B29: W Cas 5D 130
Logan Cl. WV10: Oxl 3G 27
Lomaine Dr. B30: K Nor 3A 146
Lomas Dr. B31: N'fld 4C 144
Lomas St. WV1: Wolv 5G 27
Lomas St. Hall WV1: Wolv 5G 27
Lombard Av. DY2: Neth 6F 95
Lombard St. B12: Birm 3H 117
    B70: W Brom 4A 80
Lombard St. W. B70: W Brom 4A 80
Lombardy Gdns. WV12: W'hall 2E 31
Lombardy Cft. B62: Quin 5G 113
Lomond Cl. B34: S End 3A 106
Lomond Rd. DY3: Sed 4G 59
LONDONDERRY 5B 98
Londonderry Gro. B67: Smeth 4D 98
Londonderry Ho. B4: Birm 3F 5
Londonderry La. B67: Smeth 5B 98
Londonderry Rd. B68: O'bry 5B 98
LONDON FIELDS 5B 76
London Hgts. DY1: Dud 5C 76
London Pl. WV3: Wolv 4A 170 (2G 43)
London Rd. B20: Hand 5G 83
    B75: Bass P 6F 39
    B75: Can 4E 39
    B78: Midd 1G 55
    WS14: W'frd, Can 1D 38
London St. B66: Smeth 4G 99
London St. Ind. Est. B66: Smeth 4H 99
Lones Rd. B71: W Brom 1F 99
Long Acre B7: Nech 3B 102
    WV8: Cod 5F 13
Longacre WV13: W'hall 3A 46
Long Acre Ind. Est. B7: Nech 1C 102
    (Plume Cl.)
    B7: Nech 2B 102
    (Thimble Mill La.)
Longacres B74: Lit As 5C 36
Long Acre St. WS2: Wals 6B 32
Longbank Rd. B69: Tiv 1C 96
Longboat La. DY8: Word 3C 108
Longboat Quay DY2: Neth 5F 95
Longbow Rd. B29: W Cas 6D 130
LONGBRIDGE 1D 158
Longbridge La. B31: Longb 1C 158
Longbridge Station (Rail) 1C 158
Longbrook La. CV7: Bal C 3E 169
    CV8: Fen E 3E 169
Long Cl. Wlk. B35: Cas V 4F 87
Longcroft, The B63: Hale 2G 127
    WS4: Rus 2G 33
Longcroft Av. WS10: W'bry 2G 63
Longcroft Cl. B35: Cas V 5D 86
Longdales Rd. B38: K Nor 2H 159

Longdon Av. WV4: Penn 6H 43
Longdon Cft. B93: Know 1C 166
Longdon Dr. B74: Four O 5E 37
Longdon Rd. B93: Know 3C 166
Longfellow Rd. B30: K Nor 3H 145
    DY3: Lwr G 2E 75
Longfield Cl. B28: Hall G 1F 149
Longfield Dr. B74: Lit As 5D 36
Longfield Ho. WV10: Wolv 6B 28
Longfield Rd. B31: N'fld 5C 130
    DY9: Lye .6H 109
Longford Cl. B32: Bart G 6G 129
    B93: Dorr 6D 166
    WV5: Wom 2D 72
Longford Gro. B44: K'sdng 2A 68
Longford Rd. B44: K'sdng 2A 68
    WV10: Wolv 5B 28
Long Furrow WV8: Pend 6C 14
Long Grn. Cl. B31: N'fld 5E 145
Longham Cft. B32: Harb 1D 130
Longhurst Cft. B31: Longb 2F 159
Long Hyde Rd. B67: Smeth 2D 114
Long Innage B63: Crad 5D 110
Long Knowle La. WV11: Wed 1D 28
Longlake Av. WV6: Tett 6G 25
Longlands, The WV5: Wom 1G 73
Longlands Cl. B38: K Nor 1G 159
    (off Nearhill Rd.)
Longlands Rd. B62: Hale 2E 129
Long La. B62: B'hth 2D 112
    B65: B'hth 2D 112
    WS6: Gt Wyr 2D 18
    WS11: Nort C 1D 8
    WV11: Ess .2D 18
Long La. Trad. Est.
    B62: B'hth 3D 112
Long Leasow B29: W Cas 6E 131
Longleat B43: Gt Barr 3H 65
Longleat Av. B15: Birm 2E 117
Longleat Dr. B90: Ches G 4C 164
    DY1: Dud 5A 76
Longleat Rd. WS9: A'rdge 6C 22
Long Ley WV10: Wolv 6B 28
Longley Av. B76: Min 2H 87
Longley Cres. B26: Yard 1C 136
Long Leys Ct. B46: Wat O 5D 88
Longleys Cft. B46: Wat O 5D 88
Longley Wlk. B37: Chel W 1E 123
Long Meadow B65: Row R 6C 96
Longmeadow Cl. B75: S Cold 6D 54
Longmeadow Cres. B34: S End 3A 106
Long Mdw. Dr. DY3: Sed 3F 59
Longmeadow Gro. B31: Longb 3E 159
Longmeadow Rd. WS5: Wals 3A 50
Long Mill Av. WV11: Wed 2D 28
Long Mill Nth. WV11: Wed 2D 28
Long Mill Sth. WV11: Wed 2D 28
Longmoor Cl. WV11: Wed 4H 29
Longmoor Rd. B63: Hale 2G 127
    B73: S'tly 2B 68
Longmore Av. WS2: Wals 2F 47
Longmore Cl. B73: S'tly 6A 52
Longmore Rd. B90: Shir 5A 150
Longmore St. B12: Bal H 4G 117
    WS10: W'bry 2F 63
Long Mynd B63: Hale 4F 127
Long Mynd Cl. WV12: W'hall 6B 18
Long Mynd Rd. B31: N'fld 1C 144
Long Nuke Rd. B31: N'fld 6C 130
Long Saw Dr. B31: Longb 6B 144
Longshaw Gro. B34: S End 3H 105
Longstone Cl. B90: M'path 3F 165
Longstone Rd. B42: Gt Barr 6E 67
Long St. B11: S'brk 5A 118
    WS2: Wals 2B 48
    WV1: Wolv 2C 170 (1H 43)
Long Wood B30: B'ville 2A 146
Longwood La. WS4: Wals 1A 50
    WS5: Wals 1A 50
Longwood Pathway B34: S End 4G 105
Longwood Ri. WV11: W'hall 4D 30
Longwood Rd. B45: Redn 2G 157
    WS9: A'rdge .6D 34
Lonicera Cl. WS5: Wals 2F 65

Lonsdale Cl. B33: Stech 1B 120
    WV12: W'hall 4B 30
Lonsdale Cl. B17: Harb 5G 115
Lonsdale Rd. B17: Harb 5F 115
    B66: Smeth .2B 98
    WS5: Wals .5G 49
    WV3: Wolv .4F 43
    WV14: Bils .5H 45
Loom Cl. WS6: Gt Wyr 4F 7
Lords B17: Harb 5F 115
Lords Dr. WS2: Wals 6C 32
Lordsmore Cl. WV14: Cose 4G 61
Lord St. B7: Birm 5H 101
    WS1: Wals .4B 48
    (not continuous)
    WV3: Wolv .1F 43
    (not continuous)
    WV14: Bils .2G 61
Lord St. W. WV14: Bils 2G 61
Lordswood Rd. B17: Harb 3E 115
Lordswood Sq. B17: Harb 4F 115
Lorien Cl. WV4: Penn 5A 42
Lorimer Way B43: Gt Barr 6F 51
Loriners Gro. WS1: Wals 2F 49
Lorne St. DY4: Tip 5H 61
Lorrainer Av. DY5: Brie H 3E 109
Lothians Rd. WS3: Pels 2E 21
    WV6: Tett 3C 26
Lottie Rd. B29: S Oak 4A 132
Lotus Cl. B16: Edg 2A 116
Lotus Cft. B67: Smeth 5D 98
Lotus Dr. B64: Old H 1H 111
Lotus Wlk. B36: Cas B 6B 88
Lotus Way B65: Row R 5A 96
Loughton Gro. B63: Hale 1H 127
Louisa Pl. B18: Hock 4C 100
Louisa St. B1: Birm 3A 4 (6E 101)
Louis Ct. B67: Smeth 4D 98
Louise Cl. B27: A Grn 2A 136
    B91: Sol 6C 150
Louise Cft. B14: K Hth 5G 147
Louise Lorne Rd. B13: Mose 1H 133
Louise Rd. B21: Hand 2B 100
Louise St. DY3: Gorn 4F 75
Lount Wlk. B19: Hock 4G 101
Lovatt Cl. DY4: Tip 4C 62
Lovatt St. WV1: Wolv 1F 43
Loveday Ho. B70: W Brom 4B 80
Loveday St. B4: Birm 1E 5 (5G 101)
    (not continuous)
Lovelace Av. B91: Sol 1H 165
Love La. B7: Birm 5H 101
    B47: H'wd 2G 161
    B69: Tiv 6A 78
    DY8: Stourb 2E 125
    DY9: Lye 6A 110
    WS1: Wals .4C 48
    WS6: Gt Wyr .2G 7
    WV6: Tett 3B 26
Lovell Cl. B29: W Cas 1F 145
Loveridge Cl. WV8: Cod 4F 13
Lovers Wlk. B6: Aston 1B 102
    WS10: W'bry 2F 63
Lovett Av. B69: O'bry 4D 96
Low Av. B43: Gt Barr 3B 66
Lowbridge La. B90: Tid G 5D 162
Lowbrook La. B90: Tid G 5D 162
Lowe Av. WS10: Darl 4B 46
Lowe Dr. B73: New O 2D 68
    DY6: K'wfrd 5C 92
Lwr. Beeches Rd. B31: Longb 5A 144
LOWER BRADLEY 2A 62
Lwr. Chapel St. B69: Tiv 5C 78
Lwr. Church La. DY4: Tip 2B 78
Lwr. City Rd. B69: Tiv 6C 78
Lowercroft Way B74: Four O 4E 37
Lwr. Dartmouth St. B9: Birm 1B 118
Lwr. Darwin St. B12: Birm 3H 117
Lwr. Derry St. DY5: Brie H 1H 109
Lwr. Essex St. B5: Birm 2G 117
Lwr. Forster St. WS1: Wals 1D 48
LOWER GORNAL 4H 75

Lower Grn. DY4: Tip 2G 77
    WS10: Darl .3D 46
    WV6: Tett 4C 26
Lwr. Ground Cl. B6: Aston 6H 83
    (off Emscote Rd.)
Lwr. Hall La. WS1: Wals 2C 48
Lwr. Hall St. WV13: W'hall 2B 46
    (off Walsall St.)
Lwr. High St. B64: Crad H 3E 111
    DY8: Stourb 5D 108
    WS10: W'bry 3F 63
Lwr. Higley Cl. B32: Quin 1B 130
Lwr. Hill Barn B32: Fran 4F 143
Lwr. Horseley Fld. WV1: Wolv 1A 44
Lwr. Lichfield St. WV13: W'hall 1A 46
Lwr. Loveday St. B4: Birm 5F 101
    B19: Birm 1D 4 (5F 101)
Lower Mall B5: Birm 5F 5
Lower Moor B30: B'ville 5A 132
Lwr. North St. WS4: Wals 6D 32
Lower Pde., The B72: S Cold 6A 54
LOWER PENN 6G 41
Lwr. Prestwood Rd. WV11: Wed 2E 29
Lwr. Queen St. B72: S Cold 1A 70
Lwr. Reddicroft B73: S Cold 6A 54
Lwr. Rushall St. WS1: Wals 1D 48
Lwr. Severn St. B1: Birm 5D 4 (1F 117)
Lowerstack Cft. B37: F'bri 6B 106
LOWER STONNALL 3H 23
Lower St. WV6: Tett 4C 26
Lwr. Temple St. B2: Birm 4D 4 (1F 117)
Lwr. Tower St. B19: Birm 4G 101
Lwr. Trinity St. B9: Birm 2A 118
    B70: W Brom 6B 80
    (off Glover St.)
Lwr. Valley Rd. DY5: Brie H 1E 109
Lower Vauxhall WV1: Wolv 1E 43
Lwr. Villiers St. WV2: Wolv 4G 43
Lwr. Walsall St. WV1: Wolv 2A 44
Lwr. White Rd. B32: Quin 6B 114
Lowesmoor Rd. B26: Sheld 4G 121
Lowe St. B12: Birm 3A 118
Lowe St. WV6: Wolv 5E 27
Loweswater Dr. DY3: Lwr G 4H 75
Loweswater Ho. B38: K Nor 6C 146
Lowfield Cl. B62: Quin 2G 129
LOW HILL 2A 28
Low Hill Cres. WV10: Bush 1A 28
Lowhill La. B45: Redn 3A 158
Lowland Cl. B64: Old H 2H 111
Lowlands Av. B74: S'tly 3F 51
    WV6: Tett 3C 26
Lowlands Ct. WV6: Tett 3C 26
Lowndes Rd. DY8: Woll 5C 108
Lowry Cl. B67: Smeth 3D 98
    WV6: Pert 5F 25
    WV13: W'hall 1G 45
Low St. WS6: C Hay 2D 6
Low Thatch B38: K Nor 2A 160
Low Town B69: O'bry 2G 97
Low Wood Rd. B23: Erd 2D 84
Loxdale Ind. Est. WV14: Bils 1G 61
Loxdale Sidings WV14: Bils 1H 61
Loxdale Stop (MM) 1H 61
Loxdale St. WS10: W'bry 3F 63
    WV14: Bils .1H 61
Loxley Av. B14: Yard W 4C 148
    B90: Shir 6F 149
Loxley Cl. B31: N'fld 5C 130
Loxley Rd. B67: Smeth 2D 114
    B75: R'ley 5B 38
Loxley Sq. B92: Olton 5B 136
Loxton Cl. B74: Lit As 4D 36
Loxton Ct. B7: Birm 4B 102
Loynells Rd. B45: Redn 2H 157
Loyns Cft. B37: F'bri 6B 106
LOZELLS 2D 100
Lozells Rd. B19: Loz 2D 100
Lozells St. B19: Loz 2E 101
Lozells Wood Cl. B19: Loz 2D 100
Luanne Cl. B64: Old H 2A 112
Lucas Cir. B19: Birm 4E 101
Lucas Way B90: Shir 2A 164

Luce Cl. B35: Cas V 3F 87
Lucerne Ct. B23: Erd 1D 84
Luce Rd. WV10: Bush 3A 28
Lucknow Rd. WV12: W'hall 4B 30
Lucton Ho. B30: B'vlle 2A 146
Luddington Rd. B92: Sol 5A 138
Ludford Cl. B75: S Cold 4C 54
Ludford Rd. B32: Bart G 4G 129
Ludgate Cl. B46: Wat O 4C 88
    B69: Tiv .1B 96
Ludgate Ct. WS5: Wals 4A 48
Ludgate Hill B3: Birm 2C 4 (6F 101)
Ludgate Ho. B13: Mose 1H 133
Ludgate Loft Apartments
    B3: Birm .2C 4
Ludgate St. DY1: Dud 6D 76
Ludlow Cl. B37: Chel W 1E 123
    WV12: W'hall 3B 30
Ludlow Cl. B11: S'brk 5B 118
Ludlow Ho. B13: Mose 1A 148
    WS3: Blox 3A 32
                            (off Providence La.)
Ludlow La. WS2: Wals 5G 31
Ludlow Rd. B8: Salt 6F 103
Ludlow Way DY1: Dud 5A 76
Ludmer Way B20: Hand 5E 83
Ludstone Av. WV4: Penn 6B 42
Ludstone Rd. B29: W Cas 4D 130
Ludworth Av. B37: Mars G 2D 122
Lugtrout La. B91: Sol, Cath B 1A 152
                               (not continuous)
Lukes, The DY2: Neth 2E 111
Lulworth Cl. B63: Crad 5E 111
Lulworth Rd. B28: Hall G 5G 135
Lulworth Wlk. WV4: Penn 5A 42
Lumley Gro. B37: Chel W 1F 123
Lumley Rd. WS1: Wals 2E 49
Lundy Vw. B36: Cas B 4D 106
LUNT, THE 4A 46
Lunt Gro. B32: Quin 6B 114
Lunt Pl. WV14: Bils 5A 46
Lunt Rd. WV14: Bils 5H 45
Lupin Gro. B9: Bord G 8F 103
    WS5: Wals 1F 65
Lupin Rd. DY2: Dud 6H 77
Lusbridge Cl. B63: Crad 1D 126
LUTLEY 2E 127
Lutley Av. B63: Hale 1F 127
Lutley Cl. WV3: Wolv 4C 42
Lutley Dr. DY9: Pedm 2G 125
Lutley Gro. B32: Bart G 4H 129
Lutley La. B63: Hale, Lutley 2D 126
                               (not continuous)
Lutley Mill Rd. B63: Hale 1G 127
Luton Rd. B29: S Oak 2B 132
Luttrell Rd. B74: Four O 3F 53
Lyall Gdns. B45: Fran 6E 143
Lyall Gro. B27: A Grn 3G 135
Lychgate Av. DY9: Pedm 4G 125
Lydate Rd. B62: Quin 1F 129
Lydbrook Covert B38: K Nor 1A 160
Lydbury Gro. B33: Kitts G 5E 105
Lydd Cl. WV11: Wed 4D 28
Lydd Cft. B35: Cas V 3F 87
Lyddington Dr. B62: Hale 4B 112
Lyde Grn. B63: Crad 4D 110
Lydford Gro. B24: Erd 5G 85
Lydford Rd. WS3: Blox 5H 19
Lydgate Rd. DY6: K'wfrd 3D 92
Lydget Gro. B23: Erd 6D 68
Lydham Cl. B44: K'sdng 1A 84
    WV14: Bils 1D 60
Lydia Cft. B74: Four O 3E 37
Lydian Cl. WV6: Wolv 5F 27
LYDIATE ASH 6C 156
Lydiate Ash Rd. B61: L Ash 6B 156
                               (not continuous)
Lydiate Av. B31: Longb 6B 144
Lydiates Cl. DY3: Sed 6F 59
Lydney Cl. WV12: W'hall 6D 30
Lydney Gro. B31: N'fld 4D 144
Lydon Ct. B92: Sol 1G 137
LYE 6A 110
Lye Av. B32: Bart G 3G 129

Lye Bus. Cen. DY9: Lye 5B 110
Lye By-Pass DY9: Lye 5A 110
Lye Cl. La. B32: Bart G 3F 129
    B62: Hale 3F 129
Lyecroft Av. B37: Chel W 1F 123
Lye Cross Rd. B69: Tiv 2B 96
Lye Station (Rail) 5A 110
Lye Valley Ind. Est. DY9: Lye 5B 110
Lygon Ct. B62: Hale 5B 112
Lygon Gro. B32: Quin 1C 130
Lymedene Rd. B42: P Barr 2D 82
Lyme Grn. Rd. B33: Stech 5D 104
Lymer Rd. WV10: Oxl 6G 15
Lymington Rd. WV13: W'hall 1D 46
Lymsey Cft. DY8: Word 6A 92
Lynbrook Cl. B47: H'wd 2A 162
    DY2: Neth 3F 95
Lyncourt Gro. B32: Quin 5H 113
Lyncroft Rd. B11: Tys 3F 135
Lyndale Dr. WV11: Wed 3G 29
Lyndale Rd. DY2: Dud 3G 95
    DY3: Sed .3F 59
Lyndhurst Dr. DY8: Word 2D 108
Lyndhurst Rd. B24: Erd 5F 85
    B71: W Brom 6C 64
    WV3: Wolv 4E 43
LYNDON 2B 80
Lyndon B71: W Brom 2B 80
Lyndon Cl. B20: Hand 5E 83
    B36: Cas B 1G 105
    B63: Hale 1G 127
    DY3: Sed .4A 60
Lyndon Cft. B37: Mars G 4D 122
    B92: Olton 3E 137
LYNDON GREEN 4E 121
Lyndon Gro. B71: W Brom 3B 80
    DY6: W Hth 1H 91
Lyndon Ho. B31: N'fld 4F 145
Lyndon Rd. B33: Stech 6C 104
    B45: Rub .2E 157
    B73: S Cold 6H 53
    B92: Olton 3D 136
Lyndworth Rd. B30: Stir 6E 133
Lyneham Gdns. B76: Walm 1E 87
Lyneham Way B35: Cas V 4D 86
Lynfield Cl. B38: K Nor 2B 160
Lyng La. B70: W Brom 4A 80
                               (not continuous)
Lynmouth Cl. WS9: A'rdge 4C 34
LYNN 2H 23
Lynn Gro. B29: S Oak 2G 131
Lynn La. WS14: Lynn 2H 23
Lynton Av. B66: Smeth 3E 99
    B71: W Brom 6A 64
    WV6: Tett 2C 26
Lynton Ho. B23: Erd 1B 84
Lynton Rd. B6: Aston 2A 102
Lynval Rd. DY5: Quar B 4B 110
Lynwood Av. DY6: W Hth 2H 91
Lynwood Cl. WV12: W'hall 1E 31
Lynwood Wlk. B17: Harb 1H 131
Lynwood Way B45: Lick 6G 157
Lyon Ct. B75: S Cold 6A 54
                              (off Midland Dr.)
Lyons Gro. B11: S'hll 2C 134
Lysander Rd. B45: Fran 5G 143
Lysander Way B35: Cas V 5F 87
Lysways St. WS1: Wals 3D 48
Lytham Cl. B76: Walm 1F 87
    DY8: Stourb 3E 125
Lytham Cft. B15: Birm 2F 117
Lytham Gro. WS3: Blox 3G 19
Lytham Rd. WV6: Pert 5D 24
Lythwood Dr. DY5: Brie H 3G 109
Lyttelton Rd. B16: Edg 2H 115
    B33: Stech 1B 120
    DY8: Stourb 6B 108
Lyttleton Av. B62: B'hth 4E 113
    DY2: Neth 5E 95
Lyttleton Ho. B63: Hale 3A 128
Lyttleton St. B70: W Brom 5A 80
Lytton Av. WV4: Penn 1B 58
Lytton Gro. B27: A Grn 4H 135
Lytton La. B32: Bart G 2D 130

Maas Rd. B31: N'fld 4E 145
Macarthur Rd. B64: Crad H 3E 111
Macaulay Ho. B70: W Brom 6B 80
McBean Rd. WV6: Wolv 5D 26
Macdonald Cl. B69: Tiv 5D 78
Macdonald St. B5: Birm 3G 117
    B12: Birm 3G 117
McDougall Rd. WS10: W'bry 2A 64
McGregor Cl. B6: Aston 6H 83
Machin Rd. B23: Erd 3F 85
Mackadown La. B33: Kitts G, Sheld . . .1H 121
Mackay Rd. WS3: Blox 5B 20
McKean Rd. B69: O'bry 6G 79
McKen Ct. B70: W Brom 6A 80
Mackenzie Cl. B31: N'fld 5C 130
Mackenzie Rd. B11: S'hll 3C 134
Mackmillan Rd. B65: Row R 1B 112
McLean Rd. WV10: Oxl 5G 15
Macmillan Cl. B69: Tiv 5C 78
Macrome Rd. WV6: Tett 1C 26
Madams Hill Rd. B90: Shir 2B 164
Maddocks Hill B72: W Grn 3A 70
Madehurst Rd. B23: Erd 1E 85
Madeira Av. WV8: Cod 5G 13
Madeleine Ho. B33: Stech 6C 104
Madeley Rd. B11: S'brk 6C 118
    DY6: K'wfrd 5D 92
Madin Rd. DY4: Tip 3G 77
Madison Av. B36: Hodg H 3B 104
    DY5: Brie H 6B 94
    WS2: Wals 1H 47
Madley Cl. B45: Rub 1E 157
Madresfield Dr. B63: Hale 3B 128
Maer Cl. B65: Row R 5C 96
Mafeking Rd. B66: Smeth 2E 99
Magdala St. B18: Win G 4A 100
Magdalen Cl. DY1: Dud 5C 76
Magdalen Ct. D10: Edg 2A 116
                              (off Vernon Ct.)
Magdalene Rd. WS1: Wals 4E 49
Magna Cl. WS6: C Hay 2E 7
Magness Cres. WV12: W'hall 4C 30
Magnet Wlk. B23: Erd 4C 84
Magnolia Cl. B29: W Cas 6E 131
Magnolia Dr. WS5: Wals 1D 64
Magnolia Gro. WV8: Bilb 4G 13
    WV12: W'hall 5B 30
Magnolia Way DY8: Word 3D 108
Magnum Cl. B74: S'tly 4H 51
Magpie Cl. DY2: Neth 6G 95
Magpie Ho. CV7: Bal C 2E 169
Magpie La. CV7: Bal C 2E 169
Magreal Ind. Est. B16: Birm 6B 100
Maiden Cl. WV13: W'hall 1C 46
Maidendale Rd. DY6: K'wfrd 2H 91
Maidensbridge Dr. DY6: W Hth 1A 92
Maidensbridge Gdns. DY6: W Hth 6H 73
Maidensbridge Rd. DY6: W Hth 6H 73
Maidstone Dr. DY8: Word 6C 92
Maidstone Rd. B20: Hand 6G 83
Maidwell Dr. B90: Shir 1C 164
Mailbox, The B1: Birm 6C 4 (1F 117)
Mailbox Sq. B1: Birm 5C 4 (1F 117)
Main Rd. B26: Birm A 2B 138
    CV7: Mer 4H 141
Mainstream 47 Ind. Pk.
    B7: Birm .4C 102
Mainstream Way B7: Birm 5C 102
Main St. B11: S'brk 4A 118
    WS9: Ston 4F 23
Main Ter. B11: S'brk 4A 118
Mainwaring Dr. B75: R'ley 1C 54
Maitland Dr. B34: S End 3A 106
Maitland Ho. B36: Cas B 6H 87
Maitland Rd. B8: Salt 5F 103
    DY1: Dud .6A 76
Majestic Way B65: Row R 5C 96
Major Ct. B13: Mose 3B 134
MAJOR'S GREEN 1D 162
Major St. WV2: Wolv 3A 44
Majuba Rd. B16: Edg 5G 99

Malcolm Av. B24: Erd 2A **86**
Malcolm Ct. B26: Sheld 6E **121**
  WV1: Wolv 6E **27**
Malcolm Gro. B45: Redn 2G **157**
Malcolm Rd. B90: Shir 6H **149**
Malcolmson Cl. B15: Edg 3B **116**
Malfield Dr. B27: A Grn 2C **136**
Mali Jenkins Ho. WS1: Wals 2F **49**
Malins Rd. B17: Harb 6H **115**
  WV4: E'shll 6A **44**
Malkit Cl. WS2: Wals 5F **31**
Mallaby Cl. B90: Shir 1G **163**
Mallard Cl. B27: A Grn 2A **136**
  DY5: Brie H 4G **109**
  WS3: Pels 1E **21**
Mallard Dr. B23: Erd 4B **84**
  B69: O'bry 5F **97**
Mallards Reach B92: Olton 5C **136**
Mallender Dr. B93: Know 3B **166**
Mallen Dr. B69: Tiv 6B **78**
Mallin St. B66: Smeth 2B **98**
Mallory Cres. WS3: Blox 5B **20**
Mallory Ri. B13: Mose 4C **134**
Mallory Rd. WV6: Pert 6E **25**
Mallow Cl. WS5: Wals 2E **65**
Mallow Ct. WV6: Wolv 4F **27**
Mallow Ri. B23: Erd 6B **68**
Mallows Cl. WS10: Darl 5D **46**
Malmesbury Pk. B15: Edg 4A **116**
Malmesbury Rd. B10: Small H 5E **119**
Malpas Dr. B32: Bart G 5A **130**
Malpas Gdns. WV8: Cod 3E **13**
Malpas Rd. DY5: Quar B 4B **110**
Malpas Wlk. WV10: Wolv 4C **28**
Malt Cl. B17: Harb 5H **115**
Malthouse B66: Smeth 2C **98**
Malthouse Ct. DY3: Sed 5A **60**
Malthouse Cft. B6: Aston 1G **101**
Malthouse Dr. DY1: Dud 5C **76**
Malthouse Gdns. B19: Loz 2F **101**
Malthouse Gro. B25: Yard 2C **120**
Malt Ho. La. WV13: W'hall 1A **46**
Malthouse La. B8: Salt 3E **103**
  B42: Gt Barr 5F **67**
  B61: C'wich 4B **156**
    (not continuous)
  WV6: Tett 3C **26**
Malthouse Rd. DY4: Tip 2G **77**
Malt Ho. Row B37: Mars G 3C **122**
Maltings, The B1: Birm 6B **4** (2E **117**)
  WS9: A'rdge 3E **35**
  WV1: Wolv 1C **170** (6H **27**)
  WV5: Wom 1G **73**
Malt Mill La. B62: B'hth 3C **112**
Malton Av. B69: O'bry 3D **96**
Malton Gro. B13: Mose 6B **134**
Malvern Av. DY9: Lye 6G **109**
Malvern Cl. B15: Edg 3G **115**
  B71: W Brom 2B **80**
  WV12: W'hall 5B **30**
Malvern Ct. B27: A Grn 1A **136**
  WV10: Bush 1H **27**
Malvern Cres. DY2: Dud 3B **94**
Malvern Dr. B76: Walm 5E **71**
  WS9: A'rdge 6E **23**
  WV1: Wolv 2D **44**
Malvern Hill Rd. B7: Nech 2C **102**
Malvern Ho. B63: Hale 2A **128**
    (off Pickersleigh Cl.)
Malvern Pk. Rd. B91: Sol 4H **151**
Malvern Rd. B21: Hand 6G **81**
  B27: A Grn 1A **136**
  B45: Lick 6G **157**
  B68: O'bry 3H **113**
  CV7: Bal C 6H **169**
Malvern St. B12: Bal H 6A **118**
Malvern Vw. Rd. DY3: Lwr G 3H **75**
Mamble Rd. DY8: Stourb 6C **108**
Mammoth Dr. WV10: Wolv 4H **27**
Manby Cl. WV6: Wolv 5F **27**
Manby Rd. B35: Cas V 3E **87**
Manby St. DY4: Tip 5H **61**
Mancetter Rd. B90: Shir 4A **150**

Manchester St. B6: Birm 4G **101**
  B69: O'bry 2H **97**
Mancroft Cl. DY6: K'wfrd 2H **91**
Mancroft Gdns. WV6: Tett 4A **26**
Mancroft Rd. WV6: Tett 4A **26**
Mandale Rd. WV10: Wolv 3B **28**
Mander Cen. WV1: Wolv 3B **170** (1G **43**)
Manders Ind. Est. WV1: Wolv 6B **28**
Manderley Cl. DY3: Sed 3G **59**
Manderston Cl. DY1: Dud 4A **76**
Mander Sq. WV1: Wolv 4B **170**
Mander St. WV3: Wolv 6A **170** (3F **43**)
Manderville Gdns. DY6: K'wfrd 3A **92**
Manderville Ho. B31: Longb 1D **158**
Mandeville Gdns. WS1: Wals 3D **48**
MANEY 1A **70**
Maney Cnr. B72: S Cold 1H **69**
Maney Hill Rd. B72: W Grn 2H **69**
Manfield Rd. WV13: W'hall 6E **29**
Manifoldia Grange B70: W Brom 5H **79**
Manifold Way WS10: W'bry 2C **64**
Manilla Rd. B29: S Oak 4D **132**
Manitoba Cft. B38: K Nor 1B **160**
Manley Cl. B70: W Brom 4H **79**
Manlove St. WV3: Wolv 3E **43**
Manningford Ct. B14: K Hth 5H **147**
Manningford Rd. B14: K Hth 5G **147**
Mnr. Abbey Rd. B62: Hale 2E **129**
Manor Av. WS10: W'bry 1G **7**
Manor Cl. WV4: Penn 1D **58**
  WV8: Bilb 3H **13**
  WV13: W'hall 6A **30**
Manor Ct. B27: A Grn 3B **136**
  B30: K Nor 5C **146**
  B62: Quin 4G **113**
    (off Binswood Rd.)
  B93: Dorr 6G **167**
  DY2: Neth 5E **95**
  WS2: Wals 1A **48**
Manor Dr. B73: S Cold 1H **69**
  DY3: Gorn 4F **75**
  DY3: Swind 5E **73**
Mnr. Farm Dr. WV12: W'hall 4D **30**
Mnr. Farm Rd. B11: Tys 1E **135**
Manor Fold WV8: Oaken 5D **12**
Manorford Av. B71: W Brom 4E **65**
Manor Gdns. B33: Stech 1B **120**
  WS10: W'bry 1F **63**
  WV5: Wom 6H **57**
Manor Hill B73: S Cold 1H **69**
Manor Ho. B31: N'fld 6F **131**
Manor Ho., The B44: Gt Barr 3G **67**
    (off Amblecote Av.)
Manor Ho. Cl. B29: W Cas 4D **130**
Manor Ho. Dr. B31: N'fld 6F **131**
Manor Ho. La. B26: Sheld, Yard 5D **120**
  B46: Wat O 4D **88**
Manor Ho. Pk. WV8: Bilb 3H **13**
Manor Ho. Rd. WS10: W'bry 2F **63**
Manorial Rd. B75: R'ley 6C **38**
Manor Ind. Est. WS2: Wals 2A **48**
Manor La. B61: C'wich, L Ash 4C **156**
  B62: Hale 2E **129**
  DY8: Stourb 2B **124**
Manor Pk. DY6: K'wfrd 3B **92**
Manor Pk. Cl. B13: Mose 3A **134**
Manor Pk. Gro. B31: Longb 6A **144**
Manor Pk. Rd. B36: Cas B 1D **105**
Manor Rd. B6: Aston 6H **83**
  B16: Edg 2H **115**
  B33: Stech 6C **104**
  B47: Wyt 6A **162**
  B67: Smeth 4B **98**
  B73: S Cold 6H **53**
  B74: S'tly 3A **52**
  B91: Sol 2F **151**
  B93: Dorr 6A **166**
  DY4: Tip 3H **77**
  DY8: Word 1C **108**
  WS2: Wals 1A **48**
  WS10: W'bry 3B **64**
  WV4: E'shll 6C **44**
  WV4: Penn 1D **58**
  WV10: Oxl 2G **27**

Manor Rd. Nth. B16: Edg 2H **115**
Manor Rd. Pct. WS2: Wals 1A **48**
Manor Sq. B91: Sol 4G **151**
Manor St. WV6: Tett 4A **26**
Manor Wlk. B91: Sol 4G **151**
Manor Way B62: Hale, Roms 4G **127**
  B73: S Cold 1H **69**
Mansard Cl. WV3: Wolv 3D **42**
  WV10: Bush 1D **28**
Mansard Ct. B46: Col 2H **107**
Mansell Cl. B63: Crad 4D **110**
Mansell Rd. DY4: Tip 5A **62**
Mansel Rd. B10: Small H 4E **119**
Mansfield Ho. B37: Chel W 6E **107**
Mansfield Rd. B6: Aston 1F **101**
  B25: Yard 6A **120**
Mansion Cl. DY1: Dud 4C **76**
Mansion Ct. WV5: Wom 2D **72**
    (off Heath Ho. Dr.)
Mansion Cres. B67: Smeth 5C **98**
Mansion Dr. DY4: Tip 2C **78**
  WS7: Hamm 1F **11**
Manson Dr. B64: Old H 2A **112**
Manston Dr. WV6: Pert 4E **25**
Manston Rd. B26: Sheld 4F **121**
Manton Cft. B93: Dorr 6A **166**
Manton Ho. B19: Loz 2G **101**
Manway Cl. B20: Hand 2B **82**
Manwoods Cl. B20: Hand 5D **82**
Maple Av. WS10: W'bry 1A **64**
Maple Bank B15: Edg 4C **116**
Maplebeck Cl. B91: Sol 2G **151**
Maple Bus. Pk. B7: Nech 3B **102**
Maple Cen., The WS10: Mox 2B **62**
Maple Cl. B21: Hand 6A **82**
  DY8: Stourb 3B **124**
  WV14: Cose 6C **60**
Maple Ct. B24: Erd 4F **85**
    (off Coppice Cl.)
  B66: Smeth 1B **98**
Maple Cft. B13: Mose 1H **147**
Mapledene B13: Mose 3B **134**
Mapledene Rd. B26: Sheld 5H **121**
Maple Dr. B44: K'sdng 5B **68**
  DY3: Gorn 5F **75**
  WS4: S'fld 1F **33**
  WS5: Wals 1F **65**
  WS10: Mox 1B **62**
Maple Grn. DY1: Dud 2C **76**
Maple Gro. B19: Loz 1E **101**
  B37: K'hrst 3B **106**
  DY6: K'wfrd 3C **92**
  WV3: Wolv 1A **42**
  WV14: Bils 1H **61**
Maple Leaf Dr. B37: Mars G 3D **122**
Maple Leaf Ind. Est. WS2: Wals 6G **31**
Maple Leaf Rd. WS10: W'bry 4C **62**
Maple Ri. B68: O'bry 1A **114**
Maple Rd. B30: B'vle 5A **132**
  B45: Rubery 3F **157**
  B62: B'hth 3D **112**
  B72: S Cold 2A **70**
  DY1: Dud 4E **77**
  WS3: Pels 5D **20**
  WV3: Wolv 4C **42**
Maple Row DY5: Brie H 1H **109**
Maple St. WS3: Blox 5B **20**
Mapleton Gro. B28: Hall G 6H **135**
Mapleton Rd. B28: Hall G 6H **135**
Maple Tree La. B63: Crad 5E **111**
Maple Wlk. B37: Chel W 1D **122**
    (off Chelmsley Wood Shop. Cen.)
Maple Way B31: Longb 6D **144**
Maplewood B76: Walm 5E **71**
Mapperley Gdns. B13: Mose 2E **133**
Mappleborough Rd. B90: Shir 6E **149**
Mapps Cl. B63: Crad 5E **111**
Marans Cft. B38: K Nor 2H **159**
Marbury Cl. B38: K Nor 5H **145**
Marbury Dr. WV14: Bils 5A **46**
Marbury M. DY5: Brie H 2H **109**
Marchant Rd. WV3: Wolv 1D **42**
  WV14: Bils 4E **45**
March Cl. WS6: C Hay 4D **6**

MARCH END 4G 29
March End Rd. WV11: Wed 4F 29
    (not continuous)
Marchmont Rd. B9: Bord G 1G 119
Marchmount Rd. B72: W Grn 5A 70
March Way WS9: A'rdge 6E 23
Marcliff Cres. B90: Shir 5C 148
Marcos Dr. B36: Cas B 6B 88
Marcot Rd. B92: Olton 6D 120
Marden Cl. WV13: W'hall 2H 45
Marden Gro. B31: Longb 2E 159
Marden Wlk. B23: Erd 4B 84
Mardon Rd. B26: Sheld 6F 121
Maree Gro. WV12: W'hall 6B 18
Marfield Cl. B76: Walm 1E 87
Margam Cres. WS3: Blox 5F 19
Margam Ter. WS3: Blox 5F 19
Margam Way WS3: Blox 5F 19
Margaret Av. B63: Hale 1H 127
Margaret Cl. DY5: Quar B 3A 110
Margaret Dr. DY8: Stourb 1F 125
Margaret Gdns. B67: Smeth 4C 98
Margaret Gro. B17: Harb 4G 115
Margaret Ho. B17: Harb 6F 115
Margaret Rd. B17: Harb 6G 115
    B73: New O 4D 68
    WS2: Wals 6E 31
    WS10: Darl 1C 62
Margarets Ho. B76: Walm 2D 70
Margaret St. B3: Birm 3C 4 (6F 101)
    B70: W Brom 5H 79
Margaret Va. DY4: Tip 4C 62
Margaret Vine Ct. B62: B'hth 2F 113
Marholm Cl. WV9: Pend 5D 14
Marian Cft. B26: Sheld 6H 121
Maria St. B70: W Brom 1C 98
Marie Dr. B27: A Grn 5H 135
Marigold Cres. DY1: Dud 3C 76
Marine Cres. DY8: Word 2C 108
Marine Dr. B44: K'sdng 1G 83
Marine Gdns. DY8: Word 2C 108
Mariner Av. B16: Edg 2A 116
Marion Cl. DY5: Quar B 1B 110
Marion Rd. B67: Smeth 3B 98
Marion Way B28: Hall G 6E 135
Marita Cl. DY2: Neth 6G 95
Marjoram Cl. B38: K Nor 1B 160
Marjorie Av. B30: K Nor 4D 146
Mark Av. WS10: W'bry 2E 63
Markby Rd. B18: Win G 3A 100
Mark Cl. WS1: Wals 6E 33
Market La. WV4: Lwr P 5F 41
Market Pl. B65: B'hth 2C 112
    B69: O'bry 1G 97
    (off Market St.)
    DY2: Dud 6E 77
    DY2: Neth 4E 95
    DY4: Tip 2D 78
    WS3: Blox 6H 19
    WS10: W'bry 3F 63
    WV13: W'hall 2A 46
Market Sq. B64: Crad H 3E 111
    WV3: Wolv 4A 170 (2G 43)
Market St. B69: O'bry 1G 97
    DY6: K'wfrd 3B 92
    DY8: Stourb 6E 109
    WV1: Wolv 3C 170 (1H 43)
Market Way DY9: Hag 6G 125
    WV14: Bils 6F 45
Markfield Rd. B26: Sheld 3F 121
Markford Wlk. B19: Hock 3F 101
Markham Cres. B92: Sol 4B 138
Markham Cft. WV9: Pend 5E 15
Markham Dr. DY6: K'wfrd 5C 92
Markham Rd. B73: New O 2C 68
Mark Ho. B13: Mose 3A 134
Marklew Cl. WS8: Bwnhls 2C 22
Marklin Av. WV10: Oxl 6H 15
Mark Rd. WS10: W'bry 2E 63
Marksbury Cl. WV6: Wolv 4E 27
Marlbank Rd. B68: Word 2E 109
Marlborough Cl. B74: Four O 3E 37
Marlborough Ct. B74: Four O 1F 53
    (off Vesey Cl.)

Marlborough Dr. DY8: Stourb 2E 125
Marlborough Gdns. DY8: Word 1A 108
    WV6: Wolv 5C 26
Marlborough Gro. B25: Yard 2B 120
Marlborough Rd. B10: Small H 2E 119
    B36: Cas B 1G 105
    B66: Smeth 6E 99
    DY3: Sed 6B 60
Marlborough St. WS3: Blox 6H 19
Marlbrook Cl. B92: Sol 1G 137
Marlbrook Dr. WV4: Penn 5F 43
Marlbrook La. B60: Marlb 6D 156
Marlburn Way WV5: Wom 1E 73
Marlcliff Gro. B13: Mose 1A 148
Marldon Rd. B14: K Hth 1G 147
Marlene Cft. B37: Chel W 2E 123
Marley Rd. DY6: K'wfrd 5E 93
Marling Cft. B92: Sol 6A 138
Marlin Office Village B35: Cas V 6D 86
Marlow Cl. DY2: Neth 6G 95
Marlowe Dr. WV12: W'hall 2A 30
Marlow Rd. B23: Erd 2D 84
Marlow St. B65: B'hth 2B 112
    WS2: Wals 5C 32
Marlpit La. B75: R'ley 1B 54
Marlpit Ri. B75: R'ley 6C 38
Marlpool Dr. WS3: Pels 6E 21
Marl Rd. DY2: Neth 5D 94
Marl Top B38: K Nor 5B 146
Marmion Dr. B43: Gt Barr 3B 66
Marmion Gro. DY1: Dud 1C 94
Marmion Way B70: W Brom 1F 79
Marnel Dr. WV3: Wolv 3B 42
Marquis Dr. B62: Hale 4A 112
Marriott Rd. B66: Smeth 2D 98
    DY2: Neth 5E 95
Marroway St. B16: Birm 6B 100
Marrowfat La. B21: Hand 2B 100
Mars Cl. WV14: Cose 4C 60
Marsden Cl. B92: Olton 4C 136
Marsh, The WS10: W'bry 2E 63
Marshall Cl. WS9: A'rdge 5D 34
Marshall Gro. B44: Gt Barr 6H 67
Marshall Ho. WS2: Wals 1C 96
    (off St Quentin St.)
Marshall Lake Rd. B90: Shir 1B 164
Marshall Rd. B68: O'bry 2A 114
    WV13: W'hall 2E 45
Marshalls Ind. Est. WV2: Wolv 4G 43
Marshall St. B1: Birm 6C 4 (2F 117)
    B67: Smeth 2B 98
Marsham Ct. Rd. B91: Sol 6D 136
Marsham Rd. B14: K Hth 4H 147
Marshbrook Cl. B24: Erd 3C 86
Marsh Cl. B23: Erd 2F 85
Marsh Cres. DY8: Word 6A 92
Marsh End B38: K Nor 1C 160
Marshfield B90: Dic H 4H 163
Marshfield Gdns. B24: Erd 5E 85
Marsh Gro. DY3: Swind 5E 73
Marsh Hill B23: Erd 3B 84
Marsh Ho. Farm La. B92: H Ard 4D 154
Marshland Way WS2: Wals 2E 47
Marsh La. B23: Erd 2D 84
    B46: Wat O 4D 88
    B71: W Brom 6A 64
    B76: Curd 2E 89
    B91: Sol 3A 152
    B92: H Ard 3A 152
    (not continuous)
    WS2: Wals 1B 48
    WV10: F'hses 4F 15
Marsh La. Pde. WV10: Oxl 5G 15
Marshmont Way B23: Erd 5D 68
Marsh St. WS2: Wals 1B 48
Marshwood Cft. B62: Quin 2G 129
Marsland Cl. B17: Edg 2G 115
Marsland Rd. B92: Olton 6C 136
Marston Av. WS10: Darl 5C 46
Marston Cl. DY8: Stourb 1B 124
Marston Cft. B37: Mars G 4B 122
Marston Dr. B37: K'hrst 4C 106
MARSTON GREEN 3B 122
Marston Green Station (Rail) 4B 122

Marston Gro. B43: Gt Barr 5G 65
Marston Rd. B29: W Cas 5D 130
    B73: Bold 6G 69
    DY1: Dud 1H 93
    WV2: Wolv 4F 43
Marston Rd. Ind. Est. WV2: Wolv 4G 43
Marston St. WV13: W'hall 1C 46
Martham Dr. WV6: Tett 1H 41
Martin Cl. B25: Yard 5B 120
    WV14: Cose 6F 61
Martindale Wlk. DY5: Brie H 5F 109
Martin Dr. WV12: W'hall 4C 30
Martineau Pl. B2: Birm 4E 5 (1G 117)
Martineau Twr. B19: Birm 4F 101
    (off Uxbridge St.)
Martineau Way B2: Birm 4E 5
    (off Union St.)
Martingale Cl. WS5: Wals 1D 64
Martin Gro. WS6: Gt Wyr 2G 7
Martin Hill St. DY2: Dud 1E 95
Martin Ri. B37: Mars G 3B 122
Martin Rd. DY4: Tip 2A 78
    WS5: Wals 3G 49
    WV14: Bils 2H 61
Martin St. WV4: E'shll 6B 44
Martlesham Sq. B35: Cas V 3E 87
Martley Cft. B32: Quin 1C 130
    B91: Sol 1F 165
Martley Rd. DY9: Lye 1G 125
Martley Rd. B69: O'bry 3D 96
    WS4: S'fld 6G 21
Marton Cl. B7: Nech 3B 102
Marwood Cft. B74: S'tly 1A 52
Mary Ann St. B3: Birm 1C 4 (5F 101)
    WV1: Wolv 2A 44
    (off Walsall St.)
Maryland Av. B34: Hodg H 4C 104
Maryland Dr. B31: N'fld 2F 145
Maryland Rd. DY5: Quar B 4B 110
Marylebone Cl. DY8: Amb 4E 109
Mary Macarthur Dr. B64: Crad H 2E 111
Mary Rd. B21: Hand 2A 100
    B33: Stech 6B 104
    B69: Tiv 1C 96
    B70: W Brom 6B 80
Mary Rose Cl. WS6: C Hay 4D 6
Mary St. B3: Birm 1B 4 (5E 101)
    B12: Bal H 6G 117
    WS2: Wals 6B 32
Maryvale Ct. WS1: Wals 2C 48
Mary Va. Rd. B30: B'ville, Stir 1A 146
Marywell Cl. B32: Bart G 6H 129
Masefield Av. DY1: Dud 6E 61
Masefield Cl. WV14: Bils 3H 61
Masefield M. WV10: Bush 6C 16
Masefield Ri. B62: Hale 2D 128
Masefield Rd. DY3: Lwr G 3E 75
    WS3: Blox 2C 32
    WV10: Bush 6C 16
Masefield Sq. B31: N'fld 3G 145
Masham Cl. B33: Stech 1C 120
Mashie Gdns. B38: K Nor 6H 145
Maslen Pl. B63: Hale 2B 128
Maslin Dr. WV14: Cose 4C 60
Mason Cl. B27: A Grn 3C 136
Mason Cres. WV4: Penn 6C 42
Mason Hall B15: Edg 5C 116
Mason Ho. B90: Shir 6E 149
Masonleys Rd. B31: N'fld 4B 144
Mason Rd. B24: Erd 3G 85
    WS2: Wals 4H 31
Mason's Cl. B63: Crad 5E 111
Masons Cotts. B24: Erd 2H 85
Mason St. B70: W Brom 3H 79
    WV2: Wolv 4G 43
    WV14: Cose 6D 60
Masons Vw. B24: Erd 5G 85
Mason's Way B92: Olton 3C 136
Mason Way B15: Birm 3E 117
Massbrook Gro. WV10: Wolv 3B 28
Massbrook Rd. WV10: Wolv 3B 28
Masshouse La. B5: Birm 3G 5 (6H 101)
    B38: K Nor 6B 146
Masters La. B62: B'hth 2E 113

Matchlock Cl. B74: S'tly 4G 51
Matfen Av. B73: S Cold 3F 69
Math Mdw. B32: Harb 6D 114
Matlock Cl. DY2: Neth 6F 95
  WS3: Blox 4A 20
Matlock Rd. B11: Tys 2F 135
  WS3: Blox 4A 20
Matlock Vs. B12: Bal H 6B 118
    (off Chesterton Rd.)
Matthews Cl. B65: B'hth 2B 112
Mattox Rd. WV11: Wed 3F 29
Matty Rd. B68: O'bry 5H 97
Maud Rd. B46: Wat O 4F 89
  B70: W Brom 6A 80
Maughan St. DY1: Dud 6C 76
  DY5: Quar B 3B 110
Maurice Gro. WV10: Wolv 3C 28
Maurice Rd. B14: K Hth 2G 147
  B67: Smeth 1C 114
Mavis Gdns. B68: O'bry 3H 113
Mavis Rd. B31: N'fld 6C 144
Maw St. WS1: Wals 5D 48
Maxholm Rd. B74: S'tly 3G 51
Max Rd. B32: Quin 6B 114
Maxstoke Cl. B32: Bart G 6G 129
  B73: New O 3E 69
  CV7: Mer 4H 141
  WS3: Blox 4G 19
Maxstoke Cft. B90: Shir 1A 164
Maxstoke La. CV7: Mer 3H 141
    (not continuous)
Maxstoke Rd. B73: New O 3E 69
Maxstoke St. B9: Birm 1B 118
Maxted Rd. B23: Erd 5C 68
Maxwell Av. B20: Hand 6D 82
Maxwell Rd. WV2: Wolv 6D 170 (3H 43)
Mayall Dr. B75: R'ley 5A 38
May Av. B12: Bal H 6A 118
Maybank B9: Bord G 6F 103
Maybank Pl. B44: P Barr 1G 83
Maybank Rd. DY2: Neth 6E 95
Mayberry Cl. B14: K Hth 5B 148
Maybrook Rd. B63: Hale 1A 128
Maybrook Ind. Est. WS8: Bwnhls ...2B 22
    (not continuous)
Maybrook Rd. B76: Min 2E 87
  WS8: Bwnhls 3B 22
Maybury Cl. WV8: Cod 3E 13
Maybush Gdns. WV10: Oxl 6G 15
Maydene Cft. B12: Bal H 5H 117
MAYERS GREEN 3C 80
Mayfair B37: K'hrst 4B 106
    (off Haselour Rd.)
  DY9: W'cte 3H 125
Mayfair Cl. B44: K'sdng 6B 68
  DY1: Dud 5C 76
Mayfair Dr. DY6: K'wfrd 2A 92
Mayfair Gdns. DY4: Tip 3A 78
  WV3: Wolv 1B 42
Mayfair Pde. B44: K'sdng 6B 68
May Farm Cl. B47: H'wd 3A 162
Mayfield Av. B29: S Oak 3D 132
Mayfield Cl. B91: Sol 6G 151
Mayfield Ct. B13: Mose 3A 134
Mayfield Cres. B65: Row R 6A 96
Mayfield Rd. B11: Tys 1G 135
  B13: Mose 3A 134
  B19: Hand 1E 101
  B27: A Grn 2G 135
  B30: Stir 1C 146
  B62: B'hth 2F 113
  B63: Hale 3F 127
  B73: W Grn 3G 69
  B74: S'tly 3H 51
  DY1: Dud 2D 76
  WV1: Wolv 2D 44
Mayfields Dr. WS8: Bwnhls 3F 9
Mayflower Cl. B19: Loz 3F 101
Mayflower Dr. DY5: P'ntt 2E 93
Mayford Gro. B13: Mose 1B 148
Maygrove Rd. DY6: K'wfrd 2A 92
Mayhurst Cl. B47: H'wd 2C 162
  DY4: Tip 5A 62

Mayhurst Rd. B47: H'wd 2B 162
Mayland Dr. B74: S'tly 6H 51
Mayland Rd. B16: Edg 1G 115
May La. B14: K Hth 2H 147
  B47: H'wd 2A 162
Maynard Av. DY8: Stourb 2B 124
Maynard Rd. B66: Smeth 6G 99
Mayou Ct. WS3: Pels 3E 21
Maypole Cl. B14: K Hth 6A 148
  B64: Crad H 3D 110
Maypole Ct. WV5: Wom 1G 73
Maypole Dr. DY8: Stourb 6C 108
Maypole Flds. B63: Crad 4C 110
Maypole Gro. B14: K Hth 5B 148
Maypole Hill B63: Crad 3C 110
Maypole La. B14: K Hth 5H 147
Maypole Rd. B68: O'bry 2H 113
Maypole St. WV5: Wom 6H 57
May St. WS3: Blox 3A 32
Mayswood Dr. WV6: Tett 2F 41
Mayswood Gro. B32: Quin 1B 130
Mayswood Rd. B92: Sol 3G 137
Maythorn Av. B76: Walm 1E 87
Maythorn Gdns. WV6: Tett 6A 26
  WV8: Bilb 3G 13
Maythorn Gro. B91: Sol 1F 165
Maytree Cl. B37: F'bri 1C 122
May Trees B47: H'wd 3H 161
Maywell Dr. B92: Sol 5B 138
Maywood Cl. DY6: K'wfrd 3A 92
Meaburn Cl. B29: W Cas 6E 131
Mead, The DY3: Sed 5F 59
Mead Cl. WS9: A'rdge 3D 34
Mead Cres. B9: Bord G 6H 103
Meadfoot Av. B14: K Hth 4H 147
Meadfoot Dr. DY6: K'wfrd 2H 91
Meadlands, The WV5: Wom 1E 73
Meadow Av. B71: W Brom 4D 64
Meadowbank Grange WS6: Gt Wyr ...1E 7
Meadowbrook Gdns. WV8: Bilb 3H 13
Meadow Brook Rd. B31: N'fld 2D 144
Meadowbrook Rd. B63: Hale 2F 127
Meadow Cl. B17: Harb 3F 115
  B74: S'tly 1H 51
  B76: Walm 4D 70
  B90: Shir 1B 164
  WS4: S'fld 1G 33
Meadow Ct. B17: Edg 2F 115
  B30: K Nor 5D 146
Meadow Cft. B47: Wyt 6A 162
  WV6: Pert 6D 24
Meadow Dr. B92: H Ard 1B 154
Meadowfield Rd. B45: Rub 2G 157
Meadowfields Cl. DY8: Word 1C 108
Meadow Ga. B31: N'fld 5C 144
Meadow Grange Dr. WV12: W'hall ...2C 30
Meadow Gro. B92: Olton 4B 136
  WS6: Gt Wyr 3G 7
Meadow Hill Dr. DY8: Word 1C 108
Meadow Hill Rd. B38: K Nor 5A 146
Meadowlands Dr. WS4: S'fld 1H 33
Meadow La. WV5: Wom 5G 57
  WV10: Cov H 1G 15
  WV12: W'hall 4A 30
  WV14: Cose 3D 60
    (not continuous)
Meadow Pk. Rd. DY8: Woll 3B 108
Meadow Pleck La. B90: Dic H 3G 163
Meadow Ri. B30: B'ville 6H 131
  CV7: Bal C 5H 169
Meadow Rd. B17: Harb 2F 115
  B32: Quin 5G 113
  B47: Wyt 6A 162
  B62: B'hth 3C 112
  B67: Smeth 5E 99
  B68: O'bry 1H 113
  DY1: Dud 3C 76
  WS9: A'rdge 5C 34
  WV3: Wolv 3A 42
Meadows, The DY9: Pedm 6F 125
  WS9: A'rdge 4A 34
Meadows Gro. WV8: Bilb 3G 13
Meadowside Cl. B43: Gt Barr 4A 66

Meadowside Rd. B74: Four O 5F 37
Meadow St. B64: Old H 3H 111
  WS1: Wals 3B 48
  WV1: Wolv 1F 43
Meadowsweet Av. B38: K Nor 1B 160
Meadowsweet Way DY6: K'wfrd 3D 92
Meadow Va. WV8: Bilb 5H 13
Meadow Vw. B13: Mose 5C 134
  DY3: Sed 4G 59
  WV6: Tett 5C 26
Meadow Vw. Mobile Home Pk.
  WV10: Cov H 1G 15
Meadow Vw. Ter. WV6: Tett 5C 26
Meadow Vw. Wharf WV6: Tett 5C 26
Meadow Wlk. B14: K Hth 6G 147
  B64: Crad H 3F 111
Meadow Way DY8: Word 1A 108
  WV8: Cod 5E 13
Mead Ri. B15: Edg 5B 116
Meadthorpe Rd. B44: Gt Barr 5F 67
Meadvale Rd. B45: Redn 3H 157
Meadway B33: Kitts G, Yard 1D 120
Meadway, The WV6: Tett 4G 25
Meadwood Ind. Est. WV14: Bils 6G 45
Mears Cl. B23: Erd 5D 68
Mears Coppice DY5: Quar B 5A 110
  DY9: Lye 5A 110
Mears Dr. B33: Stech 5B 104
Mease Cft. B18: Hock 4C 100
Mease Cft. B9: Birm 1B 118
Measham Gro. B26: Yard 6C 120
Measham Way WV11: Wed 2G 29
Meaton Gro. B32: Bart G 5H 129
Mecca Bingo
  Acock's Green 1H 135
  Bilston 1E 61
  Birmingham 2H 67
  Brierley Hill 1H 109
  Oldbury 2F 97
  Wednesbury 3E 63
  Wolverhampton 4A 170
Medcroft Av. B20: Hand 3A 82
Medina Cl. WV10: Bush 3B 16
Medina Rd. B11: Tys 1E 135
Medina Way DY6: K'wfrd 3A 92
Medley Gdns. DY4: Tip 3D 78
Medley Rd. B11: S'brk 6D 118
Medlicott Rd. B11: S'brk 5C 118
Medway Cl. DY5: P'ntt 3E 93
Medway Ct. B73: S Cold 6H 53
Medway Cft. B36: Cas B 2B 106
Medway Gro. B38: K Nor 1A 160
Medway Rd. WS8: Bwnhls 3G 9
Medway Twr. B7: Nech 4B 102
Medway Wlk. WS8: Bwnhls 3G 9
Meer End B38: K Nor 2H 159
Meerhill Av. B90: M'path 3E 165
Meeting Ho. La. CV7: Bal C 5H 169
Meetinghouse La. B31: N'fld 3E 145
Meeting La. DY5: Brie H 2F 109
    (not continuous)
Meeting La. Ind. Est. DY5: Brie H ...2F 109
Meeting St. DY2: Neth 4E 95
  DY4: Tip 1D 78
  WS10: W'bry 2E 63
Megabowl
  Birmingham 6F 5 (2G 117)
  Brierley Hill 1H 109
  Nechells 1D 102
    (in Star City)
Mehdi Rd. B69: O'bry 1E 97
Melbourne Av. B19: Hock 3E 101
  B66: Smeth 2F 99
Melbourne Cl. B70: W Brom 6G 63
  DY6: K'wfrd 5C 92
Melbourne Gdns. WS5: Wals 5F 49
Melbourne Rd. B34: S End 3A 106
  B63: Hale 6B 112
  B66: Smeth 2E 99
Melbourne St. WV2: Wolv ...5C 170 (2H 43)
Melbury Cl. WV3: Wolv 2E 43
Melbury Gro. B14: K Hth 2G 147

Melchett Rd. B30: K Nor 4B 146
Melcote Gro. B44: Gt Barr 5G 67
Meldon Dr. WV14: Bils 3A 62
Melford Cl. DY3: Sed 3G 59
Melford Hall Rd. B91: Sol 6D 136
Melfort Gro. B14: K Hth 4A 148
Melia Dr. WS10: W'bry 2H 63
Melksham Sq. B35: Cas V 4E 87
Mellis Gro. B23: Erd 2A 84
Mellish Ct. WS4: Wals 6E 33
(off Mellish Rd.)
Mellish Dr. WS4: Wals 6F 33
Mellish Rd. WS4: Wals 6E 33
Mellor Dr. B74: Four O 6E 37
Mellors Cl. B17: Harb 2F 131
Mellowdew Rd. DY8: Word 6A 92
Mell Sq. B91: Sol 3G 151
Melplash Av. B91: Sol 3E 151
Melrose Av. B11: S'hll 5C 118
(off Walford Rd.)
B12: Bal H 5A 118
B71: W Brom 5B 64
B73: S Cold 3E 69
DY8: Stourb 3D 124
Melrose Cl. B38: K Nor 6B 146
Melrose Cotts. WS14: Muck C 4H 11
Melrose Dr. WV6: Pert 5D 24
Melrose Gro. B19: Loz 2D 100
Melrose Pl. B66: Smeth 1B 98
Melrose Rd. B20: Hand 6G 83
Melstock Cl. DY4: Tip 2F 77
Melstock Rd. B14: K Hth 6F 133
Melton Av. B92: Olton 1E 137
Melton Dr. B15: Edg 4E 117
Melton Gro. B33: Kitts G 6A 106
Melton Rd. B14: K Hth 5ll 133
Melverley Gro. B44: K'sdng 5H 67
Melverton Av. WV10: Bush 1H 27
Melville Hall B16: Edg 2G 115
Melville Rd. B16: Edg 2G 115
Melvina Rd. B7: Birm 5B 102
Mombury Rd. B8: Salt 3D 102
Memorial Cl. WV13: W'hall 1A 46
Memory La. WS10: Darl 3D 46
WV11: Wed 4D 28
Menai Cl. WV12: W'hall 3C 30
Menai Wlk. B37: F'bri 5D 106
Mendip Av. B8: Salt 4E 103
Mendip Cl. B63: Hale 4F 127
DY3: Lwr G 4H 75
WV2: E'shll 5B 44
Mendip Rd. B8: Salt 5E 103
B63: Hale 4F 127
DY8: Amb 5F 109
Menin Cres. B13: Mose 6B 134
Menin Pas. B13: Mose 5B 134
Menin Rd. B13: Mose 5B 134
DY4: Tip 2F 77
Mentone Ct. B20: Hand 4A 82
Meon Gro. B33: Sheld 3F 121
WV6: Pert 5F 25
Meon Ri. DY9: Pedm 2G 125
Meon Way WV11: Wed 2H 29
Meranti Cl. WV12: W'hall 1C 30
Mercer Av. B46: Wat O 4C 88
Mercer Gro. WV11: Wed 2G 29
Merchants Way WS9: A'rdge 2C 34
Mercia Dr. B14: K Hth 1F 147
WV6: Pert 4E 25
Mercote Hall La. CV7: Mer 2G 155
Mere Av. B35: Cas V 4E 87
Mere Cl. WV12: W'hall 4A 30
Merecote Rd. B92: Olton 6B 136
Mere Cft. WS11: Nort C 1D 8
Meredith Rd. DY3: Lwr G 2E 75
WV11: Wed 1E 29
Merediths Pool Cl. B18: Hock 3B 100
Meredith St. B64: Crad H 2F 111
Mere Dr. B75: Four O 1H 53
MERE GREEN 6H 37
Mere Grn. Cl. B75: Four O 1A 54
Mere Grn. Rd. B75: Four O 1H 53
Mere Oak Rd. WV6: Pert 4E 25
Mere Pool Rd. B75: R'ley 1B 54

Mere Rd. B23: Erd 4C 84
DY8: Stourb 2C 124
Mereside Way B92: Olton 5C 136
Meres Rd. B63: Crad 6E 111
Mere St. B23: Erd 4E 85
Merevale Rd. B92: Sol 3F 137
Mere Vw. WS4: S'fld 1G 33
Mereways B90: Dic H 4G 163
MERIDEN .4H 141
Meriden Av. DY8: Woll 5B 108
Meriden Cl. B25: Yard 4H 119
DY8: Woll 5B 108
Meriden Dr. B37: K'hrst 3C 106
Meriden Ri. B92: Sol 2H 137
Meriden Rd. B92: H Ard 6B 140
CV7: Mer 1E 27
WV10: Oxl 1E 27
Meriden St. B5: Birm 6G 5 (1H 117)
Merino Av. B31: Longb 1E 159
Merlin Cl. B35: Cas V 4E 87
DY1: Dud 1B 94
Merlin Gro. B26: Sheld 6F 121
Merlin Wlk. B35: Cas V 3F 87
(off Merlin Way)
Merlin Way B35: Cas V 3F 87
Merrick Cl. B63: Hale 3F 127
Merrick Rd. WV11: Wed 3A 30
MERRIDALE 2D 42
Merridale Av. WV3: Wolv 2D 42
Merridale Ct. WV3: Wolv 2D 42
Merridale Cres. WV3: Wolv 1E 43
Merridale Gdns. WV3: Wolv 2E 43
Merridale Gro. WV3: Wolv 2C 42
(not continuous)
Merridale La. WV3: Wolv 1E 43
Merridale Rd. WV3: Wolv 2D 42
Merridale St. WV3: Wolv 5A 170 (2F 43)
Merridale St. W. WV3: Wolv 3E 43
Merrill Cl. WS6: C Hay 3E 7
Merrill's Hall La. WV11: Wed 5G 29
Merrington Cl. B91: Sol 1G 165
Merrions Cl. B43: Gt Barr 1A 66
Merrishaw Rd. B31: Longb 1E 159
Merritts Brook Cl. B29: W Cas 2E 145
Merritt's Brook La. B31: N'fld 3C 144
Merritt's Hill B31: N'fld 1B 144
(not continuous)
Merrivale Rd. B62: B'hth 3F 113
B66: Smeth 1E 115
Merryfield Cl. B92: Sol 6H 137
Merryfield Gro. B17: Harb 1G 131
Merryfield Rd. DY1: Dud 1H 93
MERRY HILL
DY5 . . . . .6A 94
WV3 .4B 42
Merry Hill DY5: Brie H, Quar B 2B 110
Merry Hill Cen. DY5: Brie H 6B 94
Merry Hill Ct. B66: Smeth 3H 99
Merryhill Dr. B18: Hock 3B 100
Merryhills Ent. Pk. WV10: Wolv 4B 28
Mersey Gro. B38: K Nor 1A 160
Mersey Pl. WS3: Blox 6C 20
Mersey Rd. WS3: Blox 6C 20
Merstal Dr. B92: Sol 6B 138
Merstone Cl. WV14: Bils 5E 45
Merstowe Cl. B27: A Grn 2H 135
Merton Cl. B68: O'bry 1H 113
Merton Ho. B37: F'bri 1B 122
Merton Rd. B13: Mose 2B 134
Mervyn Pl. WV14: Bils 2H 61
Mervyn Rd. B21: Hand 6A 82
WV14: Bils 2H 61
Meryhurst Rd. WS10: W'bry 6G 47
Messenger La. B70: W Brom 4B 80
Messenger Rd. B66: Smeth 3F 99
MESTY CROFT 2H 63
Metchley Abbey B17: Harb 6H 115
Metchley Ct. B17: Harb 1H 131
Metchley Cft. B90: M'path 3D 164
Metchley Dr. B17: Harb 6G 115
Metchley Gro. B18: Win G 5A 100
(off Heath Grn. Rd.)
Metchley Ho. B17: Harb 6H 115
Metchley La. B17: Harb 1H 131

Metchley Pk. Rd. B15: Edg 1H 131
Metfield Cft. B17: Harb 1H 131
DY6: K'wfrd 3D 92
Metric Wlk. B67: Smeth 4E 99
Metropolitan Ho. B16: Birm 2C 116
(off Hagley Rd.)
Metropolitan Lofts DY1: Dud 6E 77
(off Parson's St.)
Metro Triangle B7: Nech 2D 102
Metro Way B66: Smeth 2G 99
Mews, The B27: A Grn 2H 135
B44: K'sdng 6B 68
B65: Row R 1B 112
B66: Smeth 5E 99
Meynell Ho. B20: Hand 4B 82
Meyrick Rd. B70: W Brom 1G 79
Meyrick Wlk. B16: Edg 2B 116
Miall Pk. Rd. B91: Sol 2C 150
Miall Rd. B28: Hall G 5G 135
Michael Blanning Gdns.
B93: Dorr 6A 166
Michael Blanning Ho. B13: Mose 3B 134
(off Wake Grn. Pk.)
Michael Blanning Pl. CV7: Bal C 2H 169
Michael Ct. B5: Edg 5F 117
Michael Dr. B15: Edg 4E 117
Michael Rd. B67: Smeth 3C 98
WS10: Darl 4B 46
Michelle Cl. B13: Mose 2A 148
Micklehill Dr. B90: Shir 1H 163
Mickle Mdw. B46: Wat O 4D 88
Mickleover Rd. B8: W End 4A 104
Mickleton Av. B33: Sheld 3G 121
Mickleton Rd. B92: Olton 5B 136
Mickley Av. WV10: Wolv 4A 28
Midaacre WV13: W'hall 2A 46
Middle Acre Rd. B32: Bart G 3C 130
Middle Av. WV13: W'hall 3G 45
Middle Bickenhill La. B92: Bick 1A 140
Middle Cres. WS3: Wals 2E 33
Middle Cross WV1: Wolv 4D 170 (2H 43)
Middle Dr. B45: Coft H 5B 158
Middlefield B90: Pend 5C 14
Middlefield Av. B62: B'hth 3F 113
B93: Know 5D 166
Middlefield Cl. B62: B'hth 2F 113
Middlefield Gdns. B62: B'hth 3F 113
(off Hurst Grn. Rd.)
Middlefield Ho. B14: K Hth 4H 147
(off Britford Cl.)
Middle Fld. Rd. B31: N'fld 5G 145
Middlefield Rd. B69: Tiv 1A 96
Middle Gdns. WV13: W'hall 1B 46
MIDDLE HILL 1B 6
MIDDLE HILL JUNC. 1A 6
Middlehill Ri. B32: Bart G 3B 130
Middle La. B38: Head H 3E 161
B47: Wyt 3E 161
WV8: Oaken 5C 12
WV9: Coven 3D 14
Middle Leaford B34: Stech 4E 105
Middle Leasowe B32: Quin 1A 130
Middle Mdw. DY4: Tip 2B 78
Middle Mdw. Av. B32: Quin 6A 114
Middlemist Gro. B43: Gt Barr 1B 82
Middlemore Bus. Pk. WS9: A'rdge . . .4H 33
Middlemore Ind. Est. B21: Hand 1F 99
Middlemore La. WS9: A'rdge 3B 34
Middlemore La. W. WS9: A'rdge 3H 33
Middlemore Rd. B21: Hand 2F 99
B31: N'fld 5F 145
B66: Smeth 2F 99
B71: W Brom 2F 99
Middle Pk. Cl. B29: W Cas 5F 131
Middle Pk. Dr. B31: N'fld 1F 145
Middle Pk. Rd. B29: W Cas 5F 131
Middlepark Rd. DY1: Dud 1A 94
Middle Rd. B61: Wild 5A 156
Middleton Cl. WS5: Wals 6D 48
(not continuous)
WS7: Hamm 1F 11
Middleton Gdns. B30: K Nor 3H 145
Middleton Grange B31: N'fld 3G 145
Middleton Hall Rd. B30: K Nor 3H 145

Middleton Rd.—Minstead Rd.

Middleton Rd. B14: K Hth .6G 133
B74: S'tly .2A 52
B90: Shir .5G 149
WS8: Bwnhls .4C 10
Middleton Trad. Est. WV13: W'hall .1G 45
Middletree Rd. B63: Crad .4E 111
Middle Vauxhall WV1: Wolv .1E 43
Middleway B15: Birm .3D 116
Middleway Av. DY8: Word .6A 92
Middleway Grn. WV14: Bils .3E 45
Middleway Ind. Est. *B12: Birm .4H 117*
(off Moseley Rd.)
Middleway Rd. WV14: Bils .3E 45
Middleway Vw. B18: Hock .6C 100
Midford Gro. B15: Birm .3E 117
Midgley Dr. B74: Four O .1G 53
Midhill Dr. B65: Row R .3C 96
Midhurst Gro. WV6: Tett .4A 26
Midhurst Rd. B30: K Nor .4D 146
Midland Cl. B21: Hand .2C 100
Midland Ct. B3: Birm .1B 4
Midland Cft. B33: Kitts G .6H 105
Midland Dr. B72: S Cold .6A 54
Midland Karting
Walsall .5B 32
Midland Rd. B30: K Nor .2B 146
B74: S Cold .4G 53
WS1: Wals .2B 48
WS10: Darl .3C 46
Midland Sailing Club .6A 100
Midlands Art Cen. .1F 133
Midland St. B8: Birm .6C 102
B9: Birm .6C 102
Midpoint Blvd. B76: Min .2G 87
Midpoint Pk. B76: Min .3G 87
Midvale Dr. B14: K Hth .5F 147
Milburn Rd. B44: K'sdng .2A 68
Milcote Dr. B73: New O .2C 68
WV13: W'hall .2F 45
Milcote Rd. B29: W Cas .5E 131
B67: Smeth .1D 114
B91: Sol .3F 151
Milcote Way DY6: K'wfrd .2H 91
Mildenhall Rd. B42: Gt Barr .4C 66
Mildred Rd. B64: Old H .1G 111
Mildred Way B65: Row R .3C 96
Milebrook Gro. B32: Bart G .5H 129
Mile Flat DY6: K'wfrd .3E 91
Mile Oak Ct. B66: Smeth .3F 99
Milesbush Av. B36: Cas B .6H 87
Miles Gro. DY2: Dud .2H 95
Miles Mdw. Cl. WV12: W'hall .1C 30
Milestone Ct. WV6: Tett .6G 25
Milestone Cft. B63: Crad .6E 111
Milestone La. B21: Hand .1H 99
Milestone Way WV12: W'hall .1B 30
Milford Av. B12: Bal H .5A 118
WV12: W'hall .4A 30
Milford Cl. DY8: Word .6C 92
Milford Copse B17: Harb .6F 115
Milford Cft. B19: Birm .4F 101
B65: Row R .3H 95
Milford Gro. B90: M'path .2G 165
Milford Ho. B23: Erd .3C 84
Milford Pl. B14: K Hth .5G 133
Milford Rd. B17: Harb .6F 115
WV2: Wolv .4G 43
Milholme Grn. B92: Sol .5H 137
MILKING BANK .5A 76
Milking Bank DY1: Dud .5H 75
Milk St. B5: Birm .6H 5 (2H 117)
Millard Ind. Est. B70: W Brom .6G 79
Millard Rd. WV14: Cose .4D 60
Mill Bank DY3: Sed .5H 59
Millbank Gro. B23: Erd .1B 84
(not continuous)
Millbank St. WV11: Wed .6H 17
Mill Brook Dr. B31: Longb .1C 158
Millbrook Rd. B14: K Hth .1E 147
Millbrook Way DY5: Brie H .3F 109
Mill Burn Way B9: Birm .1B 118
Mill Cl. B47: H'wd .2A 162
Mill Cft. WV14: Bils .5G 45
Millcroft Cl. B32: Bart G .3C 130
Millcroft Rd. B74: S'tly .3A 52
Milldale Cres. WV10: F'hses .3H 15
Milldale Rd. WV10: F'hses .3H 15
Mill Dr. B66: Smeth .4F 99
Millennium Apartments B3: Birm .2C 4
Millennium Cl. WS3: Pels .4E 21
Millennium Gdns. B64: Old H .1H 111
Millennium Pk. B70: W Brom .2G 79
Millennium Point .3H 5 (6H 101)
Millennium Way WV8: Bilb .3H 13
Miller Ct. B33: Stech .6C 104
Miller Cres. WV14: Cose .4C 60
Millers Cl. WS2: Wals .2F 47
Millers Ct. *B66: Smeth .4F 99*
(off Corbett St.)
B90: Shir .5F 149
Millersdale Dr. B71: W Brom .3D 64
Millers Grn. Dr. DY6: W Hth .1G 91
Miller St. B6: Aston .4G 101
Millers Va. WV5: Wom .2D 72
Millers Wlk. WS3: Pels .4C 20
Mill Farm Rd. B17: Harb .2G 131
Millfield B31: N'fld .3E 145
Millfield Av. WS3: Blox .5B 20
WS4: S'fld .6F 21
Millfield Ct. *DY1: Dud .5C 76*
(off Pelham Dr.)
Millfield Rd. B20: Hand .2A 82
WS8: Bwnhls .6C 10
Millfields B33: Kitts G .6H 105
(not continuous)
Millfields Cl. B71: W Brom .4H 63
Millfields Rd. B71: W Brom .4H 63
WV4: E'shll .6C 44
WV14: Bils .6C 44
Millfields Way WV5: Wom .1E 73
Millfield Vw. B63: Hale .1G 127
Millford Cl. B28: Hall G .2G 149
Mill Gdns. B14: Yard W .2D 148
B67: Smeth .6D 98
MILL GREEN .2A 36
Mill Grn. WV10: F'hses .3H 15
Mill Gro. WV8: Bilb .4A 14
Millhaven Av. B30: Stir .1D 146
Mill Hill B67: Smeth .6D 98
Mill Ho. B8: W End .5B 104
Mill Ho. La. B75: Can .1D 38
Millhouse Rd. B25: Yard .3H 119
Millicent Pl. B12: Bal H .5A 118
Millichip Rd. WV13: W'hall .2G 45
Millington Rd. B36: Hodg H .1C 104
DY4: Tip .4H 61
WV10: Bush .3A 28
Millison Gro. B90: M'path .2E 165
Mill La. B5: Birm .6G 5 (2H 117)
B31: N'fld .6D 144
B32: Bart G .3B 130
B61: Wild .6A 156
B63: Hale .1C 128
B69: O'bry .5G 97
B91: Sol .4G 151
B93: Ben H, Dorr .5A 166
DY7: Stourt .6A 90
WS3: Wals .5D 32
WS4: Wals .5D 32
WS7: Hamm .2F 11
WS9: A'rdge .2H 35
WS9: Ston .3H 23
WV5: Swind .4D 72
WV5: Wom .6H 57
WV6: Tett .6G 25
WV8: Cod .2F 13
WV11: Wed .2C 28
WV12: W'hall .4C 30
Mill La. Arc. *B91: Sol .4G 151*
(off Touchwood Shop. Cen.)
Millmead Lodge B13: Mose .5D 134
Mill Mdw. DY8: Amb .5E 109
Millmead Rd. B32: Bart G .3C 130
Mill Pl. WS3: Wals .5C 32
Millpool, The WV5: Seis .3A 56
Mill Pool Cl. WV5: Wom .2D 72
Millpool Gdns. B14: K Hth .4H 147
Millpool Hill B14: K Hth .3H 147
Millpool Way B66: Smeth .5E 99
Millport Rd. WV4: E'shll .6B 44
Mill Race La. DY8: Amb .5E 109
Mill Rd. B64: Crad H .4G 111
WS4: S'fld .6F 21
WS8: Bwnhls .6C 10
Mills Av. B76: Walm .1C 70
Mills Cl. WV11: Wed .1D 28
Mills Cres. WV2: Wolv .3A 44
Millside B28: Hall G .4E 149
WV5: Wom .2E 73
Mills Rd. WV2: Wolv .3A 44
Millstone Cl. B76: Walm .4D 70
Mill Stream Cl. WV8: Bilb .3H 13
Mill St. B6: Birm .4H 101
B63: Crad .4E 111
B70: W Brom .3A 80
B72: S Cold .6A 54
DY4: Tip .2D 78
DY5: Brie H .1H 109
DY8: Word .1C 108
WS2: Wals .6C 32
WS10: Darl .5C 46
WV13: W'hall .1C 46
WV14: Bils .6E 45
Millsum Ho. *WS1: Wals .2D 48*
(off Paddock La.)
Mills Wlk. DY4: Tip .6H 61
Millthorpe Cl. B8: W End .4F 103
Mill Vw. B33: Kitts G .5G 105
Mill Wlk., The B31: N'fld .6D 144
Millwalk Dr. WV9: Pend .4E 15
Millward St. B9: Small H .2C 118
B70: W Brom .4G 79
Millwright Cl. DY4: Tip .2B 78
Milner Rd. B29: S Oak .4C 132
Milner Way B13: Mose .5D 134
Milnes Walker Ct. B44: Gt Barr .4G 67
Milsom Gro. B34: S End .3H 105
Milstead Rd. B26: Yard .2E 121
Milston Cl. B14: K Hth .6G 147
Milton Av. B12: Bal H .5A 118
Milton Cl. B93: Ben H .5B 166
DY8: Amb .4E 109
WS1: Wals .5B 48
WV12: W'hall .2E 31
Milton Ct. B66: Smeth .2E 115
WV6: Pert .5E 25
Milton Cres. B25: Yard .4B 120
DY3: Lwr G .2E 75
Milton Dr. DY9: Hag .6H 125
Milton Gro. B29: S Oak .2B 132
Milton Pl. WS1: Wals .5B 48
Milton Rd. B67: Smeth .4B 98
B93: Ben H .5B 166
WV10: Wolv .4C 28
WV14: Cose .5F 61
Milton St. B19: Hock .3G 101
B71: W Brom .2H 79
DY5: P'ntt .3H 93
WS1: Wals .3B 48
Milverton Cl. B63: Hale .5A 112
B76: Walm .6D 70
Milverton Ct. *B62: Quin .4G 113*
(off Binswood Rd.)
Milverton Rd. B23: Erd .3E 85
B93: Know .4E 167
Mimosa Cl. B29: W Cas .5F 131
Mimosa Wlk. DY6: K'wfrd .1C 92
Mincing La. B65: Row R .6D 96
Mindelsohn Way B15: Edg .1A 132
Minden Gro. B29: S Oak .4F 131
Minehead Rd. DY1: Dud .1H 93
WV10: Oxl .5F 15
Miner St. WS2: Wals .6A 32
Minerva Cl. WV12: W'hall .5E 31
Minewood Cl. WS3: Blox .4F 19
Minith Rd. WV14: Cose .5F 61
Miniva Dr. B76: Walm .4E 71
Minivet Dr. B12: Bal H .5G 117
Minley Av. B17: Harb .4D 114
Minories B4: Birm .3E 5 (6G 101)
Minories, The DY2: Dud .6E 77
Minstead Rd. B24: Erd .6D 84

Minster, The. WV3: Wolv 4D 42
Minster Cl. B65: Row R 6E 97
  B93: Know 1D 166
Minster Ct. B13: Mose 1A 134
  B29: W Cas 6G 131
    (off Abdon Av.)
Minster Dr. B10: Small H 4D 118
Minsterley Cl. WV3: Wolv 3C 42
Mintern Rd. B25: Yard 3A 120
Minto Ho. B12: Bal H 6G 117
Minton Cl. WV1: Wolv 2C 44
Minton Rd. B32: Quin 1D 130
MINWORTH 2H 87
Minworth Ind. Est. B76: Min 1E 87
Minworth Ind. Pk. B76: Min 1G 87
Minworth Rd. B46: Wat O 4C 88
Miraj Av. B11: S'hll 2B 134
Miranda Cl. B45: Fran 4G 143
Mirfield Cl. WV9: Pend 4E 15
Mirfield Rd. B33: Kitts G 1F 121
  B91: Sol 1E 151
Mission Cl. B64: Old H 2A 112
Mission Dr. DY4: Tip 4A 78
Mistletoe Dr. WS5: Wals 2F 65
Mitcham Cl. B29: W Cas 6G 131
    (off Abdon Av.)
Mitcham Gro. B44: K'sdng 4B 68
Mitcheldean Covert B14: K Hth 5F 147
Mitchell Av. WV14: Cose 4D 60
Mitchells Art & Craft Cen. 1C 54
Mitchel Rd. DY6: K'wfrd 5D 92
Mitford Dr. B92: Sol 6H 137
Mitre Cl. WV11: Ess 4A 18
  WV12: W'hall 2D 30
Mitre Ct. B74: S Cold 5A 54
Mitre Fold WV1: Wolv 2A 170 (6G 27)
Mitre Rd. DY9: Lye 6A 110
  WS6: C Hay 2E 6
Mitten Av. B45: Fran 6F 143
Mitton Rd. B20: Hand 5A 82
Moatbrook Av. WV8: Cod 3E 13
Moatbrook La. WV8: Cod 2C 12
Moat Coppice B32: Bart G 4H 129
Moat Cft. B37: F'bri 1C 122
  B76: Walm 6F 71
Moat Dr. B34: Hodg H 3E 105
  B62: B'hth 2E 113
Moat Farm Dr. B32: Bart G 4G 129
Moat Farm Way WS3: Pels 2E 21
Moatfield Ter. WS10: W'bry 2G 63
Moat Grn. Av. WV11: Wed 2G 29
Moat Ho. B31: Longb 1D 158
Moat Ho. La. E. WV11: Wed 2F 29
Moat Ho. La. W. WV11: Wed 2F 29
Moat Ho. Rd. B8: W End 5G 103
Moat La. B5: Birm 6F 5 (1G 117)
  B26: Yard 4C 120
  B91: Sol 1G 151
  WS6: Gt Wyr 3G 7
Moat Mdws. B32: Quin 1C 130
Moatmead Wlk. B36: Hodg H 1C 104
Moat Rd. B68: O'bry 1H 113
  DY4: Tip 6A 62
  WS2: Wals 1H 47
Moatside Cl. WS3: Pels 2E 21
Moat St. WV13: W'hall 1A 46
Moatway, The B38: K Nor 2A 160
Mobberley Rd. WV14: Cose 4C 60
Mob La. WS4: S'fld 5G 21
Mockleywood Rd. B93: Know 2D 166
Modbury Av. B32: Bart G 4B 130
Moden Cl. DY3: Up Gor 2H 75
Moden Hill DY3: Sed 1G 75
Mogul La. B63: Crad 4C 110
Moilliett Ct. B66: Smeth 3G 99
Moilliett St. B18: Win G 5H 99
Moira Cres. B14: Yard W 3C 148
Moises Hall Rd. WV5: Wom 6A 58
Moland St. B4: Birm 5G 101
Mole St. B11: S'brk 5B 118
Molineux 1A 170 (6G 27)
Molineux All. WV1: Wolv . . .1A 170 (6G 27)
    (not continuous)
Molineux Fold WV1: Wolv . . .1B 170 (6G 27)

Molineux St. WV1: Wolv 1B 170 (6G 27)
Mollington Cres. B90: Shir 4A 150
Molyneux Rd. DY2: Neth 1G 111
Monaco Ho. B5: Birm 3F 117
Monarch Dr. DY4: Tip 1C 78
Monarch Ind. Est. B11: Tys 5G 119
Monarchs Ga. B91: Sol 2A 152
Monarch Way DY2: Neth 5E 95
Mona Rd. B23: Erd 2F 85
Monastery Dr. B91: Sol 1B 150
Monckton Rd. B68: O'bry 4G 113
Moncrieffe Cl. DY2: Dud 1G 95
Moncrieffe St. WS1: Wals 2E 49
Money La. B61: C'wich 4A 156
Monica Rd. B10: Small H 4F 119
Monins Av. DY4: Tip 4A 78
Monk Cl. DY4: Tip 4B 78
Monkgate Dr. B71: W Brom 1A 80
Monk Rd. B8: W End 4H 103
Monksclose Cl. WV5: Wom 1E 73
Monkseaton Rd. B72: W Grn 3H 69
Monksfield Av. B43: Gt Barr 4H 65
Monkshood M. B23: Erd 6B 68
Monkshood Retreat B38: K Nor 1B 160
Monks Kirby Rd. B76: Walm 2D 70
MONKSPATH 3E 165
Monkspath Bus. Pk. B90: Shir 1D 164
Monkspath Cl. B90: Shir 2B 164
Monkspath Hall Rd. B90: M'path 3D 164
  B91: Sol 1F 165
Monkspath Leisure Pk. 3C 164
Monksway B38: K Nor 6D 146
Monkswell Cl. B10: Small H 4D 118
  DY5: Brie H 2H 109
Monkswood Rd. B31: N'fld 5G 145
Monkton Rd. B29: W Cas 2E 131
Monmar Ct. WV12: W'hall 4B 30
Monmer Cl. WV13: W'hall 6B 30
Monmer Cl. Ind. Est. WV13: W'hall 6C 30
Monmer La. WV13: W'hall 5B 30
Monmore Bus. Pk. WV2: Wolv 4B 44
MONMORE GREEN 3H 43
Monmore Green Stadium 3C 44
Monmore Pk. Ind. Est. WV2: E'shll 4B 44
Monmore Rd. WV1: Wolv 3C 44
Monmouth Dr. B71: W Brom 6H 63
  B73: New O, S Cold 2C 68
Monmouth Ho. B33: Kitts G 1A 122
Monmouth Rd. B32: Bart G 5B 130
  B67: Smeth 3C 114
  WS2: Wals 6E 31
Monsal Av. WV10: Wolv 5A 28
Monsaldale Cl. WS8: Clay 1H 21
Monsal Rd. B42: Gt Barr 6E 67
Mons Rd. DY2: Dud 6G 77
Montague Rd. B16: Edg 2A 116
  B21: Hand 1B 100
  B24: Erd 6G 85
  B66: Smeth 6F 99
Montague St. B6: Aston 1B 102
  B9: Birm 1A 118
Montana Av. B42: P Barr 2C 82
Montano Dr. WV10: Bush 3A 28
Monteagle Dr. DY6: K'wfrd 6B 74
Montford Gro. DY3: Sed 6H 59
Montfort Rd. B46: Col 4H 107
  WS2: Wals 5H 47
Montgomery Cres. DY5: Quar B 4B 110
Montgomery Cft. B11: S'brk 4C 118
Montgomery Rd. WS2: Wals 1E 47
Montgomery St. B11: S'brk 4B 118
Montgomery St. Bus. Cen. . . . .
  B11: S'brk 4C 118
Montgomery Wlk. B71: W Brom 3B 80
Montgomery Way B8: Salt 5G 103
Montpelier Gdns. DY1: Dud 5A 76
Montpellier St. B12: Birm 5A 118
Montreal Ho. B5: Edg 4F 117
Montrose Dr. B35: Cas V 4E 87
  DY1: Dud 1C 94
Montsford Cl. B93: Know 3B 166

Monument Av. DY9: W'cte 1A 126
Monument La. B45: Lick 5F 157
  DY3: Sed 4A 60
  DY9: Hag 6H 125
Monument Rd. B16: Birm, Edg 2B 116
    (not continuous)
Monway Ind. Est. WS10: W'bry 2E 63
Monway Ter. WS10: W'bry 2E 63
Monwood Gro. B91: Sol 5D 150
Monyhull Hall Rd. B30: K Nor 5D 146
Moodyscroft Rd. B33: Kitts G 6G 105
Moons La. WS6: C Hay 3D 6
Moor, The B76: Walm 5E 71
Moor Cen., The DY5: Brie H 6H 93
Moorcroft WV14: Bils 2A 62
Moorcroft Dr. WS10: W'bry 3C 62
Moorcroft Nine WS10: W'bry 3C 62
Moorcroft Pl. B7: Birm 5A 102
Moorcroft Rd. B13: Mose 2G 133
Moordown Av. B92: Olton 3E 137
Moore Cl. B74: Four O 3F 37
  WV6: Pert 5F 25
Moore Cres. B68: O'bry 6A 98
Moorend Av. B37: Chel W, Mars G . . .3B 122
Moor End La. B24: Erd 3G 85
Moore Rd. WV12: W'hall 1D 30
Moore's Row B5: Birm 6H 5 (2H 117)
Moore St. WV1: Wolv 2B 44
Moorfield Av. B93: Know 3A 166
Moorfield Dr. B63: Hale 5H 111
  B73: Bold 5F 69
Moorfield Rd. B34: S End 3E 105
  WV2: Wolv 4G 43
Moorfoot Av. B63: Hale 4E 127
MOOR GREEN 4E 133
Moor Grn. La. B13: Mose 4E 133
Moor Hall Dr. B75: R'ley 3A 54
Moor Hall Way B75: R'ley 2B 54
Moorhen Cl. WS8: Bwnhls 6A 10
Moorhills Cft. B90: Shir 1H 163
Moor Ho. B14: K Hth 5E 147
    (off Druids La.)
Moorings, The B18: Win G 4B 100
  B69: O'bry 1E 97
  DY5: Brie H 5B 94
  WV9: Pend 5D 14
Moorland Av. WV10: Oxl 3G 27
Moorland Rd. B16: Edg 2H 115
  WS3: Blox 1G 31
Moorlands, The B74: Four O 3F 53
Moorlands Cl. B75: S Cold 5D 54
Moorlands Ct. B65: Row R 5D 96
Moorlands Dr. B90: Shir 4A 150
Moorlands Rd. B71: W Brom 4A 64
Moor La. B6: Witt 1H 83
  B65: Row R 1A 112
Moor La. Ind. Est. B6: Witt 3A 84
Moor Leasow B31: N'fld 5G 145
Moor Mdw. Rd. B75: S Cold 4B 54
Moor Pk. WS3: Blox 4H 19
  WV6: Pert 4D 24
Moorpark Rd. B31: Longb 6E 145
Moor Pool Av. B17: Harb 5G 115
Moorpool Ter. B17: Harb 5G 115
Moors, The B36: Hodg H 1D 104
Moors Cft. B32: Bart G 4H 129
Moorside Gdns. WS2: Wals 6H 31
Moorside Rd. B14: Yard W 3C 148
Moor's La. B31: N'fld 5C 130
Moors Mill La. DY4: Tip 6D 62
Moorsom St. B6: Aston 4G 101
MOOR STREET 3G 129
Moor St. B5: Birm 5F 5
  B70: W Brom 5A 80
  DY5: Brie H 6E 93
  WS10: W'bry 3H 63
Moor St. Ind. Est. DY5: Brie H 1G 109
Moor St. Queensway
  B4: Birm 4F 5 (1G 117)
Moor St. Sth. WV1: Wolv 4G 43
Moor Street Station (Rail) 4F 5 (1G 117)
Moorville Wlk. B11: S'brk 4A 118
Morar Cl. B35: Cas V 3G 87
Moray Cl. B62: B'hth 3E 113

Morcom Rd.—Muxloe Cl.

Morcom Rd. B11: Tys . . . 6E 119
Mordaunt Dr. B75: R'ley . . . 1C 54
Morden Rd. B33: Stech . . . 6B 104
Morefields Cl. WS9: A'rdge . . . 2C 34
Moreland Cft. B76: Walm . . . 1F 87
Morelands, The B31: N'fld . . . 6F 145
Morestead Av. B26: Sheld . . . 6G 121
Moreton Av. B43: Gt Barr . . . 2E 67
WV4: E'shll . . . 1A 60
Moreton Cl. B25: Yard . . . 4H 119
B32: Harb . . . 6D 114
(not continuous)
DY4: Tip . . . 3B 62
Moreton Rd. B90: Shir . . . 5A 150
WV10: Bush . . . 6H 15
Moreton St. B1: Birm . . . 5D 100
Morford Rd. WS9: A'rdge . . . 2C 34
Morgan Cl. B64: Old H . . . 3G 111
B69: O'bry . . . 1D 96
WV12: W'hall . . . 5B 30
Morgan Ct. B24: Erd . . . 1A 86
Morgan Dr. WV14: Cose . . . 5D 60
Morgan Gro. B36: Cas B . . . 6B 88
Morgans Bus. Pk. WS11: Nort C . . . 1D 8
Morgrove Av. B93: Know . . . 3B 166
Morjon Dr. B43: Gt Barr . . . 3B 66
Morland Rd. B31: N'fld . . . 6D 144
B43: Gt Barr . . . 1E 67
Morley Gro. WV6: Wolv . . . 5G 27
Morley Rd. B8: W End . . . 3H 103
Morlich Ri. DY5: Brie H . . . 3F 109
Morning Pines DY8: Stourb . . . 1C 124
Morningside B73: S Cold . . . 5H 53
Mornington Ct. B46: Col . . . 2H 107
Mornington Rd. B66: Smeth . . . 2F 99
Morris Av. WS2: Wals . . . 1E 47
Morris Cl. B27: A Grn . . . 1B 136
Morris Ct. DY5: Brie H . . . 2F 109
Morris Cft. B36: Cas B . . . 6A 88
Morris Fld. Cft. B28: Hall G . . . 3E 149
Morrison Av. WV10: Bush . . . 1H 27
Morrison Rd. DY4: Tip . . . 3C 78
Morris Rd. B8: W End . . . 3H 103
Morris St. B70: W Brom . . . 6A 80
Morris Way B37: Mars G . . . 6F 123
B40: Mars G . . . 6F 123
Mortimers Cl. B14: K Hth . . . 6B 148
Morton Rd. DY5: Quar B . . . 4H 109
Morvale Gdns. DY9: Lye . . . 6A 110
Morvale St. DY9: Lye . . . 6A 110
Morven Rd. B73: S Cold . . . 3F 69
Morville Cl. B93: Dorr . . . 6H 165
Morville Cft. WV14: Bils . . . 1D 60
Morville Rd. DY2: Neth . . . 5F 95
Morville St. B16: Birm . . . 2C 116
(not continuous)
Mosborough Cres. B19: Birm . . . 4E 101
Mosedale Dr. WV11: Wed . . . 4H 29
Mosedale Way B15: Birm . . . 3F 117
MOSELEY
B13 . . . 2H 133
WV1 . . . 1E 45
WV10 . . . 3B 16
Moseley Bog Nature Reserve . . . 4C 134
Moseley Ct. B13: Mose . . . 3B 134
WV11: Ess . . . 4H 17
WV13: W'hall . . . 2F 45
Moseley Dovecote . . . 2G 133
Moseley Dr. B37: Mars G . . . 3B 122
Moseley Ga. B13: Mose . . . 2H 133
Moseley Old Hall . . . 2C 16
Moseley Old Hall La. WV10: F'stne . . . 2C 16
Moseley Pk. Sports Cen. . . . 3G 45
Moseley Rd. B12: Bal H, Birm . . . 6H 117
(not continuous)
WV10: Bush . . . 2B 16
WV13: W'hall . . . 2F 45
WV14: Bils . . . 2F 45
Moseley Road Swimming Pool . . . 6H 117
Moseley RUFC . . . 6B 134
Moseley St. B5: Birm . . . 2H 117
B12: Birm . . . 2H 117
DY4: Tip . . . 6C 62
WV10: Wolv . . . 5G 27
Moss Cl. WS4: Wals . . . 6E 33
WS9: A'rdge . . . 4C 34
Mossdale Way DY3: Sed . . . 6A 60
Moss Dr. B72: W Grn . . . 2A 70
Mossfield Rd. B14: K Hth . . . 6G 133
Moss Gdns. WV14: Cose . . . 2D 60
Moss Gro. B14: K Hth . . . 1F 147
DY6: K'wfrd . . . 2B 92
Moss Ho. Cl. B15: Birm . . . 2D 116
Mossley Cl. WS3: Blox . . . 6F 19
Mossley La. WS3: Blox . . . 5F 19
Mossvale Cl. B64: Old H . . . 2H 111
Mossvale Gro. B8: Salt . . . 4F 103
Moss Way B74: S'tly . . . 4H 51
Mostyn Cres. B71: W Brom . . . 6H 63
Mostyn Rd. B16: Edg . . . 1B 116
B21: Hand . . . 1B 100
Mostyn St. WV1: Wolv . . . 5F 27
Mother Teresa Ho. *B70: W Brom . . . 4H 79*
(off Baker St.)
Motorway Trad. Est.
B6: Birm . . . 4H 101
Mott Cl. DY4: Tip . . . 5C 62
Mottram Cl. B70: W Brom . . . 5G 79
Mottrams Cl. B72: W Grn . . . 3A 70
Mott St. B19: Birm . . . 1C 4 (5F 101)
Mott St. Ind. Est. B19: Birm . . . 5F 101
Motts Way B46: Col . . . 4H 107
Mounds, The B38: K Nor . . . 1A 160
Moundsley Gro. B14: K Hth . . . 4A 148
Moundsley Ho. B14: K Hth . . . 5G 147
Mount, The B23: Erd . . . 6D 84
B64: Old H . . . 2A 112
B76: Curd . . . 1E 89
Mountain Ash Dr. DY9: Pedm . . . 3G 125
Mountain Ash Rd. WS8: Clay . . . 2A 22
Mount Av. DY5: Brie H . . . 5G 93
Mountbatten Cl. B70: W Brom . . . 5D 80
Mountbatten Rd. WS2: Wals . . . 1F 47
Mount Cl. B13: Mose . . . 1H 133
DY3: Gorn . . . 5G 75
WS6: C Hay . . . 3E 7
WV5: Wom . . . 6G 57
Mount Ct. WV6: Tett . . . 1H 41
Mount Dr. WV5: Wom . . . 6G 57
Mountfield Cl. B14: K Hth . . . 5A 148
Mountford Cl. B65: Row R . . . 6C 96
Mountford Cres. WS9: A'rdge . . . 1E 35
Mountford Dr. B75: Four O . . . 3H 53
Mountford Ho. *B70: W Brom . . . 6C 80*
(off Glover St.)
Mountford La. WV14: Bils . . . 4F 45
Mountford Rd. B90: Shir . . . 6D 148
Mountford St. B11: S'hll . . . 6D 118
Mount Gdns. WV8: Cod . . . 3F 13
Mountjoy Cres. B92: Sol . . . 2G 137
Mount La. DY3: Gorn . . . 5G 75
Mt. Pleasant B10: Small H . . . 2B 118
B14: K Hth . . . 4H 133
DY5: Quar B . . . 2A 110
DY6: K'wfrd . . . 4H 91
WS6: C Hay . . . 3D 6
WV14: Bils . . . 5G 45
Mt. Pleasant Av. B21: Hand . . . 6A 82
WV5: Wom . . . 6F 57
Mt. Pleasant Ct. B10: Small H . . . 2B 118
Mt. Pleasant St. B70: W Brom . . . 5A 80
WV14: Cose . . . 5D 60
Mountrath St. WS1: Wals . . . 2C 48
Mount Rd. B21: Hand . . . 1H 99
B65: Row R . . . 6E 97
B69: Tiv . . . 1C 96
DY8: Stourb . . . 6F 109
DY8: Word . . . 1B 108
WS3: Pels . . . 3E 21
WV4: E'shll . . . 3B 60
WV4: Penn . . . 6E 43
WV5: Wom . . . 6G 57
WV6: Tett . . . 1G 41
WV13: W'hall . . . 3G 45
Mounts Rd. WS10: W'bry . . . 3F 63
Mount St. B7: Nech . . . 3C 102
B63: Hale . . . 3A 128
DY4: Tip . . . 1C 78
Mount St. DY8: Stourb . . . 6E 109
WS1: Wals . . . 3C 48
Mount St. Bus. Cen. B7: Nech . . . 3C 102
Mount St. Ind. Est. B7: Nech . . . 2D 102
Mounts Way B7: Nech . . . 2C 102
Mount Vw. B75: S Cold . . . 1C 70
Mountwood Covert WV6: Tett . . . 6H 25
Mousehall Farm Rd. DY5: Quar B . . . 3H 109
Mouse Hill WS3: Pels . . . 4D 20
MOUSESWEET . . . 6G 95
Mousesweet Brook Nature Reserve
. . . 2D 110
Mousesweet Cl. DY2: Neth . . . 5G 95
Mousesweet La. DY2: Neth . . . 6G 95
Mousesweet Wlk. B64: Crad H . . . 3D 110
Mowbray Cl. B45: Fran . . . 5G 143
Mowbray St. B5: Birm . . . 3G 117
Mowe Cft. B37: Mars G . . . 4C 122
Moxhull Cl. WV12: W'hall . . . 6C 18
Moxhull Dr. B76: Walm . . . 5C 70
Moxhull Gdns. WV12: W'hall . . . 6C 18
Moxhull Rd. B37: K'hrst . . . 4C 106
MOXLEY . . . 1B 62
Moxley Ct. WS10: Mox . . . 1A 62
Moxley Ind. Cen. WS10: Mox . . . 1C 62
Moxley Rd. WS10: Darl . . . 1B 62
Moyle Dr. B63: Crad . . . 4D 110
Moyses Cft. B66: Smeth . . . 1E 99
Muchall Rd. WV4: Penn . . . 6E 43
MUCKLEY CORNER . . . 4H 11
Mucklow Hill B62: Hale . . . 1C 128
Mucklow Hill Trad. Est. B62: Hale . . . 6C 112
Muirfield Cl. WS3: Blox . . . 4G 19
Muirfield Cres. B69: Tiv . . . 2A 96
Muirfield Gdns. B38: K Nor . . . 6H 145
Muirhead Ho. B5: Edg . . . 5E 117
Muirville Cl. DY8: Word . . . 6B 92
Mulberry Dr. B13: Mose . . . 4B 134
Mulberry Grn. DY1: Dud . . . 2B 76
Mulberry Pl. WS3: Blox . . . 6F 19
Mulberry Rd. B30: B'vlle . . . 2G 145
WS3: Blox . . . 6F 19
Mulberry Wlk. B74: S'tly . . . 3G 51
Mull Cl. B45: Fran . . . 6E 143
Mull Cft. B36: Cas B . . . 2C 106
Mullens Gro. Rd. B37: K'hrst . . . 4C 106
Mullett Rd. WV11: Wed . . . 2D 28
Mullett St. DY5: P'ntt . . . 4F 93
Mulliners Cl. B37: Chel W . . . 1E 123
Mullion Cft. B38: K Nor . . . 6A 146
Mulroy Rd. B74: S Cold . . . 5H 53
Mulwych Rd. B33: Kitts G . . . 6A 106
Munslow Gro. B31: Longb . . . 1D 158
Muntz Ho. B16: Edg . . . 2C 116
Muntz St. B10: Small H . . . 3D 118
Murcroft Rd. DY9: W'cte . . . 4H 125
Murdoch Dr. DY6: K'wfrd . . . 2A 92
Murdoch Rd. WV14: Bils . . . 5A 46
Murdock Ct. *WV12: W'hall . . . 2D 30*
(off Huntington Rd.)
Murdock Gro. B21: Hand . . . 2A 100
Murdock Pl. *B66: Smeth . . . 5F 99*
(off Corbett St.)
Murdock Rd. B21: Hand . . . 1A 100
B66: Smeth . . . 3H 99
Murdock Way WS2: Wals . . . 3F 31
Murray Ct. B73: S Cold . . . 2G 69
Murrell Cl. B5: Edg . . . 4F 117
Musborough Cl. B36: Cas B . . . 6G 87
Muscott Gro. B17: Harb . . . 6F 115
Muscovy Rd. B23: Erd . . . 4C 84
Mus. of the Jewellery Quarter . . . *4E 101*
(off Vyse St.)
Musgrave Cl. B76: Walm . . . 2C 70
Musgrave Rd. B18: Hock . . . 3B 100
MUSHROOM GREEN . . . 1D 110
Mushroom Grn. DY2: Neth . . . 2D 110
Mushroom Hall Rd. B68: O'bry . . . 4H 97
Musk La. DY3: Lwr G . . . 4F 75
Musk La. Trad. Est. DY3: Lwr G . . . 4G 75
Musk La. W. DY3: Lwr G . . . 4F 75
Musson Grn. B37: Mars G . . . 3D 122
Muswell Cl. B91: Sol . . . 2H 151
Muxloe Cl. WS3: Blox . . . 4G 19

Myatt Av. WS9: A'rdge 4B 34
  WV2: E'shll 5A 44
Myatt Cl. WV2: E'shll 5A 44
Myatt Way WS9: A'rdge 4B 34
Myddleton St. B18: Hock 5C 100
Myles Ct. DY5: Brie H 5H 93
Mynors Cres. B47: H'wd 4A 162
Myring Dr. B75: S Cold 5D 54
Myrtle Av. B12: Bal H 6A 118
  B14: K Hth 5H 147
Myrtle Cl. WV12: W'hall 2E 31
Myrtle Gro. B19: Hand 1E 101
  WV3: Wolv 5C 42
Myrtle Pl. B29: S Oak 3D 132
Myrtle Rd. DY1: Dud 4D 76
Myrtle St. WV2: E'shll 5B 44
Myrtle Ter. DY4: Tip 3B 62
Myton Dr. B90: Shir 5D 148
Mytton Cl. DY2: Dud 6G 77
Mytton Gro. DY4: Tip 2G 77
Mytton Rd. B30: B'vlle 2G 145
  B46: Wat O 4C 88
Myvod Rd. WS10: W'bry 6G 47

N

Naden Rd. B19: Hock 3D 100
Nadin Rd. B73: W Grn 5G 69
Nafford Gro. B14: K Hth 5H 147
Nagersfield Rd. DY5: Brie H 6E 93
Nailers Cl. B32: Bart G 3F 129
Nailers Row WV5: Wom 2F 73
Nailors Fold WV14: Cose 3F 61
Nailstone Cres. B27: A Grn 5A 136
Nairn Cl. B28: Hall G 2F 149
Nairn Rd. WS3: Blox 3G 19
Nally Dr. WV14: Cose 3C 60
Nanaimo Way DY6: K'wfrd 5E 93
Nansen Rd. B8: Salt 4E 103
  B11: S'hll 2C 134
Nantmel Gro. B32: Bart G 5A 130
Naomi Way WS9: Wals W 3D 22
Napier Dr. DY4: Tip 1C 78
Napier Rd. WS2: Wals 4G 31
  WV2: Wolv 4H 43
Napton Gro. B29: W Cas 3D 130
Narel Sharpe Cl. B66: Smeth 2B 98
Narraway Gro. DY4: Tip 5D 62
Narrowboat Way DY2: Dud 5C 94
  DY5: Brie H 5C 94
Narrow La. B62: B'hth 3E 113
  WS2: Wals 4H 47
  WS8: Bwnhls 6B 10
Naseby Dr. B63: Hale 3F 127
Naseby Rd. B8: Salt 4F 103
  B91: Sol 1F 151
  WV6: Pert 6F 25
Nash Av. WV6: Pert 6E 25
Nash Cl. B65: B'hth 2C 112
Nash Cft. B37: Mars G 3D 122
Nash Ho. B15: Birm 3F 117
Nash Sq. B42: P Barr 3F 83
Nash Wlk. B66: Smeth 4G 99
  (off Poplar St.)
Nately Gro. B29: S Oak 3G 131
Nathan Cl. B75: S Cold 3H 53
National Exhibition Cen. 6F 123
National Indoor Arena 4A 4 (1D 116)
National Motorcycle Mus. 3A 140
National Sea Life Cen. 4A 4 (1D 116)
Naunton Cl. B29: W Cas 6E 131
Naunton Rd. WS2: Wals 6G 31
Navenby Cl. B90: Shir 4C 148
Navigation Dr. B14: K Hth 4F 147
  B30: K Nor 1F 147
  DY5: Brie H 5C 94
Navigation La. WS10: W'bry 3D 64
Navigation Rdbt. DY4: Tip 1E 79
Navigation St. B2: Birm 5C 4 (1F 117)
  WS2: Wals 1B 48
  WV1: Wolv 2A 44
Navigation Way B18: Win G 4B 100
  B70: W Brom 5F 79

Nayland Cft. B28: Hall G 2G 149
Naylors Gro. DY3: Up Gor 3A 76
NEACHELL 5F 29
Neachells La. WV11: Wed 4F 29
  WV13: W'hall 1F 45
Neachells La. Ind. Est. WV11: Wed . . .5F 29
Neachless Av. WV5: Wom 2B 73
Neachley Gro. B33: Stech 5D 104
Neale Ho. B70: W Brom 6B 80
  WV2: Wolv 4G 43
  (off Blakenhall Gdns.)
Neale St. WS2: Wals 1A 48
Nearhill Rd. B38: K Nor 1G 159
Near Lands Cl. B32: Quin 1H 129
Nearmoor Rd. B34: S End 3H 105
Near Oak Ho. B32: Bart G 5B 130
Neasden Gro. B44: K'sdng 5B 68
Neath Rd. WS3: Blox 5F 19
Neath Way DY3: Sed 1C 76
  WS3: Blox 5F 19
Nebsworth Cl. B90: Shir 2B 150
NECHELLS 2C 102
Nechells Community Sports Cen. 4A 102
NECHELLS GREEN 4A 102
Nechells Pk. Rd. B7: Nech 3B 102
Nechell's Parkway B7: Birm 5A 102
Nechells Pl. B7: Nech 3B 102
NEC House B40: Nat E C 6F 123
Needham St. B7: Nech 2C 102
Needhill Cl. B93: Know 3B 166
NEEDLERS END 2H 169
Needlers End La. CV7: Bal C 3F 169
Needlers End Rd. CV7: Bal C 2F 169
Needless All. B2: Birm 4D 4 (1F 117)
Needwood Cl. WV2: Wolv 5F 43
Needwood Dr. WV4: E'shll 1B 60
Needwood Gro. B71: W Brom 4C 64
Needwood Ho. B27: A Grn 2B 136
Nelson Av. WV14: Bils 4E 45
Nelson Ct. B13: Mose 1H 133
Nelson Ho. DY4: Tip 6A 62
Nelson Rd. B6: Aston 6H 83
  DY1: Dud 6D 76
Nelson St. B1: Birm 6D 100
  B69: O'bry 3H 97
  B71: W Brom 2A 80
  WV2: Wolv 6B 170 (3G 43)
  WV13: W'hall 6B 30
Nene Cl. DY8: Stourb 1E 125
Nene Way B36: Cas B 1B 106
Neptune Health Pk. DY4: Tip 2G 77
Neptune Ind. Est. WV13: W'hall 3B 46
Neptune St. DY4: Tip 2G 77
Nesbit Gro. B9: Bord G 6H 103
Nesfield Cl. B38: K Nor 6G 145
Nesfield Gro. B92: H Ard 6B 140
Nesscliffe Gro. B23: Erd 6D 68
Nest Comn. WS3: Pels 2H 21
  (not continuous)
Neston Gro. B33: Stech 1A 120
Netheravon Cl. B14: K Hth 5F 147
Netherby Rd. DY3: Sed 5G 59
Nethercote Gdns. B90: Shir 4E 149
Netherdale Cl. B72: W Grn 6A 70
Netherdale Rd. B14: K Hth 6A 148
NETHEREND 4C 110
Netherend Cl. B63: Crad 4C 110
Netherend La. B63: Crad 4D 110
Netherend Sq. B63: Crad 4C 110
Netherfield Gdns. B27: A Grn 2H 135
Nethergate DY3: Up Gor 2B 76
Netherhouse Cl. B44: Gt Barr 2G 67
  (off Privet Cl.)
Netherstone Gro. B74: Four O 4F 37
NETHERTON 4E 95
Netherton Bus. Pk. DY2: Neth 5F 95
  (not continuous)
Netherton Gro. B33: Kitts G 6H 105
Netherton Hill DY2: Neth 4E 95
Netherton Lodge DY2: Neth 4E 95
Netherwood Cl. B91: Sol 1C 150
Nethy Dr. WV6: Tett 4H 25
Netley Gro. B11: Tys 2F 135
Netley Ho. B32: Harb 6D 114

Netley Rd. WS3: Blox 5E 19
Netley Way WS3: Blox 5E 19
Network Pk. B8: Salt 5C 102
Nevada Way B37: Chel W 2E 123
Neve Av. WV10: Bush 6B 16
Neve's Opening WV1: Wolv 1B 44
Neville Av. WV4: Penn 6H 43
Neville Rd. B23: Erd 4C 84
  B36: Cas B 6A 88
  B90: Shir 6F 149
Neville Wlk. B35: Cas V 5E 87
Nevin Gro. B42: P Barr 2E 83
Nevis Ct. WV3: Wolv 1C 42
Nevis Gro. WV12: W'hall 6B 18
Nevison Gro. B43: Gt Barr 1D 66
Newark Cft. B26: Sheld 5F 121
Newark Rd. DY2: Neth 1F 111
  WV12: W'hall 2C 30
New Art Gallery Walsall, The 1C 48
New Bank Gro. B9: Bord G 6G 103
New Bartholomew St.
  B5: Birm 4G 5 (1H 117)
New Birmingham Rd. B69: Tiv 5H 77
  DY2: Dud 5H 77
Newbold Cl. B93: Ben H 4B 166
Newbold Ct. B63: Hale 2B 128
Newbold Cft. B7: Birm 4B 102
NEWBOLDS .3C 28
Newbolds Rd. WV10: Wolv 3C 28
Newbolt Rd. WV14: Bils 5G 45
Newbolt St. WS5: Wals 6C 48
New Bond St. B9: Birm 2B 118
  DY2: Dud 1F 95
Newborough Gro. B28: Hall G 3F 149
Newborough Rd. B28: Hall G 3F 149
  B90: Shir 3F 149
NEWBRIDGE 6C 26
Newbridge Av. WV6: Wolv 6C 26
Newbridge Cres. WV6: Wolv 5C 26
Newbridge Dr. WV6: Wolv 5C 26
Newbridge Gdns. WV6: Wolv 5C 26
Newbridge M. WV6: Wolv 5D 26
Newbridge Rd. B9: Bord G 3H 119
  DY6: W Hth 1A 92
Newbridge St. WV6: Wolv 5D 26
Newburn Cft. B32: Quin 6H 113
Newbury Cl. B62: Hale 2D 128
  WS6: Gt Wyr 2F 7
Newbury Ho. B69: O'bry 4D 96
Newbury La. B69: O'bry 3C 96
Newbury Rd. B19: Hock 2G 101
  DY8: Word 1A 108
  WS11: Nort C 1E 9
  WV10: F'hses 5G 15
Newbury Wlk. B65: Row R 3C 96
Newby Gro. B37: F'bri 4D 106
New Canal St. B5: Birm 5G 5 (1H 117)
New Cannon Pas. B2: Birm 4E 5 (1G 117)
Newcastle Cft. B35: Cas V 4G 87
Newchurch Gdns. B24: Erd 5E 85
New Church Rd. B73: Bold, W Grn 5G 69
New Cole Hall La. B34: Stech 4F 105
New Coll. Cl. WS1: Wals 4E 49
Newcombe Rd. B21: Hand 5H 81
Newcome Cl. B24: Erd 3B 86
Newcomen Cl. WS4: Rus 2F 33
Newcomen Dr. DY4: Tip 4H 77
Newcott Cl. WV9: Pend 5D 14
New Ct. DY5: Brie H 1H 109
  (off The Promenade)
New Coventry Rd. B26: Sheld 6D 120
New Cft. B19: Loz 2G 101
Newcroft Gro. B26: Yard 4C 120
NEW CROSS 4D 28
New Cross Av. WV11: Wed, Wolv 5D 28
New Cross Ind. Est. WV1: Wolv 6C 28
New Cross St. DY4: Tip 2G 77
  WS10: Darl 6D 46
New Crown St. DY1: Dud 1D 94
Newdigate Rd. B75: S Cold 6E 55
New Dudley Rd. DY6: W Hth 1A 92
Newells Dr. DY4: Tip 6D 62
Newells Rd. B26: Yard 3E 121
New England B62: B'hth 4E 113

New England Cl.—Nine Elms La.

New England Cl. B69: O'bry 6E **79**
Newent Cl. WV12: W'hall 6D **30**
New Ent. Cen. WV1: Wolv 3C **44**
New Ent. Workshops B18: Hock 4C **100**
Newent Rd. B31: N'fld 3G **145**
Newey Bus. Pk. DY4: Tip 1F **77**
Newey Cl. B45: Redn 3G **157**
Newey Rd. B28: Hall G 1F **149**
WV11: Wed 1A **30**
Newey St. DY1: Dud 5C **76**
New Farm Rd. DY9: Lye 6G **109**
Newfield Cl. B91: Sol 1H **151**
WS2: Wals 3A **32**
Newfield Cres. B63: Hale 6A **112**
Newfield Dr. DY6: K'wfrd 5C **92**
Newfield La. B63: Hale 6A **112**
Newfield Rd. B69: O'bry 1F **97**
New Forest Rd. WS3: Wals 4C **32**
New Gas St. B70: W Brom 2G **79**
Newhall Ct. B3: Birm 2A **4** (6E **101**)
New Hall Dr. B76: Walm 1B **70**
(Lisures Dr.)
B76: Walm 3C **70**
(Walmley Rd.)
Newhall Farm Cl. B76: Walm 1B **70**
Newhall Hill B1: Birm 2A **4** (6E **101**)
Newhall Ho. *WS1: Wals* *3C* ***48***
(off Newhall St.)
New Hall Pl. WS10: W'bry 2G **63**
Newhall Pl. B3: Birm 2A **4**
Newhall Rd. B65: Row R 6C **96**
Newhall Sq. B3: Birm 3B **4** (6E **101**)
New Hall St. WV13: W'hall 1A **46**
Newhall St. B3: Birm 2B **4** (6E **101**)
B70: W Brom 5A **80**
DY4: Tip 5G **61**
WS1: Wals 3C **48**
Newhall Wlk. B3: Birm 3B **4** (6E **101**)
B72: S Cold 1A **70**
Newhampton Ho.
WV1: Wolv 1A **170** (6F **27**)
New Hampton Lofts B18: Birm 4E **101**
New Hampton Rd. E.
WV1: Wolv 1A **170** (6F **27**)
New Hampton Rd. W. WV6: Wolv 5D **26**
Newhaven Cl. B7: Birm 5A **102**
Newhay Cft. B19: Loz 2E **101**
New Heath Cl. WV11: Wed 4D **28**
New Henry St. B68: O'bry 5G **97**
New High Dr. DY4: Tip 2B **78**
Newhope Cl. B15: Birm 3F **117**
New Hope Rd. B66: Smeth 5G **99**
New Horse Rd. WS6: C Hay 2E **7**
Newhouse Cft. CV7: Bal C 3H **169**
Newhouse Farm Cl. B76: Walm 2D **70**
New Ho. Farm Dr. B31: N'fld 1F **145**
Newick Av. B74: Lit As 6B **36**
Newick Gro. B14: K Hth 3E **147**
Newick St. DY2: Neth 5E **95**
Newington Rd. B37: Mars G 3D **122**
New Inn Rd. B19: Loz 6F **83**
New Inns Cl. B21: Hand 1H **99**
New Inns La. B45: Fran, Rub 6E **143**
NEW INVENTION **2D 30**
New John St. B6: Birm 4G **101**
B62: B'hth 2C **112**
New John St. W. B19: Birm, Hock 3E **101**
New King St. DY2: Dud 6E **77**
Newland Cl. WS4: S'fld 5G **21**
Newland Ct. B23: Erd 4B **84**
Newland Gdns. B64: Crad H 4G **111**
Newland Gro. DY2: Dud 2B **94**
Newland Rd. B9: Small H 2F **119**
Newlands, The B34: S End 2G **105**
Newlands Cl. DY9: Hag 6G **125**
WV13: W'hall 2A **46**
Newlands Dr. B62: B'hth 4E **113**
Newlands Grn. B66: Smeth 5E **99**
Newlands La. B37: Mars G 5C **122**
Newlands Rd. B30: Stir 6D **132**
B93: Ben H 5B **166**
Newlands Wlk. *B68: O'bry* *5H* ***97***
(off Jackson St.)
New Landywood La. WV11: Ess 1E **19**
New Leasow B76: Walm 6E **71**
Newlyn Rd. B31: N'fld 4D **144**
B64: Crad H 3F **111**
Newman Av. WV4: E'shll 1B **60**
Newman Coll. Cl. B32: Bart G 5A **130**
Newman Ct. B21: Hand 6A **82**
Newman Pl. WV14: Bils 4H **45**
Newman Rd. B24: Erd 3F **85**
DY4: Tip 4C **62**
WV10: Bush 6C **16**
Newmans Cl. B66: Smeth 5G **99**
Newman Way B45: Redn 2G **157**
Newmarket Cl. WV6: Wolv 4E **27**
Newmarket Rd. WS11: Nort C 1E **9**
New Mkt. St. B3: Birm 3C **4** (6F **101**)
Newmarket Way B36: Hodg H 1H **103**
Newmarsh Rd. B76: Walm 1E **87**
New Mdw. Cl. B31: N'fld 5F **145**
New Meeting St. B4: Birm 4F **5** (1G **117**)
B69: O'bry 1G **97**
New Mills St. WS1: Wals 4B **48**
New Mill St. DY2: Dud 6E **77**
Newmore Gdns. WS5: Wals 6G **49**
New Moseley Rd. B12: Birm 3A **118**
Newnham Gro. B23: Erd 1E **85**
Newnham Ho. B36: Cas B 4D **106**
Newnham Ri. B90: Shir 4B **150**
Newnham Rd. B16: Edg 1G **115**
NEW OSCOTT **4C 68**
New Pool Rd. B64: Crad H 3D **110**
Newport Rd. B12: Bal H 1A **134**
B36: Hodg H 1D **104**
Newport St. WS1: Wals 2C **48**
WV10: Wolv 5A **28**
Newquay Cl. WS5: Wals 4A **50**
Newquay Rd. WS5: Wals 4H **49**
New Railway St. WV13: W'hall 1B **46**
New Rd. B18: Win G 3A **100**
B45: Rub 2F **157**
B46: Wat O 4D **88**
B47: H'wd 1H **161**
B63: Hale 1B **128**
B91: Sol 4G **151**
DY2: Dud, Neth 3E **95**
DY3: Swind 4A **72**
DY4: Tip 1D **78**
DY8: Stourb 6E **109**
WS8: Bwnhls 6B **10**
WS9: A'rdge 4C **34**
WS10: Darl 5D **46**
WV6: Wolv 5C **26**
WV10: Bush 1D **28**
WV13: W'hall 2A **46**
New Rowley Rd. DY2: Dud 2G **95**
New Royal Brierley Experience, The **4F 77**
New Shipton Cl. B76: Walm 4D **70**
New Spring Gdns. B18: Hock 5C **100**
New Spring St. B18: Hock 5C **100**
New Spring St. Nth. B18: Hock 4C **100**
Newstead Rd. B44: K'sdng 2A **68**
New St. B2: Birm 4D **4** (1F **117**)
B23: Erd 2F **85**
B36: Cas B 1F **105**
B45: Fran 5F **143**
B66: Smeth 3E **99**
B70: W Brom 6G **63**
(Norbury Rd.)
B70: W Brom 4B **80**
(St Michael St.)
DY1: Dud 6E **77**
DY3: Gorn 4G **75**
DY4: Tip 2H **77**
DY5: Quar B 3C **110**
DY6: K'wfrd 5B **92**
DY6: W Hth 1A **92**
DY8: Stourb 6D **108**
DY8: Word 1B **108**
WS1: Wals 2D **48**
WS3: Blox 6H **19**
WS4: Rus 2F **33**
WS4: S'fld 6H **21**
WS6: Gt Wyr 3G **7**
WS10: Darl 5D **46**
WS10: W'bry 4F **63**
New St. WV2: E'shll 5C **44**
WV3: Wolv 4B **42**
WV4: E'shll 6A **44**
WV11: Ess 4A **18**
WV13: W'hall 2G **45**
New St. Nth. B71: W Brom 4B **80**
New Street Station (Rail) **5D 4 (1F 117)**
New Summer St. B19: Birm 5F **101**
New Swan La. B70: W Brom 2G **79**
New Swinford Hall DY9: Lye 1G **125**
NEWTON **5G 65**
Newton Av. B74: S Cold 4H **53**
Newton Chambers *B2: Birm* *4D* ***4***
(off Cannon St.)
Newton Cl. B43: Gt Barr 4G **65**
Newton Ct. WV9: Pend 4D **14**
Newton Gdns. B43: Gt Barr 5G **65**
Newton Gro. B29: S Oak 3B **132**
Newton Ho. WV13: W'hall 2B **46**
Newton Ind. Est. B9: Bord G 1D **118**
Newton Mnr. Cl. B43: Gt Barr 5H **65**
Newton Pl. B18: Hock 2B **100**
WS2: Wals 3H **31**
Newton Rd. B11: S'hll 6B **118**
B43: Gt Barr 5G **65**
B71: W Brom 1C **80**
B93: Know 2D **166**
WS2: Wals 4H **31**
Newton Sq. B43: Gt Barr 4A **66**
Newton St. B4: Birm 2F **5** (6G **101**)
B71: W Brom 6C **64**
NEW TOWN
B70 **3E 79**
WS8 **4D 10**
NEWTOWN
B19 **3F 101**
DY2 **1E 111**
WS6 **2G 19**
New Town DY5: Brie H 5G **93**
(not continuous)
Newtown DY2: Neth 2E **111**
Newtown Dr. B19: Hock 3E **101**
Newtown La. B62: Roms 6C **142**
B64: Crad H 2F **111**
Newtown Middleway B6: Birm 4G **101**
NEW TOWN ROW **3G 101**
New Town Row B6: Aston, Birm 3G **101**
Newtown Shop. Cen. B19: Hock 3G **101**
Newtown St. B64: Crad H 1F **111**
New Village DY2: Neth 2E **111**
New Villas WV11: Wed 4C **28**
New Wood DY7: Stourt 4A **108**
New Wood Cl. DY7: Stourt 3A **108**
New Wood Dr. B31: Longb 6B **144**
New Wood Gro. WS9: Wals W 4C **22**
Next Generation Health Club
Brierley Hill **5H 93**
Ney Ct. DY4: Tip 5H **77**
Niall Cl. B15: Edg 3A **116**
Nicholas Rd. B74: S'tly 3G **51**
Nicholds Cl. WV14: Cose 4D **60**
Nicholls Fold WV11: Wed 4F **29**
Nicholls Rd. DY4: Tip 4G **61**
Nicholls St. B70: W Brom 5C **80**
Nichols Cl. B92: Sol 6B **138**
Nigel Av. B31: N'fld 2E **145**
Nigel Ct. B16: Edg 2A **116**
Nigel Rd. B8: Salt 3E **103**
DY1: Dud 5C **76**
Nightingale Av. B36: Cas B 1C **106**
Nightingale Cl. B23: Erd 6C **68**
Nightingale Ct. B91: Sol 3G **151**
Nightingale Cres. DY5: Brie H 4H **109**
WV12: W'hall 1B **30**
Nightingale Dr. DY4: Tip 2C **78**
Nightingale Pl. WV14: Bils 5F **45**
Nightingale Wlk. B15: Edg 4E **117**
Nightjar Gro. B23: Erd 1C **84**
Nighwood Dr. B74: S'tly 4H **51**
Nijon Cl. B21: Hand 6G **81**
Nimmings Cl. B31: Longb 3D **158**
Nimmings Rd. B62: B'hth 3D **112**
Nineacres Dr. B37: F'bri 1C **122**
Nine Elms La. WV10: Wolv 4A **28**

Nine Leasowes B66: Smeth 2C **98**
Nine Locks Ridge DY5: Brie H 1H **109**
Nine Pails Wlk. B70: W Brom 6B **80**
Ninestiles Community Leisure Cen.
. . . . .4H **135**
Nineveh Av. B21: Hand 2B **100**
Nineveh Rd. B21: Hand 2A **100**
Ninfield Gdns. B27: A Grn 1H **135**
Ninfield Rd. B27: A Grn 2G **135**
Nith Pl. DY1: Dud 5D **76**
Noakes Cl. WS10: Darl 4F **47**
Nocke Rd. WV11: Wed 6H **17**
Nock St. DY4: Tip 6C **62**
Noddy Pk. WS9: A'rdge 2D **34**
Noddy Pk. Rd. WS9: A'rdge 2D **34**
Noel Av. B12: Bal H 5A **118**
Noel Rd. B16: Edg 2B **116**
Nolton Cl. B43: Gt Barr 5H **65**
Nook, The DY5: P'ntt 4F **93**
  WS6: C Hay 4C **6**
Nooklands Cft. B33: Yard 1E **121**
Noose Cres. WV13: W'hall 1G **45**
Noose La. WV13: W'hall 1G **45**
Nora Rd. B11: S'hll 2C **134**
Norbiton Rd. B44: K'sdng 5A **68**
Norbreck Cl. B43: Gt Barr 4H **65**
Norbury Av. WS3: Pels 4D **20**
Norbury Cres. WV4: E'shll 1B **60**
Norbury Dr. DY5: Brie H 2H **109**
Norbury Gro. B92: Olton 2E **137**
Norbury Rd. B44: Gt Barr 2G **67**
  B70: W Brom 6G **63**
  WV10: Wolv 3B **28**
  WV14: Bils .5H **45**
Norcombe Gro. B90: M'path 4E **165**
Nordley Rd. WV11: Wed 4E **29**
Nordley Wlk. WV11: Wed 3E **29**
Norfolk Av. B71: W Brom 6B **64**
Norfolk Cl. B30: Stir 1D **146**
Norfolk Cl. B16: Edg 2H **115**
  B29: W Cas 6F **131**
Norfolk Cres. WS9: A'rdge 1D **34**
Norfolk Dr. WS10: W'bry 1B **64**
Norfolk Gdns. B75: S Cold 3H **53**
Norfolk Gro. WS6: Gt Wyr 4F **7**
Norfolk Ho. B23: Erd 2F **85**
  B30: K Nor .4C **146**
Norfolk New Rd. WS2: Wals 5G **31**
Norfolk Pl. WS2: Wals 4B **32**
Norfolk Rd. B15: Edg 4H **115**
  B23: Erd 2F **85**
  B45: Fran 5F **143**
  B68: O'bry .4A **97**
  B75: S Cold 4H **53**
  DY2: Dud 2C **94**
  DY8: Woll 3B **108**
  WV3: Wolv .3E **43**
Norfolk Twr. B18: Hock 4D **100**
Norgrave Rd. B92: Sol 3G **137**
Norlan Dr. B14: K Hth 4H **147**
Norland Rd. B27: A Grn 4A **136**
Norley Gro. B13: Mose 6C **134**
Norley Trad. Est. B33: Sheld 2G **121**
Norman Av. B32: Harb 4C **114**
Norman Ct. B23: Erd 2F **85**
Normandy Rd. B20: Hand 6F **83**
Norman Green Athletics Cen. 4E **151**
Norman Rd. B31: N'fld 4F **145**
  B67: Smeth .2B **114**
  WS5: Wals .3G **49**
Normansell Twr. B6: Aston 1B **102**
Norman St. B18: Win G 4A **100**
  DY2: Dud 1F **95**
Norman Ter. B65: Row R 5C **96**
Normanton Av. B26: Sheld 6H **121**
Normanton Twr. B23: Erd 1G **85**
Normid Ct. B31: N'fld 3G **145**
  (off Bunbury Rd.)
Norrington Gro. B31: N'fld 4A **144**
Norrington Rd. B31: N'fld 4A **144**
Norris Dr. B33: Stech 6D **104**
Norris Rd. B6: Aston 6H **83**
Norris Way B75: S Cold 6B **54**
Northampton St. B18: Birm 5E **101**

Northam Wlk. WV6: Wolv 5F **27**
Northanger Rd. B27: A Grn 3H **135**
North Av. B40: Nat E C 6G **123**
  WV11: Wed .3E **29**
Northbrook Ct. B90: Shir 2A **150**
Northbrook Rd. B90: Shir 2A **150**
Northbrook St. B16: Birm 5B **100**
Northcote Rd. B33: Stech 5B **104**
Northcote St. WS2: Wals 5B **32**
Northcott Rd. DY2: Neth 5F **95**
  WV14: Bils .1G **61**
North Cres. WV10: F'stne 1D **16**
Northcroft Way B23: Erd 3D **84**
Northdale WV6: Tett 5H **25**
Northdown Rd. B91: Sol 6D **150**
North Dr. B5: Edg 6E **117**
  B20: Hand .1D **100**
  B75: S Cold 5A **54**
NORTHFIELD 4F **145**
Northfield Gro. WV3: Wolv 4A **42**
Northfield Pool & Fitness Cen. 4E **145**
Northfield Rd. B17: Harb 2E **131**
  B30: K Nor .3H **145**
  DY2: Neth .4F **95**
Northfield Station (Rail) 5E **145**
Northfields Way WS8: Clay 1H **21**
North Ga. B17: Harb 4G **115**
Northgate B64: Crad H 3F **111**
  WS9: A'rdge 5C **22**
Northgate Cl. DY1: Dud 5D **76**
Northgate Way WS9: A'rdge 1C **34**
North Grn. WV4: Penn 5B **42**
North Holme B9: Bord G 1C **118**
Northicote Recreation & Community Cen.
. . . . .4A **16**
Northland Rd. B90: Shir 6C **150**
Northlands Rd. B13: Mose 4A **134**
Northleach Av. B14: K Hth 5F **147**
Northleigh Rd. B8: W End 3G **103**
Northmead B33: Yard 1E **121**
Northolt Dr. B35: Cas V 4E **87**
Northolt Gro. B42: Gt Barr 4R **66**
North One M. DY3: Sed 4G **59**
North Oval DY3: Up Gor 2A **76**
Northover Cl. WV9: Pend 5E **15**
North Pk. Rd. B23: Erd 3B **84**
North Pathway B17: Harb 4F **115**
North Rd. B17: Harb 5H **115**
  B20: Hand .5G **83**
  B29: S Oak .2B **132**
  DY4: Tip 5B **62**
  WV1: Wolv .5G **27**
North Rd. Halls WV1: Wolv 5G **27**
North Roundhay B33: Kitts G 5E **105**
Northside Bus. Cen. B18: Win G 4A **100**
Northside Dr. B74: S'tly 3H **51**
North Solihull Sports Cen. 6C **150**
North Springfield DY3: Sed 4A **60**
North St. B67: Smeth 4D **98**
  DY2: Dud 6F **77**
  DY5: Brie H 1G **109**
  WS2: Wals .5C **32**
  WS10: W'bry 1F **63**
  WV1: Wolv 2B **170** (1G **43**)
  (not continuous)
North St. Ind. Est. DY5: Brie H 1G **109**
Northumberland St. B7: Birm 6A **102**
North Vw. Dr. DY5: Brie H 4H **93**
North Wlk. B31: N'fld 6G **145**
Nth. Warwick St. B9: Small H 2D **118**
Northway B40: Nat E C 5H **123**
  DY3: Sed 2G **59**
  (Alderdale Av.)
  DY3: Sed 4F **59**
  (Sunningdale Rd.)
Nth. Western Arc. B2: Birm . . .3E **5** (6G **101**)
Nth. Western Rd. B66: Smeth 3D **98**
Nth. Western Ter. B18: Hock 2B **100**
Northwick Cres. B91: Sol 6F **151**
Northwood Ct. DY5: Brie H 1H **109**
Northwood Pk. Cl. WV10: Bush 4H **15**
Northwood Pk. Rd. WV10: Bush 4A **16**
Northwood St. B3: Birm 2B **4** (5E **101**)
Northwood Way DY5: Brie H 3F **109**

North Yd. B9: Birm 6H **5**
Northycote Farm 4C **16**
Northycote Farm Country Pk. 4C **16**
Northycote La. WV10: Bush 3B **16**
NORTON 2B **124**
NORTON CANES 1F **9**
NORTON CANES SERVICE AREA 2E **9**
Norton Cl. B30: K Nor 4F **147**
  B31: N'fld 4E **145**
  B66: Smeth .4G **99**
  WV4: Penn .2A **58**
Norton Cres. B9: Bord G 6H **103**
  DY2: Neth .6G **95**
  WV14: Cose 4F **61**
Norton Dr. B47: Wyt 5C **162**
Norton E. Rd. WS11: Nort C 1E **9**
Norton Ga. B38: K Nor 6A **146**
Norton Grange WS11: Nort C 1D **8**
Norton Grange Cres. WS11: Nort C . . .1D **8**
NORTON GREEN 2D **8**
Norton Grn. La. B93: Know 6E **167**
  WS11: Nort C 1C **8**
Norton Hall La. WS11: Nort C 1B **8**
Norton La. B47: Tid G, Wyt 5C **162**
  B90: Tid G .5C **162**
  B94: Earls .5C **162**
  WS6: Gt Wyr 1G **7**
  WS11: Cann, Nort C 1B **8**
Norton Rd. B46: Col 6H **89**
  DY8: Stourb 4B **124**
  WS3: Pels .1E **21**
Norton St. B18: Hock 4C **100**
Norton Ter. B30: Stir 1D **146**
  (off Warren Rd.)
Norton Twr. B1: Birm 4A **4**
Norton Vw. B14: K Hth 6F **133**
Norton Wlk. B23: Erd 4C **84**
Nortune Cl. B38: K Nor 5H **145**
Norwich Cft. B37: Mars G 2B **122**
Norwich Dr. B17: Harb 3D **114**
Norwich Rd. DY2: Neth 1F **111**
  WS2: Wals .2H **47**
Norwood Av. B64: Crad H 4G **111**
Norwood Gro. B19: Hock 2D **100**
Norwood Rd. B9: Bord G 1E **119**
  DY5: Brie H 6G **93**
Nottingham Dr. WV12: W'hall 2C **30**
Nottingham New Rd. WS2: Wals 4G **31**
Nottingham Way DY5: Quar B 1B **110**
Nova Ct. B43: Gt Barr 4D **66**
Nova Scotia St. B4: Birm 3G **5** (6H **101**)
Nowell St. WS10: Darl 6E **47**
Nuffield Ho. B36: Cas B 1C **106**
Nugent Cl. B6: Aston 2G **101**
Nugent Gro. B90: Ches G 6B **164**
Number 9 The Gallery 5A **4**
Nursery, The B29: S Oak 4C **132**
Nursery Av. B12: Bal H 6H **117**
  WS9: A'rdge 4D **34**
Nursery Cl. B30: K Nor 2B **146**
Nursery Dr. B20: Hand 6C **82**
  B30: K Nor .2B **146**
  WV5: Wom .3F **73**
Nursery Gdns. B90: Maj G 1E **163**
  DY8: Word .2D **108**
  WV8: Cod 3F **13**
Nursery La. B74: Four O 1G **53**
Nursery Rd. B15: Edg 5H **115**
  B19: Loz 3D **100**
  WS3: Blox .1H **31**
Nursery St. WV1: Wolv 1B **170** (6G **27**)
Nursery Vw. Cl. WS9: A'rdge 1G **51**
Nursery Wlk. WV6: Tett 5B **26**
NURTON 6A **24**
Nurton Bank WV6: Patt 6A **24**
Nutbush Dr. B31: N'fld 1B **144**
Nutfield Wlk. B32: Harb 6D **114**
Nutgrove Cl. B14: K Hth 6H **133**
Nuthatch Dr. DY5: Brie H 4G **109**
Nuthurst B75: S Cold 1F **71**
Nuthurst Dr. WS11: Cann 1F **7**
Nuthurst Gro. B14: K Hth 5H **147**
  B93: Ben H .5C **166**
Nuthurst Rd. B31: Longb 3D **158**

Nutley Dr. DY4: Tip 5D 62
Nutmeg Gro. WS1: Wals 1E 49
Nuttall Gro. B21: Hand 2G 99

O

Oak Av. B12: Bal H 6A 118
   B70: W Brom 4H 79
   WS2: Wals 6E 31
   WS6: Gt Wyr 4G 7
Oak Bank B18: Hock 3C 100
Oak Barn Rd. B62: B'hth 3E 113
Oak Cl. B17: Harb 5E 115
   DY4: Tip 4A 62
Oak Cotts. B7: Birm 6B 102
Oak Ct. B45: Redn 2A 158
   B63: Hale 3H 127
   B66: Smeth 1A 98
   DY8: Stourb 1E 125
   WS5: Wals 1E 65
Oak Cres. B62: Tiv 6B 78
   WS3: Blox 3B 32
Oak Cft. B37: K'hrst 6B 106
Oakcroft Rd. B13: Mose 6B 134
Oakdale Cl. B68: O'bry 1G 113
   DY5: P'nntt 2E 93
Oakdale Rd. B36: Hodg H 1C 104
   B68: O'bry 1G 113
Oakdale Trad. Est.
   DY6: K'wfrd 6B 74
Oakdene Cl. WS6: C Hay 3D 6
Oak Dr. B23: Erd 6C 68
   WV5: Seis 3A 56
OAKEN 5D 12
Oaken Covert WV8: Cod 5D 12
Oaken Dr. B91: Sol 2D 150
   WV8: Cod, Oaken 5D 12
   WV12: W'hall 2E 31
Oaken Grange WS6: Gt Wyr 4F 7
Oaken Gro. WV8: Cod 5E 13
Oakenhayes Cres.
   B76: Min 2G 87
   WS8: Bwnhls 4B 10
Oakenhayes Dr. WS8: Bwnhls 4B 10
Oaken La. WV8: Oaken 4C 12
Oaken Lanes WV8: Cod 4E 13
Oaken Pk. WV8: Cod 5G 13
Oakenshaw Rd. B90: Shir 6B 150
Oakeswell St. WS10: W'bry 2G 63
Oakeywell St. DY2: Dud 6F 77
OAKFARM 6C 74
Oak Farm Cl. B76: Walm 6E 71
Oak Farm Rd. B30: B'vlle 2H 145
Oakfield Av. B11: S'brk 5C 118
   B12: Bal H 5A 118
   B21: Hand 2H 99
   DY1: Dud 6D 60
   DY6: K'wfrd 4C 92
Oakfield Cl. B66: Smeth 3G 99
   DY8: Word 2D 108
Oakfield Ct. *DY5: Brie H* *1H 109*
   (off The Promenade)
Oakfield Dr. B45: Coft H 5B 158
   WS3: Pels 2F 21
Oakfield Rd. B12: Bal H 6G 117
   B24: Erd 4F 85
   B29: S Oak 2C 132
   B66: Smeth 3G 99
   DY8: Word 2E 109
   DY9: W'cte 3B 126
   WV8: Bilb 5H 13
Oakfields Way B91: Cath B 2D 152
Oak Grn. DY1: Dud 2C 76
   WV6: Tett 6H 25
Oak Grn. Way B69: O'bry 5G 97
Oak Gro. B31: Longb 6C 144
   WV11: Wed 2D 28
Oakhall Dr. B93: Dorr 5B 166
OAKHAM 2B 96
Oakham Av. DY2: Dud 2G 95
Oakham Ct. DY2: Dud 1G 95
Oakham Cres. DY2: Dud 2G 95
Oakham Dr. DY2: Dud 1H 95

Oakham Rd. B17: Harb 4F 115
   B69: Tiv 1G 95
   DY2: Dud 1G 95
Oakham Way B92: Olton 4E 137
Oak Hill WV3: Wolv 3A 42
Oakhill Cl. B17: Harb 3F 115
Oakhill Cres. B27: A Grn 5H 135
Oakhill Dr. B15: Edg 4A 116
Oakhill Dr. DY5: Brie H 4F 109
Oak Ho. WS6: Gt Wyr 4G 7
Oak House Mus. 5H 79
Oakhurst Rd. B27: A Grn 4H 135
   B72: W Grn 5H 69
Oak Ind. Pk. DY6: K'wfrd 6C 74
Oakington Dr. B35: Cas V 4E 87
Oakland Cl. B91: Sol 3A 152
Oakland Dr. DY3: Gorn 5F 75
Oakland Rd. B13: Mose 2A 134
   B21: Hand 1A 100
   (not continuous)
   WS3: Blox 2C 32
Oaklands B31: N'fld 3D 144
   B62: Quin 1G 129
   B76: Curd 1D 88
Oaklands, The B37: Mars G 4C 122
   WV3: Wolv 3F 43
Oaklands Av. B17: Harb 6F 115
Oaklands Cft. B76: Walm 6F 71
Oaklands Dr. B20: Hand 5B 82
   B74: S'tly 2H 51
Oaklands Grn. WV14: Bils 3F 45
Oaklands Rd. B74: Four O 3H 53
   WV3: Wolv 3F 43
Oaklands Sports & Social Cen. 1H 99
Oaklands Way B31: Longb 6H 143
   WS3: Pels 4F 21
Oak La. B70: W Brom 4H 79
   B92: Bars 6B 154
   DY6: K'wfrd 6C 74
Oaklea Dr. B64: Old H 1H 111
Oakleaf Cl. B32: Bart G 3B 130
Oak Leaf Dr. B13: Mose 2A 134
Oak Leasow B32: Quin 1H 129
Oakleigh B31: N'fld 5G 145
Oakleigh Dr. DY3: Sed 6G 59
   WV8: Bilb 4G 13
Oakleigh Rd. DY8: Stourb 3E 125
Oakleighs DY8: Word 2A 108
Oakleigh Wlk. DY6: K'wfrd 1C 92
Oakley Av. DY4: Tip 1A 78
   WS9: A'rdge 4C 34
Oakley Ct. B15: Edg 6A 116
Oakley Gro. WV4: Penn 6B 42
Oakley Rd. B10: Small H 4C 118
   (not continuous)
   B30: Stir 2D 146
   WV4: Penn 6B 42
Oak Leys WV3: Wolv 2A 42
Oakley Wood Dr. B91: Sol 3A 152
Oakmeadow Av. B24: Erd 4B 86
Oakmeadow Cl. B26: Yard 6B 120
   B33: Kitts G 1H 121
Oakmeadow Way B24: Erd 4B 86
Oakmount Cl. WS3: Pels 4D 20
Oak Mt. Rd. B74: S'tly 4A 52
Oak Pk. Ct. *B74: Four O* *6E 37*
   (off Walsall Rd.)
Oak Pk. Leisure Cen. 3B 22
Oak Pk. Rd. DY8: Word 2D 108
Oakridge Cl. WV12: W'hall 5C 30
Oakridge Dr. WS6: C Hay 3F 7
   WV12: W'hall 5C 30
Oakridge Rd. B31: N'fld 5H 145
Oak Ri. B46: Col 4H 107
Oak Rd. B68: O'bry 4H 113
   B70: W Brom 5H 79
   DY1: Dud 4E 77
   DY4: Tip 6G 61
   WS3: Pels 2D 20
   WS4: S'fld 6G 21
   WS9: Wals W 4C 22
   WV13: W'hall 1G 45
Oaks, The B17: Harb 3F 115
   B34: S End 2F 105

Oaks, The B38: K Nor 2B 160
   B67: Smeth 4D 98
   B72: W Grn 6H 69
   B76: Walm 2E 71
   WS3: Blox 6G 19
   WV3: Wolv 1E 43
Oaks Cres. WV3: Wolv 2E 43
Oaks Dr. WV3: Wolv 1E 43
   WV5: Wom 2G 73
Oakslade Dr. B92: Sol 5A 138
Oak St. B64: Crad H 2F 111
   DY2: Neth 5G 95
   DY5: Quar B 2B 110
   DY6: K'wfrd 4A 92
   WV3: Wolv 2E 43
   WV14: Cose 6D 60
Oak St. Ind. Est. *B64: Crad H* *2F 111*
   (off Oak St.)
Oak St. Trad. Est. DY5: Quar B 2B 110
Oakthorpe Dr. B37: K'hrst 4B 106
Oakthorpe Gdns. B69: Tiv 5A 78
Oak Tree Cl. B93: Ben H 5A 166
Oak Tree Ct. B28: Hall G 2G 149
   B70: W Brom 4H 79
Oak Tree Gdns. B28: Hall G 4E 149
   DY8: Word 2E 109
Oak Tree La. B29: S Oak 4A 132
   B30: B'vlle 6A 132
   B47: H'wd 3B 162
Oaktree Ri. WV8: Cod 3E 13
Oaktree Rd. WS10: W'bry 2H 63
Oak Trees B47: H'wd 3H 161
Oak Turn Dr. B38: K Nor 1H 159
Oak Vw. WS2: Wals 6E 31
Oak Wlk., The B31: Longb 6E 145
Oak Way B76: Walm 3D 70
Oakwood Cl. WS9: Wals W 3A 22
   WV11: Ess 4B 18
Oakwood Cres. DY2: Dud 3B 94
Oakwood Cft. B91: Sol 6G 151
Oakwood Dr. B14: K Hth 3F 147
   B74: S'tly 3G 51
Oakwood Pl. B11: S'hll 3E 135
Oakwood Rd. B11: S'hll 2C 134
   B47: H'wd 3A 162
   B67: Smeth 5D 98
   B73: Bold 3E 69
   WS3: Blox 2C 32
Oakwood St. B70: W Brom 2H 79
Oast Ho. B8: W End 5A 104
Oasthouse Cl. DY6: W Hth 2G 91
Oaston Rd. B36: Cas B 1H 105
Oatfield Cl. WS7: Chase 1C 10
Oatlands Wlk. B14: K Hth 5E 147
Oatlands Way WV6: Pert 6D 24
Oat Mill Cl. WS10: Darl 6E 47
Oban Rd. B92: Olton 4D 136
Oberon Cl. B45: Fran 5G 143
Oberon Dr. B90: Shir 6G 149
Occupation Rd. WS8: Wals W 3C 22
Occupation St. DY1: Dud 5C 76
Ocean Dr. WS10: W'bry 4D 62
Ockam Cft. B31: N'fld 5G 145
OCKER HILL .5C 62
Ocker Hill Rd. DY4: Tip 4B 62
O'Connor Dr. DY4: Tip 4C 62
Oddingley Cl. B23: Erd 4C 84
Oddingley Rd. B31: N'fld 5G 145
Odell Cres. WS3: Blox 2A 32
Odell Pl. B5: Edg 6E 117
Odell Rd. WS3: Blox 2H 31
Odell Way WS3: Blox 2H 31
Odensil Grn. B92: Sol 3F 137
Odeon Cinema
   Birmingham 5E 5 (1G 117)
   Brierley Hill 1A 110
Offa's Dr. WV6: Pert 4E 25
Offenham Covert B38: K Nor 1A 160
Offini Cl. B70: W Brom 5D 80
Offlow M. DY4: Tip 4H 61
Offmoor Rd. B32: Bart G 5H 129
Ogbury Cl. B14: K Hth 5E 147

Ogley Cres. WS8: Bwnhls 6C **10**
Ogley Dr. B75: S Cold 6D **54**
Ogley Hay Rd. WS7: Chase 1D **10**
   WS8: Chase, Bwnhls 3C **10**
Ogley Rd. WS8: Bwnhls 6C **10**
O'Hare Ho. WS4: Wals 6D **32**
O'Keeffe Cl. B11: S'brk 3B **118**
Okehampton Dr. B71: W Brom 1A **80**
Okement Dr. WV11: Wed 4D **28**
Old Abbey Gdns. B17: Harb 1H **131**
Oldacre Cl. B76: Walm 1A **58**
Old Acre Dr. B21: Hand 2A **100**
Oldacre Rd. B68: O'bry 3G **113**
Old Bank Pl. B72: S Cold 6A **54**
Old Bank Top B31: N'fld 5F **145**
Old Barn Rd. B30: B'vlle 1H **145**
   DY8: Word 2E **109**
Old Beeches B23: Erd 5C **68**
Old Bell Rd. B23: Erd 1H **85**
Oldberrow Cl. B90: M'path 3E **165**
Old Birchills WS2: Wals 6A **32**
Old Birmingham Rd. B45: Lick 6F **157**
Old Bri. St. B19: Hock 3E **101**
Old Bri. Wlk. B65: Row R 4H **95**
Old Bromford La. B8: W End 2H **103**
Old Brookside B33: Stech 1C **120**
OLDBURY 1G **97**
Oldbury Bus. Cen. B68: O'bry 1G **113**
Oldbury Grn. Retail Pk. B69: O'bry 1F **97**
Oldbury Leisure Cen. 3D **96**
Oldbury Pk. B69: O'bry 3H **97**
Oldbury Ringway B69: O'bry 1F **97**
Oldbury Rd. B65: Row R 1D **112**
   B66: Smeth .2A **98**
   B70: W Brom 4E **79**
Oldbury Rd. Ind. Est. B66: Smeth 2B **98**
   B70: W Brom 5F **79**
Oldbury St. WS10: W'bry 2H **63**
Old Bush St. DY5: Brie H 6A **94**
Old Camp Hill B11: S'brk 3A **118**
Old Canal Wlk. DY4: Tip 2B **78**
Old Castle Gro. WS8: Bwnhls 3B **10**
Old Chapel, The B3: Birm 2C **4** (1F **101**)
Old Chapel Rd. B67: Smeth 6D **98**
Old Chapel Wlk. B68: O'bry 5G **97**
Old Church Av. B17: Harb 6G **115**
Old Church Grn. B33: Stech 1C **120**
Old Church Rd. B17: Harb 6F **115**
   B46: Wat O .4D **88**
Old College Dr. WS10: W'bry 4G **63**
Old Ct. Cft. B9: Bord G 2C **118**
Old Ct. House, The DY1: Dud 6E **77**
              (off Priory Rd.)
Old Cft. La. B34: S End 1G **105**
   B36: Cas B .1F **105**
Old Cross B4: Birm 2G **5**
Old Cross St. DY4: Tip 2G **77**
Old Crown Cl. B32: Bart G 4H **129**
Old Damson La. B92: Sol 3B **138**
Old Dickens Heath Rd. B90: Dic H 4G **163**
Old Edwardians Sports Club 1A **150**
Olde Hall La. WS6: Gt Wyr 1F **7**
Olde Hall Rd. WV10: F'stne 1E **17**
Old End La. WV14: Cose 6E **61**
OLD FALLINGS .1A **28**
Old Fallings Cres. WV10: Bush 2A **28**
Old Fallings La. WV10: Bush 6B **16**
Old Falls Cl. WS6: C Hay 2D **6**
Old Farm Dr. WV8: Bilb 3G **13**
Old Farm Gro. B14: Yard W 2D **148**
Old Farm Mdw. WV3: Wolv 3A **42**
Old Farm Rd. B33: Stech 5C **104**
Oldfield Dr. DY8: Stourb 2E **125**
Oldfield Rd. B12: Bal H 5A **118**
   WV14: Cose 5C **60**
Oldfields B64: Crad H 3F **111**
Oldfield Trad. Est. B64: Crad H 3F **111**
Old Fire Station, The B17: Harb 5H **115**
Old Flour Mills B70: W Brom 5A **80**
Old Fordrove B76: Walm 2B **70**
Old Forest Way B34: S End 3F **105**
Old Forge Cl. WS1: Wals 3D **48**
Old Forge Trad. Est. DY9: Lye 5A **110**
Old Grange Rd. B11: S'hll 1C **134**

Old Green La. B93: Know 6B **168**
Old Gro. Gdns. DY9: W'cte 2H **125**
Old Hall Cl. DY8: Amb 3E **109**
Old Hall Ind. Est. WS3: Blox 1A **32**
Old Hall La. WS9: A'rdge 6D **50**
Old Hall St. WV1: Wolv 4C **170** (2H **43**)
Old Ham La. DY9: Pedm 3G **125**
Old Hampton La. WV10: Bush 5D **16**
Old Hawne La. B63: Hale 6A **112**
Old Heath Cres. WV1: Wolv 2C **44**
Old Heath Rd. WV1: Wolv 2C **44**
Old High St. DY5: Quar B 2B **110**
OLD HILL 3B **112**
Old Hill WV6: Tett 4B **26**
Old Hill By-Pass B64: Old H 1H **111**
Old Hill Station (Rail) 3A **112**
Old Hobicus La. B68: O'bry 4H **97**
Old Horns Cres. B43: Gt Barr 3E **67**
Oldhouse Farm Cl. B28: Hall G 1F **149**
Old House La. B62: Roms 6B **142**
Oldington Gro. B91: Sol 1F **165**
Old Kingsbury Rd. B76: Min 2G **87**
Oldknow Rd. B10: Small H 5E **119**
Old Landywood La. WV11: Ess 1C **18**
Old La. WS3: Blox 2A **32**
   WV6: Tett 1F **41**
Old Langley Hall B75: S Cold 1F **71**
Old Level Way DY2: Neth 5F **95**
Old Lime Gdns. B38: K Nor 1A **160**
Old Lindens Cl. B74: S'tly 4G **51**
Old Lode La. B92: Sol 1F **137**
Old Manor, The WV6: Tett 6A **26**
Old Masters Cl. WS1: Wals 2E **49**
Old Mdw. Rd. B31: Longb 2G **159**
Old Meeting Rd. WV14: Cose 5E **61**
Old Meeting St. B70: W Brom 2H **79**
             (not continuous)
Old Mill Cl. B90: Shir 5D **148**
Old Mill Ct. B46: Col 2H **107**
Old Mill Gdns. B33: Stech 1C **120**
   WS4: S'fld 5G **21**
Old Mill Gro. B20: Hand 5E **83**
Old Mill House Cl. WS4: S'fld 6F **21**
Old Mill Rd. B46: Col 2H **107**
Old Moat Dr. B31: N'fld 4F **145**
Old Moat Way B8: W End 3H **103**
OLD MOXLEY 1A **62**
Oldnall Cl. DY9: W'cte 1B **126**
Oldnall Rd. B63: Crad 1B **126**
   DY9: W'cte 1B **126**
Old Oak Cl. WS9: A'rdge 1D **34**
Old Oak Rd. B38: K Nor 5C **146**
OLD OSCOTT 4G **67**
Old Oscott Hill B44: Gt Barr 4G **67**
Old Oscott La. B44: Gt Barr 5G **67**
Old Park B31: N'fld 2E **145**
Old Park Cl. B6: Aston 2G **101**
Old Park La. B69: O'bry 4G **97**
Old Park Rd. DY1: Dud 3B **76**
   WS10: Darl, W'bry 5E **47**
Old Park Trad. Est. WS10: W'bry 1E **63**
Old Park Wlk. B6: Aston 2G **101**
Old Penns La. B46: Col 2H **107**
Old Pl. WS3: Blox 1A **32**
Old Pleck Rd. WS2: Wals 3H **47**
Old Port Cl. DY4: Tip 5B **78**
Old Portway B38: K Nor 2A **160**
Old Postway B19: Loz 2F **101**
Old Pump Ho., The B70: Lye 6H **109**
Old Quarry Cl. B45: Rub 1F **157**
Old Quarry Dr. DY3: Up Gor 2H **75**
Old Rectory Gdns. WS9: A'rdge 3E **35**
Old Repertory Theatre, The . . .5D **4** (1F **117**)
Old School Cl. WV13: W'hall 1A **46**
Old School Dr. B65: Row R 6B **96**
Old Scott Cl. B33: Kitts G 1G **121**
Old Smithy Pl. B18: Hock 4C **100**
Old Snow Hill B4: Birm 1D **4** (5F **101**)
Old Sq. B4: Birm 3F **5** (6G **101**)
Old Sq. Shop. Pct. WS1: Wals 2C **48**
Old Stables Wlk. B7: Nech 2C **102**
Old Station Rd. B33: Stech 5B **104**
   B92: H Ard 3H **139**
Old Stone Cl. B45: Fran 6F **143**

Old Stow Heath La. WV1: Wolv 2E **45**
OLD SWINFORD 3E **125**
Old Tokengate B17: Harb 5H **115**
Old Town Cl. B38: K Nor 5B **146**
Old Town La. WS3: Pels 4D **20**
Old Union Mill B16: Birm 1D **116**
Old Vicarage Cl. WV3: Pels 5E **21**
   WV5: Wom 6H **57**
Old Walsall Rd. B42: P Barr 1B **82**
Old Warstone La. WV11: Ess 5B **6**
Old Warwick Ct. B92: Olton 4C **136**
Old Warwick Rd. B92: Olton 4C **136**
Oldway Dr. B91: Sol 5A **152**
Old Well Cl. WS4: Rus 2F **33**
Old Wharf Rd. DY8: Amb 5D **108**
Olga Dr. DY4: Tip 4B **62**
Olinthus Av. WV11: Wed 2G **29**
Olive Av. WV4: E'shll 6A **44**
Olive Dr. B62: B'hth 3C **112**
Olive Hill Rd. B62: B'hth 3D **112**
Olive La. B62: B'hth 3C **112**
Olive Mt. B69: O'bry 1D **96**
Olive Pl. B14: K Hth 6H **133**
Oliver Cl. DY2: Dud 1G **95**
Oliver Ct. B65: Row R 1B **112**
Oliver Cres. WV14: Bils 3G **61**
Oliver Rd. B16: Birm 1B **116**
   B23: Erd 1F **85**
   B66: Smeth 6G **99**
Oliver St. B7: Birm 4A **102**
Ollerton Rd. B26: Yard 4D **120**
Ollison Dr. B74: S'tly 1H **51**
Olliver Cl. B62: Quin 2G **129**
Olorenshaw Rd. B26: Sheld 6H **121**
OLTON 4C **136**
Olton Blvd. E. B27: A Grn 3G **135**
Olton Blvd. W. B11: Tys 2F **135**
Olton Cft. B27: A Grn 2B **136**
Olton Mere B92: Olton 4C **136**
Olton Rd. B90: Shir 3H **149**
Olton Station (Rail) 4C **136**
Olton Wharf B92: Olton 3C **136**
Olympus Dr. DY4: Tip 1D **78**
Ombersley Cl. B69: O'bry 4D **96**
Ombersley Rd. B12: Bal H 5A **118**
   B63: Hale 3H **127**
Omersley Way B31: N'fld 5H **145**
One Stop Shop. Cen. B42: P Barr 4F **83**
Onibury Rd. B21: Hand 6H **81**
Onslow Cres. B92: Olton 4E **137**
Onslow Rd. B11: Tys 1G **135**
Ontario Cl. B38: K Nor 1C **160**
Oozells Sq. B1: Birm 5A **4** (1E **117**)
Oozells St. B1: Birm 5A **4** (1E **117**)
Oozells St. Nth. B1: Birm 5A **4** (1D **116**)
Open Fld. Cl. B31: N'fld 5F **145**
Openfield Cft. B46: Wat O 5E **89**
Oracle Bldg. B90: Bly P 6E **165**
Oratory, The 2B **116**
Orchard, The B37: Mars G 3B **122**
   B68: O'bry 5A **98**
   WS3: Blox 5B **20**
   WV6: Tett 3C **26**
   WV14: Bils 6G **45**
Orchard Av. B91: Sol 2H **151**
Orchard Blythe B46: Col 3H **107**
Orchard Cl. B21: Hand 5B **82**
   B46: Col 2H **107**
   B63: Crad 5E **111**
   B65: Row R .6A **96**
   B73: Bold 5G **69**
   B76: Curd 1D **88**
   WS4: Rus 4G **33**
   WS6: C Hay .2E **7**
   WV3: Wolv 4H **41**
   WV13: W'hall 2B **46**
Orchard Ct. B23: Erd 3B **84**
              (Marsh Hill)
   B23: Erd 2G **85**
             (Sutton Rd.)
   B65: Row R .6B **96**
   DY6: K'wfrd 3B **92**
Orchard Cres. WV3: Wolv 4H **41**
Orchard Dr. B31: Longb 2D **158**

Orchard Gro. B74: Four O 6F **37**
  DY3: Lwr G 4F **75**
  WS9: A'rdge 5D **34**
  WV4: Penn 1E **59**
Orchard Ho. B24: Erd 2G **85**
Orchard La. WV8: Bilb 4H **13**
Orchard Mdw. Wlk. B35: Cas V 4F **87**
Orchard Ri. B26: Yard 4D **120**
Orchard Rd. B12: Bal H 5H **117**
  B24: Erd 2G **85**
  DY2: Neth 1E **111**
  WS5: Wals 2F **65**
  WV11: Wed 2E **29**
  WV13: W'hall 2B **46**
Orchards, The B47: H'wd 2A **162**
  B74: Four O 3G **53**
  B90: Ches G 5B **164**
Orchard St. DY4: Tip 5H **77**
  DY5: Brie H 5G **93**
Orchards Way B12: Bal H 5G **117**
Orchard Way B27: A Grn 1H **135**
  B43: Gt Barr 4B **66**
  B47: H'wd 1A **162**
  B64: Old H 2H **111**
Orcheston Wlk. B14: K Hth 6F **147**
Orchid Cl. B66: Smeth 2B **98**
Orchid Dr. B19: Hock 3F **101**
Oregon Cl. DY6: K'wfrd 3D **92**
Oregon Dr. WV12: W'hall 2E **31**
Orford Gro. B23: Hand 1G **99**
Oriel Cl. DY1: Dud 5A **76**
Oriel Dr. WV10: F'hses 4H **15**
Oriel Ho. B37: F'bri 6C **106**
Oriel Vs. *B11: S'hll* *6C 118*
                (off Warwick Rd.)
Orion Bldg. B1: Birm 5C **4**
Orion Cl. B8: W End 5H **103**
  WS6: Gt Wyr 4F **7**
Orkney Av. B34: Hodg H 3D **104**
Orkney Cft. B36: Cas B 2D **106**
Orlando Cl. WS1: Wals 3C **48**
Orlando Ho. *WS1: Wals* *3D 48*
           (off Barleyfield Row)
Orme Cl. DY5: Brie H 3E **109**
Ormes La. WV6: Tett 6A **26**
Ormonde Cl. B63: Crad 4D **110**
Ormond Pl. WV14: Bils 5H **45**
Ormond Rd. B45: Fran 6E **143**
Ormsby Ct. B15: Edg 4A **116**
Ormsby Gro. B27: A Grn 6H **135**
Ormscliffe Rd. B45: Redn 3H **157**
Orphanage Rd. B24: Erd 2G **85**
  B72: W Grn 2G **85**
Orphelia Gdns. WV10: Bush 2A **28**
Orpington Rd. B44: Gt Barr 2G **67**
Orpwood Rd. B33: Yard 1E **121**
Orslow Wlk. WV10: Wolv 4C **28**
ORTON 2F **57**
Orton Av. B76: Walm 1D **86**
Orton Cl. B46: Wat O 4C **88**
Orton Gro. WV4: Penn 1B **58**
Orton La. WV4: Lwr P 2F **57**
  WV5: Wom 2F **57**
Orton Way B35: Cas V 6E **87**
Orwell Cl. DY8: Stourb 1B **124**
  WV11: Wed 4H **29**
Orwell Dr. B38: K Nor 1F **159**
  B71: W Brom 1B **80**
Orwell Pas. B5: Birm 5F **5** (1G **117**)
Orwell Rd. WS1: Wals 3F **49**
Osberton Dr. DY1: Dud 5B **76**
Osborn Ct. B73: W Grn 4H **69**
Osborne Dr. WS10: Darl 3D **46**
Osborne Gro. B19: Loz 2E **101**
Osborne Rd. B21: Hand 1B **100**
  B23: Erd 2F **85**
  B70: W Brom 4A **80**
  WV4: Penn 6D **42**
Osborne Rd. Sth. B23: Erd 3F **85**
Osborne Twr. B6: Aston 1A **102**
Osborn Rd. B11: S'brk 5C **118**
Osbourne Cl. B6: Aston 2A **102**
  DY5: Quar B 3B **110**
Osbourne Cft. B90: Ches G 4B **164**

Oscott Ct. B23: Erd 5E **69**
Oscott Gdns. B42: P Barr 4G **83**
Oscott Rd. B6: Witt 4G **83**
  B42: P Barr 4G **83**
Oscott School La. B44: Gt Barr 3G **67**
Osier Gro. B23: Erd 1B **84**
Osier Pl. WV1: Wolv 1B **44**
Osier St. WV1: Wolv 1B **44**
Osler St. B16: Birm 1B **116**
Osmaston Rd. B17: Harb 2E **131**
  DY8: Stourb 3C **124**
Osmington Gro. B63: Crad 5F **111**
Osprey Dr. DY1: Dud 6B **76**
Osprey Rd. B23: Erd 1C **84**
  B27: A Grn 3B **136**
Ostler Cl. DY6: W Hth 2G **91**
Oswald Pl. WS3: Wals 4D **32**
Oswald Rd. WS3: Wals 4D **32**
Oswin Pl. WS3: Wals 4D **32**
Othello Rd. WV10: Bush 2A **28**
Otley Gro. B9: Bord G 6A **104**
Ottawa Twr. B5: Edg 4F **117**
Otterstone Cl. DY3: Sed 3G **59**
Otter Cft. B34: S End 4H **105**
Oughton Rd. B12: Birm 4A **118**
Oundle Rd. B44: K'sdng 6H **67**
OUNSDALE 6F **57**
Ounsdale Cres. WV5: Wom 6G **57**
Ounsdale Dr. DY2: Neth 6E **95**
Ounsdale Rd. WV5: Wom 6E **57**
Ounty John La. DY8: Stourb 5E **125**
Outfields B14: K Hth 1G **147**
Outmore Rd. B33: Sheld 2F **121**
Out Wood Dr. B31: Longb 6B **144**
Oval, The B67: Smeth 6B **98**
  DY1: Dud 1A **94**
  WS10: W'bry 1F **63**
Oval Rd. B24: Erd 6E **85**
  DY4: Tip .6H **61**
Overbrook Cl. DY3: Gorn 5G **75**
Over Brunton Cl. B31: N'fld 5F **145**
Overbury Cl. B31: N'fld 4G **145**
  B63: Hale 3B **128**
Overdale Av. B76: Walm 2D **86**
Overdale Cl. WS2: Wals 6C **30**
Overdale Ct. B13: Mose 1H **133**
Overdale Dr. WS2: Wals 6C **30**
Overdale Rd. B32: Quin 1C **130**
Overend Rd. B63: Crad 4F **111**
  B64: Crad H 4F **111**
Overend St. B70: W Brom 4B **80**
Overfield Dr. WV14: Cose 2C **60**
Overfield Rd. B32: Bart G 4C **130**
  DY1: Dud 1A **94**
Over Grn. Dr. B37: K'hrst 3B **106**
Overhill Rd. WS7: Burn 1C **10**
Overlea Av. B27: A Grn 2H **135**
Overman Cl. DY9: Lye 6H **109**
Over Mill Dr. B29: S Oak 3D **132**
Over Moor Cl. B19: Loz 2E **101**
Over Pool Rd. B8: W End 3G **103**
Overseal Rd. WV11: Wed 1G **29**
Overslade Rd. B91: Sol 6D **150**
Oversley Rd. B76: Walm 1E **87**
Overstrand WV9: Pend 4D **14**
Overton Cl. B28: Hall G 1G **149**
Overton Dr. B46: Wat O 4E **89**
Overton Gro. B27: A Grn 5A **136**
Overton La. WS7: Hamm 1E **11**
Overton Pl. B7: Birm 6A **102**
  B71: W Brom 1B **80**
Overton Rd. B27: A Grn 5H **135**
Over Wood Cft. B8: Salt 6D **102**
Owen Pl. WV14: Bils 5F **45**
Owen Rd. WV3: Wolv 2E **43**
  WV13: W'hall 2C **46**
  WV14: Bils 4F **45**
Owen Rd. Ind. Est. WV13: W'hall 2C **46**
Owens Cft. B38: K Nor 6C **146**

Owens Way B64: Old H 2A **112**
Ownall Rd. B34: S End 3G **105**
Oxbarn Av. WV3: Wolv 5C **42**
Oxenton Cft. B63: Hale 3F **127**
Oxford Cl. B8: W End 4H **103**
  WS6: Gt Wyr 2F **7**
Oxford Dr. B29: W Cas 6G **131**
Oxford Dr. B27: A Grn 1B **136**
  DY8: Stourb 1D **124**
Oxford Gro. B37: Chel W 2C **122**
Oxford Ho. B31: Longb 1D **158**
Oxford Pas. DY1: Dud 6D **76**
Oxford Rd. B13: Mose 3H **133**
  B23: Erd 3F **85**
  B27: A Grn 2A **136**
  B66: Smeth 1E **99**
            (not continuous)
  B70: W Brom 4H **79**
Oxford St. B5: Birm 6G **5** (2H **117**)
  B30: Stir .6C **132**
  DY1: Dud 6D **76**
  WS2: Wals 4A **48**
  WS10: W'bry 2H **63**
  WV1: Wolv 6G **44**
  WV14: Bils 6G **45**
Oxford St. Ind. Est. WV14: Bils 6H **45**
Oxford Ter. WS10: W'bry 3H **63**
Oxford Way DY4: Tip 3F **77**
Oxhayes Cl. CV7: Bal C 6H **169**
Oxhill Rd. B21: Hand 5G **81**
  B90: Shir 5C **148**
Ox Leasow B32: Bart G 3A **130**
OXLEY 1E **27**
Oxley Av. WV10: Oxl 3G **27**
Oxley Cl. DY2: Neth 1D **110**
  WS6: Gt Wyr 4F **7**
Oxley Cl. Cvn. Pk. WV10: Oxl 1E **27**
Oxley Gro. B29: W Cas 5E **131**
Oxley La. WV1: Wolv 6G **27**
Oxley Links Rd. WV10: Oxl 1F **27**
Oxley Moor Rd. WV9: Pend 1E **27**
  WV10: Oxl 1E **27**
Ox Leys Rd. B75: S Cold 1F **71**
  B76: Walm, Wis 1F **71**
Oxley St. WV1: Wolv 5G **27**
Oxlip Cl. WS5: Wals 2E **65**
Oxpiece Dr. B36: Hodg H 1B **104**
Oxstall Cl. B76: Min 2H **87**
Ox St. DY3: Up Gor 2H **75**
Oxted Cl. WV11: Wed 4H **29**
Oxted Cft. B23: Erd 4E **85**
Oxwood La. B32: Fran 3D **142**
  B62: Hunn 3D **142**

P

Pace Cres. WV14: Bils 3A **62**
Pacific Av. WS10: W'bry 4D **62**
Packhorse La. B38: Head H 3F **161**
  B47: H'wd 3F **161**
Packington Av. B34: S End 4G **105**
Packington Ct. B74: Four O 5E **37**
Packmores B90: Dic H 4G **163**
Packwood Cl. B20: Hand 5C **82**
  B93: Ben H 5A **166**
  WV13: W'hall 3H **45**
Packwood Cotts. B93: Dorr 6G **167**
Packwood Ct. B29: W Cas 4D **130**
  B91: Sol .2G **151**
Packwood Dr. B43: Gt Barr 4H **65**
PACKWOOD GULLET 6F **167**
Packwood Rd. B26: Sheld 3F **121**
  B69: Tiv .6A **78**
Padarn Cl. DY3: Sed 4G **59**
Padbury WV9: Pend 4F **15**
Paddington Rd. B21: Hand 6G **81**
Paddington Wlk. WS2: Wals 5F **31**
Paddock WS1: Wals 2D **48**
Paddock, The B31: N'fld 3G **145**
  B76: Curd 1E **89**
  DY3: Up Gor 2A **76**
  DY9: Pedm 4F **125**
  WV4: Penn 5F **43**

Paddock, The WV5: Wom 1E 73
  WV6: Pert .5D 24
  WV8: Cod 5F 13
  WV14: Cose 4F 61
Paddock Dr. B26: Sheld 4E 121
  B93: Dorr 6H 167
Paddock La. WS1: Wals 2D 48
               (not continuous)
  WS6: Gt Wyr 2G 7
  WS9: A'rdge 4C 34
Paddocks, The B15: Edg 3D 116
  B76: Walm 1E 73
Paddocks Dr. B47: H'wd 3H 161
Paddocks Grn. B18: Hock 4C 100
Paddock Vw. WV6: Wolv 3F 27
Paddys Wide Water Ind. Est.
  DY5: Brie H 4G 93
Padgate Cl. B35: Cas V 4F 87
Padstow Rd. B24: Erd 3B 86
Paganal Dr. B70: W Brom 6C 80
Paganel Dr. DY1: Dud 4E 77
Paganel Rd. B29: W Cas 3E 131
Pagan Pl. B9: Birm 6H 5
                (off Gibb St.)
Pageant Ct. B12: Bal H 6G 117
Pages Cl. B75: S Cold 6A 54
Pages Ct. B43: Gt Barr 4A 66
Pages La. B43: Gt Barr 4A 66
Paget Cl. WV14: Cose 5D 60
Paget Ho. DY4: Tip 4B 78
Paget M. B76: Walm 3D 70
Paget Rd. B24: Erd 3B 86
  WV6: Wolv 1D 42
Paget St. WV1: Wolv 6F 27
Pagham Cl. WV9: Pend 5D 14
Pagnell Gro. B13: Mose 1C 148
Pagoda Cl. B74: S'tly 4H 51
Paignton Rd. B16: Edg 6H 99
Pailton Gro. B29: W Cas 4F 131
Pailton Rd. B90: Shir 2H 149
Painswick Cl. WS5: Wals 2F 65
Painswick Rd. B28: Hall G 6E 135
Paint Cup Row DY2: Neth 1E 111
Painters Cnr. B66: Smeth 4G 99
                (off Grove La.)
Painters Cft. WV14: Cose 4G 61
Pakefield Rd. B30: K Nor 4E 147
Pakenham Cl. B76: Walm 5D 70
Pakenham Dr. B76: Walm 5D 70
Pakenham Ho. B76: Walm 5D 70
Pakenham Rd. B15: Edg 4E 117
Pakenham Village B15: Edg 4E 117
             (off Gilldown Pl.)
Pakfield Wlk. B6: Aston 1H 101
Palace Cl. B65: Row R 5D 96
Palace Dr. B66: Smeth 1B 98
Palace Rd. B9: Small H 1E 119
Palefield Rd. B90: M'path 3D 164
Pale La. B17: Harb 3D 114
Pale St. DY3: Up Gor 2A 76
Palethorpe Rd. DY4: Tip 5A 62
PALFREY 4A 48
Palfrey Rd. DY8: Stourb 6B 108
Pallasades Shop. Cen., The
  B2: Birm 5D 4 (1F 117)
Palmcourt Av. B28: Hall G 6E 135
Palm Cft. DY5: Brie H 3G 109
Palmer Cl. WV11: Wed 6H 17
Palmers Cl. B90: Shir 2H 149
  WV8: Bilb .6A 14
PALMERS CROSS 2C 26
Palmers Gro. B36: Hodg H 1C 104
Palmerston Dr. B69: Tiv 5D 78
Palmerston Rd. B11: S'brk 5B 118
Palmer St. B9: Birm 1A 118
Palmer's Way WV8: Bilb 6A 14
Palm Ho. B20: Hand 4B 82
Palmvale Cft. B26: Sheld 5E 121
Palomino Pl. B16: Birm 1B 116
Pamela Rd. B31: N'fld 5E 145
Pan Cft. B36: Hodg H 2A 104
Panjab Gdns. B67: Smeth 3D 98
Pannel Cft. B19: Hock 3F 101
Panther Cft. B34: S End 4H 105

Paper Mill End B44: Gt Barr 1F 83
Paper Mill End Ind. Est.
  B44: Gt Barr 1F 83
Papyrus Way B36: Hodg H 6D 86
Parade B1: Birm 3A 4 (6E 101)
  B72: S Cold 1H 69
               (Holland St.)
  B72: S Cold 6A 54
             (Newhall Wlk.)
Parade, The B37: K'hrst 3C 106
  B64: Crad H 3G 111
  DY1: Dud .5D 76
  DY6: W Hth 2H 91
  WS8: Bwnhls 4A 10
Parade Vw. WS8: Bwnhls 5A 10
PARADISE 1F 95
Paradise DY2: Dud 1F 95
Paradise Cir. Queensway
  B1: Birm 3B 4 (1E 117)
Paradise Ct. B28: Hall G 1D 148
Paradise Gro. WS3: Pels 4D 20
Paradise La. B28: Hall G 1E 149
  WS3: Pels 4D 20
Paradise Pl. B3: Birm 4C 4 (1E 117)
Paradise St. B1: Birm 4C 4 (1F 117)
Pardington Cl. B92: Sol 5A 138
Pargeter Ct. WS2: Wals 1A 48
Pargeter Rd. B67: Smeth 1D 114
Pargeter St. DY8: Stourb 1D 124
  WS2: Wals 1A 48
Par Grn. B38: K Nor 6H 145
Parish Gdns. DY9: Pedm 4F 125
Park & Ride
  Bescot Cres. 6B 48
  Corser St. 2B 44
  Elmdon La. 4B 122
  Monkspath 4F 151
  Plascom .2C 44
  Priestfield 4C 44
  Science Park 3G 27
Park App. B23: Erd 5C 84
Park Av. B12: Bal H 6H 117
  B18: Hock 2C 100
  B30: K Nor 2C 146
  B46: Col .3H 107
  B65: Row R 6C 96
  B67: Smeth 5D 98
  B68: O'bry 6H 97
  B91: Sol .4H 151
  DY4: Tip 2G 77
  WV1: Wolv 1A 170 (6F 27)
  WV4: Penn 6G 43
  WV5: Wom 2F 73
  WV13: W'hall 1H 45
Park Bldgs. DY3: Lwr G 3G 75
               (off Park Rd.)
Park Cir. B6: Aston 2H 101
Park Cl. B24: Erd 2B 86
  B69: Tiv 2C 96
  B92: Sol 3H 137
  DY1: Dud .6D 60
  WS6: C Hay 2E 7
  WS8: Bwnhls 5B 10
Park Ct. B73: Bold 4F 69
Park Cres. B71: W Brom 3B 80
  WV1: Wolv 1F 43
Park Cft. B47: H'wd 4A 162
PARK DALE .6E 27
Park Dale WS5: Wals 5G 49
Parkdale DY3: Sed 5H 59
Parkdale Av. WS10: W'bry 1G 63
Parkdale Cl. B24: Erd 5F 85
Park Dale Ct. WV1: Wolv 6E 27
Parkdale Dr. B31: Longb 2E 159
Park Dale E. WV1: Wolv 6E 27
Parkdale Rd. B26: Sheld 6G 121
Park Dale W. WV1: Wolv 6E 27
Park Dr. B74: Four O 1G 53
  B74: Lit As 5C 36
  WV4: Penn 6G 43
Park Edge B17: Harb 4G 115
Park End B32: Bart G 4B 130
Parker Ho. B14: K Hth 4H 147
Parker Paul Ind. Est. WV2: Wolv 4G 43

Parker Rd. WV11: Wed 6H 17
Parkes St. B16: Edg 2B 116
  WS3: Blox 6G 19
Parkes Av. WV8: Cod 5H 13
Parkes' Hall Rd. DY1: Dud 1C 76
Parkes Ho. B69: O'bry 2G 97
Parkes La. DY3: Sed 6C 60
  DY4: Tip 5H 61
Parkes St. B67: Smeth 5D 98
  DY5: Brie H 6H 93
  WV13: W'hall 2B 46
Parkeston Cres. B44: K'sdng 4C 68
Park Farm Rd. B43: Gt Barr 1D 66
PARKFIELD .6A 44
Parkfield B32: Bart G 3F 129
Parkfield Chalet Land (Cvn. Pk.)
  WV2: Wolv 5H 43
Parkfield Cl. B15: Edg 4E 117
  B62: Quin 6G 113
Parkfield Colliery WV4: E'shll 6B 44
Parkfield Ct. B46: Col 2H 107
                (Park Rd.)
  B46: Col .3H 107
              (Sumner Rd.)
Parkfield Cres. WV2: E'shll 5A 44
Parkfield Dr. B36: Cas B 6G 87
Parkfield Gro. WV2: E'shll 5A 44
Parkfield Ho. B23: Erd 6E 85
Parkfield Pl. DY8: Stourb 6F 109
Parkfield Rd. B8: Salt 6E 103
  B46: Col .2H 107
  B68: O'bry 6G 97
  DY2: Dud 3F 95
  DY8: Stourb 6E 109
  WV4: E'shll 5H 43
Park Gdns. DY9: W'cte 2B 126
Park Gro. B10: Small H 3D 118
  B46: Wat O 4E 89
Park Hall Cl. WS5: Wals 5G 49
Park Hall Cres. B36: Cas B 1F 105
Parkhall Cft. B34: S End 2G 105
Park Hall Rd. WS5: Wals 4G 49
  WV4: Penn 1H 59
Parkhead Cres. DY2: Dud 1D 94
Parkhead Rd. DY2: Dud 1D 94
Park Hill B13: Mose 1G 133
  B65: B'hth 2B 112
  WS10: W'bry 1H 63
Park Hill Dr. B20: Hand 3B 82
Park Hill Rd. B17: Harb 5G 115
  B67: Smeth 4D 98
Parkhill Rd. B76: Walm 1D 86
Parkhill St. DY2: Dud 1G 95
Park Ho. B66: Smeth 4G 99
  WV11: Ess 4A 18
Parkhouse Av. WV11: Wed 3D 28
Parkhouse Dr. B23: Erd 2A 84
Parkhouse Gdns. DY3: Lwr G 3G 75
Parklands B45: Redn 1G 157
  B91: Sol .4E 151
Parklands, The B23: Erd 1D 84
  DY9: Pedm 2G 125
  WV3: Wolv 2B 42
Parklands Av. B20: Hand 6C 82
Parklands Ct. B45: Redn 1G 157
  WS3: Blox 6H 19
Parklands Dr. B74: Four O 3F 53
Parklands Gdns. WS1: Wals 3E 49
Parklands Rd. WS10: Darl 6E 47
  WV1: Wolv 2C 44
  WV14: Cose 3F 61
Park La. B6: Aston 2G 101
  B20: Hand 2F 81
  B21: Hand 2F 81
  B35: Cas V 3F 87
  B63: Crad 5C 110
  B69: O'bry 3G 97
  B76: Min 3G 87
  CV7: Bal C 5G 155
  DY6: K'wfrd 2C 92
  WS6: Gt Wyr 2F 7
  WS10: Darl, W'bry 4F 47
  WV10: Bush, Wolv 3A 28
Park La. E. DY4: Tip 3A 78

Park La. Ind. Est. B69: O'bry 2G 97
  B71: W Brom 6F 81
Park La. Trad. Est. WV10: Wolv 4A 28
Park La. W. DY4: Tip 2G 77
Park Lime Dr. WS4: Wals 5F 33
Park Mall WS1: Wals 1C 48
Park Mdw. Av. WV14: Bils 3E 45
Park M. B29: S Oak 4F 131
Park Mill Wlk. B7: Nech 2C 102
Park Pl. B7: Nech 2C 102
Park Retreat B66: Smeth 5F 99
Park Ridge B74: S Cold 4G 53
Park Ridge Dr. B63: Crad 5D 110
Park Ri. WV3: Wolv 1C 42
Park Rd. B6: Aston 2A 102
  B11: S'hll 2C 134
  B13: Mose 1H 133
  B18: Hock 3B 100
  B23: Erd 5C 84
  B46: Col 3H 107
  B63: Crad 6C 110
  B67: Smeth 1D 114
  B69: Tiv .1C 96
  B73: S Cold 6H 53
  B91: Sol 4G 151
  DY1: Dud 1D 76
  DY2: Neth 3E 95
  DY3: Lwr G 3G 75
  DY5: Quar B 3B 110
  DY8: Woll 6B 108
  WS3: Blox 6H 19
    (not continuous)
  WS4: Rus 4G 33
  WS5: Wals 6H 49
  WV13: W'hall 6H 29
  WV14: Bils 6E 45
Park Rd. E. WV1: Wolv 6F 27
Park Rd. Nth. B6: Aston 2A 102
Park Rd. Sth. B18: Hock 4D 100
Park Rd. W. DY8: Woll 6A 108
  WV1: Wolv 6E 27
Parkrose Ind. Est.
  B66: Smeth 1F 99
Parks Cres. WV11: Ess 3A 18
Parkside B16: Edg 6H 99
  B32: Bart G 3A 130
  B37: Mars G 4F 123
Parkside Av. WV13: W'hall 1G 45
Parkside Cl. WS10: W'bry 2H 63
Parkside Ind. Est.
  WV1: Wolv 2B 44
Parkside Rd. B20: Hand 2A 82
  B63: Crad 6F 111
Parkside Way B31: Longb 6A 144
  B74: S'tly 2A 52
Park Sq. B37: Mars G 3F 123
Parkstone Cl. WS4: S'fld 1G 33
Park St. B4: Birm 3G 5 (6H 101)
  B5: Birm 3G 5 (6H 101)
    (not continuous)
  B6: Aston 2A 102
    (not continuous)
  B64: Crad H 1G 111
  B65: B'hth 2D 112
  B69: O'bry 3F 97
  B70: W Brom 4B 80
  DY1: Dud 3B 94
  DY4: Tip 2A 78
  DY6: K'wfrd 3B 92
  DY8: Amb 3D 108
  DY9: Lye 6B 110
  WS1: Wals 1C 48
  WS6: C Hay 2E 7
  WS10: Darl 6C 46
  WS10: W'bry 2F 63
Park St. Arc. WS1: Wals 1C 48
    (off Park St.)
Park St. Sth. WV2: Wolv 5G 43
Park St. W. B65: B'hth 2D 112
Park Ter. B21: Hand 1A 100
  WS10: Darl 5B 46
Park Trad. Est. B18: Hock 3C 100
Park Tree Wlk. B24: Erd 3B 86

Park Vw. B10: Small H 4D 118
  B18: Win G 5A 100
  B73: S Cold 5G 53
  B91: Sol 5F 151
  DY8: Stourb 2E 125
  WS10: Darl 5C 46
Park View Community Leisure Cen.
  . . . . .4F 103
Parkview Ct. DY6: W'hth 1H 91
Parkview Cres. WS2: Wals 5G 31
Parkview Dr. B8: W End 3G 103
  WS8: Bwnhls 3B 10
Park Vw. Rd. B31: N'fld 4C 144
  B74: Four O 6D 36
  DY9: W'cte 1B 126
  WV14: Bils 3E 45
Park Vw. Trad. Est. B30: K Nor 4B 146
PARK VILLAGE 4B 28
Park Village Youth Media Activity Cen.
  . . . . .4B 28
Park Vs. B9: Birm 1B 118
Parkville Av. B17: Harb 1F 131
Park Wlk. DY5: Quar B 3B 110
Park Way B45: Redn 6H 143
  WV11: Wed 6A 18
Parkway, The DY4: Tip 4D 62
  WS4: S'fld 1G 33
  WV6: Pert 3D 24
Parkway Ind. Cen. B7: Birm . . .1H 5 (5A 102)
Parkway Ind. Est., The
  WS10: W'bry 4E 63
Parkway Rd. DY1: Dud 5C 76
Parkway Rdbt. WS10: W'bry 4E 63
Parkwood Cl. WS8: Wals W 2C 22
Park Wood Ct. B74: Four O 1F 53
Parkwood Cft. B43: Gt Barr 4D 66
Parkwood Dr. B73: New O 3C 68
Parkyn St. WV2: Wolv 3A 44
Parliament St. B6: Aston 3G 101
  B10: Small H 3C 118
  B70: W Brom 6B 80
Parlows End B38: K Nor 2H 159
Parry Rd. WV11: Wed 1A 30
Parsonage Dr. B45: Coft H 5B 158
  B63: Crad 4C 110
Parsonage St. B69: O'bry 2H 97
  B71: W Brom 1B 80
Parsons Hill B30: K Nor 5C 146
  B68: O'bry 2H 113
Parsons M. B30: K Nor 5D 146
Parson's St. DY1: Dud 6E 77
Parsons Way WS2: Wals 3F 31
Partons Rd. B14: K Hth 1F 147
Partridge Av. WS10: Darl 5B 46
Partridge Cl. B37: Chel W 6E 107
Partridge Ct. B4: Birm 1E 5
  WS10: W'bry 2F 63
Partridge Mill WS3: Pels 4C 20
Partridge Rd. B26: Yard 2E 121
  DY8: Stourb 1A 124
Passey Rd. B13: Mose 3D 134
Passfield Rd. B33: Yard 6E 105
Pastures, The WV6: Pert 5D 24
Pastures Wlk. B38: K Nor 2H 159
Pasture Vw. WS3: Pels 5D 20
Patent Dr. WS10: W'bry 3C 62
Patent Shaft Rdbt. WS10: W'bry 2D 62
Paternoster Row B5: Birm 4F 5 (1G 117)
  WV1: Wolv 2A 170 (1G 43)
Paterson Ct. B93: Know 3E 167
Paterson Pl. WS8: Bwnhls 2D 22
Pathlow Cres. B90: Shir 6G 149
Pathway, The B14: K Hth 2D 146
Patina Cl. DY5: Quar B 3B 110
Patman Gdns. B16: Edg 2G 115
Paton Gro. B13: Mose 3H 133
Patricia Av. B14: Yard W 3C 148
  WV4: Penn 6G 43
Patricia Cres. DY1: Dud 1D 76
Patricia Dr. DY4: Tip 5A 78
Patrick Gregory Rd. WV11: Wed 2H 29
Patrick Rd. B26: Yard 4C 120
Patriot Cl. WS1: Wals 5B 48

Patshull Av. WV10: F'hses 4F 15
Patshull Cl. B43: Gt Barr 4H 65
Patshull Gro. WV10: F'hses 4F 15
Patshull Pl. B19: Loz 2E 101
Pattenham Cl. WV12: W'hall 5D 30
Patterdale Rd. B23: Erd 3D 84
Patterdale Way DY5: Brie H 3F 109
Patterton Dr. B76: Walm 5E 71
Pattingham Rd. WV6: Pert, Tett 6A 24
Pattison Gdns. B23: Erd 5D 84
Pattison St. WS5: Wals 6C 48
Paul Byrne Ct. B20: Hand 6D 82
Paul Pursehouse Rd. WV14: Cose . . .2F 61
Pauls Coppice WS8: Bwnhls 2B 22
Paul St. WS10: W'bry 3G 63
  WV2: Wolv 6A 170 (3G 43)
  WV14: Cose 4C 60
Paul Va. DY4: Tip 2B 78
Pavenham Dr. B5: Edg 1E 133
Pavilion B40: Nat E C 1G 139
Pavilion Av. B67: Smeth 6B 98
Pavilion Cl. WS9: A'rdge 2D 34
Pavilion Dr. B6: Witt 4H 83
Pavilion Gdns. DY2: Neth 1E 111
Pavilion Rd. B6: Witt 4H 83
Pavilions, The B4: Birm 4F 5 (1G 117)
  B37: Mars G 3F 123
Pavior's Rd. WS7: Chase 1A 10
Paxford Way B31: N'fld 1D 144
Paxton Av. WV6: Pert 6E 25
Paxton Rd. B18: Hock 4C 100
  DY9: W'cte 1C 126
Payne St. B65: B'hth 2C 112
Payton Cl. B69: O'bry 6E 79
Payton Rd. B21: Hand 1H 99
PDH Ind. Est. WS10: Mox 1C 62
Peace Cl. WS6: C Hay 2E 7
Peace Wlk. B37: Chel W 2D 122
Peach Av. WS10: Darl 5C 46
Peachley Cl. B63: Hale 2B 128
Peach Ley Rd. B29: W Cas 6D 130
Peach Rd. WV12: W'hall 3A 30
Peacock Av. WV11: Wed 1A 30
Peacock Cl. DY4: Tip 3B 78
Peacock Cft. B65: Gt Wyr 3G 7
Peacock Rd. B13: Mose 1H 147
  WS10: Darl 4B 46
Peacocks Est. B64: Crad H 2E 111
Peak Cft. B36: Hodg H 1B 104
Peak Dr. DY3: Lwr G 4H 75
Peake Cres. WS8: Bwnhls 2B 22
Peake Dr. DY4: Tip 3B 78
Peake Rd. WS8: Bwnhls 2C 22
Peak Ho. Rd. B43: Gt Barr 4A 66
Peakman Cl. B45: Redn 3G 157
Peal St. WS1: Wals 2D 48
Pearce Cl. DY1: Dud 1A 94
Pearl Gro. B18: Win G 5A 100
  B27: A Grn 2H 135
Pearman Rd. B45: Fran 6D 142
  B66: Smeth 6E 99
Pearmans Cft. B47: H'wd 3A 162
Pearsall Dr. B69: O'bry 1E 97
Pearson Cl. WV12: W'hall 5D 30
Pearson St. B64: Old H 2G 111
  B70: W Brom 3H 79
  DY5: Brie H 6H 93
  DY9: Lye 1B 126
  WV2: Wolv 6B 170 (3G 43)
Pear Tree Av. DY4: Tip 2H 77
  WV13: W'hall 2B 46
Pear Tree Cl. B33: Stech 1B 120
  B43: Gt Barr 4F 65
Peartree Cl. B90: Shir 5D 148
Pear Tree Ct. B43: Gt Barr 5G 65
  B65: Row R 6D 96
Peartree Cres. B90: Shir 4C 148
Pear Tree Dr. B43: Gt Barr 5F 65
  B65: Row R 6D 96
Peartree Dr. DY8: Stourb 3E 125
Peartree Gro. B90: Shir 5C 148
Peartree Ho. B68: O'bry 4A 98
Peartree Ind. Est. DY2: Dud 3C 94

Pear Tree La. WS8: Bwnhls 3G 9
  WV11: Wed 6D 16
Peartree La. B64: Old H 2G 111
  DY2: Dud 4B 94
  WV14: Cose 5F 61
Pear Tree Rd. B34: S End 3G 105
  B43: Gt Barr 4F 65
  B67: Smeth 5C 98
Peascroft La. WV14: Bils 5G 45
Peasefield Cl. B21: Hand 1G 99
Pebble Cl. B92: Stourb 6F 109
Pebble Mill Rd. B5: Edg 1E 133
Pebworth Av. B90: M'path 3F 165
Pebworth Cl. B29: S Oak 3D 132
Pebworth Gro. B33: Sheld 3G 121
  DY1: Dud 4C 76
Peckham Rd. B44: K'sdng 3A 68
Peckingham St. B63: Hale 2B 128
Peckover Cl. B65: B'hth 2C 112
Peddimore La. B76: Min 6G 71
  B76: Min, Walm 1F 87
    (not continuous)
PEDMORE 4G 125
Pedmore Ct. Rd. DY8: Stourb 4F 125
Pedmore Gro. B44: Gt Barr 3H 67
Pedmore Hall La. DY9: Pedm 5G 125
Pedmore La. DY9: Hag, Pedm 4G 125
Pedmore M. DY8: Stourb 4F 125
Pedmore Rd. DY2: Dud 5B 94
  DY5: Brie H 6B 94
  DY9: Lye 6H 109
Pedmore Rd. Ind. Est. DY5: Brie H . .5B 94
Pedmore Wlk. B69: O'bry 4B 96
Peel Cl. B92: H Ard 1B 154
  WS10: Darl 3D 46
  WV13: W'hall 2A 46
Peel St. B18: Win G 4A 100
  B71: W Brom 2A 80
  DY2: Dud 1G 95
  DY4: Tip 3A 78
  WV3: Wolv 4A 170 (2G 43)
  WV13: W'hall 2A 46
Peel Wlk. B17: Harb 4D 114
Peel Way B69: Tiv 5C 78
Pegasus Ct. B62: Quin 6F 113
  B75: Four O 6G 37
Pegasus Wlk. B29: S Oak 4H 131
Pegleg Wlk. B14: K Hth 5E 147
Pelham Dr. DY1: Dud 5C 76
Pelham Rd. B8: W End 5H 103
Pelham St. WV3: Wolv 2E 43
PELSALL 4E 21
Pelsall La. WS3: Blox 4B 20
    (not continuous)
  WS4: Rus 1E 33
Pelsall Rd. WS8: Bwnhls 1G 21
PELSALL WOOD 3D 20
Pemberley Rd. B27: A Grn 3G 135
Pemberton Cl. B66: Smeth 6F 99
Pemberton Cres. WS10: W'bry . . .1A 64
Pemberton Rd. B70: W Brom . .1G 79
  WV14: Cose 4F 61
Pemberton St. B18: Birm 5D 100
Pembridge Cl. B32: Bart G 6G 129
  DY5: Quar B 2B 110
Pembridge Rd. B93: Dorr 6H 165
Pembroke Av. WV2: E'shll 4C 44
Pembroke Cl. B71: W Brom 4H 63
    (off Pembroke Rd.)
  WV12: W'hall 3C 30
Pembroke Cft. B28: Hall G 2G 149
Pembroke Gdns. DY8: Word 2A 108
Pembroke Ho. B36: Cas B 2C 106
  WS3: Blox 3A 32
    (off Cornwall Clo.)
Pembroke Rd. B12: Bal H 1A 134
  B71: W Brom 5H 63
Pembroke Way B8: Salt 4C 102
  B28: Hall G 2G 149
  B71: W Brom 6H 63
Pembrook Dr. B31: N'fld 1C 144
Pembury Cl. B74: S'tly 5H 51
Pembury Cft. B44: K'sdng 4A 68
Pencombe Dr. WV4: Penn 6H 43

Pencroft Rd. B34: S End 2F 105
Penda Cl. B20: Hand 1C 100
Penda Gro. WV6: Pert 4F 25
Pendeen Rd. B14: Yard W 3B 148
PENDEFORD 4E 15
Pendeford Av. WV6: Tett 1C 26
Pendeford Bus. Pk. WV9: Pend 4D 14
Pendeford Cl. WV6: Tett 1C 26
Pendeford Hall La.
  WV9: Coven, Pend 2H 13
Pendeford Hall Mobile Home Pk.
  WV9: Pend 3C 14
Pendeford La. WV9: Pend 3E 15
Pendeford Mill La. WV8: Bilb 4H 13
Pendeford Pl. WV9: Pend 4D 14
Pendene Ct. WV4: Penn 6E 43
Pendennis Cl. B30: B'vlle 2H 145
Pendennis Dr. B69: Tiv 1A 96
Penderel Cl. WV10: F'stne 1C 16
Penderel St. WS3: Blox 1A 32
Pendigo Way B40: Nat E C 1G 139
    (not continuous)
Pendinas Dr. WV8: Bilb 4H 13
Pendleton Gro. B27: A Grn 5H 135
Pendragon Rd. B42: P Barr 3E 83
Pendrel Cl. WS6: Gt Wyr 5F 7
Pendrell Cl. B37: F'bri 6C 106
  WV8: Cot 4G 13
Pendrell Ct. WV8: Cot 4G 13
Pendrill Rd. WV10: Bush 4A 16
Penfields Rd. DY8: Amb 5E 109
Penge Gro. B44: Gt Barr 2G 67
Penhallow Dr. WV4: E'shll 6A 44
Penkridge Cl. WS2: Wals 5B 32
Penkridge Gro. B33: Stech 5D 104
Penkridge St. WS2: Wals 6B 32
Penk Ri. WV6: Tett 5G 25
Penleigh Gdns. WV5: Wom 6F 57
Penley Gro. B8: W End 3H 103
Penmakers Ct. B66: Smeth 5E 99
PENN 1D 58
Pennant Cl. B65: Row R 6B 96
Pennant Gro. B29: W Cas 3E 131
Pennant Rd. B64: Crad H 2F 111
  B65: Row R 6B 96
Pennard Gro. B32: Quin 1D 130
Penn Cl. WS3: Blox 1A 32
Penn Comn. Rd. WV4: Penn 4C 58
Penncricket La. B65: Row R 6E 97
  B68: O'bry 6F 97
Penncroft La. WV4: Penn 4D 58
Penn Dale Cl. B24: Erd 1A 86
PENN FIELDS 5E 43
Penn Gro. B29: W Cas 3F 131
Pennhouse Av. WV4: Penn 6D 42
Penn Ind. Est. B64: Crad H 2F 111
Pennine Dr. DY3: Lwr G 4H 75
Pennine Way B8: Salt 4C 102
  DY8: Amb 5E 109
  WV12: W'hall 4D 30
Pennington Cl. B70: W Brom 5G 79
Penn Rd. B65: Row R 6E 97
  DY3: Sed 4D 58
  WV2: Wolv 6A 170 (4F 43)
  WV3: Wolv 4F 43
  WV4: Penn 2B 58
Penn Rd. Island WV2: Wolv . .5A 170 (2G 43)
Penn Rd. Retail Pk. WV2: Wolv 3G 43
Penns Cl. B76: Walm 6D 70
Penns Lake Rd. B76: Walm 5C 70
Penns La. B72: W Grn 6A 70
  B76: Walm 6A 70
Penn St. B4: Birm 2H 5 (6A 102)
  B64: Old H 3H 111
  WV3: Wolv 3F 43
Penns Wood Cl. DY3: Sed 3G 59
Penns Wood Dr. B76: Walm 6D 70
Pennwood Ct. WV4: Penn 5B 42
Pennwood La. WV4: Penn 2D 58
Pennyacre Rd. B14: K Hth 5F 147
Penny Ct. WS6: Gt Wyr 5F 7
Pennycress Grn. WS11: Nort C 1D 8
Pennycroft Ho. B33: Stech 6C 104

Pennyfield Cft. B33: Stech 6C 104
Pennyhill La. B71: W Brom 6C 64
Penny Royal Cl. DY3: Lwr G 5H 75
Pennyroyal Cl. WS5: Wals 2F 65
Penrice Dr. B69: Tiv 6H 77
Penrith Cl. DY5: Brie H 3F 109
Penrith Cft. B32: Bart G 5B 130
Penrith Gro. B37: Chel W 1E 123
Penryn Cl. WS5: Wals 4H 49
Penryn Rd. WS5: Wals 4H 49
Pensby Cl. B13: Mose 5D 134
Pens Cl. B66: Smeth 5E 99
Pensford Rd. B31: N'fld 4G 145
Pensham Cft. B90: M'path 3E 165
Penshaw Cl. WV9: Pend 4E 15
Penshaw Gro. B13: Mose 4D 134
Penshurst Av. B20: Hand 6F 83
PENSNETT 3G 93
Pensnett Rd. DY1: Dud 2A 94
  DY5: Brie H 4G 93
Pensnett Trad. Est. DY6: P'ntt 1D 92
Penstock Dr. B69: O'bry 5G 97
Penstone La. WV4: Lwr P 1E 57
Pentland Cft. B12: Birm 4H 117
Pentland Gdns. WV3: Wolv 1C 42
Pentos Dr. B11: S'hll 1D 134
Pentridge Cl. B76: Walm 2D 86
Penwood Gdns. WV14: Cose 5E 61
Penzer St. DY6: K'wfrd 2B 92
Peolsford Rd. WS3: Pels 3E 21
Peony Wlk. B23: Erd 4B 84
Peplins Way B30: K Nor 4D 146
Peplow Rd. B33: Stech 5E 105
Pepperbox Dr. DY4: Tip 2A 78
Peppercorn Pl. B70: W Brom 3A 80
Pepper Hill DY8: Stourb 1E 125
Pepper Wood Dr. B31: Longb 6A 144
Pepys Ct. B43: Gt Barr 4A 66
Perch Av. B37: F'bri 6C 106
Perch Cl. WV10: Wolv 5D 28
Perch Rd. WS2: Wals 5G 31
Percival Rd. B16: Edg 2G 115
Percy Bus. Pk. B69: O'bry 2F 97
Percy Rd. B11: S'hll 2D 134
Peregrine Cl. DY1: Dud 6B 76
Pereira Rd. B17: Harb 4G 115
Perimeter Rd. B40: Nat E C 1F 139
    (not continuous)
Perivale Gro. WV14: Cose 5F 61
Perivale Way DY8: Amb 3F 109
Periwinkle Cl. WS8: Clay 1H 21
Perkins Cl. DY1: Dud 1E 77
Perks Rd. WV11: Wed 6A 18
Perott Dr. B75: R'ley 1B 54
Perrins Gro. B8: W End 3G 103
Perrin's La. DY9: W'cte 1B 126
Perrins Ri. DY9: W'cte 1B 126
Perrott Gdns. DY5: Brie H 2E 109
Perrott's Folly 2B 116
Perrott St. B18: Win G 3H 99
PERRY 1G 83
Perry Av. B42: P Barr 3E 83
  WV10: Bush 1B 28
PERRY BARR 2C 82
Perry Barr Stadium (Greyhound) 4F 83
Perry Barr Station (Rail) 5F 83
PERRY BEECHES 6D 66
Perry Beeches Swimming Pool 6D 66
Perry Cl. DY2: Dud 1F 95
PERRY COMMON 5D 68
Perry Comn. Rd. B23: Erd 6D 68
Perry Ct. B68: O'bry 4H 113
Perryford Dr. B91: Sol 1G 165
Perry Hall Dr. WV12: W'hall 4B 30
Perry Hall Rd. WV11: Wed 3H 29
Perry Hill Cres. B68: O'bry 4H 113
Perry Hill Ho. B68: O'bry 3A 114
Perryhill La. B68: O'bry 4H 113
Perry Hill Rd. B68: O'bry 4H 113
Perry Pk. Cres. B42: P Barr 1E 83
Perry Pk. Rd. B64: Old H 2B 112
  B65: B'hth 2B 112
Perry St. B66: Smeth 2D 98
  DY4: Tip 3A 78

Perry St. WS10: Darl 3D **46**
    (not continuous)
  WS10: W'bry 3F **63**
  WV14: Bils 2G **61**
Perry Trad. Est. WV14: Bils 2G **61**
Perry Villa Dr. B42: P Barr 2F **83**
Perry Wlk. B23: Erd 1B **84**
Perry Well Dr. B6: Witt 3H **83**
Perry Well Rd. B6: Witt 2H **83**
Perry Wood Rd. B42: Gt Barr 5C **66**
Persehouse St. WS1: Wals 1D **48**
Pershore Av. B29: S Oak 3D **132**
Pershore Cl. WS3: Blox 5F **19**
Pershore Rd. B5: Edg, Bal H 1E **133**
  B29: S Oak 6C **132**
  B30: K Nor, Stir 3C **146**
  B63: Hale 3A **128**
  WS3: Blox 5F **19**
Pershore Rd. Sth. B30: K Nor 3B **146**
Pershore St. B5: Birm 6E **5** (2G **117**)
Pershore Way WS3: Blox 5F **19**
Pertemps Bees RUFC 3D **150**
Perth Rd. WV12: W'hall 3B **30**
PERTON .5E **25**
Perton Brook Va. WV6: Tett 1F **41**
Perton Gro. B29: W Cas 4E **131**
  WV6: Tett 1F **41**
Perton Rd. WV6: Tett 1E **41**
Petchells Cl. DY5: P'ntt 4F **93**
Peter Av. WV14: Bils 3H **61**
Peterbrook B90: Shir 6C **148**
Peterbrook Ri. B90: Shir 6D **148**
Peterbrook Rd. B90: Maj G 2D **162**
  B90: Shir 5C **148**
Peterdale Dr. WV4: Penn 2D **58**
Peterhouse M. B13: Mose 3A **134**
Peters Av. B31: N'fld 5D **144**
Petersbourne Ct. B28: Hall G 5E **135**
Petersfield Ct. B28: Hall G 5F **135**
Petersfield Dr. B65: Row R 6E **97**
Petersfield Rd. B28: Hall G 6E **135**
Petersham Pl. B15: Edg 5A **116**
Petersham Rd. B44: K'sdng 4C **68**
Peter's Hill Rd. DY5: Brie H 4G **109**
Petershouse Dr. B74: Four O 4F **37**
Peters St. B70: W Brom 6G **63**
Petford St. B64: Old H 2G **111**
Pettitt Cl. B14: K Hth 5G **147**
Pettyfield Cl. B26: Sheld 5F **121**
Pettyfields Cl. B93: Know 4B **166**
Petworth Cl. WV13: W'hall 3H **45**
Petworth Gro. B26: Yard 5C **120**
Pevensey Cl. B69: Tiv 1H **95**
Peverell Dr. B28: Hall G 6F **135**
Peveril Gro. B76: Walm 1C **70**
Peverill Rd. WV4: E'shll 2A **60**
  WV6: Pert 5F **25**
Peveril Way B43: Gt Barr 3B **66**
Pheasant Cft. B36: Cas B 1C **106**
Pheasant Rd. B67: Smeth 1B **114**
Pheasant St. DY5: Brie H 6G **93**
PHEASEY 1F **67**
Philip Ct. B76: Walm 2D **70**
Philip Rd. B63: Hale 2H **127**
  DY4: Tip 2D **78**
Philip Sidney Rd. B11: S'hll 2C **134**
Philip St. WV14: Cose 4F **61**
Philip Victor Rd. B20: Hand 6B **82**
Phillimore Rd. B8: Salt 4D **102**
Phillip Rd. WS2: Wals 5A **48**
Phillips Av. WV11: Wed 6H **17**
Phillips St. B6: Aston 3G **101**
Phillips St. Ind. Est.
  B6: Aston 3H **101**
Phipson Rd. B11: S'hll 1B **134**
Phoenix, The B90: Bly P 6D **164**
Phoenix Cl. B35: Cas V 4D **86**
Phoenix Dr. WS9: A'rdge 2C **34**
Phoenix Grn. B15: Edg 4A **116**
Phoenix Ind. Est. WV14: Bils 1H **61**
Phoenix Intl. Ind. Est.
  B70: W Brom 2F **79**
Phoenix Pk. B7: Nech 3A **102**
  B65: Row R 1E **113**

Phoenix Pas. DY2: Dud 6F **77**
    (off Hall St.)
Phoenix Ri. B23: Erd 6B **68**
  WS10: Darl 1D **62**
  WV2: Wolv 5G **43**
    (off Blakenhall Gdns.)
Phoenix Rd. DY4: Tip 1H **77**
  WV11: Wed 6F **29**
Phoenix Rd. Ind. Est. WV11: Wed 6F **29**
Phoenix St. B70: W Brom 3F **79**
  WV2: Wolv 5H **43**
Phoenix Works Ind. Est. WS10: Darl . . .4E **47**
Piccadilly Arc. B2: Birm 4D **4**
Piccadilly Cl. B37: Chel W 2E **123**
Pickenham Rd. B14: K Hth 6A **148**
Pickering Cft. B32: Bart G 4A **130**
Pickering Rd. WV11: Wed 4F **29**
Pickersleigh Cl. B63: Hale 2A **128**
Pickford St. B5: Birm 5H **5** (1H **117**)
Pickrell Rd. WV14: Cose 4D **60**
Pickwick Cl. B13: Mose 3B **134**
Pickwick Rd. B13: Mose 3C **134**
Pickwick Pl. WV14: Bils 1G **61**
Picton Cft. B37: Chel W 1F **123**
Picton Gro. B13: Mose 2B **148**
Picturedrome Way WS10: Darl 5D **46**
Piddock Rd. B66: Smeth 4E **99**
Pierce Av. B92: Olton 2C **136**
Piercy St. B70: W Brom 4G **79**
Piers Rd. B18: Hock 2C **100**
  B21: Hand 2C **100**
    (not continuous)
Pier St. WS8: Bwnhls 6B **10**
Piggotts Cft. B37: F'bri 6B **106**
Pike Cl. B20: Hand 6B **82**
Pike Dr. B37: Chel W 6E **107**
Pikehelve St. B70: W Brom 6E **63**
Pikehorne Cft. B36: Cas B 5H **87**
Pike Rd. WS2: Wals 5G **31**
Pikes, The B45: Rub 1F **157**
Pikewater Rd. B9: Bord G 1E **119**
Pilkington Av. B72: W Grn 2H **69**
Pilson Cl. B36: Hodg H 1D **104**
Pimbury Rd. WV12: W'hall 2D **30**
Pimlico Ct. DY3: Lwr G 4H **75**
Pimpernel Dr. WS5: Wals 2E **65**
Pinbury Cft. B37: Mars G 2D **122**
Pineapple Cl. B14: K Hth 1E **147**
Pineapple Gro. B30: Stir 5E **133**
Pineapple Rd. B30: Stir 6E **133**
Pine Av. B66: Smeth 2C **98**
  WS10: W'bry 6F **47**
Pine Cl. B91: Sol 5D **150**
  DY6: K'wfrd 4B **92**
  WS6: Gt Wyr 1F **7**
  WV3: Wolv 2E **43**
Pine Grn. DY1: Dud 1C **76**
Pine Gro. B14: K Hth 2A **148**
Pine Ho. B36: Hodg H 1D **104**
Pinehurst Dr. B38: K Nor 4B **146**
Pine Leigh B74: Four O 2H **53**
Pineneedle Cft. WV12: W'hall 5E **31**
Pine Rd. B69: Tiv 1A **96**
  DY1: Dud 2E **77**
Pines, The B45: Redn 6G **143**
  B90: Ches G 4B **164**
  WS1: Wals 3D **48**
  WV3: Wolv 2B **42**
Pine Sq. B37: Chel W 1D **122**
Pine St. WS3: Blox 5B **20**
Pinetree Dr. B74: S'tly 2F **51**
Pineview B31: N'fld 5D **144**
Pine Wlk. B31: N'fld 4F **145**
  DY9: W'cte 2H **125**
  WV8: Cod 5F **13**
Pinewall Av. B38: K Nor 6C **146**
Pineways B74: Four O 6C **36**
  DY8: Word 1A **108**
Pineways Dr. WV6: Wolv 5C **26**
Pinewood Cl. B44: Gt Barr 6G **67**
  B45: Rub 1D **156**
  WS5: Wals 6E **49**
  WS8: Bwnhls 3A **10**

Pinewood Cl. WV3: Wolv 3G **41**
  WV5: Wom 1G **73**
  WV12: W'hall 3D **30**
Pinewood Dr. B32: Bart G 4G **129**
Pinewood Gro. B91: Sol 5D **150**
Pine Woods B32: Bart G 3G **129**
Pinewoods B31: N'fld 5D **130**
  B62: Quin 4G **113**
Pinewood Wlk. DY6: K'wfrd 1C **92**
Pinfold Cl. WS10: Darl 6C **46**
Pinfold Cres. WV4: Penn 5B **42**
Pinfold Gdns. WV11: Wed 4F **29**
Pinfold Gro. WV4: Penn 5B **42**
Pinfold Ind. Est. WS3: Blox 1A **32**
Pinfold La. WS6: C Hay 3C **6**
  WS9: A'rdge 6C **50**
  WS11: Nort C 1C **8**
  WV4: Penn 5B **42**
Pinfold Rd. B91: Sol 2A **152**
Pinfold St. B2: Birm 4C **4** (1F **117**)
  B69: O'bry 1G **97**
  WS10: Darl 6C **46**
    (not continuous)
  WV14: Bils 6F **45**
Pinfold St. Extension
  WS10: Darl 6C **46**
Pingle Cl. B71: W Brom 4D **64**
Pingle La. WS7: Hamm 1F **11**
Pinkney Pl. B68: O'bry 6A **98**
Pink Pas. B66: Smeth 5F **99**
Pinley Gro. B43: Gt Barr 2E **67**
Pinley Way B91: Sol 1E **165**
Pinner Cl. B17: Harb 5G **115**
Pinner Gro. B32: Quin 1C **130**
Pinson Gdns. WV13: W'hall 1H **45**
Pinson Rd. WV13: W'hall 1H **45**
Pintail Dr. B23: Erd 5C **84**
Pinto Cl. B16: Birm 1B **116**
Pinza Cft. B36: Hodg H 1B **104**
Pioli Pl. WS2: Wals 4B **32**
Pioneer Way B35: Cas V 5F **87**
Piper Cl. WV6: Pert 5F **25**
Piper Pl. DY8: Amb 3D **108**
Piper Rd. WV3: Wolv 3A **42**
Pipers Grn. B28: Hall G 2F **149**
Piper's Row WV1: Wolv 3D **170** (1H **43**)
Pipes Mdw. WV14: Bils 6G **45**
Pippin Av. B63: Crad 4D **110**
Pirbright Cl. WV14: Bils 2G **61**
Pirrey Cl. WV14: Cose 4G **61**
Pitcairn Cl. B30: Stir 1D **146**
Pitcairn Dr. B62: Hale 6B **112**
Pitcairn Rd. B67: Smeth 2B **114**
Pitclose Rd. B31: N'fld 6F **145**
Pitfield Rd. B33: Kitts G 2A **122**
Pitfield Row DY1: Dud 6D **76**
Pitfields Cl. B68: O'bry 3G **113**
Pitfields Rd. B68: O'bry 3G **113**
Pitfield St. DY1: Dud 6E **77**
Pithall Rd. B34: S End 4H **105**
Pit Leasow Cl. B30: Stir 5D **132**
Pitman Rd. B32: Quin 6A **114**
Pitmaston Ct. B13: Mose 2F **133**
Pitmaston Rd. B28: Hall G 1G **149**
Pitmeadow Ho. B14: K Hth 5G **147**
    (off Pound Rd.)
Pitney St. B7: Birm 5B **102**
Pitsford St. B18: Birm, Hock 4C **100**
Pitt La. B92: Bick 3F **139**
Pitts Farm Rd. B24: Erd 2A **86**
Pitt St. B4: Birm 6A **102**
  WV3: Wolv 4A **170** (2G **43**)
Pixall Dr. B15: Edg 4D **116**
Pixhall Wlk. B35: Cas V 4F **87**
    (not continuous)
Plainview Cl. WS9: A'rdge 1G **51**
Plaistow Av. B36: Hodg H 2A **104**
Plane Gro. B37: Chel W 2D **122**
Planetary Ind. Est. WV13: W'hall 6E **29**
Planetary Rd. WV13: W'hall 5D **28**
Plane Tree Rd. B74: S'tly 3F **51**
  WS5: Wals 1F **65**
Planet Rd. DY5: Brie H 5H **93**

Plank La. B46: Wat O ... 5C 88
Planks La. WV5: Wom ... 1F 73
Plantation, The DY5: P'ntt ... 2F 93
Plantation Dr. B75: S Cold ... 5D 54
Plantation La. DY3: Himl ... 3H 73
Plantation Rd. WS5: Wals ... 1E 65
Plant Ct. DY5: Brie H ... 1H 109
(off Hill St.)
Plantsbrook Community Nature Reserve
... 3B 70
Plants Brook Cres. B24: Erd ... 4B 86
Plants Brook Nature Reserve ... 2E 87
Plants Brook Rd. B76: Walm ... 1D 86
Plants Cl. B73: New O ... 4D 68
WS6: Gt Wyr ... 5G 7
Plants Gro. B24: Erd ... 2B 86
Plants Hollow DY5: Brie H ... 2A 110
Plant St. B64: Old H ... 2F 111
DY8: Word ... 1C 108
Plant Way WS3: Pels ... 3D 20
Plascom Rd. WV1: Wolv ... 2C 44
Platts Cres. DY8: Amb ... 3C 108
Platts Dr. DY8: Amb ... 3C 108
Platts Rd. DY8: Amb ... 3C 108
Platt St. WS10: Darl ... 6D 46
Playdon Gro. B14: K Hth ... 4A 148
Pleasant Cl. DY6: K'wfrd ... 5A 92
Pleasant St. B70: W Brom ... 5A 80
(Farm St.)
B70: W Brom ... 5G 63
(Lee St.)
Pleasant Vw. DY3: Gorn ... 5H 75
PLECK ... 3H 47
Pleck Bus. Pk. WS2: Wals ... 2A 48
Pleck Ho. B14: K Hth ... 6E 147
(off Winterbourne Cft.)
Pleck Ind. Est. WS2: Wals ... 3A 48
Pleck Rd. WS2: Wals ... 3A 48
Pleck Wlk. B38: K Nor ... 6C 146
Plestowes Cl. B90: Shir ... 2H 149
Plimsoll Gro. B32: Quin ... 6A 114
Plough & Harrow Rd. B16: Edg ... 2B 116
Plough Av. B32: Bart G ... 3A 130
Ploughmans Pl. B75: R'ley ... 5B 38
Ploughmans Wlk. DY6: W Hth ... 2G 91
WV8: Pend ... 6C 14
Plover Cl. WV10: F'stne ... 1D 16
Ploverdale Cres. DY6: K'wfrd ... 2E 93
Plowden Rd. B33: Stech ... 5D 104
Plume St. B6: Aston ... 1C 102
Plummers Ho. B6: Aston ... 2G 101
Plumstead Rd. B44: K'sdng ... 5A 68
Plym Cl. WV11: Wed ... 4E 29
Plymouth Cl. B31: Longb ... 2E 159
Plymouth Rd. B30: Stir ... 6D 132
Plympton M. B71: W Brom ... 1A 80
Pocklington Pl. B31: N'fld ... 1G 145
Poets Cnr. B10: Small H ... 4D 118
Point, The B2: Birm ... 2G 101
Point 3 B3: Birm ... 2B 4 (6E 101)
Pointon Cl. WV14: Cose ... 3C 60
Polden Cl. B63: Hale ... 4E 127
Polesworth Gro. B34: S End ... 3F 105
Pollard Rd. B27: A Grn ... 4A 136
Pollards, The B23: Erd ... 5E 69
Polly Brooks Yd. DY9: Lye ... 6A 110
Polo Flds. DY9: Pedm ... 4F 125
Pomeroy Rd. B32: Bart G ... 4A 130
B43: Gt Barr ... 1F 67
Pommel Cl. WS5: Wals ... 1D 64
Pond Cres. WV2: Wolv ... 4A 44
Pond Gro. WV2: Wolv ... 4A 44
Pond La. WV2: Wolv ... 3H 43
Pool Cotts. WS7: Chase ... 1A 10
Poole Cres. B17: Harb ... 2G 131
WS8: Bwnhls ... 3G 9
WV14: Cose ... 3F 61
Poole Ho. Rd. B43: Gt Barr ... 2A 66
Pool End Cl. B93: Know ... 3B 166
Pooles La. WV12: W'hall ... 1E 31
Poole St. DY2: Dud ... 1C 124
Pool Farm Rd. B27: A Grn ... 4H 135
Pool Fld. Av. B31: N'fld ... 6C 130
Poolfield Dr. B91: Sol ... 4D 150

POOL GREEN ... 4B 34
Pool Grn. WS9: A'rdge ... 4C 34
Pool Grn. Ter. WS9: A'rdge ... 4C 34
Pool Hall Cres. WV3: Wolv ... 3F 41
Pool Hall Rd. WV3: Wolv ... 3F 41
Pool Hayes La. WV12: W'hall ... 4A 30
Pool Ho. Rd. WV5: Wom ... 1D 72
Pool La. B69: O'bry ... 5F 97
Pool Mdw. WS6: C Hay ... 4D 6
Poolmeadow B76: Walm ... 5E 71
Pool Mdw. Cl. B13: Mose ... 4C 134
B91: Sol ... 6B 152
Pool Rd. B63: Hale ... 2B 128
B66: Smeth ... 4F 99
WS7: Chase ... 1A 10
(not continuous)
WS8: Bwnhls ... 3A 10
WV11: Wed ... 3A 30
Pool St. B6: Aston ... 3H 101
DY1: Dud ... 1C 76
WS1: Wals ... 2D 48
WV2: Wolv ... 6A 170 (3G 43)
(not continuous)
Pooltail Wlk. B31: Longb ... 6B 144
Pool Vw. WS4: Rus ... 2H 33
WS6: Gt Wyr ... 1G 7
Pool Way B33: Yard ... 2E 121
Pope Rd. WV10: Bush ... 1C 28
Popes La. B30: K Nor ... 3H 145
B38: K Nor ... 3H 145
B69: O'bry ... 3H 97
WV6: Tett ... 3G 25
Pope St. B1: Birm ... 6D 100
B66: Smeth ... 3H 99
Poplar Arc. B91: Sol ... 3G 151
(off Gardeners Wlk.)
Poplar Av. B11: S'brk ... 5B 118
B12: Bal H ... 1A 134
B14: K Hth ... 5H 133
B17: Edg ... 2E 115
B19: Loz ... 1E 101
B23: Erd ... 3F 85
B37: Chel W ... 3E 123
B69: O'bry ... 5G 97
B69: Tiv ... 1B 96
B70: W Brom ... 5C 80
B75: S Cold ... 4D 54
DY4: Tip ... 2F 77
WS2: Wals ... 6D 30
WS5: Wals ... 1E 65
WS8: Bwnhls ... 5C 10
WV11: Wed ... 2D 28
Poplar Cl. B69: Tiv ... 6C 78
WS2: Wals ... 5E 31
WV5: Wom ... 1H 73
Poplar Cres. DY1: Dud ... 4D 76
DY8: Stourb ... 2C 124
Poplar Dr. B6: Witt ... 2H 83
B8: Salt ... 3D 102
Poplar Grn. DY1: Dud ... 1C 76
Poplar Gro. B19: Loz ... 1E 101
B66: Smeth ... 6F 99
B70: W Brom ... 5B 80
Poplar La. B62: Roms ... 3A 142
Poplar Ri. B42: Gt Barr ... 6D 66
B66: Smeth ... 1C 96
B74: Lit As ... 4D 36
Poplar Rd. B11: S'hll ... 6B 118
B14: K Hth ... 5G 133
B66: Smeth ... 2E 115
B69: O'bry ... 1G 97
B91: Sol ... 3G 151
B93: Dorr ... 5B 166
DY6: K'wfrd ... 4C 92
DY8: Stourb ... 2C 124
WS6: Gt Wyr ... 4F 7
WS8: Bwnhls ... 5C 10
WS10: W'bry ... 5C 46
WV3: Wolv ... 5E 43
WV14: Bils ... 4H 45
Poplars, The B11: S'brk ... 5C 118
B16: Birm ... 5B 100
DY5: P'ntt ... 2F 93
DY8: Word ... 1D 108

Poplars Dr. B36: Cas B ... 1F 105
WV8: Cod ... 5F 13
Poplars Ind. Est., The
B6: Witt ... 2H 83
Poplar St. B66: Smeth ... 4G 99
WV2: Wolv ... 5H 43
Poplar Trees B47: H'wd ... 3A 162
(off May Farm Cl.)
Poplar Way Shop. Cen. B91: Sol ... 3G 151
Poplarwoods B32: Bart G ... 3H 129
Poppy Dr. WS5: Wals ... 2D 64
Poppy Gro. B8: Salt ... 5F 103
Poppy La. B24: Erd ... 2A 86
Poppymead B23: Erd ... 5B 68
Porchester Cl. WS9: Wals W ... 4C 22
Porchester Dr. B19: Hock ... 3F 101
Porchester St. B19: Hock ... 3F 101
Porlock Cres. B31: N'fld ... 4B 144
Porlock Rd. DY8: Amb ... 5E 109
Portal Rd. WS2: Wals ... 1F 47
Portchester Dr. WV11: Wed ... 4F 29
Porter Cl. B72: W Grn ... 6H 69
Porters Cft. B17: Harb ... 3E 115
Porters Dr. B14: K Hth ... 3E 147
Porter's Fld. DY2: Dud ... 6F 77
Portersfield Ind. Est. B64: Crad H ... 4F 111
Portersfield Rd. B64: Crad H ... 3E 111
Portershill Dr. B90: Shir ... 6A 150
Porter St. DY2: Dud ... 6F 77
Porter St. Sth. DY2: Dud ... 6F 77
Porters Way B9: Bord G ... 1E 119
Portfield Dr. DY4: Tip ... 4A 78
Portfield Gro. B23: Erd ... 1G 85
Porth Kerry Gro. DY3: Sed ... 6F 59
Port Hope Rd. B11: S'brk ... 4A 118
Porthouse Gro. WV14: Cose ... 2D 60
Portia Av. B90: Shir ... 5H 149
Portland Av. WS9: A'rdge ... 4D 34
Portland Ct. WS9: A'rdge ... 4D 34
Portland Cres. DY9: Pedm ... 4F 125
Portland Dr. B69: Tiv ... 5D 78
DY9: Pedm ... 4F 125
Portland Pl. WV14: Cose ... 6D 60
Portland Rd. B16: Edg ... 6F 99
B17: Edg ... 6F 99
WS9: A'rdge ... 3D 34
Portland St. B6: Aston ... 2A 102
WS2: Wals ... 6C 32
Portland Ter. B18: Hock ... 4C 100
(off Crabtree Rd.)
Port La. WV9: Coven ... 1H 13
Portman Rd. B13: Mose ... 6H 133
PORTOBELLO ... 3G 45
Portobello Cl. WV13: W'hall ... 2F 45
Portobello Rd. B70: W Brom ... 5G 63
Portrush Av. B38: K Nor ... 6G 145
Portrush Rd. WV6: Pert ... 5D 24
Portsdown Cl. WV10: Bush ... 2B 28
Portsdown Rd. B63: Hale ... 4E 127
Portsea St. WS3: Blox ... 3A 32
Portswood Cl. WV9: Pend ... 6D 14
PORTWAY ... 4C 96
Portway, The DY6: K'wfrd ... 4C 92
Portway Cl. B91: Sol ... 6C 150
DY6: K'wfrd ... 4C 92
Portway Hill B65: Row R ... 3B 96
Portway Rd. B65: Row R ... 5B 96
B69: O'bry ... 2E 97
WV14: Bils ... 4G 45
Portway Rd. Ind. Est. B69: O'bry ... 2E 97
Portway Wlk. B65: Row R ... 3C 96
Posey Cl. B21: Hand ... 4H 81
Post Office Rd. WV5: Seis ... 2A 56
Poston Cft. B14: K Hth ... 3F 147
Potter Cl. B23: Erd ... 5D 68
Potter Ct. DY5: Brie H ... 1H 109
(off The Promenade)
Potters Brook DY4: Tip ... 2B 78
Potters La. B6: Aston ... 3G 101
WS10: W'bry ... 3E 63
Potterton Way B66: Smeth ... 1D 98
Pottery Rd. B66: Smeth ... 2E 99
B68: O'bry ... 2A 114

Pouk Hill Cl. WS2: Wals 6G **31**
Pouk La. WS14: Hilt 5G **11**
Poultney St. B70: W Brom 6F **63**
Poulton Cl. B13: Mose 3A **134**
Pound Cl. B68: O'bry 6F **97**
Pound Grn. B8: Salt 3F **103**
Pound La. B32: Fran 4F **143**
   B46: Col 5H **107**
Poundley Cl. B36: Cas B 1G **105**
Pound Rd. B14: K Hth 6G **147**
   B68: O'bry 6F **97**
                (not continuous)
   WS10: W'bry 2G **63**
Pountney St. WV2: Wolv 6A **170** (3G **43**)
Powell Av. B32: Quin 5G **113**
Powell Pl. DY4: Tip 2C **78**
   WV14: Bils 2G **61**
Powells Cl. B72: W Grn 3A **70**
Powells Ho. B73: New O 3C **68**
Powell St. B1: Birm 6D **100**
   B63: Hale 2B **128**
   WV10: Wolv 5B **28**
Power Cres. B16: Birm 1C **116**
Powerleague Soccer Cen.
   Birmingham 6C **84**
Power Way DY4: Tip 5D **62**
Powick Pl. B19: Loz 2E **101**
Powick Rd. B23: Erd 6D **84**
Powis Av. DY4: Tip 1A **78**
Powke La. B64: Old H 6H **95**
   B65: Row R 1A **112**
Powke La. Ind. Est.
   B65: Row R 1A **112**
Powlers Cl. DY9: W'cte 3A **126**
Powlett St. WV2: Wolv 5D **170** (2H **43**)
Poxon Rd. WS9: Wals W 3C **22**
Poynings, The WV6: Tett 4A **26**
Precinct, The WV12: W'hall 4B **30**
Premier Bus. Pk. WS2: Wals 2B **48**
Premier Ct. B30: K Nor 4E **147**
Premier Pk. B73: New O 3D **68**
Premier Partnership Ind. Est.
   DY6: K'wfrd 6F **93**
Premier St. B7: Nech 1D **102**
Premier Trad. Est. B7: Birm 4H **101**
Prescot Rd. DY9: Lye 1G **125**
Prescott St. B18: Hock 5D **100**
Prestbury Rd. B6: Aston 1G **101**
Preston Av. B76: Walm 2C **70**
Preston Ho. *WS1: Wals* *2D 48*
             (off Paddock La.)
Preston Rd. B18: Win G 3A **100**
   B26: Yard 5B **120**
Prestons Row WV14: Cose 2C **60**
Prestwick Cl. B75: S Cold 3A **54**
Prestwick Rd. B35: Cas V 3F **87**
   DY6: K'wfrd 3A **92**
Prestwood Av. WV11: Wed 2F **29**
Prestwood Dr. DY7: Stourt 4A **108**
Prestwood Rd. B29: W Cas 5F **131**
   WV11: Wed 4C **28**
Prestwood Rd. W. WV11: Wed 3C **28**
Pretoria Rd. B9: Bord G 6E **103**
Priam Gro. WS3: Pels 1F **21**
Price Cres. WV14: Bils 4F **45**
Price Rd. WS10: W'bry 2A **64**
Prices Rd. DY3: Gorn 4G **75**
Price St. B4: Birm 1E **5** (5G **101**)
   B66: Smeth 4F **99**
   B70: W Brom 4A **80**
   DY2: Dud 1G **95**
   WV14: Bils 6H **45**
PRIESTFIELD **5D 44**
Priestfield Cl. B44: Gt Barr 3E **67**
Priestfield Stop (MM) **4C 44**
Priestfield St. WV14: Bils 5D **44**
Priestland Rd. B34: S End 2F **105**
Priestley Cl. B20: Hand 6C **82**
   B63: Crad 5D **110**
Priestley Rd. B11: S'brk 4A **118**
   WS2: Wals 4G **31**
Priestly Wharf B7: Birm 1H **5** (5H **101**)
Priest St. B64: Old H 2H **111**

Primley Av. B36: Hodg H 2B **104**
   WS2: Wals 2H **47**
Primley Cl. WS2: Wals 1H **47**
Primrose Av. B11: S'hll 5C **118**
   DY4: Tip 5C **62**
   WV10: F'hses, Bush 4H **15**
Primrose Bank B68: O'bry 5H **97**
Primrose Cl. B64: Crad H 3D **110**
   WS3: Pels 2E **21**
Primrose Cres. DY1: Dud 3E **77**
Primrose Cft. B23: Erd 6C **68**
   B28: Hall G 2F **149**
Primrose Gdns. B38: K Nor 1B **160**
   WS8: Cod 4G **13**
PRIMROSE HILL **5F 95**
Primrose Hill B38: K Nor 1B **146**
             (not continuous)
   B67: Smeth 5B **98**
   DY8: Word 2C **108**
Primrose Hill Trad. Est. DY2: Neth . . .5F **95**
Primrose La. B28: Hall G 2F **149**
   B90: Dic H 4G **163**
   WV10: Bush 3A **16**
             (Cromwell Rd.)
   WV10: Bush 1B **28**
           (Old Fallings La.)
Primrose Pk. DY5: P'ntt 2G **93**
Primrose Rd. DY2: Neth 5E **95**
Primroses, The WS5: Wals 1F **65**
Primrose Woods B32: Bart G 3H **129**
Primsland Cl. B90: M'path 2G **165**
Prince Albert St. B9: Small H 2D **118**
             (not continuous)
Prince Andrew Cres. B45: Fran 5E **143**
Prince Charles Cl. B45: Fran 5E **143**
Prince Charles Rd. WV14: Bils 2H **61**
Prince Edward Dr. B45: Fran 5E **143**
Prince George Rd. WS10: W'bry 6G **47**
Prince of Wales La.
   B14: K Hth, Yard W 5C **148**
Prince of Wales Way
   B66: Smeth 4G **99**
Princep Cl. B43: Gt Barr 1F **67**
Prince Philip Cl. B45: Fran 5E **143**
Prince Rd. B30: K Nor 4B **146**
Princes Av. WS1: Wals 3E **49**
Princes Dr. WV8: Cod 4G **13**
PRINCES END **5H 61**
Princes End Ind. Est. DY4: Tip 4G **61**
Princes Gdns. WV8: Cod 4F **13**
Princes Ga. B70: W Brom 5C **80**
   B91: Sol 3F **151**
Princes Rd. B69: Tiv 5A **78**
   DY8: Stourb 3B **124**
Princess Alice Dr. B73: New O 3D **68**
Princess All. WV1: Wolv 3C **170** (1H **43**)
Princess Anne Dr. B45: Fran 5E **143**
Princess Anne Rd. WS2: Wals 6F **31**
   WV14: Bils 2H **61**
Princess Ct. WV10: Wolv 3C **28**
Princess Cres. B63: Hale 5G **111**
Princess Diana Way B45: Fran 5E **143**
Princess Gro. B71: W Brom 5B **64**
Princess Pde. B70: W Brom 4B **80**
Princess Sq. WV1: Wolv 2C **170** (1H **43**)
Princess Rd. B5: Edg 5G **117**
   B68: O'bry 1B **114**
Princess Sq. WV14: Bils 2H **61**
Princess Way WS10: Darl 3C **46**
Prince St. B64: Crad H 3F **111**
   DY2: Neth 3E **95**
   WS2: Wals 3A **48**
   WS9: Wals W 5B **22**
Princes Way B68: O'bry 4H **113**
   B91: Sol 3F **151**
Princethorpe Cl. B34: S End 2H **105**
   B90: Shir 5G **149**
Princethorpe Rd. B29: W Cas 4E **131**
   WV13: W'hall 3B **46**
Princeton Gdns. WV9: Pend 4E **15**
Prince William Cl. B23: Erd 5D **84**
Principal Ct. B67: Smeth 4E **99**
Princip St. B4: Birm 1E **5** (5G **101**)

Printing Ho. St. B4: Birm 2E **5** (6G **101**)
Priors Cl. CV7: Bal C 3H **169**
Priors Mill DY3: Up Gor 2A **76**
Priors Way B23: Erd 5C **68**
Priory, The 4E **77**
Priory, The DY3: Sed 5H **59**
Priory Av. B29: S Oak 3D **132**
Priory Chambers DY1: Dud 6E **77**
             (off Priory St.)
Priory Cl. B46: Col 4H **107**
   B66: Smeth 5G **99**
   B70: W Brom 5D **80**
   DY1: Dud 5D **76**
   DY8: Stourb 2F **125**
Priory Ct. B90: M'path 2F **165**
   DY1: Dud 6E **77**
   DY8: Stourb 2F **125**
   WS9: Wals W 3C **22**
   WV1: Wolv 1A **170** (6G **27**)
Priory Dr. B68: O'bry 4A **98**
Priory Fld. Cl. WV14: Cose 4B **60**
Priory Fields Nature Reserve 5D **148**
Priory Gdns. B28: Hall G 3D **148**
Priory Ho. B63: Hale 6H **111**
Priory Ho. Ind. Est. B18: Hock 4C **100**
Priory La. DY3: Sed 6H **59**
Priory New Way Ind. Est. B6: Aston . . .4G **101**
Priory Queensway, The
   B4: Birm 3E **5** (6G **101**)
Priory Rd. B5: Edg 5D **116**
   B6: Aston 1B **102**
   B14: K Hth 6E **133**
   B15: Edg 5D **116**
   B28: Hall G 2D **148**
   B62: Hale 1E **129**
   B90: Shir 2D **148**
   DY1: Dud 2E **77**
   DY8: Stourb 2F **125**
Priory Sq. Shop. Cen. B4: Birm 3F **5**
Priory St. DY1: Dud 6E **77**
Priory Wlk. B4: Birm 3F **5** (6G **101**)
   B72: W Grn 6A **70**
Priory Woods Nature Reserve *3E 81*
Pritchard Av. WV11: Wed 3G **29**
Pritchard Cl. B66: Smeth 4F **99**
Pritchard St. DY5: Brie H 6F **93**
   WS10: W'bry 2G **63**
Pritchatts Rd. B15: Edg 6A **116**
Pritchett Av. WV4: E'shll 2B **60**
Pritchett Rd. B31: Longb 2F **159**
Pritchett St. B6: Birm 4G **101**
Pritchett Twr. B10: Small H 2C **118**
Privet Cl. B44: Gt Barr 2G **67**
Privet Way B45: Coft H 5A **158**
Probert Rd. WV10: Oxl 1E **27**
Proctor St. B7: Birm 4A **102**
Proffitt Cl. WS2: Wals 5C **32**
   WS8: Bwnhls 2C **22**
Proffitt St. WS2: Wals 5C **32**
Prole St. WV10: Wolv 5A **28**
Promenade, The DY5: Brie H 1H **109**
Prospect Gdns. DY8: Stourb 1E **125**
Prospect Hill DY8: Stourb 1E **125**
Prospect La. B91: Sol 2B **150**
Prospect Pl. B12: Bal H 6H **117**
Prospect Rd. B13: Mose 4H **133**
   B62: Hale 6C **112**
   DY3: Gorn 5F **75**
Prospect Row DY2: Dud 2F **95**
   DY8: Stourb 2E **125**
Prospect St. DY4: Tip 4C **62**
   WV14: Bils 5G **45**
Prospect Trad. Est. B1: Birm 3A **4**
Prosper Mdw. DY6: K'wfrd 2C **92**
Prospero Cl. B45: Fran 5G **143**
Prosser St. WV10: Wolv 4A **28**
   WV14: Bils 6F **45**
Prossers Wlk. B46: Col 2H **107**
Prouds La. WV14: Bils 3F **45**
Provence Cl. WV10: Wolv 5B **28**
Providence Cl. WS3: Blox 2A **32**
            (not continuous)
Providence Dr. DY9: Lye 5B **110**

Providence Ind. Est. DY9: Lye 5A 110
Providence La. WS3: Blox 3A 32
Providence Row WV14: Cose 5D 60
Providence St. B64: Crad H 2F 111
  DY4: Tip 2C 78
  DY9: Lye 5A 110
Pruden Av. WV4: E'shll 2B 60
Pryor Rd. B68: O'bry 6A 98
Public, The B70: W Brom 4B 80
Pudsey Dr. B75: Four O 6A 38
Pugh Cres. WS2: Wals 1E 47
Pugh Rd. B6: Aston 2A 102
  WV14: Bils 2G 61
  WV14: Cose 3B 60
Pugin Cl. WV6: Pert 6D 24
Pugin Gdns. B23: Erd 5D 68
Pumphouse Way B69: O'bry 5F 97
Pump St. WV2: E'shll 4C 44
Puppy Grn. DY4: Tip 2A 78
Purbeck Cl. B63: Hale 4F 127
Purbeck Cft. B32: Harb 6D 114
Purbrook Rd. WV1: Wolv 3B 44
Purcel Rd. WV10: Bush 1H 27
  (not continuous)
Purdy Rd. WV14: Bils 3G 61
Purefoy Rd. B13: Mose 2C 148
Purley Gro. B23: Erd 2A 84
Purnells Way B93: Know 4C 166
Purslet Rd. WV1: Wolv 2C 44
Purslow Gro. B31: N'fld 5E 145
Putney Av. B20: Hand 6E 83
Putney La. B62: Roms 5A 142
Putney Rd. B20: Hand 6D 82
Putney Wlk. R37: F'hri 6D 106
Pype Hayes Rd. B24: Erd 3B 86
Pype Hayes Rd. B24: Erd 3B 86
Pype Marshbrook Rd.
  B24: Erd 3B 86
Pytchley Ho. B20: Hand 4B 82
Pytman Dr. B76: Walm 6E 71

Q

Quadrangle, The B30: B'vlle 1B 146
  B90: Shir .1C 164
Quadrant, The DY3: Sed 4H 59
Quadrille Lawns WV9: Pend 5D 14
Quail Grn. WV6: Tett 1F 41
Qualcast Rd. WV1: Wolv 1B 44
Quantock Cl. B45: Fran 5H 143
  B63: Hale .3F 127
  WS8: Wals W 3C 22
Quantock Rd. B8: Amb 5F 109
Quarrington Gro. B14: K Hth 4A 148
QUARRY BANK 2C 110
Quarry Brow DY3: Up Gor 2A 76
Quarry Cl. WS6: C Hay 2E 7
Quarry Hill B63: Hale 3H 127
Quarry Ho. B45: Rub 1F 157
Quarry Ho. Cl. B45: Fran 6F 143
Quarry La. B31: N'fld 4D 144
  B63: Hale .3H 127
Quarry Pk. Rd. DY8: Stourb 5E 125
Quarry Ri. B69: Tiv 1B 96
Quarry Rd. B29: W Cas 4D 130
  DY2: Neth 1D 110
Quarry Wlk. B45: Redn 2G 157
Quasar Cen. WS1: Wals 1C 48
Quatford Gdns. WV10: Wolv 4A 28
Quayle Gro. DY8: Word 6B 92
Quayside B18: Win G 4C 100
Quayside Cl. B69: O'bry 1E 97
Quayside Dr. WS2: Wals 3A 48
Quayside Wlk. DY2: Neth 5G 95
Qube B1: Birm 6E 101
  (off Edward St.)
Queen Eleanors Dr. B93: Know 1D 166
Queen Elizabeth Av. WS2: Wals 6F 31
Queen Elizabeth Ct. B19: Hock 3D 100
Queen Elizabeth Rd. B45: Fran 5E 143
Queen Mary St. WS1: Wals 5B 48
Queen Mother Ct. B30: B'vlle 5H 131

Queen Mother Gdns.
  B17: Harb .5E 115
Queen's Arc. WV1: Wolv 3B 170 (1G 43)
Queens Av. B14: K Hth 5G 133
  B18: Hock 3B 100
  B69: Tiv 6B 78
  B90: Shir .6H 149
Queensbridge Rd. B13: Mose 3F 133
Queens Cl. B24: Erd 5F 85
  B67: Smeth 4E 99
Queens Ct. B1: Birm 6B 4 (2E 117)
  B3: Birm 1C 4 (5F 101)
  B17: Harb .6E 115
  B91: Sol 3H 151
  DY5: P'ntt .3G 93
  WV10: Wolv 3C 28
Queens Ct. Trad. Est.
  B70: W Brom 4F 79
Queens Cres. DY8: Amb 4E 109
  WV14: Cose 4C 60
Queen's Cross DY1: Dud 1D 94
Queens Dr. B5: Birm 5D 4 (1F 117)
  B30: K Nor 3C 146
  B65: Row R 5D 96
  WS7: Chase 1B 10
Queens Dr., The B62: Hale 6C 112
Queens Gdns. B23: Erd 6B 68
  DY2: Neth .5E 95
  WS10: W'bry 2E 63
  WV8: Cod .4F 13
  WV14: Bils .4F 45
Queens Hall DY1: Dud 1D 94
Queen's Head Rd. B21: Hand 2A 100
Queens Hospital Cl. B15: Birm 2E 117
Queens Lea WV12: W'hall 4C 30
Queens Pde. WS3: Blox 6H 19
Queen's Pk. Rd. B32: Harb 5D 114
Queen Sq. WV1: Wolv 3B 170 (1G 43)
Queen's Ride B5: Edg 1E 133
Queens Rd. B6: Aston 1A 102
  B23: Erd 4C 84
  B26: Yard .2D 120
  B67: Smeth 5B 98
  DY3: Sed 5A 60
  DY4: Tip 2H 77
  DY8: Stourb 5D 108
  WS4: Rus 2G 33
  WS4: Rus 5F 49
Queens Sq. B70: W Brom 4B 80
Queens Twr. B7: Birm 4B 102
Queen St. B12: Bal H 6B 118
  B63: Hale .1A 128
  B64: Crad H 2F 111
  B69: O'bry .1G 97
  B70: W Brom 4B 80
  B72: S Cold 1A 70
  DY4: Tip 5H 61
  DY5: P'ntt .3G 93
  (not continuous)
  DY5: Quar B 3C 110
  (not continuous)
  DY6: K'wfrd 2B 92
  DY8: Stourb 6D 108
  DY8: Word .6B 92
  WS2: Wals .2B 48
  WS6: C Hay .2D 6
  WS7: Chase 1B 10
  WS9: Wals W 5A 22
  WS10: Darl .3D 46
  WS10: W'bry 2D 62
  WV1: Wolv 3C 170 (1H 43)
  (not continuous)
  WV14: Bils .6G 45
  (Bridge St.)
  WV14: Bils .1B 62
  (Tudor Rd.)
Queen St. Ind. Est. WS7: Chase 1B 10
Queen St. Pas. DY5: Quar B 3C 110
Queensway B6: Witt 4H 83
  B63: Hale .2A 128
  B68: O'bry .2A 98
  B74: S'tly 3A 52
  DY9: W'cte .3A 126
Queensway Cl. B68: O'bry 2H 113

Queensway Mall B63: Hale 2B 128
  (off Hagley Mall)
Queensway Trad. Est. B5: Birm 3G 5
Queenswood Rd. B13: Mose 1A 134
  B75: Four O 2H 53
Quenby Dr. DY1: Dud 4C 76
Quendale WV5: Wom 1E 73
Quentin Dr. DY1: Dud 1B 94
Queslade Cl. B43: Gt Barr 4C 66
QUESLETT 3E 67
Queslett Pk. Golf Cen. 5E 67
  (off Booth's La.)
Queslett Rd. B43: Gt Barr 4B 66
Queslett Rd. E. B74: S'tly 6G 51
Quicksand La. WS9: A'rdge 5B 34
Quigley Av. B9: Birm 1B 118
Quillets Rd. DY8: Word 6A 92
Quilter Cl. WS2: Wals 6F 31
  WV14: Cose 5C 60
Quilter Rd. B24: Erd 5H 85
Quincey Dr. B24: Erd 4A 86
Quincy Ri. DY5: Brie H 4G 109
QUINTON 5A 114
Quinton Av. WS6: Gt Wyr 2F 7
Quinton Bus. Pk. B32: Quin 6G 113
Quinton Cl. B92: Sol 2H 137
Quinton Ct. B68: O'bry 4A 114
Quintondale B90: Shir 1A 164
Quinton Expressway B32: Quin 1H 129
Quinton La. B32: Quin 5A 114
Quinton Pl. WS11: Nort C 1E 9
Quinton Rd. B17: Harb 2E 131
Quinton Rd. W. B32: Quin 6H 113
Qulsnam Ct. B13: Mose 3B 134
Uuorn Cres. DY8: Word 6A 92
Quorn Gro. B24: Erd 5H 85
Quorn Ho. B20: Hand 4B 82

R

Rabone La. B66: Smeth 3F 99
Rabone Pk. B66: Smeth 3F 99
Raby Cl. B69: Tiv 1H 95
Raby St. WV2: Wolv 6D 170 (3H 43)
Racecourse La. DY8: Stourb 3C 124
Racecourse Rd. WV6: Wolv 4E 27
Racecourse Rd. Ind. Est.
  WV6: Wolv .4E 27
Racemeadow Cres. DY2: Neth 2E 111
Raceway, The .6D 80
Rachael Gdns. WS10: W'bry 1H 63
Rachel Cl. DY4: Tip 4C 62
Rachel Gdns. B29: S Oak 3H 131
Radbourn Dr. B74: S Cold 4A 54
Radbourne Dr. B63: Crad 4C 110
Radbourne Rd. B90: Shir 4B 150
Radcliffe Dr. B62: Quin 5E 113
Radcliffe Twr. B12: Birm 3H 117
Raddens Rd. B62: Hale 2F 129
Raddington Dr. B92: Olton 5B 136
Raddlebarn Farm Dr. B29: S Oak 4B 132
Raddlebarn Rd. B29: S Oak 4A 132
Radford Cl. WS5: Wals 2E 65
Radford Dr. B74: S'fld 5G 21
Radford La. WV3: Lwr P, Wolv 5F 41
  WV4: Lwr P .5F 41
Radford Ri. B91: Sol 2A 152
Radford Rd. B29: W Cas 1E 145
  DY2: Neth .1E 111
Radley Cl. B26: Sheld 4G 121
Radley Gro. B29: W Cas 3E 131
Radley Rd. DY9: W'cte 1B 126
  WS4: Rus 2G 33
Radleys, The B33: Kitts G, Sheld 4G 121
Radley's Wlk. B33: Sheld 4G 121
Radlow Cres. B37: Mars G 3D 122
Radnell Ho. B69: O'bry 3D 96
Radnor Cl. B45: Fran 5H 143
Radnor Ct. WS9: Wals W 3B 22
Radnor Cft. WS5: Wals 2G 65
Radnor Grn. B71: W Brom 6A 64
Radnor Rd. B20: Hand 1D 100
  B68: O'bry .4H 113
  DY3: Sed 5G 59

Radnor St.—Redhall Rd.

Radnor St. B18: Hock 3C **100**
Radstock Av. B36: Hodg H 2A **104**
Radstock Rd. WV12: W'hall 6C **18**
Radway Ind. Est. B90: Shir 2C **164**
Radway Rd. B90: Shir 2C **164**
Raeburn Rd. B43: Gt Barr 1E **67**
Raford Rd. B23: Erd 1D **84**
Ragdene Rd. B33: Sheld 3H **121**
Ragees Rd. DY6: K'wfrd 5D **92**
Raglan Av. B66: Smeth 5G **99**
WV6: Pert .6F **25**
Raglan Cl. DY3: Sed 6F **59**
WS9: A'rdge 6H **35**
Raglan Rd. B5: Edg 5F **117**
B21: Hand 1G **99**
B66: Smeth 5G **99**
Raglan St. DY5: Brie H 5G **93**
WV3: Wolv 4A **170** (1F **43**)
Raglan Way B37: Chel W 1F **123**
Ragley Cl. B93: Know 2D **166**
WS3: Blox 6G **19**
Ragley Dr. B26: Sheld 5G **121**
B43: Gt Barr 3H **65**
WV13: W'hall 3H **45**
Ragley Wlk. B65: Row R 6C **96**
Ragnall Av. B33: Sheld 4H **121**
Rail Bri. Est. B70: W Brom 6G **79**
Railswood Dr. WS3: Pels 4E **21**
Railway Dr. WV1: Wolv 2D **170** (1H **43**)
WV14: Bils 6G **45**
Railway La. WV13: W'hall 2A **46**
Railway Rd. B20: Hand 5H **83**
B73: S Cold 6H **53**
Railwayside Cl. *B66: Smeth 2C 98*
(off Forest Cl.)
Railway St. B70: W Brom 3H **79**
DY4: Tip .2C **78**
WV1: Wolv 2D **170** (1H **43**)
WV14: Bils 6G **45**
Railway Ter. B7: Nech 3B **102**
B42: Gt Barr 1B **82**
WS10: W'bry 3F **63**
Railway Vw. B10: Small H 4C **118**
Railway Wlk. WS11: Nort C 1E **9**
Railwharf Sidings DY2: Neth 5F **95**
Rainbow St. WV2: Wolv 3G **43**
WV14: Cose 2F **61**
Rainford Way *B38: K Nor 1G 159*
(off Nearhill Rd.)
Rainham Cl. DY4: Tip 2F **77**
Rainsbrook Dr. B90: M'path 3D **164**
Rake Way B15: Birm 6A **4** (2D **116**)
Raleigh Cl. B21: Hand 6F **81**
Raleigh Cft. B43: Gt Barr 2A **66**
Raleigh Ind. Est. B21: Hand 6F **81**
Raleigh Rd. B9: Bord G 6D **102**
WV14: Bils 2H **61**
Raleigh St. B71: W Brom 3A **80**
WS2: Wals 1A **48**
Ralph Barlow Gdns. B44: K'sdng 5B **68**
Ralph Gdns. B44: K'sdng 5B **68**
Ralph Rd. B8: Salt 5D **102**
B90: Shir 3H **149**
Ralphs Mdw. B32: Bart G 3B **130**
Ralston Cl. WS3: Blox 3G **19**
Ramblers Way B75: R'ley 6C **38**
Ramillies Cres. WS6: Gt Wyr 4F **7**
Ramp Rd. B26: Birm A 6E **123**
Ramsay Rd. B68: O'bry 2A **114**
Ramsden Cl. B29: W Cas 6F **131**
Ramsey Cl. B45: Fran 6E **143**
B71: W Brom 5D **64**
Ramsey Ho. WS2: Wals 4A **48**
Ramsey Rd. B7: Nech 2C **102**
DY4: Tip .6G **61**
WS2: Wals 4G **31**
Randall Cl. DY6: K'wfrd 5D **92**
Randall Lines Ho. WV1: Wolv 6G **27**
Randle Dr. B75: R'ley 6A **38**
Randle Rd. DY9: Lye 1G **125**
Randwick Gro. B44: Gt Barr 4F **67**
Ranelagh Ho. *WV2: Wolv 4H 43*
(off Blakenhall Gdns.)
Ranelagh Rd. WV2: Wolv 5G **43**
Rangeview Cl. B74: S'tly 5H **51**
Rangeways Rd. DY6: K'wfrd 5D **92**
Rangoon Rd. B92: Sol 1A **138**
Ranleigh Av. DY6: K'wfrd 5D **92**
Rann Cl. B16: Birm 2C **116**
Rannoch Cl. DY5: Brie H 3F **109**
Ranscombe Dr. DY3: Gorn 5H **75**
Ransom Rd. B23: Erd 3C **84**
Ranworth Ri. WV4: Penn 1H **59**
Ratcliffe Av. B30: K Nor 4F **147**
Ratcliffe Cl. DY3: Sed 6B **60**
Ratcliffe Dr. WV13: W'hall 3B **46**
Ratcliffe Rd. B91: Sol 6G **137**
WV11: Wed 3A **30**
Ratcliff Wlk. B69: O'bry 2G **97**
Ratcliff Way DY4: Tip 1D **78**
Rathbone Cl. B5: Edg 4G **117**
WV14: Bils 6F **45**
Rathbone Rd. B67: Smeth 1D **114**
Rathlin Cl. WV9: Pend 4E **15**
Rathlin Cft. B36: Cas B 3D **106**
Rathmore Cl. DY8: Stourb 3B **124**
Rathwell Cl. WV9: Pend 5E **15**
Rattle Cft. B33: Stech 6C **104**
Ravenall Cl. B34: S End 2F **105**
Raven Cl. WS6: C Hay 3D **6**
Raven Ct. *DY5: Brie H 1H 109*
(off Lit. Potter St.)
Raven Cres. WV11: Wed 1H **29**
Ravenfield Cl. B8: W End 4F **103**
Ravenhayes La. B32: Fran 6G **129**
Raven Hays Rd. B31: Longb 5A **144**
Ravenhill Dr. WV8: Cod 4G **13**
Ravenhurst Dr. B43: Gt Barr 2A **66**
Ravenhurst M. B23: Erd 4E **85**
Ravenhurst Rd. B17: Harb 4G **115**
Ravenhurst St. B12: Birm 3A **118**
Raven Rd. WS5: Wals 5F **49**
Ravensbourne Gro. WV13: W'hall 1C **46**
Ravens Ct. WS8: Bwnhls 6B **10**
Ravenscroft DY8: Woll 5A **108**
Ravenscroft Rd. B92: Olton 5E **137**
WV12: W'hall 4B **30**
Ravensdale Cl. WS5: Wals 4F **49**
Ravensdale Gdns. WS5: Wals 5F **49**
Ravensdale Rd. B10: Small H 4F **119**
Ravenshaw B91: Sol 5D **152**
Ravenshaw La. B91: Sol 3C **152**
(not continuous)
Ravenshaw Rd. B16: Edg 1G **115**
Ravenshaw Way B91: Sol 5C **152**
Ravenshill Rd. B14: Yard W 3C **148**
Ravensholme WV6: Tett 1F **41**
Ravenside Retail Pk. B24: Erd 4C **86**
Ravensitch Wlk. DY5: Brie H 2A **110**
Ravenswood B15: Edg 3A **116**
Ravenswood Cl. B74: Four O 3H **53**
Ravenswood Dr. B91: Sol 6D **150**
Ravenswood Dr. Sth. B91: Sol 6C **150**
Ravenswood Hill B46: Col 2H **107**
Raven Wlk. B15: Edg 4E **117**
Rawdon Gro. B44: K'sdng 5B **68**
Rawlings Rd. B67: Smeth 1D **114**
Rawlins Cft. B35: Cas V 4G **87**
Rawlins St. B16: Birm 2C **116**
Raybon Cft. B45: Redn 3G **157**
Rayboulds Bri. Rd. WS2: Wals 5A **32**
Raybould's Fold DY2: Neth 4E **95**
Rayford Dr. B71: W Brom 3D **64**
Ray Hall La. B43: Gt Barr 4E **65**
Rayleigh Ho. B27: A Grn 2B **136**
Rayleigh Rd. WV3: Wolv 3E **43**
Raymond Av. B42: Gt Barr 1D **82**
Raymond Cl. WS2: Wals 4B **32**
Raymond Gdns. WV11: Wed 4G **29**
Raymond Rd. B8: Salt 5E **103**
Raymont Gro. B43: Gt Barr 1D **66**
Rayners Cft. B26: Yard 2D **120**
Raynor Rd. WV10: Wolv 3B **28**
RBSA Gallery . . . .**2B 4 (6E 101)**
Rea Av. B45: Rub 1E **157**
Reabrook Rd. B31: Longb 1D **158**
Rea Bus. Pk. B7: Birm 5C **102**
Rea Cl. B31: Longb 2E **159**
Rea Ct. B12: Birm 3A **118**
Readers Wlk. B43: Gt Barr 4B **66**
Rea Fordway B45: Fran 6F **143**
Reansway Sq. WV6: Wolv 5E **27**
Reapers Cl. WV12: W'hall 4D **30**
Reapers Wlk. WV8: Pend 6D **14**
Rea Pl. *B12: Birm 3A 118*
(off Cheapside)
Rea Rd. B31: N'fld 6D **144**
Reaside Cres. B14: K Hth 2D **146**
Reaside Cft. B12: Bal H 5G **117**
Reaside Dr. B45: Redn 1H **157**
Rea St. B5: Birm 6G **5** (2H **117**)
Rea St. Sth. B5: Birm 3G **117**
Rea Ter. B5: Birm 5H **5** (1H **117**)
Rea Twr. *B19: Birm 4E 101*
(off Mosborough Cres.)
Rea Valley Dr. B31: N'fld 5F **145**
Reaview Dr. B29: S Oak 3D **132**
Reaymer Cl. WS2: Wals 3H **31**
Reay Nadin Dr. B73: S'tly 1B **68**
Rebecca Dr. B29: S Oak 3A **132**
Rebecca Gdns. WV4: Penn 1D **58**
Recreation St. DY2: Neth 4F **95**
Rectory Av. WS10: Darl 5D **46**
Rectory Cl. DY8: Stourb 2F **125**
Rectory Flds. DY8: Word 1C **108**
Rectory Gdns. B36: Cas B 1E **105**
B68: O'bry 4H **97**
B91: Sol .4G **151**
DY8: Stourb 2F **125**
Rectory Gro. B18: Win G 3A **100**
Rectory La. B36: Cas B 1E **105**
Rectory Pk. Av. B75: S Cold 1C **70**
Rectory Pk. Cl. B75: S Cold 1C **70**
Rectory Pk. Ct. B75: S Cold 5D **54**
Rectory Pk. Rd. B26: Sheld 6F **121**
Rectory Rd. B31: N'fld 4F **145**
B75: S Cold 6A **54**
B91: Sol .4G **151**
DY8: Stourb 2F **125**
Rectory St. DY8: Word 6B **92**
Redacre Rd. B73: Bold 3F **69**
Redacres WV6: Tett 3C **26**
Red Admiral Apartments
DY8: Stourb 6D **108**
Redbank Av. B23: Erd 4C **84**
Redbourn Rd. WS3: Blox 3G **19**
Red Brick Cl. B64: Crad H 4F **111**
Redbrook Covert B38: K Nor 1A **160**
Red Brook Rd. WS2: Wals 4G **31**
Redbrooks Cl. B91: Sol 6E **151**
Redburn Dr. B14: K Hth 5F **147**
Redcar Cft. B36: Hodg H 1A **104**
Redcar Rd. WV10: F'hses 3H **15**
Redcliffe Dr. WV5: Wom 1H **73**
Redcott's Cl. WV10: Bush 1C **28**
Redcroft Dr. B24: Erd 2A **86**
Redcroft Rd. DY2: Dud 3G **95**
Red Cross Wlk. *WV1: Wolv 6G 27*
(off North Rd.)
Reddal Hill Rd. B64: Old H 2G **111**
REDDICAP HEATH **1C 70**
Reddicap Heath Rd. B75: S Cold 1C **70**
Reddicap Hill B75: S Cold 1C **70**
Reddicap Trad. Est. B75: S Cold 6B **54**
Reddicroft B73: S Cold 6A **54**
Reddings, The B47: H'wd 4A **162**
Reddings La. B11: Tys 3E **135**
B28: Hall G 3E **135**
Reddings Rd. B13: Mose 3F **133**
Redditch Ho. B33: Kitts G 1A **122**
Redditch Rd. B31: Longb 3G **159**
B38: K Nor 2G **159**
B48: Hopw 6G **159**
Redfern Cl. B92: Olton 4F **137**
Redfern Dr. WS7: Burn 1D **10**
Redfern Pk. Way B11: Tys 6G **119**
Redfern Rd. B11: Tys 6F **119**
Redfly La. DY5: P'ntt 3G **93**
Redford Cl. B13: Mose 3B **134**
Redgate Cl. B38: K Nor 5H **145**
Redhall Rd. B32: Harb 4C **114**
DY3: Gorn .5G **75**

Red Hill DY8: Stourb 1F 125
Redhill DY2: Dud 1F 95
Redhill Av. WV5: Wom 1G 73
Red Hill Cl. DY8: Stourb 1F 125
Redhill Ct. DY8: Stourb 2F 125
Redhill Gdns. B38: K Nor 1G 159
Red Hill Gro. B38: K Nor 2B 160
Redhill La. B45: Rub 4C 156
   B61: C'wich 4C 156
Redhill Pl. B62: Hunn 6A 128
Redhill Rd. B25: Yard 5G 119
   B31: Longb 1F 159
   B38: K Nor, Head H 1F 159
Red Hill St. WV1: Wolv 6G 27
Redholme Ct. DY8: Stourb 1E 125
Red Ho. Av. WS10: W'bry 2H 63
Redhouse Cl. B93: Ben H 4A 166
Redhouse Cone & Mus. 2C 108
Redhouse Ind. Est. WS9: A'rdge 3H 33
Redhouse La. WS9: A'rdge 4A 34
Red Ho. Pk. Rd. B43: Gt Barr 3A 66
Redhouse Rd. B33: Stech 6C 104
   WV6: Tett 4G 25
Redhouse St. WS1: Wals 4C 48
Redhurst Dr. WV10: F'hses 4F 15
Redlake Dr. DY9: Pedm 5F 125
Redlake Rd. DY9: Pedm 4F 125
Redlands Cl. B91: Sol 2H 151
Redlands Rd. B91: Sol 2G 151
Redlands Way B74: S'tly 2A 52
Red La. DY3: Sed 5F 59
   WV11: Ess 6C 18
Red Leasowes Rd. B63: Hale 2H 127
Redliff Av. B36: Cas B 6H 87
Red Lion Av. WS11: Nort C 1E 9
Red Lion Cl. B69: Tiv 1A 96
Red Lion Cres. WS11: Nort C 1E 9
Red Lion La. WS11: Nort C 1E 9
Red Lion St. WS2: Wals 6C 32
   WV1: Wolv 2A 170 (1G 43)
Redmead Cl. B30: K Nor 3G 145
Redmoor Gdns. WV4: Penn 6E 43
Redmoor Way B76: Min 1H 87
REDNAL 3H 157
Rednal Hill La. B45: Rub 3F 157
Rednall Dr. B75: R'ley 6A 38
Rednal Mill Dr. B45: Redn 2B 158
Rednal Pk. Ct. B38: K Nor 5B 146
Rednal Rd. B38: K Nor 1G 159
Redoak Ho. WV10: Wolv 6B 28
Redpine Crest WV12: W'hall 5D 30
Red River Rd. WS2: Wals 4G 31
Red Rock Dr. WV8: Cod 5F 13
Red Rooster Ind. Est. WS9: A'rdge 3A 34
Redruth Cl. DY6: K'wfrd 1B 92
   WS5: Wals 4H 49
Redruth Rd. WS5: Wals 4H 49
Redstone Dr. WV11: Wed 4H 29
Redstone Farm Rd. B20: Hall G 1H 149
Redstone Way DY3: Lwr G 3H 75
Redthorn Gro. B33: Stech 6B 104
Redvers Rd. B9: Small H 2E 119
Redway Ct. B75: S Cold 1C 70
Redwing Cl. WS7: Hamm 1F 11
Redwing Gro. B23: Erd 6B 68
Red Wing Wlk. B36: Cas B 1C 106
Redwood Av. DY1: Dud 2B 76
Redwood Bus. Pk. B66: Smeth 2A 98
Redwood Cl. B30: K Nor 3A 146
   B74: S'tly 1H 51
Redwood Cft. B14: K Hth 6G 133
Redwood Dr. B69: Tiv 5B 78
Redwood Gdns. B27: A Grn 6H 119
Redwood Ho. B37: K'hrst 4C 106
Redwood Rd. B30: K Nor 3A 146
   WS5: Wals 1F 65
   WV14: Cose 3F 61
Redwood Way WV12: W'hall 1B 30
Redworth Ho. B45: Rub 1F 157
   (off Deelands Rd.)
Reedham Gdns. WV4: Penn 6B 42
Reedly Rd. WV12: W'hall 6C 18
Reedmace Cl. B38: K Nor 1B 160
Reedswood Cl. WS2: Wals 6A 32

Reedswood Gdns. WS2: Wals 6A 32
Reedswood La. WS2: Wals 6A 32
Reedswood Retail Pk. WS2: Wals 5H 31
Reedswood Way WS2: Wals 5G 31
Rees Dr. WV5: Wom 6H 57
Reeves Cl. DY4: Tip 5B 78
Reeves Gdns. WV8: Cod 3G 13
Reeves Rd. B14: K Hth 1E 147
Reeves St. WS3: Blox 1H 31
Reflex Ind. Pk. WV13: W'hall 6H 29
Reform St. B70: W Brom 4B 80
Regal Cft. B36: Hodg H 1H 103
Regal Dr. WS2: Wals 3A 48
Regan Av. B90: Shir 6G 149
Regan Ct. B75: S Cold 6G 55
Regan Cres. B23: Erd 1E 85
Regan Dr. B69: O'bry 1D 96
Regency Cl. B9: Small H 2D 118
Regency Ct. DY3: Lwr G 4A 76
   WV1: Wolv 1A 170 (6G 27)
Regency Dr. B38: K Nor 5B 146
Regency Gdns. B14: Yard W 4C 148
Regency Wlk. B74: Four O 4D 36
Regent Av. B69: Tiv 6A 78
Regent Cl. B5: Edg 5F 117
   B63: Hale 1A 128
   B69: Tiv 1A 96
   DY6: K'wfrd 3B 92
Regent Ct. B62: Quin 4G 113
   (off Binswood Rd.)
   B66: Smeth 4E 99
Regent Dr. B69: Tiv 6A 78
Regent Gro. WS2: Wals 6B 32
   (off Green La.)
   WV1: Wolv 2A 170 (6F 27)
Regent Pde. B1: Birm 1A 4 (5E 101)
Regent Pk. Rd. B10: Small H 3C 118
Regent Pl. B1: Birm 1A 4 (5E 101)
   B69: Tiv 5B 78
Regent Rd. B17: Harb 5H 115
   B21: Hand 1H 99
   B69: Tiv 1A 96
   WV4: Penn 6E 43
Regent Row B18: Birm 1A 4 (5E 101)
Regents, The B15: Edg 3H 115
Regent St. B1: Birm 1A 4 (5E 101)
   B30: Stir 6C 132
   B64: Old H 1H 111
   B66: Smeth 3E 99
   DY1: Dud 1E 77
   DY4: Tip 5G 61
   WV13: W'hall 6A 30
   WV14: Bils 5F 45
Regents Way B75: S Cold 5D 54
Regent Wlk. B8: W End 2H 103
Regina Av. B44: Gt Barr 5F 67
Regina Cl. B45: Fran 5E 143
Regina Cres. WV6: Tett 5H 25
Regina Dr. B42: P Barr 4E 83
   WS4: Wals 5F 33
Reginald Rd. B8: Salt 5D 102
   B67: Smeth 1D 114
Regis Beeches WV6: Tett 4A 26
Regis Gdns. B65: Row R 1C 112
Regis Heath Rd. B65: Row R 1D 112
Regis Rd. B65: Row R 2C 112
   WV6: Tett 4H 25
Regus Bldg. B90: Bly P 6D 164
Reid Av. WV12: W'hall 3D 30
Reid Rd. B68: O'bry 2A 114
Reigate Av. B8: W End 5H 103
Reliance Trad. Est. WV14: Bils 6D 44
Relko Dr. B36: Hodg H 2A 104
Remembrance Rd. WS10: W'bry 2A 64
Remington Pl. WS2: Wals 4A 32
Remington Rd. WS2: Wals 3H 31
Renaissance Ct. B12: Birm 2A 118
Renfrew Cl. DY8: Word 6A 92
Renfrew Sq. B35: Cas V 3F 87
Rennie Gro. B32: Quin 6B 114
Rennison Dr. WV5: Wom 1G 73
Renown Cl. DY5: P'ntt 1F 93
Renton Gro. WV10: Oxl 6E 15
Renton Rd. WV10: Oxl 6E 15

Repington Way B75: S Cold 5F 55
Repton Av. WV6: Pert 6E 25
Repton Gro. B9: Bord G 6H 103
Repton Ho. B23: Erd 1F 85
Repton Rd. B9: Bord G 6H 103
Reservoir Cl. B31: N'fld 2B 144
   WS2: Wals 3H 47
Reservoir Pas. WS10: W'bry 2F 63
Reservoir Pl. WS2: Wals 3H 47
Reservoir Retreat B16: Edg 2B 116
Reservoir Rd. B16: Edg 1B 116
   B23: Erd 3D 84
   B29: S Oak 2F 131
   B45: Coft H 6A 158
   B65: Row R 6C 96
   B68: O'bry 5A 98
   B92: Olton 5D 136
   WS2: Wals 3H 47
Reservoir St. WS2: Wals 3H 47
Retallack Cl. B66: Smeth 1F 99
Retford Dr. B76: Walm 1C 70
Retford Gro. B25: Yard 5A 120
Retreat, The B64: Crad H 4G 111
Retreat Gdns. DY3: Sed 6A 60
Retreat St. WV3: Wolv 6A 170 (3F 43)
Revesby Wlk. B7: Birm 5A 102
Revival St. WS3: Blox 6H 19
Reynards Cl. DY3: Sed 6C 60
Reynolds Cl. DY3: Swind 5E 73
Reynolds Gro. WV6: Pert 4F 25
Reynolds Ho. B19: Loz 2G 101
   (off Newbury Rd.)
Reynolds Rd. B21: Hand 2A 100
Reynoldstown Rd. B36: Hodg H 1A 104
Reynolds Wlk. WV11: Wed 1B 30
Rhayader Rd. B31: N'fld 2C 144
Rhodes Cl. DY3: Lwr G 3E 75
Rhone Cl. B11: S'hll 2C 134
Rhoose Cft. B35: Cas V 4F 87
Rhys Thomas Cl. WV12: W'hall 5D 30
Rian Ct. B64: Crad H 3F 111
Ribbesford Av. WV10: Oxl 1F 27
Ribbesford Cl. B63: Crad 6F 111
Ribbesford Cres. WV14: Cose 4F 61
Ribble Ct. B73: S Cold 6H 53
Ribblesdale Rd. B30: Stir 6C 132
Ribble Wlk. B36: Cas B 1B 106
Richard Lighton Ho. B1: Birm 3B 4
Richard Parkes Ho. WS10: W'bry 2E 63
Richard Pl. WS5: Wals 3G 49
Richard Rd. WS5: Wals 3G 49
Richards Cl. B31: Longb 3D 158
   B65: Row R 5E 97
Richards Ho. B69: O'bry 5D 96
   WS2: Wals 6B 32
   (off Burrowes St.)
Richardson Dr. DY8: Amb 3C 108
Richards Rd. DY4: Tip 4H 61
Richards St. WS10: Darl 3D 46
Richard St. B6: Aston 4H 101
   B7: Birm 4H 101
   B70: W Brom 4H 79
Richard St. Sth. B70: W Brom 5A 80
Richard St. W. B70: W Brom 5H 79
Richard Wattis Dr. WS10: W'bry 6F 47
Richard Williams Rd.
   WS10: W'bry 3H 63
Richborough Dr. DY1: Dud 4A 76
Riches St. WV6: Wolv 6D 26
Richford Gro. B33: Kitts G 1H 121
Richmere Ct. WV6: Tett 6H 25
Richmond Ashton Dr. DY4: Tip 2A 78
Richmond Av. B12: Bal H 6H 117
   WV3: Wolv 2D 42
Richmond Cl. B20: Hand 4C 82
   B47: H'wd 2B 162
Richmond Ct. B15: Edg 3D 116
   (off Enfield Rd.)
   B29: W Cas 6G 131
   B63: Hale 2G 127
   B68: O'bry 4A 98
   B70: W Grn 6H 69
   DY9: Pedm 4F 125
   (off Redlake Rd.)
Richmond Cft. B42: Gt Barr 1B 82

Richmond Dr. B75: S Cold 5D **54**
WV3: Wolv 2C **42**
WV6: Pert 5F **25**
Richmond Gdns. DY8: Amb 4D **108**
WV5: Wom 2G **73**
Richmond Gro. DY8: Woll 3C **108**
Richmond Hill B68: O'bry 4A **98**
Richmond Hill Gdns. B15: Edg 4A **116**
Richmond Hill Rd. B15: Edg 5A **116**
Richmond Ho. B37: Chel W 2E **123**
Richmond Pk. DY6: W Hth 1A **92**
Richmond Pl. B14: K Hth 5H **133**
Richmond Rd. B18: Hock 3D **100**
B33: Stech 1B **120**
B45: Rub 2E **157**
B66: Smeth 1E **115**
B73: S Cold 5H **53**
B92: Olton 4C **136**
DY2: Dud 1E **95**
DY3: Sed 6A **60**
WV3: Wolv 1C **42**
Richmond St. B63: Hale 1A **128**
B70: W Brom 1F **79**
WS1: Wals 2D **48**
Richmond St. Sth.
B70: W Brom 2E **79**
Richmond Way B37: Chel W 6E **107**
Rickard Cl. B93: Know 4A **166**
Rickman Dr. B15: Birm 3F **117**
Rickyard Cl. B25: Yard 2B **120**
B29: W Cas 1E **145**
Rickyard Piece B32: Quin 1C **130**
Riddfield Rd. B36: Hodg H 1C **104**
Ridding La. WV3: W'bry 3F **63**
Riddings, The B33: Stech 5C **104**
B76: Walm 5F **71**
DY9: W'cte 3H **125**
WV10: Bush 2C **28**
Riddings Cres. WS3: Pels 3D **20**
Riddings Hill CV7: Bal C 5H **169**
RIDGACRE .5B **114**
Ridgacre Ent. Pk. B71: W Brom 1H **79**
Ridgacre La. B32: Quin 5H **113**
Ridgacre Rd. B32: Quin 5H **113**
(not continuous)
B71: W Brom 1H **79**
Ridgacre Rd. W. B32: Quin 5G **113**
Ridge Cl. B13: Mose 1C **148**
WS2: Wals 6D **30**
Ridgefield Rd. B62: B'hth 3C **112**
Ridge Gro. DY9: Lye 6G **109**
Ridge Hill DY8: Word 6D **92**
Ridge La. WV11: Wed 2F **29**
Ridgemount Dr. B38: K Nor 2H **159**
Ridge Rd. DY6: K'wfrd 4H **91**
Ridge St. DY8: Woll 5A **108**
Ridgewater Cl. B45: Redn 3H **157**
Ridgeway B17: Edg 1F **115**
B32: Quin 1G **129**
WS9: A'rdge 5D **34**
Ridgeway, The B23: Erd 1A **84**
DY3: Sed 1H **75**
WS7: Burn 1C **10**
Ridgeway Av. B62: Quin 5G **113**
Ridgeway Ct. WS2: Wals 2F **47**
Ridgeway Dr. WV4: Penn 2D **58**
Ridgeway Rd. DY4: Tip 5A **62**
DY8: Word 1D **108**
Ridgewood B34: S End 3F **105**
Ridgewood Av. DY8: Woll 4A **108**
Ridgewood Cl. WS1: Wals 3D **48**
Ridgewood Dr. B75: Four O 2H **53**
Ridgewood Gdns. B44: Gt Barr 6H **67**
Ridgmont Cft. B32: Quin 6C **114**
Riding Cl. B71: W Brom 5D **64**
Riding Way WV12: W'hall 3D **30**
Ridley St. B1: Birm 6B **4** (2E **117**)
Ridpool Rd. B33: Kitts G 6F **105**
Rifle St. WV14: Cose 5C **60**
Rigby St. WS10: W'bry 4F **63**
Riland Av. B75: S Cold 6B **54**
Riland Ct. B72: W Grn 6A **70**
Riland Gro. B75: S Cold 6A **54**
Riland Ind. Est. B75: S Cold 6B **54**

Riland Rd. B75: S Cold 6B **54**
Riley Cres. WV3: Wolv 5D **42**
Riley Dr. B36: Cas B 6C **88**
Riley Rd. B14: Yard W 4D **148**
Riley St. WV13: W'hall 1B **46**
Rilstone Rd. B32: Harb 6D **114**
Rindleford Av. WV4: Penn 5A **42**
Ring, The B25: Yard 3A **120**
Ringhills Rd. WV8: Bilb 5H **13**
Ringinglow Rd. B44: Gt Barr 3E **67**
Ringmere Av. B36: Cas B 1F **105**
Ring Rd. Nth. B15: Edg 1B **132**
Ring Rd. St Andrews
WV1: Wolv 3A **170** (1F **43**)
Ring Rd. St Davids
WV1: Wolv 3D **170** (1H **43**)
Ring Rd. St Georges
WV2: Wolv 5C **170** (2H **43**)
Ring Rd. St Johns
WV2: Wolv 5A **170** (2G **43**)
Ring Rd. St Marks
WV3: Wolv 4A **170** (2F **43**)
Ring Rd. St Patricks
WV1: Wolv 1C **170** (6H **27**)
Ring Rd. St Peters
WV1: Wolv 2A **170** (1G **43**)
Ring Rd. Sth. B15: Edg 1B **132**
Ringswood Rd. B92: Olton 1C **136**
Ringway Bus. Pk. B7: Birm 4A **102**
Ringwood Av. WS9: A'rdge 4D **34**
Ringwood Dr. B45: Fran 6G **143**
Ringwood Rd. WV10: Bush 6H **15**
Ripley Cl. B69: Tiv 1H **95**
Ripley Gro. B23: Erd 2B **84**
Ripon Dr. B71: W Brom 4B **64**
Ripon Rd. B14: Yard W 3C **148**
WS2: Wals 1H **47**
WV10: Oxl 2G **27**
Rippingille Rd. B43: Gt Barr 1E **67**
Ripple Rd. B30: Stir 6D **132**
Risborough Ho. B31: Longb 1D **158**
Rischale Way WS4: Rus 1H **33**
Rise, The B37: Mars G 4C **122**
B42: Gt Barr 5C **66**
B48: Hopw 5F **159**
DY6: K'wfrd 4C **92**
Rise Av. B45: Redn 2G **157**
Riseley Cres. B5: Edg 5F **117**
Rising Brook WV6: Tett 5H **25**
Rissington Av. B29: S Oak 5C **132**
Ritchie Cl. B13: Mose 4A **134**
Rivendell Ct. B28: Hall G 4E **135**
Rivendell Gdns. WV6: Tett 4H **25**
Riverbank Rd. WV13: W'hall 1D **46**
River Brook Dr. B30: Stir 5D **132**
River Lee Rd. B11: Tys 6E **119**
Rivermead Pk. B34: S End 4E **105**
Riversdale Rd. B14: Yard W 4D **148**
Riverside Ct. B38: K Nor 4H **145**
B46: Col 2H **107**
(off Prossers Wlk.)
Riverside Cres. B28: Hall G 3D **148**
Riverside Dr. B29: S Oak 2E **133**
B33: Stech 5B **104**
B91: Sol 5A **152**
Riverside Gdns. WV8: Bilb 3H **13**
Riversleigh Dr. DY8: Word 3C **108**
River St. B5: Birm 5H **5** (1A **118**)
River Wlk. WS10: W'bry 4G **63**
Riverway WS10: W'bry 3H **63**
Rivington Cl. DY8: Stourb 1C **124**
Rivington Cres. B44: K'sdng 4C **68**
Roach Cl. B37: Chel W 6E **107**
DY5: Brie H 4H **93**
Roach Cres. WV11: Wed 1H **29**
Roach Pool Cft. B16: Edg 1G **115**
Robert Av. B23: Erd 1E **85**
Robert Cl. B13: Mose 3B **134**
Robert Lucas Pl. B67: Smeth 5D **98**
Robert Rd. B20: Hand 6D **82**
DY4: Tip 1H **77**
Roberts Cl. WS9: Wals W 5B **22**
WS10: Mox 1B **62**
Roberts Ct. B24: Erd 1A **86**

Roberts Grn. Rd. DY3: Up Gor 3A **76**
Roberts La. DY9: Pedm 5F **125**
Robertson Knoll B36: Hodg H 2D **104**
Robertsons Bus. B7: Nech 2C **102**
Roberts Rd. B27: A Grn 2A **136**
WS3: Wals 4D **32**
WS10: W'bry 2C **64**
Robert St. DY3: Lwr G 3H **75**
Robert Wynd WV14: Cose 4B **60**
Robeson Cl. DY4: Tip 2F **77**
Robin Cl. B36: Cas B 1C **106**
DY6: K'wfrd 3E **93**
Robin Gro. WV11: Wed 2E **29**
Robin Hood Crematorium B90: Shir . .2H **149**
Robin Hood Cres. B28: Hall G 6E **135**
Robin Hood Cft. B28: Hall G 1F **149**
Robin Hood Island B28: Hall G 2G **149**
(off Stratford Rd.)
Robin Hood La. B28: Hall G 6D **134**
Robin Hood Rd. DY5: Quar B 1B **110**
Robin Rd. B23: Erd 3E **85**
Robins Cl. DY8: Stourb 2E **125**
WS6: C Hay 4D **6**
Robins Ct. B14: K Hth 4H **133**
Robinsfield Dr. B31: Longb 2E **159**
Robinsons Way B76: Min 2H **87**
Robin Wlk. WS2: Wals 6F **31**
Robottom Cl. WS2: Wals 3H **31**
Robson Cl. WS8: Bwnhls 2C **22**
Rocester Av. WV11: Wed 2G **29**
Rochdale Wlk. B10: Small H 4C **118**
Roche Rd. WS3: Blox 6F **19**
Rochester Cft. WS2: Wals 5G **31**
Rochester Rd. B31: N'fld 3E **145**
Roche Way WS3: Blox 6F **19**
Rochford Cl. B45: Rub 2E **157**
B63: Hale 3H **127**
B76: Walm 5E **71**
WS2: Wals 4A **48**
Rochford Ct. B90: M'path 3E **165**
Rochford Gro. WV4: Penn 6B **42**
Rock, The WV6: Tett 4B **26**
Rock Av. B45: Redn 2A **158**
Rocket Pool Dr. WV14: Bils 3H **61**
Rockface, The 6H **101**
Rockford Rd. B42: Gt Barr 6C **66**
Rock Gro. B92: Olton 2C **136**
Rockingham Cl. B93: Dorr 6H **165**
DY3: Gorn 4F **75**
WS3: Blox 6H **19**
Rockingham Dr. WV6: Pert 6E **25**
Rockingham Gdns. B74: S Cold 5H **53**
Rockingham Hall Gdns. DY9: Hag . . .6H **125**
Rockingham Rd. B25: Yard 3B **120**
Rockland Dr. B33: Stech 5C **104**
Rockland Gdns. WV13: W'hall 3H **45**
Rocklands Dr. B75: S Cold 3H **53**
Rockley Gro. B45: Redn 2H **157**
Rockley Rd. B65: Row R 3A **96**
Rockmead Av. B44: Gt Barr 3H **67**
Rockmoor Cl. B37: K'hrst 6A **106**
Rock Rd. B92: Olton 2C **136**
WV14: Cose 5B **60**
Rockrose Gdns. WV10: F'stne 1D **16**
Rocks Hill DY5: Brie H 2H **109**
Rock St. DY3: Up Gor 2A **76**
Rockville Rd. B8: Salt 5G **103**
Rocky La. B6: Aston 3A **102**
B7: Nech 3B **102**
B42: Gt Barr, P Barr 1C **82**
Rocky La. & Chelsea Trad. Ests.
B7: Nech 3A **102**
Rodborough Rd. B26: Sheld 5F **121**
B93: Dorr 6F **167**
Rodbourne Rd. B17: Harb 2G **131**
Roddis Cl. B23: Erd 5D **68**
Roderick Dr. WV11: Wed 2F **29**
Roderick Rd. B11: S'brk 6C **118**
Rodlington Av. B44: Gt Barr 4H **67**
Rodman Cl. B15: Edg 3H **115**
Rodney Cl. B16: Birm 1C **116**
B92: Olton 4F **137**
Rodney Rd. B92: Olton 4F **137**

Rodway Cl. B19: Loz 2G **101**
. DY5: Quar B 4H **109**
. WV4: E'shll 2H **59**
Rodwell Gro. B44: K'sdng 5A **68**
Roebuck Cl. B34: S End 4A **106**
Roebuck Glade WV12: W'hall 5E **31**
Roebuck La. B66: Smeth 2C **98**
. B70: W Brom 6C **80**
Roebuck Pl. WS3: Blox 3C **32**
Roebuck Rd. WS3: Blox 3C **32**
Roebuck St. B70: W Brom 6D **80**
Roedean Cl. B44: K'sdng 6B **68**
Roford Ct. DY3: Up Gor 1A **76**
Rogerfield Rd. B23: Erd 1G **85**
Rogers Cl. WV11: Wed 6A **18**
Rogers Rd. B8: W End 4H **103**
Rokeby Cl. B76: Walm 1C **70**
Rokeby Rd. B43: Gt Barr 3B **66**
Rokeby Wlk. B34: Hodg H 3D **104**
Rokewood Cl. DY6: K'wfrd 6B **74**
Roland Gdns. B19: Loz 1E **101**
Roland Gro. B19: Loz 1E **101**
Rolan Dr. B90: Maj G 1E **163**
Roland Rd. B19: Loz 1E **101**
Roland Vernon Way DY4: Tip 6C **62**
Rolfe St. B66: Smeth 3E **99**
Rollason Rd. B24: Erd 4G **85**
. DY2: Dud 1F **95**
Rollesby Dr. WV13: W'hall 3H **45**
Rollingmill Bus. Pk. WS2: Wals 2A **48**
Rollingmill St. WS2: Wals 2A **48**
Rolling Mill Cl. B5: Edg 4G **117**
Rolling Mill Rd. WS11: Nort C 1E **9**
Rollingmill St. WS2: Wals 2A **48**
Rollswood Dr. B91: Sol 3D **150**
Roman Cl. WS8: Bwnhls 3A **10**
Roman Ct. B38: K Nor 1C **160**
Roman Grange B74: Lit As 4C **36**
Roman La. B74: Lit As 5B **36**
Roman Pk. B46: Col 6H **89**
. B74: Lit As 5B **36**
Roman Pl. D74: Lit As 1B **52**
Roman Rd. B74: Lit As 4C **36**
. DY7: Stourb 2A **124**
. DY8: Stourb 2A **124**
. . . .(not continuous)
Roman Vw. WS11: Cann 1F **7**
Roman Way B15: Edg 4H **131**
. B46: Col .5G **89**
. B65: Row R 5C **96**
Romany Rd. B45: Fran 6D **142**
Romany Way DY8: Stourb 2A **124**
Roma Rd. B11: Tys 6E **119**
Romford Cl. B26: Sheld 5F **121**
Romilly Av. B20: Hand 5D **82**
Romilly Cl. B76: Walm 1E **71**
. DY8: Woll 5C **108**
Romney Cl. B28: Hall G 6F **135**
Romney Ho. Ind. Est. WS10: Darl . . .4B **46**
. . . .(off Wolverhampton St.)
Romney Way B43: Gt Barr 1F **67**
Romsey Gro. WV10: F'hses 4G **15**
Romsey Rd. WV10: F'hses 4G **15**
Romsey Way WS3: Blox 4F **19**
ROMSLEY 3A **142**
Romsley Cl. B45: Rub 1E **157**
. B63: Hale 3B **128**
. WS4: S'fld 5G **21**
ROMSLEY HILL 5A **142**
Romsley Rd. B32: Bart G 5H **129**
. B68: O'bry 1H **113**
. DY9: Lye .6G **109**
Romulus Cl. B20: Hand 4D **82**
Ronald Gro. B36: Cas B 6H **87**
Ronald Pl. B9: Bord G 1E **119**
Ronald Rd. B9: Bord G 1D **118**
Ron Davis Cl. B66: Smeth 4F **99**
ROOD END 3A **98**
Rood End Rd. B68: O'bry 3A **98**
. B69: O'bry 2A **98**
Rooker Av. WV2: E'shll 4A **44**
Rooker Cres. WV2: E'shll 5A **44**
Rookery, The B62: Quin 3G **129**
Rookery Av. DY5: Brie H 1E **109**
. WV4: E'shll 2C **60**

Rookery La. WS9: A'rdge 3D **34**
. WV2: Wolv 5E **43**
Rookery Pde. WS9: A'rdge 3D **34**
Rookery Pk. DY5: P'ntt 4F **93**
Rookery Ri. WV5: Wom 1H **73**
Rookery Rd. B21: Hand 1A **100**
. B29: S Oak 3B **132**
. WV4: E'shll 2C **60**
. WV5: Wom 1H **73**
Rookery St. WV11: Wed 4E **29**
Rookwood Dr. WV6: Tett 1F **41**
Rookwood Rd. B27: A Grn 1H **135**
Rooth St. WS10: W'bry 1H **63**
Roper Wlk. DY3: Sed 1B **76**
Roper Way DY3: Sed 1B **76**
Rope Wlk. WS1: Wals 2E **49**
Rosafield Av. B62: Quin 5F **113**
Rosalind Av. DY1: Dud 6D **60**
Rosalind Gro. WV11: Wed 4A **30**
Rosamond St. WS1: Wals 4B **48**
Rosary Rd. B23: Erd 4D **84**
Rosary Vs. B11: S'hll 6B **118**
Rose Av. B68: O'bry 4B **114**
. DY6: K'wfrd 4D **92**
Rose Bank B74: Lit As 4D **36**
Rose Bank Dr. WS3: Wals 5C **32**
Rosebay Av. B38: K Nor 1B **160**
Rosebay Gro. WV5: Wom 1E **73**
Roseberry Rd. B66: Smeth 5G **99**
Roseberry St. B18: Hock 5C **100**
. WV3: Wolv 2F **43**
Rosebriars B90: Maj G 2E **163**
Rose Cl. B66: Smeth 4G **99**
Rose Cott. Dr. DY8: Word 1H **107**
. . . .(off Barnett La.)
Rose Cotts. B29: S Oak 3B **132**
. B30: Stir .1C **146**
Rose Ct. CV7: Bal C 1H **169**
Rosecroft Rd. B26: Sheld 5G **121**
Rosedale Av. B23: Erd 4E **85**
. B66: Smeth 4G **99**
Rosedale Gro. B25: Yard 3A **120**
Rosedale Pl. WV13: W'hall 3A **46**
Rosedale Rd. B25: Yard 3A **120**
Rosedale Wlk. DY6: K'wfrd 1C **92**
. . . .(off Birchwood Wlk.)
Rosedene Dr. B20: Hand 5B **82**
Rose Dr. WS8: Clay 1A **22**
Rosefield Ct. B67: Smeth 5E **99**
Rosefield Cft. B6: Aston 2H **101**
Rosefield Rd. B67: Smeth 5E **99**
Rosefields B31: N'fld 2F **145**
Rosegardens, The
. B63: Hale 3B **127**
Rosehall Cl. B91: Sol 6D **150**
Rose Hill B45: Coft H, Lick 6G **157**
. DY5: Quar B 2C **110**
. WV13: W'hall 3A **46**
Rose Hill Cl. B36: Cas B 1F **105**
Rosehill Ct. DY1: Dud 6E **77**
. . . .(off Wolverhampton St.)
Rose Hill Gdns. WV13: W'hall 2A **46**
Rose Hill Rd. B21: Hand 2C **100**
Rosehip Cl. WS5: Wals 2E **65**
Roseland Av. DY2: Dud 6H **77**
Roseland Way B15: Birm 2D **116**
Rose La. B69: Tiv 5C **78**
Roseleigh Rd. B45: Redn 3H **157**
Rosemary Av. WS6: C Hay 2D **6**
. WV4: Penn 5G **43**
. WV14: Bils 5H **45**
Rosemary Cl. WS8: Clay 1H **21**
Rosemary Cres. WV11: Wed 2H **29**
Rosemary Cres. DY1: Dud 1B **76**
. WV4: Penn 6G **43**
Rosemary Cres. W. WV4: Penn 6F **43**
Rosemary Dr. B74: Lit As 6C **36**
Rosemary Hill Rd. B74: Four O 6C **36**
Rosemary La. DY8: Stourb 2B **124**
Rosemary Nook B74: Lit As 4D **36**
Rosemary Rd. B33: Stech 1D **120**
. B63: Hale 3F **127**
. DY4: Tip .1A **78**
. WS6: C Hay 1D **6**

Rosemoor Dr. DY5: Brie H 4F **109**
Rosemount B32: Quin 1C **130**
Rose Pl. B18: Birm 1A 4 (5E **101**)
Rose Rd. B17: Harb 5H **115**
. B46: Col .1H **107**
Rose St. WV14: Bils 3H **61**
ROSEVILLE 6D **60**
Roseville Ct. WV14: Cose 5E **61**
. . . .(off Castle St.)
Roseville Gdns. WV8: Cod 3G **13**
Roseville Pct. WV14: Cose 5E **61**
. . . .(off Castle St., not continuous)
Rosewood Cl. B74: Lit As 4D **36**
Rosewood Ct. WV14: Cose 5E **61**
. . . .(off Bayer St.)
Rosewood Dr. B23: Erd 5D **84**
Rosewood Gdns. WV11: Ess 4B **18**
Rosewood Pk. WS6: C Hay 3D **6**
Rosewood Rd. DY1: Dud 2D **76**
Roshven Rd. B12: Bal H 1A **134**
Roslin Gro. B19: Hock 3E **101**
Roslyn Cl. B66: Smeth 3E **99**
Rosneath Gdns. WV4: E'shll 6B **44**
Ross B65: Row R 1B **112**
Ross Cl. WV3: Wolv 1C **42**
Ross Dr. DY6: K'wfrd 2A **92**
Rosse Ct. B92: Sol 5B **138**
Rossendale Cl. B63: Crad 5F **111**
Ross Hgts. B65: Row R 6B **96**
Rosslyn Rd. B76: Walm 1D **86**
Ross Rd. WS3: Wals 3D **32**
Rostrevor Rd. B10: Small H 2F **119**
Rotary Ho. DY1: Dud 6B **76**
Rotherby Gro. B37: Mars G 4D **122**
Rotherfield Rd. B26: Sheld 3F **121**
Rothesay Cft. B32: Bart G 6H **129**
Rothesay Dr. DY8: Word 6A **92**
Rothesay Gdns. WV4: E'shll 6A **44**
Rothesay Way WV12: W'hall 3B **30**
Rothley Wlk. B38: K Nor 1G **159**
Rothwell Dr. B91: Shir 2B **150**
Rotton Pk. Rd. B16: Edg 5H **99**
. . . .(not continuous)
Rotton Pk. St. B16: Birm 6B **100**
ROTTON ROW 5E **167**
Rough Coppice Wlk. B35: Cas V 5E **87**
ROUGH HAY 4C **46**
Rough Hay Pl. WS10: Darl 4C **46**
Rough Hay Rd. WS10: Darl 4C **46**
Rough Hill Dr. B65: Row R 3H **95**
Rough Hills Cl. WV2: E'shll 5B **44**
Rough Hills Rd. WV2: E'shll 5B **44**
Roughlea Av. B36: Hodg H 2D **104**
ROUGHLEY 6A **38**
Roughley Dr. B75: R'ley 1A **54**
Roughley Farm Rd. B75: R'ley 6C **38**
Rough Rd. B44: K'sdng 2A **68**
Rough Wood Country Pk. 3E **31**
Rouncil Cl. B92: Sol 6H **137**
Roundabout, The B31: Longb 6B **144**
Round Cl. B90: Dic H 3G **163**
Round Cft. WV13: W'hall 1A **46**
Round Hill DY3: Sed 3H **59**
Round Hill Av. DY9: Pedm 4G **125**
Roundhill Cl. B76: Walm 2C **70**
Roundhill Ho. DY6: K'wfrd 6B **74**
Roundhills Rd. B62: B'hth 3F **113**
Roundhill Ter. B62: B'hth 2E **113**
Roundhouse Rd. DY3: Up Gor 3A **76**
Roundlea Cl. WV12: W'hall 1B **30**
Roundlea Rd. B31: N'fld 5C **130**
Round Moor Wlk. B35: Cas V 4E **87**
ROUND OAK 5H **93**
Round Rd. B24: Erd 5H **85**
Roundsaw Cft. B45: Rub 1F **157**
ROUND'S GREEN 2E **97**
Round's Grn. Rd. B69: O'bry 2E **97**
Rounds Hill Rd. WV14: Cose 5F **61**
Rounds Rd. WV14: Cose 2F **61**
Round St. DY2: Neth 3E **95**
Rounds Wharf DY4: Tip 2G **77**
Roundway Down WV6: Pert 6E **25**

Rounton Cl. B74: Four O 5D **36**
Rousay Cl. B45: Fran 6F **143**
Rousdon Gro. B43: Gt Barr 5H **65**
Rover Dr. B27: A Grn 1B **136**
  B36: Cas B 6B **88**
Rovex Bus. Pk. B11: Tys 6F **119**
Rowallan Rd. B75: R'ley 2B **54**
Rowan Cl. B47: H'wd 4B **162**
  B76: Walm 3D **70**
Rowan Ct. B30: K Nor 5C **146**
  B66: Smeth 1B **98**
Rowan Cres. WV3: Wolv 4C **42**
  WV14: Cose 4D **60**
Rowan Dr. B28: Hall G 2G **149**
  WV11: Ess 4B **18**
Rowan Ri. DY6: K'wfrd 3C **92**
Rowan Rd. B72: S Cold 3A **70**
  DY3: Sed 4B **60**
  WS5: Wals 1D **64**
Rowantrees B45: Redn 4H **157**
Rowan Way B31: Longb 6D **144**
  B37: Chel W 2E **123**
Roway La. B69: O'bry 6E **79**
Rowbrook Cl. B90: Maj G 1E **163**
Rowchester Ct. B4: Birm 2E **5**
Rowcroft Covert B14: K Hth 4E **147**
Rowdale Rd. B42: Gt Barr 6E **67**
Rowden Dr. B23: Erd 1G **85**
  B91: Sol 5C **150**
Rowena Gdns. DY3: Sed 3G **59**
Rowheath Ho. B30: B'vlle 1A **146**
Rowheath Rd. B30: K Nor 3B **146**
Rowington Av. B65: Row R 6D **96**
Rowington Rd. B34: S End 3A **106**
Rowland Gdns. WS2: Wals 6A **32**
Rowland Hill Dr. DY4: Tip 2C **78**
Rowlands Av. WS2: Wals 6E **31**
  WV1: Wolv 1D **44**
Rowlands Cl. WS2: Wals 5E **31**
Rowlands Cres. B91: Sol 5F **137**
Rowlands Rd. B26: Yard 4C **120**
Rowland St. WS2: Wals 6A **32**
Rowley Gro. B33: Kitts G 6H **105**
Rowley Hall Av. B65: Row R 5C **96**
Rowley Hill Vw. B64: Crad H 3H **111**
Rowley Pl. WS4: Rus 2F **33**
ROWLEY REGIS 6C **96**

Rowley Regis Crematorium
  B65: Row R 1A **112**
Rowley Regis Station (Rail) 1E **113**
Rowley St. WS1: Wals 1D **48**
Rowley Vw. B70: W Brom 4H **79**
  WS10: Darl 1C **62**
  WV14: Bils 2A **62**
Rowley Village B65: Row R 6C **96**
Rowney Cft. B28: Hall G 2E **149**
Rowood Dr. B91: Sol 6G **137**
  B92: Sol 6H **137**
Rowthorn Cl. B74: S'tly 4A **52**
Rowthorn Dr. B90: M'path 3E **165**
Rowton Av. WV6: Pert 6E **25**
Rowton Dr. B74: S'tly 6H **51**
Roxburgh Gro. B43: Gt Barr 1E **67**
Roxburgh Rd. B73: S Cold 2G **69**
Roxby Gdns. WV6: Wolv 4E **27**
Royal Arch Apartments B1: Birm 6B **4**
Royal Cl. B65: Row R 4C **96**
  DY5: Brie H 3G **109**
Royal Ct. B72: W Grn 3H **69**
Royal Gro. B23: Erd 6B **68**
Royal Oak Rd. B62: Quin 1F **129**
  B65: Row R 4H **95**
Royal Rd. B72: S Cold 6A **54**
Royal Scot Gro. WS1: Wals 6C **48**
Royal Star Cl. B33: Kitts G 1G **121**
Royal, The Stop (MM) 2A **44**
Royal Way DY4: Tip 5A **78**
Roydon Rd. B27: A Grn 5A **136**
Roylesden Cres. B73: New O 3C **68**
Royston Chase B74: Lit As 6B **36**
Royston Ct. B13: Mose 3B **134**
  (off Wake Grn. Pk.)
Royston Cft. B12: Bal H 5H **117**
Royston Way DY3: Sed 5G **59**

RSPB Sandwell Valley Nature Reserve
  . . . . .1G **81**
Rubens Cl. DY3: Up Gor 2H **75**
RUBERY 2F **157**
Rubery By-Pass B45: Rub 2E **157**
Rubery Cl. WS10: Darl 4C **46**
Rubery Farm Gro. B45: Rub 1F **157**
Rubery Fld. Cl. B45: Redn 6G **143**
Rubery La. B45: Fran 6F **143**
Rubery La. Sth. B45: Rub 1F **157**
Rubery St. WS10: Darl 3D **46**
Ruckley Av. B19: Loz 2E **101**
Ruckley Rd. B29: W Cas 5E **131**
Rudd Gdns. WV10: Wolv 5D **28**
Ruddington Way B19: Hock 4G **101**
Rudge Av. WV1: Wolv 6D **28**
Rudge Cl. WV12: W'hall 5C **30**
Rudge Cft. B33: Kitts G 5E **105**
Rudge Wlk. B18: Hock 6C **100**
Rudgewick Cft. B6: Aston 3H **101**
Rudyard Cl. WV10: Bush 3A **16**
Rudyard Gro. B33: Kitts G 6F **105**
Rudyngfield Dr. B33: Stech 6D **104**
Rufford Cl. B23: Erd 5D **68**
Rufford Rd. DY9: Lye 1G **125**
Rufford St. DY9: Lye 5H **109**
Rufford Way WS9: A'rdge 2A **34**
Rugby Rd. DY8: Woll 4B **108**
Rugby St. WV1: Wolv 6F **27**
Rugeley Av. WV12: W'hall 1D **30**
Rugeley Cl. DY4: Tip 2G **77**
Rugeley Gro. B7: Nech 3B **102**
Ruislip Cl. B35: Cas V 3E **87**
RUITON 3H **75**
Ruiton St. DY3: Lwr G 3H **75**
Rumbow B63: Hale 1B **128**
RUMBUSH 6E **163**
Rumbush La. B90: Dic H 3G **163**
  (not continuous)
  B90: Dic H, Tid G 6E **163**
  B94: Earls 6E **163**
Runcorn Cl. B37: F'bri 5E **107**
Runcorn Rd. B12: Bal H 6H **117**
Runnymede Dr. CV7: Bal C 6H **169**
Runnymede Rd. B11: S'hll 2E **135**
Rupert St. B7: Birm, Nech 4A **102**
  WV3: Wolv 1E **43**
RUSHALL 2F **33**
Rushall Cl. DY8: Word 3C **108**
  WS4: Wals 5F **33**
Rushall Ct. B43: Gt Barr 6A **66**
  (off West Rd.)
Rushall Mnr. Cl. WS4: Wals 5F **33**
Rushall Mnr. Rd. WS4: Wals 5F **33**
Rushall Rd. WV10: Bush 5A **16**
Rushbrook Cl. B92: Olton 3C **136**
  WS8: Clay 1A **22**
Rushbrooke Cl. B13: Mose 1H **133**
Rushbrooke Dr. B73: New O 2C **68**
Rushbrook Gro. B14: K Hth 4E **147**
Rushbury Cl. B90: Shir 3B **150**
  WV14: Bils 6D **44**
Rushden Cft. B44: K'sdng 4H **67**
Rushes Mill WS3: Pels 4C **20**
Rushey La. B11: Tys 6G **119**
Rushford Av. WV5: Wom 1G **73**
Rushford Cl. B90: M'path 2E **165**
Rush Grn. B32: Bart G 3C **130**
Rushleigh Rd. B90: Maj G 1E **163**
Rushmead Gro. B45: Redn 2G **157**
Rushmere Rd. DY4: Tip 5A **62**
Rushmoor Cl. B74: S Cold 5H **53**
Rushmore Ho. B45: Rub 1F **157**
Rushton Cl. CV7: Bal C 5H **169**
Rushwater Cl. WV5: Wom 1E **73**
Rushwick Cft. B34: S End 3H **105**
Rushwick Gro. B90: M'path 3E **165**
Rushwood Cl. WS4: Wals 6E **33**
Rushy Piece B32: Bart G 2B **130**
Ruskin Av. B65: Row R 1D **112**
  DY3: Lwr G 2E **75**
  WV4: E'shll 3B **60**
Ruskin Cl. B6: Aston 2H **101**

Ruskin Ct. B66: Smeth 2B **98**
  B68: O'bry 3H **113**
Ruskin Gro. B27: A Grn 3H **135**
Ruskin Hall Gro. B6: Aston 2H **101**
Ruskin Rd. WV10: Bush 1B **28**
Ruskin St. B71: W Brom 2A **80**
Russell Bank Rd. B74: Four O 5E **37**
Russell Cl. B69: Tiv 5D **78**
  DY4: Tip 4C **62**
  WV11: Wed 6H **17**
Russell Ct. B74: Four O 6D **36**
  WV3: Wolv 2F **43**
Russell Ho. WS10: W'bry 3F **63**
  WV8: Cod 3E **13**
Russell Rd. B13: Mose 2F **133**
  B28: Hall G 3E **135**
  WV14: Bils 4H **45**
Russells, The B13: Mose 2F **133**
RUSSELL'S HALL 6B **76**
Russells Hall Rd. DY1: Dud 6A **76**
Russell St. DY1: Dud 6D **76**
  WS10: W'bry 3F **63**
  WV3: Wolv 2F **43**
  WV13: W'hall 1B **46**
Russett Cl. WS5: Wals 3A **50**
Russett Way DY5: P'ntt 2F **93**
Russet Wlk. WV8: Pend 6C **14**
Russet Way B31: N'fld 1C **144**
Ruston St. B16: Birm 2D **116**
Ruthall Cl. B29: W Cas 6G **131**
Ruth Cl. DY4: Tip 3C **62**
Rutherford Rd. B23: Erd 6E **69**
  WS2: Wals 3G **31**
Rutland Av. WV4: Penn 1B **58**
Rutland Cl. B29: W Cas 6G **131**
Rutland Cres. WS9: A'rdge 6D **22**
  WV14: Bils 4F **45**
Rutland Dr. B26: Yard 4C **120**
Rutland Pas. DY1: Dud 6E **77**
Rutland Pl. DY8: Woll 3B **108**
Rutland Rd. B66: Smeth 2E **115**
  B71: W Brom 6A **64**
  WS10: W'bry 1A **64**
  WV3: Wals 4C **32**
Rutland Ter. B18: Hock 4C **100**
  (off Crabtree Rd.)
Rutley Gro. B32: Quin 1D **130**
Rutters Mdw. B32: Quin 1H **129**
Rutter St. WS1: Wals 4B **48**
Ryan Av. WV11: Wed 1A **30**
Ryan Pl. DY2: Neth 3E **95**
Rycroft Gro. B33: Kitts G 1G **121**
Rydal Cl. B74: S'tly 1H **51**
  WV11: Wed 2E **29**
Rydal Dr. WV6: Pert 5F **25**
Rydal Ho. B69: O'bry 4D **96**
Rydal Way B28: Hall G 6F **135**
Rydding La. B71: W Brom 5H **63**
Rydding Sq. B71: W Brom 5H **63**
Ryde Gro. B27: A Grn 4G **135**
Ryde Pk. Rd. B45: Redn 3A **158**
Ryders Grn. Rd. B70: W Brom 3E **79**
Ryders Hayes La.
  WS3: Pels 3E **21**
Ryder St. B4: Birm 2F 5 (6G **101**)
  B70: W Brom 2F **79**
  DY8: Word 1B **108**
Ryebank Cl. B30: B'vlle 2G **145**
Ryeclose Cft. B37: Chel W 6F **107**
RYECROFT 5B **32**
Rye Cft. B27: A Grn 6A **120**
  B47: H'wd 4A **162**
  DY9: W'cte 2A **126**
Ryecroft Av. WV4: Penn 6F **43**
Ryecroft Cl. DY3: Sed 5G **59**
Ryecroft Pk. WS2: Wals 6C **32**
Ryecroft Pl. WS3: Wals 3D **32**
Ryecroft St. WS2: Wals 6C **32**
Ryefield WV8: Pend 5C **14**
Ryefield Cl. B91: Sol 2C **150**
Ryegrass Rd. B45: Redn 3A **92**
Rye Grass Wlk. B35: Cas V 4F **87**
Rye Gro. B11: Tys 1F **135**
Ryemarket DY8: Stourb 6E **109**

Ryhope Wlk. WV9: Pend 4E 15
    (not continuous)
Ryknild Cl. B74: Four O 3F 37
Ryknild Dr. B74: S'tly 4A 52
Ryland Cl. B63: Hale 3G 127
DY4: Tip 2B 78
Ryland Ho. B19: Birm 4F 101
    (off Gt. Hampton Row)
Ryland Rd. B11: S'hll 1D 134
B15: Edg 4E 117
B24: Erd 6F 85
Rylands Dr. WV4: Penn 1D 58
Ryland St. B16: Birm 2D 116
Ryle St. WS3: Blox 5B 20
Rymond Rd. B34: Hodg H 3C 104
Ryton Cl. B73: S Cold 6H 53
WV10: Wolv 4C 28
Ryton End La. B92: Bars 6C 154
Ryton Gro. B34: S End 2H 105

S

Sabell Rd. B67: Smeth 3D 98
Sabrina Rd. WV6: Tett 2E 41
Saddlers Cen. WS1: Wals 2C 48
Saddlers Cl. B63: Crad 6D 110
Saddlers Ct. WS2: Wals 4H 47
Saddlers Ct. Ind. Est. WS2: Wals . . .2G 31
Saddlers M. B91: Sol 6G 151
Saddleworth Rd. WS3: Blox 3G 19
Sadler Cres. B11: S'hll 1D 134
    (off Lea Rd.)
Sadler Rd. B75: S Cold 4D 54
WS8: Bwnhls 6C 10
Sadlers Mill WS8: Bwnhls 6C 10
Sadlers Wlk. B16: Edg 2C 116
Saffron Gdns. WV4: Penn 1E 59
Saffron Ho. B38: K Nor 1A 160
Sage Cft. B31: N'fld 2D 144
St Agatha's Rd. B8: W End 4H 103
St Agnes Cl. B13: Mose 3B 134
St Agnes Rd. B13: Mose 3B 134
St Aidans Wlk. B10: Small H 3C 118
St Albans Cl. B67: Smeth 3D 98
WV11: Wed 1A 30
St Albans Ho. B32: Harb 6D 114
St Albans Rd. B13: Mose 2A 134
B67: Smeth 3C 98
St Alphege Cl. B91: Sol 4G 151
St Ambrose Cl. B65: B'hth 3B 112
St Andrew's Av. WS3: Pels 2E 21
St Andrews Cl. B32: Bart G 2E 131
DY3: Lwr G 4E 75
DY8: Stourb 3D 124
WV6: Wolv 5E 27
St Andrews Dr. B69: Tiv 2B 96
WV6: Pert 4D 24
St Andrew's Ho. WV6: Wolv 5F 27
St Andrews Ind. Est. B9: Bord G 1C 118
St Andrews Rd. B9: Birm 1B 118
B75: S Cold 4A 54
St Andrews Stadium 2C 118
St Andrews St. B9: Birm 1B 118
DY2: Neth 4E 95
St Annes Cl. B20: Hand 3B 82
WS7: Chase 1A 10
St Annes Ct. B13: Mose 1G 133
B44: K'sdng 6A 68
B64: Crad H 2E 111
WV13: W'hall 2B 46
St Annes Gro. B93: Know 3C 166
St Annes Ind. Est. WV13: W'hall 6B 30
St Annes Rd. DY2: Crad H 2E 111
WV10: Oxl 5G 15
WV13: W'hall 6B 30
St Anne's Way B44: K'sdng 1A 84
St Ann's Ter. WV13: W'hall 6B 30
St Anthony's Dr. WS3: Pels 2F 21
St Athan Cft. B35: Cas V 4F 87
St Audries Ct. B91: Sol 5D 150
St Augustine's Rd. B16: Edg 2H 115
St Augustus Cl. B70: W Brom 5D 80
St Austell Rd. WS5: Wals 4A 50

St Bartholomew's Ter.
WS10: W'bry 2F 63
St Benedict's Cl. B70: W Brom 5D 80
St Benedicts Rd. B10: Small H 4F 119
WV5: Wom 1G 73
St Bernards Rd. B72: W Grn 3A 70
B92: Olton 2B 150
St Blaise Av. B46: Wat O 5D 88
St Blaise Rd. B75: R'ley 6B 38
St Brades Cl. B69: Tiv 2C 96
St Brides Cl. DY3: Sed 5G 59
WV5: Wom 1F 73
Saintbury Dr. B91: Sol 2G 165
St Caroline Cl. B70: W Brom 5D 80
St Catharines Cl. WS1: Wals 4E 49
St Catherines Cl. B15: Birm 2F 117
B75: S Cold 4D 54
DY2: Dud 6A 78
St Catherine's Ct. B91: Sol 3F 151
St Catherine's Cres. WV4: Penn 1D 58
St Chads WV14: Cose 6D 60
St Chads Cir. Queensway
    B4: Birm 2D 4 (6F 101)
St Chad's Cl. DY3: Lwr G 4F 75
St Chads Ind. Est. B19: Birm 4F 101
St Chad's Queensway
    B4: Birm 1E 5 (5G 101)
St Chads RC Cathedral 1D 4 (5G 101)
St Chads Rd. B45: Rub 2F 157
B75: S Cold 6C 54
WV10: Bush 1B 28
WV14: Bils 4H 45
St Christopher Dr. WS10: W'bry 2C 64
St Christopher Cl. B70: W Brom 5D 80
St Christophers B20: Hand 3B 82
St Clements Av. WS3: Blox 2B 32
St Clements Cl. B63: Hale 2A 128
St Clements La. B71: W Brom 3B 80
St Clements Rd. B7: Nech 3C 102
St Columbas Dr. B45: Redn 2A 158
St Cuthbert's Cl. B70: W Brom 5D 80
St Cuthberts Pl. B35: Cas V 4F 87
St David Dr. WS10: W'bry 2C 64
St David's Cl. B70: W Brom 5D 80
WS3: Pels 2F 21
St Davids Ct. B69: O'bry 2G 97
St Davids Dr. B32: Quin 6H 113
St Davids Gro. B20: Hand 3B 82
St Davids Pl. WS3: Blox 5B 20
St Denis Rd. B29: W Cas 1E 145
St Dennis Ho. B16: Edg 2H 115
    (off Melville Rd.)
St Dominic's Rd. B24: Erd 6E 85
    (not continuous)
St Edburgh's Rd. B25: Yard 2C 120
St Edmund's Cl. B70: W Brom 5D 80
WV6: Wolv 6D 26
St Edwards Rd. B29: S Oak 3B 132
St Eleanors Cl. B70: W Brom 5D 80
St Francis Av. B91: Sol 1C 150
St Francis' Cl. WS3: Pels 2F 21
St Francis Dr. B30: K Nor 4F 147
St Francis Factory Est.
    B70: W Brom 5B 80
St George Dr. B66: Smeth 2E 99
St Georges Av. B23: Erd 2G 85
St Georges Cl. B15: Edg 4C 116
B75: S Cold 5D 54
WS10: Darl 4D 46
St Georges Ct. B30: B'ville 6A 132
B74: Four O 4E 37
WS1: Wals 1D 48
    (off Persehouse St.)
WS10: Darl 4D 46
    (off St George's St.)
St George's Pde.
WV2: Wolv 4C 170 (2H 43)
St Georges Pd. B70: W Brom 4A 80
WS1: Wals 1D 48
St Georges Rd. B90: Shir 1B 164
DY2: Dud 3F 95
DY8: Stourb 3B 124
St George's St. B19: Birm 5F 101
WS10: Darl 4D 46

St Gerards Ct. B91: Sol 5C 150
St Gerards Rd. B91: Sol 5C 150
St Giles Av. B65: Row R 5B 96
St Giles Cl. B65: Row R 5C 96
St Giles Ct. B65: Row R 6D 96
WV13: W'hall 2B 46
St Giles Cres. WV1: Wolv 1C 44
St Giles Rd. B33: Kitts G 1H 121
WV1: Wolv 1C 44
WV13: W'hall 2B 46
St Giles Row DY8: Stourb 5E 109
    (off Lwr. High St.)
St Giles St. DY2: Neth 4E 95
St Helens Av. DY4: Tip 2C 78
St Helens Pas. B1: Birm . . .1A 4 (6E 101)
St Heliers Rd. B31: N'fld 3C 144
St Ives Rd. WS5: Wals 4H 49
St James Av. B65: Row R 5B 96
St James Cl. B70: W Brom 5D 80
WS3: Pels 2F 21
St James Gdns. B68: O'bry 6G 97
WS8: Bwnhls 6B 10
St James Pl. B7: Birm 6A 102
B15: Edg 3D 116
B90: Shir 5H 149
WS11: Nort C 1C 8
St James Rd. B15: Edg 3D 116
B21: Hand 1H 99
B69: O'bry 1D 96
B75: Four O 1A 54
St James's Rd. DY1: Dud 5D 76
St James's Ter. DY1: Dud 5C 76
St James St. DY3: Lwr G 4H 75
WS10: W'bry 3E 63
WV1: Wolv 2A 44
St James Wlk. WS8: Bwnhls 6B 10
    (off Short St.)
St John Bosco Cl.
    B71: W Brom 6H 63
St John Cl. B75: R'ley 5B 38
St John's Arc. WV1: Wolv 3B 170 (1G 43)
St Johns Av. B65: Row R 5B 96
St John's Cl. B70: W Brom 5D 80
B93: Know 3D 166
DY3: Swind 5D 72
WS9: Wals W 4B 22
St Johns Ct. B17: Harb 5F 115
B31: N'fld 6F 145
DY5: Brie H 1H 109
    (off Hill St.)
WS3: Blox 6H 19
WS10: W'bry 3F 63
St Johns Gro. B37: K'hrst 6B 106
St John's Ho. B70: W Brom 5A 80
St Johns Retail Pk.
    WV2: Wolv 6B 170 (2G 43)
St Johns Rd. B11: S'hll 6C 118
B17: Harb 5H 115
B63: Hale 1G 127
B68: O'bry 4A 98
DY2: Dud 1G 95
DY4: Tip .6H 61
DY8: Stourb 5E 109
WS2: Wals 3H 47
WS3: Pels 2F 21
WS8: Bwnhls 2C 22
WS10: Darl 6C 46
WV11: Ess 4A 18
St John's Sq. WV2: Wolv 5B 170 (2G 43)
St John's St. DY2: Neth 4E 95
St Johns Wlk. B5: Birm 6E 5 (2G 117)
B42: P Barr 3F 83
St John's Way B93: Know 3E 167
St Johns Wood B45: Redn 4H 157
St Joseph's Av. B31: N'fld 3F 145
St Joseph's Cl. WS3: Pels 3E 21
St Joseph's Ct. WV4: Penn 5A 42
St Joseph's Rd. B8: W End 4A 104
St Joseph St. DY2: Dud 6F 77
St Judes Cl. B14: K Hth 5H 147
B75: S Cold 5D 54
St Jude's Cl. WV6: Wolv 6D 26
St Judes Pas. B5: Birm 6D 4 (2F 117)

St Jude's Rd. WV6: Wolv 6D **26**
St Jude's Rd. W. WV6: Wolv 6D **26**
St Katherines Rd. B68: O'bry 1H **113**
St Kenelms Av. B63: Hale 4G **127**
St Kenelm's Cl. B70: W Brom 5D **80**
St Kenelm's Rd. B62: Roms 3A **142**
St Kilda's Rd. B8: Salt 5E **103**
St Laurence M. B31: N'fld 4E **145**
St Laurence Cl. B31: N'fld 2F **145**
St Lawrence Cl. B93: Know 4D **166**
St Lawrence Ho. B16: Edg 2H **115**
(off Melville Rd.)
St Lawrence Way WS10: Darl 4D **46**
St Leonard's Cl. B37: Mars G 4C **122**
St Loye's Cl. B62: B'hth 3D **112**
St Lukes Cl. B65: Row R 5B **96**
St Luke's Rd. B5: Birm 3F **117**
(not continuous)
WS10: W'bry 2G **63**
St Lukes St. B64: Crad H 2F **111**
St Luke's Ter. DY1: Dud 1C **94**
St Margaret's B74: Four O 6C **36**
St Margarets Av. B8: W End 3H **103**
St Margaret's Ct. B92: Olton 4C **136**
St Margarets Dr. B63: Hale 3H **127**
St Margarets Rd. B8: W End 3G **103**
B43: Gt Barr 3B **66**
B92: Olton 4C **136**
WS3: Pels 3E **21**
St Marks Cl. WS6: Gt Wyr 1F **7**
St Marks Cres. B1: Birm 6C **100**
St Mark's Factory Cen. DY9: Lye 6H **109**
St Marks Rd. B67: Smeth 6B **98**
DY2: Dud 5H **77**
DY4: Tip 5H **61**
DY9: Lye 6H **109**
WS3: Pels 3E **21**
WS8: Bwnhls 2C **22**
WV3: Wolv 2E **43**
(not continuous)
St Marks St. B1: Birm 6D **100**
WV3: Wolv 4A **170** (2F **43**)
St Martin's Church 5F **5** (1G **117**)
St Martins Cl. B70: W Brom 5D **80**
WV2: E'shll 5A **44**
St Martins Dr. DY4: Tip 2A **78**
St Martin's Ga. B2: Birm 4E **5**
St Martins Ind. Est. B69: O'bry 3H **97**
St Martin's Queensway
B2: Birm 5E **5** (1G **117**)
St Martin's Rd. B75: S Cold 6D **54**
St Martin's St. B15: Birm 2D **116**
St Martin's Ter. WV14: Bils 1G **61**
St Marys Cl. B24: Erd 3B **86**
B27: A Grn 2H **135**
DY3: Sed 5B **60**
St Marys Cl. DY5: Brie H 1H **109**
WV13: W'hall 1A **46**
(off Wolverhampton St.)
St Mary's Hall WV2: Wolv 5C **170**
St Mary's La. DY8: Stourb 2F **125**
St Mary's Mobile Home Pk.
B47: Wyt 6G **161**
St Mary's Rd. B17: Harb 6G **115**
B67: Smeth 2D **114**
WS10: W'bry 2F **63**
St Marys Row B4: Birm 2E **5** (6G **101**)
B13: Mose 2H **133**
St Mary's St. WV1: Wolv 2C **170** (1H **43**)
St Mary's Vw. B23: Erd 5D **68**
St Marys Way WS9: A'rdge 4C **34**
St Matthews Cl. WS1: Wals 2D **48**
WS3: Pels 2F **21**
St Matthews Rd. B66: Smeth 4G **99**
B68: O'bry 1G **113**
(not continuous)
St Matthews St. WV1: Wolv 2B **44**
St Mawes Rd. WV6: Pert 6F **25**
St Mawgan Cl. B35: Cas V 3G **87**
St Michaels Cl. WS3: Pels 5E **21**
St Michaels Ct. B70: W Brom 4A **80**
WV6: Tett 4C **26**
St Michaels Gdns. B71: O'bry 5F **97**
St Michael's Gro. DY2: Dud 6A **78**

St Michael's Hill B18: Hock 2C **100**
St Michael's M. B69: Tiv 5A **78**
St Michael's Rd. B18: Hock 2C **100**
B73: Bold 5F **69**
DY3: Lwr G 2D **74**
St Michael St. B70: W Brom 4A **80**
WS1: Wals 3C **48**
St Michaels Way DY4: Tip 4A **78**
St Nicholas Cl. WS3: Pels 3E **21**
St Nicholas Gdns. B38: K Nor 5B **146**
St Nicholas Wlk. B76: Curd 1D **88**
St Oswald's Ct. B10: Small H 3E **119**
St Oswald's Rd. B10: Small H 3E **119**
St Patricks Cl. B14: K Hth 2G **147**
St Paul's Av. B12: Bal H 6A **118**
St Paul's Cl. WS1: Wals 1C **48**
St Pauls Ct. B46: Wat O 4D **88**
B65: B'hth 2D **112**
St Paul's Cres. B46: Col 2H **107**
B70: W Brom 6E **63**
WS3: Pels 3F **21**
St Pauls Dr. B62: B'hth 2D **112**
DY4: Tip 3B **78**
St Paul's Rd. B12: Bal H 5H **117**
B66: Smeth 2B **98**
DY2: Neth 4F **95**
WS10: W'bry 6H **47**
St Paul's Sq. B3: Birm 2B **4** (6E **101**)
St Paul's St. WS1: Wals 1C **48**
St Pauls Ter. B3: Birm 1B **4** (5E **101**)
St Peter Cft. WS10: W'bry 2C **64**
St Peters Cl. B28: Hall G 1D **148**
B46: Wat O 5D **88**
B72: W Grn 2H **69**
DY4: Tip 3D **78**
WS9: Ston 3G **23**
WV1: Wolv 2B **170** (1G **43**)
St Peters Ct. WS3: Blox 6H **19**
St Peter's Dr. WS3: Pels 3E **21**
St Peters La. B92: Bick 4F **139**
St Peters Rd. B17: Harb 6F **115**
B20: Hand 6E **83**
DY2: Dud, Neth 3F **95**
DY9: Pedm 4G **125**
St Peter's Sq. WV1: Wolv 2B **170** (1G **43**)
St Peters Ter. WS2: Wals 5C **32**
St Philips Av. WV3: Wolv 4D **42**
St Philips Cathedral 3D **4** (6F **101**)
St Philips Gro. WV3: Wolv 4D **42**
St Philips Pl. B3: Birm 3E **5** (6G **101**)
St Phillips Ct. B46: Col 2H **107**
St Quentin St. WS2: Wals 3A **48**
St Saviours Cl. WV2: E'shll 5B **44**
St Saviour's Rd. B8: Salt 5D **102**
St Silas' Sq. B19: Loz 2D **100**
St Simons Cl. B75: S Cold 5D **54**
St Stephens Av. WV13: W'hall 1H **45**
St Stephen's Cen. B21: Hand 3A **100**
St Stephen's Ct. WV13: W'hall 2H **45**
St Stephens Gdns.
WV13: W'hall 1A **46**
St Stephens Rd. B29: S Oak 5D **132**
B71: W Brom 6F **81**
St Stephen's St. B6: Aston 3G **101**
St Thomas Cl. B75: S Cold 6D **54**
WS3: Wals 3C **32**
WS9: A'rdge 6D **22**
St Thomas' Rd. B23: Erd 4D **84**
St Thomas St. DY2: Neth 4E **95**
DY8: Stourb 6D **108**
St Valentines Cl. B70: W Brom 5D **80**
St Vincent Cres. B70: W Brom 1F **79**
St Vincent St. B16: Birm 1D **116**
St Vincent St. W. B16: Birm 1C **116**
Saladin Av. B69: O'bry 4E **97**
Salcombe Av. B26: Sheld 6G **121**
Salcombe Dr. DY5: Brie H 4G **109**
Salcombe Gro. WV14: Cose 4F **61**
Salcombe Rd. B66: Smeth 4F **99**
Saldavian Ct. WS2: Wals 5H **47**
Salem St. DY4: Tip 2D **78**
Salford Circ. B6: Aston 6D **84**
Salford St. B6: Aston 1C **102**
Salford Trad. Est. B6: Aston 1C **102**

Salisbury Cl. B13: Mose 1G **133**
DY1: Dud 4B **76**
Salisbury Ct. B91: Sol 3G **151**
Salisbury Dr. B46: Wat O 4E **89**
Salisbury Gro. B72: W Grn 6A **70**
Salisbury Pl. Ind. Est. WV3: Wolv 2F **43**
(off Rosebery St.)
Salisbury Rd. B8: Salt 4E **103**
B13: Mose 1G **133**
B19: Loz 1F **101**
B66: Smeth 5F **99**
B70: W Brom 6C **80**
Salisbury St. WS10: Darl 4E **47**
WV3: Wolv 2F **43**
Salisbury Twr. B18: Hock 6C **100**
Sallow Gro. WS8: Bwnhls 4B **10**
Sally Ward Dr. WS9: Wals W 3C **22**
Salop Cl. B71: W Brom 1H **79**
Salop Dr. B68: O'bry 1A **114**
B68: O'bry 6A **98**
Salop Rd. B12: Birm 3H **117**
B69: O'bry 6E **79**
DY1: Dud 5D **76**
WV3: Wolv 4A **170** (2G **43**)
WV14: Bils 1G **61**
Salstar Cl. B6: Aston 3G **101**
Saltash Gro. B25: Yard 2A **120**
Saltbrook Rd. B63: Crad 4C **110**
Saltbrook Trad. Est. B63: Crad 4C **110**
Salter Rd. DY4: Tip 6H **61**
Salter's La. B71: W Brom 3C **80**
Salter's Rd. WS9: Wals W 3C **22**
SALTER STREET 6A **164**
Salter St. B94: Earls, H'ley H 6A **164**
Salter Va. B70: W Brom 6C **80**
SALTLEY 4D **102**
Saltley Bus. Pk. B8: Salt 3D **102**
Saltley Cotts. B24: Erd 6F **85**
Saltley Ga. B8: Salt 4D **102**
Saltley Ind. Cen. B8: Salt 5C **102**
Saltley Leisure Cen. 6G **103**
Saltley Rd. B7: Birm 4B **102**
Saltley Trad. Est. B8: Salt 3D **102**
Saltley Viaduct B7: Birm 4C **102**
B8: Salt 4C **102**
Saltney Cl. B24: Erd 2B **86**
Saltwells La. DY2: Neth 1B **110**
DY5: Brie H, Quar B 1B **110**
Saltwells Nature Reserve 6C **94**
Saltwells Rd. DY2: Neth 1D **110**
Salwarpe Gro. B29: W Cas 3D **130**
Sambourn Cl. B91: Sol 1A **152**
Sambourne Dr. B34: S End 2H **105**
Sambrook Rd. WV10: Wolv 3C **28**
Sampson Cl. B21: Hand 6G **81**
B69: Tiv 2C **96**
Sampson Rd. B11: S'brk 4B **118**
Sampson Rd. Nth. B11: S'brk 3B **118**
Sampson St. WS10: W'bry 2H **63**
Sams La. B70: W Brom 5A **80**
Samuels Rd. B32: Quin 6G **113**
Samuel St. WS3: Blox 6H **19**
Sanda Cft. B36: Cas B 3D **106**
Sandalls Cl. B31: Longb 6B **144**
Sandal Ri. B91: Sol 4A **152**
Sandals Ri. B62: Hale 2D **128**
Sandalwood Cl. WV12: W'hall 1B **30**
Sandbank WS3: Blox 6G **19**
Sandbarn Cl. B90: M'path 3D **164**
Sandbeds Rd. WV12: W'hall 5C **30**
Sandbourne Rd. B8: W End 5G **103**
Sanderling Ri. DY6: K'wfrd 3E **93**
Sanders Cl. DY2: Dud 2G **95**
Sanders St. DY4: Tip 2B **78**
Sandfield Bri. DY5: P'ntt 6F **75**
Sandfield Cl. B90: Shir 1G **163**
Sandfield Farm Home Pk.
WS8: Bwnhls 4D **10**
Sandfield Gro. DY3: Gorn 5F **75**
Sandfield Rd. B71: W Brom 4C **64**
DY8: Word 1D **108**
Sandfields Av. B10: Small H 3B **118**

Sandfields Rd. B68: O'bry 1A 114
Sandford Av. B65: Row R 6C 96
Sandford Ri. WV6: Tett 3C 26
Sandford Rd. B13: Mose 1A 134
   DY1: Dud 6A 76
Sandgate Rd. B28: Hall G 3F 149
   DY4: Tip .5A 62
Sandham Grange B34: Hodg H 2E 105
Sandhill Farm Cl. B19: Loz 2F 101
Sandhills Cres. B91: Sol 1F 165
Sandhill St. WS3: Blox 6G 19
Sandhurst Av. B36: Hodg H 3B 104
   DY9: W'cte 3H 125
Sandhurst Ct. *B66: Smeth* 1E 115
   (off Bearwood Rd.)
Sandhurst Dr. WV4: Penn 1E 59
Sandhurst Gro. DY8: Word 6C 92
Sandhurst Ho. B38: K Nor 6C 146
Sandhurst Rd. B13: Mose 3G 133
   B74: Four O 4F 37
   DY6: K'wfrd 5E 93
Sandland Cl. WV14: Bils 5H 45
Sandland Rd. WV12: W'hall 1D 30
Sandmartin Cl. DY2: Neth 1E 111
Sandmeadow Pl. DY6: K'wfrd 4A 92
Sandmere Gro. B14: Yard W 4D 148
Sandmere Ri. WV10: Bush 6A 16
Sandmere Rd. B14: Yard W 4D 148
Sandon Gro. B24: Erd 3H 85
Sandon Rd. B17: Edg 1E 115
   B66: Edg, Smeth 1E 115
   B66: Smeth 1E 115
   DY9: W'cte 1B 126
   WV10: F'hses 5F 15
Sandown Av. WS6: C Hay 2E 7
Sandown Ct. B29: W Cas 6G 131
Sandown Dr. WV6: Pert 5F 25
Sandown Rd. B36: Hodg H 1B 104
Sandown Twr. B31: N'fld 6E 145
Sandpiper Cl. DY9: W'cte 6B 110
Sandpiper Gdns. B38: K Nor 2D 160
Sandpiper Way B23: Erd 1C 84
Sandpit Cl. WS10: W'bry 3C 64
Sand Pits B1: Birm 3A 4 (6D 100)
Sandpits, The B30: B'vlle 5A 132
Sandpits Cl. B76: Curd 1D 88
Sandpits Ind. Est. B1: Birm 6D 100
Sandra Cl. WS9: A'rdge 4D 34
Sandringham Av. WV12: W'hall 2B 30
Sandringham Ct. B43: Gt Barr 4B 66
Sandringham Dr. B65: Row R 5C 96
   WS9: A'rdge 6D 22
Sandringham Pl. DY8: Word 2B 108
Sandringham Rd. B42: P Barr 1D 82
   B62: Hale 4B 112
   DY8: Word 2A 108
   WV4: Penn 1E 59
   WV5: Wom 1F 73
Sandringham Way DY5: Brie H 3G 109
Sandstone Av. B45: Rub 1G 157
Sandstone Cl. DY3: Lwr G 3H 75
Sand St. B70: W Brom 3E 79
Sandway Gdns. B8: Salt 3D 102
Sandway Gro. B13: Mose 6C 134
SANDWELL 1E 99
Sandwell Av. WS10: Darl 6B 46
Sandwell Bus. & Technology Cen.
   B68: O'bry 6G 97
   (off Wolverhampton Rd.)
Sandwell Bus. Development Cen.
   B66: Smeth 2A 98
Sandwell Bus. Pk. B66: Smeth 1A 98
Sandwell Cen. B70: W Brom 4B 80
Sandwell Ct. B21: Hand 1A 98
Sandwell & Dudley Station (Rail) 6G 79
Sandwell Ind. Est. B66: Smeth 1A 98
Sandwell Pk. Farm 4D 80
Sandwell Pl. B66: Smeth 1E 99
   WV12: W'hall 2D 30
Sandwell Rd. B21: Hand 6H 81
   B70: W Brom 3A 80
   WV10: Oxl 6F 15
Sandwell Rd. Nth. B71: W Brom 3B 80
Sandwell Rd. Pas. B70: W Brom 3A 80

Sandwell St. WS1: Wals 3D 48
Sandwell Valley Country Pk. 3D 80
Sandwell Wlk. WS1: Wals 3D 48
Sandwood Dr. B44: Gt Barr 5H 67
Sandy Acre Way DY8: Stourb 6F 109
Sandy Cres. WV11: Wed 1A 30
Sandy Cft. B13: Mose 6C 134
Sandycroft B72: W Grn 2A 70
Sandyfields Rd. DY3: Lwr G, Sed 2D 74
Sandy Gro. WS8: Bwnhls 4B 10
Sandy Hill Ri. B90: Shir 3G 149
Sandy Hill Rd. B90: Shir 3G 149
Sandy Hollow WV6: Tett 1A 42
Sandy La. B6: Aston 2B 102
   B42: Gt Barr 5E 67
   B61: L Ash, Wild 4A 156
   DY8: Stourb 1B 124
   WS10: W'bry 2D 64
   WV6: Tett 3C 26
   WV8: Cod 3F 13
   WV10: Bush 4A 16
Sandy Mt. WV5: Wom 6H 57
Sandymount Rd. WS1: Wals 3D 48
Sandy Rd. DY8: Stourb 4B 124
Sandys Gro. DY4: Tip 2G 77
Sandy Way B15: Birm 6A 4 (2D 116)
Sangwin Rd. WV14: Cose 6E 61
Sansome Ri. B90: Shir 5F 149
Sansome Rd. B90: Shir 5F 149
Sanstone Cl. WS3: Blox 4A 20
Sanstone Rd. WS3: Blox 4H 19
Santolina Dr. WS5: Wals 2E 65
Sant Rd. B31: Longb 2F 159
Sapcote Bus. Pk. B10: Small H 5E 119
Sapcote Trad. Cen. B64: Old H 6H 95
Saplings, The B76: Walm 5C 53
Sapphire Ct. B3: Birm 1B 4 (5E 101)
   B92: Olton 4D 136
Sapphire Hgts. B1: Birm 6D 100
Sapphire Ho. E. B91: Sol 3E 151
Sapphire Ho. W. B91: Sol 3E 151
Sapphire Twr. *B6: Aston* 3H 101
   (off Park La.)
Saracen Dr. B75: S Cold 5D 54
   CV7: Bal C 3E 169
Sara Cl. B74: Four O 6G 37
Sarah Cl. WV14: Bils 4G 61
Sarah Ct. B73: New O 4D 68
Sarah Gdns. WS5: Wals 1D 64
Sarah St. B9: Birm 1B 118
Saredon Cl. WS3: Pels 6E 21
Saredon Rd. WS6: C Hay 1B 6
   WV10: Share 1A 6
   (not continuous)
Sarehole Mill Gdns. B13: Mose 1H 133
Sarehole Mill Mus. 5D 134
Sarehole Rd. B28: Hall G 6D 134
Sargent Cl. B43: Gt Barr 1F 67
Sargent Ho. B16: Birm 1D 116
Sargent's Hill WS5: Wals 5G 49
Sargent Turner Trad. Est. DY9: Lye . .5B 110
Sark Dr. B36: Cas B 3D 106
Satellite Ind. Pk. WV13: W'hall 5F 29
Saturday Bri. B1: Birm 6B 4
Saunton Rd. WS3: Blox 4G 19
Saunton Way B29: S Oak 4G 131
Saveker Dr. B76: Walm 1C 70
Savernake Cl. B45: Fran 5G 143
Saville Cl. B45: Redn 2H 157
Savoy Cl. B32: Harb 6D 114
Saw Mill Cl. WS4: Wals 6C 32
Saxelby Cl. B31: K Hth 5G 145
Saxelby Ho. B14: K Hth 5G 147
   (not continuous)
Saxon Cl. WS6: Gt Wyr 3G 7
Saxon Ct. WV6: Tett 4A 26
Saxondale Av. B26: Sheld 5D 120
Saxon Dr. B65: Row R 5C 96
Saxonfields WV6: Tett 4A 26
Saxons Way B14: K Hth 5A 148
Saxon Way B37: K'hrst 6B 106
Saxon Wood Cl. B31: N'fld 3E 145
Saxon Wood Rd. B90: Ches G 4B 164
Saxton Dr. B74: Four O 3F 37

Scafell Dr. B23: Erd 2D 84
   WV10: Bush 4H 45
Scafell Rd. DY8: Amb 5F 109
Scampton Cl. WV6: Pert 4E 25
Scarborough Cl. WS2: Wals 3H 47
Scarborough Rd. WS2: Wals 3H 47
Scarecrow La. B75: R'ley 5C 38
Scarsdale Rd. B42: Gt Barr 5F 67
Schofield Av. B71: W Brom 5H 63
Schofield Rd. B37: K'hrst 4C 106
Scholars Cl. B21: Hand 2C 100
Scholars Ga. B33: Kitts G 1F 121
Scholars Wlk. WS4: Rus 2F 33
Scholefield Twr. *B19: Birm* 4F 101
   (off Uxbridge St.)
Schoolacre Ri. B74: S'tly 2G 51
Schoolacre Rd. B34: S End 3F 105
School Av. WS3: Blox 1A 32
   WS8: Bwnhls 5B 10
School Cl. B31: N'fld 5C 144
   B35: Cas V 4F 87
   B37: K'hrst 3C 106
   B69: Tiv .2C 96
   WV3: Wolv 4H 41
   WV5: Try 5C 56
   WV8: Cod 3G 13
School Dr. B34: S End 4A 106
   B47: Wyt 6A 162
   DY8: Amb 3D 108
   WV14: Bils 3A 62
School Dr., The DY2: Dud 2F 95
Schoolgate Cl. B8: W End 3G 103
   WS4: S'fld 6H 21
School Grn. WV14: Bils 3E 45
Schoolhouse Cl. B38: K Nor 5D 146
School La. B33: Yard 2D 120
   B34: S End 3F 105
   B63: Hale 3H 127
   B91: Sol 2H 151
   DY5: Brie H 5F 93
   DY9: Hag 6H 125
   WS3: Lit Wyr 3C 8
   WS3: Pels 3D 20
   WS11: Lit Wyr 3C 8
   WV3: Wolv 4A 170 (2G 43)
   WV10: Bush 5H 15
School Pas. DY5: Quar B 2C 110
School Rd. B13: Mose 4H 133
   B14: Yard W 3B 148
   B28: Hall G 5F 135
   B45: Rub 3E 157
   B90: Shir 5H 149
   DY3: Himl 4H 73
   DY5: Quar B 1C 110
   WS10: W'bry 3B 64
   WV5: Try 5C 56
   WV5: Wom 6G 56
   WV6: Tett 3C 26
   WV11: Wed 3D 28
School St. B64: Crad H 2F 111
   DY1: Dud 6D 76
   (not continuous)
   DY3: Sed 5A 60
   DY5: P'ntt 2H 93
   DY8: Stourb 5D 108
   WS4: S'fld 6H 21
   WS10: Darl 5C 46
   (Alma St.)
   WS10: Darl 6E 47
   (Nowell St., not continuous)
   WV3: Wolv 4A 170 (2G 43)
   WV13: W'hall 1H 45
   WV14: Cose 5E 61
School St. W. WV14: Cose 5E 61
School Ter. B29: S Oak 3B 132
School Wlk. WV14: Bils 3E 45
Scorers Cl. B90: Shir 1H 149
Scotchings, The B36: Hodg H 1C 104
Scotland La. B32: Bart G 5H 129
Scotland Pas. B70: W Brom 4B 80
SCOTLANDS 1C 28
Scotland St. B1: Birm 3A 4 (6E 101)
Scott Arms Shop. Cen.
   B42: Gt Barr 4B 66

Scott Av. WS10: W'bry 3H 63
WV4: Penn 1C 58
Scott Cl. B71: W Brom 2B 80
Scott Gro. B92: Olton 2C 136
Scott Ho. B43: Gt Barr 6B 66
Scott Rd. B43: Gt Barr 3B 66
B92: Olton 2C 136
WS5: Wals 5H 49
SCOTT'S GREEN 1C 94
Scotts Grn. Cl. DY1: Dud 1B 94
Scotts Grn. Island DY1: Dud 2B 94
Scott's Rd. DY8: Stourb 5D 108
Scott St. DY4: Tip 2C 78
Scotwell Cl. B65: Row R 6B 96
Scout Cl. B33: Kitts G 1G 121
Scribbans Cl. B66: Smeth 5F 99
Scriber's La. B28: Hall G 3D 148
Scribers Mdw. B28: Hall G 3E 149
Scrimshaw Ho. WS2: Wals 4A 48
(off Pleck Rd.)
Seacroft Av. B25: Yard 2C 120
Seafield Cl. DY6: K'wfrd 5C 92
Seaforth Gro. WV12: W'hall 6B 18
Seagar St. B71: W Brom 3C 80
Seagers La. DY5: Brie H 1H 109
Seagull Bay Dr. WV14: Cose 4F 61
Seal Cl. B76: Walm 1C 70
Seals Grn. B38: K Nor 2H 159
Seamless Dr. WV11: Wed 5F 29
Sear Hills Cl. CV7: Bal C 3H 169
Sear Retail Pk. B90: Shir 6B 150
Seaton Cl. WV11: Wed 4H 29
Seaton Gro. B13: Mose 4F 133
Seaton Pl. DY8: Word 1A 108
Seaton Rd. B66: Smeth 4F 99
Second Av. B6: Witt 4H 83
B9: Bord G 2E 119
B29: S Oak 2D 132
DY6: P'ntt 2D 92
WS8: Bwnhls 4C 10
WV10: Bush 2A 28
Second Exhibition Av.
B40: Nat E C 1F 139
Security Ho. WV1: Wolv 4B 170
Sedge Av. B38: K Nor 4B 146
Sedgeberrow Covert B38: K Nor 1A 160
Sedgeberrow Rd. B63: Hale 3A 128
Sedgebourne Way B31: Longb 6A 144
Sedgefield Cl. DY1: Dud 4A 76
Sedgefield Gro. WV6: Pert 5F 25
Sedgeford Cl. DY5: Brie H 3H 109
Sedgehill Av. B17: Harb 1F 131
Sedgemere Gro. CV7: Bal C 6H 169
WS4: S'fld 1G 33
Sedgemere Rd. B26: Yard 2D 120
Sedgfield Way WS11: Nort C 1E 9
SEDGLEY .5G 59
Sedgley Gro. B20: Hand 3A 82
Sedgley Hall Av. DY3: Sed 5G 59
Sedgley Hall Est. DY3: Sed 4G 59
Sedgley Rd. DY1: Dud 1D 76
WV4: Penn 2C 58
Sedgley Rd. E. DY4: Tip 3A 78
Sedgley Rd. W. DY4: Tip 1F 77
Sedgley St. WV2: Wolv 4G 43
Seedhouse Ct. B64: Old H 3A 112
Seeds La. WS8: Bwnhls 5B 10
Seeleys Rd. B11: Tys 6D 118
Sefton Dr. B65: Row R 3H 95
Sefton Gro. DY4: Tip 3C 62
Sefton Rd. B16: Edg 1B 116
Segbourne Rd. B45: Rub 1E 157
Segundo Cl. WS5: Wals 1D 64
Segundo Rd. WS5: Wals 1D 64
SEISDON .2A 56
Seisdon Hollaway WV5: Seis 2A 56
Seisdon Rd. WV5: Seis, Try 3A 56
Selborne Cl. WS1: Wals 2E 49
Selborne Gro. B13: Mose 2C 148
Selborne Rd. B20: Hand 5C 82
DY2: Dud 2F 95
Selborne St. WS1: Wals 2E 49
Selbourne Cres. WV1: Wolv 2D 44
Selby Cl. B26: Yard 2D 120

Selby Gro. B13: Mose 2B 148
Selby Ho. B69: O'bry 3D 96
Selby Way WS3: Blox 5E 19
Selcombe Way B38: K Nor 2B 160
Selco Way B76: Min 2E 87
Selcroft Av. B32: Harb 6D 114
Selecta Av. B44: Gt Barr 3F 67
Selkirk Cl. B71: W Brom 1A 80
Selly Av. B29: S Oak 3C 132
Selly Cl. B29: S Oak 3D 132
Selly Hall Cft. B30: B'vlle 1C 146
Selly Hill Rd. B29: S Oak 3B 132
SELLY OAK 3H 131
Selly Oak Ind. Est.
B29: S Oak 4A 132
Selly Oak Rd. B30: B'vlle, K Nor 6A 132
Selly Oak Station (Rail) 3A 132
SELLY PARK 3D 132
Selly Pk. Rd. B29: S Oak 2C 132
Selly Wharf B29: S Oak 3A 132
Selly Wick Dr. B29: S Oak 3D 132
Selly Wick Rd. B29: S Oak 3C 132
Sellywood Rd. B30: B'vlle 6H 131
Selma Gro. B14: Yard W 2D 148
Selman's Hill WS3: Blox 4A 20
Selman's Pde. WS3: Blox 5A 20
Selsdon Cl. B47: Wyt 4C 162
Selsdon Rd. WS3: Blox 4F 19
Selsey Av. B17: Edg 6F 99
Selsey Rd. B17: Edg 6F 99
Selston Rd. B6: Aston 2G 101
Selvey Av. B43: Gt Barr 2D 66
Selworthy Rd. B36: Cas B 2B 106
Selwyn Cl. WV2: Wolv 4G 43
Selwyn Ho. B37: Chel W 6F 107
Selwyn Rd. B16: Edg 6H 99
WV14: Bils 5H 45
Selwyn Wlk. B74: Lit As 5C 36
Senior Cl. WV11: Ess 4A 18
Senneley's Pk. Rd. B31: N'fld 5C 130
Sennen Cl. WV13: W'hall 2H 45
Sensall Rd. DY9: W'cte 2B 126
Sentry Way B75: S Cold 5D 54
Serpentine Rd. B6: Aston 6A 84
B17: Harb 5G 115
B29: S Oak 2C 132
Servite Ct. B14: K Hth 5A 148
Servite Ho. B44: Gt Barr 3H 67
B92: Olton 6B 136
Seth Somers Track 3C 128
Settle Av. B34: Hodg H 3E 105
Settle Cft. B37: F'bri 2B 122
Setton Dr. DY3: Sed 6A 60
Seven Acres Rd. B31: N'fld 6G 145
B62: Quin 6G 113
Sevendwellings Vw. DY5: Brie H 2G 109
Seven Star Rd. B91: Sol 2E 151
Seven Stars Rd. B69: O'bry 2G 97
Severn Cl. B36: Cas B 2B 106
DY4: Tip 2H 77
WV12: W'hall 2A 30
Severn Ct. B23: Erd 4B 84
B73: S Cold 6H 53
Severn Dr. DY5: P'ntt 2F 93
WV6: Pert 5E 25
Severne Gro. B27: A Grn 4A 136
Severne Rd. B27: A Grn 5A 136
Severn Gro. B11: S'brk 5C 118
B19: Loz 2E 101
(not continuous)
Severn Ri. B65: Row R 1B 112
Severn Rd. B63: Crad 6D 110
DY8: Stourb 2D 124
WS3: Blox 6C 20
WS8: Bwnhls 3G 9
Severn St. B1: Birm 6C 4 (2F 117)
Severn St. Pl. B1: Birm 6C 4
Severn Twr. B7: Nech 4B 102
Severn Way B47: Wyt 6G 161
Sevington Cl. B91: Sol 1G 165
Seymour Cl. B29: S Oak 3C 132
WS6: C Hay 4D 6
Seymour Gdns. B74: Four O 6E 37

Seymour Rd. B69: O'bry 2A 98
DY4: Tip 4C 62
DY9: W'cte 6B 110
Shackleton Dr. WV6: Pert 4E 25
Shackleton Hall B15: Edg 5C 116
Shackleton Rd. WS3: Blox 5B 20
Shadowbrook La. B92: H Ard 5F 139
Shadwell Dr. DY3: Lwr G 4H 75
Shadwell St. B4: Birm 1D 4 (5F 101)
Shady La. B44: Gt Barr 3F 67
Shadymoor Dr. DY5: Brie H 3G 109
Shaftesbury Av. B63: Crad 4D 110
DY9: Pedm 2G 125
Shaftesbury Rd. WS10: W'bry 3H 63
Shaftesbury Sq. B71: W Brom 2A 80
Shaftesbury St. B70: W Brom 3A 80
B71: W Brom 3A 80
Shaftmoor Ind. Est. B28: Hall G 3F 135
Shaftmoor La. B27: A Grn 3E 135
B28: Hall G 3E 135
Shaftsbury Cl. WV14: Bils 4H 45
Shaftsbury Rd. B26: Sheld 6G 121
Shahjalal Rd. B8: Salt 4D 102
Shakespeare Cl. WV14: Cose 3F 61
Shakespeare Cres. WS3: Blox 1C 32
(not continuous)
Shakespeare Dr. B90: Shir 6G 149
Shakespeare Ho. B31: Longb 1E 159
Shakespeare Pl. WS3: Blox 2C 32
Shakespeare Rd. B23: Erd 4B 84
B67: Smeth 5C 98
B90: Shir 6B 150
DY3: Lwr G 3E 75
DY4: Tip 5A 62
Shakespeare St. B11: S'hll 6C 118
WV1: Wolv 2A 44
Shaldon Wlk. B66: Smeth 4F 99
Shales, The WV5: Wom 2E 73
Shale St. WV14: Bils 6E 45
Shalford Rd. B92: Olton 1C 136
Shallcross La. DY3: Lwr G 4H 75
Shalnecote Gro. B14: K Hth 2E 147
Shambles, The WS10: W'bry 3F 63
Shandon Cl. B32: Bart G 2D 130
Shanklin Cl. WS6: Gt Wyr 2F 7
Shannon Dr. WS8: Bwnhls 3G 9
Shannon Rd. B38: K Nor 2H 159
Shannon Wlk. WS8: Bwnhls 3G 9
Shanti Niketan WV2: Wolv 4H 43
(off Dudley Rd.)
Shapinsay Dr. B45: Fran 6F 143
SHARD END 3G 105
Shard End Cres. B34: S End 3G 105
Shardlow Rd. WV11: Wed 1G 29
Shardway, The B34: S End 4G 105
(not continuous)
Sharesacre St. WV13: W'hall 6B 30
Sharington Cl. DY2: Dud 1G 95
Sharman Rd. WV10: Bush 3A 28
SHARMANS CROSS 3C 150
Sharmans Cross Rd. B91: Sol 3C 150
Sharon Cl. WV4: E'shll 6A 44
Sharps Cl. B45: Redn 2G 157
Sharrat Fld. B75: R'ley 1B 54
Sharrocks St. WV1: Wolv 2A 44
SHAVER'S END 4D 76
Shawberry Av. B35: Cas V 4E 87
Shawberry Rd. B37: K'hrst 4B 106
SHAWBROOK 5H 161
Shawbrook Gro. B14: K Hth 4A 148
Shawbury Gro. B12: Birm 3H 117
WV6: Pert 4E 25
Shawbury Rd. WV10: Wolv 4B 28
Shaw Dr. B33: Yard 1C 120
Shawfield B47: H'wd 4A 162
Shaw Hall La. WV10: Cov H 1F 15
Shawhellier Av. DY5: Brie H 1A 110
Shaw Hill Gro. B8: W End 5G 103
Shaw Hill Rd. B8: W End 5G 103
Shawhurst Cft. B47: H'wd 2A 162
Shawhurst Gdns. B47: H'wd 2B 162
Shawhurst La. B47: H'wd 4A 162
Shaw La. WV6: Tett 6H 25
Shawley Cft. B27: A Grn 1C 136

Shaw Pk. Bus. Village—Shottery Cl.

Shaw Pk. Bus. Village WV10: Bush 3H **27**
Shaw Rd. DY2: Dud 2D **94**
(not continuous)
DY4: Tip 3C **78**
WV2: Wolv 5G **43**
WV10: Bush 3G **27**
(not continuous)
WV14: Cose 4D **60**
Shawsdale Rd. B36: Hodg H 2D **104**
Shaws La. WS6: Gt Wyr 3G **7**
Shaw's Pas. B5: Birm 5G **5** (1H **117**)
Shaw St. B70: W Brom 5E **63**
WS2: Wals 1B **48**
Shayler Gro. WV2: Wolv 4H **43**
Sheaf La. B26: Sheld 6F **121**
Sheapecote Ho. B71: W Brom 3D **64**
Shearers Pl. B75: R'ley 6C **38**
Shearwater Cl. B45: Rub 3F **157**
Shearwater Dr. DY5: Brie H 4G **109**
Shearwater Wlk. B23: Erd 6B **68**
Sheaves Cl. WV14: Cose 2D **60**
Shedden St. DY2: Dud 1F **95**
Sheddington Rd. B23: Erd 6D **68**
Sheen Rd. B44: Gt Barr 1G **67**
Sheepclose Dr. B37: F'bri 6C **106**
Sheepcote St. B16: Birm 6A **4** (1D **116**)
Sheepfold Cl. B65: Row R 5A **96**
Sheepmoor Cl. B17: Harb 3D **114**
Sheepwash La. DY4: Tip 2D **78**
Sheepwash Nature Reserve 3D 78
Sheffield Rd. B73: Bold 6G **69**
Sheffield St. DY5: Quar B 2C **110**
Shefford Rd. B6: Aston 4H **101**
Sheila Av. WV11: Wed 2G **29**
Shelah Rd. B63: Hale 5H **111**
Shelbourne Cl. B69: Tiv 5D **78**
SHELDON .6H 121
Sheldon Av. WS10: W'bry 1G **63**
Sheldon Cl. WV14: Bils 2F **61**
Sheldon Country Pk. 4H 121
Sheldon Dr. B31: Longb 5B **144**
Sheldonfield Rd. B26: Sheld 6H **121**
Sheldon Gro. B26: Sheld 6F **121**
Sheldon Hall Av. B33: Kitts G 6H **105**
(not continuous)
Sheldon Health Leisure Cen. 3G 121
Sheldon Heath Rd. B26: Yard, Sheld . . .2E **121**
Sheldon Rd. B71: W Brom 5C **64**
WV10: Oxl .6E **15**
Sheldon Wlk. B33: Sheld 2G **121**
SHELFIELD .6G 21
Shelfield Rd. B14: K Hth 4E **147**
Shelley Av. DY4: Tip 5A **62**
Shelley Cl. DY3: Lwr G 2E **75**
DY8: Amb 3E **109**
Shelley Dr. B23: Erd 4B **84**
B74: Four O 3F **37**
Shelley Rd. WV10: F'hses 5H **15**
WV12: W'hall 2E **31**
Shelley Twr. B31: N'fld 4G **145**
Shelly Cl. B37: F'bri 1B **122**
Shelly Cres. B90: M'path 2F **165**
Shelly Cft. B33: Kitts G 6E **105**
Shelly Ho. B68: O'bry 5H **97**
Shelly La. B90: M'path 3F **165**
Shelly Manor Mus. 5B 132
Shelly Shop. Cen. B90: M'path 2F **165**
Shelsley Av. B69: O'bry 4D **96**
Shelsley Dr. B13: Mose 4B **134**
Shelsley Way B91: Sol 6F **151**
Shelton Cl. WS10: W'bry 6A **48**
Shelton La. B63: Crad 6G **111**
Shelwick Gro. B93: Dorr 5A **166**
Shenley Av. DY1: Dud 1D **76**
Shenley Court Leisure Cen. 6C 130
SHENLEY FIELDS 1C 144
Shenley Flds. Dr. B31: N'fld 5C **130**
Shenley Flds. Rd.
B29: S Oak, W Cas 6D **130**
Shenley Gdns. B29: W Cas 6E **131**
Shenley Hill B31: N'fld 1C **144**
Shenley La. B29: W Cas 4D **130**
Shenley Lane Community & Sports Cen. .1E 145
Shenstone Av. B62: Hale 6E **113**
DY8: Stourb 2B **124**
Shenstone Cl. B74: Four O 3E **37**
Shenstone Ct. B90: Shir 5D **148**
WV3: Wolv 5E **43**
Shenstone Dr. CV7: Bal C 3G **169**
WS9: A'rdge 1C **34**
Shenstone Flats B62: Quin 6F **113**
Shenstone Rd. B14: K Hth 6A **148**
B16: Edg .6G **99**
B43: Gt Barr 5A **66**
Shenstone Trad. Est. B63: Hale 1C **128**
Shenstone Valley Rd. B62: Quin 5E **113**
Shenstone Wlk. B62: Hale 6D **112**
SHENSTONE WOODEND 1G 37
Shenton Wlk. B37: K'hrst 4C **106**
Shepheard Rd. B26: Sheld 6H **121**
Shepherd Dr. WV12: W'hall 4C **30**
Shepherds Brook Rd. DY9: Lye 6H **109**
Shepherds Fold B65: Row R 1B **112**
Shepherds Gdns. B15: Birm 2D **116**
Shepherds Grn. Rd. B24: Erd 5F **85**
Shepherds La. CV7: Mer 2G **141**
Shepherds Pool Rd. B75: R'ley 1C **54**
Shepherds Standing B34: S End 3F **105**
Shepherds Wlk. WV8: Pend 5D **14**
Shepherds Way B23: Erd 5C **68**
Shepley Rd. B45: Redn 3H **157**
Sheppey Dr. B36: Cas B 4D **106**
SHEPWELL GREEN 1C 46
Shepwell Grn. WV13: W'hall 2C **46**
Sherard Cft. B36: Cas B 3D **106**
Sheraton Cl. WS9: A'rdge 3D **34**
Sheraton Grange DY8: Stourb 3D **124**
Sherborne Cl. B46: Col 5H **107**
WS3: Blox .2A **32**
Sherborne Gdns. WV8: Cod 4G **13**
Sherborne Gro. B1: Birm 6C **100**
Sherborne Lofts B16: Birm 1D **116**
Sherborne Rd. WV10: Bush 6H **15**
Sherborne St. B16: Birm 1D **116**
Sherborne Wharf B16: Birm 1D **116**
Sherbourne Ct. B27: A Grn 1A **136**
Sherbourne Dr. B27: A Grn 1A **136**
Sherbourne Rd. B12: Bal H 4G **117**
B27: A Grn 1A **136**
B64: Old H 3A **112**
DY8: Stourb 1F **125**
Sherbourne Rd. E. B12: Bal H 5H **117**
Sherdmore Cft. B90: M'path 3E **165**
Sheridan Cl. WS2: Wals 4H **47**
Sheridan Gdns. DY3: Lwr G 2D **74**
Sheridan St. B71: W Brom 3B **80**
WS2: Wals 4H **47**
Sheridan Wlk. B35: Cas V 4E **87**
Sheriff Dr. DY5: Quar B 1B **110**
Sherifoot La. B75: Four O 5H **37**
Sheringham B15: Edg 3A **116**
Sheringham Rd. B30: K Nor 4D **146**
Sherington Dr. WV4: Penn 6H **43**
Sherlock Cl. WV12: W'hall 4D **30**
Sherlock St. B5: Birm 4G **117**
Sherrans Dell WV4: E'shll 2A **60**
Sherratt Cl. B76: Walm 5D **70**
Sherringham Dr. WV11: Ess 6C **18**
Sherron Gdns. B12: Bal H 6H **117**
Sherston Covert B30: K Nor 5E **147**
Shervale Cl. WV4: Penn 5E **43**
Sherwin Av. WV14: Cose 3C **60**
Sherwood Av. DY4: Tip 3H **77**
Sherwood Cl. B28: Hall G 2F **149**
B92: Olton .6D **136**
Sherwood Dr. DY5: Quar B 2B **110**
Sherwood M. B28: Hall G 1E **149**
Sherwood Rd. B28: Hall G 6E **135**
B67: Smeth 2E **115**
DY8: Woll .4C **108**
Sherwood St. WV1: Wolv 6G **27**
Sherwood Wlk. B45: Fran 4H **143**
WS9: A'rdge 2A **34**
Shetland Cl. B16: Birm 1B **116**
WV6: Wolv .4F **27**
Shetland Dr. B66: Smeth 2B **98**
Shetland Wlk. B36: Cas B 3D **106**
Shidas La. B69: O'bry 2E **97**
Shifnal Rd. WV7: Alb 6A **12**
Shifnal Wlk. B31: Longb 1D **158**
Shifrall Way B75: S Cold 4D **54**
Shillcock Gro. B19: Birm 4G **101**
Shilton Cl. B90: M'path 3D **164**
Shilton Gro. B29: W Cas 5D **130**
Shinwell Cres. B69: Tiv 5D **78**
Shipbourne Cl. B32: Harb 6D **114**
Shipley Flds. B24: Erd 4G **85**
Shipley Gro. B29: W Cas 5E **131**
Shipston Rd. B31: N'fld 6F **145**
Shipton Cl. DY1: Dud 4A **76**
Shipton Rd. B72: S Cold 2A **70**
Shipway Rd. B25: Yard 4G **119**
Shirebrook Cl. B6: Aston 1G **101**
Shire Brook Ct. B19: Loz 1F **101**
Shire Cl. B16: Birm 1B **116**
B68: O'bry 1H **113**
Shireland Brook Gdns. B18: Win G 5H **99**
Shireland Cl. B20: Hand 4A **82**
Shireland Rd. B66: Smeth 5F **99**
Shire Lea WS8: Bwnhls 1D **22**
SHIRE OAK .2B 22
Shire Oak Pk. (Nature Reserve) 3D 22
Shire Ridge WS9: Wals W 3C **22**
Shirestone Rd. B33: Kitts G 1H **121**
Shireview Gdns. WS3: Pels 3F **21**
Shireview Rd. WS3: Pels 3E **21**
Shirland Rd. B37: Mars G 2C **122**
SHIRLEY 4H 149
Shirleydale B90: Shir 6A **150**
Shirley Dr. B72: S Cold 1A **70**
SHIRLEY HEATH 1H 163
Shirley Pk. Rd. B90: Shir 5H **149**
Shirley Rd. B27: A Grn 4H **135**
B28: Hall G 1G **149**
B30: K Nor 2C **146**
B68: O'bry 3A **98**
DY2: Dud .1G **95**
Shirley Station (Rail) 6F 149
SHIRLEY STREET 5H 149
Shirley Trad. Est. B90: Shir 1D **164**
Shirrall Dr. B78: Dray B 5G **39**
Shirrall Gro. B37: K'hrst 4B **106**
Sholing Cl. WV8: Pend 6D **14**
Shooters Cl. B5: Edg 5F **117**
Shooters Hill B72: S Cold 3B **70**
Shop La. WV6: Tres 4B **40**
WV8: Oaken 6C **12**
Shopton Rd. B34: S End 2E **105**
Shoreham Cl. WV13: W'hall 2F **45**
Short Acre St. WS2: Wals 6B **32**
SHORT CROSS 1H 127
Shorters Av. B14: K Hth 3B **148**
Shortfield Cl. CV7: Bal C 2H **169**
SHORT HEATH
B23 . . . . .1D 84
WV12 . . . . .4D 30
Short Heath Ct. B23: Erd 2F **85**
Short Heath Rd. B23: Erd 1D **84**
Shortland Cl. B93: Know 2C **166**
Shortlands Cl. B30: K Nor 5C **146**
Shortlands La. WS3: Pels 3D **20**
Short La. WS6: C Hay 2E **7**
Short Rd. B67: Smeth 6B **98**
WV10: Bush 6A **16**
Short St. B63: Hale 1H **127**
B65: B'hth 2C **112**
B65: B'hth, Row R 1C **112**
(not continuous)
B90: Dic H 4G **163**
DY1: Dud .5C **76**
DY4: Tip .5G **61**
DY8: Stourb 6D **108**
WS2: Wals 2B **48**
WS8: Bwnhls 5B **10**
WS10: Darl 4F **47**
WS10: W'bry 2E **63**
WV1: Wolv 2C **170** (1H **43**)
WV12: W'hall 4C **30**
WV14: Bils 5F **45**
Shorwell Pl. DY5: Brie H 3G **109**
Shottery Cl. B76: Walm 4D **70**

Shottery Gro. B76: Walm 4D **70**
Shottery Rd. B90: Shir 6H **149**
Shotteswell Rd. B90: Shir 2H **163**
Showcase Cinema
  Birmingham 5B **86**
  Dudley .5G **77**
  Walsall .2G **47**
Showell Cir. WV10: Bush 2A **28**
SHOWELL GREEN 1A **134**
Showell Grn. La. B11: S'hll 2B **134**
Showell Ho. B69: O'bry 2G **97**
Showell La. WV4: Lwr P 2G **57**
Showell Rd. WV10: Bush 2H **27**
Showell Rd. Ind. Est. WV10: Wolv 3H **27**
Showells Gdns. B7: Nech 2C **102**
Shrawley Cl. B45: Rub 2F **157**
  B63: Hale 3A **128**
Shrawley Rd. B31: N'fld 5G **145**
Shrewley Cres. B33: Kitts G 2A **122**
Shrewsbury Cl. WS3: Blox 6F **19**
Shrewton Av. B14: K Hth 6F **147**
Shropshire Way B71: W Brom 6A **64**
Shrubbery, The B16: Birm 6B **100**
  DY1: Dud 5D **76**
  DY4: Tip 1C **78**
Shrubbery Av. DY4: Tip 2F **77**
Shrubbery Cl. B76: Walm 1B **86**
  WS1: Wals 2F **49**
Shrublands Av. B68: O'bry 4H **113**
Shrub La. B24: Erd 3H **85**
Shugborough Cl. WS3: Blox 6H **19**
Shugborough Dr. DY1: Dud 5A **76**
Shustoke La. WS5: Wals 1F **65**
Shustoke Rd. B34: S End 3G **105**
  B91: Sol 2H **151**
SHUT END 6E **75**
Shutlock La. B13: Mose 4F **133**
Shyltons Cft. B16: Birm 1C **116**
Sibdon Gro. B31: Longb 1E **159**
Sidaway Cl. B65: Row R 3C **96**
Sidaway St. B64: Old H 2G **111**
Sidbury Gro. B93: Dorr 6A **166**
Sidcup Cl. WV14: Cose 2D **60**
Sidcup Rd. B44: K'sdng 4A **68**
Siddeley Wlk. B36: Cas B 6B **88**
Siddons Factory Est.
  B70: W Brom 5F **63**
Siddons Rd. WV14: Cose 3F **61**
Siddons Way B70: W Brom 6G **63**
Sidenhill Cl. B90: Shir 1H **163**
Sidestrand WV9: Pend 4D **14**
Sidford Gdns. B24: Erd 4A **86**
Sidford Gro. B23: Erd 6E **69**
Sidings, The B20: Hand 1E **101**
  B23: Erd 4E **85**
  B70: W Brom 5A **80**
Sidlaw Cl. B63: Hale 3F **127**
  WV10: Oxl 3G **27**
Sidney St. WV2: Wolv 6A **170** (3G **43**)
Sidwick Cres. WV2: E'shll 5D **44**
Sigmund Cl. WV1: Wolv 6D **28**
Signal Gro. WS3: Blox 6G **19**
Signal Hayes Rd. B76: Walm 3D **70**
  (not continuous)
Silesbourne Cl. B36: Cas B 1G **105**
Silhill Hall Rd. B91: Sol 1E **151**
Silva Av. DY6: K'wfrd 5D **92**
Silver Birch Cl. B8: Salt 3D **102**
Silver Birch Coppice B74: Four O 4D **36**
Silverbirch Ct. B24: Erd 1H **85**
Silver Birch Rd. B47: H'wd 3B **162**
Silver Birch Rd. B24: Erd 1H **85**
  B37: K'hrst 3B **106**
  B74: S'tly 2H **51**
  WS11: Nort C 1F **9**
  WV2: Wolv 4H **43**
Silverbirch Rd. B91: Sol 4A **152**
Silver Ct. WS8: Bwnhls 6B **10**
Silver Ct. Gdns. WS8: Bwnhls 6B **10**
Silvercroft Av. B20: Hand 4G **81**
Silverdale Dr. WV10: Wolv 5A **28**
Silverdale Gdns. DY8: Word 6A **92**
Silverdale Rd. B24: Erd 2B **86**
SILVER END 2F **109**

Silver End Bus. Pk. DY5: Brie H 2G **109**
Silver End Ind. Est. DY5: Brie H 2F **109**
Silverfield Cl. B14: K Hth 5G **133**
Silver Innage B63: Crad 4E **111**
Silverlands Av. B68: O'bry 6H **97**
Silverlands Cl. B28: Hall G 4F **135**
Silvermead Ct. B47: Wyt 4H **161**
Silvermere Rd. B26: Sheld 5H **121**
Silvers Cl. WS3: Pels 2D **20**
Silverstone Cl. WS2: Wals 6E **31**
Silverstone Dr. B74: S'tly 5H **51**
SILVER STREET 4G **161**
Silver St. B14: K Hth 5G **133**
  B38: Head H 4F **161**
  B47: Wyt 4G **161**
  DY5: Brie H 2G **109**
  WS8: Bwnhls 6A **10**
Silverthorne Av. DY4: Tip 2F **77**
Silverthorne La. B64: Crad H 2D **110**
Silverton Cres. B13: Mose 4D **134**
Silverton Hgts. B67: Smeth 3D **98**
Silverton Rd. B67: Smeth 3C **98**
Silverton Way WV11: Wed 4H **29**
Silvertrees Rd. DY4: Tip 2G **77**
Silvester Ct. B70: W Brom 4B **80**
Silvester Rd. WV14: Bils 5G **45**
Silvester Way DY5: Brie H 3F **109**
Silvington Cl. B29: W Cas 6G **131**
Simcox Gdns. B32: Bart G 3B **130**
Simcox Rd. WS10: W'bry 6F **47**
Simeon Bissell Cl. DY4: Tip 2A **78**
Simeon's Wlk. DY5: Quar B 4B **110**
Simmonds Cl. WS3: Blox 4B **20**
Simmonds Pl. WS3: Blox 4B **20**
  WS10: Darl 4E **47**
Simmonds Rd. WS3: Blox 4B **20**
Simmonds Way WS8: Bwnhls 2C **22**
Simmons Dr. B32: Quin 1A **130**
Simmons Leasow B32: Bart G 3B **130**
Simmons Rd. WV11: Wed 6B **18**
Simms La. B47: H'wd 4A **162**
  (not continuous)
  DY2: Neth 4E **95**
Simon Cl. B71: W Brom 4C **64**
Simon Rd. B47: H'wd 2A **162**
Simpkins Cl. WS9: Wals W 4C **22**
Simpson Gro. WV10: Bush 3A **28**
Simpson Rd. B72: W Grn 4A **70**
  WS2: Wals 4H **31**
  WV10: Bush 3A **28**
Simpson St. B69: O'bry 2G **97**
Sinclair Cl. B13: Mose 1G **133**
Singer Cft. B36: Cas B 6B **88**
Singh Cl. B21: Hand 6A **82**
Sion Cl. DY5: Brie H 6H **93**
Sir Alfred's Way B76: Walm 2C **70**
Sir Harrys Rd. B5: Edg 5D **116**
  B15: Edg 5D **116**
Sir Hilton's Rd. B31: Longb 2F **159**
Sir Johns Rd. B29: S Oak 2E **133**
Sir Richards Dr. B17: Harb 4D **114**
Sisefield Rd. B38: K Nor 6C **146**
Siskin Cl. B68: O'bry 1A **114**
Siskin Dr. B12: Bal H 5G **117**
Siskin Rd. DY9: W'cte 2H **125**
Sister Dora Bldgs. WS1: Wals 2C **48**
  (off The Bridge)
Sister Dora Gdns. WS1: Wals 2C **48**
Siviters Cl. B65: Row R 6C **96**
Siviters La. B65: Row R 6B **96**
Siviter St. B63: Hale 1B **128**
Six Acres B32: Quin 1A **130**
Sixes Sports Cen. 6C **74**
Six Foot Rd. DY2: Neth 4E **95**
Six Towers Rd. WS2: Wals 5A **32**
Six Ways B23: Erd 3F **85**
Skelcher Rd. B90: Shir 3G **149**
Skemp Cl. WV14: Bils 2F **61**
Sketchley Cl. B66: Smeth 4E **99**
Skidmore Av. WV3: Wolv 3D **42**
Skidmore Dr. B70: W Brom 4G **79**
Skidmore Rd. WV14: Cose 3F **61**

Skinner La. B5: Birm 2G **117**
Sky Lark Cl. WV1: Wolv 3A **170** (1G **43**)
Skip La. WS5: Wals 6H **49**
Skipton Grn. WV6: Wolv 4E **27**
Skipton Rd. B16: Edg 2C **116**
Skomer Cl. B45: Fran 6E **143**
Skye Cl. B36: Cas B 3D **106**
Skye Wlk. B64: Old H 2G **111**
Skylark Cl. B23: Erd 6C **68**
Skywalk B40: Nat E C 1F **139**
Slack La. B20: Hand 5A **82**
Slackey La. WS3: Blox 6C **20**
Slade Cl. B71: W Brom 3D **64**
Sladefield Rd. B8: W End 4G **103**
Slade Gdns. WV8: Cod 3G **13**
Slade Gro. B93: Know 3B **166**
Slade Hill WV6: Wolv 6D **26**
Slade La. B28: Hall G 4E **149**
  B75: R'ley 6E **39**
Slade Lanker B34: Stech 4E **105**
Sladepool Farm Rd. B14: K Hth 4H **147**
Slade Rd. B23: Erd 3D **84**
  B63: Crad 5E **111**
  B75: R'ley, Can 6C **38**
  WV10: F'hses 4G **15**
Slaithwaite Rd. B71: W Brom 3C **80**
Slaney Ct. WS2: Wals 4A **48**
Slaney Rd. WS2: Wals 5H **47**
Slatch Ho. Rd. B67: Smeth 1C **114**
Slate La. WV8: Cod 2D **12**
Slateley Cres. B90: M'path 3E **165**
Slater Cl. B64: Old H 2H **111**
Slate Row WS3: Pels 4E **21**
Slater Rd. B93: Ben H 5A **166**
Slater's La. WS2: Wals 4H **47**
Slater's Pl. WS2: Wals 4H **47**
Slater St. DY4: Tip 3A **78**
  (Crompton Rd.)
  DY4: Tip 4D **46**
  (Sheepwash La.)
  WS10: Darl 4D **46**
  WV13: W'hall 6C **30**
  WV14: Bils 1G **61**
Sleaford Gro. B28: Hall G 6G **135**
Sleaford Rd. B28: Hall G 6H **135**
Sledmore Rd. DY2: Dud 2F **95**
Slieve, The B20: Hand 4C **82**
Slim Av. WV14: Bils 2G **61**
Slimbridge Cl. B90: M'path 3E **165**
Slim Rd. WS2: Wals 1E **47**
Slims Ga. B63: Hale 1A **128**
Sling, The DY2: Neth 3E **95**
Slingfield Rd. B31: N'fld 5G **145**
Slitting Mill Cl. B21: Hand 1G **99**
Sloane Ho. B1: Birm 2A **4**
Sloane St. B1: Birm 3A **4** (6E **101**)
Slough La. B38: Head H 1G **161**
  B47: H'wd 1G **161**
Smallbrook La. WV5: Wom 6H **57**
Smallbrook Queensway
  B5: Birm 6D **4** (2F **117**)
Small Cl. B67: Smeth 4B **98**
Smalldale Rd. B42: Gt Barr 6F **67**
SMALL HEATH 3D **118**
Small Heath Bri. B10: Small H 3B **118**
  B11: S'brk 4B **118**
Small Heath Bus. Pk.
  B10: Small H 4F **119**
Small Heath Highway
  B10: Small H 3B **118**
Small Heath Leisure Cen. 3D **118**
Small Heath Station (Rail) 4D **118**
Small Heath Trad. Est.
  B11: Small H 5D **118**
Smallshire Cl. WV11: Wed 4H **29**
Smallshire Way DY8: Word 3B **108**
Small St. B71: W Brom 1H **79**
  WS1: Wals 3C **48**
Smallwood Cl. B24: Erd 4B **86**
  B76: Walm 2C **70**
Smallwood Rd. WV8: Pend 5C **14**
Smarts Av. WS14: Shen W 2G **37**
Smeaton Gdns. B18: Win G 5A **100**

Smeed Gro. B24: Erd 4H 85
SMESTOW 3D 72
Smestow Ga. DY3: Swind 2B 72
Smestow La. DY3: Swind 3C 72
Smestow St. WV10: Wolv 5H 27
Smestow Valley Local Nature Reserve
. . . . .3D 26
SMETHWICK 4E 99
Smethwick Galton Bridge Station (Rail)
. . . . .2C 98
Smethwick New Ent. Cen.
B66: Smeth 3E 99
Smethwick Rolfe Street Station (Rail)
. . . . .3E 99
Smethwick Swimming Cen. 1D 114
Smirrells Rd. B28: Hall G 2E 149
Smith Av. WS10: Darl 1D 62
Smith Cl. B67: Smeth 6B 98
WV14: Cose 4C 60
Smithfield Rd. WS3: Blox 6B 20
Smithfields DY8: Stourb 6E 109
Smithfield St. B5: Birm 6G 5 (2G 117)
Smithmoor Cres. B71: W Brom 5D 64
Smith Pl. DY4: Tip 3B 78
Smith Rd. WS2: Wals 5A 48
WS10: W'bry 4E 63
Smiths Cl. B32: Bart G 3H 129
Smiths La. B93: Know 3A 166
Smith St. B19: Birm 4E 101
DY2: Dud 2F 95
WV14: Bils 6F 45
Smiths Way B46: Wat O 4C 88
SMITH'S WOOD 2C 106
Smithy, The B26: Sheld 5G 121
Smithy Dr. WS3: Pels 3E 21
Smithy La. DY5: P'ntt 6F 75
Smout Cres. WV14: Cose 3B 60
Snapdragon Dr. WS5: Wals 2D 64
Snape Rd. WV11: Wed 6A 18
Sneyd Hall Cl. WS3: Blox 1G 31
Sneyd Hall Rd. WS3: Blox 6G 19
Sneyd La. WS3: Blox 6F 19
WV11: Ess 5R 18
Snowberry Dr. DY5: P'ntt 6G 75
Snowberry Gdns. B27: A Grn 6A 120
Snowdon Gro. B63: Hale 4F 127
Snowdon Ri. DY3: Sed 1H 75
Snowdon Rd. DY8: Amb 5F 109
Snowdon Way WV10: Oxl 3F 27
WV12: W'hall 6B 18
Snowdrop Cl. WS8: Clay 1H 21
Snowford Cl. B90: Shir 6F 149
Snow Hill Junc.
WV2: Wolv 5C 170 (2H 43)
Snow Hill Queensway
B4: Birm 2D 4 (6G 101)
Snow Hill Station (Rail & MM)
. . . . .3E 5 (6F 101)
Snowshill Dr. B90: Ches G 4B 164
Snowshill Gdns. DY1: Dud 3B 76
Soberton Cl. WV11: Wed 2H 29
SOHO 2G 99
Soho Av. B18: Hock 2C 100
Soho Benson Road Stop (MM) 3B 100
Soho Cl. B66: Smeth 4G 99
Soho Hill B19: Hock 2C 100
Soho Ho. B66: Smeth 4G 99
Soho Pool Way B18: Hock 3C 100
Soho Rd. B21: Hand 1A 100
Soho St. B66: Smeth 3G 99
Soho Way B66: Smeth 3F 99
Solari Cl. DY4: Tip 5C 62
Solent Cl. WV9: Pend 5D 14
Solent St. B73: S Cold 6H 53
SOLIHULL 4G 151
Solihull Arden Club 3D 150
Solihull By-Pass B91: Sol 2G 151
Solihull Ice Rink 2F 137
Solihull La. B28: Hall G 1G 149
SOLIHULL LODGE 5C 148
Solihull Moors FC 4B 138
Solihull Parkway B37: Mars G 4F 123

Solihull Retail Pk. B90: Shir 6B 150
Solihull Rd. B11: S'hll 2D 134
B90: Shir 4A 150
B92: H Ard 1E 153
Solihull Station (Rail) 3E 151
Soliway Cl. WS10: W'bry 1A 64
Solly Gro. DY4: Tip 6D 62
Solva Cl. WV1: Wolv 2D 44
Soma Ho. B75: S Cold 6G 55
Somerby Dr. B91: Sol 1E 165
Somercotes Rd. B42: Gt Barr 5F 67
Somerdale Rd. B31: N'fld 3G 145
Somerfield Cl. WS4: S'fld 6G 21
Somerfield Rd. WS3: Blox 1H 31
Somerford Cl. WS6: Gt Wyr 4E 7
Somerford Gdns. WV10: Bush 5A 16
Somerford Pl. WV13: W'hall 2H 45
Somerford Rd. B29: W Cas 5D 130
Somerford Way WV14: Cose 5D 60
Somerland Rd. B26: Yard 2E 121
Somerset Cres. WS10: W'bry 1B 64
Somerset Dr. B31: Longb 2D 158
DY8: Woll 4B 108
Somerset Rd. B15: Edg 5A 116
B20: Hand 5B 82
B23: Erd 1F 85
B71: W Brom 1B 80
WS4: Wals 5E 33
WV13: W'hall 1D 46
Somers Rd. B62: Hale 6C 112
CV7: Mer 4F 141
WS2: Wals 4G 47
Somers Wood Cvn. & Camping Pk.
CV7: Mer 4F 141
Somerton Dr. B23: Erd 1G 85
B37: Mars G 4C 122
Somerville Ct. B73: S Cold 3G 69
Somerville Dr. B73: S Cold 1G 69
Somerville Ho. B37: Chel W 6F 107
Somerville Rd. B10: Small H 3D 118
B73: S Cold 1G 69
Somery Rd. B29: W Cas 3E 131
DY1: Dud 4E 77
Sommerfield Rd. B32: Bart G 3A 130
Sonning Dr. WV9: Pend 5D 14
Sopwith Cft. B35: Cas V 5E 87
Sorrel Cl. B69: Tiv 5B 78
Sorrel Dr. WS5: Wals 2E 65
Sorrel Gro. B24: Erd 4B 86
Sorrel Ho. B24: Erd 4B 86
Sorrell Dr. B27: A Grn 3H 135
Sorrel Wlk. DY5: Brie H 5F 109
Sorrento Ct. B13: Mose 2A 134
Sot's Hole Nature Reserve 2C 80
Souters Ho. B32: Bart G 5B 130
Southacre Av. B5: Birm 3G 117
(not continuous)
Southall Cres. WV14: Cose 4E 61
Southall Rd. WV11: Wed 1A 30
Southalls La. DY1: Dud 6D 76
Southam Cl. B28: Hall G 6E 135
Southam Dr. B73: W Grn 4H 69
Southam Ho. B13: Mose 6A 134
Southampton St.
WV1: Wolv 1D 170 (6H 27)
Southam Rd. B28: Hall G 5E 135
South Av. DY8: Stourb 1D 124
WV11: Wed 4E 29
Southbank Rd. B64: Old H 2G 111
Southbank Vw. DY6: K'wfrd 5C 92
Southbourne Av. B34: Hodg H 3B 104
WS2: Wals 2H 47
Southbourne Cl. B29: S Oak 3C 132
Southbourne Pl. WV10: F'hses 4G 15
Sth. Car Pk. Rd. B40: Nat E C 2G 139
Southcote Gro. B38: K Nor 6H 145
Southcott Av. DY5: Brie H 3H 109
South Cres. WV10: F'stne 1D 16
Southcroft Rd. B23: Erd 4E 85
South Dene B67: Smeth 4D 98
Southdown Av. B18: Hock 3C 100
South Dr. B5: Edg 1E 133
B46: Col 2F 107
B75: S Cold 5A 54

Sth. Eastern Arc. B2: Birm 1G 117
(off Corporation St.)
Southern Cl. DY6: K'wfrd 6D 92
Southerndown Rd. DY3: Sed 6F 59
Southern Dr. B30: K Nor 4F 147
Southern Rd. B8: W End 4A 104
Southern Way WS10: Mox 2C 62
Southey Cl. B91: Sol 1F 165
WV12: W'hall 1E 31
Southfield Av. B16: Edg 6H 99
B36: Cas B 1E 105
Southfield Cl. WS9: A'rdge 3C 34
Southfield Dr. B28: Hall G 2G 149
Southfield Gro. WV3: Wolv 4A 42
Southfield Rd. B16: Edg 6H 99
WV11: Wed 4H 29
Southfields Cl. B46: Col 5H 107
Southfields Rd. B91: Sol 6D 150
Southfield Way WS6: Gt Wyr 3F 7
Southgate B64: Crad H 3F 111
WV1: Wolv 1F 43
Southgate Rd. B44: Gt Barr 3G 67
Southgate Way DY1: Dud 5D 76
South Grn. WV4: Penn 6B 42
South Gro. B6: Aston 1F 101
B19: Hand 1D 100
B23: Erd 2F 85
South Holme B9: Bord G 1C 118
Southlands Rd. B13: Mose 4A 134
Southminster Dr. B14: K Hth 1G 147
South Oval DY3: Up Gor 2A 76
South Pde. B72: S Cold 6A 54
South Pk. M. DY5: Brie H 1G 109
South Range B11: Bal H 5B 118
B14: K Hth 5G 133
B18: Hock 2C 100
B23: Erd 3F 85
B31: N'fld 5D 144
B67: Smeth 4D 98
DY4: Tip 5B 62
DY8: Stourb 1B 124
South Rd. Av. B18: Hock 3C 100
South Roundhay B33: Kitts G 6E 105
Southside B5: Birm 6E 5
Southside Bus. Cen. B12: Bal H . . .6A 118
(off Ladypool Rd.)
Sth. Staffordshire Bus. Pk.
WS11: Cann 1C 6
South Staffordshire Golf Course . . .2B 26
South St. B17: Harb 6H 115
DY5: Brie H 1G 109
WS1: Wals 3B 48
WV10: Oxl 3G 27
WV13: W'hall 2H 45
South St. Gdns. WS1: Wals 3B 48
South Twr. B7: Birm 5B 102
South Vw. B43: Gt Barr 6A 66
South Vw. Cl. WV8: Bilb 5H 13
WV10: F'stne 1D 16
Southview Ridge DY5: Brie H 4H 109
South Vw. Rd. DY3: Sed 5G 59
Southville Bungs. B14: K Hth 3B 148
South Wlk. B31: N'fld 6G 145
South Way B40: Nat E C 2H 139
Southway Ct. DY6: K'wfrd 5D 92
Southwell Wlk. B70: W Brom 5A 80
Southwick Pl. WV14: Bils 4F 45
Southwick Rd. B62: B'hth 3D 112
Southwold Av. B30: K Nor 4E 147
Southwood Av. B34: S End 2F 105
Southwood Cl. DY6: K'wfrd 4C 92
Southwood Covert B14: K Hth 5F 147
SOUTH YARDLEY 5A 120
Sovereign Ct. B1: Birm 2A 4 (6E 101)
Sovereign Dr. DY1: Dud 5A 76
Sovereign Hgts. B31: Longb 6A 144
Sovereign Rd. B30: K Nor 3B 146
Sovereign Wlk. WS1: Wals 1E 49
Sovereign Way B13: Mose 1H 133
Sowerby March B24: Erd 3B 86
Sowers Cl. WV12: W'hall 4D 30
Sowers Ct. B75: R'ley 5B 38
Sowers Gdns. WV12: W'hall 4D 30

Spa Gro. B30: Stir 5E 133
SPARKBROOK 4B 118
SPARKHILL 1C 134
Sparkhill Pool & Fitness Cen. 1C 134
Spark St. B11: S'brk 4A 118
Sparrey Dr. B30: Stir 5C 132
Sparrow Cl. WS10: W'bry 6H 47
Spartan Ind. Cen. B70: W Brom 1E 79
Speakers Ct. B69: Tiv 2B 96
Speed Rd. DY4: Tip 1G 77
Speedwell Cl. B25: Yard 5G 119
WS9: A'rdge 4B 34
WV11: Wed 4G 29
Speedwell Dr. CV7: Bal C 3G 169
Speedwell Gdns. DY5: Brie H 5F 109
Speedwell Ho. B38: K Nor 6C 146
Speedwell Rd. B5: Edg 5F 117
B25: Yard 5G 119
Speedwell Trad. Est.
B11: Tys 5G 119
Spelter Works WS3: Blox 2G 31
Spencer Av. WV14: Cose 5E 61
Spencer Cl. B24: Erd 3B 86
B69: Tiv 1B 96
B71: W Brom 5D 64
DY3: Lwr G 3E 75
Spencer St. B18: Birm 1A 4 (4E 101)
(not continuous)
Spenser Av. WV6: Pert 5F 25
Spernall Gro. B29: W Cas 4E 131
Spey Cl. B5: Edg 5F 117
Spiceland Rd. B31: N'fld 1D 144
Spiers Cl. B93: Know 3C 166
Spies Cl. B62: Quin 5F 113
Spies La. B62: Quin 6F 113
Spills Mdw. DY3: Up Gor 2A 76
Spilsbury Cft. B91: Sol 1E 165
Spindle La. B90: Dic H 3G 163
(not continuous)
Spindles, The WS6: Gt Wyr 4F 7
Spinners End Dr. B64: Crad H 2F 111
Spinners End Ind. Est.
B64: Crad H 3F 111
Spinney, The B15: Edg 6A 116
B20: Hand 3A 82
B38: K Nor 6B 146
B47: Wyt 5B 162
B74: Lit As 4B 36
B91: Sol 1G 165
DY3: Gorn 5G 75
WV3: Wolv 2B 42
Spinney Cl. B31: N'fld 4E 145
DY8: Word 6A 92
WS3: Pels 5E 21
Spinney Dr. B90: Ches G 5B 164
Spinney Wlk. B76: Walm 6D 70
Spiral Cl. B62: B'hth 3E 113
Spiral Ct. B24: Erd 5E 85
B76: Walm 2D 70
DY3: Lwr G 4H 75
(off Yorkdale Cl.)
DY8: Stourb 1E 125
WV11: Wed 2F 29
Spiral Grn. B24: Erd 3A 86
Spitfire Pk. B24: Erd 5B 86
Spitfire Rd. B24: Erd 5A 86
Spitfire Way B35: Cas V 5E 87
Spondon Rd. B34: S End 4G 105
Spondon Rd. WV11: Wed 1G 29
Spon La. B70: W Brom 6B 80
Spon La. Ind. Est. B66: Smeth 1B 98
Spon La. Sth. B66: Smeth 1B 98
B70: Smeth, W Brom 1B 98
Spon La. Trad. Est.
B70: W Brom 5B 80
Spoon Dr. B38: K Nor 5H 145
Spooner Cft. B5: Birm 3G 117
Spooners Cl. B92: Sol 6B 138
Spouthouse La. B43: Gt Barr 6A 66
Spout La. WS1: Wals 4C 48
(not continuous)
Spreadbury Cl. B17: Harb 3D 114
Sprig Cft. B36: Hodg H 1A 104
Spring Av. B65: Row R 1C 112

Spring Avon Cft. B17: Harb 5F 115
SPRING BANK 6B 30
Springbank B9: Bord G 6F 103
Spring Bank Ho. WV13: W'hall 6A 30
Springbank Rd. B15: Edg 4E 117
Springbrook Cl. B36: Cas B 6H 87
Spring Cl. B91: Sol 4D 150
WS4: S'fld 5G 21
Spring Coppice Dr. B93: Dorr 6C 166
Spring Ct. B66: Smeth 4G 99
B70: W Brom 5B 80
WS1: Wals 4E 49
Spring Cres. B64: Crad H 4H 111
Springcroft Rd. B11: Tys 3F 135
Spring Dr. WS6: Gt Wyr 3G 7
Spring Dr. Ind. Est.
WV4: E'shll 1C 60
SPRINGFIELD
B13 . . . . .4D 134
B65 . . . . .3H 95
WV10 . . . . .5A 28
Springfield B23: Erd 4D 84
Springfield Av. B12: Bal H 5A 118
B68: O'bry 5A 98
DY3: Sed 4A 60
DY9: W'cte 1A 126
Springfield Cl. B65: Row R 4A 96
Springfield Ct. B28: Hall G 5F 135
B75: S Cold 6G 55
Springfield Cres. B70: W Brom 6C 80
B76: Walm 1E 71
B92: Sol 2G 137
DY2: Dud 1H 95
Springfield Dr. B14: K Hth 4G 133
B62: B'hth 4D 112
Springfield Grn. DY3: Sed 4A 60
Springfield Gro. DY3: Sed 4H 59
Springfield La. B65: Row R 4H 95
WV10: F'hses 3H 15
Springfield Rd. B13: Mose 4D 134
B14: K Hth 5H 133
B36: Cas B 1H 105
B62: B'hth 4D 112
B68: O'bry 5A 98
B75: S Cold 1F 71
B76: Walm 3D 70
DY5: Brie H 1F 109
WV10: Wolv 5A 28
WV14: Bils 4G 45
Springfields B46: Col 4H 107
WS4: Rus 2F 33
Springfield St. B18: Hock 6C 100
Springfield Ter. B65: Row R 4H 95
Spring Gdns. B21: Hand 2A 100
B66: Smeth 6F 99
DY2: Dud 1F 95
DY3: Gorn 5G 75
Spring Gro. B19: Hock 3D 100
Spring Gro. Gdns. B18: Hock 3B 100
Spring Head WS10: W'bry 3F 63
SPRING HILL 1A 58
SPRINGHILL
WS14 . . . . .6G 11
WV11 . . . . .2D 18
Spring Hill B1: Birm 6D 100
B18: Hock 5C 100
B24: Erd 4F 85
Springhill Av. WV4: Penn 2A 58
Springhill Cl. WS4: S'fld 6H 21
WV12: W'hall 2D 30
Springhill Ct. WS1: Wals 3E 49
Springhill Gro. WV4: Penn 1A 58
Spring Hill Ind. Est.
B18: Hock 6C 100
Springhill La. WV4: Lwr P 6F 41
WV4: Penn 2A 58
Springhill Pk. WV4: Penn 2H 57
Spring Hill Pas. B18: Hock 6C 100
Springhill Rd. WS1: Wals 2D 48
WS8: Bwnhls 6C 10
WV11: Wed 1G 29
Spring Hill Ter. WV4: Penn 5E 43
Spring Ho. B37: K'hrst 4D 106

Spring La. B24: Erd 4G 85
WS4: S'fld 5G 21
WV12: W'hall 5B 30
Spring Mdw. B63: Hale 3H 127
B64: Old H 2H 111
DY4: Tip 1C 78
WS6: C Hay 4D 6
Springmeadow Gro. B19: Hock 3F 101
Springmeadow Rd. B15: Edg 4F 117
DY2: Neth 1E 111
Spring Mdws. Cl. WV8: Bilb 3H 13
Spring Parklands DY1: Dud 1C 94
Spring Rd. B11: Tys 2F 135
B15: Edg 4F 117
B66: Smeth 1B 98
DY2: Neth 3F 95
WS4: S'fld 6H 21
WV4: E'shll 6C 44
Spring Rd. Ind. Est. WV4: E'shll 1C 60
Spring Road Station (Rail) 3G 135
Springs, The B64: Old H 2A 112
Springslade B32: Harb 6D 114
Springslade Dr. B24: Erd 4B 86
SPRINGS MIRE 1A 94
Spring St. B15: Birm 3F 117
B63: Crad 5E 111
DY4: Tip 2A 78
(Alexandra Rd.)
DY4: Tip 5C 62
(Oaker Hill Rd.)
DY9: Lye 1A 126
Springthorpe Grn. B24: Erd 3A 86
Springthorpe Rd. B24: Erd 3B 86
(Pype Hayes Rd.)
B24: Erd 3B 86
(Woodcote Rd.)
SPRING VALE 1D 60
Springvale Av. WS5: Wals 4G 49
WV14: Bils 1D 60
Springvale Bus. Cen. WV14: Bils 1D 60
Spring Va. Cl. WV14: Cose 4C 60
Spring Va. Ind. Pk. WV14: Bils 6E 45
Spring Va. Rd. B65: Row R 4A 96
Springvale St. WV13: W'hall 6B 30
Springvale Way WV14: Bils 1E 61
Spring Vs. B63: Hale 2A 128
Spring Wlk. B63: Hale 4F 127
B69: O'bry 4G 97
WS2: Wals 6H 31
Sproat Av. WS10: Darl 6C 46
Spruce Gro. B24: Erd 5H 85
Spruce Rd. WS5: Wals 2F 65
Spruce Way WV3: Wolv 2B 42
Spur Tree Av. WV3: Wolv 2G 41
Squadron Cl. B35: Cas V 3G 87
Square, The B15: Birm 2D 116
B17: Harb 6G 115
(off High St.)
B17: Harb 5F 115
(Carless Av.)
B91: Sol 4G 151
DY2: Dud 3B 94
DY4: Tip 6D 62
WS9: A'rdge 3D 34
WV2: Wolv 6D 170 (3H 43)
WV8: Cod 3F 13
WV12: W'hall 1D 30
Square Cl. B32: Bart G 2A 130
Square on the Square, The B3: Birm . . .1B 4
Squires Ct. DY5: Brie H 5G 109
Squires Cft. B76: Walm 4E 71
Squires Ga. WV13: W'hall 1B 46
Squires Ga. Wlk. B35: Cas V 4E 87
Squires Wlk. WS10: W'bry 2F 63
Squirrel Hollow B76: Walm 3E 71
Squirrels Hollow B68: O'bry 4B 114
Squirrel Wlk. B74: Lit As 4C 36
WV4: Penn 1E 59
Stable Ct. DY3: Sed 1A 76
Stable Cft. B71: W Brom 6D 64
Stableford Cl. B32: Bart G 2D 130
Stables, The B29: S Oak 3C 132
Stablewood Gro. WS1: Wals 4E 49
Stacey Cl. B64: Old H 2G 111

Stacey Dr. B13: Mose 2A 148
Stacey Grange Gdns. B45: Redn . . .3G 157
Stackhouse Cl. WS9: Wals W 3C 22
Stackhouse Dr. WS3: Pels 3E 21
Staddlestones, The WV6: Pert 5D 24
Stadium Cl. WV13: W'hall 6B 30
Stadium Dr. DY2: Neth 2E 111
Stadium Way B42: P Barr 2E 83
Stafford Cl. WS3: Blox 5H 19
Stafford Ct. B43: Gt Barr 6A 66
(off West Rd.)
WV10: F'hses 2G 15
Stafford Dr. B71: W Brom 1H 79
Stafford Ho. B33: Kitts G 1A 122
Stafford La. WV8: Cod 6D 12
Stafford Rd. B21: Hand 1B 100
WS3: Blox 1G 19
WS6: Gt Wyr 1G 19
WS10: Darl 5C 46
WV10: Cov H 1H 15
WV10: F'hses, Oxl, Wolv 1G 27
Staffordshire Pool Cl. B6: Aston 6H 83
(off Emscote Rd.)
Stafford St. DY1: Dud 6D 76
WS2: Wals 6C 32
WS10: W'bry 3E 63
WV1: Wolv 1C 170 (5G 27)
WV13: W'hall 1A 46
(not continuous)
WV14: Bils 6F 45
Stafford St. Junc.
WV1: Wolv 1B 170 (6G 27)
Stafford Twr. B4: Birm 2F 5 (6H 101)
Stafford Way R43: Gt Barr 6A 66
Staff Way B23: Erd 3E 85
Stag Cres. WS3: Blox 3C 32
Stag Hill Rd. WS3: Blox 2C 32
Stag Ind. Est. WV14: Bils 1H 61
Stag Wlk. B76: Walm 6B 70
Stainsby Av. B19: Birm 4E 101
Stainsby Cft. B90: M'path 4F 165
Stallings La. DY6: K'wfrd 1B 92
Stambermill Cl. DY9: Lye 6H 109
Stambermill Ho. DY9: Lye 6A 110
Stambermill Ind. Est.
DY9: Lye 5G 109
Stamford Cft. B91: Sol 5F 151
Stamford Gro. B20: Hand 6E 83
Stamford Rd. B20: Hand 6E 83
DY5: Brie H 4G 109
DY8: Amb 6F 109
Stamford St. DY8: Amb 4D 108
Stamford Way WS9: A'rdge 5D 22
Stanbrook Rd. B90: M'path 3E 165
Stanbury Av. WS10: Darl 5B 46
Stanbury Rd. B14: K Hth 3B 148
Stancroft Gro. B26: Yard 3E 121
Standard Way B24: Erd 1F 103
Standbridge Way DY4: Tip 2A 78
Standhills Rd. DY6: K'wfrd 3C 92
Standlake Av. B36: Hodg H 2B 104
Standleys Twr. B23: Erd 1G 85
Stanfield Rd. B32: Quin 4B 114
B43: Gt Barr 6F 51
Stanford Av. B42: Gt Barr 6C 66
Stanford Dr. B65: Row R 5B 96
Stanford Gro. B63: Hale 4E 127
Stanford Rd. WV2: Wolv 4G 43
Stanford Way B69: O'bry 5E 97
(off Kempsey Cl.)
Stanhoe Cl. DY5: Brie H 3H 109
Stanhope Rd. B67: Smeth 6D 98
Stanhope St. B12: Birm 4H 117
DY2: Neth 5G 95
WV3: Wolv 4A 170 (2F 43)
Stanhope Way B43: Gt Barr 1F 67
B46: Col 6H 89
Stanhurst Way B71: W Brom 3E 65
Stanier Cl. WS4: Rus 2F 33
Stanier Gro. B20: Hand 5D 82
Staniforth St. B4: Birm 1F 5 (5G 101)
Stanley Av. B32: Harb 4C 114
B75: S Cold 1D 70
B90: Shir 3H 149

Stanley Cl. B28: Hall G 2G 149
WV11: Wed 1H 29
Stanley Ct. B13: Mose 3B 134
(off Wake Grn. Pk.)
WV6: Pert 5E 25
Stanley Dr. DY3: Swind 5E 73
Stanley Gro. B11: S'brk 5B 118
Stanley Pl. B13: Mose 2H 133
WS4: Rus 3F 33
WV14: Bils 6D 44
Stanley Rd. B7: Nech 2C 102
B14: K Hth 6F 133
B68: O'bry 3A 114
B71: W Brom 6C 64
DY8: Stourb 2D 124
WS4: Rus 3F 33
WS10: Darl 6D 46
WV10: Bush 6H 15
(not continuous)
Stanley St. WS3: Blox 1A 32
Stanmore Gro. B62: Quin 2G 129
Stanmore Rd. B16: Edg 2G 115
Stansbury Ho. WS2: Wals 3A 48
(off St Quentin St.)
Stanton Av. DY1: Dud 1B 76
Stanton Gro. B26: Yard 3D 120
B90: Shir 3G 149
DY4: Tip 2A 78
Stanton Ho. B71: W Brom 4D 64
Stanton Rd. B43: Gt Barr 6H 65
B90: Shir 3G 149
WV1: Wolv 1B 44
Stanville Rd. B26: Sheld 5G 121
Stanway Gdns. B71: W Brom 1B 80
Stanway Gro. B44: Gt Barr 2H 67
Stanway Rd. B71: W Brom 1B 80
B90: Shir 4H 149
Stanwell Gro. B23: Erd 1E 85
Stanwick Av. B33: Kitts G 6A 106
Stapenhall Rd. B90: M'path 3E 165
Stapleford Cft. B14: K Hth 5E 147
Stapleford Gro. DY8: Word 6C 92
Staplehall Rd. B31: N'fld 5F 145
Staplehurst Rd. B28: Hall G 5F 135
Staple Lodge Rd. B31: N'fld 6F 145
Stapleton Cl. B76: Walm 1F 87
Stapleton Dr. B37: F'bri 6D 106
Stapleton Rd. WS9: A'rdge 4B 34
Stapylton Av. B17: Harb 6F 115
Stapylton Ct. B17: Harb 6F 115
(off Old Church Rd.)
Starbank Rd. B10: Small H 3G 119
Starbold Cl. B93: Know 3D 166
Starbold Cres. B93: Know 4C 166
Star City 1D 102
Star Cl. DY4: Tip 2C 78
WS2: Wals 5F 31
Starcrest Ind. Est. DY5: Brie H 2A 110
Starcross Rd. R27: A Grn 3A 136
Star Hill B15: Edg 3D 116
Starkey Rd. B37: Chel W 1E 123
Starkie Dr. B68: O'bry 5A 98
Starley Way B37: Mars G 5E 123
Star St. DY9: Lye 6B 110
WV3: Wolv 3C 42
Start Point Trad. Est.
B11: S'hll 1D 134
Statham Dr. B16: Edg 1G 115
Station App. B73: S Cold 5H 53
B74: Four O 3F 37
B91: Sol 3E 151
B93: Dorr 6G 167
Station Av. B16: Edg 2G 115
Station Bldgs. B46: Wat O 4D 88
(off Minworth Rd.)
Station Cl. WS3: Blox 1H 31
WV8: Cod 4F 13
Station Dr. B28: Hall G 4F 135
B46: Wat O 4D 88
B74: Four O 3H 53
B92: Olton 4C 136
DY4: Tip 3B 78
DY5: Brie H 2F 109
(Meeting La.)

Station Dr. DY5: Brie H 1A 110
(The Boulevard)
DY9: Lye 5A 110
Station Link Rd. B26: Birm A 1F 139
B40: Nat E C 1F 139
Station M. B17: Harb 5G 115
Station Pl. WS3: Blox 1H 31
Station Rd. B6: Aston 6H 83
B14: K Hth 5F 133
B17: Harb 5G 115
B21: Hand 1G 99
B23: Erd 2F 85
B27: A Grn 2A 136
B30: K Nor 2A 146
B31: N'fld 5E 145
B33: Stech 5B 104
B37: Mars G 3B 122
B38: K Nor 3B 146
B46: Col 1H 107
B47: Wyt 6A 162
Station Rd. B64: Old H 2H 111
B65: Row R 1D 112
B69: O'bry 4G 97
B73: Bold, W Grn 4G 69
B91: Sol 3F 151
B92: H Ard 6B 140
B93: Dorr, Know 6C 166
CV7: Bal C 3G 169
DY5: Brie H 5G 93
DY9: Lye 5A 110
WS3: Pels 4E 21
WS4: Rus 3E 33
WS6: Gt Wyr 1F 7
WS7: Hamm 2G 11
WS9: A'rdge 4C 34
WV5: Wom 5G 57
WV8: Cod 4E 13
WV14: Bils 6G 45
Station Rd. Ind. Est. B65: Row R 1D 112
Station St. B5: Birm 6D 4 (2F 117)
B64: Crad H 3E 111
B73: S Cold 6H 53
DY4: Tip 2B 78
WS2: Wals 2B 48
WS3: Blox 1H 31
WS6: C Hay 2E 7
WS10: Darl 5E 47
Station Ter. WV14: Cose 4E 61
Station Way B37: Mars G 2F 139
B40: Nat E C 1F 139
Staulton Grn. B69: O'bry 5E 97
Staveley Rd. B14: K Hth 1F 147
WV1: Wolv 5G 27
Stead Cl. DY4: Tip 4B 62
WS2: Wals 4A 32
Steadman Cft. DY4: Tip 5D 62
STECHFORD 1C 120
Stechford Cascades 6C 104
Stechford La. B8: W End 4A 104
Stechford Retail Pk. B33: Stech 5C 104
Stechford Rd. B34: Hodg H 4B 104
Stechford Station (Rail) 6B 104
Stechford Trad. Est. B33: Stech 6C 104
Steel Bright Rd. B66: Smeth 3G 99
Steel Dr. WV10: Bush 1H 27
Steel Gro. B25: Yard 4A 120
Steelhouse La. B4: Birm . . .2E 5 (6G 101)
WV2: Wolv 2A 44
Steelmans Rd. WS10: Darl 4F 47
Steelpark Rd. B62: Hale 4B 112
Steelpark Way WV11: Wed 5F 29
Steel Rd. B31: N'fld 5D 144
Steene Gro. B31: N'fld 4B 144
Steeples, The DY8: Stourb 2F 125
Steepwood Cft. B30: K Nor 3H 145
Stella Cft. B37: Chel W 1E 123
Stella Rd. B43: Gt Barr 5F 65
Stella Rd. DY4: Tip 1H 77
Stenbury Cl. WV10: Bush 3B 16
Stencills Dr. WS4: Wals 6F 33
Stencills Rd. WS4: Wals 5F 33
Stennels Av. B62: Hale 1E 129
Stephens Cl. WV11: Wed 1H 29

Stephens Ind. Est. B11: Tys 1F 135
Stephenson Av. WS2: Wals 3G 31
Stephenson Dr. B37: Chel W 6D 106
    WV6: Pert 3E 25
Stephenson Pl. B2: Birm 4E 5 (1G 117)
Stephenson Sq. WS2: Wals 4H 31
Stephenson St. B2: Birm 4D 4 (1F 117)
    WV3: Wolv 2F 43
Stephenson Twr. B5: Birm 5D 4
Stephens Rd. B76: Walm 1E 71
Stepping Stone Cl. WS2: Wals 5F 31
Stepping Stones DY8: Stourb 6F 109
Steppingstone St. DY1: Dud 6D 76
Sterling Pk. DY5: Brie H 5B 94
Sterndale B42: Gt Barr 1E 83
Steven Dr. WV14: Bils 4G 61
Stevens Av. B32: Bart G 3B 130
Stevens Ga. WV2: Wolv 6B 170 (3G 43)
Stevens Dr. DY9: W'cte 3H 125
Steward St. B18: Hock 6C 100
Stewart Rd. DY6: K'wfrd 5B 92
    WS9: Wals W 4C 22
Stewarts Rd. B62: B'hth 4D 112
Stewart St. WV2: Wolv 6B 170 (3G 43)
Stewkins DY8: Word 3C 108
Steyning Rd. B26: Yard 6C 120
St Georges Stop (MM) 4C 170 (2H 43)
Stickley La. DY3: Lwr G 3G 75
Stilehouse Cres. B65: Row R 1C 112
Stilthouse Gro. B45: Redn 2G 157
STIRCHLEY 1C 146
Stirchley Indoor Bowling Cen. 6C 132
Stirchley Trad. Est. B30: Stir 6D 132
Stirling Ct. B16: Edg 2B 116
Stirling Cres. WV12: W'hall 3B 30
Stirling Rd. B16: Edg 2A 116
    B73: New O 3D 68
    B90: Shir 1C 164
    DY2: Dud 3G 95
    WV14: Bils 2H 61
Stirrup Cl. WS5: Wals 1D 64
Stockbridge Cl. WV6: Tett 1F 41
Stockdale Pl. B15: Edg 3H 115
Stock Exchange Bldg.
    B3: Birm 3C 4
STOCKFIELD 1B 136
Stockfield Rd. B25: Yard 1H 135
    B27: A Grn 1H 135
Stockhill Dr. B45: Rub 3F 157
Stocking St. DY9: Lye 6B 110
Stockland Cl. B74: S'tly 3A 52
STOCKLAND GREEN 3C 84
Stockland Green Community Leisure Cen.
    . . . . .3C 84
Stockland Rd. B23: Erd 3D 84
Stockley Cres. B90: Shir 4B 150
Stockmans Cl. B38: K Nor 1A 160
Stocks Wood B30: B'vlle 5B 132
Stockton Cl. B76: Min 2G 87
    B93: Know 5D 166
    WS2: Wals 5B 32
Stockton Ct. WV14: Cose 5D 60
Stockton Gro. B33: Kitts G 2H 121
Stockwell Av. DY5: Quar B 3H 109
STOCKWELL END 4B 26
Stockwell End WV6: Tett 3B 26
Stockwell Ri. B92: Sol 6H 137
Stockwell Rd. B21: Hand 5A 82
    WV6: Tett 4B 26
Stokes Av. DY4: Tip 5A 62
    WV13: W'hall 3H 45
Stokesay WV6: Pert 6F 25
Stokesay Cl. WV14: Cose 1A 96
Stokesay Gro. B31: Longb 1D 158
Stokesay Ho. B23: Erd 1F 85
Stokesay Ri. DY1: Dud 4A 76
Stokes St. WS3: Blox 1H 31
Stoke Way B15: Birm 6A 4 (2E 117)
Stom Rd. WV14: Bils 6D 44
Stoneacre Cl. WV3: Wolv 2G 41
Stone Av. B75: S Cold 6E 55
Stonebow Av. B91: Sol 1F 165
STONEBRIDGE 3C 140
Stonebridge Cres. B37: K'hrst 4B 106

Stonebridge Rd. B46: Col 2H 107
    (not continuous)
Stonebrook Way B29: W Cas 3D 130
Stonebury B15: Edg 3H 115
Stonechat Dr. B23: Erd 5C 84
Stone Cl. B38: K Nor 5B 146
Stonecroft Av. B45: Redn 2G 157
Stonecrop Cl. B38: K Nor 1B 160
    WS8: Clay 1H 21
Stonecross B46: Wat O 4D 88
Stonedown Cl. WV14: Cose 2C 60
Stonefield Dr. DY5: P'ntt 2E 93
Stonefield Rd. WV14: Bils 6F 45
Stonefield Wlk. WV14: Bils 6F 45
    (off Stonefield Rd.)
Stoneford Rd. B90: Shir 3G 149
Stonehaven Gro. B28: Hall G 5H 135
Stonehenge Cft. B14: K Hth 6F 147
Stone Hill Cft. B90: M'path 3D 164
Stonehouse Av. WV13: W'hall 5H 29
Stonehouse Cres. WS10: W'bry 3H 63
Stonehouse Dr. B74: Lit As 5C 36
Stonehouse Gro. B32: Bart G 3B 130
Stonehouse Hill B29: W Cas 2E 131
Stonehouse La. B32: Bart G 3B 130
Stonehurst Rd. B43: Gt Barr 1E 67
Stone Lea WS9: A'rdge 4D 34
Stoneleigh Cl. B71: W Brom 5C 64
Stoneleigh Cl. B74: Four O 3F 53
Stoneleigh Gdns. WV8: Cod 3F 13
Stoneleigh Ho. B32: Harb 6C 114
Stoneleigh Rd. B20: Hand 6G 83
    B91: Sol 2B 150
Stoneleigh Way DY3: Up Gor 1H 75
Stonepine Pl. DY3: Up Gor 1A 76
Stone Rd. B15: Edg 4F 117
Stonerwood Av. B28: Hall G 5E 135
Stones Grn. B23: Erd 1F 85
Stone St. B69: O'bry 2G 97
    DY1: Dud 6E 77
    WV14: Bils 6G 45
Stoneton Cres. CV7: Bal C 3G 169
Stoneton Gro. B29: W Cas 5E 131
Stone Yd. B12: Birm 6H 5 (2H 117)
    B64: Crad H 3E 111
Stoneybrook Leys WV5: Wom 2E 73
Stoney Cl. B92: Sol 6A 138
Stoneycroft Twr. B36: Hodg H 1C 104
Stoneyford Gro. B14: Yard W 3B 148
Stoneyhurst Rd. B24: Erd 6F 85
Stoney La. B12: Bal H 6B 118
    B25: Yard 3C 120
    B32: Quin 5H 113
    B71: W Brom 3B 80
    DY2: Neth 6E 95
    WS3: Blox 4H 19
    (not continuous)
    WV4: Penn 6F 43
Stoney Leasow B72: W Grn 3H 69
Stoneymoor Dr. B36: Cas B 6G 87
Stoneythorpe Cl. B91: Sol 6F 151
Stonnal Gro. B23: Erd 1G 85
STONNALL 3G 23
Stonnall Ga. WS9: A'rdge 1E 35
Stonnall Rd. WS9: A'rdge 1E 35
Stonor Pk. Rd. B91: Sol 2D 150
Stonor Rd. B28: Hall G 2G 149
Stony La. B67: Smeth 4D 98
Stony St. B67: Smeth 3D 98
Stornoway Rd. B35: Cas V 3F 87
Storrs Cl. B9: Small H 2D 118
Storrs Pl. B10: Small H 2D 118
Storrs Way, The B32: Bart G 6H 129
Stotfold Rd. B14: K Hth 5H 147
STOURBRIDGE 6E 109
Stourbridge Crematorium
    DY8: Stourb 1B 124
Stourbridge Ind. Est. DY8: Amb 5E 109
Stourbridge Junction Station (Rail) . . .2F 125
Stourbridge Lawn Tennis & Squash Club
    . . . . .4A 124
Stourbridge Rd. B63: Hale 6G 111
    DY1: Dud 4A 94

Stourbridge Rd. DY3: Himl 3A 74
    DY5: Brie H 4A 94
    DY9: Hag 6G 125
    DY9: Lye 6G 109
    WV4: Penn, Wom 4B 58
    WV5: Himl, Wom 2H 73
Stourbridge Rugby Football Club 5A 108
Stourbridge Town Station (Rail) 6E 109
Stour Cl. B63: Hale 5G 111
Stour Ct. B63: Hale 6B 112
Stourdale Rd. B64: Crad H 4E 111
Stourdell Rd. B63: Crad 5G 111
Stour Hill DY5: Quar B 4C 110
Stourmore Cl. WV12: W'hall 3D 30
Stour St. B18: Hock 6C 100
    B70: W Brom 4E 79
Stourton Cl. B76: Walm 1D 70
    B93: Know 2D 166
Stourton Dr. WV4: Penn 6A 42
Stourton Rd. B32: Quin 6H 113
Stour Va. Rd. DY9: Lye 5B 110
Stour Valley Cl. DY5: Quar B 4H 109
Stourville Ind. Est. DY9: Lye 5B 110
Stow Dr. DY5: Brie H 5F 109
Stowell Rd. B44: K'sdng 6H 67
Stowe St. WS3: Blox 2A 32
Stow Gro. B36: Hodg H 2C 104
STOW HEATH 4D 44
Stowheath La. WV1: Wolv 4D 44
Stow Heath Pl. WV1: Wolv 4D 44
STOW LAWN 3E 45
Stowmans Cl. WV14: Cose 2D 60
St Pauls Stop (MM) 1C 4 (5F 101)
Straight Rd. WV12: W'hall 3D 30
STRAITS, THE 3E 75
Straits, The DY3: Lwr G 2D 74
Straits Est. DY3: Lwr G 3E 75
Straits Grn. DY3: Lwr G 3F 75
Straits Rd. DY3: Lwr G 4F 75
Stratford Cl. DY1: Dud 5A 76
Stratford Ct. B72: S Cold 2H 69
    B90: Shir 1B 164
Stratford Dr. WS9: A'rdge 1E 35
Stratford Pl. B12: Birm 3A 118
Stratford Rd.
    B11: Hall G, S'brk, S'hll 4A 118
    B28: Hall G 3E 135
    B90: M'path, Shir 3C 164
    B94: H'ley H 6F 165
Stratford St. B11: S'hll 6C 118
    (not continuous)
Stratford St. Nth. B11: S'brk 3A 118
Stratford Wlk. B36: Hodg H 2A 104
Strathdene Gdns. B29: S Oak 4G 131
Strathdene Rd. B29: S Oak 3G 131
Strathern Dr. WV14: Cose 4C 60
Strathfield Wlk. WV4: Penn 5A 42
Strathmore Cres. WV5: Wom 4G 57
Strathmore Rd. DY4: Tip 5A 62
Stratton St. WV10: Wolv 5A 28
Strawberry Cl. B69: Tiv 2C 96
Strawberry Flds. CV7: Mer 4H 141
Strawberry La. WS6: Gt Wyr 5E 7
    WV13: W'hall 6E 29
Strawberry La. Ind. Est.
    WV13: W'hall 1E 45
Strawmoor La. WV8: Oaken, Cod 5B 12
Stray, The DY5: P'ntt 3G 93
Stream Mdw. WS4: S'fld 6G 21
Stream Pk. DY6: K'wfrd 5C 92
Stream Rd. DY6: K'wfrd 4B 92
    (Greenfields Rd.)
    DY6: K'wfrd 5C 92
    (Lesley Dr.)
    DY8: Word 4B 92
Streamside Way B92: Sol 1H 137
    WS4: S'fld 1H 33
Streatham Gro. B44: K'sdng 3A 68
Streather Rd. B75: R'ley 2A 54
STREETLY 2H 51
Streetly Crematorium WS9: A'rdge 1F 51
Streetly Cres. B74: Four O 6D 36
Streetly Dr. B74: Four O 6D 36
Streetly La. B74: Four O 1C 52

Streetly Rd. B23: Erd 2D **84**
Streetly Wood B74: S'tly 1A **52**
Streetly Youth & Sports Cen. 2A **52**
Streetsbrook Rd. B90: Shir, Sol 1H **149**
   B91: Sol .2C **150**
Streets Cnr. Gdns. WS9: Wals W 3C **22**
Streets La. WS6: Gt Wyr 5E **7**
Strensham Ct. B13: Mose 1G **133**
Strensham Hill B13: Mose 1G **133**
Strensham Rd. B12: Bal H 1G **133**
Stretton Ct. B24: Erd 5E **85**
Stretton Gdns. WV8: Cod 3F **13**
Stretton Gro. B8: W End 3A **104**
   B11: S'brk 5C **118**
     (off Sydenham Rd.)
   B19: Loz .2E **101**
Stretton Pl. DY2: Neth 5F **95**
   WV14: Cose 4C **60**
Stretton Rd. B90: Shir 1H **163**
   WV12: W'hall 1C **30**
Stringer Cl. B75: Four O 5G **37**
Stringes Cl. WV13: W'hall 6C **30**
Stringes La. WV13: W'hall 1B **46**
Strode Rd. WV2: Wolv 5G **43**
Stronsay Cl. B45: Fran 6F **143**
Stroud Av. WV12: W'hall 5C **30**
Stroud Cl. WV12: W'hall 5C **30**
Stroud Rd. B90: Shir 5F **149**
Strutt Cl. B15: Edg 3H **115**
Stuart Cres. DY2: Dud 6G **77**
Stuart Ho. B46: Col 2H **107**
Stuart Rd. B62: Quin 6F **113**
   B65: Row R 5C **96**
Stuarts Dr. B33: Stech 2B **120**
Stuarts Grn. DY9: Pedm 5F **125**
Stuarts Rd. B33: Stech 1B **120**
Stuart St. B7: Nech 2C **102**
   WS3: Blox 1H **31**
Stuarts Way B32: Bart G 6G **129**
STUBBERS GREEN 1A **34**
Stubbers Grn. Rd.
   WS4: K'rdge 6H **21**
   WS9: A'rdge 6H **21**
Stubbington Cl. WV13: W'hall 2F **45**
Stubbs Rd. WV3: Wolv 4E **43**
Stubby La. WV11: Wed 3H **29**
Stubley Dr. WV10: Wolv 3A **28**
Studland Rd. B28: Hall G 5G **135**
Stud La. B33: Stech 6D **104**
Studley Cft. B92: Sol 1H **137**
Studley Dr. DY5: Brie H 3G **109**
Studley Ga. DY8: Stourb 1B **124**
Studley Rd. WV3: Wolv 3A **42**
Studley St. B12: Bal H 5B **118**
Studley Twr. B12: Birm 4H **117**
     (off Canford Cl.)
Sturman Dr. B65: B'hth 2B **112**
Suckling Grn. La. WV8: Cod 5F **13**
Sudbury Cl. WV11: Wed 1G **29**
Sudbury Gro. B44: K'sdng 3B **68**
Sudeley Cl. B36: Cas B 6F **87**
Sudeley Gdns. DY1: Dud 5H **75**
Suffield Gro. B23: Erd 2B **84**
Suffolk Cl. B68: O'bry 5H **97**
   WV11: Wed 2E **29**
Suffolk Dr. DY5: Brie H 4G **109**
Suffolk Gro. WS9: A'rdge 1D **34**
Suffolk Ho. B23: Erd 2F **85**
Suffolk Pl. B1: Birm 6D **4** (2F **117**)
   WS2: Wals 4B **32**
Suffolk Rd. DY2: Dud 2C **94**
   WS10: W'bry 2A **64**
Suffolk St. Queensway
   B1: Birm 5C **4** (1F **117**)
Suffrage St. B66: Smeth 4F **99**
Sugar Loaf La. DY7: I'ley 5A **124**
Sugden Gro. B5: Birm 3G **117**
Sulgrave Cl. DY1: Dud 4B **76**
Sumburgh Cft. B35: Cas V 4E **87**
Summercourt Dr. DY6: K'wfrd 3A **92**
Summercourt Ho. B29: S Oak 4F **131**
Summercourt Sq. DY6: K'wfrd 4A **92**
Summer Cft. B19: Hock 3F **101**
Summer Dr. DY3: Lwr G 4G **75**

Summerfield Av. B70: W Brom 3A **80**
     (not continuous)
   DY6: W Hth 2A **92**
Summerfield Cen. 5A **100**
Summerfield Ct. B15: Edg 3G **115**
Summerfield Cres. B16: Edg 6A **100**
Summerfield Dr. B29: W Cas 6E **131**
Summerfield Gro. B18: Win G 5A **100**
Summerfield Ind. Est. B18: Win G . . .5C **100**
Summerfield Rd. B16: Edg 6A **100**
   B92: Olton 3E **137**
   DY2: Dud 2F **95**
   WV1: Wolv 1F **43**
Summerhills Av. B62: B'hth 3F **113**
Summergate DY3: Lwr G 4G **75**
SUMMER HILL 5A **62**
SUMMERHILL 5G **11**
Summer Hill B63: Hale 2B **128**
     (not continuous)
   DY6: K'wfrd 3A **92**
Summer Hill Ind. Pk. B1: Birm 6D **100**
     (off Anderton St.)
Summer Hill Rd. B1: Birm 6D **100**
   WV14: Cose 4F **61**
Summerhill Rd. DY4: Tip 6H **61**
Summer Hill St. B1: Birm 6D **100**
Summer Hill Ter. B1: Birm 3A **4** (6D **100**)
Summerhouse Rd. WV14: Cose 4C **60**
Summer La. B19: Birm, Hock . . .1D **4** (5F **101**)
   B76: Min 1H **87**
   DY3: Lwr G 4G **75**
   WS4: S'fld 5G **21**
Summerlee Rd. B24: Erd 5H **85**
Summer Rd. B15: Edg 4E **117**
     (not continuous)
   B23: Erd .2F **85**
   B27: A Grn 3G **135**
   B65: Row R 6D **96**
   DY1: Dud 3C **76**
Summer Row B31: Birm 3B **4** (6E **101**)
Summer St. B71: W Brom 3B **80**
   DY6: K'wfrd 3B **92**
   DY8: Stourb 6D **108**
   DY9: Lye .6A **110**
   WV13: W'hall 1H **45**
Summerton Rd. B69: O'bry 6D **78**
Summerville Ter. B17: Harb 6G **115**
Summit, The DY9: W'cte 1H **125**
Summit Cres. B66: Smeth 1C **98**
Summit Gdns. B63: Hale 2H **127**
Summit Pl. DY3: Gorn 5F **75**
Sumner Rd. B46: Col 3H **107**
Sunbeam Cl. B36: Cas B 6B **88**
Sunbeam Dr. WS6: Gt Wyr 2F **7**
Sunbeam St. WV2: Wolv 4G **43**
Sunbeam Way B33: Kitts G 1G **121**
Sunbury Cl. WV14: Cose 4G **61**
Sunbury Cotts. B31: N'fld 3E **145**
Sunbury Rd. B31: Longb 2C **158**
   B63: Hale 1H **127**
Suncroft B32: Quin 6A **114**
Sunbury Ri. B31: N'fld 2F **145**
Sunderland Dr. DY8: Amb 3E **109**
Sunderton Rd. B14: K Hth 2G **147**
Sundew Cft. B36: Hodg H 1B **104**
Sundial La. B43: Gt Barr 4B **66**
Sundour Cres. WV11: Wed 6D **16**
Sundridge Ct. B44: Gt Barr 2G **67**
Sundridge Rd. B44: Gt Barr 1G **67**
Sundridge Wlk. WV4: Penn 5A **42**
Sun Ho. B2: Birm 4D **4**
Sunleigh Gro. B27: A Grn 1C **136**
Sunningdale B62: Hale 1E **129**
Sunningdale Av. WV6: Pert 4D **24**
Sunningdale Cl. B20: Hand 3A **82**
   B73: W Grn 3A **69**
   DY8: Stourb 3D **124**
Sunningdale Dr. B69: Tiv 2A **96**
Sunningdale Rd. B11: Tys 2G **135**
   DY3: Sed 5F **59**
Sunningdale Way WS3: Blox 4G **19**
Sunny Av. B12: Bal H 6A **118**
Sunnybank Av. B44: K'sdng 6B **68**
Sunnybank Cl. WS9: A'rdge 1G **51**

Sunnybank Ct. B68: O'bry 4A **114**
Sunnybank Rd. B68: O'bry 4A **114**
   B73: Bold, W Grn 5G **69**
   DY3: Up Gor 2B **76**
Sunnydale Wlk. B71: W Brom 3A **80**
Sunnydene B8: W End 4G **103**
Sunny Hill Cl. WV5: Wom 1H **73**
Sunnymead Rd. B26: Sheld 5D **120**
Sunnymead Way B74: S'tly 4H **51**
Sunnymede Rd. DY6: K'wfrd 5E **93**
Sunnyside B69: Tiv 2B **96**
   WS9: Wals W 5C **22**
Sunnyside Av. B23: Erd 4E **85**
Sunnyside Cl. CV7: Bal C 5H **169**
Sunnyside La. CV7: Bal C 5H **169**
Sunnyside Ter. CV7: Bal C 5H **169**
Sunridge Av. B19: Hock 3F **101**
Sunrise Ct. B15: Edg 4F **117**
Sunrise Wlk. B68: O'bry 6A **98**
Sunset Cl. WS6: Gt Wyr 2F **7**
Sunset Pl. WV4: E'shll 2B **60**
Sun St. DY5: Quar B 2B **110**
   WS1: Wals 4B **48**
     (not continuous)
   WV1: Wolv 1A **44**
   WV10: Wolv 1A **44**
Surfeit Hill Rd. B64: Crad H 3F **111**
Surrey Cres. B71: W Brom 5G **63**
Surrey Dr. DY6: K'wfrd 5D **92**
   WV3: Wolv 2C **42**
Surrey Rd. B44: Gt Barr 1G **67**
   DY2: Dud 2C **94**
Surrey Wlk. WS9: A'rdge 6C **22**
Sussex Av. B71: W Brom 1A **80**
   WS9: A'rdge 1C **34**
   WS10: W'bry 1B **64**
Sussex Ct. B29: W Cas 6G **131**
Sussex Dr. WV3: Wolv 2C **42**
Sutherland Av. B90: Shir 4A **150**
   WV2: Wolv 3B **44**
Sutherland Cl. B43: Gt Barr 1F **67**
Sutherland Dr. B13: Mose 1H **133**
   WV5: Wom 5G **57**
Sutherland Gro. WV6: Pert 5F **25**
Sutherland Ho. WV1: Wolv 1E **43**
Sutherland Pl. WV2: Wolv . . .5D **170** (2H **43**)
Sutherland Rd. B64: Old H 3G **111**
   WS6: C Hay 2E **7**
   WV4: Penn 6F **43**
Sutherland St. B6: Aston 1B **102**
Sutton App. B8: W End 5G **103**
Sutton Arts Theatre 1A **70**
SUTTON COLDFIELD 6A **54**
Sutton Coldfield By-Pass
   B75: Bass P, S Cold 1F **55**
   B76: Min, Wis 1G **87**
Sutton Coldfield Crematorium
   B75: S Cold 1E **55**
Sutton Coldfield Station (Rail) 6H **53**
Sutton Coldfield Tennis & Squash Club
   . . . . .3H **69**
Sutton Ct. B43: Gt Barr 6A **66**
   B75: S Cold 4A **54**
   WV4: E'shll 3A **60**
Sutton Cres. B70: W Brom 4G **79**
Sutton Lodge B91: Sol 4E **151**
Sutton New Rd. B23: Erd 3F **85**
Sutton Oak Cnr. B73: S'tly 6A **52**
Sutton Oak Rd. B73: S'tly 1A **68**
Sutton Pk. 4E **53**
Sutton Pk. Ct. B72: W Grn 3H **69**
Sutton Pk. Vis. Cen. 6G **53**
Sutton Rd. B23: Erd 2G **85**
   WS1: Wals 3D **48**
   WS5: Wals 3F **49**
   WS10: Mox 6A **46**
Suttons Dr. B43: Gt Barr 1B **66**
Sutton Sq. B76: Min 1A **88**
Sutton St. B1: Birm 2F **117**
   B6: Aston 3H **101**
   DY8: Word 2C **108**
Suttton Rd. WS9: A'rdge 2A **50**
Swains Gro. B44: Gt Barr 1H **67**

Swale Gro. B38: K Nor 6B 146
WV13: W'hall 1D 46
Swale Rd. B76: Walm 4E 71
Swallow Av. B36: Cas B 1C 106
Swallow Cl. B12: Bal H 6B 118
DY2: Neth 1F 111
WS10: W'bry 1H 63
Swallow Ct. WV10: Bush 2H 27
Swallowdale WS9: Wals W 3D 22
WV6: Tett 1F 41
Swallowfall Av. DY8: Stourb 1A 124
Swallowfields Rd. DY3: Sed 3G 59
Swallows Cl. WS3: Pels 2E 21
Swallows Ind. Est., The B90: Shir . . .1B 164
Swallows Mdw. B90: Shir 1B 164
(not continuous)
Swallows Ri. Bus. Pk. DY5: Brie H . . .6A 94
Swallow St. B2: Birm 5C 4 (1F 117)
B70: W Brom 3G 79
Swanage Rd. B10: Small H 3D 118
Swan Av. B66: Smeth 2C 98
Swan Bank WV4: Penn 1D 58
Swan Cl. B8: Salt 3F 103
WS6: C Hay 3D 6
Swan Copse B25: Yard 6A 120
Swancote Dr. WV4: Penn 5A 42
Swancote Rd. B33: Stech 4D 104
DY1: Dud 6D 76
Swancote St. DY1: Dud 1C 94
Swan Courtyard B26: Yard 5B 120
Swan Cres. B69: O'bry 5F 97
Swancroft Rd. DY4: Tip 5H 61
Swan Dr. WS8: Bwnhls 6A 10
Swanfield Rd. DY8: Word 2D 108
Swanhurst Community Leisure Cen.
. . . . .6A 134
Swan Island B25: Yard 5B 120
Swan La. B70: W Brom 2G 79
DY8: Word 1D 108
Swan La. Ind. Est. B70: W Brom 2G 79
Swanley Cl. B62: Quin 2G 129
Swanmore Cl. WV3: Wolv 3C 42
Swann Rd. WV14: Cose 3C 60
Swann Wlk. DY4: Tip 5A 62
Swan Pool Gro. WS4: S'fld 6H 21
Swan Rdbt. B70: W Brom 2F 79
Swansbrook Gdns. B38: K Nor 5E 147
Swan Shop. Cen., The B25: Yard 5B 120
Swanshurst La. B13: Mose 5C 134
Swan St. DY2: Neth 3E 95
DY5: P'ntt 2G 93
DY8: Stourb 6C 108
WV1: Wolv 1B 44
Swanswell Rd. B92: Olton 5B 136
Swanswood Gro. B37: Chel W 6E 107
SWAN VILLAGE
B70 .2G 79
WV14 . . . . .6D 60
Swan Village B70: W Brom 2G 79
Swan Village Ind. Est. B70: W Brom . . .2G 79
Swarthmore Rd. B29: W Cas 6E 131
Sweetbriar La. WV12: W'hall 4D 30
Sweetbriar Rd. WV2: E'shll 4C 44
Sweetbrier Dr. DY8: Word 2C 108
Sweetman Pl. WV6: Wolv 6E 27
Sweetman St. WV6: Wolv 5D 26
(not continuous)
Sweetmoor Cl. B36: Cas B 1G 105
Swift Cl. B36: Cas B 1C 106
Swinbrook Gro. B44: Gt Barr 4G 67
Swinbrook Way B90: Shir 3B 150
Swincross Rd. DY8: Stourb 1F 125
Swindell Rd. DY9: Pedm 4G 125
SWINDON 5E 73
Swindon Rd. B17: Edg 6F 99
DY6: K'wfrd 1F 91
Swinford Gro. B93: Dorr 6A 166
Swinford Leys WV5: Wom 2D 72
Swinford Rd. B29: W Cas 2E 131
DY8: Stourb 3E 125
WV10: Wolv 4A 28
Swin Forge Way DY3: Swind 5E 73
Swiss Dr. DY8: Word 1D 108

Swynnerton Dr. WV11: Ess 3H 17
Sycamore Av. B12: Bal H 6A 118
Sycamore Cl. B24: Erd 4F 85
B76: Walm 3D 70
DY8: Stourb 3B 124
WS4: S'fld 1F 33
Sycamore Ct. B23: Erd 6C 68
B30: K Nor 3A 146
Sycamore Cres. B24: Erd 4F 85
B37: Mars G 3C 122
DY4: Tip 6H 61
Sycamore Dr. B47: H'wd 4A 162
WV3: Wolv 2B 42
(not continuous)
Sycamore Grn. DY1: Dud 2B 76
Sycamore Ho. B13: Mose 2A 134
B31: N'fld 4F 145
(off Rectory Rd.)
Sycamore Ind. Est. B21: Hand 2H 99
Sycamore Paddock DY8: Word 2E 109
Sycamore Pl. B67: Smeth 5D 98
WV14: Bils 2A 62
Sycamore Rd. B6: Aston 1A 102
B21: Hand 2H 99
B23: Erd 6F 69
B30: B'vlle 6B 132
B43: Gt Barr 2A 66
B66: Smeth 6F 99
B69: O'bry 5G 97
DY6: K'wfrd 3C 92
WS4: S'fld 1F 33
WS5: Wals 6D 48
WS10: W'bry 3G 63
Sycamores, The WV10: Bush 1B 28
Sycamore Ter. B14: K Hth 1E 147
Sycamore Way B27: A Grn 1A 136
Sydenham Rd. B11: S'brk 5C 118
B66: Smeth 2E 99
WV1: Wolv 1D 44
Sydney Cl. B70: W Brom 6G 63
Sydney Rd. B9: Bord G 1C 118
B64: Crad H 2E 111
B67: Smeth 1C 114
Sydney Way B34: S End 3A 106
Sylvan Av. B31: N'fld 4D 144
Sylvan Grn. B62: Hale 6D 112
Sylvan Grn. B90: Shir 2H 149
Sylvia Av. B31: Longb 1F 159
Symphony Ct. B16: Birm 1D 116
(off Delius Ho.)
Sytch La. WV5: Wom 2G 73

T

Tack Farm Rd. DY8: Word 2B 108
Tackford Cl. B36: Cas B 6G 87
Tackley Cl. B90: Shir 1H 163
Tadmore Cl. WV14: Bils 6E 45
Tadworth Cl. WV1: Wolv 1C 44
Tait Cft. B92: Sol 5B 138
Talaton Cl. WV9: Pend 5E 15
Talbot Av. B74: Lit As 6B 36
Talbot Cl. B23: Erd 5D 68
WS2: Wals 3A 32
Talbot Pas. DY8: Stourb 6E 109
(off Talbot St.)
Talbot Pl. WV14: Bils 5E 45
Talbot Rd. B66: Smeth 6E 99
DY2: Neth 5D 94
WV2: Wolv 5G 43
Talbots La. DY5: Brie H 2A 110
Talbot St. B18: Hock 3B 100
B63: Crad 5E 111
DY5: Brie H 6H 93
(Adelaide St.)
DY5: Brie H 6H 93
(Albion St.)
DY8: Stourb 6E 109
DY9: Lye 6B 110
Talbot Way B10: Small H 4F 119
Talfourd St. B9: Small H 2D 118
Talgarth Covert B38: K Nor 2A 160
Talke Rd. WS5: Wals 6D 48

Talladale B32: Bart G 6H 129
Tallington Rd. B33: Sheld 4G 121
Tall Trees Cl. B74: Four O 5D 36
WV12: W'hall 3D 30
Tall Trees Dr. DY9: Pedm 3H 125
Talton Cl. B90: M'path 4E 165
Tamar Cl. WS8: Bwnhls 3G 9
Tamar Dr. B36: Cas B 1B 106
B76: Walm 6F 71
DY3: Sed 1B 76
Tamar Gro. WV6: Pert 5E 25
WV13: W'hall 1C 46
Tamarisk Cl. B29: W Cas 5F 131
Tamar Ri. DY8: Amb 3E 109
Tame Av. WS10: W'bry 1H 63
Tame Bri. WS5: Wals 1D 64
Tame Bri. Factory Est. WS5: Wals . . .3F 65
Tamebridge Ind. Est. B42: P Barr 3G 83
Tame Bridge Parkway Station (Rail) . . .3D 64
Tame Cl. WS1: Wals 5C 48
Tame Cres. B71: W Brom 1A 80
Tame Crossing WS10: W'bry 4G 63
Tame Dr. WS3: Pels 6E 21
Tame Ri. B68: O'bry 3H 113
Tame Rd. B6: Witt 5A 84
B68: O'bry 3G 113
DY4: Tip 2C 78
Tame Rd. Ind. Est. B6: Witt 6A 84
Tamerton Rd. B32: Bart G 4B 130
Tameside Dr. B6: Witt 3H 83
B35: Cas V 6D 86
Tameside Way B42: P Barr 2G 83
Tame St. B70: W Brom 5F 63
WS1: Wals 5C 48
WV14: Bils 6H 45
Tame St. E. WS1: Wals 5D 48
Tamworth Cl. WS8: Bwnhls 3B 10
Tamworth Rd. B75: Bass P 1F 55
B75: S Cold 4A 54
Tanacetum Dr. WS5: Wals 2F 65
Tandy Ct. B14: K Hth 4H 147
Tandy Dr. B14: K Hth 4H 147
Tanfield Cl. WV6: Tett 6H 25
Tanfield Rd. B33: Stech 6D 104
DY2: Dud 2D 94
Tanford Rd. B92: Sol 2G 137
Tanglewood Cl. B32: Quin 6H 113
B34: S End 4G 105
Tanglewood Gro. DY3: Sed 3G 59
Tangmere Cl. WV6: Pert 4E 25
Tangmere Dr. B35: Cas V 5D 86
Tangmere Sq. B35: Cas V 4D 86
Tanhouse Av. B43: Gt Barr 6G 65
Tanhouse Farm Rd. B92: Sol 3G 137
Tanhouse La. B63: Crad 5D 110
Tanners Cl. B75: S Cold 4D 54
Tanners Ct. WS1: Wals 3C 48
Tanners Cl. WS2: Wals 6B 32
Tansey B74: Four O 4F 37
Tansey Ct. DY5: P'ntt 2F 93
TANSEY GREEN 2F 93
Tansey Grn. Rd. DY5: P'ntt 6E 75
Tansey Grn. Trad. Est. DY5: P'ntt 1F 93
Tansley Cl. B93: Dorr 5B 166
Tansley Gro. B44: K'sdng 4H 67
Tansley Hill Av. DY2: Dud 1H 95
Tansley Hill Rd. DY2: Dud 1G 95
Tansley Rd. B44: K'sdng 5H 67
Tansley Vw. WV2: Wolv 4H 43
Tantallon Dr. B32: Bart G 4B 130
Tantany La. B71: W Brom 3A 80
Tantarra St. WS1: Wals 2D 48
(not continuous)
Tanwood Cl. B91: Sol 1F 165
Tanworth Gro. B12: Bal H 5H 117
Tanworth La. B90: Shir 2H 163
Tanyards B27: A Grn 2A 136
Tapestries Av. B70: W Brom 3G 79
Tapton Cl. WS3: Blox 4A 20
Tarmac Rd. WV4: E'shll 6D 44
Tarragon Gdns. B31: Longb 5A 144
Tarrant Gro. B32: Harb 6D 114
Tarrington Covert B38: K Nor 1A 160
Tarry Hollow Rd. DY5: P'ntt 1F 93

Tarry Rd. B8: Salt 5E 103
Tarvin M. DY5: Brie H 2H 109
Taryn Dr. WS10: Darl 4D 46
Tasker St. B70: W Brom 3E 79
   WS1: Wals 3B 48
TAT BANK 3H 97
Tat Bank Rd. B68: O'bry 2G 97
   B69: O'bry 2G 97
Taunton Av. WV10: F'hses 3H 15
Taunton Cl. B31: Longb 4A 144
Taunton Rd. B12: Bal H 1A 134
Taverners Cl. WV12: W'hall 6C 18
Taverners Grn. B20: Hand 4B 82
Tavistock Rd. B27: A Grn 6A 136
Taw Cl. B36: Cas B 1B 106
Tay Cft. B37: F'bri 5E 107
Tay Gro. B38: K Nor 1B 160
   B62: B'hth 3E 113
Taylor Av. WS3: Blox 1B 32
Taylor Ho. WS2: Wals 4A 48
           (off Oxford St.)
Taylor Rd. B13: Mose 2H 147
   DY2: Neth 1G 111
   WV4: E'shll 6B 44
Taylors La. B67: Smeth 4D 98
   B69: O'bry 2E 97
   B71: W Brom 3B 80
Taylors Orchard B23: Erd 3B 84
Taylor St. WV11: Wed 4F 29
Taylor Way B69: Tiv 1B 96
Taynton Covert B30: K Nor 4E 147
Tay Rd. B45: Fran 6H 143
Taysfield Rd. B31: N'fld 1C 144
Taywood Dr. B10: Small H 4C 118
Tealby Gro. B29: S Oak 4C 132
Teal Dr. B23: Erd 4B 84
Teal Gro. WS10: Mox 2B 62
Teall Ct. B27: A Grn 2A 136
Teall Rd. B8: Salt 4E 103
Tean Cl. B11: Tys 2G 135
Teasdale Rd. WV11: Wed 1H 125
Teasel Rd. WV11: Wed 4G 29
Teazel Av. B30: B'vlle 1H 145
Tebworth Cl. WV9: Pend 5D 14
Tedbury Cres. B23: Erd 1E 85
Tedder Rd. WS2: Wals 1F 47
Teddesley Gro. B33: Kitts G 5G 105
Teddesley St. WS4: Wals 6D 32
Teddington Cl. B73: S Cold 3G 69
Teddington Gro. B42: P Barr 2E 83
Tedstone Rd. B32: Quin 6C 114
Teesdale Av. B34: Hodg H 3D 104
Teesdale Cl. WV1: Wolv 1C 44
Tees Gro. B38: K Nor 1B 160
Teignmouth Rd. B29: S Oak 3B 132
Telford Av. WS6: Gt Wyr 2F 7
Telford Cl. B67: Smeth 2B 114
   B71: W Brom 5G 63
   WS2: Wals 4G 31
Telford Gdns. WV3: Wolv 4B 42
Telford Rd. WS2: Wals 4G 31
Telford Way B66: Smeth 2D 98
Teme Gro. WV13: W'hall 1D 46
Teme Rd. B63: Crad 6D 110
   DY8: Stourb 2D 124
Tempest St. WV2: Wolv 4C 170 (2H 43)
Templars, The B69: O'bry 4E 97
Templars Wlk. WV13: W'hall 6A 30
Temple Av. B28: Hall G 1G 149
   CV7: Bal C 3F 169
TEMPLE BALSALL 5C 168
Temple Bar WV13: W'hall 1A 46
Temple Ct. B46: Col 6H 89
Templefield Gdns. B9: Bord G 2C 118
Templefield Sq. B15: Edg 4D 116
Templefield St. B9: Bord G 2C 118
Temple La. B93: Know 6A 168
Temple Mdws. Rd.
   B71: W Brom 2C 80
Templemore Dr. B43: Gt Barr 6A 66
Temple Pas. B2: Birm 4D 4 (1F 117)
Temple Rd. B93: Dorr 6C 166
   WV13: W'hall 6A 30

Temple Row B2: Birm 4D 4 (1F 117)
Temple Row W. B2: Birm 3D 4 (1F 117)
Temple Sq. WV13: W'hall 6B 30
Temple St. B2: Birm 4D 4 (1F 117)
   B70: W Brom 3A 80
   DY3: Lwr G 4H 75
   WV2: Wolv 4B 170 (2G 43)
   WV14: Bils 6G 45
Templeton Cl. B93: Dorr 6C 166
Templeton Rd. B44: Gt Barr 3G 67
Temple Way B46: Col 6G 89
   B69: Tiv 5C 78
Tempus Dr. WS2: Wals 2G 47
Tempus Ten WS2: Wals 2G 47
Tenacre La. DY3: Up Gor 1A 76
Ten Acre M. B30: Stir 5D 132
TEN ACRES 5D 132
Ten Acres End B30: Stir 5D 132
Ten Ashes La. B45: Coft H 5A 158
Tenbury Cl. WS2: Wals 6D 30
   WS9: A'rdge 1E 35
Tenbury Ct. WV4: Penn 6B 42
Tenbury Gdns. WV4: Penn 1B 58
Tenbury Ho. B63: Hale 2A 128
         (off Highfield La.)
Tenbury Rd. B14: K Hth 1F 147
Tenby Ct. B29: W Cas 6G 131
         (off Tugford Rd.)
Tenby Rd. B13: Mose 4D 134
Tenby St. B1: Birm 1A 4 (5D 100)
Tenby St. Nth. B1: Birm 1A 4 (5D 100)
Tenby Twr. B31: N'fld 6E 145
Tenlands Rd. B63: Hale 2H 127
Tennal Dr. B32: Harb 5D 114
Tennal Gro. B32: Harb 5D 114
Tennal La. B32: Harb 6C 114
Tennal Rd. B32: Harb 5C 114
Tennant St. B15: Birm 6A 4 (2D 116)
Tennis Ct. B30: K Nor 3H 145
Tennis Ct., The B15: Edg 6C 116
Tennis Ct. Flats B15: Edg 6C 116
Tennscore Av. WS6: C Hay 2E 7
Tennyson Av. B74: Four O 3F 37
Tennyson Ho. B31: Longb 1E 159
   B68: O'bry 5A 98
Tennyson Rd. B10: Small H 4E 119
   DY3: Lwr G 2E 75
   WS3: Blox 1C 32
   WV10: Bush 6C 16
   WV12: W'hall 1E 31
Tennyson St. DY5: P'ntt 3H 93
Tenter Cl. B63: Hale 1B 128
Tenter Dr. B63: Hale 1B 128
Tenterfields B63: Hale 1B 128
Tern Cl. WV4: E'shll 2H 59
Terrace, The B64: Crad H 3G 111
   WV3: Wolv 2A 42
Terrace Rd. B15: Edg 2B 132
   B19: Hock 2C 100
Terrace St. B65: Row R 2B 112
   DY5: Brie H 4A 94
   WS10: W'bry 2G 63
Terret Cl. WS1: Wals 1D 48
Terry Dr. B76: Walm 4D 70
Terrys La. B24: Erd 4A 86
Terry St. DY2: Dud 6F 77
Tessall La. B31: Longb 6H 143
         (not continuous)
Tetbury Gro. B31: N'fld 4B 144
Tetley Av. WS4: Wals 5F 33
Tetley Rd. B11: S'hll 2E 135
Tetnall St. DY2: Dud 1F 95
TETTENHALL 5A 26
Tettenhall Rd. WV1: Wolv 5C 26
   WV3: Wolv 5C 26
   WV6: Wolv 5C 26
TETTENHALL WOOD 6H 25
Teviot Gdns. DY5: P'ntt 3E 93
   WV13: W'hall 2G 13
Teviot Gro. B38: K Nor 1B 160
Teviot Twr. B19: Birm 4E 101
      (off Mosborough Cres.)
Tewkesbury Dr. DY2: Neth 6F 95

Tewkesbury Rd. B20: Hand 6G 83
   WS3: Blox 5E 19
Tew Pk. Rd. B21: Hand 2A 100
Thackeray Rd. B30: B'vlle 2H 145
Thames Cl. DY5: P'ntt 2F 93
Thames Ct. B47: Wyt 6G 161
        (off Chapel La.)
   B73: S Cold 6H 53
Thames Gdns. WV14: Cose 4C 60
Thames Rd. WS3: Blox 1B 32
Thames Twr. B7: Nech 4B 102
Thanet Cl. DY6: K'wfrd 3A 92
Thanet Gro. B42: P Barr 3E 83
Thatchers, The B62: B'hth 3E 113
Thatchway Gdns. B38: K Nor 2A 160
Thaxted Rd. B33: Kitts G 6A 106
The . . . .
   Names prefixed with 'The' for example
   'The Academy' are indexed under the
   main name such as 'Academy, The'
Theatre App. B5: Birm 6E 5 (2G 117)
Thelbridge Rd. B31: Longb 3C 158
Thelma Rd. DY4: Tip 2G 77
Thelma St. WS1: Wals 4B 48
Thelsford Way B92: Sol 5H 137
Theodore Cl. B17: Harb 1H 131
   B69: O'bry 6E 79
Theresa Rd. B11: S'brk 4B 118
Thetford Cl. DY4: Tip 2F 77
Thetford Gdns. WV11: Wed 3F 29
Thetford Rd. B42: Gt Barr 6D 66
Thetford Way WS5: Wals 2G 65
Thickett Cl. WS2: Wals 3H 47
Thicknall Dr. DY9: Pedm 3F 125
Thimble Dr. B76: Walm 4D 70
THIMBLE END 4D 70
Thimble End Ct. B76: Walm 3E 71
Thimble End Rd. B76: Walm 2D 70
Thimble La. B93: Know 3E 167
Thimble Mill La. B6: Aston 2B 102
   B7: Nech 2B 102
Thimblemill Rd. DG7: Smeth 5B 98
Thinktank 3H 5 (6H 101)
Third Av. B6: Witt 4H 83
   B9: Bord G 1F 119
   B29: S Oak 2E 133
   DY6: P'ntt 1D 92
   WS8: Bwnhls 4C 10
   WV10: Bush 2A 28
Third Exhibition Av. B40: Nat E C 1F 139
Third Rd. B61: Wild 5A 156
Thirlmere Cl. WV6: Tett 1B 26
Thirlmere Dr. B13: Mose 5C 134
   WV11: Ess 5A 18
Thirlmere Gro. WV6: Pert 5F 25
Thirlmere Ho. B15: Edg 2H 131
Thirlmere Rd. WV6: Tett 1B 26
Thirlmere Wlk. DY5: Brie H 4F 109
Thirsk Cft. B36: Hodg H 1A 104
Thirston Cl. WV11: Wed 4A 30
Thistle Cl. DY3: Sed 1B 76
   WV11: Wed 4F 29
Thistle Down Cl. B74: S'tly 1A 52
Thistledown Rd. B34: S End 2G 105
Thistledown Wlk. DY3: Sed 4G 59
Thistle Grn. B38: K Nor 2A 160
Thistlegreen Cl. B65: Row R 4H 95
Thistlegreen Rd. DY2: Neth 5G 95
Thistle Ho. B36: Hodg H 1B 104
Thistle La. B32: Bart G 5H 129
Thomas Benson Pl. B12: Birm 4H 117
Thomas Cres. B66: Smeth 4G 99
Thomas Guy Rd. B70: W Brom 6E 63
Thomas Ho. WS3: Blox 4B 20
Thomas Mason Cl. WV11: Wed 2F 29
Thomas St. B6: Aston 3H 101
   B66: Smeth 4F 99
   B70: W Brom 5B 80
   WS2: Wals 1B 48
   WV2: Wolv 6B 170 (3G 43)
Thomas Wlk. B35: Cas V 4F 87
Thompson Av. WV2: Wolv 4H 43
Thompson Cl. DY2: Neth 1D 110
   WV13: W'hall 6A 30

Thompson Dr. B24: Erd 1F 103
Thompson Gdns. B67: Smeth 5D 98
Thompson Ho. DY4: Tip 5C 62
Thompson Rd. B67: Smeth 5D 98
  B68: O'bry 5H 97
Thompson St. WV13: W'hall 6A 30
  WV14: Bils 6F 45
Thomson Av. B38: K Nor 6G 145
Thoresby Cft. DY1: Dud 4B 76
Thornberry Dr. DY1: Dud 1H 93
Thornberry Wlk. B7: Nech 3C 102
Thornbridge Av. B42: Gt Barr 6E 67
Thornbridge Gro. WS9: Wals W 4B 22
Thorn Brook Cl. WS4: Wals 6D 32
                              (off Butts Rd.)
Thornbury Ct. WV6: Pert 6G 25
Thornbury Rd. B20: Hand 5F 83
Thornby Av. B91: Sol 2F 151
Thornby Rd. B23: Erd 5C 68
Thorncliffe Rd. B44: Gt Barr 3G 67
Thorn Cl. WS10: W'bry 1F 63
Thorncroft Way WS5: Wals 1F 65
Thorne Av. WV10: Bush 2A 28
Thorne Pl. B65: Row R 1C 112
Thorne Rd. WV13: W'hall 6A 30
THORNES .4G 23
Thornes Cft. WS9: Ston 3G 23
Thorne St. WV2: E'shll 4C 44
Thorneycroft La. WV10: Wolv 4C 28
Thorneycroft Pl. WV14: Bils 2B 62
Thorneycroft Rd. WV14: Bils 2A 62
Thorney Rd. B74: S'tly 2H 51
Thornfield Cft. DY3: Sed 6A 60
Thornfield Rd. B27: A Grn 3A 136
Thorngrove Av. B91: Sol 1G 165
Thornham Way B14: K Hth 6F 147
Thornhill Gro. B21: Hand 1B 100
Thornhill Pk. B74: S'tly 3A 52
Thornhill Rd. B11: S'hll 2D 134
  B21: Hand 2B 100
  B63: Hale 2G 127
  B74: S'tly 5A 52
  B91: Sol .6G 137
  DY1: Dud 3E 77
  DY5: Quar B 2A 110
Thornhurst Av. B32: Quin 4C 114
Thornleigh DY3: Up Gor 2H 75
Thornleigh Trad. Est. DY2: Dud 2C 94
Thornley Cl. B13: Mose 4A 134
  WV11: Wed 6H 17
Thornley Cft. WS6: C Hay 4D 6
Thornley Gro. B76: Min 1G 87
Thornley Rd. WV11: Wed 6H 17
Thornley St. WV1: Wolv . . . 2C 170 (1H 43)
Thorn Rd. B30: B'ville 6A 132
Thorns Av. DY5: Quar B 2A 110
Thornsett Gro. B90: Shir 1H 149
Thorns Leisure Cen. 3A 110
Thorns Rd. DY5: Quar B 4A 110
Thornthwaite Cl. B45: Fran 5H 143
Thornton Cl. B69: Tiv 5C 78
Thornton Dr. DY5: Brie H 2A 110
Thornton Ho. B19: Hock 4G 101
                         (off Ruddington Way)
Thornton Rd. B8: W End 4H 103
  B90: M'path 3D 164
  WV1: Wolv 2D 44
Thornwood Cl. B68: O'bry 4A 98
Thornyfield Cl. B90: Shir 4A 150
Thornyfield Rd. B90: Shir 4A 150
Thornyhurst La.
  WS14: Hilt, Lynn . . . . . . .6H 11 & 1H 23
Thorpe Cl. B75: S Cold 3A 54
Thorpe Ct. B91: Sol 1D 150
Thorpe Rd. WS1: Wals 4C 48
Thorp St. B5: Birm 6D 4 (2F 117)
Three Acres La. B90: Dic H 3F 163
Three Cnr. Cl. B90: Maj G 1E 163
THREE MAYPOLES 3H 163
Three Oaks Rd. B47: Wyt 5B 162
Three Shires Oak Rd. B67: Smeth . . .1D 114
Three Tuns La. WV10: Oxl 5G 15
Three Tuns Pde. WV10: Oxl 5G 15
Threshers Dr. WV12: W'hall 3D 30

Threshers Way WV12: W'hall 3D 30
Throne Cl. B65: Row R 4C 96
Throne Cres. B65: Row R 4D 96
Throne Rd. B65: Row R 4C 96
Throstles Cl. B43: Gt Barr 6A 66
Thrushel Wlk. WV11: Wed 4E 29
Thrush Rd. B68: O'bry 1F 113
Thruxton Cl. B14: K Hth 4H 147
Thunderbolt Way DY4: Tip 1F 77
Thurcroft Cl. B8: W End 5F 103
Thuree Rd. B67: Smeth 1C 114
Thurleigh Cl. DY9: Pedm 3G 125
Thurloe Cres. B45: Fran 6E 143
Thurlstone Dr. WV4: Penn 1D 58
Thurlstone Rd. WS3: Blox 4H 19
Thursfield Rd. B71: W Brom 5C 64
  DY4: Tip .1A 78
Thurston Av. B69: O'bry 3F 97
Thynne St. B70: W Brom 5C 80
Tibbats Cl. B32: Bart G 2A 130
Tibberton Cl. B63: Hale 2C 128
  B91: Sol .1E 165
  WV3: Wolv 4B 42
Tibbets La. B17: Harb 1E 131
Tibbington Rd. DY4: Tip 6G 61
Tibbington Ter. DY4: Tip 6G 61
Tibbits Ho. WS2: Wals 6B 32
                          (off Burrowes St.)
Tiddlestone B90: Dic H 4G 163
Tiberius Cl. B46: Col 6H 89
Tibland Rd. B27: A Grn 4A 136
TIDBURY GREEN 5E 163
Tiddington Cl. B36: Cas B 6F 87
Tideswell Rd. B42: Gt Barr 1E 83
Tidmarsh Cl. CV7: Bal C 3G 169
Tidworth Cft. B14: K Hth 4A 148
Tierney Dr. DY4: Tip 1C 78
Tiffany La. WV9: Pend 5D 14
Tiffield Rd. B25: Yard 6A 120
Tigley Av. B32: Bart G 4B 130
Tilbury Cl. WV3: Wolv 3G 41
Tilbury Gro. B13: Mose 4F 133
Tildasley St. B70: W Brom 2H 79
Tildesley Dr. WV12: W'hall 4B 30
TILE CROSS 1G 121
Tile Cross Rd. B33: Kitts G 2H 121
Tile Cross Trad. Est.
  B33: Kitts G 2H 121
Tiled Ho. La. DY5: P'ntt 4F 93
Tile Gro. B37: K'hrst 4C 106
TILEHOUSE GREEN 2B 166
Tilehouse Grn. La. B93: Know 2B 166
Tilehouse La. B90: Tid G 5E 163
Tilesford Cl. B90: M'path 4E 165
Tiller Gro. B75: R'ley 5B 38
Tilley St. WS10: Darl 5E 47
Tillyard Cft. B29: S Oak 4G 131
Tilshead Cl. B14: K Hth 4G 147
Tilsley Gro. B23: Erd 2B 84
Tilston Dr. DY5: Brie H 2H 109
Tilton Rd. B9: Bord G 2C 118
                         (not continuous)
Timbercombe Way B21: Hand 1H 99
Timberdine Cl. B63: Crad 5F 111
Timberlake Cl. B90: M'path 3F 165
Timberley Cft. B34: S End 4H 105
Timberley La. B34: S End 3G 105
Timber Mill Ct. B17: Harb 5F 115
Timbers Way B11: S'brk 5A 118
  B24: Erd .3D 86
Timbertree Cres. B64: Crad H 4G 111
Timbertree Rd. B64: Crad H 4G 111
Times Sq. Av. DY5: Brie H 1A 110
Timmins Cl. B91: Sol 2A 152
Timmins Rd. WV14: Cose 2D 60
Timmis Rd. DY9: Lye 5G 109
Timothy Rd. B69: Tiv 2C 96
Tinacre Hill WV6: Tett 1E 41
Tinchbourne St. DY1: Dud 6E 77
Tindal St. B12: Bal H 6H 117
Tinker's Farm Gro. B31: N'fld 4C 144
Tinker's Farm Rd. B31: N'fld 4C 144

Tinmeadow Cres. B45: Redn 2A 158
Tinsley Av. B64: Old H 2G 111
Tinsley St. DY4: Tip 2E 79
Tintagel Cl. WV6: Pert 6F 25
Tintagel Dr. DY1: Dud 5A 76
Tintagel Way WS9: A'rdge 3A 34
Tintern Cl. B74: S'tly 4A 52
Tintern Ct. WV6: Pert 5E 25
Tintern Cres. WS3: Blox 4F 19
Tintern Ho. B32: Harb 6D 114
Tintern Rd. B20: Hand 6G 83
Tintern Vs. B12: Bal H 6B 118
                      (off Chesterton Rd.)
Tintern Way WS3: Blox 5F 19
Tipperary Cl. B36: Hodg H 1C 104
Tipperary Wlk. B69: O'bry 2F 97
Tipper Trad. Est. DY9: Lye 6C 110
Tippity Grn. B65: Row R 5B 96
Tipps Stone Cl. DY4: Tip 3G 77
TIPTON 2F 77
Tipton Ind. Est. WV14: Cose 6F 61
Tipton Leisure Cen. 4A 62
Tipton Rd. B69: Tiv 4B 78
  DY1: Dud 3G 77
  DY3: Sed .6A 60
Tipton Station (Rail) 1H 77
Tipton St. DY3: Sed 6A 60
Tipton Swimming Cen. 2H 77
Tipton Trad. Est. WV14: Cose 6F 61
Tirley Rd. B33: Stech 4E 105
Titania Cl. B45: Fran 4H 143
Titchfield Cl. WV10: Bush 3A 16
Titford Cl. B69: O'bry 5F 97
Titford La. B65: Row R 5E 97
Titford Rd. B69: O'bry 5F 97
                        (not continuous)
Tithe Cft. WV10: Wolv 6B 28
Tithe Rd. WV11: Wed 3F 29
Titterstone Rd. B31: Longb 1E 159
Tiverton Cl. DY6: K'wfrd 6D 92
Tiverton Dr. B71: W Brom 1A 80
Tiverton Gro. B67: Smeth 3D 98
                          (off Dibble Rd.)
Tiverton Rd. B29: S Oak 3B 132
  B66: Smeth 4F 99
Tiverton Road Pool & Fitness Cen. . . .3B 132
TIVIDALE 6A 78
Tividale Rd. B69: Tiv 5H 77
  DY4: Tip .5H 77
Tividale St. DY4: Tip 4A 78
Tivoli, The B25: Yard 5B 120
                          (off Church Rd.)
Tixall Rd. B28: Hall G 2E 149
Toadnest La. WV6: Pert 6A 24
Toberland WS2: Wals 2H 31
Tobruk Wlk. DY5: Brie H 6H 93
  WV13: W'hall 2G 45
Toll End Rd. DY4: Tip 6C 62
Tollgate Cl. B31: Longb 1D 158
Tollgate Dr. B20: Hand 2C 100
Tollgate Pct. B67: Smeth 3D 98
Toll Ho. Rd. B45: Redn 2A 158
Tollhouse Way B66: Smeth 2D 98
  WV5: Wom 6E 57
Tolworth Gdns. WV2: Wolv 4A 44
Tolworth Hall Rd. B24: Erd 4H 85
Tomey Rd. B11: S'brk 6D 118
Tomlan Rd. B31: Longb 2G 159
Tomlinson Rd. B36: Cas B 6H 87
Tompstone Rd. B71: W Brom 5D 64
Tonadine Cl. WV11: Wed 6A 18
Tonbridge Rd. B24: Erd 6G 85
Tong Ct. WV1: Wolv 5G 27
                       (off Boscobel Cres.)
Tong St. WS1: Wals 2E 49
Topcroft Rd. B23: Erd 6F 69
Topfield Ho. B14: K Hth 6G 147
Top Fld. Wlk. B14: K Hth 5F 147
Topland Gro. B31: Longb 3A 144
Top Rd. B61: Wild 4A 156
Topsham Cft. B14: K Hth 2F 147
Topsham Rd. B67: Smeth 3C 98
Torfield WV8: Pend 5C 14
Tor Lodge Dr. WV6: Tett 1H 41

Toronto Gdns. B32: Harb 5C **114**
Torre Av. B31: N'fld 5C **144**
Torrey Gro. B8: W End 5A **104**
Torridge Dr. WV11: Wed 4E **29**
Torridon Cft. B13: Mose 2F **133**
Torridon Rd. WV12: W'hall 6B **18**
Torvale Rd. WV6: Tett 1G **41**
Tor Way WS3: Pels 4D **20**
Totnes Gro. B29: S Oak 3B **132**
Totnes Rd. B67: Smeth 3D **98**
Tottenham Cres. B44: K'sdng 3B **68**
Touchwood Hall Cl. B91: Sol 3G **151**
Touchwood Shop. Cen. B91: Sol 4G **151**
Tourist Info. Cen.
  Birmingham International 1F **139**
  Birmingham, Broad St.
  . . . . .4A **4** (1E **117**)
  Birmingham, Corporation St.
  . . . . .4E **5** (1G **117**)
  Birmingham, St Martin's Queensway
  . . . . .5E **5** (1G **117**)
  Dudley 6F **77**
  Solihull 4G **151**
  Wolverhampton 3B **170** (1G **43**)
Towcester Cft. B36: Hodg H 1B **104**
Tower Cft. B37: F'bri 5D **106**
TOWER HILL 1D **82**
Tower Hill B42: Gt Barr 1C **82**
Tower Ri. B69: Tiv 2C **96**
Tower Rd. B6: Aston 2H **101**
  (not continuous)
  B23: Erd 4E **85**
  B69: Tiv 2B **96**
  B75: Four O 6H **37**
Tower St. B19: Dirm 4F **101**
  DY1: Dud 6E **77**
  DY3: Sed 4H **59**
  WS1: Wals 1C **48**
  WV1: Wolv 3C **170** (1H **43**)
Tower Vw. Rd. WS6: Gt Wyr 5F **7**
Tower Works Ind. Est. WV3: Wolv 2E **43**
Town End Sq. WS1: Wals 1C **48**
  (off Park St.)
Townend St. WS2: Wals 1C **48**
Town Fold WS3: Pels 3E **21**
Town Ga. Retail Pk. DY1: Dud 5H **77**
Town Hall Stop (MM) 4A **80**
Townley Gdns. B6: Aston 6G **83**
Townsend Av. DY3: Sed 5H **59**
Townsend Dr. B76: Walm 6D **70**
Townsend Pl. WV4: W'frd 3B **92**
Townsend Way B1: Birm 3A **4** (6D **100**)
Townshend Gro. B37: K'hrst 5B **106**
Townson Rd. WV11: Wed 1A **30**
Townwell Fold WV1: Wolv 3A **170** (1G **43**)
Town Wharf Bus. Pk. WS2: Wals 2B **48**
Town Yd. WV13: W'hall 2A **46**
Towpath Cl. B9: Birm 1B **118**
Towpath Way B14: K Hth 3E **147**
Towyn Rd. B13: Mose 3D **134**
Toy's La. B63: Crad 6E **111**
Tozer St. DY4: Tip 6H **61**
Traceys Mdw. B45: Redn 2G **157**
Tractor Spares Ind. Est.
  WV13: W'hall 1F **45**
Trafalgar Ct. B69: Tiv 6B **78**
Trafalgar Gdns. B25: Yard 5G **119**
Trafalgar Rd. B13: Mose 2H **133**
  B21: Hand 1A **100**
  B24: Erd 4F **85**
  B66: Smeth 5F **99**
  B69: Tiv 6B **78**
Trafalgar Ter. B66: Smeth 5F **99**
Trajan Hill B46: Col 6H **89**
Tram Way B66: Smeth 2A **98**
Tramway WS10: Darl 4E **47**
  WV14: Bils 4H **45**
Tranter Rd. B8: W End 4G **103**
Tranwell Cl. WV9: Pend 5D **14**
Traquain Dr. DY1: Dud 4C **76**
Travellers Way B37: Chel W 6F **107**
Treaford La. B8: W End 5H **103**
Treddles La. B70: W Brom 4B **80**
Tredington Cl. B29: W Cas 6E **131**

Tree Acre Gro. B63: Crad 1E **127**
Treeford Cl. B91: Sol 6D **150**
Treeside Way B31: N'fld 5E **145**
Trees Rd. WS1: Wals 5D **48**
Treeton Cft. B33: Yard 1E **121**
Tree Tops WV5: Wom 5E **57**
Treetops Dr. WV12: W'hall 4E **31**
Trefoil Cl. B29: W Cas 6E **131**
  (not continuous)
Trefoil Gdns. DY8: Amb 5E **109**
Tregaron Dr. B31: N'fld 1C **144**
Tregarron Rd. B63: Crad 6E **111**
Tregea Ri. B43: Gt Barr 6G **65**
Trehern Cl. B93: Know 4C **166**
Trehernes Dr. DY9: Pedm 4F **125**
Trehurst Av. B42: Gt Barr 5E **67**
Trejon Rd. B64: Crad H 3G **111**
Tremaine Gdns. WV10: Wolv 5H **27**
Tremont Ho. WV10: Wolv 6A **28**
Tremont St. WV10: Wolv 6A **28**
Trenchard Cl. B75: S Cold 6D **54**
Trent Cl. DY8: Stourb 1E **125**
  WV6: Pert 5E **25**
Trent Ct. B73: S Cold 6H **53**
Trent Cres. B47: Wyt 6G **161**
Trent Dr. B36: Cas B 1B **106**
Trentham Av. WV12: W'hall 4A **30**
Trentham Gro. B26: Yard 6C **120**
Trentham Ho. WV2: E'shll 4B **44**
Trent Pl. WS3: Blox 1B **32**
Trent Rd. WS3: Pels 6E **21**
Trent St. B5: Birm 5H **5** (1H **117**)
Trent Twr. B7: Birm 5A **102**
Trenville Av. B11: S'hll 6B **118**
  B12: Bal H 6B **118**
Tresco Cl. B45: Fran 6E **143**
TRESCOTT 4B **40**
Trescott Rd. B31: N'fld 4B **144**
Tresham Rd. B44: Gt Barr 4G **67**
  DY6: K'wfrd 1B **92**
Trevanie Av. B32: Quin 5A **114**
Trevelyan Ho. B37: Chel W 2E **123**
Trevor Av. WS6: Gt Wyr 2G **7**
Trevorne Cl. B12: Bal H 5H **117**
Trevor Rd. WS3: Pels 3D **20**
Trevor St. B7: Nech 3C **102**
Trevor St. W. B7: Nech 3C **102**
Trevose Cl. WS3: Blox 4F **19**
Trevose Retreat B12: Bal H 6H **117**
Trewman Cl. B76: Walm 5D **70**
Treyamon Rd. WS5: Wals 4H **49**
Treynham Cl. WV1: Wolv 2E **45**
TRIANGLE 1D **10**
Triangle, The B18: Hock 3A **100**
Trickley Dr. B75: S Cold 5D **54**
Tricorn Ho. B16: Edg 2C **116**
Trident Blvd. B35: Cas V 5F **87**
Trident Cen. DY1: Dud 6E **77**
Trident Cl. B23: Erd 6G **69**
  B76: Walm 6D **70**
Trident Ct. B20: Hand 4C **82**
  B37: Mars G 3G **123**
Trident Dr. B68: O'bry 4H **97**
  WS10: W'bry 2D **62**
Trident Ho. B15: Birm 6A **4** (2E **117**)
Trident Retail Pk. B9: Birm 1A **118**
Trident Rd. B26: Birm A 1E **139**
Trigen Ho. B90: Bly P 6D **164**
Trigo Cft. B36: Hodg H 1C **104**
Trimpley Cl. B93: Dorr 6A **166**
Trimpley Gdns. WV4: Penn 2C **58**
Trimpley Rd. B32: Bart G 5H **129**
Trinder Rd. B67: Smeth 1B **114**
Trindle Cl. DY2: Dud 6F **77**
Trindle Rd. DY2: Dud 6F **77**
Trinity Cl. DY8: Word 1B **108**
Trinity Cen. B64: Old H 1G **111**
Trinity Cl. B92: Olton 4F **137**
  DY8: Word 1B **108**
Trinity Ct. B6: Aston 6F **83**
  B13: Mose 3B **134**
  B64: Old H 2G **111**
  WV3: Wolv 1E **43**
  WV13: W'hall 2G **45**

Trinity Gro. WS10: W'bry 2G **63**
Trinity Hill B72: S Cold 6A **54**
Trinity Pk. B37: Mars G 2F **139**
Trinity Pl. B72: S Cold 6A **54**
Trinity Rd. B6: Aston 6F **83**
  B75: Four O 2H **53**
  DY1: Dud 6E **77**
  DY8: Amb 3E **109**
  WV12: W'hall 3D **30**
Trinity Rd. Nth. B70: W Brom 6B **80**
  (not continuous)
Trinity Rd. Sth. B70: W Brom 6B **80**
Trinity St. B64: Old H 2G **111**
  B67: Smeth 3E **99**
  B69: O'bry 4G **97**
  B70: W Brom 5B **80**
  DY5: Brie H 6H **93**
Trinity Ter. B11: S'brk 3A **118**
Trinity Way B20: Hand 6D **82**
  B70: W Brom 6B **80**
Trinity Way Stop (MM) 6B **80**
Trippleton Av. B32: Bart G 5H **129**
Tristram Av. B31: N'fld 6F **145**
Triton Cl. WS6: Gt Wyr 4F **7**
Trittiford Rd. B13: Mose 1B **148**
Triumph Wlk. B36: Cas B 6C **88**
Tromans Cl. B64: Crad H 4G **111**
Tromans Ind. Est. DY2: Neth 6F **95**
Troon Cl. B75: S Cold 3B **54**
  WS3: Blox 4G **19**
Troon Ct. WV6: Pert 4D **24**
Troon Pl. DY8: Word 6A **92**
Trostrey Rd. B14: K Hth 4F **147**
  B30: K Nor 4F **147**
Trotter's La. B71: W Brom 6G **63**
Trouse La. WS10: W'bry 2F **63**
Troutbeck Dr. DY5: Brie H 3F **109**
Troy Gro. B14: K Hth 3F **147**
Truck Stop Bus. Pk. B11: Tys 6H **119**
Truda St. WS1: Wals 4B **48**
TRUEMAN'S HEATH 2C **162**
Trueman's Heath La. B47: H'wd 2B **162**
  B90: Maj G 2B **162**
Trundalls La. B90: Dic H 4G **163**
Truro Cl. B65: Row R 5E **97**
Truro Rd. WS5: Wals 4H **49**
Truro Twr. B16: Birm 1C **116**
Truro Wlk. B37: Chel W 1C **122**
Trustin Cres. B92: Sol 5A **138**
Tryon Pl. WV14: Bils 5G **45**
TRYSULL .4C **56**
Trysull Av. B26: Sheld 1G **137**
Trysull Gdns. WV3: Wolv 4B **42**
Trysull Holloway WV5: Try 1C **56**
Trysull Rd. WV3: Wolv 4B **42**
  WV5: Wom 5E **57**
Trysull Way DY2: Neth 6E **95**
Tudbury Rd. B31: N'fld 3B **144**
Tudman Cl. B76: Walm 6E **71**
Tudor Cl. B13: Mose 1H **147**
  B14: K Hth 6A **148**
  B73: New O 3D **68**
  CV7: Bal C 3G **169**
  WS6: C Hay 2E **7**
Tudor Coppice B91: Sol 5F **151**
Tudor Ct. B1: Birm 3A **4**
  B72: S Cold 6A **54**
  B74: Four O 1G **53**
  DY4: Tip 3A **78**
  WV11: Ess 4H **17**
Tudor Cres. WV2: Wolv 5F **43**
Tudor Cft. B37: F'bri 2B **122**
Tudor Gdns. B23: Erd 4E **85**
  DY8: Stourb 6C **108**
Tudor Grange Pk. 4E **151**
Tudor Grange Sports Cen. 4F **151**
Tudor Gro. B74: S'tly 3A **52**
TUDOR HILL 5H **53**
Tudor Hill B73: S Cold 5G **53**
Tudor Ind. Est. B11: Tys 6H **119**
Tudor Pk. Ct. B74: Four O 6F **37**
Tudor Pl. DY3: Up Gor 1A **76**
Tudor Rd. B13: Mose 3H **133**
  B65: Row R 4C **96**

Tudor Rd. B68: O'bry 5A 98
  B73: S Cold 6H 53
  DY3: Up Gor 1A 76
  WV10: Wolv 5C 28
  WV14: Bils 1B 62
Tudors Cl. B10: Small H 3C 118
Tudor St. B18: Win G 5H 99
  DY4: Tip 3A 78
Tudor Ter. B17: Harb 5G 115
  DY2: Dud 6G 77
Tudor Va. DY3: Up Gor 1A 76
Tudor Way B72: W Grn 3H 69
  WS6: C Hay 4D 6
Tufnell Gro. B8: W End 2G 103
Tugford Rd. B29: W Cas 6G 131
Tulip Gro. B74: S'tly 4H 51
Tulips Gdns. B29: W Cas 6D 130
Tulip Wlk. B37: Chel W 3E 123
Tulsi Cen. B19: Birm 5E 101
Tulyar Cl. B36: Hodg H 1A 104
Tumbler Gro. WV10: Wolv 6B 28
Tunnel La. B14: K Hth 3E 147
  B30: K Nor, K Hth 3D 146
Tunnel Rd. B70: W Brom 5G 63
Tunnel St. WV14: Cose 5E 61
Tunstall Rd. DY6: K'wfrd 4E 93
Turchill Dr. B76: Walm 5E 71
Turf Cl. WS11: Nort C 1E 9
Turfpits La. B23: Erd 1D 84
Turf Pitts La. B75: Can 6D 38
          (not continuous)
Turks Head Way B70: W Brom 5A 80
Turley St. DY1: Dud 1C 76
Turls Hill Rd. DY3: Sed 5A 60
  WV14: Cose 5A 60
Turls St. DY3: Sed 5A 60
Turnberry Cl. WV6: Pert 4D 24
Turnberry Rd. B42: Gt Barr 5D 66
  WS3: Blox 4F 19
Turner Av. WV14: Cose 3B 60
Turner Dr. DY5: Quar B 4H 109
Turner Gro. WV6: Pert 5G 25
Turners Cft. B71: W Brom 5E 65
Turners Gro. DY3: Lwr G 3G 75
TURNER'S HILL 3B 96
Turner's Hill B65: Row R 3B 96
Turners Hill Rd. DY3: Lwr G 3G 75
Turner's La. DY5: Brie H 3G 109
Turner St. B11: S'brk 5A 118
  B70: W Brom 3G 79
  DY1: Dud 1D 94
  DY3: Lwr G 4H 75
  DY4: Tip 6H 61
Turney Rd. DY8: Stourb 5D 108
Turnham Grn. WV6: Pert 6E 25
Turnhouse Rd. B35: Cas V 4C 86
Turnley Rd. B34: S End 3G 105
Turnpike Cl. B11: S'brk 5A 118
  CV7: Bal C 2H 169
Turnpike Dr. B46: Wat O 4E 89
Turnstone Dr. WV10: F'stne 1D 16
Turton Cl. WS3: Blox 3G 19
Turton Rd. B70: W Brom 5H 79
  DY4: Tip 4H 61
Turtons Cft. WV14: Cose 2D 60
TURVES GREEN 1E 159
Turves Grn. B31: Longb, N'fld 2D 158
Turves Green Leisure & Adult Education Cen.
  . . . . .6E 145
Turville Rd. B20: Hand 6E 83
Tustin Gro. B27: A Grn 5A 136
Tutbury Av. WV6: Pert 6F 25
Tuxford Cl. WV10: Wolv 5A 28
Twatling Rd. B45: B Grn, Lick 6G 157
Tweeds Well B32: Bart G 6H 129
Tweed Twr. B20: Hand 5F 83
Twickenham Ct. DY8: Woll 4A 108
Twickenham Dr. B13: Mose 3G 133
Twickenham Rd. B44: K'sdng 4B 68
Two Gates B63: Crad 6D 110
Two Gates La. B63: Crad 6E 111
Two Locks DY5: Brie H 5B 94
Two Woods La. DY5: Brie H 2A 110
Twycross Gro. B36: Hodg H 2B 104

Twydale Av. B69: Tiv 5C 78
Twyford Cl. WS9: A'rdge 4D 34
Twyford Gro. WV11: Wed 2H 29
Twyford Rd. B8: W End 4A 104
Twyning Rd. B16: Edg 5H 99
  B30: Stir 6D 132
Tybalt Cl. WV10: Bush 3A 28
Tyber Dr. B20: Hand 4D 82
Tyberry Cl. B90: Shir 6G 149
TYBURN 4D 86
Tyburn Av. B24: Erd 4B 86
Tyburn Gro. B24: Erd 4B 86
Tyburn Rd. B24: Erd 6D 84
  WV1: Wolv 2E 45
Tyburn Sq. B24: Erd 4B 86
Tyburn Trad. Est. B35: Cas V 5B 86
Tyebeams B34: S End 4G 105
Tye Gdns. DY9: Pedm 4F 125
Tyler Ct. B24: Erd 4F 85
Tyler Gdns. WV13: W'hall 2B 46
Tyler Gro. B43: Gt Barr 4C 66
Tyler Rd. WV13: W'hall 3A 46
Tylers Gro. B90: M'path 3D 164
Tylers Grn. B38: K Nor 5D 146
Tylney Cl. B5: Edg 4F 117
Tyndale Cres. B43: Gt Barr 2E 67
Tyndall Wlk. B32: Bart G 3G 129
Tyne Cl. B37: F'bri 5D 106
  WS8: Bwnhls 3G 9
Tyne Ct. B73: S Cold 6H 53
Tynedale Cres. WV4: E'shll 2A 60
Tynedale Rd. B11: Tys 2F 135
Tyne Gro. B25: Yard 3B 120
Tyne Pl. DY5: Quar B 1B 110
Tyning Cl. WV9: Pend 5E 15
Tyninghame Av. WV6: Tett 3B 26
Tynings La. WS9: A'rdge 4C 34
Tyrley Cl. WV6: Tett 1H 41
Tyrol Cl. DY8: Woll 6B 108
TYSELEY 6G 119
Tyseley Hill Rd. B11: Tys 1G 135
Tyseley Ind. Est. B11: Tys 6E 119
Tyseley La. B11: Tys 1G 135
Tyseley Station (Rail) 6G 119
Tysoe Dr. B76: Walm 1D 70
Tysoe Rd. B44: K'sdng 6H 67
Tythebarn Dr. DY6: W Hth 2G 91
Tythe Barn La. B90: Dic H 3E 163
          (not continuous)
Tyzack Cl. DY5: Brie H 1G 109

U

Udall Rd. WV14: Cose 2F 61
Uffculme Rd. B30: Stir 5F 133
Uffmoor Est. B63: Hale 3G 127
Uffmoor La. B62: Roms, Hale 6F 127
  B63: Hale 4G 127
Uffmoor Wood Nature Reserve 6G 127
Ufton Cl. B90: Shir 4C 150
Ufton Cres. B90: Shir 4B 150
Ullenhall Rd. B76: Walm 4D 70
  B93: Know 3C 166
Ullenwood B21: Hand 2A 100
Ulleries Rd. B92: Olton 3D 136
Ullrick Grn. B24: Erd 5F 85
Ullswater Cl. B32: Bart G 3D 130
Ullswater Gdns. DY6: K'wfrd 3B 92
Ullswater Ho. B69: O'bry 4D 96
Ullswater Ri. DY5: Brie H 4H 93
Ullswater Rd. WV12: W'hall 6B 18
Ulster Dr. DY6: K'wfrd 5C 92
Ulverley Cl. B92: Olton 5D 136
Ulverley Cres. B92: Olton 5D 136
ULVERLEY GREEN 5D 136
Ulverley Grn. Rd. B92: Olton 4C 136
Umberslade Rd. B29: S Oak 4B 132
  B30: Stir 6C 132
Uncle Ben's Cl. B69: O'bry 5F 97
Underhill La. WV10: Bush 4B 16
Underhill Rd. B8: Salt 6F 103
  DY4: Tip 1C 78
Underhill St. B69: O'bry 4G 97

Underhill Wlk. B69: O'bry 4G 97
Underley Cl. DY6: W Hth 2H 91
Underpass, The
  B40: Nat E C 1F 139
Underwood Cl. B15: Edg 2H 131
  B23: Erd 3C 84
Underwood Rd. B20: Hand 2A 82
Unett Ct. B66: Smeth 4G 99
Unett St. B19: Birm 4E 101
  B66: Smeth 5G 99
Unett St. Nth. B19: Birm, Hock 4E 101
Unett Wlk. B19: Birm 4E 101
Union Cen. WS10: W'bry 3F 63
Union Dr. B73: Bold 3F 69
Union La. WV5: Try 4D 56
Union Mill St. WV1: Wolv 1A 44
Union Pas. B2: Birm 4E 5 (1G 117)
Union Pl. B29: S Oak 3D 132
Union Rd. B6: Aston 1B 102
  B69: O'bry 6E 79
  B70: W Brom 5F 79
  B90: Shir 5A 150
  B91: Sol 3G 151
Union Row B21: Hand 1B 100
Union St. B2: Birm 4E 5 (1G 117)
  B65: B'hth 2C 112
  B70: W Brom 1B 98
  DY2: Dud 6E 77
  DY4: Tip 5H 61
           (Attwell Rd.)
  DY4: Tip 1H 77
           (Unity Wlk.)
  DY8: Stourb 6E 109
  DY9: Lye 6A 110
  WS1: Wals 1D 48
  WS10: W'bry 3F 63
  WV1: Wolv 3D 170 (1H 43)
  WV13: W'hall 1A 46
  WV14: Bils 6E 45
Unisant Trad. Est. B64: Old H 1H 111
Unitt Dr. B64: Old H 3G 111
Unity Cl. WS10: Darl 1C 62
Unity Pl. B29: S Oak 3B 132
  B69: O'bry 1G 97
Unity Wlk. DY4: Tip 2G 77
University of Aston
  Chemical Engineering Building
  . . . . .6H 101
University of Birmingham
  Edgbaston Pk. Rd. 6B 116
  Selly Oak Campus 5H 131
  University Rd. E. 1B 132
University of Central England
  Bournville Campus 6A 132
  Department of Art 3C 4 (6F 101)
  Gosta Green Campus . . .1G 5 (5H 101)
  Hamstead Campus 5A 82
  Perry Barr Campus 4G 83
  School of Jewellery . . .1A 4 (5E 101)
  Sycamore Rd. 6B 132
  Westbourne Campus 3C 116
University of Wolverhampton
  City Campus 2B 170 (1G 43)
  Walsall Campus 4E 49
University Rd. E. B15: Edg 1B 132
University Rd. W. B15: Edg 1A 132
University Station (Rail) 1A 132
Unketts Rd. B67: Smeth 6C 98
Unwin Cres. DY8: Stourb 6C 108
Upavon Cl. B35: Cas V 3E 87
Upland Rd. B29: S Oak 3C 132
Uplands B63: Hale 3F 127
Uplands, The B67: Smeth 4D 98
Uplands Av. B65: Row R 6D 96
  WV3: Wolv 3B 42
  WV13: W'hall 2F 45
Uplands Cl. DY2: Dud 2H 95
Uplands Dr. DY3: Sed 5H 59
  WV3: Wolv 3C 42
  WV5: Wom 1G 73
Uplands Gro. WV13: W'hall 2E 45
Uplands Rd. B21: Hand 5H 81
  DY2: Dud 2G 95
  WV13: W'hall 2E 45

Up. Ashley St. B62: B'hth 2C **112**
Up. Balsall Heath Rd.
  B12: Bal H 5H **117**
Up. Brook St. WS2: Wals 2B **48**
Up. Castle St. WS10: Darl 3D **46**
Up. Chapel St. B69: Tiv 5B **78**
Up. Church La. DY4: Tip 5H **61**
Up. Clifton Rd. B73: S Cold 6H **53**
Upper Cl. B32: Bart G 2B **130**
Up. Conybere St. B12: Birm 4H **117**
Up. Dean St. B5: Birm 6E **5** (2G **117**)
Up. Ettingshall Rd. WV14: Cose 5C **60**
Up. Forster St. WS4: Wals 6D **32**
UPPER GORNAL 2A **76**
Up. Gough St. B1: Birm 6C **4** (2F **117**)
Up. Grn. WV6: Tett 4B **26**
Up. Grosvenor Rd. B20: Hand 5D **82**
Upper Hall La. WS1: Wals 2C **48**
Up. Highgate St. B12: Birm 4H **117**
Up. High St. B64: Crad H 2F **111**
  WS10: W'bry 2F **63**
Up. Holland Rd. B72: S Cold 1A **70**
UPPER LANDYWOOD 5E **7**
Up. Landywood La.
  WS6: C Hay, Gt Wyr 4D **6**
Up. Lichfield St. WV13: W'hall 1A **46**
Upper Mall B5: Birm 5F **5**
Up. Mall E. B5: Birm 5F **5** (1G **117**)
Up. Mall W. B5: Birm 5E **5** (1G **117**)
Up. Marshall St. B1: Birm 6C **4** (2F **117**)
Up. Meadow Rd. B32: Quin 6A **114**
Up. Navigation St. WS2: Wals 1B **48**
Up. Portland St. B6: Aston 2A **102**
Up. Rushall St. WS1: Wals 2D **48**
Up. Russell St. W310. W'bry 3F **63**
Up. St Mary's Rd. B67: Smeth 2D **114**
Up. Short St. WS2: Wals 2B **48**
Up. Sneyd Rd. WV11: Ess 5B **18**
Up. Stone Cl. B76: Walm 1C **70**
Upper St. WV6: Tett 4B **26**
Up. Sutton St. B6: Aston 2H **101**
Up. Thomas St. B6: Aston 2H **101**
  (not continuous)
Up. Trinity St. B9: Birm 2A **118**
Upper Vauxhall WV1: Wolv 1E **43**
Up. Villiers St. WV2: Wolv 5G **43**
Up. William St. B1: Birm 6A **4** (2E **117**)
Up. Zoar St. WV3: Wolv 3F **43**
Upton Ct. B23: Erd 4B **84**
  (off Alwynn WLk.)
Upton Gdns. WV14: Bils 6E **45**
Upton Gro. B33: Stech 2A **120**
Upton Rd. B33: Stech 1A **120**
Upton St. DY2: Neth 4E **95**
Upwey Av. B91: Sol 3E **151**
Urban Ga. B23: Erd 3D **84**
Urton Grn. WV10: F'hses 4F **15**
USAM Trad. Est. WV10: F'hses 5H **15**
Usk Cl. WS3: Blox 1B **32**
Usk Way B36: Cas B 1B **106**
Uttoxeter Cl. WV6: Wolv 3F **27**
Uxbridge Cl. DY3: Lwr G 4H **75**
Uxbridge Cl. WS7: Chase 1A **10**
Uxbridge St. B19: Birm 4F **101**

V

Valbourne Rd. B14: K Hth 3E **147**
Vale, The B11: S'hll 3C **134**
  B15: Edg 5C **116**
Vale Av. DY3: Up Gor 1H **75**
  WS9: A'rdge 6F **35**
Vale Cl. B32: Bart G 2D **130**
Vale Ct. B64: Crad H 4F **111**
Vale Head Dr. WV6: Tett 1G **41**
Valencia Cft. B35: Cas V 3F **87**
Valentine Cl. B74: S'tly 5H **51**
Valentine Ct. B14: K Hth 4H **133**
Valentine Rd. B14: K Hth 4G **133**
  B68: O'bry 1A **114**
Valepits Rd. B33: Sheld 2G **121**
Valerian B74: Four O 5F **37**
Valerie Gro. B43: Gt Barr 5G **65**

Vale Rd. DY2: Neth 5G **95**
Vale Row DY3: Up Gor 2H **75**
Vales Cl. B76: Walm 6C **70**
Vale St. B71: W Brom 1C **80**
  DY3: Up Gor 2H **75**
  DY8: Amb 3E **109**
  WV2: E'shll 5C **44**
Vale Vw. WS9: A'rdge 5D **34**
Valiant Ho. B35: Cas V 2F **87**
Valiant Way B92: Sol 5G **137**
Vallian Cft. B36: Hodg H 2D **104**
Valley Farm Rd. B45: Rub 3F **157**
Valley Grn. WS6: C Hay 3E **7**
Valley Rd. B43: Gt Barr 6G **65**
  B62: B'hth 3F **113**
  B64: Crad H 4G **111**
  B67: Smeth 6D **98**
  B74: S'tly 4H **51**
  B92: Sol 2G **137**
  DY3: Up Gor 1A **76**
  DY9: Lye 6B **110**
  WS3: Blox 1A **32**
  WV10: Wolv 4B **28**
Valleyside WS3: Pels 5D **20**
Valley Vw. WS8: Bwnhls 6C **10**
Vanborough Wlk. DY1: Dud 5C **76**
Vanbrugh Ct. WV6: Pert 6E **25**
Van Diemans Rd. WV5: Wom 2E **73**
Vanguard Cl. B36: Hodg H 1C **104**
Vanguard Rd. B26: Birm A 1E **139**
Vann Cl. B10: Small H 3C **118**
  (not continuous)
Vantage Point B70: W Brom 5A **80**
  (off Blacksmith Way)
Vantage Way B24: Erd 6B **86**
Varden Cft. B5: Edg 4H **117**
Vardon Way B38: K Nor 6H **145**
Varley Rd. B24: Erd 3B **86**
Varley Va. B24: Erd 3B **86**
Varlins Way B38: K Nor 2H **159**
Varney Av. B70: W Brom 5B **80**
Vaughan Cl. B74: Four O 3F **37**
Vaughan Gdns. WV8: Cod 3F **13**
Vaughan Rd. WV13: W'hall 2F **45**
Vaughan Trad. Est.
  DY4: Tip 3B **78**
Vaughton Dr. B75: S Cold 5C **54**
Vaughton Ho. B15: Edg 4E **117**
Vaughton St. B12: Birm 3H **117**
  B12: Birm 3G **117**
Vaughton St. Sth. B5: Birm 3G **117**
  B12: Birm 3G **117**
VAUXHALL .4B **102**
Vauxhall Av. WV1: Wolv 1E **43**
Vauxhall Bus. Pk. B7: Birm 4C **102**
Vauxhall Cres. B36: Cas B 6B **88**
Vauxhall Gdns. DY2: Dud 2G **95**
Vauxhall Gro. B7: Birm 6B **102**
Vauxhall Ho. WV1: Wolv 1E **43**
  (off Upper Vauxhall)
Vauxhall Pl. B7: Birm 6A **102**
Vauxhall Rd. B7: Birm 6A **102**
  DY8: Stourb 6E **109**
Vauxhall St. DY1: Dud 1D **94**
Vauxhall Ter. B7: Birm 5B **102**
Vauxhall Trad. Est. B7: Birm 5B **102**
Vector Ind. Pk. B71: W Brom 1A **80**
Velsheda Rd. B90: Shir 5G **149**
Venetia Rd. B9: Bord G 1C **118**
Venice Ct. B13: Mose 3B **134**
Venning Gro. B43: Gt Barr 6H **65**
Ventnor Av. B19: Hock 2E **101**
  B36: Hodg H 2B **104**
Ventnor Cl. B68: O'bry 4A **114**
Ventnor Rd. B92: Sol 2G **137**
Venture Ct. WV10: F'hses 2H **15**
Venture Way B7: Birm 1H **5** (5H **101**)
Vera Rd. B26: Yard 4C **120**
Verbena Gdns. B7: Birm 4A **102**
Verbena Rd. B31: N'fld 1D **144**
Vercourt B74: Lit As 6B **36**
Verdun Cres. DY2: Dud 5H **77**
Vere St. B5: Birm 3F **117**
Verity Wlk. DY8: Word 2C **108**
Verney Av. B33: Sheld 4H **121**

Vernier Av. DY6: K'wfrd 4E **93**
Vernolds Cft. B5: Birm 3G **117**
Vernon Av. B20: Hand 3B **82**
  DY4: Tip 3G **77**
  WS8: Bwnhls 5C **10**
Vernon Cl. B62: B'hth 3C **112**
  B74: Four O 4E **37**
  WV11: Ess 3H **17**
  WV13: W'hall 2G **45**
Vernon Ct. B16: Edg 2A **116**
Vernon Rd. B16: Edg 2H **115**
  B62: B'hth 3C **112**
  B68: O'bry 3A **98**
  WV14: Bils 5H **45**
Vernon St. B70: W Brom 4E **79**
Vernon Trad. Est. B62: B'hth 3C **112**
Vernon Way WS3: Blox 6D **18**
Veronica Av. WV4: E'shll 6A **44**
Veronica Rd. DY6: K'wfrd 3E **93**
Verstone Cft. B31: N'fld 5E **145**
Verstone Rd. B90: Shir 3A **150**
Verwood Cl. WV13: W'hall 2F **45**
Vesey Cl. B46: Wat O 5D **88**
  B74: Four O 1F **53**
Vesey Rd. B73: W Grn 4H **69**
Vesey St. B4: Birm 1E **5** (5G **101**)
Vestry Cl. B64: Old H 2H **111**
Vestry Ct. DY8: Woll 5C **108**
Viaduct Dr. WV6: Wolv 3F **27**
Viaduct St. B7: Birm 6A **102**
Vibart Rd. B26: Yard 3D **120**
Vicarage Cl. B30: Stir 6E **133**
  B42: Gt Barr 6F **67**
  DY4: Tip 2G **77**
  DY5: Brie H 3G **109**
  WS8: Bwnhls 6C **10**
  (not continuous)
Vicarage Gdns. B65: B'hth 2C **112**
  B76: Walm 6D **70**
Vicarage Gro. B28: Hall G 5H **135**
Vicarage La. B46: Wat O 5D **88**
  DY5: P'ntt 1H **93**
Vicarage Pl. WS1: Wals 2C **48**
Vicarage Prospect DY1: Dud 6D **76**
Vicarage Rd. B6: Aston 2A **102**
  (not continuous)
  B14: K Hth 1E **147**
  B15: Edg 3B **116**
  B17: Harb 6F **115**
  B18: Hock 2C **100**
  B33: Yard 2C **120**
  B62: B'hth 2C **112**
  B67: Smeth 4D **98**
  B68: O'bry 5H **97**
  B71: W Brom 1B **80**
  B94: Earls 6A **164**
  DY3: Up Gor 2B **76**
  DY5: Brie H 4G **109**
  DY8: Amb 4E **109**
  DY8: Woll 4A **108**
  DY9: Lye 6B **110**
  WS3: Pels 5E **21**
  WS8: Bwnhls 6B **10**
  WS10: W'bry 2F **63**
  WV2: Wolv 6D **170** (3H **43**)
  WV4: Penn 2B **58**
  WV11: Wed 3D **28**
  WV14: Cose 6E **61**
Vicarage Rd. Sth. DY9: Lye 6A **110**
Vicarage Rd. W. DY1: Dud 1D **76**
Vicarage St. B68: O'bry 4H **97**
Vicarage Ter. WS2: Wals 3A **48**
Vicarage Wlk. WS1: Wals 2C **48**
Vicar St. DY2: Dud 6E **77**
  DY3: Sed 5H **59**
  WS10: W'bry 2G **63**
Vicars Wlk. DY9: W'cte 3A **126**
Viceroy Cl. B5: Edg 5E **117**
  DY6: K'wfrd 4E **93**
Victor Cl. WV2: E'shll 5D **44**
Victoria Arc. WV1: Wolv 3B **170**
Victoria Av. B10: Small H 3D **118**
  B21: Hand 1B **100**

Victoria Av. B62: Quin 5F 113
  B66: Smeth 4E 99
  WS3: Blox 6H 19
Victoria Bldgs. B16: Birm 6A 100
          (off Barford Rd.)
Victoria Ct. B11: S'brk 5C 118
  B13: Mose 1H 133
  B62: Quin 4G 113
         (off Binswood Rd.)
  B66: Smeth 3F 99
  DY5: Brie H 6H 93
  WS11: Nort C 1F 9
Victoria Fold WV1: Wolv 4A 170 (2G 43)
Victoria Gdns. B64: Old H 1H 111
Victoria Gro. B18: Win G 5A 100
  WV5: Wom 5G 57
Victoria Ho. B16: Birm 1D 116
          (off Bellcroft)
  WS3: Blox 1B 32
  SC10: Darl 5C 46
         (off Factory St.)
Victoria M. B69: O'bry 6F 97
  WS4: Wals 6E 33
Victoriana Way B20: Hand 6C 82
Victoria New Works WS10: Darl 3D 46
Victoria Pk. Rd. B66: Smeth 4F 99
Victoria Pas. DY8: Stourb 6E 109
  WV1: Wolv 3B 170 (1G 43)
Victoria Rd. B6: Aston 2G 101
        (not continuous)
  B17: Harb 6F 115
  B21: Hand 2A 100
  B23: Erd .4D 84
  B27: A Grn 3A 136
        (not continuous)
  B30: Stir 6C 132
  B33: Stech 6B 104
  B62: B'hth 2D 112
  B64: Old H 1H 111
  B68: O'bry 3A 98
  B72: S Cold 6A 54
  DY3: Sed 5A 60
  DY4: Tip 2H 77
  DY5: Quar B 2C 110
  WS3: Pels 4E 21
  WS10: Darl 5D 46
  WV3: Wolv 4C 42
  WV6: Tett 4C 26
  WV10: Wolv 4B 28
  WV11: Wed 3D 28
Victoria Sq. B2: Birm 4C 4 (1F 117)
  WV1: Wolv 3C 170
Victoria St. B9: Small H 2D 118
  B63: Hale 1A 128
  B70: W Brom 2F 79
         (Phoenix St.)
  B70: W Brom 4A 80
         (Price St.)
  DY5: Brie H 6H 93
  DY5: P'ntt 2G 93
  DY6: W Hth 6H 73
  DY8: Stourb 6E 109
  WS10: W'bry 3E 63
  WV1: Wolv 4B 170 (2G 43)
  WV13: W'hall 6A 30
Victoria Ter. WS4: Wals 6E 33
Victor Rd. B18: Win G 3A 100
  B92: Sol 2H 137
Victor St. WS1: Wals 4C 48
  WS3: Pels 6E 21
Victor Twr. B7: Nech 3B 102
Victory Av. B65: Row R 1B 112
  WS10: Darl 1C 62
Victory Ho. B13: Mose 1H 133
Victory La. WS2: Wals 5G 31
Victory Ri. B71: W Brom 2A 80
View Dr. DY2: Dud 1G 95
Viewfield Cres. DY3: Sed 6H 59
Viewlands Dr. WV6: Tett 1G 41
View Point B69: Tiv 1B 96
VIGO 4B 22
Vigo Cl. WS9: Wals W 5B 22
Vigo Pl. WS9: A'rdge 1B 34
Vigo Rd. WS9: Wals W 5B 22

Vigo Ter. WS9: Wals W 5B 22
Viking Ri. B65: Row R 5C 96
VILLAGE, THE 2C 92
Village, The DY6: K'wfrd 2C 92
Village M. B32: Quin 5G 113
Village M., The WV6: Tett 4A 26
Village Rd. B6: Aston 6A 84
Village Sq. B31: Longb 5A 144
Village Wlk. WS10: W'bry 2H 63
  WS2: Wals 1G 47
  WV14: Bils 6E 45
Villa Pk. 6H 83
Villa Rd. B19: Hock 2C 100
Villa St. B19: Hock, Loz 2D 100
        (not continuous)
  DY8: Amb 3E 109
Villette Gro. B14: Yard W 3C 148
Villiers Av. WV14: Bils 4F 45
Villiers Ho. WV2: Wolv 4G 43
      (off Blakenhall Gdns.)
Villiers Pl. WV14: Bils 4F 45
Villiers Sq. WV14: Bils 4F 45
Villiers St. WS1: Wals 4C 48
  WV13: W'hall 1A 46
Villiers Trad. Est. WV2: Wolv 4F 43
Vimy Rd. B13: Mose 6B 134
  WS10: W'bry 1G 63
Vimy Ter. WS10: W'bry 1G 63
Vincent Cl. B12: Bal H 5H 117
Vincent Dr. B15: Edg 2H 131
Vincent Pde. B12: Bal H 5H 117
Vincent Rd. B75: S Cold 4C 54
Vincent St. B12: Bal H 6H 117
        (not continuous)
  WS1: Wals 4D 48
Vince St. B66: Smeth 6E 99
Vinculum Way WV13: W'hall 3B 46
Vine Av. B12: Bal H 6A 118
Vine Cl. WV10: F'hses 4H 15
Vine Cres. B71: W Brom 1B 80
Vine Gdns. B64: Old H 1H 111
Vine La. B63: Hale 2B 128
Vineries, The B27: A Grn 1B 136
Vine St. B6: Aston 2B 102
  DY5: Brie H 4A 94
  DY8: Word 2C 108
Vine Ter. B17: Harb 6G 115
Vineyard Cl. B18: Hock 2B 100
Vineyard Rd. B31: N'fld 2D 144
Vinnall Gro. B32: Bart G 5H 129
Vintage Cl. B34: Stech 4E 105
Violet Cft. DY4: Tip 4C 62
Virgin Active 6D 164
Virginia Dr. WV4: Penn 1D 58
Viscount Cl. B35: Cas V 5E 87
Viscount Dr. B35: Cas V 5F 87
Viscount Ho. B26: Birm A 1E 139
Vista, The DY3: Sed 4H 59
Vista Grn. B38: K Nor 6C 146
        (not continuous)
Vittoria St. B1: Birm 1A 4 (5E 101)
  B66: Smeth 3H 99
Vivian Cl. B17: Harb 6G 115
Vivian Rd. B17: Harb 6G 115
Vixen Cl. B76: Walm 6B 70
Vowles Rd. B71: W Brom 1B 80
Vue Cinema
  Nechells 1D 102
        (in Star City)

W

Wadbarn B90: Dic H 4G 163
Waddell Cl. WV14: Cose 3B 60

Waddens Brook La. WV11: Wed 4G 29
Waddington Av. B43: Gt Barr 4A 66
Wades Cl. DY4: Tip 2G 77
Wadesmill Lawns WV10: Bush 3A 16
Wadham Cl. B65: Row R 3C 96
Wadham Rd. B37: Chel W 6E 107
Wadhurst Rd. B17: Edg 1F 115
Wadley's Rd. B91: Sol 1D 150
Waen Cl. DY4: Tip 5B 62
Waggoners La. B78: Hints 2H 39
Waggon St. B64: Old H 1H 111
Waggon Wlk. B38: K Nor 1G 159
        (not continuous)
Wagoners Cl. B8: Salt 3F 103
Wagon La. B92: Olton 1D 136
Wagstaff Cl. WV14: Cose 5F 61
Wagstaff Way B37: Mars G 3C 122
Waine Ho. WS8: Bwnhls 1C 22
Wainwright Cl. DY6: W Hth 1G 91
Wainwright St. B6: Aston 2A 102
Waite Rd. WV13: W'hall 3G 45
Wakefield Cl. B73: Bold 3G 69
Wakefield Ct. B13: Mose 3B 134
  B29: W Cas 6G 131
        (off Abdon Av.)
Wakefield Gro. B46: Wat O 4D 88
Wakeford Rd. B31: N'fld 6G 145
WAKE GREEN 3A 134
Wake Grn. Pk. B13: Mose 3B 134
Wake Grn. Rd. B13: Mose 2H 133
  DY4: Tip .4A 62
Wakelam Gdns. B43: Gt Barr 4H 65
Wakelams Fold DY3: Gorn 4G 75
Walcot Cl. B75: Four O 6H 37
Walcot Dr. B43: Gt Barr 1B 82
Walcot Gdns. WV14: Bils 1D 60
Walcot Grn. B93: Dorr 6H 167
Waldale Cl. WV11: Ess 6C 18
Walden Gdns. WV4: Penn 5C 42
Walden Rd. B11: Tys 2G 135
Waldeve Gro. B92: Sol 5B 138
Waldley Gro. B24: Erd 4A 86
Waldon Wlk. B36: Cas B 1B 106
Waldron Av. DY5: Brie H 1F 109
Waldron Cl. WS10: W'bry 5F 47
Waldrons Moor B14: K Hth 2E 147
Walford Av. WV3: Wolv 3D 42
Walford Dr. B92: Sol 2H 137
Walford Grn. B32: Bart G 6H 129
Walford Rd. B11: S'brk 5B 118
Walford St. B69: Tiv 5A 78
Walhouse Cl. WS1: Wals 1D 48
Walhouse Rd. WS1: Wals 1D 48
        (not continuous)
Walk, The DY3: Sed 4H 59
Walker Av. B69: Tiv 2C 96
  DY5: Quar B 4H 109
  DY9: W'cte 2H 125
  WV10: Bush 1A 28
Walker Dr. B24: Erd 1E 103
Walker Grange DY4: Tip 6H 61
Walker Pl. WS3: Blox 1C 32
Walker Rd. WS3: Blox 1B 32
Walkers Fold WV12: W'hall 3D 30
WALKER'S HEATH 5C 146
Walkers Heath Rd. B38: K Nor 6D 146
Walker St. DY2: Neth 5E 95
  DY4: Tip .6B 62
Walk La. WV5: Wom 6G 57
Walkmill La. WS11: Cann 1D 6
Wallace Cl. B69: O'bry 3D 96
  WS11: Nort C 1D 8
Wallace Ct. WS6: C Hay 4D 6
Wallace Ho. B69: O'bry 4D 96
Wallace Ri. B64: Crad H 4G 111
Wallace Rd. B29: S Oak 3D 132
  B69: O'bry 3D 96

Wallace Rd. WS8: Bwnhls 5A 10
  WV14: Bils 2A 62
Wall Av. B46: Col 4H 107
Wallbank Ct. B8: W End 3G 103
Wallbank Rd. B8: W End 3G 103
WALLBROOK 5F 61
Wallbrook St. WV14: Cose 5F 61
Wall Cl. B67: Smeth 5B 98
Wall Cft. WS9: A'rdge 2D 34
Wall Dr. B74: Four O 5F 37
Wall End Cl. WS2: Wals 2G 31
Wallface B71: W Brom 6G 63
WALL HEATH 1H 91
Wallheath Cres. WS9: Ston 2G 23
Wall Heath La. WS9: Ston 2H 23
Walling Cft. WV14: Cose 2D 60
Wallington Cl. WS3: Blox 5H 19
WALLINGTON HEATH 5G 19
Wallington Heath WS3: Blox 5H 19
Wallis Ct. B13: Mose 3B 134
Wallows Ind. Est., The DY5: Brie H ...4H 93
Wallows La. WS1: Wals 5A 48
  WS2: Wals 5A 48
Wallows Pl. DY5: Brie H 4G 93
Wallows Rd. DY5: Brie H 5G 93
Wallows Wood DY3: Lwr G 3E 75
Wall St. WV1: Wolv 1D 44
Wall Well B63: Hale 2H 127
Wall Well La. B63: Hale 2H 127
Walmead Cft. B17: Harb 4D 114
Walmer Gro. B23: Erd 2B 84
Walmer Mdw. WS9: A'rdge 2D 34
Walmers, The WS9: A'rdge 2D 34
Walmers Wlk., The B31: Longb ...6B 144
Walmer Way B37: Chel W 6C 107
Walmesley Way B31: N'fld 4C 144
WALMLEY 5D 70
WALMLEY ASH 2D 86
Walmley Ash La. B76: Min, Walm ...1F 87
Walmley Ash Rd. B76: Walm, Min ...6D 70
Walmley Cl. B63: Crad 4D 110
  B76: Walm 5D 70
Walmley Rd. B76: Walm 1C 70
Walnut Av. WV8: Bilb 4G 13
Walnut Cl. B37: Chel W 2D 122
  DY9: Pedm 4F 125
Walnut Dr. B66: Smeth 4F 99
  WV3: Wolv 2B 42
Walnut Ho. B20: I'land 4B 82
Walnut La. WS10: W'bry 3G 63
Walnut Rd. WS5: Wals 1E 65
Walnut Way B31: Longb 1D 158
Walpole St. WV6: Wolv 6E 27
Walpole Wlk. B70: W Brom 6B 80
WALSAL END 4A 154
Walsal End La. B92: H Ard 4H 153
WALSALL 2D 48
Walsall Bus. Pk. WS9: A'rdge ...6A 34
Walsall Enterprise Pk. WS2: Wals ...3A 48
Walsall FC 5B 48
Walsall Gala Baths 1D 48
Walsall Library & Mus. 1D 48
  (off Lichfield St.)
Walsall Local History Cen. 5C 32
Walsall New Firms Cen., The
  WS1: Wals 3B 48
Walsall Rd. B42: Gt Barr, P Barr ...4B 66
  B71: W Brom 6B 64
  B74: Four O 5D 36
  B74: Lit As 3C 36
  WS3: Pels 5E 21
  WS5: Wals 1D 64
  WS6: Gt Wyr 1F 7
  WS9: A'rdge 6A 34
  WS9: S'fld, Wals W 6H 21
  WS10: Darl 5D 46
  WS10: W'bry 3C 64
  WS11: Nort C 2D 8
  WS14: Hilt, Lynn, Muck C ...6F 11
  WV13: W'hall 1B 46
Walsall Station (Rail) 2C 48
Walsall St. B70: W Brom 4B 80
  WS10: Darl 4D 46
  WS10: W'bry 2F 63

Walsall St. WV1: Wolv 2A 44
  WV13: W'hall 2B 46
  WV14: Bils 5F 45
WALSALL WOOD 3C 22
Walsall Wood Rd. WS9: A'rdge ...5C 22
Walsgrave Cl. B92: Sol 1H 151
Walsgrave Dr. B92: Sol 6H 137
Walsham Cft. B34: S End 4G 105
Walsh Dr. B76: Walm 1D 70
Walsh Gro. B23: Erd 5D 68
Walsingham St. WS1: Wals 2E 49
Walstead Cl. WS5: Wals 6G 49
Walstead Rd. WS5: Wals 6D 48
Walstead Rd. W. WS5: Wals 6C 48
Walt Dene Cl. B43: Gt Barr 3A 66
Walter Burden Ho. B66: Smeth ...6G 99
Walter Cobb Dr. B73: W Grn 4G 69
Walter Rd. B67: Smeth 3C 98
  WV14: Bils 2G 61
Walters Cl. B31: Longb 3D 158
Walters Rd. B68: O'bry 4G 113
Walters Row DY1: Dud 6C 76
Walter St. B7: Nech 3B 102
  B70: W Brom 5C 80
  WS3: Pels 6E 21
Waltham Gro. B44: K'sdng 3B 68
Waltham Ho. B38: K Nor 6C 146
  B70: W Brom 4B 80
Walthamstow Ct. DY5: Brie H ...2H 109
Walton Av. B65: B'hth 3B 112
Walton Cl. B63: Hale 3H 127
  B65: Row R 5A 96
Walton Ct. B63: Hale 2H 127
Walton Cres. WV4: E'shll 6A 44
Walton Cft. B91: Sol 6F 151
Walton Dr. DY9: Lye 6G 109
Walton Gdns. WV8: Cod 3F 13
Walton Gro. B30: K Nor 5D 146
Walton Heath WS3: Blox 4F 19
Walton Ho. B16: Birm 1D 116
Walton Rd. B68: O'bry 1H 113
  DY8: Amb 5E 109
  WS9: A'rdge 6C 22
  WS10: W'bry 3A 64
  WV4: E'shll 6A 44
Walton St. DY4: Tip 2H 77
Wanderers Av. WV2: Wolv 5G 43
Wanderer Wlk. B36: Hodg H 6C 86
Wandle Gro. B11: Tys 2G 135
Wandsworth Rd. B44: Gt Barr ...2G 67
Wansbeck Gro. B38: K Nor 1A 160
Wansbeck Wlk. DY3: Sed 1B 76
Wanstead Gro. B44: K'sdng 4A 68
Wantage Rd. B46: Col 6G 89
Ward Cl. B8: W End 4G 103
Warden Av. B73: Bold 5F 69
Ward End Cl. B8: Salt 3F 103
Ward End Hall Gro. B8: W End ...3G 103
Ward End Ho. B8: W End 3G 103
Ward End Pk. Rd. B8: Salt 4F 103
Wardend Rd. B8: W End 3G 103
Warden Rd. B73: Bold 5F 69
Ward Gro. WV4: E'shll 2A 60
Wardle Cl. B75: Four O 5G 37
Wardle La. WS6: Gt Wyr 3F 7
Wardlow Cl. WV4: Penn 5F 43
Wardlow Rd. B7: Birm 4B 102
Wardour Dr. B37: Chel W 1E 123
Wardour Gro. B44: K'sdng 5C 68
Ward Rd. WV4: Penn 6H 43
  WV8: Cod 4F 13
Ward St. B19: Birm 5G 101
  B23: Erd 3E 85
  WS1: Wals 1D 48
  WV1: Wolv 1A 44
  (not continuous)
  WV2: E'shll 4D 44
  WV13: W'hall 6B 30
  WV14: Cose 5D 60
Wareham Cl. WS3: Wals 4D 32
Wareham Ho. B28: Hall G 4E 149
Wareham Rd. B45: Fran 5H 143
Wareing Dr. B23: Erd 5D 68

Warewell Cl. WS1: Wals 1D 48
Warewell St. WS1: Wals 2D 48
Waring Cl. DY4: Tip 5G 61
Waring Rd. DY4: Tip 5A 62
Warings, The WV5: Wom 3F 73
War La. B17: Harb 6F 115
Warley Cft. B68: O'bry 3C 114
Warley Hall Rd. B68: O'bry ...3B 114
Warley Rd. B68: O'bry 4A 98
WARLEY WOODS 2C 114
Warmington Dr. B73: S Cold ...1H 69
Warmington Rd. B26: Sheld ...6G 121
  B47: H'wd 3A 162
Warmley Cl. B91: Sol 2H 151
  WV6: Wolv 4F 27
Warner Dr. DY5: Brie H 2H 109
Warner Pl. WS3: Wals 3D 32
Warner Rd. WS3: Wals 3D 32
  WS10: W'bry 3A 64
  WV8: Cod 4F 13
Warner St. B12: Birm 3A 118
Warners Wlk. B10: Small H 3C 118
Warnford Wlk. WV4: Penn 5A 42
Warple Rd. B32: Quin 6A 114
Warren Av. B13: Mose 3H 133
  WV10: Wolv 4B 28
Warren Dr. DY4: Tip 6H 61
Warren Dr. B65: Row R 4H 95
  B93: Dorr 6C 166
  DY3: Sed 4G 59
Warren Farm Rd. B44: K'sdng ...5H 67
Warren Gdns. DY6: K'wfrd 3A 92
Warren Gro. B8: Salt 3E 103
Warren Hill Rd. B44: K'sdng ...1H 83
Warren Ho. Ct. B76: Walm 4D 70
Warren Ho. Wlk. B70: Walm 1D 70
Warren La. B45: Lick 6H 157
Warren Pl. WS8: Bwnhls 6C 10
Warren Rd. B8: Salt 3E 103
  B30: Stir 6C 132
  B44: K'sdng 1A 84
Warrens Cft. WS5: Wals 6H 49
Warrens End B38: K Nor 1B 160
Warrens Hall Nature Reserve ...3G 95
Warrens Hall Rd. DY2: Dud 2F 95
Warrington Cl. B76: Walm 4E 71
Warrington Dr. B23: Erd 5D 68
Warsash Cl. WV1: Wolv 3D 44
WARSTOCK 4B 148
Warstock La. B14: K Hth 2A 148
Warstock Rd. B14: K Hth 4A 148
Warston Av. B32: Bart G 3B 130
WARSTONE 6B 6
Warstone Ct. B18: Birm ...1A 4 (5E 101)
Warstone Dr. B71: W Brom 5C 80
Warstone La. B18: Birm ...1A 4 (5D 100)
Warstone M. B18: Birm 1A 4
Warstone Pde. E. B18: Birm ...5D 100
Warstone Rd. WV10: Share 3A 6
  WV11: Ess 3A 6
Warstones Cres. WV4: Penn 6B 42
Warstones Dr. WV4: Penn 5A 42
Warstones Gdns. WV4: Penn 5A 42
Warstones Ho. WV4: Penn 5B 42
Warstones Rd. WV4: Penn 5A 42
Warstone Ter. B21: Hand 1A 100
Warstone Twr. B36: Hodg H ...1A 104
Wartell Bank DY6: K'wfrd 2B 92
Wartell Bank Ind. Est.
  DY6: K'wfrd 2C 92
Warwards La. B29: S Oak 4C 132
Warwell La. B26: Yard 5B 120
Warwick Av. WS10: W'bry 1A 64
  WV6: Pert 6F 25
  WV13: W'hall 1D 46
Warwick Cl. B68: O'bry 1H 113
  B70: W Brom 6E 63
  DY3: Lwr G 4H 75
Warwick Ct. B13: Mose 3A 134
  B29: W Cas 6F 131
  B37: Chel W 1F 123
  B91: Sol 2F 151
Warwick Crest B15: Edg 4D 116
Warwick Cft. B36: Hodg H ...1A 104

Warwick Dr. WV8: Cod 3E 13
Warwick Gdns. B69: Tiv 5C 78
Warwick Grange B91: Sol 6D 136
Warwick Gro. B92: Olton 4C 136
Warwick Pk. Ct. B92: Olton 5D 136
Warwick Pas. B2: Birm 4E 5 (1G 117)
Warwick Rd. B6: Witt 5G 83
(not continuous)
  B11: S'hll, Tys 6C 118
  B27: A Grn 6C 118
  B68: O'bry 4B 114
  B73: New O 3C 68
  B91: Sol 2E 151
  B92: Olton 5D 136
  B93: Know 6C 152
(not continuous)
  DY2: Neth 6G 95
  DY8: Word 2B 108
Warwick Rd. Trad. Est. B11: S'hll . . .1D 134
Warwickshire County Cricket Club . . .6F 117
Warwick St. B12: Birm 2A 118
  WS4: Wals 6D 32
  WV1: Wolv 2A 44
  WV14: Bils 6G 45
Warwick Wlk. WS9: A'rdge 6C 22
Wasdale Dr. DY6: K'wfrd 3C 92
Wasdale Rd. B31: N'fld 3D 144
  WS8: Clay 1H 21
Waseley Hills Country Pk. 6C 142
Waseley Hills Country Pk. Vis. Cen.
. . . . .6C 142
Waseley Rd. B45: Rub 1E 157
Washbrook La. WS11: Nort C . . .1A 8 & 1C 8
Washbrook Rd. B8: W End 3G 103
Washford Gro. B25: Yard 3H 119
Washington Cen. DY2: Neth 6F 95
Washington Ct. B1: Birm 6B 4
  WV3: Wolv 2B 42
Washington Dr. B20: Hand 4D 82
Washington St. B1: Birm . . .6B 4 (2E 117)
  DY2: Neth 6F 95
Washington St. Ind. Est. DY2: Neth . .6F 95
Washington Wharf B1: Birm . . .6B 4 (2E 117)
Wash La. B25: Yard 4A 120
WASHWOOD HEATH 3E 103
Washwood Heath Rd.
  B8: Salt, W End 4D 102
Wasperton Cl. B36: Cas B 1F 105
Wassell Cl. B63: Hale 3G 127
Wassell Gro. La. DY9: Hag 5B 126
Wassell Rd. B63: Hale 3G 127
  DY9: W'cte 3B 126
  WV14: Bils 4F 45
West Hill Gro. B38: K Nor 2B 160
West Hills La. B38: Hopw 5H 159
  B48: Hopw 5H 159
Wastwater Ri. WV6: Pert 5F 25
Watchbury Cl. B36: Cas B 6G 87
Watchman Av. DY5: Quar B 4B 110
Waterbridge La. WV5: Wom 6E 57
Water Dale WV3: Wolv 1C 42
Waterdale B90: Ches G 4B 164
  WV5: Wom 2E 73
Waterfall Cl. B66: Smeth 2C 98
Waterfall La. B64: Old H 2A 112
  B65: B'hth 2A 112
Waterfall La. Trad. Est. B64: Old H . . .2A 112
Waterfall Rd. DY5: Brie H 4G 109
Waterfield Cl. DY4: Tip 2E 77
Waterfield Ho. WV5: Wom 6H 57
Waterfield Way B26: Sheld 4G 121
Waterford Ct. B23: Erd 3B 84
Waterford Pl. B33: Kitts G 6G 105
Waterford Rd. DY6: K'wfrd 2B 92
Waterfront, The DY5: Brie H 5A 94
Waterfront Bus. Pk. DY5: Brie H 6H 93
Waterfront E. DY5: Brie H 5A 94
Waterfront Wlk. B1: Birm . . .6B 4 (2E 117)
Waterfront Way DY5: Brie H 5A 94
  WS2: Wals 1B 48
Waterfront W. DY5: Brie H 5A 94
Waterglade La. WV13: W'hall 2A 46
Waterhaynes Cl. B45: Redn 3G 157

Waterhead Cl. WV10: Bush 5C 16
Waterhead Dr. WV10: Bush 5C 16
Water La. B71: W Brom 6D 64
Water Lily Gro. WS8: Bwnhls 6A 10
Waterlinks Blvd. B6: Aston 2A 102
Waterlinks Ho. B7: Birm 4H 101
(off Richard St.)
Waterloo Av. B37: F'bri 5D 106
Waterloo Ind. Est. B37: F'bri 4D 106
Waterloo Pas. B2: Birm 4D 4
Waterloo Rd. B14: K Hth 5G 133
  B25: Yard 5H 119
  B66: Smeth 5A 98
  WV1: Wolv 2A 170 (1G 43)
Waterloo Rd. Junc.
  WV1: Wolv 2A 170 (1G 43)
Waterloo St. B2: Birm 4C 4 (1F 117)
  DY1: Dud 1C 94
  DY4: Tip 2G 77
Waterloo St. E. DY4: Tip 2H 77
Waterloo Ter. WV1: Wolv 6F 27
Watermarque B16: Birm 1D 116
Watermead Grange WS8: Bwnhls 6A 10
Watermeadow Dr. WS4: S'fld 6H 21
Watermere WS4: S'fld 1H 33
Water Mill Cl. B29: S Oak 2H 131
Watermill Cl. WV10: F'hses 4H 15
Water Mill Cres. B76: Walm 4D 70
WATER ORTON 4D 88
Water Orton La. B76: Min 2H 87
Water Orton Rd. B36: Cas B 1G 105
Water Orton Station (Rail) 4C 88
Water Rd. DY3: Gorn 5G 75
Waters Dr. B74: Four O 6D 36
Waters Edge, The B1: Birm . . .5A 4 (1E 117)
Waterside B15: Birm 2E 117
  B43: Gt Barr 6A 66
  B90: Dic H 4G 163
Waterside Av. WS10: W'bry 4G 63
Waterside Bus. Pk. DY5: Brie H 2F 109
Waterside Cl. B9: Birm 1C 118
  B24: Erd 2E 87
  B69: O'bry 5F 97
  WV2: Wolv 4H 43
Waterside Ct. B16: Birm 1H 116
(off Vincent St.)
Waterside Dr. B18: Win G 4B 100
(not continuous)
Waterside Est. DY2: Neth 6E 95
Waterside Ind. Est. B65: Row R 5H 95
  WV2: E'shll 5C 44
Waterside Orchard Cvn. Pk.
  B48: Hopw 6F 159
Waterside Pk. WV4: Tip 6D 62
Waterside Vw. B18: Hock 4C 100
  DY5: Brie H 3F 109
Waterside Way WS8: Bwnhls 3G 9
  WV9: Pend 4E 15
Waterson Cft. B37: Chel W 6F 107
Water St. B3: Birm 2C 4 (6F 101)
  B70: W Brom 5B 80
  DY6: K'wfrd 2B 92
  WV10: Wolv 6H 27
Waters Vw. WS3: Pels 2F 21
Waterward Cl. B17: Harb 6G 115
Waterway Ct. B14: Yard W 4C 148
Waterways Dr. B69: O'bry 6E 79
Waterways Gdns. DY8: Word 2C 108
Waterworks Cotts. B71: W Brom 6C 64
Waterworks Dr. B31: N'fld 2B 144
Waterworks Rd. B16: Edg 2B 116
Waterworks St. B6: Aston 1B 102
Watery La. B32: Quin 2B 129
  B48: A'chu, Hopw 6A 160
  B67: Smeth 4E 99
  B93: Know 5G 167
  B94: Earls 5A 164
  DY4: Tip 2H 77
(not continuous)
  DY8: Word 1C 108
  WS1: Wals 4B 48
(not continuous)
  WV8: Cod 3G 13
  WV13: W'hall 6F 29

Watery La. Ind. Est. WV13: W'hall . . .6G 29
Watery La. Middleway
  B9: Birm 1B 118
WATFORD GAP 3F 37
Watford Gap Rd. WS14: Lit H 2G 37
Watford Rd. B30: K Nor 2B 146
Wathan Av. WV14: Cose 3B 60
Watkins Gdns. B31: N'fld 4F 145
Watkins Rd. WV12: W'hall 4C 30
Watland Grn. B34: Stech 4E 105
Watling St. WS7: Muck C 3E 11
  WS8: Bwnhls 3D 8
  WS8: Muck C 3E 11
  WS11: Bwnhls 3D 8
  WS11: Cann, Nort C 1F 7
(not continuous)
  WS14: Muck C 3E 11
Watling St. Bus. Pk. WS11: Bwnhls . . .3E 9
Watney Gro. B44: K'sdng 5C 68
Watson Cl. B72: W Grn 3A 70
Watson Rd. B7: Nech 1D 102
  B8: W End 4F 103
  WS10: Mox 6A 46
  WV10: F'hses 5F 15
  WV14: Cose 3C 60
Watson Rd. E. B7: Nech 2D 102
Watsons Cl. DY2: Dud 1G 95
Watson's Grn. Flds. DY2: Dud 1H 95
Watson's Grn. Rd. DY2: Dud 6G 77
Watson Way CV7: Bal C 5H 169
Wattisham Sq. B35: Cas V 3E 87
Wattis Rd. B67: Smeth 1E 115
Wattle Grn. B70: W Brom 4F 79
Wattle Rd. B70: W Brom 4F 79
Watton Cl. WV14: Cose 4C 60
Watton Grn. B35: Cas V 5E 87
(not continuous)
Watton La. B46: Wat O 5E 89
Watton St. B70: W Brom 5B 80
Watt Rd. B23: Erd 3E 85
  DY4: Tip 5B 62
Watts Cl. DY4: Tip 2E 77
Watt's Rd. B10: Small H 3D 118
Watt St. B21: Hand 2H 99
  B66: Smeth 3F 99
Wattville Av. B21: Hand 1G 99
Wattville Rd. B21: Hand 1G 99
  B66: Hand, Smeth 2F 99
Watwood Rd. B28: Hall G 4F 149
  B90: Hall G, Shir 4F 149
Waugh Cl. B37: Chel W 1D 122
Waugh Dr. B63: Hale 5F 127
Wavell Rd. B8: Salt 4E 103
  DY5: Quar B 4B 110
  WS2: Wals 1E 47
Waveney Av. WV6: Pert 5E 25
Waveney Cft. B36: Cas B 1B 106
Wavenham Cl. B74: Four O 4E 37
Waverhill Rd. B21: Hand 2B 100
Waverley Av. B43: Gt Barr 1D 66
Waverley Cres. B62: Roms 3A 142
  WV2: Penn 5F 43
  WV4: E'shll 2B 60
Waverley Gdns. WV5: Wom 6H 57
Waverley Gro. B91: Sol 4D 150
Waverley Rd. B10: Small H 4D 118
  WS3: Blox 5F 19
  WS10: Darl 5D 46
Waverley Sq. DY2: Dud 1C 94
Wavers Marston B37: Mars G 3C 122
Waxland Rd. B63: Hale 3B 128
Wayfield Cl. B90: Shir 5A 150
Wayfield Rd. B90: Shir 4A 150
Wayford Dr. B72: W Grn 6B 70
Wayford Glade WV13: W'hall 3H 45
Wayford Gro. B8: W End 5H 103
Waynecroft Rd. B43: Gt Barr 3A 66
Wayside B37: Mars G 3B 122
  WV8: Pend 5C 14
Wayside Acres WV8: Cod 5F 13
Wayside Dr. B74: Lit As 6C 36
  B75: R'ley 6C 38
Wayside Gdns. WV12: W'hall 5E 31
Wayside Wlk. WS2: Wals 6G 31

Wealden Hatch WV10: Bush 3A **16**
Wealdstone Dr. DY3: Lwr G 5H **75**
Weaman St. B4: Birm 2E **5** (6G **101**)
Weates Yd. B27: A Grn 1A **136**
Weatheroak Rd. B11: S'hll 6C **118**
Weather Oaks B17: Harb 6F **115**
Weatheroaks B62: Quin 4G **113**
  WS9: Wals W 3D **22**
Weaver Av. B26: Sheld 5F **121**
  B76: Walm 4E **71**
Weaver Cl. DY5: P'ntt 3F **93**
Weaver Ct. B75: R'ley 6C **38**
Weaver Gro. WV13: W'hall 1D **46**
Weavers Cl. WS6: Gt Wyr 4F **7**
Weavers Ri. DY2: Neth 6F **95**
Webb Av. WV6: Pert 4E **25**
Webb Ct. DY8: Stourb 6D **108**
  (off Drury La.)
Webbcroft Rd. B33: Stech 5C **104**
Webb La. B28: Hall G 1E **149**
Webb Rd. DY4: Tip 6C **62**
Webb St. WV13: W'hall 1H **45**
  WV14: Cose 3E **61**
Webley Ri. WV10: Bush 3B **16**
Webnor Ind. Est. WV2: E'shll 5C **44**
Webster Cl. B11: S'brk 5B **118**
  B72: W Grn 6H **69**
Webster Rd. WS2: Wals 4B **32**
  WV13: W'hall 6A **30**
Webster Way B76: Walm 4E **71**
Weddell Wynd WV14: Bils 4G **61**
Wedgbury Cl. WS10: W'bry 4G **63**
Wedgbury Way DY5: Brie H 2F **109**
Wedge Ct. WS1: Wals 2D **48**
  (off Union St.)
Wedge St. WS1: Wals 1D **48**
Wedgewood Av. B70: W Brom 6F **63**
Wedgewood Cl. WV5: Wom 6F **57**
Wedgewood Ct. WS4: S'fld 6G **21**
  (off Green La.)
Wedgewood Ho. B37: F'bri 5D **106**
Wedgewood Pl. B70: W Brom 6F **63**
Wedgewood Rd. B32: Quin 6A **114**
Wedgwood Cl. WV1: Wolv 2C **44**
Wedgwood Dr. B20: Hand 5D **82**
Wedmore Rd. B73: Bold 4F **69**
WEDNESBURY 3F **63**
Wednesbury Great Western Street Stop (MM)
  . . . . .3E **63**
Wednesbury Leisure Cen. 2E **63**
Wednesbury Mus. & Art Gallery . . .3F **63**
Wednesbury New Ent. Cen.
  WS10: Mox 2C **62**
Wednesbury Oak Rd. DY4: Tip 4A **62**
Wednesbury Parkway Stop (MM) 3D **62**
Wednesbury Rd. WS1: Wals 4A **48**
  WS2: Wals 4A **48**
Wednesbury Trad. Est. WS10: W'bry . .1E **63**
WEDNESFIELD 4F **29**
Wednesfield High Sports Cen. 4G **29**
Wednesfield Rd.
  WV10: Wolv 1D **170** (6H **27**)
  WV13: W'hall 6A **30**
Wednesfield Way WV10: Wolv 5C **28**
  WV11: Wed 5F **29**
Wednesfield Way Ind. Est.
  WV11: Wed 5F **29**
Weeford Dell B75: R'ley 6C **38**
Weeford Dr. B20: Hand 3B **82**
Weeford Rd. B75: R'ley 1C **54**
Weirbrook Cl. B29: W Cas 6F **131**
Weland Cl. B46: Wat O 5D **88**
Welbeck Av. WV10: Bush 2H **27**
Welbeck Cl. B62: Quin 6E **113**
Welbeck Dr. WS4: Rus 2H **33**
Welbeck Gro. B23: Erd 2B **84**
Welbury Gdns. WV6: Wolv 4D **26**
Welby Ga. CV7: Bal C 4H **169**
Welby Rd. B28: Hall G 4F **135**
Welch Cl. DY4: Tip 6B **62**
Welches Cl. B31: N'fld 2F **145**
Welcombe Dr. B76: Walm 6D **70**
Welcombe Gro. B91: Sol 4D **150**
Welford Av. B26: Yard 3D **120**

Welford Gro. B74: Four O 6F **37**
Welford Rd. B20: Hand 1C **100**
  B73: New O 4E **69**
  B90: Shir 3A **150**
Welham Cft. B90: M'path 3E **165**
Welland Dr. DY8: Amb 3E **109**
Welland Gro. B24: Erd 4A **86**
  WV13: W'hall 1C **46**
Welland Rd. B63: Hale 3A **128**
Welland Way B76: Walm 6E **71**
Well Cl. B36: Hodg H 1C **104**
Wellcroft Rd. B34: S End 2E **105**
Wellcroft St. WS10: W'bry 2F **63**
Weller Ct. WV3: Wolv 2B **42**
Wellesbourne Cl. WV3: Wolv 3H **41**
Wellesbourne Dr. WV14: Cose 6D **60**
Wellesbourne Rd. B20: Hand 6D **82**
Wellesley Rd. B5: Birm 3G **117**
Wellesley Dr. DY4: Tip 2H **77**
Wellesley Gdns. B13: Mose 4D **134**
Wellesley Rd. B68: O'bry 3H **97**
Wellfield Gdns. DY2: Dud 3G **95**
Wellfield Rd. B28: Hall G 1H **149**
  WS9: A'rdge 1D **34**
Wellhead La. B42: P Barr 5G **83**
Wellhead Way B6: Witt 5G **83**
Wellington Av. WV3: Wolv 4D **42**
Wellington Cl. DY6: K'wfrd 5C **92**
Wellington Ct. B20: Hand 5E **83**
  B32: Harb 6D **114**
  B64: Old H 1H **111**
  (off Vine Gdns.)
Wellington Cres. B20: Hand 5D **82**
Wellington Gro. B91: Sol 1D **150**
Wellington Ho. B32: Quin 1D **130**
Wellington Ind. Est.
  WV14: Cose 6E **61**
Wellington Pas. B2: Birm 4D **4**
Wellington Pl. WV13: W'hall 6H **29**
Wellington Rd. B15: Edg 5D **116**
  B20: Hand 5D **82**
  B67: Smeth 6E **99**
  DY1: Dud 1D **94**
  DY4: Tip 3A **78**
  WS5: Wals 5G **49**
  WV14: Bils 4D **44**
Wellington St. B18: Win G 3H **99**
  B64: Old H 1H **111**
  B66: Smeth 3H **99**
  B69: O'bry 3H **97**
  B71: W Brom 3A **80**
  WS2: Wals 4H **47**
Wellington St. Sth. B70: W Brom 3A **80**
Wellington Ter. B19: Loz 2D **100**
  WV13: W'hall 6H **29**
Wellington Twr. B31: N'fld 6E **145**
Wellington Way B35: Cas V 5F **87**
Well La. B5: Birm 5F **5** (1H **117**)
  WS3: Blox 2C **32**
  WS6: Gt Wyr 4G **7**
  WV11: Wed 5E **29**
Wellman Cft. B29: S Oak 4H **131**
Wellman's Rd. WV13: W'hall 2C **46**
Well Mdw. B45: Redn 3G **157**
Wellmeadow Gro. B92: H Ard 6A **140**
Wellmead Wlk. B45: Rub 1F **157**
Well Pl. WS3: Blox 1C **32**
Wells Av. WS10: Darl 5B **46**
Wells Cl. DY4: Tip 4A **62**
  WV6: Pert 5D **24**
Wells St. B71: W Brom 5B **64**
  DY2: Neth 4E **95**
  (off Meeting St.)
Wellsford Av. B92: Olton 1E **137**
WELLS GREEN 6F **121**
Wells Grn. Rd. B92: Olton 1D **136**
Wells Grn. Shop. Cen.
  B26: Sheld 1F **137**
Wells Rd. B65: Row R 5E **97**
  B92: Sol 1G **137**
  DY5: Brie H 6F **93**
  WV4: Penn 6D **42**
  WV14: Bils 2G **61**
Wells Twr. B16: Birm 1C **116**

Well St. B19: Birm 4E **101**
  WS10: Darl 5E **47**
Wells Wlk. B37: Mars G 2C **122**
Welney Gdns. WV9: Pend 4E **15**
Welsby Av. B43: Gt Barr 6A **66**
Welsh Ho. Farm Rd.
  B32: Quin, Harb 1D **130**
Welshmans Hill B73: New O 3B **68**
Welton Cl. B76: Walm 3E **71**
Welwyndale Rd. B72: W Grn 1A **86**
Wembley Gro. B25: Yard 3A **120**
Wem Gdns. WV11: Wed 3F **29**
Wendell Crest WV10: Bush 3B **16**
Wendover Ho. B31: Longb 1D **158**
Wendover Rd. B23: Erd 6C **68**
  B65: Row R 4A **96**
  WV4: E'shll 3B **60**
Wendron Gro. B14: K Hth 3F **147**
Wenlock Av. WV3: Wolv 3C **42**
Wenlock Cl. B63: Hale 3F **127**
  DY3: Sed 6G **59**
Wenlock Gdns. WS3: Wals 4C **32**
Wenlock Rd. B20: Hand 6H **83**
  DY8: Amb 5F **109**
Wenman St. B12: Bal H 5H **117**
Wensley Cft. B90: Shir 1H **149**
Wensleydale Rd. B42: P Barr 1C **82**
Wensley Rd. B26: Sheld 5D **120**
Wentbridge Rd. WV1: Wolv 2E **45**
Wentworth Av. B36: Cas B 1F **105**
Wentworth Ct. B24: Erd 5F **85**
  B74: Four O 2H **53**
Wentworth Dr. B69: Tiv 2A **96**
Wentworth Ga. B17: Harb 5F **115**
Wentworth Gro. WV6: Pert 4D **24**
Wentworth Pk. Av. B17: Harb 5F **115**
Wentworth Ri. B62: Hale 1D **128**
Wentworth Rd. B17: Harb 5F **115**
  B74: Four O 4G **53**
  B92: Olton 2D **136**
  DY8: Woll 4B **108**
  WS3: Blox 3F **19**
  WV10: Bush 5A **16**
Wentworth Way B32: Bart G 2D **130**
Wenyon Cl. DY4: Tip 3B **78**
Weoley Av. B29: S Oak 3G **131**
WEOLEY CASTLE 4D **130**
Weoley Castle 3E **131**
Weoley Castle Rd. B29: W Cas 4D **130**
Weoley Hill B29: S Oak 5G **131**
Weoley Pk. Rd. B29: S Oak 4F **131**
WERGS .3F **25**
Wergs Dr. WV6: Tett 2G **25**
Wergs Hall WV8: Tett 2F **25**
Wergs Hall Rd. WV6: Tett 1F **25**
  WV8: Cod 6F **13**
Wergs Rd. WV6: Tett 3G **25**
Werneth Gro. WS3: Blox 3G **19**
Wesley Av. B63: Crad 3D **110**
  WS6: C Hay 2D **6**
  WV8: Bilb 5H **13**
Wesley Cl. B64: Old H 2H **111**
  WV5: Wom 2F **73**
Wesley Ct. B16: Edg 6H **99**
  B64: Old H 3H **111**
  WV13: W'hall 2G **45**
Wesley Gro. WS10: W'bry 2E **63**
Wesley Ho. WS2: Wals 4A **48**
  (off Oxford St.)
Wesley Pl. DY4: Tip 6C **62**
Wesley Rd. B23: Erd 2F **85**
  DY5: P'ntt 4F **93**
  WV8: Bilb 5H **13**
  WV12: W'hall 3C **30**
Wesley's Fold WS10: Darl 5D **46**
Wesley St. B69: O'bry 1G **97**
  B70: W Brom 4H **79**
  WV2: E'shll 5C **44**
  WV14: Bils 3G **61**
Wessex Cl. WS8: Bwnhls 6B **10**
Wessex Rd. WV2: E'shll 5B **44**
Wesson Gdns. B63: Hale 2A **128**
Wesson Rd. WS10: Darl 3C **46**
Westacre WV13: W'hall 2H **45**

Westacre Cres. WV3: Wolv 3H 41
Westacre Dr. DY5: Quar B 3B 110
Westacre Gdns. B33: Stech 6D 104
West Av. B20: Hand 3B 82
   B36: Cas B 1H 105
   B69: Tiv 2B 96
   WV11: Wed 3E 29
West Blvd. B32: Quin, Bart G 5C 114
Westbourne Av. B34: Hodg H 3C 104
   WS6: C Hay 1E 7
Westbourne Ct. WS4: Wals 6E 33
               (off Lichfield Rd.)
Westbourne Cres. B15: Edg 3C 116
Westbourne Gdns. B15: Edg 4C 116
Westbourne Gro. B21: Hand 2B 100
Westbourne Rd. B15: Edg 4B 116
   B21: Hand 6H 81
   B62: B'hth 4E 113
   B70: W Brom 5H 79
   B92: Olton 5D 136
   WS4: Wals 5D 32
   WS10: Darl 4F 47
   WV4: Penn 6E 43
Westbourne St. WS4: Wals 6D 32
WEST BROMWICH 4B 80
West Bromwich Albion FC 6F 81
West Bromwich Central Stop (MM) . . .5A 80
W. Bromwich Crematorium
   B71: W Brom 6E 65
W. Bromwich Parkway B70: W Brom . .4H 79
             (Dartmouth St.)
   B70: W Brom 6C 80
             (Springfield Cres.)
W. Bromwich Ringway B70: W Brom . .4B 80
                (New St.)
   B70: W Brom 4A 80
             (St Michael St.)
W. Bromwich Rd. WS1: Wals 5C 48
            (not continuous)
   WS5: Wals 5C 48
W. Bromwich St. B69: O'bry 6F 79
   WS1: Wals 3C 48
Westbrook Av. WS9: A'rdge 4A 34
Westbrook Way WV5: Wom 2F 73
Westbury Av. WS10: W'bry 5F 47
Westbury Ct. DY5: Brie H 1H 109
            (off Lit. Potter St.)
Westbury Rd. B17: Edg 6F 99
   WS10: W'bry 5F 47
Westbury St. WV1: Wolv 2C 170 (1H 43)
Westcliffe Pl. B31: N'fld 3D 144
Westcombe Gro. B32: Bart G 4G 129
W. Coppice Rd. WS8: Bwnhls 5G 9
Westcote Av. B31: Longb 5A 144
Westcote Cl. B92: Olton 3E 137
Westcott Cl. DY6: K'wfrd 6D 92
Westcott Rd. B26: Yard 3E 121
WESTCROFT 6C 16
Westcroft Av. WV10: Bush 6C 16
Westcroft Gro. B38: K Nor 4G 145
Westcroft Rd. DY3: Sed 3F 59
   WV6: Tett 3F 25
Westcroft Way B14: K Hth 6B 148
W. Cross Shop. Cen. B66: Smeth 2B 98
Westdean Cl. B62: Hale 1C 128
West Dr. B5: Edg 6E 117
   B20: Hand 1D 100
West End Av. B66: Smeth 2B 98
Westerdale Cl. DY3: Sed 6C 60
Westerham Cl. B93: Know 3B 166
Westeria Cl. B36: Cas B 1G 105
Westering Parkway WV10: Bush 3A 16
Westerings B20: Hand 5E 83
Western Av. B19: Loz 2E 101
   B62: Hale 1E 129
   DY3: Sed 5F 59
   DY5: Brie H 1F 109
   WS2: Wals 6D 30
Western Bus. Pk. B62: Hale 4B 112
Western Cl. WS2: Wals 6D 30
Western Ct. B9: Birm 2A 118
            (off Bromley St.)
Western Rd. B18: Win G 5B 100
   B24: Erd 4G 85

Western Rd. B64: Crad H 3G 111
   B69: O'bry 4H 97
   B73: W Grn 4G 69
   DY8: Stourb 1D 124
Western Way WS10: Mox, W'bry 1C 62
Westfield Av. B14: K Hth 6B 148
Westfield Cl. B93: Dorr 6F 167
Westfield Dr. WS9: A'rdge 3C 34
   WV5: Wom 6F 57
Westfield Grange B14: K Hth 4G 133
Westfield Gro. WV3: Wolv 3A 42
Westfield Hall B16: Edg 2G 115
Westfield Ho. B36: Cas B 2C 106
Westfield Mnr. B75: Four O 5G 37
Westfield Rd. B14: K Hth 5F 133
   B15: Edg 3G 115
   B27: A Grn 2H 135
   B62: B'hth 2E 113
   B67: Smeth 5D 98
   DY2: Dud 2F 95
   DY3: Sed 4H 59
   DY5: Quar B 3B 110
   WV13: W'hall 3G 45
   WV14: Bils 4D 44
Westford Gro. B28: Hall G 4E 149
West Ga. B1: Birm 6D 100
   B16: Edg 6A 100
Westgate B15: Edg 1A 132
   B69: O'bry 5E 97
   WS9: A'rdge 2H 33
Westgate Cl. DY3: Sed 6A 60
West Ga. Plaza B70: W Brom 5A 80
Westgate Trad. Est. WS9: A'rdge 3A 34
West Grn. WV4: Penn 6A 42
West Grn. Cl. B15: Edg 3D 116
West Gro. Av. B90: M'path 3D 164
Westhall Ga. WS3: Blox 5H 19
Westham Ho. B37: F'bri 5D 106
Westhaven Dr. B31: N'fld 6C 130
Westhaven Rd. B72: S Cold 5A 54
Westhay Rd. B28: Hall G 6H 135
WEST HEATH 6F 145
W. Heath Rd. B18: Win G 5H 99
   B31: N'fld 5F 145
Westhill WV3: Wolv 1A 42
Westhill Cl. B29: S Oak 4H 131
   B92: Olton 5C 136
W. Hill Ct. B14: K Hth 3E 147
Westhill Rd. B38: K Nor 4B 146
West Holme B9: Birm 1C 118
Westholme Cft. B30: B'vlle 6A 132
Westhorpe Gro. B19: Birm 4E 101
Westhouse Gro. B14: K Hth 3F 147
Westland Av. WV3: Wolv 1D 42
West Land Cl. B23: Erd 2F 85
Westland Gdns. DY8: Amb 4D 108
   WV3: Wolv 1E 43
Westland Rd. WV3: Wolv 1D 42
Westlands Est. DY8: Word 2C 108
Westlands Rd. B13: Mose 4A 134
   B76: Walm 1D 86
Westland Wlk. B35: Cas V 5D 86
Westleigh Rd. WV5: Wom 2F 73
Westley Brook Cl. B26: Sheld 6F 121
Westley Cl. B28: Hall G 1H 149
Westley Ct. B71: W Brom 1B 80
Westley Rd. B27: A Grn 2H 135
Westley St. B9: Birm 1A 118
   DY1: Dud 1D 94
Westmead Cres. B24: Erd 3A 86
W. Mead Dr. B14: K Hth 1G 147
Westmede Cen. B68: O'bry 5H 97
West M. B44: Gt Barr 3F 67
W. Mill Cft. B38: K Nor 2A 160
Westminster Av. WV4: Penn 6F 43
Westminster Cl. DY1: Dud 5C 76
Westminster Ct. B20: Hand 5D 82
Westminster Cres. B20: Hand 6E 83
Westminster Dr. B14: K Hth 1G 147
Westminster Ind. Est. DY2: Neth 1F 111
Westminster Pl. B31: Longb 1F 159
Westminster Rd. B20: Hand 5E 83
   B29: S Oak 4C 132

Westminster Rd. B71: W Brom 4B 64
   DY8: Word 1A 108
   WS4: Rus 2F 33
Westmore Way WS10: W'bry 6B 48
Westmorland Cl. B71: W Brom 6B 64
Westmorland Rd. B71: W Brom 6B 64
Weston Av. B11: S'brk 5C 118
   B69: Tiv 6B 78
Weston Cl. B93: Dorr 6H 167
   WS1: Wals 5C 48
Weston Ct. WV1: Wolv 5G 27
             (off Boscobel Cres.)
Weston Cres. WS9: A'rdge 4D 34
Weston Dr. DY4: Tip 3C 62
   WS6: Gt Wyr 5E 7
   WV14: Bils 1D 60
Weston Ho. B19: Hock 3G 101
Weston Ind. Est. B11: Tys 1E 135
Weston La. B11: Tys 1E 135
Weston Rd. B19: Hock 2D 100
   B67: Smeth 1D 114
Weston St. WS1: Wals 5C 48
Weston Ter. B19: Loz 1F 101
            (off New Inn Rd.)
Westover Rd. B20: Hand 3A 82
West Pk. Av. B31: N'fld 5C 144
West Pk. Cl. WS9: A'rdge 4A 34
West Pk. Ct. WV1: Wolv 1E 43
West Pk. Rd. B67: Smeth 2B 98
West Pathway B17: Harb 5G 115
West Point B15: Edg 3G 115
Westport Cres. WV11: Wed 4H 29
Westray Cl. B45: Fran 6E 143
Westridge DY3: Sed 5G 59
Westridge Rd. B13: Mose 6C 134
West Ri. B75: S Cold 5A 54
West Rd. B6: Witt 5G 83
   B43: Gt Barr 6A 66
   B63: Crad 5D 110
   DY4: Tip 5B 62
West Rd. Sth. B63: Crad 5D 110
Westside Dr. B32: Bart G 4B 130
WEST SMETHWICK 2B 98
West St. B65: B'hth 2C 112
   DY3: Gorn 4H 75
   DY5: Quar B 3B 110
   DY8: Stourb 6D 108
   WS3: Blox 2A 32
   WV10: Wolv 4G 27
West Vw. B8: W End 5A 104
West Vw. Ct. B75: S Cold 5C 54
West Vw. Dr. DY6: K'wfrd 4C 92
West Vw. Rd. B75: S Cold 5C 54
Westville Rd. WS2: Wals 6G 31
Westward Cl. B44: K'sdng 5H 67
West Way B31: Longb 2F 159
   WS4: S'fld 5F 21
Westwick Cl. WS9: Ston 3G 23
Westwood Av. B11: Tys 1D 134
   DY8: Stourb 2A 124
Westwood Bus. Pk. B6: Witt 6B 84
Westwood Ct. B73: S'tly 1B 68
Westwood Dr. B45: Redn 6H 143
Westwood Gro. B91: Sol 5D 150
Westwood Rd. B6: Witt 6A 84
   B73: S'tly 1A 68
Westwood St. DY5: Brie H 2E 109
Westwood Vw. B24: Erd 4A 86
Wetherby Cl. B36: Hodg H 1B 104
   WV10: F'hses 3H 15
Wetherby Rd. B27: A Grn 3A 136
   WS3: Blox 3G 19
Wetherfield Rd. B11: Tys 2G 135
Wexford Cl. DY1: Dud 5B 76
Wexler Lofts B1: Birm 2A 4
Weybourne Rd. B44: Gt Barr 3C 67
Weycroft Rd. B23: Erd 6B 68
Weyhill Cl. WV9: Pend 5D 14
Weymoor Rd. B17: Harb 2E 131
Weymouth Dr. B74: Four O 5F 37
Wharf, The B1: Birm 5B 4 (1E 117)
Wharf App. WS9: A'rdge 2B 34
Wharfdale Rd. B11: Tys 6G 119
Wharfedale Cl. DY6: W Hth 2H 91

Wharfedale St. WS10: W'bry 3F 63
Wharf La. B18: Hock 3C 100
B91: Sol 1H 151
WS7: Chase 2C 10
Wharf Rd. B11: Tys 6H 119
B30: K Nor 5C 146
Wharf Rd. Ind. Est. B11: Tys 6H 119
Wharfside B69: O'bry 2F 97
Wharfside Leisure Complex 2D 146
Wharfside St. B1: Birm 6C 4 (2F 117)
Wharf St. B6: Aston 2A 102
B18: Hock 3C 100
WV1: Wolv 2A 44
Whar Hall Rd. B92: Sol 5A 138
Wharton Av. B92: Sol 6A 138
Wharton Rd. B66: Smeth 2G 99
Wharton St. B7: Nech 1D 102
Wharwell La. WS6: Gt Wyr 4G 7
Whatcote Grn. B92: Sol 5H 137
Whatecroft, The B17: Harb 5F 115
Whateley Av. WS3: Wals 3D 32
Whateley Cres. B36: Cas B 1H 105
Whateley Grn. B36: Cas B 1G 105
B74: Four O 3G 53
Whateley Hall Cl. B93: Know 2E 167
Whateley Hall Rd. B93: Know 2D 166
Whateley Lodge Dr. B36: Cas B 1G 105
Whateley Pl. WS3: Wals 3D 32
Whateley Rd. B21: Hand 1A 100
WS3: Wals 3D 32
Wheatcroft Cl. B62: B'hth 3F 113
B75: R'ley 6C 38
Wheatcroft Dr. B37: Chel W 2E 123
Wheatcroft Gro. D32: Dud 6H 77
Wheatcroft Rd. B33: Yard 1D 120
Wheaten Cl. B37: Chel W 6F 107
Wheatfield Cl. B36: Cas B 2C 106
Wheatfield Vw. B31: N'fld 1B 144
Wheat Hill WS5: Wals 3A 50
Wheathill Cl. WV4: Penn 2C 58
Wheatland Gro. WS9: A'rdge 5D 34
Wheatlands, The WV6: Pert 6D 24
Wheatlands Cft. B33: Kitts G 6A 106
Wheatley Cl. D68: O'bry 3R 114
B75: Four O 6A 38
B92: Sol 5A 138
Wheatley Grange B46: Col 3H 107
Wheatley Gro. WS6: Gt Wyr 3G 7
Wheatley Rd. B68: O'bry 3A 114
Wheatley St. B70: W Brom 4G 79
WV2: E'shll 5A 44
Wheatmoor Ri. B75: S Cold 5C 54
Wheatmoor Rd. B75: S Cold 4D 54
Wheaton Cl. WV10: Oxl 2G 27
Wheaton Va. B20: Hand 4A 82
Wheatridge Cl. DY6: W Hth 1G 91
Wheats Av. B17: Harb 2F 131
Wheatsheaf Cl. B75: R'ley 5C 38
Wheatsheaf Rd. D16: Edg 1H 115
B69: Tiv 1A 96
WV8: Pend 6C 14
Wheatstone Cl. DY3: Sed 1A 76
Wheatstone Gro. B33: Stech 4D 104
WHEATSTONE PARK 2D 12
Wheel Av. WV8: Cod 4F 13
Wheel Ct., The WV8: Cod 4F 13
Wheeler Cl. WV8: Cod 3E 13
Wheeler Ho. B69: O'bry 2G 97
Wheeler Rd. WV11: Wed 1E 29
Wheeler's Fold WV1: Wolv ..3C 170 (1H 43)
(off Lwr. High St.)
Wheeler's Hill DY8: Stourb 5D 108
(off Lwr. High St.)
Wheeler's La. B13: Mose 1G 147
Wheeler St. B19: Hock, Loz 1H 101
DY8: Stourb 6D 108
Wheeler St. Shop. Cen.
B19: Hock 3F 101
Wheeley Moor Rd. B37: K'hrst 4C 106
Wheeley Rd. B92: Sol 6H 137
Wheeley's La. B15: Birm 3E 117
Wheeley's Rd. B15: Edg 4D 116
Wheelfield WV8: Cod 4F 13
Wheelock Cl. B74: S'tly 4H 51
Wheels Pk. 1C 118

Wheelwright Cl. WS10: Darl 5C 46
Wheelwright Ct. B24: Erd 5E 85
Wheelwright Rd. B24: Erd 5E 85
Wheldrake Av. B34: S End 4G 105
Whernside Dr. WV6: Wolv 4E 27
Wherretts Well La. B91: Sol 2A 152
Whetstone Cl. B15: Edg 6B 116
Whetstone Grn. WV10: Bush 6H 15
Whetstone Gro. WV10: Bush 1H 27
Whetstone La. WS9: A'rdge 5D 34
Whetstone Rd. WV10: Bush 1H 27
Whetty Bri. Rd. B45: Rub 3E 157
Whetty La. B45: Rub 2E 157
Whichbury Ct. B65: Row R 5D 96
Whichford Cl. B76: Walm 1B 86
Whichford Gro. B9: Bord G 1H 119
While Rd. B72: S Cold 1H 69
Whilmot Cl. WV10: F'stne 1D 16
Whinberry Ri. DY5: P'ntt 6G 75
Whisley Brook La. B28: Hall G 3F 135
Whistler Gro. WV10: Bush 1C 28
Whiston Av. WV11: Wed 2A 30
Whiston Gro. B29: W Cas 5F 131
Whiston Ho. WS1: Wals 2D 48
Whitacre La. WS14: Lynn 6G 11
Whitacre Rd. B9: Bord G 6E 103
B93: Know 2D 166
Whitbourne Cl. B12: Bal H 6B 118
Whitburn Av. B42: P Barr 2C 82
Whitburn Cl. WV9: Pend 5E 15
Whitby Cl. WS3: Blox 4F 19
Whitby Rd. B12: Bal H 1A 134
Whitchurch La. B90: Dic H 3F 163
Whitcot Gro. B31: Longb 1D 158
Whitebeam Cl. DY3: Lwr G 3G 75
WS8: Clay 1A 22
Whitebeam Cft. B38: K Nor 6A 146
Whitebeam Rd. B37: Chel W 3E 123
White City Rd. DY5: Quar B 2C 110
White Cl. DY9: Pedm 3G 125
Whitecrest B43: Gt Barr 3B 66
White Falcon Ct. B91: Sol 5D 150
White Farm Rd. B74: Four O 4E 37
Whitefield Av. B17: Harb 5E 115
Whitefield Cl. WV8: Bilb 5H 13
Whitefields Cres. B91: Sol 5F 151
Whitefields Ga. B91: Sol 6E 151
Whitefields Rd. B91: Sol 6E 151
(not continuous)
Whitefriars Dr. B63: Hale 1A 128
Whitegates Rd. WV14: Cose 2F 61
Whitehall Dr. B63: Hale 1B 128
DY1: Dud 5C 76
Whitehall Ind. Pk. DY4: Tip 2E 79
Whitehall Rd. B9: Small H 1D 118
B21: Hand 2C 100
B63: Hale 1B 128
B64: Crad H 2E 111
B70: W Brom 2E 79
DY4: Tip 2D 78
DY6: K'wfrd 3A 92
DY8: Stourb 3F 125
WS1: Wals 4C 48
WV4: Penn 1F 59
White Hart, The WS1: Wals 3C 48
(off Caldmore Grn.)
Whitehead Dr. B76: Min 1H 87
Whitehead Gro. CV7: Bal C 2H 169
Whitehead Rd. B6: Aston 2G 101
Whiteheath Ct. B69: O'bry 5E 97
(off Birchfield La.)
White Hill B31: N'fld 2F 145
Whitehill La. B29: W Cas 2E 145
White Hollies WS3: Pels 3D 20
White Horse Rd. WS8: Bwnhls 3A 10
Whitehouse Av. WS10: Darl 4B 46
WS10: W'bry 2F 63
WV3: Wolv 3B 42
WV11: Wed 2H 29
White Ho. Cl. B91: Sol 4D 150
WHITEHOUSE COMMON 4D 54
Whitehouse Comn. Rd. B75: S Cold ..3C 54
Whitehouse Ct. B75: S Cold 6D 54

Whitehouse Cres. B75: S Cold 3C 54
WV11: Wed 6H 17
Whitehouse Dr. B66: Smeth 2E 99
WHITEHOUSE GATE 5E 97
White Ho. Grn. B91: Sol 4D 150
Whitehouse La. DY3: Stourt, Swind ..6A 72
WV8: Cod, Cod W 1B 12
Whitehouse Pl. B45: Rub 3F 157
White Ho's. La. WV10: F'stne 1C 16
(not continuous)
Whitehouse St. B6: Aston 3H 101
DY4: Tip 5A 78
WS2: Wals 6B 32
WV14: Cose 5E 61
White Row WV5: Try 4C 56
Whites Dr. DY3: Sed 5A 60
Whiteslade Cl. B93: Know 2C 166
Whitesmiths Cl. DY3: Sed 5H 59
Whitesmiths Cft. B14: K Hth 5G 133
Whites Rd. B71: W Brom 1A 80
White Stitch La. CV7: Mer 2H 141
WHITE STITCH 1H 141
Whitestone Rd. B63: Hale 5A 112
White St. B12: Bal H 6A 118
WS1: Wals 3C 48
Whites Wood WV5: Wom 2G 73
Whitethorn Cres. B74: S'tly 2F 51
Whitethorn Rd. DY8: Word 2E 109
Whitewood Glade WV12: W'hall 5E 31
Whitford Dr. B90: M'path 2F 165
Whitgreave Av. WV10: Bush 1A 28
WV10: F'stne 1D 16
Whitgreave Ct. B70: W Brom 4E 79
WV10: F'stne 1D 16
Whitgreave St. B70: W Brom 4E 79
Whitland Cl. B45: Redn 3H 157
Whitland Dr. B14: K Hth 4H 147
Whitley Cl. WV6: Tett 1H 41
Whitley Ct. B20: Hand 4A 82
Whitley Ct. Rd. B32: Quin 5A 114
Whitley Dr. B74: S'tly 3A 52
Whitley St. WS10: W'bry 2E 63
Whitlock Gro. B14: K Hth 4A 148
Whitminster Av. B24: Erd 4H 85
Whitminster Cl. WV12: W'hall 5C 30
Whitmore Hill WV1: Wolv 2A 170 (1G 43)
Whitmore Ho. WV6: Wolv 5E 27
WHITMORE REANS 5D 26
Whitmore Rd. B10: Small H 3C 118
DY8: Stourb 6B 108
Whitmore St. B18: Hock 4D 100
WS1: Wals 5B 48
WV1: Wolv 2C 170 (1H 43)
Whitnash Cl. CV7: Bal C 3G 169
Whitney Av. DY8: Woll 5B 108
Whittaker St. WV2: E'shll 5A 44
Whittall St. B4: Birm 2E 5 (6G 101)
Whittimere St. WS1: Wals 1D 48
Whittingham Gro. WV11: Wed 3H 29
Whittingham Rd. B63: Hale 6A 112
Whittington Cl. B14: K Hth 2G 147
B71: W Brom 5D 64
Whittington Gro. B33: Yard 1D 120
Whittington Hall La. DY7: Kinv 1A 124
Whittington Oval B33: Yard 1E 121
Whittington Rd. DY8: Stourb 2B 124
Whittleford Gro. B36: Cas B 6G 87
Whitton St. WS10: Darl 5E 47
Whitwell Cl. B90: M'path 4E 165
Whitworth Cl. WS10: Darl 4E 47
Whitworth Dr. B71: W Brom 4C 64
Whitworth Ind. Pk. B9: Bord G 1C 118

Whyle St. B63: Hale 1B **128**
Whyley St. B70: W Brom 3G **79**
Whyley Wlk. B69: O'bry 4G **97**
Whynot St. B63: Crad 6D **110**
Wibert Cl. B29: S Oak 4C **132**
Wichnor Rd. B92: Olton 6D **120**
Wicketts Twr. B5: Edg 6E **117**
Wickham Gdns. WV11: Wed 3D **28**
Wickham Sq. B70: W Brom 5H **79**
Wicklow Cl. B63: Hale 4F **127**
Wideacre Dr. B44: Gt Barr 6G **67**
Wide Acres B45: Fran 6F **143**
Widney Av. B29: S Oak 3G **131**
 WS9: A'rdge 6D **22**
Widney Cl. B93: Ben H 4B **166**
Widney La. B91: Sol 6C **150**
Widney Mnr. Rd. B91: Sol 5G **151**
Widney Manor Station (Rail) 1G **165**
Widney Rd. B93: Ben H, Know 4A **166**
Wiggin Cotts. B17: Harb 6G **115**
Wiggin Ho. WS3: Blox 4A **20**
Wiggins Cft. B76: Walm 2D **70**
Wiggins Hill Rd. B76: Min, Wis 1B **88**
Wigginsmill Rd. WS10: W'bry 4D **62**
Wiggin St. B16: Birm 6B **100**
Wight Cft. B36: Cas B 3D **106**
WIGHTWICK 2F **41**
Wightwick Bank WV6: Tett 2G **41**
Wightwick Cl. WS3: Blox 6H **19**
Wightwick Ct. WV6: Tett 1G **41**
Wightwick Gro. WV6: Tett 1G **41**
Wightwick Hall Rd. WV6: Tett 2E **41**
Wightwick Leys WV6: Tett 1F **41**
Wightwick Manor 2F **41**
Wigland Way B38: K Nor 6C **146**
Wigmore Gro. B44: K'sdng 5B **68**
Wigmore La. B71: W Brom 5E **65**
 (not continuous)
Wigorn La. DY9: Pedm 5F **125**
Wigorn Rd. B67: Smeth 2D **114**
Wilberforce Way B92: Sol 6B **138**
Wilcote Gro. B27: A Grn 5A **136**
Wildacres DY8: Woll 5F **109**
Wilday Cl. DY4: Tip 2A **78**
Wilde Cl. B14: K Hth 3F **147**
Wilden Cl. B31: N'fld 4A **144**
Wilderness La. B43: Gt Barr 3H **65**
Wildfell Rd. B27: A Grn 3B **136**
WILDMOOR 5A **156**
Wildmoor La. B61: Cats, Wild 6A **156**
Wildmoor Rd. B90: Shir 2H **149**
Wildside Activity Cen. 4D **26**
Wildtree Av. WV10: Bush 5C **16**
Wiley Av. WS10: Darl 5C **46**
Wiley Av. Sth. WS10: Darl 6C **46**
Wilford Gro. B76: Walm 1F **87**
 B91: Sol 5F **151**
Wilford Rd. B71: W Brom 1B **80**
Wilkes Av. WS2: Wals 1F **47**
Wilkes Cl. WS3: Pels 4C **20**
Wilkes Cft. DY3: Sed 6H **59**
Wilkes Rd. WV8: Cod 3F **13**
Wilkes St. B71: W Brom 6C **64**
 WV13: W'hall 2A **46**
Wilkin, The WS8: Bwnhls 3G **9**
Wilkin Rd. WS8: Bwnhls 3G **9**
Wilkins Ho. WS3: Blox 6G **19**
 (off Sandbank)
Wilkinson Av. WV14: Bils 2G **61**
Wilkinson Cl. B73: W Grn 3H **69**
Wilkinson Cft. B8: W End 3A **104**
Wilkinson Rd. WS10: Mox 6A **46**
Wilkins Rd. WV14: Bils 4F **45**
Wilks Grn. B21: Hand 4H **81**
Willard Rd. B25: Yard 5A **120**
Willaston Rd. B33: Sheld 4H **121**
Willclare Rd. B26: Sheld 5E **121**
Willcock Rd. WV2: Wolv 4A **44**
WILLENHALL 1B **46**
Willenhall Ind. Est. WV13: W'hall 6C **30**
Willenhall La. WS2: Wals 2F **31**
 WS3: Blox 2F **31**
Willenhall La. Ind. Est. WS3: Blox 1G **31**

Willenhall Leisure Cen. 2B **46**
Willenhall Library & Mus. 2B **46**
Willenhall Rd. WS10: Darl 2D **46**
 WV1: Wolv 2C **44**
 WV13: W'hall 2C **44**
 WV14: Bils 5H **45**
Willenhall St. WS10: Darl 3C **46**
Willerby Fold WV10: Bush 3B **16**
Willersey Rd. B13: Mose 5D **134**
Willes Ct. B62: Quin 4G **113**
 (off Binswood Rd.)
Willes Rd. B18: Win G 3A **100**
Willett Av. WS7: Chase 1A **10**
Willett Rd. B71: W Brom 5C **64**
Willetts Dr. B63: Crad 1D **126**
Willetts Rd. B31: N'fld 6E **145**
Willey Gro. B24: Erd 5H **85**
William Bentley Ct. WV11: Wed 4E **29**
William Booth La. B4: Birm 1D **4** (5F **101**)
William Cook Rd. B8: W End 4H **103**
William Ct. B13: Mose 1H **133**
 B16: Edg 2A **116**
William Edward St. B12: Birm 3H **117**
William Grn. Rd. WS10: W'bry 2A **64**
William Harper Rd. WV13: W'hall 2B **46**
William Henry St. B7: Nech 3A **102**
William Kerr Rd. DY4: Tip 2C **78**
William Paget Ho. WS10: W'bry 2E **63**
William Rd. B31: N'fld 6D **144**
 B67: Smeth .6B **98**
William Savage Way B66: Smeth 5G **99**
William's Cl. WV12: W'hall 4C **30**
Williamson St. WV3: Wolv 6A **170** (3F **43**)
William St. B15: Birm 6A **4** (2E **117**)
 B70: W Brom 2E **79**
 DY5: Brie H .6G **93**
 WS4: Wals 6D **32**
William St. Nth. B19: Birm 5F **101**
William St. W. B66: Smeth 2F **99**
William Wiggin Av. WS3: Blox 5H **19**
Willingsworth Rd. WS10: W'bry 4C **62**
Willingworth Cl. WV14: Cose 2C **60**
Willis Pearson Av. WV14: Bils 3H **61**
Willmore Gro. B38: K Nor 1B **160**
Willmore Rd. B20: Hand 5F **83**
Willmott Cl. B75: R'ley 6B **38**
Willmott Rd. B75: R'ley 6B **38**
Willoughby Dr. B91: Sol 6F **151**
Willoughby Gro. B29: W Cas 4E **131**
Willow Av. B17: Edg 1E **115**
 WS10: W'bry 1F **63**
 WV11: Wed .1C **28**
Willow Bank WV3: Wolv 2A **42**
Willowbank Rd. B93: Know 3B **166**
Willow Cl. B21: Hand 1H **99**
 B64: Old H 2G **111**
Willow Coppice B32: Bart G 4A **130**
Willow Ct. B13: Mose 2A **134**
 B66: Smeth .1B **98**
 DY9: Lye 6H **109**
Willowdale Grange WV6: Tett 4C **26**
Willow Dr. B21: Hand 6G **81**
 B69: Tiv 2C **96**
 B90: Ches G 5B **164**
 WV8: Bilb 4H **13**
Willow End DY9: W'cte 2H **125**
Willow Gdns. B16: Birm 5B **100**
Willow Gro. WV11: Ess 4B **18**
 WV13: W'hall 2B **46**
Willow Hgts. B64: Crad H 3A **112**
Willowherb Cl. WS5: Wals 2E **65**
Willowherb Way B90: Dic H 4G **163**
Willow Ho. B7: Birm 5A **102**
 (off Vauxhall Rd.)
Willow M. B29: S Oak 4F **131**
Willow Pk. Dr. DY8: Stourb 3E **125**
Willow Ri. DY5: Brie H 2G **109**
Willow Rd. B30: B'vlle 5B **132**
 B43: Gt Barr .4B **66**
 B91: Sol 5C **150**
 DY1: Dud 3C **76**
 WV3: Wolv 3B **42**

Willows, The B27: A Grn 3H **135**
 B47: H'wd 3A **162**
 B74: Four O .1F **53**
 B76: Walm 3D **70**
 DY2: Neth 4G **95**
 WV5: Wom 2F **73**
Willowsbrook Rd. B62: B'hth 3F **113**
Willows Cres. B12: Bal H 6F **117**
Willowside WS4: S'fld 1G **33**
Willows Rd. B12: Bal H 6G **117**
 WS1: Wals 2E **49**
 WS4: S'fld 1G **33**
Willow Wlk. B76: Walm 6D **70**
Willow Way B37: Chel W 1D **122**
Wills Av. B71: W Brom 5H **63**
Willsbridge Covert B14: K Hth 5F **147**
Wills Ho. B70: W Brom 5A **80**
Willson Cft. B28: Hall G 4D **148**
Wills St. B19: Loz 2D **100**
Wills Way B66: Smeth 5G **99**
Wilmcote Cl. B12: Bal H 5G **117**
Wilmcote Dr. B75: Four O 6H **37**
Wilmcote Rd. B91: Sol 1D **150**
Wilmcote Twr. B12: Birm 4H **117**
Wilmington Rd. B32: Quin 5H **113**
Wilmore La. B47: Wyt 5H **161**
Wilmot Av. B46: Col 3H **107**
Wilmot Cl. CV7: Bal C 1H **169**
Wilmot Dr. B23: Erd 1G **85**
 DY4: Tip 1G **77**
Wilmot Gdns. DY1: Dud 5C **76**
Wilnecote Gro. B42: P Barr 3F **83**
Wilner's Vw. WS3: Pels 2D **20**
Wilsford Cl. B14: K Hth 6F **147**
 WS4: S'fld 1G **33**
Wilson Dr. B69: Tiv 4C **78**
 B75: S Cold .6E **55**
 (not continuous)
Wilson Rd. B19: Loz 1F **101**
 B66: Smeth .6F **99**
 B68: O'bry 3B **114**
 DY5: Brie H .5G **93**
 WV4: Cose 6E **61**
Wilsons Rd. B93: Know 3E **167**
Wilson St. DY4: Tip 2A **78**
 WV1: Wolv 6H **27**
Wilton Cl. DY3: Sed 6A **60**
Wilton Rd. B11: S'hll 6B **118**
 B20: Hand 6D **82**
 B23: Erd 2G **85**
 CV7: Bal C 3H **169**
Wilton St. B19: Loz 1F **101**
Wiltshire Cl. WS2: Wals 5B **32**
Wiltshire Ct. B29: W Cas 6G **131**
 (off Tugford Rd.)
Wiltshire Dr. B63: Crad 4D **110**
Wiltshire Way B71: W Brom 6A **64**
Wimbledon Dr. DY8: Stourb 3F **125**
Wimborne Rd. WV10: Wolv 3C **28**
Wimbourne Rd. B16: Edg 6H **99**
 B76: Walm 1E **71**
Wimhurst Mdw. WV10: Bush 3B **16**
Wimperis Way B43: Gt Barr 1E **67**
Wimpole Gro. B44: K'sdng 6B **68**
Wincanton Cft. B36: Hodg H 1A **104**
Winceby Rd. WV6: Pert 6F **25**
Winchcombe Cl. B92: Olton 3F **137**
 DY1: Dud 4A **76**
Winchcombe Rd. B92: Olton 3F **137**
Winchester Cl. B65: Row R 5E **97**
 DY9: Hag 6E **125**
Winchester Ct. B74: Four O 1F **53**
 (off Vesey Cl.)
Winchester Dr. B37: Chel W 1C **122**
 DY8: Stourb .2E **125**
Winchester Gdns. B31: N'fld 4E **145**
Winchester Gro. B21: Hand 1G **99**
Winchester M. WS9: A'rdge 5D **34**
Winchester Ri. DY1: Dud 5C **76**
Winchester Rd. B20: Hand 6F **83**
 B71: W Brom 5H **63**
 WV10: F'hses 4G **15**
Winchfield Dr. B17: Harb 3D **114**
Wincote Dr. WV6: Tett 5A **26**

Wincrest Way. B34: S End 4G 105
Windermere Dr. B74: S'tly 6H 35
  DY6: K'wfrd 3B 92
Windermere Ho. B15: Edg 2H 131
  (off Vincent Rd.)
  B69: O'bry 4D 96
Windermere Rd. B13: Mose 4B 134
  B21: Hand 5A 82
  WV6: Tett 1B 26
Windfall Ct. B24: Erd 3B 86
Winding Mill Nth. DY5: Quar B 4A 110
Winding Mill Sth. DY5: Quar B 4A 110
Windlass Cft. B31: N'fld 2D 144
Windleaves Rd. B36: Cas B 1A 106
Windley Cl. B19: Birm 4E 101
Windley Ho. B73: New O 3C 68
Windmill Av. B45: Rub 1E 157
  B46: Col .2H 107
Windmill Bank WV5: Wom 6G 57
Windmill Cl. B31: N'fld 2G 145
Windmill Cres. B66: Smeth 4G 99
  WV3: Wolv 2G 41
Windmill End DY2: Neth 5G 95
Windmill Fold WV5: Wom 6G 57
Windmill Gro. DY6: W Hth 1H 91
Windmill Hill B31: N'fld 2F 145
  B63: Crad 5E 111
Windmill La. B66: Smeth 5F 99
  WV3: Wolv 2G 41
Windmill Pct. B66: Smeth 4F 99
Windmill Rd. B90: Shir 5E 149
Windmill St. B1: Birm 6D 4 (2F 117)
  DY1: Dud .5C 76
  DY3: Up Gor 2H 75
  WS1: Wals 3C 48
  WS10: W'bry 2G 63
Windmill Ter. WS10: W'bry 2G 63
Windmill Vw. DY1: Dud 6D 60
Windridge Cres. B92: Sol 5B 138
Windrow, The WV6: Pert 5D 24
Windrush Cl. B92: Olton 3E 137
  WS3: Pels 6E 21
Windrush Gro. B29: S Oak 5C 132
Windruch Rd. B47: H'wd 2B 162
Windsor Arc. B4: Birm 3E 5 (6G 101)
Windsor Av. B68: O'bry 6G 97
  WV4: Penn 5C 42
Windsor Cl. B31: Longb 3E 159
  B45: Fran 5G 143
  B63: Hale 2H 127
  B65: Row R 5C 96
  DY3: Gorn 6F 75
Windsor Ct. B38: K Nor 6B 146
Windsor Cres. DY2: Dud 3F 95
Windsor Dr. B24: Erd 2A 86
  B92: Sol .2F 137
Windsor Gdns. WV3: Wolv 4G 41
  WV8: Cod 4F 13
Windsor Ga. WV12: W'hall 5C 30
Windsor Gro. DY8: Word 2C 108
  WS4: S'fld .5G 21
Windsor Ho. B23: Erd 1F 85
Windsor Ind. Est. B7: Birm 4A 102
Windsor Lodge B92: Olton 5B 136
Windsor Pl. B7: Birm 6A 102
  B23: Erd .4E 85
Windsor Rd. B30: Stir 2B 146
  B36: Cas B 2B 106
  B63: Hale 1H 127
  B65: Row R 5C 96
  B68: O'bry 6G 97
  B71: W Brom 5H 63
  B73: New O 4D 68
  DY4: Tip 5A 62
  DY8: Stourb 2B 124
  WS6: C Hay 1E 7
  WV4: E'shll 6B 44
  WV5: Wom 1F 73
Windsor St. B7: Birm 4H 101
  WS1: Wals 4C 48
  WV14: Bils 5E 45
Windsor St. Sth. B7: Birm 5A 102
Windsor Ter. B16: Edg 2B 116
Windsor Vw. B32: Bart G 6H 129

Windsor Wlk. WS10: Darl 3D 46
Windsor Way WS4: Rus 2H 33
Winds Point DY9: Hag 6E 125
Windward Way B36: Cas B 1B 106
Windward Way Ind. Est.
  B36: Cas B 1B 106
Windy Mnr. Rd. B93: Know 5G 151
Windyridge Rd. B76: Walm 1D 86
Windyridge Av. DY6: K'wfrd 5C 92
Wingate Cl. B30: K Nor 3B 146
Wingate Ct. B74: Four O 5E 37
Wingate Rd. WS2: Wals 1E 47
Wing Cl. WS2: Wals 5F 31
Wingfield Cl. B37: F'bri 6B 106
Wingfield Ho. B37: K'hrst 4B 106
Wingfield Rd. B42: Gt Barr 6E 67
  B46: Col .4H 107
Wingfoot Av. WV10: Bush 1A 28
Wingfoot Cl. B24: Erd 6A 86
Wingfoot Way B24: Erd 6A 86
Wing Yip Cen. B7: Nech 3B 102
Winifride Ct. B17: Harb 6F 115
Winkle St. B70: W Brom 3H 79
Winleigh Rd. B20: Hand 5B 82
Winnall Cl. WV14: Cose 3F 61
Winn Ho. WS2: Wals 6B 32
  (off Burrowes St.)
Winnie Rd. B29: S Oak 4A 132
Winnington Rd. B8: W End 2G 103
Winnipeg Rd. B38: K Nor 1C 160
Winrush Cl. DY3: Gorn 4H 75
Winscar Cft. DY3: Lwr G 4A 76
Winsford Cl. B63: Hale 5A 112
  B76: Walm 2C 70
  CV7: Bal C 3G 169
Winsham Gro. B21: Hand 1A 100
Winslow Av. B8: W End 5H 103
Winslow Dr. WV6: Wolv 5D 26
Winslow Ho. B29: S Oak 4F 131
WINSON GREEN 4A 100
Winson Green/ Outer Circle Stop (MM)
  . . . . .2A 100
Winson Grn. Rd. B18: Win G 4A 100
Winson St. B18: Win G 5H 99
Winspear Cl. CV7: Mer 4H 141
Winstanley Rd. B33: Stech 1B 120
Winster Av. B93: Dorr 5A 166
Winster Gro. B44: Gt Barr 3F 67
Winster Gro. Ind. Est. B44: Gt Barr . . .3F 67
Winster Rd. B43: Gt Barr 5H 65
  WV1: Wolv 2D 44
Winston Churchill Ct. WV14: Bils 3E 45
Winston Dr. B20: Hand 6D 82
  B62: Roms 3A 142
Winston Rd. DY3: Swind 5E 73
Winterbourne Cft. B14: K Hth 6E 147
Winterbourne Rd. B91: Sol 3D 150
Winterdene CV7: Bal C 2H 169
Winterley Gdns. DY3: Sed 1A 76
Winterley La. WS4: Rus 2G 33
Winterton Rd. B44: K'sdng 2A 68
Winthorpe Dr. B91: Sol 1G 165
Wintney Cl. B17: Harb 4E 115
Winton Gro. B76: Walm 1E 87
Winwood Rd. B65: Row R 6E 97
Winwoods Gro. B32: Bart G 5G 129
Wiremill Cl. B44: Gt Barr 1G 83
Wirral Rd. B31: N'fld 1D 144
Wiseacre Cft. B90: Shir 5E 149
Wiseman Gro. B23: Erd 4D 68
Wisemeadows B90: Shir 5E 149
Wisemore WS1: Wals 1C 48
  WS2: Wals 1C 48
Wishaw Cl. B90: Shir 5E 149
Wishaw Gro. B37: K'hrst 4B 106
Wishaw La. B76: Curd 1D 88
  B76: Min, Wis 1H 87
Wisley Way B32: Harb 6D 114
Wistaria Cl. B31: N'fld 1E 145
Wisteria Dr. WS5: Wals 1D 64
  WS8: Bwnhls 3G 9
Wisteria Gro. B44: Gt Barr 3G 67
Wistmans Cl. DY1: Dud 5A 76
Wistwood Hayes WV10: Bush 3B 16

Witham Cl. B76: Walm 4E 71
Witham Cft. B91: Sol 6G 151
Withdean Cl. B11: S'brk 6D 118
Witherford Cl. B29: S Oak 5G 131
Witherford Cft. B91: Sol 5B 150
Witherford Way B29: S Oak 5G 131
Withern Way DY3: Gorn 4G 75
Withers Rd. WV8: Bilb 4H 13
Withers Way B71: W Brom 3B 80
Withington Covert B14: K Hth 5F 147
Withington Gro. B93: Ben H, Dorr 5A 166
Withybrook Rd. B90: Shir 1H 163
Withy Gro. B37: K'hrst 4B 106
Withy Hill Rd. B75: S Cold 4D 54
Withymere La. WV5: Wom 5A 58
Withymoor Rd. DY2: Neth 5G 95
  DY8: Amb 4E 109
WITHYMOOR VILLAGE 2H 109
Withy Rd. WV14: Bils 2E 61
Withy Rd. Ind. Est. WV14: Bils 2E 61
Withywood Cl. WV12: W'hall 6C 18
Witley Av. B63: Hale 1G 127
  B91: Sol .5G 151
Witley Cres. B69: O'bry 4E 97
Witley Farm Cl. B91: Sol 5G 151
Witley Rd. B31: N'fld 5H 145
Witney Dr. B37: F'bri 1B 122
Witney Gro. WV10: F'hses 4F 15
Wittersham Ct. WV13: W'hall 1B 46
  (off Birmingham St.)
WITTON 6H 83
Witton Bank B62: Quin 4F 113
Witton La. B6: Aston 6H 83
  B71: W Brom 5G 63
Witton Lodge Rd. B23: Erd 6B 68
Witton Rd. B6: Aston, Witt 1G 101
  WV4: Penn 5E 43
Witton Station (Rail) 6H 83
Witton St. B9: Birm 1B 118
  DY8: Stourb 1C 124
Wixford Cft. B34: S End 2E 105
Wixford Gro. B90: Shir 5B 150
Wobaston Rd. WV9: Pend 4B 14
  WV10: F'hses 3E 15
Woburn Av. WV12: W'hall 3B 30
Woburn Cres. B43: Gt Barr 4H 65
Woburn Dr. B62: Hale 4B 112
  DY5: Brie H 4F 109
Woburn Gro. B27: A Grn 4A 136
Woburn Ho. B15: Edg 4E 117
  (off Woodview Dr.)
Wodehouse Cl. WV5: Wom 1E 73
Wodehouse La. DY3: Sed 5A 58
  WV5: Wom 5A 58
Woden Av. WV11: Wed 3E 29
Woden Cl. WV5: Wom 6F 57
Woden Cres. WV11: Wed 3E 29
Woden Pas. WS10: W'bry 3F 63
Woden Rd. WV10: Wolv 5A 28
Woden Rd. E. WS10: W'bry 1H 63
Woden Rd. Nth. WS10: W'bry 6E 47
Woden Rd. Sth. WS10: W'bry 4F 63
Woden Rd. W. WS10: Darl 1D 62
Wodensfield Twr. WV11: Wed 4E 29
Woden Way WV11: Wed 3E 29
Wolcot Gro. B6: Witt 2H 83
Wold Wlk. B13: Mose 1B 148
Wolfsbane Dr. WS5: Wals 2E 65
WOLLASTON 5B 108
Wollaston Ct. DY8: Woll 5A 108
  WS1: Wals 1D 48
  (off Lwr. Rushall St.)
Wollaston Cres. WV11: Wed 3F 29
Wollaston Rd. DY7: Stourt 4A 108
  DY8: Amb 4C 108
Wollerton Gro. B75: S Cold 5D 54
WOLLESCOTE 6B 110
Wollescote Bus. Pk. DY9: Lye 6B 110
Wollescote Dr. B91: Sol 6F 151
Wollescote Rd. DY9: W'cte 2G 125
  (not continuous)
Wolmer Rd. WV11: Wed 5H 17
Wolseley Av. B27: A Grn 1B 136
Wolseley Bank WV10: Bush 2B 28

Wolseley Cl. B36: Cas B 6C **88**
WV10: Bush 2B **28**
Wolseley Dr. B8: W End 2G **103**
Wolseley Ga. WV10: Bush 2B **28**
Wolseley Rd. B70: W Brom 6E **63**
WV14: Bils 4D **44**
Wolseley St. B9: Birm 1B **118**
(not continuous)
Wolston Cl. B90: Shir 2H **149**
WOLVERHAMPTON 4D **170** (1H **43**)
Wolverhampton (Rail) 2D **170** (1H **43**)
Wolverhampton Art Gallery & Mus.
. . . . .2C **170**
Wolverhampton Cricket Ground . . .3A **26**
Wolverhampton Race Course 3E **27**
Wolverhampton Rd. B68: O'bry 6G **97**
B69: O'bry 2D **96**
DY3: Sed 4H **59**
DY6: W Hth 6A **74**
WS2: Wals 1G **47**
(not continuous)
WS3: Blox 6H **19**
WS3: Pels 4C **20**
WS6: C Hay 4B **6**
WS11: Cann 1B **6**
(not continuous)
WV4: Sed 2H **59**
WV6: Patt 6A **24**
WV8: Cod 3F **13**
(not continuous)
WV10: Share 3A **6**
(Saredon Rd., not continuous)
WV10: Share 4B **6**
(Warstone Rd.)
WV10: Wolv 6B **28**
WV11: Ess 4H **17**
WV11: Wed 4E **29**
Wolverhampton Rd. E. WV4: Penn 6H **43**
Wolverhampton Rd. Sth. B32: Quin . . .4C **114**
Wolverhampton Rd. W. WS2: Wals . . .1C **46**
WV13: W'hall 1C **46**
Wolverhampton Science Pk.
WV10: Wolv 3G **27**
Wolverhampton Sports Arena 4E **27**
Wolverhampton St. DY1: Dud 5D **76**
WS2: Wals 1B **48**
WS10: Darl 4B **46**
WV13: W'hall 2H **45**
WV14: Bils 5E **45**
Wolverhampton Wanderers FC
. . . . .1A **170** (6G **27**)
Wolverley Av. B78: Woll 5A **108**
WV4: Penn 6B **42**
Wolverley Cres. B69: O'bry 4D **96**
Wolverley Rd. B32: Bart G 5H **129**
B63: Hale 3H **127**
B92: Sol 3H **137**
Wolverson Cl. WV12: W'hall 5C **30**
Wolverson Rd. WS9: Wals W 3C **22**
Wolverton Rd. B37: Mars G 4D **122**
B45: Redn 3A **158**
DY2: Dud 6G **77**
WOMBOURNE 2F **73**
Wombourne Cl. DY3: Sed 5G **59**
Wombourne Ent. Pk. WV5: Wom 2D **72**
Wombourne Leisure Cen. 6F **57**
Wombourne Pk. WV5: Wom 2F **73**
Wombourne Rd. DY3: Swind 5E **73**
Wombrook Bus. Cen.
WV5: Wom 1E **73**
Wombrook Dale WV5: Wom 1D **72**
Woodacre Rd. B24: Erd 3A **86**
Woodall Rd. B6: Aston 6H **83**
Woodall St. B64: Crad H 2E **111**
WS3: Blox 6A **20**
(not continuous)
Woodard Rd. DY4: Tip 6C **62**
Wood Av. DY3: Lwr G 3G **75**
WV11: Wed 3F **29**
Wood Bank Rd. WV3: Wolv 3G **41**
Woodbank Rd. DY3: Sed 6G **59**
Woodberry Dr. B76: Walm 3E **71**
Woodberry Wlk. B27: A Grn 2B **136**
Woodbine Av. B10: Small H 3D **118**

Woodbine Cft. B26: Sheld 5E **121**
Woodbine Wlk. B37: Chel W 1F **123**
Woodbourne B15: Edg 3H **115**
(not continuous)
Woodbourne Rd. B15: Edg 3F **115**
B17: Harb 3F **115**
B67: Smeth 1C **114**
Woodbridge Cl. WS3: Blox 4G **19**
WS4: S'fld 6H **21**
Woodbridge Rd. B13: Mose 2H **133**
Woodbrooke Gro. B31: N'fld 1G **145**
Woodbrooke Rd. B30: B'vlle 6H **131**
Woodbrook Ho. B37: Chel W 1D **122**
Woodburn Rd. B66: Smeth 2H **99**
Woodbury Cl. B34: Hodg H 3E **105**
B62: B'hth 3F **113**
DY5: Brie H 1A **110**
Woodbury Gro. B91: Sol 6F **151**
Woodbury Rd. B62: B'hth 3F **113**
B62: Quin 4F **113**
Woodchester Rd. B93: Dorr 6F **167**
Woodchurch Grange B73: Bold 5F **69**
Wood Cl. B46: Col 2H **107**
Woodclose Rd. B37: F'bri 6B **106**
Woodcock Cl. B31: Longb 6A **144**
WOODCOCK HILL 6C **130**
Woodcock La. B27: A Grn 2B **136**
(not continuous)
B31: N'fld 6C **130**
Woodcock La. Nth. B27: A Grn 1B **136**
Woodcock Sports Cen. 5H **101**
(off Woodcock St.)
Woodcock St. B7: Birm 1G **5** (5H **101**)
Woodcombe Cl. DY5: Brie H 4F **109**
Wood Comn. Grange WS3: Pels 3D **20**
Woodcote Dr. B8: Salt 4F **103**
B93: Dorr 6H **167**
Woodcote Pl. B19: Loz 2E **101**
Woodcote Rd. B24: Erd 2B **86**
WV6: Tett 5A **26**
Woodcote Way B18: Hock 4C **100**
B74: S'tly 5H **51**
Wood Ct. B20: Hand 5C **82**
Wood Cft. B47: H'wd 3B **162**
Woodcroft Av. B20: Hand 4A **82**
DY4: Tip 2E **77**
Woodcroft Cl. B64: Old H 3H **111**
WOODCROSS 3B **60**
Woodcross La. WV14: Cose 3C **60**
Woodcross St. WV14: Cose 3B **60**
WOOD END 2E **29**
Woodend B20: Hand 1A **82**
Wood End Farm WS5: Wals 2H **49**
Wood End La. B24: Erd 4F **85**
Woodend Pl. WV6: Tett 5H **25**
Wood End Rd. B24: Erd 4F **85**
WS5: Wals 3H **49**
WV11: Wed 1E **29**
Woodend Way WS9: A'rdge 6D **22**
Woodfall Av. B30: K Nor 2B **146**
Woodfield Av. B64: Crad H 3F **111**
B69: O'bry 5G **97**
DY5: P'ntt 2F **93**
DY9: W'cte 3B **126**
WV4: Penn 5D **42**
Woodfield Cl. B74: Four O 3H **53**
WS5: Wals 6A **50**
Woodfield Cres. B12: Bal H 5A **118**
Woodfield Hgts. WV6: Tett 5B **26**
Woodfield Rd. B12: Bal H 5A **118**
B13: K Hth 5H **133**
B91: Sol 1F **151**
DY3: Lwr G 3G **75**
Woodfield Social & Sports Club 5E **43**
Woodfold Cft. WS9: A'rdge 2D **34**
Woodford Av. B36: Cas B 1F **105**
Woodford Cl. WV9: Pend 5D **14**
Woodford Grn. Rd. B28: Hall G 5G **135**
Woodford La. WV5: Try, Wom 5C **56**
Woodford Way WV5: Wom 1D **72**
Woodfort Rd. B43: Gt Barr 6A **66**
WOODGATE 5H **129**
Woodgate Bus. Pk. B32: Bart G 3H **129**
(not continuous)

Woodgate Dr. B32: Bart G 4G **129**
Woodgate Gdns. B32: Bart G 3G **129**
Woodgate La. B32: Bart G 3G **129**
Woodgate Valley Country Pk. 3A **130**
Woodgate Valley Country Pk. Vis. Cen.
. . . . .3H **129**
Woodgate Valley Urban Farm 3G **129**
Woodglade Cft. B38: K Nor 5A **146**
WOOD GREEN 6H **47**
Wood Grn. WS6: C Hay 1E **7**
Wood Grn. Rd. B18: Win G 5H **99**
WS10: W'bry 1G **63**
Woodgreen Rd. B68: O'bry 4A **114**
Woodhall Cl. DY4: Tip 5A **62**
Woodhall Cft. B92: Olton 2D **136**
Woodhall Ho. WS3: Blox 1A **32**
(off Woodhall Rd.)
Woodhall Rd. WV4: Penn 1C **58**
Woodham Cl. B45: Fran 6E **143**
Woodhaven WS4: S'fld 6H **21**
WOOD HAYES 1E **29**
Wood Hayes Cft. WV10: Bush 5E **17**
Wood Hayes Rd. WV10: Bush 5D **16**
WV11: Wed 5D **16**
Woodhill Cl. WV5: Wom 1F **73**
Wood Hill Dr. WV5: Wom 2F **73**
Wood Ho. WS1: Wals 4D **48**
Woodhouse Ct. DY5: Quar B 2C **110**
Woodhouse Fold WV11: Wed 4F **29**
Woodhouse Rd. B32: Quin 5C **114**
WV6: Tett 5H **25**
Woodhouse Rd. Nth. WV6: Tett 5H **25**
Woodhouse Way B64: Crad H 2E **111**
Woodhurst Rd. B13: Mose 1A **134**
Wooding Cres. DY4: Tip 4B **62**
Woodington Rd. B75: S Cold 6E **55**
Woodland Av. DY1: Dud 4E **77**
DY5: Quar B 2C **110**
WV6: Tett 6H **25**
Woodland Cl. DY9: Pedm 4H **125**
WV12: W'hall 3D **30**
Woodland Ct. WS14: Shen W 2G **37**
Woodland Cres. WV3: Wolv 4B **42**
Woodland Dr. B66: Smeth 2C **98**
WS6: C Hay 1E **7**
Woodland Gro. B43: Gt Barr 2A **66**
DY3: Gorn 4F **75**
Woodland Ri. B64: Crad H 3H **111**
B73: S Cold 1H **69**
Woodland Rd. B21: Hand 1G **99**
B31: N'fld 4F **145**
B62: B'hth 3D **112**
WV3: Wolv 4B **42**
Wood Lands, The B75: S Cold 5E **55**
Woodlands, The B64: Crad H 4A **112**
DY8: Stourb 3E **125**
WV8: Cod 5G **13**
Woodlands Av. B46: Wat O 5D **88**
WS5: Wals 6A **50**
Woodlands Cen., The WV12: W'hall . . .2E **31**
Woodlands Cotts. WV4: Penn 1C **58**
Woodlands Crematorium B46: Col 4F **107**
Woodlands Cres. WS3: Pels 2D **20**
Woodlands Farm Rd. B24: Erd 3D **86**
Woodlands La. B90: Shir 1H **163**
Woodlands Paddock WV4: Penn 1C **58**
Woodlands Pk. Rd.
B30: B'vlle, K Nor 1G **145**
Woodlands Rd. B8: Salt 5F **103**
B11: S'hll 2B **134**
B45: Rub 2D **156**
WV5: Wom 2G **73**
Woodlands St. B66: Smeth 4G **99**
Woodlands Wlk. WV4: Penn 6C **42**
Woodlands Way B37: Chel W 6F **107**
Wood La. B17: Harb 5E **115**
B20: Hand 5C **82**
B24: Erd 6G **85**
B32: Bart G 4G **129**
(not continuous)
B37: Mars G 3C **122**
B70: W Brom 4G **79**
B74: S'tly 2G **51**

Wood La. B92: Bars 5G 153
  WS3: Pels 2D 20
  WS9: A'rdge 6H 23
  WS14: Foot 6H 23
  WV10: F'hses 6H 15
  WV12: W'hall 2E 31
Wood La. Cl. WV12: W'hall 2E 31
Woodlawn B91: Sol 3A 152
Woodlawn Gro. DY6: K'wfrd 4B 92
Woodlea Dr. B24: Erd 5F 85
  B91: Sol 2C 150
Wood Leasow B32: Bart G 3B 130
Wood Leaves B47: H'wd 1H 161
Woodleigh Av. B17: Harb 1H 131
Woodleigh Cl. B63: Hale 5A 112
Woodleigh Ct. B38: K Nor 6B 146
Woodleigh Rd. B72: W Grn 4A 70
Woodleys, The B14: K Hth 3A 148
Woodloes Rd. B90: Shir 1H 163
Woodman Cl. B63: Hale 2C 128
  WS10: W'bry 1H 63
Woodman Gro. B75: R'ley 6C 38
Woodman La. WS6: C Hay 1E 7
Woodman Rd. B14: K Hth 6A 148
  B63: Hale 2C 128
Woodman Wlk. B23: Erd 2A 84
Woodmeadow Rd. B30: K Nor 4D 146
Woodnorton Dr. B13: Mose 3G 133
Woodnorton Rd. B65: Row X 1F 113
Woodpecker Gro. B36: Cas B 2C 106
Woodpecker Rd. B33: Stech 5D 104
Woodperry Av. B91: Sol 6G 151
Woodridge B6: Aston 6G 83
Woodridge Av. B32: Quin 1H 129
Woodridge Rd. B63: Hale 6A 112
Wood Rd. DY3: Lwr G 4G 75
  WV5: Wom 5H 57
  WV6: Tett 6H 25
  WV8: Cod 2D 12
Woodrough Dr. B13: Mose 3H 133
Woodrow Cres. B93: Know 4C 166
Woodrow La. B61: Cats 6B 156
Woodruff Way WS5: Wals 1D 64
Woodrush Dr. B47: H'wd 4A 162
WOODS, THE 1A 64
Woods, The B14: K Hth 4H 133
WOODS BANK 5D 46
Woods Bank Est., The WS10: Darl 1D 62
Woods Bank Ter. WS10: Darl 6C 46
Woods Cres. DY5: Quar B 2C 110
WOODSETTON 1B 76
Woodsetton Cl. DY1: Dud 1D 76
Woodshires Rd. B92: Olton 6C 136
WOODSIDE 3B 94
Wood Side WV11: Wed 1A 30
Woodside B37: K'hrst 4A 106
  B74: Four O 1E 53
Woodside Cl. WS5: Wals 5H 49
Woodside Cres. B93: Know 5D 166
Woodside Dr. B74: Lit As 4C 36
Woodside Gro. WV8: Bilb 4H 13
Woodside Ho. B34: S End 4A 106
Woodside Ind. Est. DY5: Brie H 4H 109
Woodside Rd. B29: S Oak 4C 132
  (not continuous)
  DY2: Dud 3B 94
  WS5: Wals 5H 49
Woodside Way B32: Bart G 5G 129
  B91: Sol 2C 150
  WS9: A'rdge 4D 34
  WV12: W'hall 2E 31
Woods La. B64: Crad H 3E 111
  DY5: Brie H 4H 109
Woodsome Gro. B23: Erd 6C 68
Woodsorrel Rd. DY1: Dud 3B 76
Woodstile Cl. B75: R'ley 6B 38
Woodstile Way B34: S End 3F 105
Woodstock Cl. DY1: Dud 1C 94
  DY8: Word 2A 108
  WS5: Wals 2E 65
Woodstock Cres. B93: Dorr 6B 166
Woodstock Dr. B74: Four O 5D 36
  DY8: Word 2A 108
Woodstock Ho. B13: Mose 6A 134

Woodstock Rd. B13: Mose 1A 134
  B21: Hand 1B 100
  WV1: Wolv 2D 44
Woodston Gro. B91: Sol 1G 165
Wood St. B16: Birm 1C 116
  DY2: Dud 3B 94
  DY4: Tip 1G 77
  DY8: Woll 4B 108
  DY9: Lye 6B 110
  WS10: Darl 5F 47
  WV4: E'shll 2C 60
  WV10: Wolv 4B 28
  WV13: W'hall 1A 46
  WV14: Bils 6F 45
Woodthorne Cl. DY3: Gorn 5H 75
Woodthorne Rd. WV6: Tett 3G 25
Woodthorne Rd. Sth. WV6: Tett 5G 25
Woodthorne Wlk. DY6: K'wfrd 1C 92
Woodthorpe Dr. DY9: W'cte 2H 125
Woodthorpe Gdns. B14: K Hth 2G 147
Woodthorpe Rd. B14: K Hth 2F 147
Woodvale Dr. B28: Hall G 3E 149
Woodvale M. B14: K Hth 2B 148
Woodvale Rd. B28: Hall G 3E 149
  B32: Bart G 4G 129
Woodview Dr. B15: Edg 4E 117
Woodville Ct. B23: Erd 5E 85
  (off Gravelly Hill)
Woodville Gdns. DY3: Sed 4B 60
Woodville Rd. B14: K Hth 5H 133
  B17: Harb 5E 115
Woodward Pl. DY9: Lye 1G 125
Woodwards Cl. WS2: Wals 3H 47
Woodwards Pl. WS2: Wals 3H 47
Woodwards Rd. WS2: Wals 3H 47
Woodward St. B71: W Brom 3C 80
Woodway B24: Erd 2H 85
Woodwells Rd. B8: W End 4G 103
Woody Bank WS6: C Hay 3E 7
Woolacombe Lodge Rd.
  B29: S Oak 3G 131
Woolmore Rd. B23: Erd 3C 84
Woolpack All. WV1: Wolv 3B 170
Woolpack Cl. B65: Row R 5A 96
Woolpack St. WV1: Wolv 3B 170 (1G 43)
Wooton Gro. B44: K'sdng 5C 68
Wootton Av. WV11: Wed 2F 29
Wootton Cl. DY5: Brie H 3F 109
WOOTTON GREEN 6G 155
Wootton Grn. La. CV7: Bal C 6G 155
Wootton La. CV7: Bal C 6E 155
Wootton Rd. B31: Longb 2E 159
  WV3: Wolv 4B 42
Woottons Sq. WV14: Bils 3G 61
Worcester Arc. B2: Birm 1G 117
  (off New St.)
Worcester Bar B1: Birm 1E 117
Worcester Cl. B75: R'ley 6B 38
Worcester Ct. WV3: Wolv 5E 43
Worcester Grn. B71: W Brom 6A 64
Worcester Gro. WV6: Pert 5D 24
Worcester Ho. B36: Cas B 1C 106
  B63: Hale 2A 128
  (off Hill St.)
Worcester La. B75: R'ley 6B 38
  DY8: Stourb 4F 125
  DY9: Hag, Pedm 4F 125
Worcester Ri. B29: S Oak 4D 132
Worcester Rd. B6: Witt 5H 83
  B68: O'bry 3G 113
  DY2: Neth 6G 95
  DY9: Hag 6F 125
  WV13: W'hall 1D 46
Worcester St. B2: Birm 5E 5
  DY8: Stourb 1D 124
  WV2: Wolv 5A 170 (2G 43)
Worcester Wlk. B2: Birm 5E 5 (1G 117)
  B37: Mars G 3B 122
Word Hill B17: Harb 4D 114
WORDSLEY 1B 108
Wordsley Cl. DY8: Word 6B 92
Wordsley Grn. DY8: Word 1B 108
  (not continuous)

Wordsley Grn. Shop. Cen.
  DY8: Word 1B 108
Wordsworth Av. WV4: E'shll 1A 60
  WV6: Pert 5E 25
Wordsworth Cl. DY4: Tip 5A 62
Wordsworth Ho. B31: Longb 1E 159
  B68: O'bry 5A 98
Wordsworth Rd. B10: Small H 4D 118
  DY3: Lwr G 2F 75
  WS3: Blox 1C 32
  WV10: Bush 1C 28
  WV12: W'hall 2E 31
Wordsworth St. B71: W Brom 2A 80
Worfield Cl. WS4: Wals 5E 33
Worfield Gdns. WV3: Wolv 5D 42
Works Rd. B26: Birm A 2B 138
WORLDS END 6D 136
Worlds End Av. B32: Quin 5B 114
Worlds End La. B32: Quin 5B 114
Worlds End Rd. B20: Hand 4C 82
Worley's Wharf Av. WS10: W'bry 3C 64
Worsey Dr. DY4: Tip 1D 78
Worthen Gro. B31: Longb 1E 159
Worthings, The B30: Stir 1D 146
Worthy Down WV11: Wed 4H 29
Worthy Down Wlk. B35: Cas V 4F 87
Wortley Av. WV10: Wolv 3A 28
Worton Rd. DY9: W'cte 3A 126
Wragby Cl. WV9: Pend 4F 15
Wrekin Cl. B63: Hale 4E 127
Wrekin Dr. DY9: W'cte 1H 125
  WV3: Wolv 3C 42
  WV6: Tett 4G 25
Wrekin Gro. WV12: W'hall 6B 18
Wrekin La. WV6: Tett 4G 25
Wrekin Rd. B44: K'sdng 1H 83
  B73: Bold 4G 69
Wrekin Vw. WS8: Bwnhls 2C 22
  WV1: Wolv 2A 170 (1G 43)
Wrekin Vw. Rd. DY3: Sed 5G 59
  (not continuous)
Wren Av. WV6: Pert 6D 24
Wrenbury Dr. WV14: Bils 4A 46
Wrens Av. DY4: Tip 2E 77
  DY6: K'wfrd 5E 93
Wrens Hill Rd. DY1: Dud 2C 76
WREN'S NEST 3C 76
Wren's Nest Geological Nature Reserve
  . . . . .3D 76
Wren's Nest La. B90: Dic H 4G 163
Wrens Nest Pl. DY1: Dud 2C 76
Wrens Nest Rd. DY1: Dud 3C 76
Wrens Pk. Av. B76: Walm 6C 70
Wren St. DY1: Dud 1D 76
  DY2: Neth 4D 94
Wrentham St. B5: Birm 3F 117
Wretham Ct. B19: Hock 2D 100
Wretham Rd. B19: Hock 3D 100
Wrexham Av. WS2: Wals 2F 47
Wright Av. WV11: Wed 2F 29
Wrighton Cl. WV12: W'hall 1C 30
Wrighton Dr. DY5: P'ntt 6G 75
Wright Rd. B8: Salt 4E 103
Wright St. B10: Small H 3D 118
  B63: Hale 1B 128
  WV10: Wolv 5H 27
  WV14: Bils 1G 61
Wrottesley Pk. Rd. WV6: Pert 1D 40
  WV8: Pert, Wrot P 6D 24
Wrottesley Rd. B43: Gt Barr 4H 65
  WV6: Tett 4H 25
Wrottesley Rd. W. WV6: Tett 3F 25
Wrottesley St. B5: Birm 6E 5 (2G 117)
Wroxall Cl. DY5: Brie H 3F 109
Wroxall Gro. B13: Mose 1A 148
Wroxall Rd. B91: Sol 1C 150
Wroxham Glen WV13: W'hall 4H 45
Wroxton Rd. B26: Yard 3C 120
Wulfruna Ct. WV3: Wolv 2F 43
Wulfruna Gdns. WV3: Wolv 2D 42
Wulfruna St. WV1: Wolv 2B 170 (1G 43)
Wulfrun Cen. WV1: Wolv 4B 170 (2G 43)
Wulfrun Sq. WV1: Wolv 4C 170 (2H 43)

Wulfrun Trad. Est. WV10: Wolv 4G 27
Wulfrun Way WV1: Wolv 4B 170 (2G 43)
Wyatt Cl. B5: Edg 6E 117
Wyatt Rd. B75: S Cold 5F 55
Wychall Dr. WV10: Bush 3A 16
Wychall La. B31: K Nor 5H 145
Wychall Pk. Gro. B38: K Nor 5H 145
Wychall Rd. B31: N'fld 4F 145
Wychbold Cl. WV12: W'hall 6D 18
Wychbold Ct. DY9: Pedm 5G 125
Wychbold Cres. B33: Kitts G 6G 105
Wychbold Way WV12: W'hall 6D 18
Wychbury B76: Walm 4E 71
Wychbury Ct. B63: Hale 2A 128
Wychbury Dr. DY9: Hag 6G 125
Wychbury Rd. B32: Bart G 5G 129
DY5: Quar B 3A 110
DY9: W'cte 4H 125
WV3: Wolv 4A 42
Wyche Av. B14: K Hth 3F 147
Wychelm Farm Rd. B14: K Hth 6A 148
Wych Elm Rd. WS8: Clay 2A 22
Wycherley Way B64: Old H 3G 111
Wychnor Gro. B71: W Brom 3C 64
Wychwood Av. B93: Know 1D 166
Wychwood Cres. B26: Sheld 5D 120
Wyckham Cl. B17: Harb 1E 131
Wyckham Rd. B36: Cas B 1A 106
Wycome Rd. B28: Hall G 1F 149
Wye Cliff Rd. B20: Hand 1D 100
Wye Cl. B76: Walm 6E 71
WV6: Pert 5F 25
Wyegate Cl. B36: Cas B 1B 106
Wyemanton Cl. B43: Gt Barr 4G 65
Wye Rd. WS3: Blox 6C 20
Wykeham Gro. WV6: Pert 6D 24
Wyken Cl. B93: Dorr 6F 167
Wyld Cl. B71: W Brom 5G 63
Wylde Cres. B65: Row R 5C 96
WYLDE GREEN 4A 70
Wylde Grn. Rd. B72: W Grn 4A 70
B76: Walm 4A 70
Wylde Green Station (Rail) 4H 69
Wymering Av. WV11: Wed 2H 29
Wynall La. WV9: W'cte 1B 126
Wynall La. Sth. DY9: W'cte 2C 126
Wynbrook Gro. B90: M'path 3F 165
Wynchcombe Av. WV4: Penn 1B 58
Wynd, The DY3: Sed 4H 59
Wyndcliff Rd. B9: Small H 2D 118
Wyndham Gdns. B30: K Nor 3H 145
Wyndham Rd. B16: Edg 2B 116
Wyndhurst Rd. B33: Stech 5C 104
Wyndley Cl. B74: Four O 3F 37
Wyndley Dr. B73: S Cold 1H 69
Wyndley Gro. B72: W Grn 3A 70
Wyndley La. B73: S Cold 1G 69
Wyndley Leisure Cen. 6G 53
Wyndley Mnr. B74: Four O 3G 37
Wyndley Swimming Baths 1G 69
Wyndmill Cres. B71: W Brom 4D 64
Wynds Covert B14: K Hth 5F 147
Wynds Point B31: N'fld 2F 145
Wyne Cres. WV4: Penn 2A 58
Wynfield Gdns. B14: K Hth 2H 147
Wynford Rd. B27: A Grn 6A 120
Wynford Rd. Ind. Est. B27: A Grn 6A 120
Wynn Griffith Dr. DY4: Tip 4A 78
Wynn Rd. WV4: Penn 5D 42
Wynn St. B15: Birm 3F 117
Wynstead Covert B14: K Hth 5E 147
Wyntor La. B71: W Brom 5H 63
Wyre Cl. B45: Fran 6H 143
WS9: Wals W 3B 22
Wyre Rd. DY8: Woll 5C 108
Wyrley Cl. WS8: Bwnhls 2B 10
WV12: W'hall 2D 30
Wyrley Ho. B23: Erd 1D 84
DY4: Tip 4B 78

Wyrley La. WS3: Lit Wyr 4C 8
Wyrley Rd. B6: Witt 4A 84
B75: R'ley 2B 54
WV11: Wed 3A 30
Wyrley St. WV10: Wolv 1B 44
Wyrley Trad. Est. B6: Witt 5B 84
Wyrley Way B23: Erd 1A 84
WYTHALL 6A 162
Wythall Grn. Way B47: Wyt 5G 161
Wythall Rd. B63: Hale 3A 128
Wythall Station (Rail) 5C 162
Wythwood Cl. DY9: Pedm 4H 125
Wythwood Gro. B47: H'wd 3C 162
DY4: Tip 5A 62
Wythwood Rd. B47: H'wd 3B 162
Wyton Av. B68: O'bry 1A 114
Wyvern Cl. B68: O'bry 5H 97
B74: S Cold 4H 53
WV12: W'hall 2A 30
Wyvern Gro. B29: S Oak 3G 131
Wyvern Rd. B74: S Cold 4H 53
Wyvis Cl. WV3: Wolv 1C 42

Y

Yale Dr. WV11: Wed 4G 29
Yale Rd. WV13: W'hall 3A 46
YARDLEY .3B 120
Yardley Cl. B68: O'bry 2H 113
Yardley Crematorium B25: Yard 6B 120
Yardley Flds. Rd. B33: Stech 1B 120
Yardley Grn. Rd. B9: Bord G 2F 119
B33: Stech 2F 119
Yardley Rd. B25: Yard 1A 136
B27: A Grn 1A 136
Yardley St. DY9: Lye 5G 109
WS10: Darl 4C 46
YARDLEY WOOD 4D 148
Yardley Wood Rd. B13: Mose 2B 134
B14: Yard W 2B 148
B90: Shir 2B 148
Yardley Wood Station (Rail) 2D 148
Yare Gro. WV13: W'hall 1D 46
Yarnborough Hill DY8: Stourb 3E 125
Yarnbury Cl. B14: K Hth 6G 147
Yarn Cl. B47: H'wd 4A 162
Yarner Cl. DY1: Dud 5A 76
Yarnfield Rd. B11: Tys 2G 135
Yarningale Cl. B30: K Nor 4F 147
Yarningale Rd. B14: K Hth 3E 147
Yarningdale B90: Shir 6A 150
Yarn La. B90: Dic H 3G 163
Yarrow Cl. WS3: Pels 2E 21
WV11: Wed 4H 29
Yarrow Dr. B38: K Nor 1B 160
Yarwell Cl. WV10: Wolv 5H 27
Yateley Av. B42: Gt Barr 6C 66
Yateley Cres. B42: Gt Barr 6C 66
Yateley Rd. B15: Edg 4A 116
Yatesbury Av. B35: Cas V 4D 86
Yates Cft. B74: Four O 3F 37
Yates La. B65: Row R 1F 113
Yeadon Gdns. WV3: Wolv 3B 42
Yeames Cl. B43: Gt Barr 1E 67
Yelverton Cl. WS3: Blox 3H 19
Yelverton Dr. B15: Edg 3A 116
Yeman Rd. B68: O'bry 6B 98
Yems Cft. WS4: Rus 3E 33
Yemscroft WS6: Gt Wyr 5G 7
Yemscroft Flats WS4: Rus 3E 33
Yenton Cl. B24: Erd 1H 85
Yenton Gro. B24: Erd 1A 86
Yeomanry Cl. B75: S Cold 5E 55
Yeomans Grange B75: S Cold 5D 54
(off Yeomans Way)
Yeomans Way B75: S Cold 5D 54
Yeovil Ct. DY5: Brie H 1H 109
(off Hill St.)

Yerbury Gro. B23: Erd 3B 84
Yew Cft. Av. B17: Harb 5E 115
Yewdale B17: Harb 1G 131
Yewhurst Rd. B91: Sol 3C 150
YEW TREE .1F 65
Yew Tree Gdns. WS5: Wals 1F 65
WV8: Cod 3G 13
Yew Tree Hills DY2: Neth 5E 95
Yew Tree La. B26: Yard 4C 120
B32: Fran 4D 142
B65: Row R 1B 112
B91: Sol 2A 152
WS10: W'bry 3G 63
WV6: Tett 3G 25
Yewtree La. WV14: Cose 4F 61
Yew Tree Pl. B62: Roms 2A 142
WS3: Blox 4B 20
Yew Tree Retail Pk. B25: Yard 3B 120
Yew Tree Ri. B76: Walm 2D 70
Yew Tree Rd. B6: Aston 6A 84
B13: Mose 3F 133
B15: Edg 3E 117
B36: Cas B 1A 106
B63: Hale 2H 127
B67: Smeth 5C 98
B73: Bold 6G 69
B74: S'tly 3F 51
DY2: Neth 5E 95
WS4: S'fld 6F 21
WS5: Wals 6E 49
Yew Wlk. B37: Chel W 1D 122
Yockleton Rd. B33: Kitts G 6G 105
York Av. WS2: Wals 1H 47
WV3: Wolv 2C 42
WV13: W'hall 1D 46
Yorkbrook Dr. B26: Sheld 6F 121
York Cl. B30: B'vlle 2C 146
DY4: Tip 3F 77
York Cres. B34: S End 4A 106
B70: W Brom 1G 79
DY8: Woll 4B 108
WS10: Darl 5D 46
WV3: Wolv 2C 42
Yorkdale Cl. DY3: Lwr G 4H 75
York Dr. B36: Hodg H 1H 103
Yorke Av. DY5: Brie H 2E 109
York Gdns. WV3: Wolv 2C 42
York Ho. B73: W Grn 2H 69
Yorklea Cft. B37: F'bri 1B 122
Yorkminster Dr. B37: Chel W 1E 123
York Rd. B14: K Hth 5G 133
B16: Edg 2A 116
B21: Hand 1B 100
B23: Erd 3F 85
B28: Hall G 3E 135
B65: Row R 6E 97
DY2: Neth 6G 95
WS4: Rus 2G 33
WV3: Wolv 3H 41
York St. B17: Harb 5H 115
WV1: Wolv 2A 44
Yorks Wood Dr. B37: K'hrst 3B 106
York Ter. B18: Birm 4E 101
Young St. B70: W Brom 4G 79
Yoxall Gro. B33: Kitts G 6E 105
Yoxall Rd. B90: Shir 5B 150

Z

Zion Cl. WS6: C Hay 2D 6
Zions Cl. B64: Old H 2H 111
Zion St. DY4: Tip 5H 61
Zoar St. DY3: Gorn 4G 75
WV3: Wolv 2F 43
Zouche Cl. DY8: Amb 3C 108

HOSPITALS and HOSPICES
covered by this atlas.

N.B. Where Hospitals and Hospices are not named on the map, the reference
given is for the road in which they are situated.

ACORNS CHILDREN'S HOSPICE (SELLY OAK) 5A **132**
103 Oak Tree Lane
Selly Oak
BIRMINGHAM
B29 6HZ
Tel: 0121 2484850

ACORNS CHILDREN'S HOSPICE (WALSALL) 6D **48**
Walstead Road
WALSALL
WS5 4NL
Tel: 01922 422500

BIRMINGHAM CHEST CLINIC 3C **4** (6F **101**)
151 Gt. Charles Street Queensway
BIRMINGHAM
B3 3HX
Tel: 0121 4241950

BIRMINGHAM CHILDREN'S HOSPITAL
    (DIANA, PRINCESS OF WALES HOSPITAL)
. . . . .2F **5** (6G **101**)
Steelhouse Lane
BIRMINGHAM
B4 6NH
Tel. 0121 3339999

BIRMINGHAM DENTAL HOSPITAL 1E **5** (6G **101**)
St Chad's Queensway
BIRMINGHAM
B4 6NN
Tel: 0121 2368611

BIRMINGHAM HEARTLANDS HOSPITAL 1H **119**
Bordesley Green East
BIRMINGHAM
B9 5ST
Tel: 0121 4242000

BIRMINGHAM NUFFIELD HOSPITAL 6B **116**
22 Somerset Road
Edgbaston
BIRMINGHAM
B15 2QQ
Tel: 0121 4562000

BIRMINGHAM ST MARY'S HOSPICE 4C **132**
176 Raddlebarn Road
BIRMINGHAM
B29 7DA
Tel: 0121 4721191

BIRMINGHAM WOMEN'S HOSPITAL 1H **131**
Metchley Park Road
BIRMINGHAM
B15 2TG
Tel: 0121 4721377

BLOXWICH HOSPITAL 1H **31**
Reeves Sreet
WALSALL
WS3 2JJ
Tel: 01922 858600

BUSHEY FIELDS HOSPITAL 2A **94**
Bushey Fields Road
DUDLEY
DY1 2LZ
Tel: 01384 457373

CITY HOSPITAL (BIRMINGHAM) .5B **100**
Dudley Road
BIRMINGHAM
B18 7QH
Tel: 0121 554 3801

COMPTON HOSPICE 1A **42**
4 Compton Road West
WOLVERHAMPTON
WV3 9DH
Tel: 0845 2255497

CORBETT HOSPITAL 4E **109**
Vicarage Road
STOURBRIDGE
DY8 4JB
Tel: 01384 456111

DOROTHY PATTISON HOSPITAL .2H **47**
Alumwell Close
WALSALL
WS2 9XH
Tel: 01922 858000

EDWARD STREET HOSPITAL 4A **80**
Edward Street
WEST BROMWICH
B70 8NL
Tel: 0845 146 1800

GOOD HOPE HOSPITAL 5B **54**
Rectory Road
SUTTON COLDFIELD
B75 7RR
Tel: 0121 3782211

GUEST HOSPITAL 4G **77**
Tipton Road
DUDLEY
DY1 4SE
Tel: 01384 456111

HALLAM STREET HOSPITAL 2C **80**
Hallam Street
WEST BROMWICH
B71 4HH
Tel: 0845 146 1800

HEATH LANE HOSPITAL 6B **64**
Heath Lane
WEST BROMWICH
B71 2BG
Tel: 0845 146 1800

HIGHCROFT HOSPITAL 3D **84**
Reservoir Road
Erdington
BIRMINGHAM
B23 6DJ
Tel: 0121 6235500

JOHN TAYLOR HOSPICE 2A **86**
76 Grange Road
Erdington
BIRMINGHAM
B24 0DF
Tel: 0121 4652000

KINGS HILL DAY UNIT 6E **47**
School Street
WEDNESBURY
WS10 9JB
Tel: 0121 526 4405

LITTLE ASTON SPIRE HOSPITAL 4B **36**
Little Aston Hall Drive
Little Aston
SUTTON COLDFIELD
B74 3UP
Tel: 0845 8502444

LITTLE BLOXWICH DAY HOSPICE 4B **20**
Stoney Lane
WALSALL
WS3 3DW
Tel: 01922 858735

MANOR HOSPITAL (WALSALL) 2A **48**
Moat Road
WALSALL
WS2 9PS
Tel: 01922 721172

MARIE CURIE HOSPICE, SOLIHULL, THE 3H **151**
911-913 Warwick Road
SOLIHULL
B91 3ER
Tel: 0121 2547800

MARY STEVENS HOSPICE, THE 3F **125**
221 Hagley Road
STOURBRIDGE
DY8 2JR
Tel: 01384 443010

MOSELEY HALL HOSPITAL 2G **133**
Alcester Road
BIRMINGHAM
B13 8JL
Tel: 0121 4424321

MOSELEY HALL MENTAL HEALTH UNIT 2G **133**
Alcester Road
BIRMINGHAM
B13

MOSSLEY DAY UNIT 6G **19**
Sneyd Lane
WALSALL
WS3 2LW
Tel: 01922 858680

NEW CROSS HOSPITAL (WOLVERHAMPTON) 4D **28**
Wolverhampton Road
Heath Town
WOLVERHAMPTON
WV10 0QP
Tel: 01902 307999

NHS WALK-IN CENTRE (BIRMINGHAM) 4E **5** (1G **117**)
Boots The Chemists
66 High Street
BIRMINGHAM
B4 7TA
Tel: 0121 255 4500

NHS WALK-IN CENTRE (WALSALL) 2C **48**
The Market Square, Unit 19-21 Digbeth
WALSALL
WS1 1QZ
Tel: 01922 858550

PARKWAY SPIRE HOSPITAL 2A **152**
1 Damson Parkway
SOLIHULL
B91 2PP
Tel: 0845 850 1451

PENN HOSPITAL 1C **58**
Penn Road
WOLVERHAMPTON
WV4 5HN
Tel: 01902 444141

PRIORY BMI HOSPITAL, THE 6D **116**
Priory Road
Edgbaston
BIRMINGHAM
B5 7UG
Tel: 0121 4402323

QUEEN ELIZABETH HOSPITAL 1A **132**
Edgbaston
BIRMINGHAM
B15 2TH
Tel: 0121 4721311

QUEEN ELIZABETH PSYCHIATRIC HOSPITAL (SOUTH BUILDING)
....2A **132**
Vincent Drive
BIRMINGHAM
B15

QUEEN ELIZABETH PSYCHIATRIC HOSPITAL
(SPECIALTIES BUILDING) 2A **132**
Vincent Drive
BIRMINGHAM
B15

ROWLEY REGIS COMMUNITY HOSPITAL 1B **112**
Moor Lane
ROWLEY REGIS
B65 8DA
Tel: 0121 607 3465

ROYAL ORTHOPAEDIC HOSPITAL, THE 2F **145**
  Bristol Road South
  Northfield
  BIRMINGHAM
  B31 2AP
  Tel: 0121 685 4000

RUSSELLS HALL HOSPITAL 2H **93**
  Pensnett Road
  DUDLEY
  DY1 2HQ
  Tel: 01384 456111

ST DAVID'S HOUSE (DAY HOSPITAL) 1F **73**
  Planks Lane
  Wombourne
  WOLVERHAMPTON
  WV5 8DU
  Tel: 01902 326001

SANDWELL GENERAL HOSPITAL 2B **80**
  Lyndon
  WEST BROMWICH
  B71 4HJ
  Tel: 0121 553 1831

SELLY OAK HOSPITAL 4B **132**
  Raddlebarn Road
  BIRMINGHAM
  B29 6JD
  Tel: 0121 6271627

SHELDON UNIT 6B **144**
  11 Sheldon Drive
  BIRMINGHAM
  B31 5EJ
  Tel: 0121 475 6100

SHOWELL GREEN MENTAL HEALTH UNIT
  SHOWELL GREEN LANE 2C **134**
  Showell Green Lane
  BIRMINGHAM
  B11

SOLIHULL HOSPITAL 3G **151**
  Lode Lane
  SOLIHULL
  B91 2JL
  Tel: 0121 4242000

SUTTON COLDFIELD COTTAGE HOSPITAL 1H **69**
  27a Birmingham Road
  SUTTON COLDFIELD
  B72 1QH
  Tel: 0121 465 5400

WALSALL HOSPICE 1D **32**
  (Due open 2009)
  Goscote Lane
  WALSALL
  WS3 1SJ

WEST HEATH HOSPITAL 1G **159**
  Rednal Road
  BIRMINGHAM
  B38 8HR
  Tel: 0121 6271627

WEST MIDLANDS CAPIO HOSPITAL 6F **111**
  Colman Hill
  HALESOWEN
  B63 2AH
  Tel: 01384 560123

WEST PARK REHABILITATION HOSPITAL 1E **43**
  Park Road West
  WOLVERHAMPTON
  WV1 4PW
  Tel: 01902 444000

WOLVERHAMPTON NUFFIELD HOSPITAL 5A **26**
  Wood Road
  WOLVERHAMPTON
  WV6 8LE
  Tel: 01902 754177

WOODBOURNE PRIORY HOSPITAL 3G **115**
  21 Woodbourne Road
  Harborne
  BIRMINGHAM
  B17 8BY
  Tel: 0121 4344343

A-Z Digital Mapping

With the familiar look of our printed maps and atlases, A-Z Digital maps are accurate and easy to use. For detailed system requirements and information please refer to our website, **www.a-zmaps.co.uk**

Copy maps to:

A-Z Memory-Map CD-ROM

● High quality seamless maps taken from our original paper version are displayed full screen.

● Fully searchable indexes to features such as towns, cities, streets, postcodes, district names, railway stations, hospitals, sports and leisure facilities and selected places of interest. Indexed map features vary on each CD-ROM.

● Connect a GPS reciever and the map will pin-point your location and follow your movement.

● Print maps for personal use

● Draw routes to calculate distance of travel.

● Visualise maps in a 3D landscape.

● **Range includes:** Greater London, Greater Manchester, Merseyside, West Midlands, Bristol & Bath, West Yorkshire, South Yorkshire, Glasgow & Edinburgh also Great Britain Road Atlas.

Pocket A-Z downloadable mapping

● Full screen mapping. Move the map around the screen using the stylus and zoom in/out.

● Connect a GPS reciever and Pocket A-Z will choose the best map, pin-point your location and follow your movement.

● Windows Mobile Compatible. Maps can be downloaded to any Windows Mobile based Pocket PC (including phone edition).

● Fully indexed. Easily search for streets, postcodes, towns, districts, stations, places of interest. Individual map indexes vary.

● **Range includes:** London, Birmingham, Manchester, Liverpool, Edinburgh, Brighton, Great Britain Road Atlas and many more.

Mobile Phone downloadable mapping

● Easy to read mapping. Move the map around the screen using the navigation button.

● Connect a GPS reciever and the map will pin-point your location and follow your movement.

● Symbian™ Compatible Maps can be downloaded to any Symbian 3rd edition phone from PC. No air time or subscription required.

● Fully indexed. Easily search for streets, postcodes, towns, districts, stations, places of interest. Individual map indexes vary.

● **Range includes:** London and Birmingham, also Great Britain Road Atlas. Additional cities coming soon.